Sisymote, Bigé

THE DEVELOPING CHILD

THE DEVELOPING CHILD

SEVENTH EDITION

HELEN BEE

HarperCollins*CollegePublishers*

Acquisitions Editor: Jill Lectka
Developmental Editor: Rebecca Kohn
Project Editor: Robert Ginsberg
Creative Director: Teresa D. Rodriguez
Cover Designer: Kay Petronio
Art Studio: Ed Smith Design
Photo Researcher: Rosemary Hunter
Electronic Production Manager: Michael Kemper
Electronic Desktop Manager: Heather A. Peres
Manufacturing Manager: Joseph Campanella
Electronic Page Makeup: RR Donnelley Barbados
Printer and Binder: RR Donnelly :
Cover Printer: Coral Graphic Services, Inc.

For permission to use copyrighted material, grateful acknowledgment is made to the copyright holders on pp. 531–532, which are hereby made part of this copyright page.

The Developing Child, Seventh Edition

Library of Congress Cataloging-in-Publication Data
Bee, Helen L.
    The developing child / Helen Bee.—7th ed.
        p. cm.
    Includes bibliographical references and indexes.
    ISBN 0-06-501737-4
    1. Child psychology. 2. Child development. I. Title.
BF721.B336 1995
155.4—dc20   94-10633
                                                                                CIP

94 95 96 97 98 7 6 5 4 3 2 1

For all my children, adopted and step
Thomas
Rex
Lisa
Peter
Adam
Arwen

CONTENTS IN BRIEF

Detailed Contents   ix
To the Student   xix
To the Instructor   xxi

PART ONE   INTRODUCTION   1
Chapter 1   Basic Questions   3

PART TWO   THE BEGINNINGS OF LIFE   37
Chapter 2   Prenatal Development   39
Chapter 3   Birth and the Newborn Child   71

PART THREE   THE PHYSICAL CHILD   101
Chapter 4   Physical Development   103
Chapter 5   Perceptual Development   134

PART FOUR   THE THINKING CHILD   161
Chapter 6   Cognitive Development I: Cognitive Power   163
Chapter 7   Cognitive Development II: Structure and Process   190
Chapter 8   The Development of Language   227

PART FIVE   THE SOCIAL CHILD   257
Chapter 9   Personality Development: Alternative Views   259
Chapter 10   The Concept of Self in Children   288
Chapter 11   The Development of Social Relationships   313
Chapter 12   Thinking About Relationships: The Development
                of Social Cognition   344

PART SIX   THE WHOLE CHILD   371
Chapter 13   The Ecology of Development: The Child Within
                the Family System   373
Chapter 14   Beyond the Family: The Impact of the Broader
                Culture   402
Chapter 15   Atypical Development   434
Chapter 16   Putting It All Together: The Developing Child   462

Glossary   485
References   491
Credits   531
Name Index   533
Subject Index   545

DETAILED CONTENTS

To the Student   xix
To the Instructor   xxi

PART ONE: INTRODUCTION   1

1   Basic Questions   3

Nature and Nurture: An Ancient Debate   4
The Nature Side of the Equation   5
Inborn Biases and Constraints   5
Maturation   5
Behavior Genetics   6
• **Research Report:** *How Do Behavior Geneticists Identify Genetic
  Effects?* **7**
The Nurture Side of the Equation   7
Models of Environmental Influence   7
The Timing of Experience   9
Internal Models of Experience   10
The Ecological Perspective   11
Interactions of Nature and Nurture   14
Vulnerability and Resilience   14
The Nature of Developmental Change   15
Stages and Sequences   16
Theories of Development   16
Biological Theories   17
Learning Theories   17
Psychoanalytic Theories   20
Cognitive-Developmental Theories   21
Contrasting the Theories   22
Finding the Answers: Research on Development   23
Research Design   24
Cross-sectional Designs   24
Longitudinal Designs   26
Cross-cultural or Cross-context Designs   26
• **Cultures and Contexts:** *An Example of a Cross-cultural
  Comparison Study* **27**
Experimental Designs   27
Research Methods   29
Research Analysis   30
• **Research Report:** *Ethical Issues in Research on Development*   **31**
A Final Word   32

Summary   33
Key Terms   34
Suggested Readings   35

PART TWO: THE BEGINNINGS OF LIFE   37

2   Prenatal Development   39

Conception   40
The Basic Genetics of Conception   41
Dominant and Recessive Genes   42
Males and Females   44
Twins and Siblings   44
Genotypes and Phenotypes   45
Development from Conception to Birth   46
The Germinal Stage: From Conception to Implantation   46
The Embryonic Stage   47
The Fetal Stage   48
Prenatal Sexual Differentiation   49
An Overview of Prenatal Development   51
Genetic Errors   51
Single-Gene Defects   53
• **The Real World: *Prenatal Diagnosis of Genetic Errors   54***
Teratogens: Diseases and Drugs   54
Diseases of the Mother   55
• **The Real World: *Rh Factor: Another Type of Genetic Problem   56***
Drugs Taken by the Mother   57
• **Research Report: *Streissguth's Study of Prenatal Alcohol Exposure   59***
Other Teratogens   60
Other Influences on Prenatal Development   61
• **The Real World: *Weight Gain and Diet During Pregnancy   62***
An Overview of Risks and Long-Term Consequences of
   Prenatal Problems   65
Sex Differences in Prenatal Development   66
Social Class Differences in Prenatal Development   67
Summary   67
Key Terms   69
Suggested Readings   69

3   Birth and the Newborn Child   71

Birth   72
The Stages of Labor   72
The First Greeting: Parents and Newborns   73
Birth Choices   74
Problems at Birth   78
Assessing the Newborn   81
Adapting to the Newborn   82
• **The Real World: *Postpartum Depression   82***
The Newborn: What Can He Do?   82
Reflexes   83

Perceptual Skills: What the Newborn Sees, Hears, and Feels 85

Motor Skills: Moving Around 85

Learning and Habituation 86

Social Skills 88

The Daily Life of Infants 89

Sleeping 90

Crying 91

Eating 92

• **Cultures and Contexts: *Cultural and Social Class Differences in Patterns of Breast-feeding, and Their Consequences* 92**

Individual Differences Among Babies 93

Health and Death in the First Year 93

Variations in Crying Patterns 94

Temperament 95

• **Cultures and Contexts: *Cultural Differences in Infant Temperament* 96**

Sex Differences 96

Summary 97

Key Terms 98

Suggested Readings 99

PART THREE: THE PHYSICAL CHILD   101

4   Physical Development   103

Four Reasons for Studying Physical Development 104

Basic Sequences and Common Patterns 105

Size and Shape 105

Bones 106

Muscles 107

Fat 108

Other Body Changes 108

Development of the Nervous System 108

Hormones 110

Development of Sexual Maturity 112

Sexual Development in Girls 113

Sexual Development in Boys 114

Using the Body: The Effects of Physical Changes on Behavior 115

Motor Development in the Early Years 115

• **The Real World: *Sports for Children* 117**

Adolescent Sexuality and Pregnancy 118

• **The Real World: *Which Teenage Girls Get Pregnant?* 119**

Big or Fast Versus Slow or Small: Some Individual Differences in Physical Development 120

Differences in Rate 120

Social Class and Racial Differences in Physical Development 123

Health and Illness in Childhood and Adolescence 123

• **Research Report: *An Australian Study Illustrating Sex Differences in Body Image Among Adolescents* 126**

• **The Real World: *How to Get Your Teenager to Stop Smoking, or Not to Start* 127**

Determinants of Growth: Explanations of Physical Development 128

Maturation 128

Heredity 128
Environmental Effects 129
Summary 131
Key Terms 132
Suggested Readings 133

5 Perceptual Development 134

Basic Sensory Skills 136
Seeing 136
Hearing 138
Other Senses 138
Complex Perceptual Skills: Preferences, Discriminations, and Patterns 140
Looking 140
• **Research Report:** *Langlois' Studies of Babies'*
Preferences for Attractive Faces 143
Listening 144
Cross-modal Transfer: Combining Information from Several Senses 146
Ignoring Perceptual Information: The Perceptual Constancies 147
The Object Concept 148
Object Perception 149
Object Permanence 150
• **Cultures and Contexts:** *Object Permanence in Zambian Infants 152*
Individual Differences in Perception: Speed and Efficiency 152
Explanations of Perceptual Development 153
Nativism Versus Empiricism 153
An Alternative Theoretical Approach: Eleanor Gibson's Views 155
Perceptual Development: A Summing-Up 156
Summary 157
Key Terms 158
Suggested Readings 158

PART FOUR: THE THINKING CHILD 161

6 Cognitive Development I: Cognitive Power 163

Three Views of Intelligence 164
Measuring Intellectual Power: IQ Tests and Other Measures 165
The First IQ Tests 165
Modern IQ Tests 167
Achievement Tests 167
• **The Real World:** *Performance Tests: A New Way to Measure School*
Achievement 169
Stability and Predictive Value of IQ Tests 169
Stability of Test Scores 170
What IQ Tests Predict 171
Limitations of Traditional IQ Tests 173
An Alternative View: Sternberg's Triarchic Theory of Intelligence 173
Explaining Differences in IQ 175
Evidence for the Importance of Heredity 175
Evidence for the Importance of Environment 175
Specific Family Characteristics and IQ 176

• **Cultures and Contexts:** *Maternal "Responsiveness" in Different Cultures*   **178**
School Experience and Special Interventions   179
Interaction of Heredity and Environment   181
Group Differences in IQ: Race and Sex Differences   182
Racial Differences in IQ   182
• **Cultures and Contexts:** *IQ Testing of Blacks in the Schools*   **183**
• **Cultures and Contexts:** *How Asian Teachers Teach Math and Science So Effectively*   **184**
Sex Differences in IQ   185
The Measurement of Intelligence: A Last Look   186
Summary   187
Key Terms   188
Suggested Readings   188

7   Cognitive Development II: Structure and Process   190

Piaget's Basic Ideas   191
The Processes of Adaptation   191
The Four Stages   193
• **The Real World:** *Young Children's Play*   **196**
• **Research Report:** *An Illustration of Classification Ability*   **198**
Lasting Influences from Piaget's Ideas   199
Cognitive Development in Infancy   200
Imitation   200
Memory in Infancy   202
Cognitive Development in the Preschool Period   203
Perspective Taking   204
Appearance and Reality   204
• **Cultures and Contexts:** *Understanding of Appearance and Reality in Other Cultures*   **205**
Theories of Mind   205
Other Aspects of Preschool Thought: Conservation and Classification   206
Overview of the Preschool Child's Thinking   207
Cognitive Development in the School-Age Child   208
Direct Tests of Piaget's Ideas   208
New Themes: Memory and Strategy Development   208
• **The Real World:** *Memory and the Child as Witness*   **211**
Expertise   212
Overview of the Thinking of the Schoolchild   213
Cognitive Development in Adolescence   213
Why Doesn't Every Teenager Use Formal Logic?   215
Preliminary Conclusions and Questions   215
Information Processing in Children   217
Developmental Approaches to Information Processing   217
Individual Differences in Information Processing   221
Putting the Three Approaches Together   222
Summary   223
Key Terms   225
Suggested Readings   225

8   The Development of Language   227

What Is Language Anyway?   228

Before the First Word: The Prelinguistic Phase   229
Early Perception of Language   230
Early Sounds   230
Early Gestures   231
• **Research Report:** *Early Gestural "Language" in the Children of Deaf Parents   231*
The First Words   232
The Naming Explosion   233
• **Cultures and Contexts:** *Early Words by Children in Many Cultures   234*
Later Word Learning   234
Speaking in Sentences: The Development of Grammar   235
First Sentences: 18 to 27 Months   235
Grammar Explosion: 27 to 36 Months   237
Complex Sentences: 30 to 48 Months   238
• **The Real World:** *Bilingual Children   239*
The Development of Word Meaning   239
Which Comes First, the Meaning or the Word?   239
Extending the Class   240
Constraints on Word Learning   241
Using Language: Communication and Self-Direction   243
Explaining Language Development   244
Imitation and Reinforcement   244
Newer Environmental Theories: Talking to the Child   245
• **Research Report:** *The Importance of Reading to the Child   245*
Innateness Theories   246
• **Cultures and Contexts:** *Universals and Variations in Early Language   247*
Constructivist Theories   247
Individual Differences in Language Development   248
Differences in Rate   248
Differences in Style   250
An Application of the Basic Knowledge: Learning to Read   252
Summary   253
Key Terms   255
Suggested Readings   255

PART FIVE: THE SOCIAL CHILD   257

9   **Personality Development: Alternative Views   259**

The Major Alternative Views of Personality   260
A Biological Approach: Temperament   261
Basic Propositions   261
The Evidence   263
• **Research Report:** *The Inheritance of Personality Patterns: Evidence from Adults   264*
• **Research Report:** *Temperament and Behavior Problems   266*
Strengths, Weaknesses, and Implications   266
Learning Approaches to Personality   267
Basic Propositions   267
• **The Real World:** *Applying Learning Principles at Home   268*
Evidence and Applications   269
Strengths, Weaknesses, and Implications   271

Psychoanalytic Approaches to Personality   273
Basic Propositions   273
Some Differences Between Freud and Erikson   274
Freud's Psychosexual Stages   274
Erikson's Psychosocial Stages   276
Other Psychoanalytic Views: Bowlby's Model of Attachment   279
Evidence and Applications   280
• **The Real World:** *The Effects of Divorce: One Test of Psychoanalytic Theory*   281
Strengths, Weaknesses, and Implications   281
A Tentative Synthesis   283
Summary   285
Key Terms   286
Suggested Readings   287

10 The Concept of Self in Children   288
The Concept of Self: Developmental Patterns   289
The First Step: The Subjective Self   289
The Second Step: The Objective Self   289
Self-concept at School Age and Adolescence   291
Identity in Adolescence   292
• **Cultures and Contexts:** *Ethnic Identity in Adolescence*   295
Individual Differences in the Self-concept: Self-esteem   296
Consistency of Self-esteem over Time   297
Consequences of Variations in Self-esteem   298
Origins of Differences in Self-esteem   298
The Self-concept: A Summing-Up   299
The Development of Gender and Sex-Role Concepts   300
Some Definitions   300
Developmental Patterns   301
• **Cultures and Contexts:** *Sex-Role Stereotypes Around the World*   303
Explaining Sex-Role Development   304
• **The Real World:** *Sex Stereotyping on TV*   307
Individual Differences in Sex-Typing and Sex-Role Stereotypes   307
Summary   310
Key Terms   312
Suggested Readings   312

11 The Development of Social Relationships   313
Attachment Theory: Concepts and Terminology   314
The Formation of the Parents' Bond to the Child   315
The Initial Bond   315
Meshing of Attachment Behaviors   316
• **The Real World:** *Child Abuse and Other Consequences of Failure of Bonding*   317
Father-Child Bonds   318
The Attachment Process: Child to Parent   319
• **Cultures and Contexts:** *Attachment in a Very Different Cultural System*   320
Attachments in the Preschool and Elementary-School Years   321
Parent-Child Relationships at Adolescence   322
Attachments to Mothers and Fathers   324
Individual Differences in the Quality of Infants' Attachments   325
Secure and Insecure Attachments   325

• **Cultures and Contexts:** *Secure and Insecure Attachments in Different Cultures* **327**
Horizontal Relationships: The Child's Relationships with Other Children 329
Developmental Changes in Peer Relationships 330
• **The Real World:** *Homosexuality Among Adolescents* **334**
Prosocial Behavior and Aggression 335
• **The Real World:** *Rearing Helpful and Altruistic Children* **337**
Individual Differences in Peer Relationships 338
Popularity and Rejection 338
Sex Differences 340
Summary 341
Key Terms 343
Suggested Readings 343

12 Thinking About Relationships: The Development of Social Cognition 344

Some General Principles and Issues 345
The Cognitive Side of Social Cognition 345
The Social Side of Social Cognition 346
• **Research Report:** *The Link Between a Child's Popularity and His Ability to Read Others' Intentions or Emotions* **346**
Thinking About Other People: Feelings and Qualities 346
Reading Others' Feelings 347
Describing Other People 351
Thinking About Relationships 352
Thinking About What People *Ought* to Do 354
Kohlberg's Stages of Moral Development 355
Eisenberg's Model of Prosocial Reasoning 361
Gilligan's Ethic of Caring 363
Social Cognition and Behavior 364
• **The Real World:** *Application of Kohlberg's Theory to Education* **367**
Social Cognition and General Cognitive Development 368
Summary 369
Key Terms 370
Suggested Readings 370

PART SIX: THE WHOLE CHILD 371

13 The Ecology of Development: The Child Within the Family System 373

Theoretical Approaches 374
Systems Theory 375
Bronfenbrenner's Ecological Approach 375
Dimensions of Family Interaction 377
The Emotional Tone of the Family 377
Responsiveness 377
• **Research Report:** *The Long-term Consequences of Hostility and Abuse* **378**
Methods of Control 378

- **The Real World:** *To Spank or Not to Spank*   **380**
Communication Patterns   *381*
Patterns or Styles of Child Rearing   381
A Research Example: The Work of Steinberg and Dornbusch   *383*
Adding Up What We Know About Parental Style   386
Other Aspects of Family Dynamics   386
The Child's Characteristics   *387*
Siblings: Treated the Same or Differently?   *387*
- **Cultures and Contexts: China's One-Child Policy**   **388**
The Parents' Characteristics   *389*
Family Structure: Divorce and Other Variations   *389*
- **Cultures and Contexts:** *The Benefits of Extended Families*   **392**
Some Exosystem Effects: The Impact of Parents' Work and Social Support on
   Family Functioning   395
The Impact of Parents' Jobs on the Family and the Child   *395*
- **The Real World:** *Softening the Effects of Divorce*   **396**
Social Support for Parents   *398*
Summary   398
Key Terms   400
Suggested Readings   400

14   Beyond the Family: The Impact of the Broader Culture   402

The Child's Experience of Day Care   403
Who Is Taking Care of the Children?   *403*
Effects of Day Care on Cognitive Development   *404*
Effects of Day Care on Personality   *406*
Effects of Day Care on Children's Attachment to Parents   *406*
- **Soap Box:** *The Need for a Family Policy in the United States*   **408**
The Impact of Schools   408
School and Self-Judgments   *409*
School Quality   *412*
Joining the Work World: The Impact of Jobs on Teenagers   414
Causal Effects or Self-selection?   *415*
The Impact of the Mass Media   416
- **Research Report:** *Family Viewing Patterns*   **417**
Positive Educational Effects of TV   *417*
Negative Effects of TV on Cognitive Skills   *417*
Television and Aggression   *418*
Macrosystem Effects: The Impact of the Larger Culture   420
Economic Variations: Social Class and Poverty   *421*
- **Soap Box: Children in Danger**   **424**
Ethnicity   *424*
The Culture as a Whole   *430*
Summary   432
Key Terms   433
Suggested Readings   433

15   Atypical Development   434

How Common Are Such Problems?   435
Developmental Psychopathology: A New Approach   436

• **Cultures and Contexts:** *Problem Behaviors Among Children in Kenya and Thailand* **437**
The Psychopathologies of Childhood 438
Externalizing Problems 438
Internalizing Problems: The Example of Depression 442
• **The Real World:** *Adolescent Suicide and Its Prevention* **444**
Vulnerability and Resilience 446
Developmental Psychopathology: A Reprise 446
Intellectually Atypical Development 447
Mental Retardation 447
Learning Disorders 450
Giftedness 452
Physically Atypical Development 454
The Deaf Child 454
The Blind Child 454
Sex Differences in Atypical Development 455
• **Research Report:** *Basic Attachments Between Blind Babies and Their Mothers* **456**
The Impact of an Atypical Child on the Family 458
A Final Point 459
Summary 459
Key Terms 461
Suggested Readings 461

16 Putting It All Together: The Developing Child 462

Transitions, Consolidations, and Systems 463
Age Periods in Perspective 463
From Birth to 18 Months 463
The Preschool Years: From 18 Months to 6 Years 466
The Elementary-School Years: From 6 to 12 468
Adolescence: From 12 to 20 470
Returning to Some Basic Questions 475
What Are the Major Influences on Development? 475
Does Timing Matter? 476
What Is the Nature of Developmental Change? 478
Individual Differences 480
A Final Point: The Joy of Development 481
Summary 483
Key Terms 484
Suggested Readings 484
Glossary 485
References 491
Credits 531
Name Index 533
Subject Index 545

TO THE STUDENT

Hello and welcome. Let me invite you into the study of a fascinating subject—children and their development. This is a bit like inviting you into my own home, since I have lived in the world of the study of children for a great many years. Unfortunately, I cannot know each of you individually, but by writing this book as if it were a conversation between you and me, I hope I can make the reading, and the studying of this subject, as personal a process as possible.

Because such personal involvement is one of my goals, you will find that I often write in the first person and that I have included a number of anecdotes about my own life. (One of the amusing side effects of this style of writing is that I often meet students from around the country who, having read this book, know all kinds of personal things about me and feel that they know me well, even though we have never met.)

Welcome, too, to the adventure of science. From the very first edition of this book, one of my goals has been to try to convey a sense of excitement about scientific inquiry. I want each of you to take away some feeling for the way psychologists think, the kinds of questions we ask, and the ways we go about trying to answer those questions. I also want you to take away with you some sense of the theoretical and intellectual ferment that is part of any science. Think of psychology as a kind of detective story. We discover clues after hard, often painstaking work; we make new guesses or hypotheses; and then we search for new clues to check on those hypotheses.

Of course, I also want you to come away from reading this book with a firm grounding of knowledge in the field. There is much that we do not yet know or understand. But a great many facts and observations have accumulated. These facts and observations will be of help to you professionally if you are planning (or are already in) a career with children—such as teaching, nursing, social work, medicine, or psychology; the information will also be useful to you as parents, now or in the future. There is much to be learned. In the midst of all that learning, though, I hope you enjoy the reading as much as I have enjoyed the writing.

Helen Bee

TO THE INSTRUCTOR

Working on a revision of a book that has been through as many editions as has *The Developing Child* is a task with many pleasant benefits. The basic structure is familiar and well established; some sections become more and more polished over time, and require little new work; editors have long since given up trying to make my writing style sound like anything other than what it is—personal and informal.

At the same time, there are also pitfalls and problems for any revision. One of the most acute is how to deal with the massive, continuous inflow of new data, new theories, new concepts. I subscribe to 20 journals, and read at least another dozen on a regular basis; my office overflows with new edited volumes. One cannot handle this new information simply by adding new sections to the text, edition after edition. One must cut and trim and reshape entire chapters to try to reflect the current state of our thinking and our knowledge. In the process, one must work very hard not to get stuck in old ruts, to use old structures or patterns of talking about a particular subject simply because they are familiar, rather than adopting a newer structure that works better with current data.

▶ Basic Goals

As I struggle with these dilemmas, I try to keep my basic goals in mind:

1. To find that difficult but essential balance among theory, research, and practical application
2. To make the study of child development relevant not just for psychologists but also for students in the many other fields in which this information is needed: nursing, medicine, social work, education, home economics
3. To keep all discussions as current as humanly possible, so that students can encounter the very latest thinking, the most recent research
4. To write to the student in as direct a way as possible, so that the book is more like a conversation than a traditional text; such a personal style need not clash with either theoretical clarity or research rigor, both of which I continue to work hard to achieve

▶ Additional Goals of the Seventh Edition

In this edition, two additional goals have guided my work.

A Cultural Perspective. First and most important, I wanted to enrich the book throughout with discussions of the impact of culture on development. In the past, I think many of us have operated with the implicit assumption that we were studying or searching for basic developmental processes that would be the same for all children in all cultures. In such a search, it doesn't matter which specific children you study. There may well be some such basic processes, and certainly we will go on attempting to uncover them. But it has become more and more evident that we will understand development fully only when we also understand the immensely complex way in which the basic biological and psychological processes are embedded in the family, the neighborhood, an ethnic group, and the larger culture. My central goal in this revision was to infuse the entire book with this perspective. Indeed, most of the major changes in the book flow directly from this goal:

- The chapter on the ecology of development (Chapter 13 in the sixth edition) has been divided into two chapters in this edition so that I could greatly expand the discussion of cultural and subcultural effects.
- The boxes have been divided into several subtypes, including one group called *cultures and contexts,* many of which are new in this edition.
- Throughout the text, I have drawn examples from research in countries other than the United States, and have repeatedly raised the question of cross-cultural validity.
- I have added a discussion of cross-cultural research in the methods section of Chapter 1.

Reducing the Length. My second specific goal in this edition has been, perhaps paradoxically, to reduce the overall length of the book. The first edition of *The Developing Child,* in 1975, ran 400 pages; the sixth edition was half again as long. Certainly there is more to talk about, and adding substantial coverage of culture expands the range still further. But I was convinced that I had to buck the trend of ever-longer texts. And despite the addition of another full chapter, this book *is* shorter. Even if, in the process of tightening, cutting, and choosing, I have omitted some of your favorite sections, the payoff for the student is worth all the effort. Students do not need an encyclopedic text; they need a text that lays out the issues clearly. That I think I have done.

▶ Other Changes in the Seventh Edition

The expansion of coverage of cultural comparisons throughout the text, including the addition of Chapter 14 (Beyond the Family: The Impact of Broader Cultures), is the largest single change in this edition. Naturally, every topic has also been updated, with new research examples and new discussions. One-fifth of all the citations, in fact, are 1992 or later. In addition, there are a number of changes in the pedagogy that may have significant implications for the way you teach from this text.

Critical Thinking Questions and Projects. In this edition, the *critical thinking questions* no longer appear at the end of the chapter, but instead appear in the margins at strategic points. Each chapter has 7 to 10 such questions. Some ask the students to pause and consider a point before going on, or they ask the reader to consider how the material may apply to his or her own life. In other cases, they ask the student to think about how one could design a piece of research to answer a particular question. In still other instances they ask theoretical questions, or ask the student to consider her or his own point of view on the subject at issue. These questions may be useful for provoking class discussion; it is also my hope that they will make the reading process more active and thus provide for deeper learning.

Another significant change is that the *student projects*, so long a feature of this text, no longer appear in the text itself, but instead are provided in the Instructor's Manual. This change was suggested by a number of instructors who felt they could maintain far better control over the process of obtaining informed consent for the projects if they were in the IM, rather than in the text itself. The Instructor's Manual includes three types of projects:

Fourteen *research projects*, each of which involves students' observing or testing one or more individual subjects of some age, such as listening to the language of a 2-year-old, or observing on a playground, or testing 5- or 6-year-olds with conservation problems.

Four *at home projects*, each of which involves some analysis that can be done at home, without having to locate individual subjects or obtain any informed consent, such as analyzing aggression or sex roles on TV programs.

Four *investigative projects*, each of which is designed for a single student or a small group of students to determine the availability of certain kinds of services within your own community, such as day-care options, birth options, or the like.

In order to make it possible for each instructor to select appropriate projects and to tailor the projects or the project instructions to his or her own needs, Harper-Collins will also provide a computer disk containing all the projects.

Boxes. The boxes have also changed in a number of ways: There are twice as many of them (54 versus 26 in the sixth edition); two-thirds of them contain entirely new material; they are shorter; and they have been subdivided into several types.

Cultures and contexts boxes focus on two aspects of cross-cultural or cross-ethnic group research: evidence showing that basic developmental processes are the *same* in children or adults of every culture, and research cataloging the variations in life experience or developmental patterns as a function of culture or subcultural differences. An example of the first type is a box on common patterns of early language development around the world in Chapter 8; an example of the second type is the discussion of China's one-child policy in Chapter 13.

Research reports are more detailed descriptions of individual research projects or highly specific research areas, such as Anne Streissguth's studies of fetal alcohol exposure (Chapter 2), or an Australian study of sex differences in body image among adolescence (Chapter 4), or a discussion of Kenneth Dodge's work on the social-cognitive processes of children with conduct disorders (Chapter 12).

The *real world* boxes all explore some practical application of research or theory, such as a discussion of how much weight a woman should gain in pregnancy (Chapter 2), or the child as a witness in court (Chapter 7), or how to rear helpful or altruistic children (Chapter 11).

Soap boxes are the last and least-common type. There are only two, both in Chapter 14, when I couldn't resist inserting my own views on some pressing social policy issue.

▶ Supplements

Naturally there are a variety of supplements available to the instructor and the student.

Instructor's Manual (ISBN:0-06-502171-1). I totally rewrote and expanded the IM for the sixth edition. For this edition, I have added new material for virtually every chapter. As in the version for the sixth edition, it lays out a whole course using *The Developing Child,* including the preplanning, a sample syllabus, the organization of lectures, and lecture material for each chapter. For those of you who have taught this course many times, much of the planning detail will not be needed, though I hope you may still find the lecture suggestions helpful. For those of you approaching the teaching of this course for the first time, the manual may be a timely form of assistance.

Included with the Instructor's Manual is also a set of transparency masters, some of which duplicate figures that appear in the text—to make it easier to review some figures in class. Many of the transparencies provide new data, designed to illustrate particular points you may cover in lecture. About a quarter of these are new for the seventh edition.

Finally, there is a new film/video guide included in the Manual.

Text Bank. Written by Darryl Dietrich of the College of St. Scholastica, the test bank contains approximately 2,000 questions, 60 percent of which are new for this edition. Each of these multiple-choice and essay questions is referenced to page number, topic, and skill. Some also appear in the student study guide or SuperShell II software tutorial and are referenced as such.

Study Guide (ISBN 0-06-502169-X). Also written by Darryl Dietrich, each chapter of the comprehensive study guide contains a brief chapter outline, learning objectives, a definition of key terms, lists of key concepts and individuals, and three practice tests containing multiple-choice, matching, and fill-in-the-blank questions with their answers.

SuperShell II Student Tutorial (ISBN 0-06-502447-8). Darryl Dietrich has written this interactive computerized tutorial for IBM and IBM-compatible computers. In addition to chapter outlines and glossary terms, SuperShell provides immediate correct answers to multiple-choice, true-false, and short-answer questions. All of the material is referenced to the text page. It contains material not found in the study guide and provides a running score for students.

Software. Two forms of software are available with the test bank. TestMaster Computerized Testing System is a flexible, easy-to-master computerized test bank that includes all the test items in the printed test bank. The TestMaster software allows instructors to edit existing questions and add their own items. It is available in IBM (ISBN 0-06-502173-8) or Macintosh (ISBN 0-06-502174-7) formats.

QuizMaster is a new software program, available to instructors, that allows students to take TestMaster-generated tests on computer. QuizMaster gives the students their scores right away as well as a diagnostic report at the end of the test. This report lets the students know what topics or objectives they may need to study to improve their scores. Test scores can be saved on disk, allowing instructors to keep track of scores for individual students, class sections, or whole courses.

▶ Some Bouquets

As always, my work has been greatly aided by the comments of excellent reviewers, who almost unanimously rejected one of my notions about how this seventh edition ought to be reorganized, but provided valuable insight and support for other changes. I want them to know that I listened!

Janette B. Benson, University of Denver

Marvin W. Berkowitz, Marquette University

Kenneth S. Bordens, Indiana University/Purdue University at Fort Wayne

Mary Lou Brotherson, St. Thomas University

Rebecca Bigler, The University of Texas at Austin

Joan Cook, County College of Morris

Joan Coughlin, Palo Alto College

Marlynn M. Griffin, Georgia Southern University

John Hensley, Tulsa Junior College

E. Romayne Hertweck, Mira Costa College

Harry W. Hoeman, Bowling Green State University

Robert J. Keller, Kishwaukee College

Eleanor A. Ryan, Elmhurst College

Nicholas R. Santilli, John Carroll University

George Vesprani, University of Cincinnati

Special bouquets, also, to the HarperCollins staff, who have been especially marvelous this time around. My acquisitions editor, Jill Lectka, has been efficient, flexible, and enormously helpful. Rosemary Hunter, the photo researcher, has once again done stellar work, on a tight schedule. She has also adapted wonderfully to a new way of working, sending me reams of photos to choose from at the beginning of the revision process, so that I could select photos as I went along. And when I needed a photo we didn't yet have, she was diligent in her search for something appropriate. I think you will agree that the quality of the photos in this edition reflects not only the advantages of this system, but also the quality of Rosemary's work.

The jewel in the crown has been Becky Kohn, developmental editor extraordinaire. It took a while for HarperCollins to persuade me of the usefulness of developmental editors, but now I could not get along without one. Or, more specifically, I could not get along without Becky. She has read and commented on every word I've written, answered endless questions, and dealt with a difficult time schedule with aplomb, humor, and always helpful support. I am immensely grateful, and hope I have told her so often enough.

Finally, I need to express my thanks to my husband, Carl de Boor, who spent two days converting all my old bibliographic lists to a format that could be read by a fancy new reference database program, and to my Madison friends, Diane Edie, Sarah Brooks, Tilli de Boor, and Miriam Schneider. They have all offered steady and loving support in myriad ways.

Helen Bee

THE DEVELOPING CHILD*

Seventh Edition

Helen L. Bee
Ph.D., Stanford University

ISBN 0-06-501737-4

Widely acknowledged as the most readable, personal, and engaging text in the field, *The Developing Child* combines research and practice to create a cohesive look at child development, from conception through adolescence. The text features a topical organization which reinforces core concepts, and cutting-edge research that is balanced with applications centered around real-life situations. *The Developing Child, 7e* also includes a unique chapter on atypical development; helpful boxes that amplify chapter material; and a summary chapter which reviews child development by age rather than by topic. The seventh edition emphasizes the role of culture in development, thereby offering a wide-ranging, contemporary assessment of the subject.

*A new text, *The Growing Child,* offers the same features as *The Developing Child* but in a chronological organization.

▶ The Impact of Schools

Another vitally important "microsystem," one experienced by virtually all children in every culture, is school. School begins at age 5 or 6 or 7, and in industrialized countries, typically continues through age 16 or older. During these 10 or more years, the child learns an enormous number of facts and develops new and much more complex forms of thinking, many of which I talked about in Chapter 7. In fact, we have good evidence from studies in many different countries—Mexico, Peru, Colombia, Liberia, Zambia, Nigeria, Uganda, Hong Kong, and others—that school experiences are *causally* linked to the emergence of such advanced cognitive skills (Stevenson & Chen, 1989; Stevenson et al., 1991). Children who do not attend schools not only do not learn many complex concepts and strategies, they are also not as good at generalizing a learned concept or principle to some new setting. So attending school helps children learn to think—precisely what it is intended to do.

But this is quite obviously not the only effect that school experience has on the child. During those 10 or 12 formative years, children hone their social skills in the context of peer contacts and establish crucial beliefs and attitudes about their own abilities, a central part of the self-scheme. These beliefs and attitudes then shape or limit the choices they will make later in childhood and adulthood.

School and Self-Judgments

Kindergarten and first-grade children seem to judge themselves and their abilities mostly on direct experience of their own success or failure. They pay relatively little attention to how well others do at a particular task; in fact the great majority will confidently tell you that they are the smartest kid in their class. But by third grade or so, children begin to compare themselves with others, and judge themselves accordingly. They notice whether their classmates finish a test sooner than they did, or whether someone else got a better grade or more corrections on his spelling paper. Teachers' behavior shows a similar change: In the first few grades, teachers emphasize effort and work habits. Gradually they begin

TABLE 14.1
Ideal Characteristics of a Day-Care Setting

- **A low teacher/child ratio:** For children younger than 2, the ratio should be no higher than 1:4; for 2-to-3-year-olds, ratios between 1:4 and 1:10 appear to be okay.
- **A small group size.** The smaller the number of children cared for together—whether in one room in a day-care center or in a home—the better for the child. For infants, a maximum of 6 to 8 per group appears best; for 1-to-2-year-olds, [...] older children, groups as large as 15 or 20 [...]

ROLE OF CULTURE IN DEVELOPMENT

A special focus of the book, this material tracks the similarities and differences in child development across cultures, broadening the scope of the field and making the material more meaningful to a wider variety of students.

amount, but that boys use their arm muscles more in various sports activities than girls do. Still, there does seem to be a basic hormonal difference as well, because we know that very fit girls and women are still not as strong as very fit boys and men.

Fat
Another major component of the body is fat, most of which is stored immediately under the skin. This *subcutaneous fat* is first laid down beginning at about 34 weeks prenatally, and has an early peak at about 9 months after birth (the so-called "baby fat"); the thickness of this layer of fat then declines until about age 6 or 7, after which it rises until adolescence.

Once again there is a sex difference in these patterns. From birth, girls have slightly more fat tissue than boys do, and this difference becomes gradually more marked during childhood. At adolescence, the difference grows still further. The size of the change is illustrated nicely in the results of a large study of Canadian teenagers (Smoll & Schutz, 1990). Between seventh and twelfth grades, the percentage of body weight made up of fat rose from 21.8 to 24 percent among girls in this group, but dropped from 16.1 to 14.0 percent among boys. So during and after puberty, proportions of fat rise among girls and decline among boys, while the proportion of weight that is muscle rises in boys and declines in girls.

Of course, as with muscle tissue, this sex difference in fat may be partially a life-style or activity-level effect; girls and women who are extremely athletic, such as long-distance runners or ballet dancers, typically have body fat levels that approximate those of the average boy. But if we compare equally fit boys and girls, boys have lower fat levels.

Other Body Changes
Puberty also brings important changes in other body organs. In particular, the heart and lungs increase considerably in size and the heart rate drops. Both of these changes are more marked for boys than for girls—another of the factors that increases the capacity for sustained effort for boys relative to girls. Before about age 12, boys and girls have similar physical strength, speed, and endurance, although even at these earlier ages, when there is a difference it favors the boys because of their lower levels of body fat. After puberty, boys have a clear advantage in all three (Smoll & Schutz, 1990).

Development of the Nervous System
Growth in height and weight involves changes you can see. Even the changes in muscles, bones, and fat can be detected fairly easily in the child's longer legs, greater strength, or softness or leanness of body. But there are two enormously important types of developmental changes in the body that are not so easy to per-

Suppose you were a member of a local school board, faced with a decision about whether to have teenage boys and girls play on the same competitive teams, such as volleyball, soccer, or baseball. Given what you have read so far, how would you decide the issue, and why?

Figure 7.2
This 3-month-old baby in one of Rovee-Collier's memory experiments will quickly learn to kick her foot in order to make the mobile move. And she will remember this connection between kicking and the mobile several days later. (*Source*: Rovee-Collier, 1993, page 131.)

the setting in which the observation occurred (the laboratory), suggests that Piaget was simply wrong about when we are first able to use some kind of internal representation to remember actions and events.

Memory in Infancy
The same point emerges from Carolyn Rovee-Collier's fascinating studies of memory in very young infants (1993). She has used an ingenious variation of an operant conditioning procedure to demonstrate that babies as young as 3 months of age can remember particular objects and their actions with those objects over periods of as long as a week. And if you "remind" them in between times, they can remember their earlier actions over six weeks.

Rovee-Collier first hangs an attractive mobile over the baby's crib, and watches to see how the baby responds. In particular, she is interested in how often the baby normally kicks his legs while looking at the mobile. Then after three minutes of observation, she attaches a string from the mobile to the baby's leg, as you can see in Figure 7.2, so that each time the baby kicks his leg, the mobile moves. Babies quickly learn to kick repeatedly in order to make this interesting new thing happen. Within three to six minutes, 3-month-olds double or triple their kick rates, showing that learning clearly occurred. She then tests the baby's memory of this learning by coming back some days later, hanging the same mobile over the crib, and counting the rate of the baby's kicks without attaching the string to his foot. If the baby remembers the previous occasion, he should kick at

PHOTO PROGRAM

Carefully chosen to illustrate specific topics throughout the book, the photos give the text a streamlined, visually dynamic presentation.

Figure 2.1
The moment of conception when a single sperm has pierced the shell of the ovum.

Most parents find the nine months of a pregnancy to be a time of delighted anticipation. It is also a time in which the genetic patterning for the child (the genotype) is established, and in which complex maturational sequences unfold.

harmful. Even more, I was struck by how long the list of "don'ts" had become, and how hard it is for a conscientious woman to be sure of what is okay and what is not.

So what do we now know? What does the list of dos and don'ts look like today? It's an important practical question for any of you who plan to be parents, and to answer it I need to explore what we know about the basic processes of development from conception to birth, as well as what we have learned about what can interfere with those basic processes. And of course beyond this practical issue, it is also essential for any complete understanding of child development that we begin our search at the beginning—at conception and pregnancy.

Conception

The first step in the development of a single human being is that moment of conception when a single sperm cell from the male pierces the wall of the ovum of the female—a moment captured stunningly in the photo in Figure 2.1. Ordinarily, a woman produces one **ovum** (egg cell) per month from one of her two ovaries. This occurs roughly midway between two menstrual periods. If it is not fertilized, the ovum travels from the ovary down the **fallopian tube** toward the **uterus**, where it gradually disintegrates and is expelled as part of the next menstruation.

But if a couple has intercourse during the crucial few days when the ovum is in the fallopian tube, one of the millions of sperm ejaculated as part of each male

TABLE 8.3 Sentences Examples of Daniel's Stage I and Stage II	
Stage I (simple) sentences (age 21 months)	Stage II (more complex) sentences (age 23 months)
A bottle	A little boat
Broke-it	Doggies here
Here (the) bottle	Give you the book
Hi daddy	It's a boy
Horse doggie	It's a robot
Broke it	Little box there
Kitty cat	No book
Poor Daddy	Oh cars
That monkey	That flowers
Want bottle	Where going?

Source: Reprinted by permission of the publisher. D. Ingram, Early patterns of grammatical development, in R. E. Stark (Ed.), *Language behavior in infancy and early childhood*, Tables 6 and 7, pp. 344–345. Copyright 1981 by Elsevier Science Publishing Co., Inc.

EXHIBITS/TABLES

Exhibits and Tables conveniently organize key chapter concepts for quick and easy comprehension and review.

meanings in their early word combinations, and there does not seem to be a fixed order in which these meanings or constructions are acquired, but all children appear to express at least several of these patterns in their earliest, simplest sentences (Maratsos, 1983).

Grammar Explosion: 27 to 36 months
Just as there is a vocabulary explosion following an early, slow beginning, so there is also a grammar explosion following these first simple sentences. Beginning some time in the third year, most children rather quickly add many of the inflections and function words, a process Roger Brown refers to as stage II grammar. Within a few months, children use plurals, past tenses, auxiliary verbs such as *is* or *does*, prepositions, and the like. They also begin to create negative sentences, and to ask questions with the auxiliary verb in the correct order. You can get a feeling for the sound of the change from Table 8.3, which lists some of the sentences of a little boy named Daniel, recorded by David Ingram (1981). The left-hand column lists some of Daniel's sentences at about 21 months of age, when he was still using the simplest forms; the right-hand column lists some of his sentences only 2 1\2 months later (age 23 to 24 months), when he had shifted into higher gear.

Adding Inflections.   You can get some sense from the table that Daniel did not add all the inflections at once. In this sample, he uses only a few, such as the *s* for plural, although there is the beginning of a negative construction in "no book" and the beginning of a question form in "where going?" although he does not yet have the auxiliary verb added to the question. Within each language community, children seem to add inflections and more complex word orders in

"CULTURE AND CONTEXT" BOXES

These boxes focus on two aspects of cross-cultural or cross-ethnic group research: evidence showing that basic developmental processes are the same in children of every culture, and research cataloging the variations in life experience or developmental patterns as a function of cultural or subcultural differences.

CULTURES AND CONTEXTS
Early Words by Children in Many Cultures

Children in every culture studied by linguists have shown the same tendency to learn words for people or things before they learn words for actions or other parts of speech. Here are some (translated) samples from the very early vocabularies of one child from each of four cultures, all studied by Dedre Gentner (1982).

German boy	English girl	Turkish girl	Chinese girl
Some of the words for people or things			
Mommy	Mommy	Mama	Momma
Papa	Daddy	Daddy	Papa
Gaga	babar	Aba	grandmother
baby	baby	baby	horse
dog	dog	food	chicken
bird	dolly	apple	uncooked rice
cat	kitty	banana	cooked rice
milk	juice	bread	noodles
ball	book	ball	flower
nose	eye	pencil	wall clock

German boy	English girl	Turkish girl	Chinese girl
moon	moon	towel	lamp
Total percentage of naming words:			
67%	69%	57%	59%
Some of the nonnaming words			
cry	run	cry	go
come	all gone	come	come
eat	more	put on	pick up
sleep	bye-bye	went pooh	not want
want	want	want	afraid
no	no	hello	thank you

Isn't it impressive how very similar these early vocabularies are? Of course there are some variations, but all these children had names for Mommy and Daddy, for some other relative, for other live creatures, and for food. All but the Chinese child had words for toys or clothes. All four had also learned more naming words than any other type, with very similar proportions. They don't know the *same* words, but the pattern is remarkably similar.

been found in studies of children learning other languages as well, as you can see in the cultures and contexts box.

However, just as all children do not show a vocabulary spurt, all children do not follow a noun-before-verb pattern either. Katherine Nelson (1973) first noticed that some toddlers use what she called an **expressive style.** For them, most early words are linked not to objects but to social relationships. They often learn pronouns (*you, me*) early, and use many more of what Nelson calls "personal-social" words, such as *no, yes, want,* or *please.* Their early vocabulary may also include some multiword strings, like *love you* or *do it* or *go away.* This is in sharp contrast to the children who use what Nelson calls a **referential style,** whose early vocabulary is made up predominantly of nominals.

I'll talk further about such style differences at the end of the chapter. For now, I only want to point out that while nounlike terms are the most common early words, they are not the only ones, and some children use them relatively infrequently in the early months.

Later Word Learning

During the preschool years, there is yet another spurt in vocabulary growth, even more astonishing in speed. Children in this age range add as many as 5 to 10 words *a day.* They can accomplish this feat because at this point they seem to pay attention to words in whole groups, such as words that name objects in a single

THE REAL WORLD
Sex Stereotyping on TV

In modern cultures, one obvious source for children to acquire information for their sex-role schemas is through TV. From early preschool age, children in the United States spend an average of two to four hours a day in the presence of a TV set that is running. (I put it that way because we don't know how much of the time children actually *watch* the moving image.) Before they begin school, children have already been exposed to thousands of hours of TV; by the time they are 18, the average child has spent more time in front of a TV set than in a classroom (Calvert & Huston, 1987). How are men and women portrayed in all those TV programs and commercials?

Highly stereotypically (Huston, 1983; Huston et al., 1990). Males outnumber females by two to one or three to one on virtually every kind of programming except commercials, but in the latter, the "voice-over" is nearly always male. Women are more often shown at home or in romantic situations; men more often appear in work settings, with cars, or playing sports. Men are shown solving problems, being more active, aggressive, and independent. Women are shown as sex objects, or showing emotions, and are more passive and deferential. Females generally play the "handmaiden" roles—they hand the male character his coat, type his reports, and listen to his troubles.

A continuous exposure to these stereotyped males and females does seem to have at least a small effect on child's vision of men and women and their roles. In two longitudinal studies, Morgan (1982; 1987) has found that among elementary and high school students, those who watched a lot of TV at the beginning

of the study reported more traditional sex-role stereotyping a year later. They were more likely, for example, to think that household chores should be done by women than by men. Even more persuasive is an experiment by Emily Davidson (Davidson, Yasuna, & Tower, 1979), who deliberately exposed some 5- and 6-year-olds to highly sex-stereotyped cartoons. Those who had seen such cartoons, compared to control children who had seen neutral cartoons, later gave more stereotyped answers to questions about the qualities of men and women.

At a more subtle level, Aletha Huston and her colleagues, in several studies (Huston et al., 1984) have found that toy commercials aimed at boys, and those aimed at girls, are simply designed differently. Boys' commercials are fast, sharp, and loud—lots of quick cuts, loud music, activity. Girls' commercials are gradual, soft, and fuzzy. They have camera fades and dissolves rather than sharp cuts, and use softer background music. Children as young as first grade notice these differences, too. They can watch a commercial of some nonstereotyped toy and tell you whether the *style* of the commercial is suited to a boys' or girls' toy.

TV is clearly not the only source of information children have about sex roles, nor is it likely to be the most crucial source. We know that children growing up without TV nonetheless acquire sex-role stereotypes. Yet TV does have an impact on children's ideas about men and women. Current TV programming appears to foster more stereotyped (and thus inaccurate) sex-role concepts in children than would occur normally.

"THE REAL WORLD" BOXES

Each "Real World" Box explores a practical application of research or theory.

order, for rules that help to make sense of their experiences. And a rule about "what men do" and "what women do" is a helpful schema for children. Like grammatical rules, children first apply this new rule too rigidly, and then later learn the exceptions. But the rule-learning process seems to be a natural one.

Gender schema theory is surely not the last word. It, too, has limitations. For example, when researchers have measured preschool children's understanding of gender and then looked at how sex-typed their behavior is, they often find only very weak connections (Bussey & Bandura, 1992; Martin, 1993). So 3-year-olds who show the clearest preferences for same-sex playmates are not necessarily the same ones who have the most advanced cognitive understanding of gender. Ultimately, some combination of social learning theory and gender schema theory may be devised that will handle the data better.

Individual Differences in Sex-Typing and Sex-Role Stereotypes

The developmental patterns I have been describing seem to hold for virtually all children. Nonetheless, as usual, we also see quite a lot of variation from child to child in the rigidity of the rule they develop, or in the sex-typing of their behav-

"RESEARCH REPORT" BOXES

"Research Reports" contain detailed descriptions of individual research projects or highly specific research areas.

RESEARCH REPORT
The Inheritance of Personality Patterns: Evidence from Adults

In the past decade, a number of methodologically careful new studies of adult twins have repeatedly demonstrated that identical twins are more like one another than are fraternal twins on a whole host of measures of personality.

For example, Robert Plomin and his colleagues (Plomin et al., 1988) have taken advantage of the existence of an amazingly extensive and up-to-date twin registry in Sweden that includes 25,000 pairs of twins born between 1886 and 1958. From this set, they were able to identify 99 pairs of identical twins and 229 pairs of fraternal twins reared together, and could then compare these with similar groups of twins reared together. On measures of emotionality and activity, identical twins were more similar than fraternal twins, whether they had been reared together or not. The results were less clear for sociability.

A smaller but much more famous study in the United States is the Minnesota Twin Study (Bouchard, 1984; Lykken et al., 1992; Tellegen et al., 1988)—a study that has been the subject of a great many articles in the popular press. These researchers have been particularly interested in identical twins reared apart, frequently arranging for them to meet one another for the first time. On standard personality tests they find the now-familiar pattern: identical twins are simply much more like one another than are fraternal twins, even when the identical twins did not grow up together. This was true on measures such as positive and negative emotionality (which may be similar to Buss and Plomin's dimension of emotionality), but also on less-obvious measures, such as

a sense of "social potency" or a sense of well-being. Even a measure of "traditionalism"—an affinity for traditional values and a strong allegiance to established authority—shows slightly higher correlations among identical than among fraternal twins.

What has intrigued the popular press much more, though, are the less-precise but far more striking descriptions of the similarities in clothing preferences, interests, posture and body language, speed and tempo of talking, favorite jokes, and hobbies in pairs of identical twins reared apart:

> One male pair who had never previously met arrived in England sporting identical beards, haircuts, wire-rimmed glasses and shirts. . .One pair had practically the same items in their toilet cases, including the same brand of cologne and a Swedish brand of toothpaste. . .[One pair] had the same fears and phobias. Both were afraid of water and had adopted the same coping strategy: backing into the ocean up to their knees. (Holden, 1987, p. 18)

It is difficult to imagine what sort of genetic process could account for similar preferences in hairstyles or for a particular brand of toothpaste. But we can't merely dismiss the results because they are hard to explain. At the very least, these findings certainly point to strong genetic components in many of the elements of personal style and emotional responsiveness that temperament researchers are trying to identify and track in children.

TABLE 9.2 Similarity of Identical and Fraternal Twins on Buss and Plomin's Temperament Dimensions		
	Twin correlations	
Temperament scale	Identical	Fraternal
Emotionality	.63	.12
Activity	.62	−.13
Sociability	.53	−.03

Source: Buss & Plomin, 1984, Table 9.2, p. 122.

1990) have reported correlations in the range of .60 between a measure of behavioral inhibition in children aged 2 to 5 and a series of physiological measures, such as muscle tension, heart rate, dilation of the pupil of the eye, and the chemical composition of both urine and saliva, all of which strongly suggests that temperament is not simply a set of learned habits.

SOAP BOX
The Need for a Family Policy in the United States

In a recent paper, Louise Silverstein (1991) makes a number of compelling points:

> In 1990, fewer than 7% of American families reflected the two-parent model of husband as breadwinner and mother as homemaker (Braverman, 1989). Thus, the question of whether mothers should work is essentially irrelevant to modern family life. Mothers do work, and "child care is now as essential to family life as the automobile and the refrigerator" (Scarr et al., 1990, p. 26).

> However, the United States remains the only one of 75 industrialized nations that does not have a government-sponsored family policy that provides some form of paid maternity benefits, parental leave, and subsidized child care. (p. 1025)

Silverstein's central argument is that psychologists have contributed to this lack of official support for the modern family by continuing to focus so much research attention on the question of the potential ill effects of mothers' employment, or of day care.

Instead, she argues, we must devote our research attention to the "negative consequences of the lack of affordable, government-subsidized, high-quality programs" (p. 1030).

A panel convened by the National Academy of Sciences to study child care in the United States echoes these concerns. Their basic conclusions include the following:

> 1. Existing child care services in the United States are inadequate to meet current and likely future needs of children, parents, and society as a whole. . . . The general accessibility of high-quality, affordable child care has immediate and long-term implications for the health and well-being of children, parents, and society as a whole. . . .

> 2. Of greatest concern is the large number of children who are presently cared for in settings that do not protect their health and safety and do not provide appropriate developmental stimulation. (Hayes et al., 1990, p. xii)

Assuming that these statements are accurate, what do you think we ought to do about it? What new policies or programs would we need?

"SOAP BOXES"

In the text's two "Soap Boxes", featured in Chapter 14, the author expresses her personal views on pressing social policy issues.

---

pears to, as suggesting that these children are "emotionally insecure" (p. 69). Others have concluded that there may indeed be a link between some aspect of day care and security of attachment, but that we simply don't yet know what the link might be (Lamb et al., 1992).

One can also argue that Belsky is asking the wrong question. For the vast majority of families, the question is not "Should I put my child in day care?" but rather "Given that I have to work to help support my family, how do I find good-quality, affordable care for my child?"

We do know that the quality of the child's care makes a difference. Indeed, most of the positive outcomes of day care I have been describing are found *only* in good-quality programs, while inconsistent care, or poor-quality custodial care, can be actively detrimental to the child. In Table 14.1, I've listed the characteristics of good-quality programs, a list that might serve as a starting point in your evaluation of alternatives if and when you face this choice with your own children.

▷ The Impact of Schools

Another vitally important "microsystem," one experienced by virtually all children in every culture, is school. School begins at age 5 or 6 or 7, and in industrialized countries, typically continues through age 16 or older. During these 10 or more years, the child learns an enormous number of facts and develops new and much more complex forms of thinking, many of which I talked about in Chapter 7. In fact, we have good evidence from studies in many different countries—Mex-

PRENATAL DEVELOPMENT

2

Conception

The Basic Genetics of Conception
   Dominant and Recessive Genes
   Males and Females
   Twins and Siblings
   Genotypes and Phenotypes

Development from Conception to Birth
   The Germinal Stage: From Conception to Implantation
   The Embryonic Stage
   The Fetal Stage

Prenatal Sexual Differentiation

An Overview of Prenatal Development

Genetic Errors
   Single-Gene Defects
   • *The Real World:* Prenatal Diagnosis of Genetic Errors

Teratogens: Diseases and Drugs
   Diseases of the Mother

• *The Real World:* Rh Factor: Another Type of Genetic Problem
   Drugs Taken by the Mother
• *Research Report:* Streissguth's Study of Prenatal Alcohol Exposure
   Other Teratogens

Other Influences on Prenatal Development
   • *The Real World:* Weight Gain and Diet During Pregnancy

An Overview of Risks and Long-Term Consequences of Prenatal Problems

Sex Differences in Prenatal Development

Social Class Differences in Prenatal Development

Summary

Key Terms

Suggested Readings

At a family gathering a decade or so ago, my then four-months-pregnant sister-in-law Nancy complained of a headache. Having heard warnings about the possible ill effects of various kinds of drugs during pregnancy, she was very reluctant to take any aspirin. We tried all the usual home remedies (shoulder rubs, warm baths, herb tea) but the headache persisted. Finally she took a nonaspirin pain medicine, which did the trick.

This incident brought home to me very clearly just how sensitized most women are today to the various hazards (*teratogens*) during pregnancy, including ....d by Nancy's determination to avoid doing anything

In the midst of a recession, Sam McKenzie's company had to lay off workers, and six months ago Sam, aged 35, lost his job as a machinist. Sam's wife Edith still has her job as a clerk in the local grocery store, but Sam's unemployment compensation is running out. Money is tight. Sam has tried hard to persuade himself that these things happen to people, but mostly he blames himself and his lack of education. He also finds it very difficult to have to rely so much on his wife's income, since he thinks it is the man's job to support the family. And he most definitely does not think it is a man's job to get the kids off to school or put the meat loaf in the oven at 5:00 so that dinner will be ready when his wife comes home from work. Over the months, he has become increasingly gloomy and irritable. He drinks more, has trouble sleeping, and he and Edith have been arguing more. The kids have also felt the change—not just in the things they can't buy now, but in the whole atmosphere at home. Sam snaps at them often and most of the time is much stricter with them—though there are times, too, when he seems to pay no attention at all. The kids also notice that he hugs them a lot less. David, who is 13, has started yelling back much more frequently than he used to, and has been spending more and more time with his school buddies. Nine-year-old Jennifer has reacted differently: she's become quite withdrawn and depressed, and no longer spends much time with her friends. Both the children have had a lot more colds and other sicknesses than usual, too.

What the McKenzie family has experienced is fairly typical of families when the father loses his job (Crouter & McHale, 1993). It also illustrates two important points—points that I made in a preliminary way in Chapter 1, but that may have gotten a bit lost in all the intervening chapters.

First, to understand the child's development we must go beyond the child himself and whatever intrinsic developmental patterns may exist; we must go beyond the dyad of child and mother, or child and father. We need to look at the whole ecology of development—at the pattern of interaction within the family, and at the influences of the larger culture on that family. David and Jennifer McKenzie have been affected by Sam's job loss both directly and indirectly, and some of those effects may be very long-lasting. Glen Elder's studies (1974; 1981; 1984), for example, show that some children whose families experienced major financial upheavals during the Great Depression in the 1930s continued to show the emotional scars well into adult life.

Second, the McKenzie's story illustrates that there is a *system* of influences at work. Sam's job loss was not just an economic event. It affected Sam's attitudes, his self-esteem, his behavior, and it reverberated through the entire family system, affecting every other person and every relationship.

In th.... ....I want to explore this larger psychological ....ent occurs....

**Key Terms take inventory of
important terminology in each
chapter, while Annotated
Suggested Readings present
lists of works related to chapter
material, giving students an
opportunity to extend their study
and build their knowledge.**

18. Some difficulties in prenatal development can produce permanent disabilities
or deformities, such as Down syndrome or deafness from rubella. Other lasting problems, such as learning disabilities, may also be caused by teratogens.
But many disorders associated with prenatal problems can be overcome if the
child is reared in a supportive and stimulating environment.

19. Sex differences in prenatal development are few in number. Boys are slower
to develop, bigger at birth, and more vulnerable to most forms of prenatal
stress.

20. Nearly all potential problems of prenatal development are more common
among poor women, but these increased risks can be greatly reduced with
good diet and adequate prenatal care.

▶ **Key Terms**

alpha-fetoprotein
test (15)

amniocentesis
(19)

amnion (21)

autosomes (27)

axon (19)

chorionic villus
sampling (29)

chromosome (15)

dendrites (26)

deoxyribonucleic
acid (22)

Down syndrome
(15)

embryo (19)

fallopian tube
(28)

fetal alcohol
syndrome (FAS)
(15)

fetus (22)

gametes (25)

gene (15)

genotype (15)

glial cells (21)

neuron (18)

ovum (15)

phenotype (24)

placenta (19)

rubella (24)

sex chromosomes
(15)

synapse (19)

ultrasound (22)

uterus (22)

▶ **Suggested Readings**

The Boston Women's Health Collective. (1992). *The new our bodies, ourselves: A book by and for
women.* New York: Simon & Schuster.

This recent revision of a popular book is really focused on the adult female's body, rather than on
prenatal development, but it has an excellent discussion of health during pregnancy. This is a
strongly feminist book; some of you may not be entirely in sympathy with all of the political
views included. But it is nonetheless a very good compact source of information on all facets of
pregnancy and childbirth.

Nightingale, E. O., & Goodman, M. (1990). *Before birth: Prenatal testing for genetic disease.* Cambridge, MA: Harvard University Press.

---

sured when the baby was 5 to 10 days old, and the security of the child's attachment to the mother was measured when the child was 12 months old. We might
expect that irritable babies would be more likely to be insecurely attached, merely because they are more difficult to care for. In fact, Crockenberg found a small
effect of this kind (see Table 9.5). But Crockenberg didn't stop there. She also
measured the level of the mother's social support—the degree to which she had
family and friends who were sufficiently helpful to assist her in dealing with the
strains of a new child or other life changes she might be experiencing. The results
of the study show that insecure attachment in the child was most likely when the
mother had *both* an irritable infant *and* low levels of support. If the baby was irritable but the mother had good support, the child's attachment nearly always
developed securely. Only when two difficult conditions occurred together did a
poor outcome result for the child.

In a later study, Crockenberg (1987) found that a higher level of anger and
noncompliant behavior was common in toddlers who had been irritable as infants
and whose mothers were angry and punitive toward them. Furthermore, such
angry and punitive behavior in the mother was more likely if the mother had
experienced rejection in her own childhood, and if she experienced little support
from her partner. We are dealing here with a *system* of effects.

Finally, I have included arrow 8 in the diagram to underline the *transactional*
elements of the system. Once the child's unique pattern of behaviors and attitudes
(personality) is formed, this affects the environment she will encounter, the experiences she will choose, and the responses of the people around her, which in turn
affect her behavior (Scarr & McCartney, 1983; Sroufe et al., 1993).

No doubt even this fairly complex system underestimates the intricacy of the
process of personality development in the child. Most of our research does not yet
encompass all the pieces of the puzzle. But the very fact that developmental psychologists are turning toward such complex models seems to me to be a very good
thing. Development *is* this complex, and we will not be able to describe it or
explain it until we begin to examine and try to measure all these separate forces.

▶ **Summary**

1. The word *personality* refers to the unique, individual, relatively enduring pattern of relating to others and responding to the world that is characteristic of
each individual. *Personality* is a more inclusive term than *temperament*; the
latter refers primarily to inborn style of response to the environment.

2. The origins of personality differences have been described in three distinct
theoretical approaches: temperament theories (a primarily biological approach), learning theories, and psychoanalytic theories.

3. Temperament theory proposes that each child is born with innately determined patterns or styles of reacting to people and objects. These patterns
shape the child's interactions with the world, and affect others' responses to
the child.

**Chapter Summaries review the
main topics covered in each
chapter, helping to reinforce
students' comprehension.**

BASIC QUESTIONS

1

Nature and Nurture: An Ancient Debate

The Nature Side of the Equation
 Inborn Biases and Constraints
 Maturation
 Behavior Genetics
 • *Research Report:* How Do Behavior Geneticists Identify Genetic Effects?

The Nurture Side of the Equation
 Models of Environmental Influence
 The Timing of Experience
 Internal Models of Experience
 The Ecological Perspective

Interactions of Nature and Nurture
 Vulnerability and Resilience

The Nature of Developmental Change
 Stages and Sequences

Theories of Development
 Biological Theories
 Learning Theories

Psychoanalytic Theories
Cognitive-Developmental Theories
Contrasting the Theories

Finding the Answers: Research on Development

Research Design
 Cross-sectional Designs
 Longitudinal Designs
 Cross-cultural or Cross-Context Designs
 • *Cultures and Contexts:* An Example of a Cross-cultural Comparison Study
 Experimental Designs

Research Methods
 • *Research Report:* Ethical Issues in Research on Development

Research Analysis
 A Final Word

Summary

Key Terms

Suggested Readings

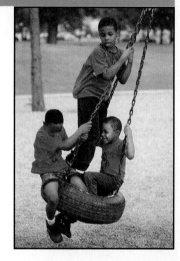

Each summer, I spend several months at an unusual camp in the state of Washington, where adults of all ages as well as families with young children come each year to live for a short time in a kind of temporary community. Because many of the same people come back year after year, bringing their children (and often later their grandchildren), I see these growing children in once-a-year snapshots. When a family arrives, I am quite naturally struck by how much the children have changed, and I find myself saying to the kids, "Good grief, you've grown a foot," or "Last time I saw you, you were only this big." (I say these things, even remembering full well how much I hated it when people said these things to me at the same age. Of *course* I had grown. And because I was always taller than anyone my age, I didn't like to be reminded of this peculiarity.)

At the same time, I am also struck by the consistency in these children from year to year. Sweet-tempered young Malcolm and ebullient Crystal always give me many hugs; Malcolm's older brother Elliot, far shier, still gazes at me silently from some measured distance. He warms up as the days go by, but his behavior is quite different from his brother's, and remains noticeably constant from year to year, just as 13-year-old Stacey remains dreamy and a little slow-moving. Each of these children has a particular style, a particular set of skills, a particular personality, and these qualities appear to be at least somewhat consistent from year to year, perhaps even into adult life.

These simple examples illustrate one of the key points about human development: it involves both change and continuity. To understand development, we will need to look at both. Equally important, we need to understand which developmental changes, and which types of consistency or continuity, are shared by individuals in all cultures, and which are unique to a given culture, to a group within a culture, or to a particular individual. For example, you probably know that in the first weeks after they are born, babies do not sleep through the night; they wake every two hours or so to be fed. But by about 6 weeks of age, most babies are able to string several two-hour stretches together, and begin to show something approximating a day/night sleeping pattern (Bamford et al., 1990). That certainly sounds like a basic biological change, one that would occur pretty much regardless of the child's environment. But according to one study (Super & Harkness, 1982), babies in rural Kenya who are carried about by their mothers in a sling all day and fed on demand at night do not show any shift toward a nighttime sleep pattern over the first eight months of life. So what seems like a universal, biological process turns out not to be universal at all. It is affected by culture—by attitudes and values expressed through variations in care and handling. This issue of what is universal and what is not will be a persistent theme.

This example also illustrates the point that to understand how development works, we will need to explore both *nature* and *nurture,* both biology and culture, and how they interact to explain both consistency and change. Throughout these chapters, I will be trying to sort out the relative impacts of nature and nurture in each domain of development and at each age. But that task will be a great deal easier if you have at least a grounding in some of the basic concepts and theories that form the framework for such an analysis. So let me take you on a quick tour of current ideas about nature and nurture, and an equally brief look at the major theoretical approaches to explaining both consistency and individuality in development.

◗ Nature and Nurture: An Ancient Debate

The argument about nature versus nurture, also referred to as heredity versus environment or nativism versus empiricism, is one of the oldest and most central theoretical issues within philosophy as well as psychology. When asked by developmental psychologists, the question is basically whether a child's development is governed by a pattern built in at birth, or whether it is shaped by experiences af-

In many parts of Kenya, babies are carried in slings all day, and allowed to nurse on demand at night. This cultural pattern, quite different from what we see in most Western societies, seems to have an effect on the baby's sleep/wake cycle.

ter birth. Historically, the nativist/nature side of the controversy was represented principally by Plato and (in the more modern era) René Descartes, both of whom believed that at least some ideas were innate. On the other side of the philosophical argument was found a group of British philosophers called "empiricists," such as John Locke, who insisted that at birth the mind is a blank slate, in Latin a *tabula rasa*. All knowledge, they argued, is created by experience.

No developmental psychologist today would cast this issue in such black-and-white terms. We agree that a child's development is a product of some interaction of nature and nurture. In every culture, puberty occurs sometime between roughly age 9 and age 16, but the timing is affected by such environmental factors as diet. Some temperamental patterns may be inherited, but they can be and are modified by the parents' style of caregiving. And so on. No aspect of development is entirely one or the other. Nonetheless, there is still a good deal of disagreement about the relative importance of these two factors.

Because of this disagreement, and because it is easier to introduce the various concepts separately, I'll begin by talking about each of the two halves of this dichotomy, saving for later the question of how nature and nurture interact.

▶ The Nature Side of the Equation

Inborn Biases and Constraints

Descartes' notion of inborn ideas has not totally disappeared from our thinking. The most modern version of it is the concept of "inborn biases," sometimes expressed as "constraints" on development. The argument is not that infants are born knowing many things, or that they have built-in concepts, but rather that the baby is "programmed" in some fashion to pay more attention to certain kinds of information, or to respond in particular ways to objects. For example, Dan Slobin (1985b), who studies early language learning, proposes that children are born with certain "operating principles" that govern the way they listen to and try to make sense out of the flow of sounds coming at them. One such principle, according to Slobin, is the tendency to pay special attention to the beginnings and ends of strings of sounds. Similarly, in the study of infants' perceptual skills a number of researchers and theorists have emphasized built-in "rules babies look by" (Haith, 1980), such as paying attention to movement or to shifts between dark and light. Unlike Descartes, current theorists do not propose that these built-in response patterns are the end of the story; rather they are seen as the starting point. What then develops is a result of experience filtered through these initial biases. But those biases *constrain* the number of developmental pathways that are possible (Campbell & Bickhard, 1992).

Maturation

Nature can shape processes after birth in other ways as well, most clearly through genetic programming that may determine whole sequences of later development. Arnold Gesell (1925; Thelen & Adolph, 1992) used the term **maturation** to describe such genetically programmed sequential patterns of change, and this term is still uniformly used today. Changes in body size and shape, changes in hormones at puberty, changes in muscles and bones, and changes in the nervous system all may be programmed in this way. You can probably remember your own

Think about your own patterns of behavior for a moment. Which ones do you think are the *mostly* governed by basic human biology (nature)? Which ones seem to be mostly a product of your environment, including your upbringing?

physical changes during adolescence. The timing of these pubertal changes differs from one teenager to the next, but the basic sequence is essentially the same for all children. Such sequences, which begin at conception and continue until death, are shared by all members of our species. The instructions for these sequences are part of the specific hereditary information that is passed on at the moment of conception.

In its pure form, as Gesell described it, maturationally determined development occurs regardless of practice or training. You don't have to practice growing pubic hair; you don't have to be taught how to walk. In fact it would take almost herculean efforts to *prevent* such sequences from unfolding. But even confirmed maturational theorists agree that experience has some effect. These powerful, apparently automatic, maturational patterns require at least some minimal environmental support, such as adequate diet and opportunity for movement and experimentation.

Specific experience may also interact with maturational patterns in intricate ways. For example, Greenough (1991) points to the fact that one of the proteins required for the development of the visual system is controlled by a gene whose action is only triggered by visual experience. So *some* visual experience is needed for the genetic program to operate. In normal development, of course, every (nonblind) child will have some such experience. But examples like this one tell us that maturational sequences do not simply "unfold" automatically. The system appears to be "ready" to develop along particular pathways, but it requires experience to trigger the movement.

I should point out that the term *maturation* does not mean quite the same thing as *growth*, although the two terms are sometimes used as if they were synonyms. *Growth* refers to some kind of step-by-step change in quantity, as in size, and it can occur either with or without an underlying maturational process. A child's body could grow because her diet has significantly improved, or it could grow because she is getting older. The first of these has no maturational component, while the second does. To put it another way, the term *growth* is a *description* of change, while the concept of maturation is one *explanation* of change.

Behavior Genetics

Both of the "nature" concepts I have described so far (inborn biases and maturation) are designed to account for patterns and sequences of development that are the same for all children. But nature can also contribute to variations from one individual to the next, since genetic inheritance is individual as well as collective. The study of genetic contributions to individual behavior, called **behavior genetics,** has become a particularly vibrant and influential research area in recent years.

Using two primary research techniques, the study of identical and fraternal twins, and the study of adopted children—both of which I have described more fully in the research report on page 7—behavior geneticists have shown that specific heredity affects a remarkably broad range of behaviors. Included in the list are not only obvious physical differences such as height, body shape, or a tendency to skinniness or obesity, but also cognitive abilities such as general intelligence (about which I will have a great deal more to say in Chapter 6), and more specific cognitive skills like spatial visualization ability (Plomin & Rende, 1991).

RESEARCH REPORT
How Do Behavior Geneticists Identify Genetic Effects?

There are two basic ways of searching for a genetic influence on a trait. You can study identical and fraternal twins, or you can study adopted children.

Identical twins share exactly the same genetic patterning, because they develop from the same fertilized ovum. Fraternal twins each develop from a separate ovum, separately fertilized. They are therefore no more alike than are any other pair of siblings, except that they have shared the same prenatal environment, and grow up in the same sequential niche within the family. If identical twins turn out to be more like one another on any given trait than fraternal twins, that would be evidence for the influence of heredity on that trait.

An even more powerful variant of the twin strategy is to study twins who have been reared apart from one another. If identical twins are still more like one another on some dimension, despite having grown up in different environments, we have even clearer evidence of a genetic contribution for that trait.

In the case of adopted children, the strategy is to compare the degree of similarity between the adopted child and his birth parents (with whom he shares genes but not environment) with the degree of similarity between the adopted child and his adoptive parents (with whom he shares environment but not genes). If the child should turn out to be more similar to his birth parents than to his adoptive parents, or if his behavior or skill is better predicted by the characteristics of his birth parents than by the characteristics of his adoptive parents, that would again demonstrate the influence of heredity.

Let me give you one example of each type. Bouchard and McGue (1981) have combined the results of dozens of twin studies on the heritability of IQ scores, with the following results (p. 1056, from Figure 1):

Identical twins reared together	.85
Identical twins reared apart	.67
Fraternal twins reared together	.58
Siblings (including fraternal twins) reared apart	.24

The numbers here are correlations—a statistic I'll explain more fully later in this chapter. For now, you need to know only that a correlation can range from 0 to +1.00 or −1.00. The closer it is to 1.00, the stronger the relationship it describes. In this case, the number reflects how similar the IQs are of the two members of a twin pair. You can see that identical twins reared together have IQs that are highly similar, much more similar than what occurs for fraternal twins reared together. You can also see, though, that environment plays a role since identical twins reared apart are less similar than are those reared together.

IQ has also been the focus of adoption studies of heritability. Here are some results from a study of roughly one hundred adopted children by Scarr & Weinberg (1983, Table 1, p. 262), again expressed in terms of correlations between the child's IQ and the parents' IQs:

The natural mother's IQ	.33
The natural father's IQ	.43
The adoptive mother's IQ	.21
The adoptive father's IQ	.27

Because the children's IQs were *more* similar to the IQs of their natural parents than to their adoptive parents, these results, like the results of twin studies of IQ, tell us that there is indeed a substantial genetic component in what we measure with an IQ test.

Newer research is also showing that many aspects of pathological behavior are genetically influenced, including alcoholism, schizophrenia, excessive aggressiveness, even anorexia (Plomin, Rende, & Rutter, 1991). Finally, and importantly, behavior geneticists have found a significant genetic influence on children's temperament, including such dimensions as emotionality (the tendency to get distressed or upset easily), activity (the tendency toward vigorous, rapid behavior), and sociability (the tendency to prefer the presence of others to being alone) (Buss & Plomin, 1984; 1986).

▶ The Nurture Side of the Equation

Models of Environmental Influence

Concepts on the nurture side of this ancient dispute have also become considerably more subtle and complex. One particularly helpful analysis of the potential impact of environment has come from Richard Aslin (1981a), who suggests five

Roles of early experience

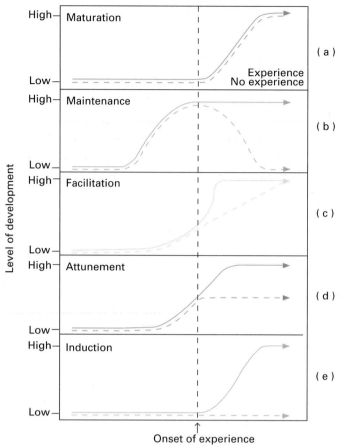

Figure 1.1
Five models of possible relationships between maturation and environment, as proposed by Aslin. The top model shows a purely maturational effect; the bottom model (induction) shows a purely environmental effect. The other three show interactive combinations: *maintenance*, in which experience prevents the deterioration of a maturationally developed skill; *facilitation*, in which experience speeds up the development of some maturational process; and *attunement*, in which experience increases the ultimate level of some skill or behavior above the "normal" maturational level. (*Source:* Aslin, 1981a, p. 50.)

models of influence, shown schematically in Figure 1.1. In each drawing the dashed line represents the path of development of some skill or behavior that would occur without a particular experience; the solid line represents the path of development if the experience were added.

For comparison purposes, the first of the five models actually shows a maturational pattern with *no* environmental effect. The second model, which Aslin calls *maintenance*, describes a pattern in which some environmental input is necessary to sustain a skill or behavior that has already developed maturationally. For example, kittens are born with full binocular vision, but if you cover one of their eyes for a period of time, binocular skill declines. Similarly, muscles will atrophy if not used.

The third model shows a *facilitation* effect of the environment in which a skill or behavior develops earlier than it normally would because of some experience. For example, children whose parents talk to them more often, using more complex sentences, in the first 18–24 months of life appear to develop two-word sentences and other early grammatical forms somewhat earlier than do children talked to less. But less-talked-to children catch up shortly thereafter, so there is no permanent gain.

When a particular experience does lead to a permanent gain or to a higher level of performance, Aslin would call it *attunement,* which is his fourth model. There is some indication, for example, that children growing up in families in which their parents talk to them a great deal have slightly higher IQs later than do children who receive less early verbal stimulation.

Aslin's final model, *induction,* describes a pure environmental effect; without some experience a particular behavior would not develop at all. Giving a child tennis lessons, or exposing her to a second language, would fall into this category.

These five models illustrate the greater complexity of current thinking about nature/nurture issues. But they still do not take us far enough. At least three other aspects of the environmental side of the equation are also significant in current thinking about development: the timing of experience, the child's own interpretation of experience, and the total ecological/cultural system in which experiences occur.

The preschool program Head Start was designed, several decades ago, to improve the school preparation of children growing up in poor families. Which of Aslin's models do you think best describes what the designers of Head Start thought (or hoped) would be the result of the program?

The Timing of Experience

Just as the importance of nature may vary from one time in development to another, so the timing of specific experiences may matter as well. The impact of day care on an infant may be quite different when he is 6 months old than when he is 16 months old; moving from one school to another may have a different effect if it coincides with puberty than if it does not, and so forth.

Our thinking about the importance of timing was stimulated, in part, by research on other species which showed that specific experiences had different or stronger effects at some points in development than at others. The most famous example is that baby ducks will become *imprinted* (become attached to and follow) any duck or any other quacking, moving object that happens to be around them 15 hours after they hatch. If nothing is moving or quacking at that critical point, they don't become imprinted at all (Hess, 1972). So the period just around 15 hours after hatching is a **critical period** for the duck's development of a proper following response.

We can see similar critical periods in the action of various **teratogens** in prenatal development. A teratogen is some outside agent, such as a disease organism or chemical, which, if present during prenatal development, adversely affects the process of that development. While some teratogens can have negative consequences at any time in gestation, most have effects only during some critical period. For example, if a mother contracts the disease rubella (commonly called German measles) during a narrow range of days in the first three months of pregnancy, some damage or deformity occurs in the fetus. Infection with the same virus after the third month of pregnancy has no such effect.

In the months after birth, too, there seem to be critical periods in brain development—specific weeks or months during which the child needs to encounter certain types of stimulation or experience for the nervous system to develop normally and fully (Hirsch & Tieman, 1987).

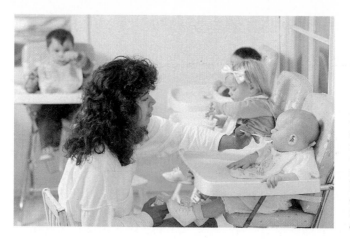

If the first year of life is a sensitive period for the establishment of a secure attachment (as some contend), then is it risky for a child of this age to be separated from her parents every day in day care? There is a hot debate among psychologists on this point.

The broader and somewhat looser concept of a **sensitive period** has also been widely used. A sensitive period is a span of months or years during which a child may be particularly responsive to specific forms of experience, or particularly influenced by their absence. For example, the period from 6 to 12 months of age may be a sensitive period for the formation of a core attachment to the parents. Other periods may be particularly significant for intellectual development or language (Tamis-LeMonda & Bornstein, 1987).

Internal Models of Experience

Another concept appearing more and more prominently in our theoretical repertoire is that of an internal model of experience. The key idea is that the effect of some experience lies in an individual's *interpretation* of it, the *meaning* the individual attaches to it, rather than any objective properties of the experience. You can easily come up with everyday examples from your own life. For instance, if a friend says something to you that he thinks is innocuous but that you take as a criticism, what matters for your experience is how you interpreted the comment, now how he meant it. If you regularly hear criticism in other people's comments, we would say that you have an internal model of yourself and others that includes a basic expectation that might be like this: "I usually do things wrong, so other people criticize me."

Theorists who emphasize the importance of such meaning systems argue that each child creates a set of internal models—a set of assumptions or conclusions about the world, about himself, and about relationships with others—through which all subsequent experience is filtered (Epstein, 1991). John Bowlby (1969; 1980) expressed this idea when he talked about the child's "internal working model" of attachment. A child with a secure model of attachment may assume that someone will come when he cries, and that affection and attention are reliably available. A child with a less secure model may assume that if a grown-up frowns it probably means she will be yelled at. These expectations are based on actual experiences, to be sure, but once formed into a internal model, they generalize beyond the original experience and affect the way the child interprets future experiences. A child who expects adults to be reliable and affectionate will be more likely to interpret the behavior of new adults in this way and will re-create friendly and affectionate relationships with others outside the family; a child who expects hostility will read hostility into otherwise fairly neutral encounters.

Such a view of the pathway or mechanism of environmental effects is not dominant in developmental psychology, but has gained importance in recent years.

The Ecological Perspective

A third facet of current thinking about environmental effects is a growing emphasis on casting a wider environmental net. Until quite recently, most research on environmental influences focused on a child's family (frequently only the child's mother), perhaps on playmates, or on some proximate inanimate stimulation such as toys. If we looked at a larger family context at all it was usually in terms of the general wealth or poverty of the family.

In the past 10 or 15 years, however, there has been a strong push to widen our scope. One key figure has been Urie Bronfenbrenner (1979; 1989), who used the phrase *ecology of development* to describe his approach. Recently, the term *context* has been used to describe the same kind of variation.

Bronfenbrenner emphasizes that each child grows up in a complex social environment (a social ecology) with a distinct cast of characters: brothers, sisters, one or both parents, grandparents, baby-sitters, pets, schoolteachers, friends. And this cast is itself embedded within a larger social system: the parents have jobs that they may like or dislike; they may have close and supportive friends or they may be quite isolated; they may be living in a safe neighborhood or one full of dangers; the local school may be excellent or poor; and the parents may have good or poor relationships with the school. Bronfenbrenner's argument is that we must not only include descriptions of these more extended aspects of the environment in our research, we must also understand the ways in which all the components of this complex system interact with one another.

How would you describe the "ecology" of your own childhood? What sort of family? What sort of neighborhood and school? What other significant people were in your life? What significant events affected your parents' lives?

A particularly nice example of research that examines such a larger system of influences is Gerald Patterson's work on the origins of antisocial behavior in children (Patterson, DeBaryshe, & Ramsey, 1989). His studies show that parents who use poor discipline techniques and poor monitoring of the child are more likely to have noncompliant or antisocial children. Once established, however, the child's antisocial behavior pattern has repercussions in other areas of his life, leading both to rejection by peers and to academic difficulty. These problems, in turn, are likely to push the young person toward a deviant peer group and still further delinquency (Dishion et al., 1991; Vuchinich, Bank, & Patterson, 1992). So a pattern that began in the family is maintained and exacerbated by interactions with peers and with the school system.

But it is not enough even to look at these settings. We also have to understand which parents are likely to use poor disciplinary techniques, and why. Patterson finds that those parents who were themselves raised using poor disciplinary practices are more likely to use those same poor strategies with their children. But even parents who possess good basic child-management skills may fall into poor patterns when the stresses in their own lives are increased. A recent divorce or period of unemployment increases the likelihood that poor disciplinary practices

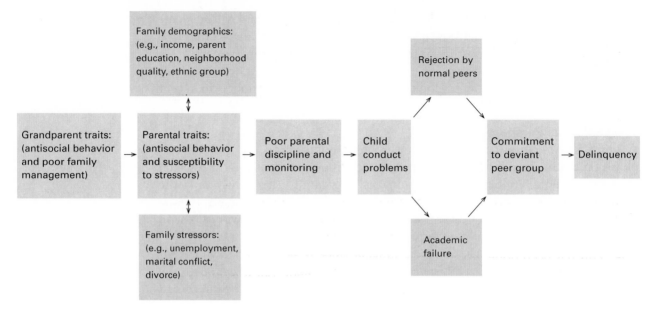

Figure 1.2
Patterson's model describes the many factors that influence the development of delinquency. The core of the process, in this model, is the interaction between the child and the parent. One might argue that the origin of delinquency lies in that relationship. But Patterson argues that there are larger ecological or contextual forces that are also "causes" of the delinquency. (*Source:* Patterson, DeBaryshe, & Ramsey, 1989, Figures 1 and 2, pp. 331, 333.)

will be used, and thus increases the likelihood that the child will develop a pattern of antisocial behavior. Figure 1.2 shows Patterson's conception of how these various components fit together. Clearly, by taking into account the larger social ecological system in which the family is embedded, our understanding of the process is greatly enhanced.

Cultural Influences.   Bronfenbrenner's formulation does not include the still-broader concept of **culture.** There is no commonly agreed-upon definition for this term, but in essence it describes some *system of meanings and customs,* including values, attitudes, goals, laws, beliefs, morals, as well as physical artifacts of various kinds—tools, forms of dwellings, and the like. Furthermore, to be called a culture, this system of meanings and customs must be *shared by some identifiable group,* whether that group is a subsection of some population or a larger unit, and *transmitted from one generation of that group to the next* (Betancourt & Lopez, 1993; Cole, 1992). Families and children are clearly embedded in culture, just as they are located within an ecological niche in the culture.

My awareness of the power of even quite small cultural variations was greatly enhanced by a year spent living in Germany in 1992–1993. My goal had been to learn German, which is my husband's native tongue, but I learned a lot more about culture than about language. Even in a culture so outwardly similar to U.S. culture, small differences in cultural patterns often left me feeling dislocated and uncertain. One fairly trivial example: As an American, I quite naturally smiled at strangers I might pass while out walking on one of the many special paths crisscrossing the country. Yet those I met rarely made eye contact and never smiled at me. Indeed, they often seemed quite put off by my friendliness. I experienced their behavior as coldness, even when my logical mind told me that it was merely a different cultural pattern. Experiences like this convinced me that Sapir was right when he said: "The worlds in which different societies live are distinct worlds, not merely the same world with different words attached" (Sapir, 1929, p. 209).

Studying culture is important for our understanding of child development for a whole host of reasons, but two are particularly clear. First, if we are going to uncover those developmental patterns or processes that are truly universal, it is not enough to study white American middle-class children and assume that what we see in their development is true for all children. When we think we have uncovered some basic sequence or process, we need to observe or test other children, from other subcultural or cultural groups, from as wide an array of cultures as possible. This has been done in some areas already, such as cross-cultural studies of language development, moral development, and attachment. But it is only beginning in most other areas.

As part of this first task, we also need to discover whether or not the _relationship_ between some environmental event and the outcome for the child is the same in all cultures. For example, in a recent study in Egypt, Ted Wachs and his colleagues (1993) found that in those families in which the parents talked a lot to their babies, the children were later rated as more competent—a result that closely parallels the relationship between these two variables found in studies in the United States.

In the Hispanic-American subculture, families like the Limons, shown here at their annual reunion, are tightly knit, with frequent contact and support. Such a cultural pattern may have wide repercussions.

But in other cases, the same relationships may _not_ hold across cultures or subcultures. For example, an African-American pediatrician, Ronald David, has recently pointed out (Lambert, 1993) that the relationship between the availability of prenatal care and the rate of infant mortality is not the same in the Mexican-American subculture as in the African-American subculture. Among Mexican-Americans, he reports, poverty is _not_ associated with high infant mortality, while among African-Americans it is. Such a difference obviously has implications not only for our understanding of culture, but also at a practical level for any attempt to design an appropriate intervention to reduce infant mortality.

A second reason to study culture is that if we are to understand "nurture," surely we must understand culture as part of the environment in which the child is growing up. How is children's development changed by cultural variations, as in the example of "sleeping through the night" I already mentioned? How do different cultural values affect the way children experience their childhood and adolescence? For instance, one feature of American culture is a powerful emphasis on individual freedom, independence, and achievement. Some have argued that a consequence of this value is a much higher level of tolerance of aggression and violence than is true in other cultures (Lore & Schultz, 1993). Such tolerance, in turn, may well be one factor in creating the "war zones" we see in many of our inner cities.

To achieve understanding of cultural variations it will not be enough simply to catalog a whole series of cultural patterns and describe the children in each setting. Ultimately, we will need to develop theories about the *ways* cultural variations affect children.

As yet we have relatively little cross-cultural research to draw on, so most of the time I base what I say entirely on studies done in the United States, mostly on middle-class white children. But the database is growing, and I will bring it in whenever I can.

▶ Interactions of Nature and Nurture

The ecological/cultural approach underlines the importance of understanding the interactions among many different environmental influences. Equally, we need to understand the interactions among various internal and external influences, between nature and nurture.

There are at least two ways we could look at this interaction. On the one hand, we could look for the common or normative patterns of interaction between nature and nurture. What skills is every child born with, how is the basic system "wired," and how does it mature? And how are those skills altered or shaped by specific experience? This is basically the approach taken by most of those who have studied perceptual development and language development, and by some who have studied cognitive development. I'll be describing the current conclusions drawn from this work in later chapters.

Alternatively, we might look for ways in which nature/nurture interactions *vary* from one child to another. The basic idea is that the same environment may have quite different effects on children who are born with different characteristics. One influential approach of this type is the study of *vulnerable* and *resilient* children.

Vulnerability and Resilience

A baby born weighing only two pounds, a child born into a highly impoverished family, a baby who has an unusually cranky or difficult temperament, all seem to start life with several strikes against them, while a child with a particularly sunny disposition begins the developmental journey with certain advantages. In recent years, theorists and researchers such as Norman Garmezy and Michael Rutter (Garmezy, 1993; Garmezy & Rutter, 1983; Rutter, 1987) have argued that such variations in children's qualities or assets are highly important, making some children highly vulnerable to the stresses of childhood, while others are buffered from the worst consequences.

In their writings, Garmezy and Rutter have largely emphasized social origins of vulnerability, such as inadequately loving relationships with parents. Frances Horowitz uses the same term, but focuses primarily on inborn kinds of vulnerability, such as premature birth, or a "difficult" temperament. In Horowitz's model, shown in Figure 1.3, the child's inborn vulnerability or resilience interacts in a particular way with the "facilitativeness" of the environment (Horowitz, 1987; 1990). A highly facilitative environment is one in which the child has loving and responsive parents and is provided with a rich array of stimulation. If the relationship between vulnerability and facilitativeness were merely additive, we would find that the best outcomes occurred for resilient infants reared in optimum environments, the worst outcomes for vulnerable infants in poor environments, and the other combinations would lie somewhere in between. But that is not what

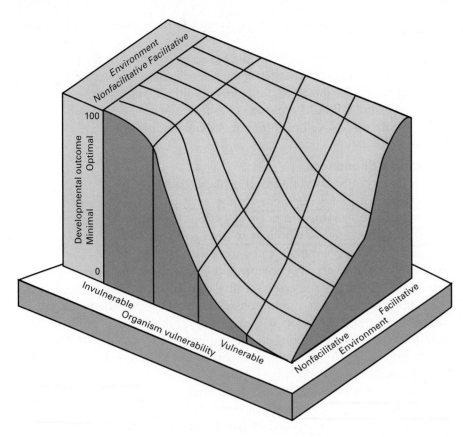

Figure 1.3
Horowitz's model describes one possible type of interaction between the vulnerability of the child and the quality of the environment. The height of the surface is the goodness of the developmental outcome (such as IQ or skill in social relationships). In this model, only the combination of a vulnerable infant and a nonfacilitative environment will result in really poor outcomes. (*Source:* Horowitz, 1987, Figure 1.1, p. 23.)

Horowitz proposes. Instead she is suggesting that a resilient child in a poor environment may do quite well, since such a child can take advantage of all the stimulation and opportunities available; similarly, she suggests that a vulnerable child may do quite well in a highly facilitative environment. According to this model it is only the double whammy—the vulnerable child in a poor environment—that leads to really poor outcomes for the child.

In fact, as you will see throughout the book, a growing body of research shows precisely this pattern. For example, very low IQ scores are most common among children who were low-birth-weight children *and* reared in poverty-level families, while low-birth-weight children reared in middle-class families have essentially normal IQs, as do normal-weight infants reared in poverty-level families (Werner, 1986). We are beginning to understand that the same environment can have very different effects, depending on the qualities or capacities the child brings to the equation.

▶ The Nature of Developmental Change

The nature/nurture controversy is not the only "big question" in developmental psychology. An equally central dispute concerns the nature of developmental change itself: Is a child's expanding ability just "more of the same," or does it reflect a new kind of activity? For example, a 2-year-old is likely to have no individual friends among her playmates, while an 8-year-old is likely to have several. We could think of this as a *quantitative* change (a change in amount) from zero friends to some friends. Or we could think of it as a *qualitative* change (a change in kind

[Handwritten margin notes:]
quantitative change — increase or decrease some peculiar chrstics it measure by quantity

Another possible variation of this same idea: Do you think it is possible that girls and boys, beginning in infancy, respond differently to the *same* environments? If this is true, what would be the ramifications of such a pattern?

qualitative change — involve dvlpt of new process that develope. eg. how much hair, teeth or type) from disinterest in peers to interest, or from one *sort* of peer relationship to another. Where a given researcher or theorist stands on this question has a profound effect on the way he or she perceives children and their behavior. Does a child simply get better and better at things, such as walking or running, or reading? That is, are the *processes* the same and only the efficiency or the speed different, or are there different processes at different ages? Or do older children use different strategies, develop different understandings, organize their behavior differently?

Stages and Sequences

A very important related question concerns the existence of *stages* in the course of development. If development consists only of additions (quantitative change) then the concept of stages is not needed. But if development involves reorganization or the emergence of wholly new strategies or skills (qualitative change), then the concept of stages may become attractive. Certainly we hear a lot of "stage-like" language in everyday conversation about children: "He's just in the terrible twos," or "It's only a stage she's going through." Although there is not always agreement on just what would constitute evidence for the existence of discrete stages, the usual description is that a stage shift involves not only a change in skills but some discontinuous change in underlying *structure* (McHale & Lerner, 1990). The child in a new stage approaches tasks differently, sees the world differently, is preoccupied with different issues.

As we move through the following chapters, you will see that stage theories are common in studies of development, although the concept has come under considerable recent attack. John Flavell, a major thinker in the area of cognitive development, points out that research on children's thinking in the past several decades has yielded only limited evidence of stages. What one does see are *sequences* of development in each of a large number of content areas. There are sequences in the development of concepts of gender, sequences in the development of memory strategies, sequences in the acquisition of language skills. Each of these sequences appears to be common across children and to reflect qualitative as well as quantitative changes, but they do not seem to be organized into cohesive wholes that we might think of as broad stages (Flavell, 1982; 1985; 1992). A child might be very advanced in one sequence and only average in several others, for example, rather than being equally fast or slow in all areas. Thus the idea of stages of development, which seems at first blush to be a tidy way of organizing information, a simple way of describing changes with age, has turned out to be slippery and difficult to sustain. You should keep that in mind as you encounter the various stage theories that are still part of our theoretical language. You should also keep in mind, however, that it is not necessary to assume stages in order to argue that the nature of developmental change is qualitative as well as (or instead of) quantitative. Qualitative change may be gradual as well as abrupt, sequential rather than stagelike.

▶ Theories of Development

In principle, any of the many logical combinations of answers to the various questions I have been asking about nature versus nurture, or about the nature of development, might form the basis of a theory of development. But certain patterns

Is this boy behaving like this because he is in a "stage" in which tantrums are common? What other explanations can you come up with?

of answers have been much more prominent than others. Of these, four families of theories have been most influential—not just in studies of development but also in psychology as a whole: biological, learning, psychoanalytic, and cognitive-developmental theories. Since you will meet members of these four theoretical families again and again through the book, and since I will be examining all four in much greater detail in later chapters, let me describe them only briefly here, pointing out the ways in which they differ in their answers to the key questions.

Biological Theories

The most basic proposition of biological theories of development is that both our common patterns of development and our unique individual behavioral tendencies are partially or wholly programmed in the genes, or are influenced by such physiological processes as hormone changes. Biologically oriented theorists do not argue that environment is unimportant—no one takes such an extreme position. But genetic programming is seen by many psychologists as a powerful framework, affecting both shared and individual patterns of development. You have already met the two most significant variations of this view: Gesell's maturational theory, and the behavior geneticists' emphasis on the genetic component in most, if not all, behavior and development.

Learning Theories

Learning theorists have started from the other end of the nature/nurture argument, emphasizing the dominant role of experience. Albert Bandura, a leading theorist, puts it this way:

> . . . human nature is characterized by a vast potentiality that can be fashioned by direct and vicarious experience into a variety of forms within biological limits. (Bandura, 1989, p. 51)

Clearly Bandura is not rejecting biology, any more than biological theorists reject environment. But he sees human behavior as enormously plastic, shaped by predictable processes of learning. Two of those processes are classical conditioning and operant conditioning. If you have encountered these concepts in earlier courses, you can skim the next section. But for those of you who lack such a background, a brief description is needed.

Classical Conditioning.   This type of learning, made famous by Pavlov's experiments with his salivating dog, involves the acquisition of new signals for existing responses. If you touch a baby on the cheek, he will turn toward the touch and begin to suck. In the technical terminology of **classical conditioning,** the touch on the cheek is the **unconditioned stimulus;** the turning and sucking are **unconditioned responses.** The baby is already programmed to do all that; these are automatic reflexes. Learning occurs when some *new* stimulus is hooked into the system. The general model is that other stimuli that are present just before or at the same time as the unconditioned stimulus will eventually trigger the same responses. In the typical home situation, for example, a number of stimuli occur at about the same time as the touch on the baby's cheek before feeding. There is the sound of the mother's footsteps approaching, the kinesthetic cues of being picked up, and the tactile cues of being held in the mother's arms. All of these stimuli may eventually become **conditioned stimuli** and may trigger the infant's response of turning and sucking, even without any touch on the cheek.

Classical conditioning is of special interest in our study of child development because of the role it plays in the development of emotional responses. For example, things or people present when you feel good will become conditioned stimuli for that same sense of goodwill, while those previously associated with some uncomfortable feeling may become conditioned stimuli for a sense of unease or anxiety. This is especially important in infancy, since a child's mother or father is present so often when nice things happen—when the child feels warm, comfortable, and cuddled. In this way mother and father usually come to be a conditioned stimulus for pleasant feelings, a fact that makes it possible for the parents' mere presence to reinforce other behaviors as well. But a tormenting older sibling might come to be a conditioned stimulus for angry feelings, even after the sibling has long since stopped the tormenting. These classically conditioned emotional responses are remarkably powerful. They begin to be formed very early in life, continue to be formed throughout childhood and adulthood, and profoundly affect each individual's emotional experiences.

Operant Conditioning. The second major type of learning is most often called **operant conditioning,** although you will also see it referred to as *instrumental conditioning.* Unlike classical conditioning, which involves attaching an old response to a new stimulus, operant conditioning involves attaching a new response to an old stimulus, achieved by the application of appropriate principles of reinforcement. Any behavior that is reinforced will be more likely to occur again in the same or in a similar situation. There are two types of reinforcements. A **positive reinforcement** is any event which, following some behavior, increases the chances that the behavior will occur again in that situation. There are certain classes of pleasant consequences, such as praise, a smile, food, a hug, or attention, that serve as reinforcers for most people most of the time. But strictly speaking, a reinforcement is defined by its effect; we don't know something is reinforcing unless we see that its presence increases the probability of some behavior.

A daily achievement chart, like this one for 5-year-old Aaron, can be highly reinforcing for many children.

The second major type is a **negative reinforcement,** which occurs when something an individual finds *unpleasant* is *stopped.* Suppose your little boy is whining and begging you to pick him up. At first you ignore him, but finally you do pick him up. What happens? He stops whining. So your picking-up behavior has been *negatively reinforced* by the cessation of his whining, and you will be *more* likely to pick him up the next time he whines. At the same time, his whining has probably been *positively reinforced* by your attention, so he will be more likely to whine on similar occasions.

Both positive and negative reinforcements strengthen behavior. **Punishment,** in contrast, is intended to weaken some undesired behavior. Sometimes punishments involve eliminating nice things (like "grounding" a child, or taking away TV privileges, or sending her to her room); often they involve administering unpleasant things such as a scolding or a spanking. What is confusing about the idea of punishment is that it doesn't always do what it is intended to do: it does not always suppress the undesired behavior. If your child has thrown his milk glass at you to get your attention, spanking him may be a positive reinforcement instead of the punishment you intended.

In laboratory situations, experimenters can be sure to reinforce some behavior every time it occurs, or to stop reinforcements completely so as to produce extinction of the response. But in the real world, consistency of reinforcement is the exception rather than the rule. Much more common is a pattern of **partial reinforcement,** in which some behavior is reinforced on some occasions but not others. Studies of partial reinforcement show that children and adults take longer to learn some behavior under partial reinforcement conditions, but once established, such behaviors are much more resistant to extinction. If you smile at your daughter only every fifth or sixth time she brings a picture to show you (and if she finds your smile reinforcing), she'll keep on bringing pictures for a very long stretch, even if you quit smiling altogether.

Additional Processes in Bandura's Theory. Bandura, whose variation of learning theory is by far the most influential among developmental psychologists today, suggests several other key forms of learning (Bandura, 1977; 1982; 1989). First, he argues that learning does not always require direct reinforcement. Learning may also occur merely as a result of watching someone else perform some action. Learning of this type, called **observational learning** or **modeling,** is involved in a wide range of behaviors. Children learn ways of hitting from watching other people in real life and on TV. They learn how to be generous by watching others donate money or goods.

Bandura also calls attention to another class of reinforcements called **intrinsic reinforcements** or intrinsic rewards, such as pride or discovery. These are reinforcements internal to the individual, such as the pleasure a child feels when she finally figures out how to draw a star, or the sense of satisfaction you may experience after strenuous exercise.

Third, and perhaps most important, Bandura has gone far toward bridging the gap between learning theory and cognitive-developmental theory by emphasizing important *cognitive* (mental) elements in observational learning. Indeed he now even refers to his theory as "social cognitive theory" (Bandura, 1986; 1989). For example, Bandura now stresses the fact that modeling can be the vehicle for learning abstract as well as concrete skills or information. The observer extracts a rule that may be the basis of the model's behavior, and learns the rule as well as the specific behavior. In this way a child or adult can acquire attitudes, values, ways of solving problems, even standards of self-evaluation through modeling.

Think again about your own upbringing. What values or attitudes do you think you learned through modeling? How were those values and attitudes displayed (modeled) by your parents or others?

Learning to use chopsticks through modeling is only one of the myriad skills, attitudes, beliefs, and values that are learned in this way.

Collectively, these additions to traditional learning theory make the system far more flexible and powerful, although it is still not a strongly *developmental* theory. That is, Bandura has little to say about changes with age in what or how a child may learn from modeling. In contrast, psychoanalytic theories are strongly developmental, emphasizing sequential, often stagelike qualitative change.

Psychoanalytic Theories

The word *psyche*, in Greek, refers to the soul, spirit, or mind. So psychoanalysis is the analysis of the mind or spirit. All the theorists in this general tradition have been interested in explaining human behavior by understanding the underlying processes of the mind and the personality. And nearly all psychoanalytic theorists have begun by studying and analyzing adults or children who are disturbed in some way. Many believed they could come to understand the normal processes by analyzing how they had gone wrong.

As with learning theories, there is a whole family of theories called "psychoanalytic," beginning with Freud's and continuing with theories by Carl Jung (1916; 1939), Alfred Adler (1948), Erik Erikson (1963; 1964; 1974), and many others.

Sigmund Freud (1905; 1920) is usually credited with originating the psychoanalytic approach, and his terminology and many of his concepts have become part of our intellectual culture, even while his explicit influence upon developmental psychologists has waned. Among current theorists in this tradition, Erik Erikson (1963; 1980) is probably the most influential, although there are other important thinkers whose work has been strongly influenced by psychoanalytic theory, such as John Bowlby and Jane Loevinger.

The most distinctive and central assumption of the psychoanalytic approach is that behavior is governed by *unconscious* as well as conscious processes. Some of these unconscious processes are present at birth, others develop over time. For example, Freud proposed the existence of a basic unconscious, instinctual sexual drive he called the **libido.** He argued that this energy is the motive force behind virtually all our behavior. Freud also proposed that unconscious material is created over time through the functioning of the various defense mechanisms—those automatic, normal, unconscious strategies for reducing anxiety that we all use on a daily basis, such as repression, or denial, or projection.

A second basic assumption is that personality has a structure, and that such a structure develops over time. Freud proposed three parts: the **id,** which is the center of the libido, the **ego,** a much more conscious element, the executive of the personality, and the **superego,** which is the center of conscience and morality, since it incorporates the norms and moral strictures of the family and society. In Freud's theory, these three parts are not all present at birth. The infant is all id, all instinct, all desire, without the restraining influence of the ego or the superego. The ego begins to develop in the years from 2 to about 4 or 5 as the child learns to adapt his instant-gratification strategies. Finally the superego begins to develop just before school age, as the child incorporates the parents' values and cultural mores.

Psychoanalytic theorists also see development as fundamentally stagelike, with each stage centered on a particular form of tension, or a particular task. The child moves through these stages, resolving each task, reducing each tension as best as he can. So there is direction to this development, an ideal sequence.

The stages themselves are conceived somewhat differently in the various theories in this tradition. Freud thought they were strongly influenced by maturation. In each of Freud's five *psychosexual stages*, the libido is invested in that part of the body that is most sensitive at that age. In a newborn, the mouth is the most sensitive part of the body, so libidinal energy is focused there. The stage is therefore called the *oral* stage. As neurological development progresses the infant has more sensation in the anus (hence the *anal* stage), and later the genitalia (the *phallic* and eventually the *genital* stages).

The stages Erikson proposed, called *psycho**social** stages*, are much less influenced by maturation and much more by common cultural demands for children of a particular age, such as the demand that the child become toilet trained at about 2, or that the child learn school skills at age 6 or 7. In Erikson's view, each child moves through a fixed sequence of tasks or dilemmas, each centered on the development of a particular facet of identity. For example, the first task, central to the first 12 to 18 months of life, is to develop a sense of basic trust. If the child's caregivers are not responsive and loving, however, the child may instead develop a sense of mistrust, which will affect her responses at all of the later stages.

In both theories, however, the critical point is that the degree of success a child experiences in meeting the demands of these various stages will depend very heavily on the interactions he has with the people and objects in his world. This *interactive* element in Freud's and all subsequent psychoanalytic theories is absolutely central. Basic trust cannot be developed unless the parents or other caregivers respond to the infant in a loving, consistent manner. The oral stage cannot be fully completed unless the infant is given sufficient gratification of the desire for oral stimulation. And when any one stage is not fully resolved, the old patterns or the unmet need is carried forward, affecting the individual's ability to handle later tasks or stages. So, for example, a young adult who developed a sense of mistrust in the first years of life may have a more difficult time establishing secure intimate relationships with a partner or friends.

Does this make sense to you—this idea that one carries unresolved issues forward into adulthood? Can you think of any examples in your own experience?

Cognitive-Developmental Theories

In psychoanalytic theories, the quality and character of a child's relationships with a few key people are seen as central to the child's whole development. The child's encounters with the inanimate world—with toys and objects, with sights and sounds—are rarely discussed. Cognitive-developmental theorists, whose interest has been primarily in cognitive development rather than personality, reverse this order of importance, emphasizing the centrality of the child's explorations of objects. But cognitive-developmental theorists share with their psychoanalytically inclined colleagues the assumption that the cause or source of change is internal as well as external. The child is an active participant in the process of development.

The central figure in cognitive-developmental theory has been Jean Piaget (1952; 1970; 1977; Inhelder & Piaget, 1969), a Swiss psychologist whose theories shaped the thinking of several generations of developmental psychologists. Piaget, along with other early cognitive theorists such as Lev Vygotsky (1962) and Heinz Werner (1948), was struck by the great regularities in the development of children's thinking. He noticed that all children seemed to go through the same kinds of sequential discoveries about their world, making the same sorts of mistakes and arriving at the same solutions. For example, 3- and 4-year-olds all seem to think that if you pour water from a short, fat glass into a tall, thin one, there is now more water, since the water level is higher in the thin glass than it was in the fat glass. But most 7-year-olds realize that there is still the same amount of water in either case. If a 2-year-old loses her shoe, she may look for it briefly and haphazardly, but she is unable to undertake a systematic search. A 10-year-old, in contrast, is likely to use such good strategies as retracing her steps or looking in one room after another.

Piaget's detailed observations of children's thinking led him to several assumptions, the most central of which is that it is the nature of the human organism to *adapt* to its environment. This is an active process. In contrast to many learning theorists, Piaget does not think that the environment *shapes* the child. Rather the child (like the adult) actively seeks to understand his environment. In the process, he explores, manipulates, and examines the objects and people in his world.

The process of adaptation, in Piaget's view, is made up of several important subprocesses— *assimilation, accommodation,* and *equilibration*—all of which I will define fully in Chapter 7. For now, the key idea is that the child's exploration of the environment leads over a period of time to a series of fairly distinct "understandings" or "theories" about the way the world works, each of which comprises a specific stage. Since Piaget thought that virtually all infants begin with the same skills and built-in strategies, and since the environments children encounter are highly similar in important respects, the stages through which their thinking moves are also similar. Piaget proposes a fixed sequence of four major stages, each growing out of the one that preceded it, and each consisting of a more-or-less complete system or organization of concepts, strategies, and assumptions.

Contrasting the Theories

No doubt by now your head is swimming with theories. But we can make some order out of the array by returning to some of the central issues I discussed earlier in the chapter, and see how the various theories differ along these dimensions— an analysis you can see in Table 1.1. In this table, as in my descriptions of the theories, I have intentionally made the contrasts as great as possible to help you keep the alternatives clearly separate. But as we go along you will find that many current theories involve very interesting mixtures of these approaches. You've already seen this in the cognitive elements now contained in Bandura's theories, and in the ecological concepts added to a basic learning theory approach in Patterson's work. But there are many more examples, such as newer theories of the child's attachment to her parents, which combine basic psychoanalytic concepts with clearly cognitive themes such as the notion of an internal working model. And in virtually every area of study we see a return to an emphasis on biological roots. Having distinctly separate theories may be tidy, but I find the new blends, the new syntheses, far more intriguing.

Issue	Biological Theory	Learning Theory	Psychoanalytic Theory	Cognitive-Developmental Theory
TABLE 1.1 Comparison of Developmental Theories on Some of the Key Questions About Development				
What is the major influence on development?	Primarily nature	Primarily nurture	Both	The child's own internal processing of experience
Is developmental change qualitative or quantitative?	Both	Both in Bandura's version	Qualitative	Qualitative
Are there stages or sequences?	Sequences	No stages	Stages	Piaget said stages
Examples of research questions emerging from that theoretical tradition	Temperamental differences and their effects; role of heredity and environment in intelligence	Impact of TV on behavior; origins of social behaviors such as aggression	Attachment; fantasies	Development of logic; gender concepts; moral development

▶ Finding the Answers: Research on Development

I've asked an enormous number of questions already in this chapter. But before you can understand the answers—before I can get to the really interesting stuff you are probably most curious about—you need one more tool, namely at least a modicum of familiarity with the methods researchers use when they explore questions about development. Let me walk you through the various alternative methods by using a concrete example with clear practical ramifications.

Imagine that you are a social scientist. One day you get a call from your local state representative. She has become seriously concerned about the apparently rising levels of crime and lawlessness among teenagers, and wants to propose new legislation to respond to this problem. First, though, she wants to have some answers to a series of basic questions:

— Does the same problem exist everywhere in the world, or only in the United States? If the latter, then what is it about our culture that promotes or supports such behavior?
— At what age does the problem begin to be visible?
— Which children are most at risk for such delinquent behavior, and why?

How would you, could you, go about designing one or more studies that might answer such questions? You would face a number of decisions:

• In order to answer the question about the age at which delinquent acts begin to occur, should you compare groups of children and teenagers of different ages, or should you select a group of younger children and follow them over time, as they moved into adolescence? And should you study young people in many settings or cultures, or in only one setting, such as inner city youth in the U.S.? These are questions of *research design*.

- How will you measure delinquent behavior? Can you observe it? Can you ask about it? Can you rely on official records? What other things about each young person might you want to know in order to begin to answer the "why" question? Family history and relationships? Peer contacts and relationships? Self-esteem? These are questions of *research methodology*.

- How will you analyze the data you collect and how will you interpret your findings? Suppose you find that young people whose families live in poverty were considerably more likely to be delinquent. Would you be satisfied to stop there, or would you want to analyze the results separately for each of several ethnic groups, or for children growing up with single mothers, or in other ways that might clarify the meaning of your results? These are questions of *research analysis*.

▌ Research Design

Choosing a research design is crucial for any research, but especially so when the subject matter you are trying to study is change (or continuity) with age. You have basically three choices: (1) You can study *different* groups of people of different ages, called a **cross-sectional** design. (2) You can study the *same* people over a period of time, called a **longitudinal** design. (3) Or you can combine the two in some fashion, using what is called a **sequential** design (Schaie, 1983). And if you want to know whether the same patterns hold across different cultures or contexts, you will need to do some kind of **cross-cultural** research, in which equivalent or parallel methods are used in more than one context.

Cross-sectional Designs

The key feature of a cross-sectional design is that separate age groups are assessed, with each subject tested only once. To study delinquency cross-sectionally you might select groups of subjects at each of a series of ages, such as 8, 10, 12, 14, and 16. You would then assess each child or teen's delinquent behavior, along with measuring whatever other characteristics you had decided were important. To get some feeling for what the results from such a study might look like, take a look at Figure 1.4, which shows the rate of "conduct disorders" in a large random sample of all children between the ages of 4 and 16 in the province of Ontario, Canada (Offord, Boyle, & Racine, 1991). (A conduct disorder is akin to what is often called delinquency in everyday language.) It is clear that conduct disorders in this sample were far more common in adolescents, and in boys, results that are typical (in Western cultures, at least, in which this work has been done).

Cross-sectional research is often enormously useful. It is relatively quick to do, and when age differences are indeed found, it may suggest new hypotheses about developmental processes. And when the investigators collect a rich array of additional information about each subject, it can yield highly interesting results. In the Ontario study, for example, Offord and his colleagues found that the probability of a conduct disorder was four times as high in low-income families, nearly three times as high in "dysfunctional" families, three times as high in families

Figure 1.4
In this cross-sectional comparison from the Ontario study of conduct disorders, boys and teenagers showed higher rates of problem behavior. (*Source:* Offord, Boyle, & Racine, 1991, from Table 2.4, p. 40.)

with domestic violence, and so forth. Thus a research design of this type can begin to tell us *which* children are at risk, and give us some hints about whys.

At the same time, there are three major problems or limitations with any cross-sectional design. First of all, there is the "cohort problem."

The Cohort Problem.   Social scientists use the word **cohort** to describe groups of individuals born within some fairly narrow band of years, who share the same cultural/historical experiences at the same times in their lives. Within any given culture, successive cohorts may have quite different life experiences. Children growing up in the U.S. in the 1970s and 1980s, for example, were much more likely to experience a divorce between their parents than were kids growing up in the 1950s and 1960s. When we compare different age groups in a single study, as we do in any cross-sectional design, we are also inevitably comparing cohorts to some degree. Thus *cohort* and *age* are totally confounded, and we cannot tell whether some apparent age difference is really attributable to age, or only to cohort differences. When the age groups we are comparing are close in age, as is true in most studies of children, this is not usually a major problem since we can assume roughly similar life circumstances. But over age ranges of as much as 10 years, the cohort differences may be significant.

The Time of Measurement Problem.   A related difficulty is that any study is done at some specific time, and the results may simply not generalize to other time periods. The Ontario study was done in 1982 and 1983; would we find the same results if we were to repeat the study today? Might all the problem rates be higher? Would the same family characteristics predict conduct disorders now as predicted them then? This problem of generalizing across time periods is especially acute in any society or culture undergoing rapid change, as is the case in many Western cultures today.

Origins, Sequences, and Consistency.   Finally and perhaps most importantly, cross-sectional research cannot tell us much about *sequences of development*, or about the cumulative development of some pattern over time. The Ontario study doesn't tell us what happens—in children or in families—to lead to increased rates of conduct disorders in adolescence. It also doesn't tell us if there is some typical sequence through which a child passes, from minor misbehavior to more serious lawlessness. To give you another example, a cross-sectional study of

Make a list of all the differences you can think of between the likely childhood experiences of the cohort born (in your country) in 1960 and the cohort born in 1980. How might those differences affect the behavior of the children in each group?

children's gender concepts might show that 2-year-olds have a different idea of gender than 4-year-olds. But this won't tell us whether there are steps in between or whether every child acquires this concept in the same sequence. Similarly, cross-sectional studies will not tell us anything about the consistency of individual behavior over time. For example, it won't tell us if the children who show conduct disorders at 6 or 7 or 8 are likely to show the same kind of problem in adolescence.

Longitudinal Designs

Two of these three problems can be addressed with longitudinal designs, in which the *same* individuals are studied over a period of time. These designs allow us to look at sequences of change and individual consistency or inconsistency. And because they compare performances by the same people at different ages, they get around the cohort problem. Because of these advantages, they have become extremely common in developmental research. Several famous older longitudinal studies, in which children were followed from birth to adulthood, have also yielded rich veins of information.

As one example, Patterson's model of the development of aggressive and delinquent behavior, shown in Figure 1.2, is buttressed by a number of longitudinal studies in which boys at high risk for later delinquency were followed from fourth grade through junior high school (Patterson, Capaldi, & Bank, 1991; Vuchinich et al., 1992).

But longitudinal designs are not a panacea. Because they are time-consuming and expensive, researchers often study quite small samples, so that it is hard to generalize the findings to broader groups. This design also does not solve the time of measurement problem, because each study involves only one group, growing up in a particular historical context.

One solution to this problem is to repeat a longitudinal study several times, each time with a new cohort. This particular strategy, called a *cohort-sequential design,* is one of a family of research designs called sequential designs, which involve either combinations of cross-sectional, or combinations of longitudinal designs, or both. I know of no large cohort-sequential studies in which cohorts as widely apart as 10 or more years have been followed through childhood, but shorter-term versions of this design are becoming much more common.

Cross-cultural or Cross-Context Designs

Finally, to address the questions of universality or cultural specificity, we would need to compare across cultures. Several varieties of cross-cultural studies can be and have been done.

One variety is what anthropologists call an *ethnography*—a detailed description of a single culture or context, based on extensive observation. Often the observer lives within the culture for a period of time, perhaps as long as several years. Information from several different ethnographies may then be compared, to see if similar developmental patterns exist in varying cultures (Whiting & Edwards, 1988). For example, are girls and boys always given different tasks, and are those gender assignments similar from one context, one culture, to the next?

Alternatively, researchers can use standardized assessment instruments or methods to study some aspect of children's development or behavior in other cul-

---

CULTURES AND CONTEXTS
An Example of a Cross-cultural Comparison Study

Mark Bornstein and his colleagues (Bornstein, Tal, & Tamis-LeMonda, 1991; Bornstein et al., 1992) videotaped 24 mothers in each of three different cultures, Japan, France, and the United States, interacting in their homes with their 5-month-old infants. They noted that the *babies* behaved very similarly, which suggests that any differences in the mothers' behavior can't be attributed to varying signals or responses from the babies. And in some ways, the mothers responded similarly, too. In particular, they all showed similar rates of nurturance toward their infants, and similar levels of imitation. Nonetheless, there were some intriguing differences.

First of all, American mothers simply provided much more stimulation to their babies than did either Japanese or French mothers. They pointed, named, described, touched, and positioned their babies more. Furthermore, there were differences in the relative weight mothers in these three cultures gave to various types of stimulation. American mothers and French mothers were both more likely to focus efforts on getting their babies to interact with objects, and less on getting their babies to interact with Mom. For Japanese mothers, the two were nearly in balance. A third difference was that American mothers were a lot more likely to use a special, high-pitched sort of speech toward their infants—a form of speech sometimes called "motherese." Both the French and Japanese mothers used motherese occasionally, but much less often than the American mothers. They were more likely to talk to their baby using ordinary adult conversational tones. Such a finding does not— or does not necessarily— mean that the *process* of development is different in these different cultures. Babies in every culture may respond similarly to motherese, for example. Rather, these results suggest some of the subtle but significant ways that babies may be shaped into the cultural pattern in which they are growing.

---

tural settings, and then compare their results to existing U.S. or Western data. This is precisely what Wachs and his colleagues did in the Egyptian study I mentioned earlier. As such a body of research in any one area accumulates, it is possible to compare results across many cultures.

Finally, there are studies in which the same investigator compares two or more samples of children or families, each from a different culture or context, using the same instruments or measures or direct translations of those measures. Such comparative research has become quite common within the United States, as we begin to explore the impact of ethnic variations and neighborhood effects on children's development. But of course we can and eventually must reach beyond borders to compare children in quite different cultural milieus. Such studies are growing in number as well (Bornstein, 1991).

This is immensely difficult research to do well. Among the many difficulties, perhaps the most troublesome is the problem of equivalence of measurement (Helms, 1992). Is it enough just to translate some test into another language? Will the same measure or assessment technique be equally valid in all cultures? Do behaviors have the same *meaning* in other contexts, other cultures? I'll come back to this set of issues often as I talk about various facets of development, so I will not belabor the point here. For the moment, it is enough to point out that the amount of cross-cultural and cross-context research is still small, but growing.

What other problems can you think of that would make it hard to do good cross-cultural research?

Experimental Designs

Most of the research designs I have described so far are alternative ways to look at changes with age. But if we are interested in examining a basic process—such as learning or memory— or in *explaining* any observed phenomena, we may do **experiments.**

An experiment is normally designed to test a specific hypothesis, a particular causal explanation. For example, Patterson hypothesized that the beginning of the chain of causal events implicated in aggressive and delinquent behavior lies in the family discipline patterns. To test this, he could devise an intervention experiment in which some families of aggressive children were given training in better discipline techniques, and other families, with similar children, were given no training. He could then check at the end of the training, and perhaps some months or years later, to see if the children whose families had had the training were less likely to show aggression or delinquency.

A key feature of an experiment, then, is that subjects are assigned *randomly* to participate in one of several groups. Subjects in the **experimental group** receive the treatment the experimenter thinks will produce an identified effect (such as training in disciplinary strategies), while those in the **control group** receive either no special treatment or a neutral treatment. The presumed causal element in the experiment is called the **independent variable** (in this case the training), and any behavior on which the independent variable is expected to have an effect is called a **dependent variable** (in this case aggression or delinquency).

Problems with Experiments in Studying Development.   Experiments like this are essential for our understanding of many aspects of development. But two special problems in studying child or adult development limit the use of experimental designs.

First, many of the questions we want to answer have to do with the effects of particular unpleasant or stressful experiences on individuals—abuse, prenatal influences such as the mother's drinking, family poverty, or parental unemployment. For obvious ethical reasons, we cannot manipulate these variables. We cannot ask one set of pregnant women to have two alcoholic drinks a day and others to have none; we cannot randomly assign adults to become unemployed. So, to study the effects of such experiences we must rely on nonexperimental designs, including longitudinal and sequential studies.

Second, the independent variable in which we are often most interested is age itself, and *we cannot assign subjects randomly to age groups.* We can compare 4-year-olds and 6-year-olds in their approach to a particular task, such as searching for a lost object, but the children differ in a host of ways in addition to their ages. Older children have had more and different experiences. Thus, unlike psychologists studying other aspects of behavior, developmental psychologists *cannot* systematically manipulate many of the variables we are most interested in.

To get around this problem, we can use any one of a series of strategies that are sometimes called *quasi experiments*, in which we compare groups without assigning the subjects randomly. Cross-sectional comparisons are a form of quasi experiment. So are studies in which we select naturally occurring groups that differ in some dimension of interest, such as children whose parents choose to place them in day-care programs compared to children whose parents rear them at home, or children in single-parent families versus those in two-parent families.

Such comparisons have built-in problems, because groups that differ in one way are likely to be different in other ways as well. Families who place their children in day care, compared to those who rear them at home, are also likely to be poorer, may more often be single-parent families, and may have different values or religious backgrounds. If we find that the two groups of children differ in some fashion, is it because they have spent their daytime hours in different places or because of these other differences in their families? We can make such comparisons a bit cleaner if we select our comparison groups initially so that they are matched on those variables we think might matter, such as income or marital status or religion. But quasi experiments, by their very nature, will always yield more ambiguous results than will a fully controlled experiment.

▶ Research Methods

Choosing a research design is only the first crucial decision an investigator must make. Equally important is deciding what subjects to study, and how one will study them.

Choosing the Subjects.   Because we would like to uncover basic developmental patterns that are true for all children, all adolescents, or all adults, the ideal strategy would be to select a random sample of all people in the world to study. Clearly impractical. Borrowing techniques widely used by sociologists and epidemiologists, more and more developmental psychologists are selecting large samples that are representative of some subgroup or population—such as the Ontario study I've already described.

More commonly, psychologists choose to study much smaller groups in greater depth and detail, in an attempt to uncover very basic processes. For instance, Alan Sroufe and his colleagues (Sroufe, 1989; Sroufe, Egeland, & Kreutzer, 1990) have studied a group of 267 children and families, beginning before the birth of the child. Families were deliberately chosen from among those thought to be at high risk for later caregiving problems, such as low-education, single mothers with unplanned pregnancies. The children have now been repeatedly studied, each time in considerable detail. The sample is not representative of the population as a whole, but it is enormously informative nonetheless, and may tell us more about the process of emotional and social development than we could possibly glean from larger samples studied more broadly. Neither strategy is better than the other; both are useful. In either case, we need to remember that the conclusions we can draw will be limited by the sample we studied.

Collecting the Information from Your Subjects.   Having chosen your basic design and the subjects you wish to study, you then need to decide how to assess them—how to *describe* their behavior, attitudes, or values in some way. How does a 2-year-old or a 4-year-old react to the presence of a strange adult? How often does a teenager show delinquent behavior? The two time-honored ways of trying to answer questions like these,. are observing people and asking them questions. Because infants and young children are not particularly good at answering questions, observation has been an especially prominent research strategy among developmental psychologists.

Observation.   Any researcher planning to use observation to collect information about children or their environments will have to make at least three further decisions: What shall I observe? Where shall I observe? How shall I record the observations?

The decision about what to observe can be divided still further: Should you try to observe everything a child does, or focus only on selected behaviors? Should you observe only the child, or also the immediate environment, such as the responses of the people around the child, or the quality of the home? Which I choose will depend largely on the basic question I am trying to address. If I am interested in the child's first words I would not need to pay much attention to how close the child was sitting to an adult, or whether the child exchanged mutual gazes with the adults in his vicinity. But I might want to make note of what the child was playing with, whether other people were present, and what they said to the child. On the other hand, if I were interested in the development of attachment, I would want to make note of mutual gazes as well as how close or far away from the parent the child might be standing or sitting.

It is also no simple matter to decide *where* we will observe. We can observe in a natural setting, such as a child's home or school, in which case we are introducing an enormous amount of variability into the system and increasing the complexity of the observation immensely. Or we can choose a controlled setting, keeping it the same for each child observed. For example, the most commonly used measure of the security of a child's attachment to an adult is obtained in what is called the Strange Situation: the child is observed in a series of episodes in a laboratory setting, including periods with the mother, with the mother and a stranger, alone with a stranger, and reunited with the mother. By standardizing the situation, we gain the enormous advantage of having comparable information for each child, but we may lose some ecological validity. We cannot be sure that what we observe in this strange laboratory is representative of the child's behavior in more accustomed settings.

Questionnaires and Interviews.   Among researchers studying older children, questionnaires and interviews provide an excellent alternative to observation. They have been widely used in studies of children's moral development, for example (which you'll read about in Chapter 12), as well as studies of peer relationships among elementary-school- and high-school-age children. Assessments of parent-child relationships are also often done with questionnaires.

Each of these alternatives has costs and benefits. Structured laboratory tests give the experimenter excellent control over the situation so that each subject is confronted with the same task, the same stimuli. But because they are artificial, such tests may not give us an accurate portrayal of how individuals behave in the more complex natural environment. Interviews, especially very open-ended ones in which the subject is only guided toward general topics, may give a rich picture of an individual's thoughts and feelings, but how do you reduce the answers to a set of scores that would allow you to compare groups or individuals with one another? Questionnaires solve some of this problem, but the trade-off may be the richness and individuality of replies. Often the best strategy—although one not always possible because of cost in time or money—is to collect many different kinds of information from or about each subject.

Careful observation of children in both natural and experimentally created settings has formed the backbone of our knowledge about early development.

▶ Research Analysis

Finally, you need to analyze the results of your research. In studies of development, there are two broad forms of analysis.

First, we can compare different age groups by simply calculating the average score of each group on some measure, just as the Ontario researchers did in com-

---

RESEARCH REPORT
Ethical Issues in Research on Development

Anytime we try to understand human behavior by observing, testing, asking questions, we are probing into personal lives. If we go into people's homes to observe the way they interact with their children, we are invading their privacy. We may even inadvertently give the impression that there must be something wrong with the way they are raising their family. If we give adults or children laboratory tests, some subjects will do very well, others will not. How will the less-successful subject interpret this experience? What is the risk that some subject will become depressed over what he perceives as a poor performance?

Any research on human behavior involves some risks, and raises some ethical questions. Because of this, psychologists and other social and biological scientists have established clear procedures and guidelines that must be followed before any observation can be undertaken, any test given. In every school or college—the settings in which most such research is done—there is a committee of peers who must approve any research plan involving human subjects. The most basic guideline is that subjects must always be protected from any potential mental or physical harm. More specific principles include:

Informed Consent

Each adult subject must give written consent to participate. In the case of research on children, informed consent must be obtained from the parent or guardian. In every case, the procedure and its possible consequences must be explained in detail. If there are potential risks, these must be described. For example, if you were

studying patterns of communication between teenagers and their parents, you might want to observe each family while they talked about some unresolved issue between them. As part of your informed-consent request, you would have to explain to each family that while such discussions often lead to greater clarity, they also occasionally increase tension. And you would need to provide support and debriefing at the end of the procedure, to assist any family who found the task stressful or destabilizing.

Right of Privacy

Subjects must be assured that highly personal information they may provide will be kept entirely private—including information about income, or attitudes, or illegal behavior like drug taking. Researchers can use the information *collectively,* but they cannot report it individually in any way that will associate a subject's name with some piece of data—unless the subject has specifically given permission for such use.

In virtually all cases, it is also considered unethical to observe through a one-way mirror without the subject's knowledge, or to secretly record behavior.

Testing Children

These principles are important for any research, but particularly so for research on children. Any child who balks at being tested or observed must *not* be tested or observed; any child who becomes distressed must be comforted; any risk to the child's self-esteem must be avoided.

---

paring rates of conduct disorders for each age or gender group in Figure 1.4. You will see *many* examples of exactly this kind of analysis as you go through the book.

A second strategy allows us to look at relationships between two separate variables, most often using a statistic called a **correlation.** A correlation is simply a number ranging from −1.00 to +1.00, that describes the strength of a relationship between two variables. A zero correlation indicates that there is no linear relationship between those variables. For instance, you might expect to find a zero or near-zero correlation between the length of big toes and IQ. People with toes of all sizes have high IQs, and those with toes of all sizes have low IQs. The closer a correlation comes to −1.00 or +1.00, the stronger the relationship being described. If the correlation is positive, it indicates that high scores on the two dimensions tend to go together, and low scores tend to go together, such as length of big toes and shoe size, for example. Height and weight are also strongly positively correlated, as (probably) are age and memory span.

If the correlation is negative, it describes a relationship in which high scores on one variable are associated with low scores on the other. There is a negative correlation between the amount of disorder and chaos in a family and the child's later IQ (high chaos is associated with lower IQ, and low chaos with higher IQ).

Perfect correlations (−1.00 or +1.00) do not happen in the real world, but correlations of .80 or .70 do occur and correlations of .50 are common in psychological research, indicating a relationship of moderate strength.

Correlations are an enormously useful descriptive tool. They can tell us about consistency over time, or about links between two environmental variables, or between the child's behavior and some experience he may have had. Useful as they are, though, correlations have a major limitation: they do not tell us about *causal* relationships. For example, several researchers have found a moderate positive correlation between the "difficultness" of a child's temperament and the amount of punishment the child receives from his parents: The more difficult the temperament the more punishment the child experiences. But which way does the causality run? Do difficult children *elicit* more punishment? Or does a greater rate of punishment lead to a more difficult temperament? Or is there some third factor that may cause both, such as perhaps some genetic contribution both to the child's difficultness and to the parent's personality? The correlation alone does not allow us to choose among these alternatives. Stating the point more generally: No correlation, standing alone, can prove causality. A correlation may point in a particular direction, or suggest possible causal links, but to discover the causes, we must then explore such possibilities with other techniques, including experiments.

A Final Word

It may seem to you that these details about research design are of interest and value only to professional researchers. But that is not true. There are many practical, daily applications for knowledge of this kind, even if you never take another course in psychology. An example:

An issue of *Time* magazine I read recently included an article about a new system for providing stimulation for the unborn baby. The pregnant woman apparently wears a belt full of audio equipment, on which is played tapes of various complex patterns of heartbeat sounds. The article reported that the maker of this gadget had done some "research" to demonstrate that this procedure produces smarter, faster-developing babies. To quote *Time:* "Last year 50 of the youngsters [whose mothers had worn the belt], ranging in age from six months to 34 months, were given standardized language, social and motor-skills tests. Their overall score was 25% above the national norm" (September 30, 1991, p. 76).

I hope you would not go out and buy this apparatus on the basis of that finding! After reading what I've said about research design, you should be able to see immediately that self-selection is a major problem here. What kind of mothers will buy such a gadget? In fact this reported "research" tells us nothing. It isn't even a quasi experiment because there is no comparison group. There are equivalent reports of research on children, on adolescents, on adults in the newspapers and popular magazines every day. Obviously I want you to be critical analysts of the research I'll talk about in this book. But if nothing else, I want you to become very critical consumers of popularly presented research information. Some of it is very good. A lot of it is bunk, or at the very least inconclusive. I hope you are now in a better position to tell the difference.

⟩ Summary

1. To understand children's development, we must understand both change and consistency, both universality and individuality.

2. Both nature and nurture, biology and culture, are involved in all aspects of development, although there has been long-standing disagreement on the relative importance of these factors. ⟩

3. Current thinking about the nature side of the equation emphasizes not only the role of maturation but also points to potential inborn strategies of perceiving or responding to the environment.

4. Current thinking about the nurture side of the equation emphasizes not only the potential importance of the timing of some experience and the significance of a child's interpretation of some experience, but also the importance of examining the entire ecological system in which development occurs, including culture. ⟩

5. Nature and nurture may not interact in precisely the same way for each child. Children with different inborn qualities (vulnerability or resilience) may be affected differently by the same environment. ⟩

6. Another key question concerns the nature of developmental change itself, whether it is qualitative or quantitative, continuous or stagelike. ⟩

7. Four families of theories represent different combinations of positions on these issues: biological, learning, psychoanalytic, and cognitive-developmental.

8. Biological theorists, such as Gesell or behavior geneticists, generally assume that the most significant influences on development are internal (nature) and that developmental change is primarily quantitative. ⟩

9. Learning theorists generally place strongest emphasis on environmental influences, thought to produce largely quantitative change. Bandura's influential version of learning theory includes more cognitive elements and the crucial concept of modeling. ⟩

10. Psychoanalytic theorists such as Freud and Erikson have primarily studied the development of personality, emphasizing the interaction of internal instincts and environmental influences in producing shared stages of development as well as individual differences in personality. ⟩

11. Cognitive-developmental theorists such as Piaget and his many followers emphasize the child's own active exploration of the environment as a critical ingredient leading to shared stages of development. These theorists strongly emphasize qualitative change. ⟩

12. A first major question in planning research is the basic research design. Cross-sectional studies compare different children of different ages; longitudinal studies observe the same children as they develop over time; sequential studies combine some of these features; and cross-cultural studies compare children, their rearing, or nature/nurture relationships in differing cultures or subcultures.

13. Each of these designs has particular strengths and drawbacks.

14. To study causal connections, researchers normally use experimental designs. In an experiment, the researcher controls (manipulates) one or more relevant variables and assigns subjects randomly to different treatment and control groups.

15. In a quasi experiment, subjects are not randomly assigned to separate groups; rather, existing groups are compared. Quasi experiments are needed in developmental research because subjects cannot be randomly assigned either to age groups or to experience such negative treatments as poverty or abuse or poor attachment.

16. Decisions about research methods include the choice of subjects to be studied, and the methods to be used to observe or assess them.

17. When research results are analyzed, the two most common methods are comparing average scores between groups, and describing relationships among variables with the statistic called a correlation. It can range from +1.00 to −1.00, and describes the strength of relationship.

▶ Key Terms

behavior genetics (6)

classical conditioning (17)

cohort (25)

conditioned stimulus (17)

control group (28)

correlation (31)

critical period (9)

cross-cultural research (24)

cross-sectional study (24)

culture (12)

dependent variable (28)

ego (20)

experiment (27)

experimental group (28)

id (20)

independent variable (28)

intrinsic reinforcements (19)

libido (20)

longitudinal study (24)

maturation (5)

modeling (19)

negative reinforcement (18)

observational learning (19)

operant conditioning (18)

partial reinforcement (19)

positive reinforcement (18)

punishment (18)

sensitive period (10)

sequential designs (24)

superego (20)

teratogen (9)

unconditioned response (17)

unconditioned stimulus (17)

▶ Suggested Readings

Bornstein, M. H. (Ed.). (1987). *Sensitive periods in development: Interdisciplinary perspectives*. Hillsdale, NJ: Erlbaum .

Bornstein's own paper in this collection of reports is an excellent introduction to the concept of sensitive periods, but the book also contains a number of reports of research exploring potential sensitive periods both in humans and in other animals.

Cole, M. (1992). Culture in development. In M. H. Bornstein & M. E. Lamb (Eds.), *Developmental psychology: An advanced textbook* (3rd ed.) (pp. 731–738). Hillsdale, NJ: Erlbaum.

Not at all easy reading, but the best analysis I have yet seen on this very complicated subject.

Plomin, R., & McClearn, G. E. (Eds.). (1993). *Nature, nurture & psychology*. Washington, DC: American Psychological Association.

If you think the "great debate" about nature and nurture is an old issue, this book will quickly persuade you otherwise. The controversy is alive and well, although the papers in this book reflect the efforts of many people to recast it in more useful terms.

Seitz, V. (1988). Methodology. In M. H. Bornstein & M. E. Lamb (Eds.), *Developmental psychology: An advanced textbook* (2nd ed.) (pp. 51–84). Hillsdale, NJ: Lawrence Erlbaum Associates.

A very good source for a further exploration of various methods of research. Well organized and clearly written.

Thomas, R. M. (Ed.). (1990). *The encyclopedia of human development and education: Theory, research, and studies*. Oxford: Pergamon Press.

This is a very useful volume. It includes brief descriptions of virtually all the theories I have described in this chapter as well as a helpful chapter on the concept of stages. Each chapter is quite brief but covers many of the critical issues.

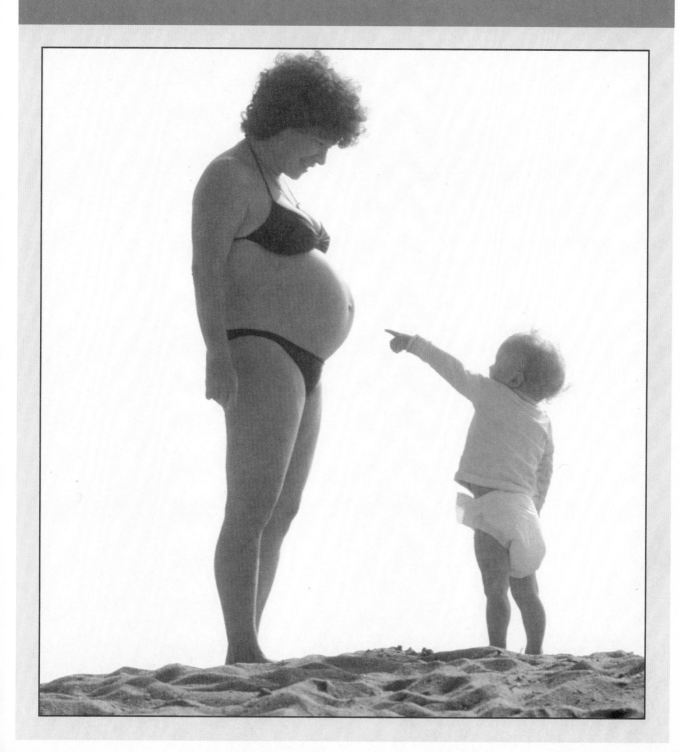

PRENATAL DEVELOPMENT

2

Conception

The Basic Genetics of Conception
  Dominant and Recessive Genes
  Males and Females
  Twins and Siblings
  Genotypes and Phenotypes

Development from Conception to Birth
  The Germinal Stage: From Conception to Implantation
  The Embryonic Stage
  The Fetal Stage

Prenatal Sexual Differentiation

An Overview of Prenatal Development

Genetic Errors
  Single-Gene Defects
  • *The Real World:* Prenatal Diagnosis of Genetic Errors

Teratogens: Diseases and Drugs
  Diseases of the Mother

• *The Real World:* Rh Factor: Another Type of Genetic Problem
Drugs Taken by the Mother
• *Research Report:* Streissguth's Study of Prenatal Alcohol Exposure
Other Teratogens

Other Influences on Prenatal Development
• *The Real World:* Weight Gain and Diet During Pregnancy

An Overview of Risks and Long-Term Consequences of Prenatal Problems

Sex Differences in Prenatal Development

Social Class Differences in Prenatal Development

Summary

Key Terms

Suggested Readings

At a family gathering a decade or so ago, my then four-months-pregnant sister-in-law Nancy complained of a headache. Having heard warnings about the possible ill effects of various kinds of drugs during pregnancy, she was very reluctant to take any aspirin. We tried all the usual home remedies (shoulder rubs, warm baths, herb tea) but the headache persisted. Finally she took a nonaspirin pain medicine, which did the trick.

This incident brought home to me very clearly just how sensitized most women are today to the various hazards (*teratogens*) during pregnancy, including drugs. I was impressed by Nancy's determination to avoid doing anything

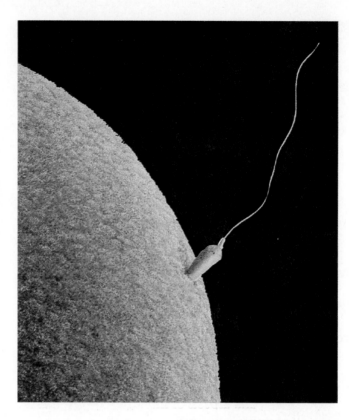

Figure 2.1
The moment of conception
when a single sperm has
pierced the shell of the
ovum.

harmful. Even more, I was struck by how long the list of "don'ts" had become, and
how hard it is for a conscientious woman to be sure of what is okay and what is
not.

So what do we now know? What does the list of dos and don'ts look like today? It's an important practical question for any of you who plan to be parents,
and to answer it I need to explore what we know about the basic processes of development from conception to birth, as well as what we have learned about what
can interfere with those basic processes. And of course beyond this practical issue, it is also essential for any complete understanding of child development that
we begin our search at the beginning—at conception and pregnancy.

▶ Conception

The first step in the development of a single human being is that moment of conception when a single sperm cell from the male pierces the wall of the ovum of
the female—a moment captured stunningly in the photo in Figure 2.1. Ordinarily, a woman produces one **ovum** (egg cell) per month from one of her two
ovaries. This occurs roughly midway between two menstrual periods. If it is not
fertilized, the ovum travels from the ovary down the **fallopian tube** toward the
uterus, where it gradually disintegrates and is expelled as part of the next menstruation.

But if a couple has intercourse during the crucial few days when the ovum is
in the fallopian tube, one of the millions of sperm ejaculated as part of each male

orgasm may travel the full distance through the woman's vagina, cervix, uterus, and fallopian tube, and penetrate the wall of the ovum. A child is conceived. The now-fertilized ovum then continues on its journey down the fallopian tube, where instead of disintegrating, it implants itself in the wall of the uterus.

One of the surprising things about this very early part of the process is just how often it works imperfectly. Experts now estimate that only about one-half to two-thirds of fertilized ova eventually result in a live baby. One current study (Wilcox et al., 1988) suggests that about a quarter of the losses occur within the first few days; typically these women do not even know that they are pregnant. Of those pregnancies that continue for three to four weeks, including implantation, perhaps a third are subsequently spontaneously aborted—an event usually called a *miscarriage* in everyday language.

The Basic Genetics of Conception

The genetic events accompanying conception are of vital importance. The combination of genes from the father in the sperm and from the mother in the ovum create a unique genetic blueprint—the **genotype**—that characterizes each individual. To understand how that occurs, I need to back up a few steps.

The nucleus of each cell of our bodies contains a set of 46 **chromosomes,** arranged in 23 pairs. These chromosomes include all the necessary genetic information, including that controlling highly individual characteristics like hair color, height, body shape, temperament, and aspects of intelligence, as well as all those characteristics shared by all members of our species, such as patterns of physical development, or "built-in biases" of various kinds.

The only cells that do *not* contain 46 chromosomes are the sperm and the ovum, collectively called **gametes** or germ cells. In the early stages of development, gametes divide as all other cells do (a process called *mitosis*), with each set of 23 chromosome pairs "unzipping" and duplicating itself. But in gametes there is a final step, called *meiosis*, in which each new cell receives only one chromosome from each original pair. Thus each gamete has only 23 chromosomes, instead of 23 *pairs*. When a child is conceived, the 23 chromosomes in the ovum and the 23 in the sperm combine to form the 23 *pairs* that will be part of each cell in the newly developing body.

The chromosomes, in turn, are composed of long strings of molecules of a chemical called **deoxyribonucleic acid** (DNA). In an insight for which they won the Nobel Prize, James Watson and Francis Crick (1953) deduced that DNA is in the shape of a *double helix*, a kind of twisted ladder. The remarkable feature of this ladder is that the rungs are made up in such a way that the whole thing can "unzip" and then each half can guide the duplication of the missing part, thus allowing multiplication of cells so that each new cell contains the full set of genetic information.

The string of DNA that makes up each chromosome can be further subdivided into segments, called **genes,** each of which controls or influences some specific feature or a portion of some developmental pattern. A gene controlling a specific characteristic, such as your blood type or your hair color, always appears in the same place (the *locus*) on the same chromosome in every individual of the

Most parents find the nine months of a pregnancy to be a time of delightful anticipation. It is also a time in which the genetic patterning for the child (the genotype) is established, and in which complex maturational sequences unfold.

same species. The locus of the gene that determines whether you have type A, B, or O blood is on chromosome 9; the locus of the gene that determines whether you have the Rh factor in your blood is on chromosome 1, and so forth (Scarr & Kidd, 1983). Geneticists have made remarkable strides in recent years in mapping the loci for a great many features or characteristics—a scientific achievement that has allowed similarly giant strides in our ability to diagnose various genetic defects or inherited diseases before a child is born.

Dominant and Recessive Genes

Because each individual inherits *two* of each chromosome (one from each parent), the genetic instructions at any given locus may be either the same (*homozygous*) or contradictory (*heterozygous*). If you receive a gene for blue eyes from both parents, your inheritance is homozygous and you will have blue eyes. But what if you receive heterozygous information, such as a gene for blue eyes from one parent and a brown-eye gene from the other?

Heterozygosity is resolved in several different ways, depending on the particular genes involved. Sometimes the two signals appear to blend, resulting in some intermediate characteristic. For example, the children of one tall parent and one short parent generally have height that falls in between. Another, rarer, outcome is that the child expresses *both* characteristics. For example, type AB blood results from the inheritance of a type A gene from one parent and a type B gene from the other. The most common outcome of heterozygosity, however, is that one of the two genes is *dominant* over the other, and only the dominant gene is actually expressed. The "weaker" gene, called a *recessive* gene, continues to be part of the genotype and can be passed on to offspring through meiosis, but it has no effect on visible characteristics or behavior.

A large number of specific diseases appear to be transmitted through the operation of dominant and recessive genes, such as Tay-Sachs disease, sickle-cell anemia, and cystic fibrosis. Figure 2.2 shows how this might work in the case of sickle-cell anemia, which is caused by a *recessive* gene. For an individual to have this disease, she or he must inherit the disease gene from *both* parents. A "carrier" is someone who inherits the disease gene from only one parent. Such a person does not actually have the disease, but can pass the disease gene on to his or her children. If two carriers have children together (example III in the figure), or if a carrier and someone with the disease have children (example IV in the figure), their offspring may inherit disease genes from both parents and thus have the disease.

Unlike this simple example, most human characteristics are affected by many more than one gene. Temperament, intelligence, rate of growth, even apparently simple characteristics such as eye color, all involve the interaction of multiple genes. Very exciting new genetic research has also pointed toward totally unexpected additional complexities. For example, researchers studying muscular dystrophy, a recessive gene disease, have observed that this disease often becomes more severe from one generation to the next, apparently through some kind of multiplication of the DNA in the section of the chromosome that signals the disease (Fu et al., 1992). Other genetic researchers have discovered that, contrary to the long-accepted theory, the outcome may be different if a particular gene comes

In the inheritance of eye color, brown is dominant over blue. Can you figure out what your parents' genotype for eye color has to be, based on the color of your eyes, your siblings' eyes, and that of your grandparents? What is your *own* eye color genotype likely to be?

Figure 2.2
Some examples of how a recessive gene disease, like sickle-cell anemia, is transmitted. In section I, a mother who has the disease passes her sickle-cell disease gene to all her children, but since her partner is normal, none of the children actually express the disease. In section II, a normal mother and a carrier father have no children with the disease, but each of their children has a 50/50 chance of carrying the SCA gene. The child can inherit the actual disease either of three ways: with two carrier parents (section III), with one carrier parent and one affected parent (section IV), or with two affected parents (not shown in the figure).

from the mother rather than from the father, even though the genes appear to signal precisely the same genotypic characteristic (McBride, 1991; Rogers, 1991). Research like this is beginning to unlock the secrets of genetic transmission, but there is an enormous amount that we still do not know.

Males and Females

Still another complexity comes from the fact that there are actually two types of chromosomes. In 22 of the pairs, called **autosomes,** the members of the pair look alike and contain exactly matching genetic loci. But the twenty-third pair, which determines the child's gender and is therefore called the **sex chromosomes,** is unique. Sex chromosomes come in two types, referred to by convention as the X and the Y chromosomes. A normal human female has two X chromosomes on this twenty-third pair (an XX pattern), while the normal human male has one X and one Y (an XY pattern). The X chromosome is considerably larger than the Y and contains many genetic loci not matched on the Y.

Note that the sex of the child is determined by the X or Y chromosome from the sperm. Since the mother has *only* X chromosomes, every ovum carries an X. But the father has both X and Y chromosomes. When the father's gametes divide, half the sperm will carry an X, half a Y. If the sperm that fertilizes the ovum carries an X, then the child inherits an XX pattern and will be a girl. If the fertilizing sperm carries a Y, then the combination is XY, and the infant will be a boy.

Geneticists have recently pushed this understanding a step further. They have discovered that only one very small section of the Y chromosome actually determines maleness—a segment referred to as *TDF,* or *testis-determining factor* (Page et al., 1987). Fertilized ova that are genetically XY, but that lack the TDF, develop physically as female. The mother does have some indirect effect on the gender of the child, because the relative acidity or alkalinity of the mucus in the vagina affects the survival rate of X-carrying or Y-carrying sperm. This chemical balance varies from one woman to the next, and in all women over the course of their monthly cycle. So the timing of intercourse, or a woman's typical chemical balance, can sharply alter the probability of conceiving a child of a particular gender, even though it is still true that the X or Y in the sperm is the final determining factor.

One important consequence of the difference between X and Y chromosomes is that a boy inherits many genes from his mother on his X chromosome that are not matched by, or counteracted by, equivalent genetic material on the Y chromosome. Since the X chromosome contains the loci for genes that, when abnormal, cause specific diseases, such as hemophilia and muscular dystrophy, a boy may inherit these if his mother carries the (recessive) gene for the disease, since there is no equivalent gene on the Y chromosome to counteract the effect (see Figure 2.3). A girl, in contrast, could not inherit such a disease unless she received the gene signaling that disease on both of her X chromosomes, one from her mother and one from her father. Such *sex-linked* inheritance patterns occur for many characteristics in addition to diseases.

Twins and Siblings

In the great majority of cases, babies are conceived and born one at a time. But multiple births occur roughly once in a hundred cases. The most common type of

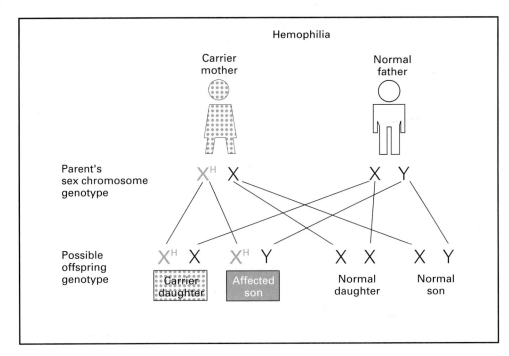

Figure 2.3
Compare the pattern of sex-linked transmission of a recessive disease with the patterns already shown in Figure 2.2. In the inheritance of a sex-linked disease such as hemophilia, a carrier mother can pass on the disease to half her sons (on average) because there is no offsetting gene on the Y chromosome. But a daughter of a carrier mother will not inherit the disease itself unless her father has the disease.

multiple birth is *fraternal twins*, when more than one ovum has been produced and both have been fertilized, each by a separate sperm. Such twins, also called *dizygotic* twins, are no more alike genetically than any other pair of siblings, and need not even be of the same sex. In rarer cases, a single fertilized ovum may divide and each half may develop into a separate individual. These are *identical* or *monozygotic* twins, and have identical genetic heritages because they come from precisely the same original fertilized ovum. You'll remember from Chapter 1 that comparisons of the degree of similarity of these two types of twins is one of the two major research strategies in the important field of behavior genetics.

Genotypes and Phenotypes

Using such strategies, behavior geneticists have made great strides in identifying those skills, characteristics, or traits that are influenced by heredity. But no geneticist proposes that an inherited combination of genes fully *determines* any outcome for a given individual. Geneticists (and psychologists) make an important distinction between the genotype, which is the specific set of "instructions" contained in a given individual's genes, and the **phenotype,** which is the actual observed characteristics of the individual. The phenotype is a product of three things: the genotype, all the environmental influences from the time of conception onward, and the interaction between the environment and the genotype. A child might have a genotype associated with high IQ, but if his mother drinks too much alcohol during pregnancy, there may be damage to the fetal nervous system, resulting in mild retardation. Another child may have a genotype for a "difficult" temperament, but have parents who are particularly sensitive and thoughtful, so that the child learns other ways to handle herself.

Can you think of other examples where the phenotype would be different from the genotype?

This distinction between the genotype and the phenotype is crucial. It reminds us that genetic codes are not irrevocable signals for this or that pattern of development, or this or that disease. They are all affected by the specific experiences the individual may have from conception onward.

▶ Development from Conception to Birth

If we assume that conception takes place two weeks after a menstrual period, when ovulation normally occurs, then the period of gestation of the human infant is 38 weeks (about 265 days). Most physicians calculate gestation as 40 weeks, counting from the last menstrual period. All the specifications of weeks of gestation I've given here are based on the 38-week calculation, counting from the presumed time of conception.

These 38 weeks have been subdivided in several different ways. Physicians typically talk in terms of three equal three-month periods, called *trimesters*. In contrast, biologists and embryologists typically divide the weeks of gestation into three unequal subperiods, linked to specific changes within the developing organism. These are the *germinal,* which lasts roughly two weeks; the *embryonic*, which continues until about 8 to 12 weeks after conception; and the *fetal* stage, which makes up the remaining 26 to 30 weeks.

The Germinal Stage: From Conception to Implantation

Sometime during the first 24 to 36 hours after conception, cell division begins; within two to three days there are several dozen cells and the whole mass is about the size of a pinhead. This initial mass of cells is undifferentiated until about four days after conception. At that point the organism, now called a *blastocyst*, begins to subdivide. A cavity begins to appear within the ball of cells, and the mass divides into two parts. The outer cells will form the various structures that will support the developing organism, while the inner mass will form the embryo itself. When it touches the wall of the uterus, the outer shell of cells in the blastocyst breaks down at the point of contact. Small tendrils develop and attach the cell

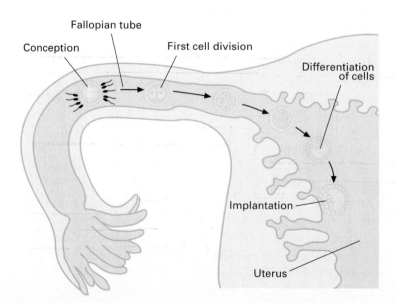

Figure 2.4
This schematic shows the normal progression of development for the first 10 days of gestation, from conception to implantation. (*Source:* Smith & Stenchever, 1978, p. 43.)

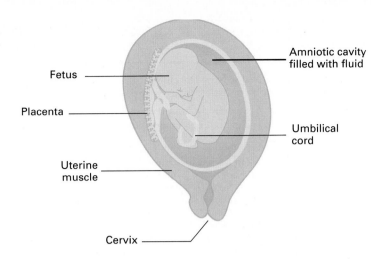

Fetus

Placenta

Uterine
muscle

Cervix

Amniotic cavity
filled with fluid

Umbilical
cord

Figure 2.5
You can see here how the various structures are organized during the fetal period. Note especially the placenta and the umbilical cord, and the fact that the fetus floats in the amniotic fluid.

mass to the uterine wall, a process called *implantation*. When implantation occurs, normally 10 days to 2 weeks after conception, there are perhaps 150 cells in the blastocyst (Tanner, 1978). You can see this whole sequence schematically in Figure 2.4.

The Embryonic Stage

The embryonic stage begins when implantation is complete and continues until the various support structures are fully formed and all the major organ systems have been laid down in at least rudimentary form, a process that normally takes another 6 to 10 weeks.

Development of Support Structures. Two of the key support structures that develop out of the outer layer of cells are the **amnion,** which is the sac or bag, filled with liquid (amniotic fluid) in which the baby floats, and that marvelous organ, the **placenta,** a platelike mass of cells that lies against the wall of the uterus. The placenta is fully developed by about four weeks after gestation, and serves as liver, lungs, and kidneys for the **embryo** and later the **fetus.** The embryo's circulatory system is connected to the placenta through a third support structure, the *umbilical cord.* Thus the placenta lies between the mother's circulatory system and the embryo's, and can serve as a sort of filter. Nutrients such as oxygen, proteins, sugars, and vitamins from the maternal blood can pass through the placental filter, while digestive wastes and carbon dioxide from the infant's blood pass back through to the mother, whose own body can eliminate them (Rosenblith & Sims-Knight, 1989). At the same time, many (but not all) harmful substances, such as viruses the mother may carry, are filtered out because they are too large to pass through the various membranes in the placenta. The same is true of most of the mother's hormones. Most drugs and anesthetics, however, do pass through the placental barrier, as do some disease organisms. You can see all of these separate structures in Figure 2.5.

Development of the Embryo. While these support structures are developing, the mass of cells that will form the embryo is itself differentiating further into several types of cells that form the rudiments of skin, sense receptors, nerve cells, muscles, circulatory system, and internal organs. Such differentiation is remarkably swift. By the eighth week of gestation, the embryo is roughly 1 1/2 inches long, has a heart that beats, a primitive circulatory system, the beginnings of eyes

TABLE 2.1 Major Milestones of Fetal Development	
Gestational Age	Major New Developments
12 weeks	Sex of child can be determined; muscles are developed more extensively; eyelids and lips are present; feet have toes and hands have fingers.
16 weeks	First fetal movement is usually felt by the mother at about this time; bones begin to develop; fairly complete ear is formed.
20 weeks	Hair growth begins; child is very human-looking at this age and thumb-sucking may be seen.
24 weeks	Eyes are completely formed (but closed); fingernails, sweat glands, and taste buds are all formed; some fat deposit beneath skin. The infant is capable of breathing if born prematurely at this stage but survival rate is still low for infants born this small.
28 weeks	Nervous system, blood, and breathing systems are all well enough developed to support life, although prematures born at this stage have poor sleep/wake cycles and irregular breathing.
29–40 weeks	Interconnections between individual nerve cells (neurons) develop rapidly; weight is added; general "finishing" of body systems takes place.

and ears, a mouth that opens and closes, legs, arms, and a primitive spinal cord. When this *organogenesis* is complete, a new stage, that of the fetus, begins.

The Fetal Stage

The seven months of the fetal stage involve primarily a process of refining all the primitive organ systems already in place, much like what happens in constructing a house: the framework is created quickly, but the finishing work takes much more time. Table 2.1 lists some of the milestones of fetal development; you can see the changes even more vividly in the series of photos in Figure 2.6.

Development of the Nervous System.   The nervous system is one of the least well developed elements at the end of the embryonic period. It is composed of two basic types of cells, **neurons** and **glial cells.** The glial cells are the glue that holds the whole system together, providing firmness and structure to the brain, helping to remove debris after neuronal death or injury, segregating neurons from one another (Kandel, 1985). It is the neurons that do the job of receiving and sending messages from one part of the brain to another, or from one part of the body to another.

Neurons have four main parts, which you can see in the drawing in Figure 2.7: (1) a cell body; (2) branchlike extensions of the cell body called **dendrites,** which are the major *receptors* of nerve impulses; (3) a tubular extension of the cell body called the **axon,** which can extend as far as 1 meter in length in humans (about three feet); and (4) terminal fibers at the end of the axon, which form the primary *transmitting* apparatus of the nervous system. Because of the branchlike appearance of dendrites, physiologists describe these structures in a language intriguingly reminiscent of botany, speaking of the "dendritic arbor" or of "pruning" of the arbor.

Figure 2.6
This sequence of photos shows the changes in the fetal period much more graphically. Photo 1 shows a fetus at 9 to 10 weeks, photo 2 a fetus at 14 to 16 weeks. Fingers and toes are clearly present, as are many facial features. Photo 3 was taken at perhaps 18 to 20 weeks, and photo 4 shows a fetus at about 32 weeks gestation, an age at which most infants now survive if born prematurely, although lungs and nervous system are still quite immature at this stage.

The point at which two neurons connect, where the axon's transmitting fibers come into close contact with another neuron's dendrites, is called a **synapse**. Synapses can also be formed between neurons and other kinds of cells, such as muscle cells. The number of such synapses in a single human is vast. One cell in the part of the brain that controls vision, for instance, may have as many as 10,000 to 30,000 synaptic inputs to its dendrites (Greenough, Black, & Wallace, 1987).

Glial cells begin to develop at about 13 weeks after conception and continue to be added until perhaps two years after birth. Neurons begin to appear at about 12 weeks, and are virtually all present by 28 weeks. But at this early stage the neurons consist largely of the cell body. Axons are short, and there is little dendritic development. It is in the last two months before birth, and the first few years after birth, that the lengthening of the axons and the major growth of the "dendritic arbor" occurs, making possible the vast numbers of synapses necessary for all aspects of human functioning (Parmelee & Sigman, 1983).

Can you think of any practical consequences of the fact that all the neurons one is ever going to have are present by about 28 weeks of gestation?

Development of Length and Weight.   Similarly, the major growth in fetal size occurs late in the fetal period, with the gain in length occurring earlier than the major gain in weight. The fetus is about half her birth length by about 20 weeks gestation, but she does not reach half her birth weight until nearly three months later, at about 32 weeks.

▶ Prenatal Sexual Differentiation

I've already said that the sex of the child is determined at the moment of conception by the XX or XY combination of chromosomes. But this is not the end of the story. As I pointed out in the discussion of genotypes and phenotypes, the basic

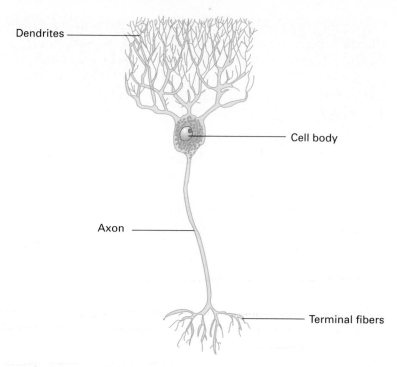

Figure 2.7
The structure of a single developed neuron. The cell bodies are the first to be developed, primarily during the second trimester of prenatal development. Axons and dendrites develop later and continue to increase in size and complexity for several years after birth.

genetic patterning does not *guarantee* a particular outcome. In this case it does not guarantee that the newborn infant will have the appropriate sexual characteristics, or that he or she will have the behaviors and sexual preferences typical for his or her genetic pattern.

Prenatal gender differentiation is also significantly influenced by the action of a series of hormones (Hines, 1982). Simplifying a bit, it seems that for the development of a male child, both the genetic programming (XY) *and* a particular pattern of hormone action are required for normal gender development. Sometime between four and eight weeks after conception, the male hormone *testosterone* begins to be secreted by the rudimentary testes in the male embryo. If this hormone is not secreted or is secreted in inadequate amounts, the embryo will be "demasculinized" (to use John Money's term [Money, 1987]), even to the extent of developing female genitalia. Normal development of the girl does not require any additional hormonal input, but the accidental presence of testosterone at the critical time (such as from some drug the mother may take) acts to "defeminize" or masculinize the female fetus, possibly resulting in malelike genitalia.

There is also growing speculation among physiologists and psychologists, based primarily on studies with other animals, that such prenatal hormones may affect not just the development of genitalia but also the pattern of brain development (Hines, 1982; Meyer-Bahlburg, Ehrhardt, & Feldman, 1986). Such functions as the pattern of growth-hormone secretions in adolescence, the level of aggressive behavior, or the relative dominance of the right and left hemispheres of the brain might be affected. The research evidence on such points is still fairly confusing; it is clear that whatever role prenatal hormones play is highly complex. But the possibilities are intriguing—and yet another example of the growing importance of biological explanations of children's development.

An Overview of Prenatal Development

One of the most important points about prenatal development is how remarkably regular and predictable it is. If the embryo has survived the early, risky period, development usually proceeds smoothly, with the various changes occurring in what is apparently a fixed order, at fixed time intervals. Maturation seems clearly at work. The fetus doesn't learn to grow fingernails, nor does it have to be stimulated from the outside to grow them. The eyes, the ears, the internal organs, the nervous system are all apparently controlled in some fashion by the developmental codes contained in the genes.

However, this sequence of development is not immune to modification or outside influence. Indeed, as psychologists and biologists have looked more carefully at various kinds of teratogens, it has become clear the sequence is more vulnerable than had earlier appeared. Still, it takes a fairly sizable intervention to make a large difference in the outcome.

Before I begin talking about the things that can go wrong, I want to reemphasize that the maturational system is really quite robust. Normal prenatal development requires an adequate environment, but "adequate" seems to be a fairly broad range. *Most* children are quite normal. The list of things that *can* go wrong is long (and getting longer as our knowledge expands), but many of these possibilities are quite rare. More important, a very great number of them are partially or wholly preventable, and many of the remaining problems need not have permanent consequences for the child.

The potential problems can be grouped into two classes: genetic errors, and teratogens. Genetic errors occur at the moment of conception, and there is little that can be done about them. Teratogens are numerous, and many are controllable or preventable.

Genetic Errors

In perhaps 3 to 8 percent of all fertilized ova (Kopp, 1983), the genetic material itself contains errors because either the sperm or the ovum has failed to divide correctly, so that there are either too many or too few chromosomes. Current estimates are that perhaps 90 percent of these abnormal conceptuses are spontaneously aborted. Only about 1 percent of live newborns have such abnormalities.

Over 50 different types of chromosomal anomaly have been identified, many of them very rare. The most common is **Down syndrome** (also called *mongolism* and *trisomy 21*), in which the child, because of a failure of proper meiosis in either sperm or ovum, has three copies of chromosome 21 rather than the normal two. Other forms of trisomy also occur, of course, but Down syndrome is by far the

Note the distinctive facial characteristics of this Down syndrome child.

most frequent. Estimates of the incidence of this abnormality differ, but the frequency is somewhere between 1 in 600 and 1 in 1000 (Nightingale & Goodman, 1990). These children have distinctive facial features (as you can see in the photo) and are typically retarded.

The risk of bearing a child with this deviant pattern is greatest for mothers over 35. Among women aged 35–39, the incidence of Down syndrome is about 1 in 280 births; among 40-year-olds it is roughly 1 in 100; and for mothers aged 45 it is 1 in 30 births (D'Alton & DeCherney, 1993). Recent research by epidemiologists is also revealing a link between exposure to environmental toxins of various kinds and the risk of offspring with Down syndrome. For example, one large study in Canada shows that men who work as mechanics, farm laborers, or sawmill workers, who are regularly exposed to solvents, oils, lead, and pesticides, are at higher risk for fathering Down syndrome children than are men who work in cleaner environments (Olshan, Baird, & Teschke, 1989). Findings like these suggest that chromosomal anomalies may not be purely random events, but may themselves be a response to various teratogens.

Sex-Chromosome Anomalies.   Other types of genetic anomalies are caused by an incomplete or incorrect division of either sex chromosome, which occurs in roughly 1 out of every 400 births (Berch & Bender, 1987). The most common is an XXY pattern, called *Klinefelter's syndrome*, which may occur as often as once in 500 births. This pattern results in boys who often have very long legs, poor coordination, poorly developed testes, sterility, and sometimes mild mental retardation. Not quite as common is the XYY pattern. These children also develop as boys, are typically unusually tall, and have mild retardation. A single-X pattern (XO), called *Turner's syndrome*, and a triple-X pattern (XXX) may also occur, and in both cases the child develops as a girl. Girls with Turner's syndrome are exceptions to the usual rule that embryos with too few chromosomes do not survive. These girls show stunted growth, are usually sterile, and often perform particularly poorly on tests that measure spatial ability. On tests of verbal skill, however, Turner's syndrome girls are at or above normal levels (Scarr & Kidd, 1983). Girls with an XXX pattern are of normal size but are slower than normal in physical development. They also have markedly poor verbal abilities (Rovet & Netley, 1983). As a general rule, children with sex chromosome anomalies are not as severely affected as what we see in Down syndrome, but they do show unusual physical features and some cognitive deficits.

Fragile-X Syndrome.   A quite different type of genetic anomaly involves not an improper amount of chromosomal material, but rather an abnormal section of DNA at a specific location on the X chromosome (Dykens, Hodapp, & Leckman, 1994). This is an *inherited* disorder, following the sex-linked inheritance pattern illustrated earlier in Figure 2.3. Thus both boys and girls may inherit a fragile X (ordinarily from a carrier mother), but boys, lacking the potentially overriding influence of a normal X, are much more susceptible to the negative intellectual or behavioral consequences. The affected child appears to have a considerably heightened risk of mental retardation; current estimates are that among males, 5 to 7 percent of all retardation is caused by this syndrome (Zigler & Hodapp, 1991).

TABLE 2.2   Some of the Major Inherited Diseases

Phenylketonuria	A metabolic disorder that prevents metabolism of a common amino acid (phenylalanine). Treatment consists of a special phenylalanine-free diet. The child is not allowed many types of food, including milk. If not placed on the special diet shortly after birth, the child usually becomes very retarded. Affects only 1 in 8000 children. Diagnostic tests for this disorder are now routinely given at birth; cannot be diagnosed prenatally.
Tay-Sachs disease	An invariably fatal degenerative disease of the nervous system; virtually all victims die within the first three to four years. This gene is most common among Jews of Eastern European origin, among whom it occurs in approximately 1 in 3500 births. Can be diagnosed prenatally.
Sickle-cell anemia	A sometimes fatal blood disease, with joint pain, increased susceptibility to infection, and other symptoms. The gene for this disease is carried by about 2 million Americans, most often blacks. Can now be diagnosed prenatally.
Cystic fibrosis	A fatal disease affecting the lungs and intestinal tract. Many children with CF now live into their twenties. The gene is carried by over 10 million Americans, most often whites. Carriers cannot be identified before pregnancy, and affected children cannot be diagnosed prenatally. If a couple has had one CF child, however, they know that their chances of having another are 1 in 4.
Muscular dystrophy	A fatal muscle-wasting disease, carried on the X chromosome, thus found almost exclusively among boys. The gene for the most common type of MD, Duchenne's, has just been located, so prenatal diagnosis may soon be available.

Single-Gene Defects

As I have already indicated, problems can also occur at conception if the child inherits a gene for a specific disease. In a few cases, such diseases may be caused by a dominant gene. The best-known example is Huntington's disease, a severe neurological disorder resulting in rapid loss of both mental and physical functioning, with symptoms usually appearing only at midlife. Dominant-gene diseases are relatively rare because the affected parent would almost always know that he or she was suffering from the disorder and would be unable or unwilling to reproduce.

Far more common are recessive-gene diseases, some of which I've listed in Table 2.2. The few examples listed in the table do not begin to convey the diversity of such disorders. Among known causes of mental retardation, for example, there are 141 diseases or disorders with known genetic loci and 361 more whose locus has not yet been identified (Wahlström, 1990).

Geneticists estimate that the average adult carries genes for four different recessive diseases or abnormalities (Scarr & Kidd, 1983), but for any one disease the distribution of genes is not random. For example, sickle-cell genes are more common among blacks; Tay-Sachs is most common among Jews of Eastern European origin.

THE REAL WORLD
Prenatal Diagnosis of Genetic Errors

Not so many years ago children were born with whatever deformities, diseases, or anomalies happened to come along. The parents had no choices. Today, parents have access to many types of genetic information, as well as tests to detect fetal abnormalities, which increase choice but may also create difficult decisions.

Prepregnancy Genetic Testing

Prepregnancy blood tests can tell you and your spouse whether you are carriers of genes for those specific diseases for which the loci are known, such as Tay-Sachs or sickle-cell anemia. This may be an important step if you and your spouse belong to a subgroup known to be likely to carry particular recessive genes.

Prenatal Diagnosis of the Fetus

Four prenatal diagnostic strategies are now available. Two of these, the **alpha-fetoprotein test** (AFP) and ultrasound, are primarily used to detect problems in the formation of the *neural tube,* the structure that becomes the brain and spinal cord. If the tube fails to close at the bottom end, a disability called *spina bifida* occurs. Children with this defect are often partially paralyzed, and many (but not all) are retarded.

Alpha-fetoprotein is a substance produced by the fetus and detectable in the mother's blood. If the blood test, normally done between 16 and 18 weeks of gestation, shows an abnormally high AFP level, it suggests that there may be some problem with the spinal cord or brain. It does not mean there is definitely a problem; it means there is a higher *risk* of problems and further tests are indicated.

One such further test is **ultrasound,** which involves the use of sound waves to provide an actual "moving picture" of the fetus. With this method it is frequently possible to detect, or rule out, neural tube defects or other physical abnormalities. The procedure is not painful, and gives parents an often-delightful chance to see their unborn child moving, but it cannot provide information about the presence of chromosomal anomalies or inherited diseases.

If you want the latter information, you have two choices: **amniocentesis,** or **chorionic villus sampling** (CVS). In both cases, a needle is inserted and cells are taken from the developing embryo. In CVS, the sample is taken from what will become the placenta; in amniocentesis, the sample is from the amniotic fluid. Of the two, amniocentesis was developed earlier and is the more widely used. Its major drawback is that because the amniotic sac must be large enough to allow a sample of fluid to be taken with very little danger to the fetus, the test cannot be done until the sixteenth week of gestation and the results are not typically available for several more weeks. If the test reveals an abnormality, and the parents decide to abort, it is quite late for an abortion to be performed. CVS, in contrast, is done between the ninth and eleventh weeks of gestation. Neither of these procedures is without risk. Both procedures sometimes cause miscarriages, and there has been a recent flurry of concern about *possible* links between CVS and slight increases in physical defects in the infant (Report of National Institute, 1993). Both procedures are recommended only for women known to be at high risk, such as those older than 35, or those who have borne a previous child with defects or chromosomal anomaly.

By the time you are facing this choice, there may be still newer and safer options using maternal blood samples. But no matter what technique you may select, the moral and ethical choices you may be called upon to make are far from easy.

For example, consider the case of diseases that can occur in mild or moderate as well as severe forms—such as sickle-cell anemia. Prenatal tests can tell you if the child will inherit the disease, but they cannot tell you how severely the child will be affected. Genetic counselors may play a very helpful role, but ultimately each couple has to make its own decisions.

▶ Teratogens: Diseases and Drugs

Deviant prenatal development can also result from variations in the environment in which the embryo/fetus is nurtured. I pointed out in Chapter 1 that the effect of any teratogen depends heavily on the *timing* of the intervention or interference (Vorhees & Mollnow, 1987), an example of *critical periods,* or *sensitive periods.* The general rule is that each organ system—the nervous system, heart, ears, reproductive system, and so on—is most vulnerable to disruption at the time when it is developing most rapidly (Moore, 1988). At that point it is maximally sensitive to outside interference, whether that be from a disease organism that passed

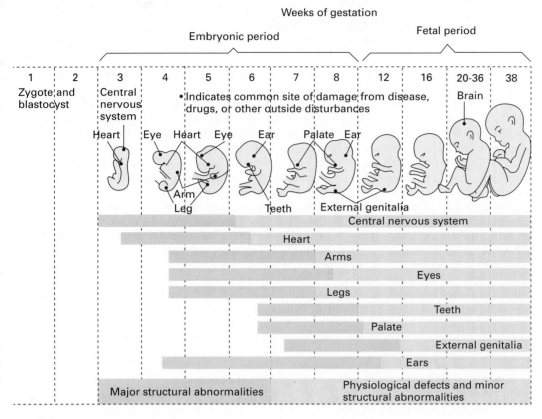

Figure 2.8
Critical periods in the prenatal development of various body parts. The blue portion of each line signifies the period during which any teratogen is likely to produce a major structural deformity in that particular body part. The yellow part of each line shows the period in which more minor problems may result. The embryonic period is generally the time of greatest vulnerability. (*Source:* Moore, 1988, Figure 8-14, p. 136.)

through the placental barrier, inappropriate hormones, drugs, or whatever. Since the most rapid development of most organ systems occurs during the first 12 weeks of gestation, this is the period of greatest risk. Figure 2.8 shows the maximum times of vulnerability for different parts of the body.

Because most organ systems develop most rapidly during the first 12 weeks of gestation, this is the period of greatest risk for most teratogens. Of the many teratogens, the most critical are probably drugs the mother may take and diseases she may have or may contract during the pregnancy.

Diseases of the Mother
There are at least three mechanisms by which a disease in the mother can affect the embryo or fetus. Some diseases, particularly viruses, can attack the placenta, reducing the nutrients available to the embryo. Some others have molecules small enough to pass through the placental filters and attack the embryo or fetus

THE REAL WORLD
Rh Factor: Another Type of Genetic Problem

Another possible problem, Rh factor incompatibility, is neither a genetic defect nor a teratogenic effect, but an interesting interaction of heredity and environment. One of the many factors in the blood is the presence or absence of a red cell antigen, called the Rh factor because rhesus monkeys have it. Humans who have this factor are called Rh+ (Rh positive), while those who lack it are Rh− (Rh negative). Only about 15 percent of whites and 5 percent of blacks in the United States are Rh−; it is quite rare among Asians and Native Americans.

Problems arise if the mother is Rh− and the baby is Rh+. Because Rh+ is dominant, a baby with an Rh+ father could inherit an Rh+ gene from him, even though the mother is Rh−. If the mother's and fetus's blood mix in the uterus, the mother's body considers the baby's Rh+ factor to be a foreign substance, and her immune system tries to fight it off by producing antibodies. These antibodies cross the placenta and attack the baby's blood, producing a chemical substance in the baby called bilirubin. Ba-

bies with high levels of bilirubin look quite yellow; if the condition is untreated, brain damage can occur.

Without treatment, the risk of damage to the fetus increases with each succeeding pregnancy in which an Rh− mother carries an Rh+ baby. Normally, the placenta keeps the two blood systems separate, but during birth some mixing usually occurs. So after the first baby, the mother produces some antibodies. With a second incompatible baby, these antibodies attack the infant's blood, producing negative effects.

This problem used to be treated with rather heroic measures, such as complete exchange of the infant's blood shortly after birth to remove all the antibodies. Fortunately, scientists have now discovered a much simpler and safer treatment. Within three days of the birth of her first child, an Rh− mother with an Rh+ baby can be injected with a substance called rhogam, which prevents the buildup of antibodies, and thus protects subsequent infants, even if they are also Rh+.

directly. Examples of this type include rubella and rubeola (both forms of measles), cytomegalovirus (CMV), syphilis, diphtheria, influenza, typhoid, serum hepatitis, and chicken pox. The third transmission method occurs during birth: disease organisms present in the mucous membranes of the birth canal may infect the infant. Genital herpes, for example, is transmitted this way. So far as researchers now know, AIDS is transmitted in both the second and third ways, as well as through breast milk after birth (Van de Perre et al., 1991). Among the riskiest of these diseases for the infant are rubella, AIDS, CMV, and genital herpes.

Rubella.   **Rubella** (also called *German measles*) is most risky during the first month of gestation. Half of infants exposed in this time show abnormalities of the ears, eyes, or heart, while only a quarter show effects if they are exposed in the second month (Berg, 1974; Kopp, 1983). Deafness is the most common outcome.

Fortunately, rubella is preventable. Vaccination is available and should be given to all children as part of a regular immunization program. Adult women who were not vaccinated as children can be vaccinated later, but it must be done at least three months before a pregnancy to provide complete immunity.

AIDS.   At present, there are approximately 3000 infants in the United States with AIDS, a relatively low rate in comparison to many other diseases of childhood. But because the number of infected women of childbearing age continues to grow, the number of infants born infected with the HIV virus will also grow. In areas with a high population of drug users, as many as 3 to 5 percent of all pregnant women are now HIV-infected (Heagarty, 1991). The only good news in all of this is that not all infants born to HIV-infected mothers themselves become infected. Estimates range from 13 percent in a European study (European

Women readers: Have you been vaccinated for rubella? If you don't know, find out; if you have not been, arrange for such a vaccination—but only if you are sure you are not pregnant!

Collaborative Study, 1991) to 30 percent in U.S. studies (Hutto et al., 1991). Researchers are still searching for good explanations for this pattern of transmission.

CMV.   A much less well known but remarkably widespread and potentially serious disease is cytomegalovirus (CMV), a virus in the herpes group. As many as 60 percent of *all* women have antibodies to CMV, but most have no recognized symptoms. One to 2 percent of babies whose mothers have CMV antibodies become infected prenatally. When the mother's disease is in an active phase, the transmission rate is more like 40 to 50 percent (Blackman, 1990). As with AIDS, researchers have not yet uncovered all the details of the mechanisms of transmission. Nor have they understood why only about 5 to 10 percent of babies infected prenatally show clear symptoms of the disease at birth. But the 2500 babies born each year in the United States who do display symptoms of the disease have a variety of serious problems, often including deafness and widespread damage to the central nervous system. Most are mentally retarded. In fact, CMV is now thought to be the single most important known infectious cause of both congenital mental retardation and deafness.

Herpes Simplex.   Like CMV, this form of herpes, also known as *genital herpes*, may be transmitted to the fetus during delivery if the mother's disease is in the active phase at that time. Not only will the child then periodically experience the genital sores characteristic of the disease, but other complications are also possible, most notably a potentially serious inflammation of the brain and spinal cord called *meningoencephalitis*. Because of this increased risk, many physicians now recommend surgical delivery (cesarean section) of infants of mothers with herpes, although vaginal delivery is possible if the disease is inactive.

Drugs Taken by the Mother

Ten or 15 years ago, the average pregnant woman in the U.S. took six to seven prescribed drugs and another three or four over-the-counter drugs (such as aspirin) during the course of her pregnancy (Stewart, Cluff, & Philp, 1977). Today that number is doubtless lower, but it is not zero. What are the effects of any of these drugs on the embryo or fetus?

There is now a huge literature on the effects of prenatal drugs, involving everything from aspirin to antibiotics to alcohol and cocaine. Sorting out their effects has proven to be an immensely challenging task, not only because it is clearly not possible to assign women randomly to various drug groups, but also because in the real world most women who use one drug are highly likely to use others as well. Women who drink alcohol are also more likely to smoke; those who use cocaine are also likely to take other illegal drugs, or to smoke or drink to excess. The task is made still more difficult by the fact that the effects of drugs may be subtle, visible only many years after birth in the form of minor learning disabilities or increased risk of behavior problems. Still, we are creeping toward some fairly clear conclusions in several areas. Let me give you some examples.

Smoking.   One of the most extensive bodies of research is on the effect of smoking. One consistent result stands out: Infants of mothers who smoke are on average about half a pound lighter at birth than are infants of nonsmoking mothers (Floyd et al., 1993; Vorhees & Mollnow, 1987). This does not mean that every

Before you read further, make a list of all the drugs you have taken in the past year, including over-the-counter drugs (aspirin? decongestants?), prescription drugs, and such "recreational" drugs as alcohol, nicotine, or cocaine. How many are there? How hard would it be to give them all

Figure 2.9
These three children, from three racial backgrounds (from left: Native American, black, and white) have all been diagnosed as having fetal alcohol syndrome (FAS). All are mentally retarded and have relatively small heads. Note also the short nose and low nasal bridge typical of FAS children. (*Source:* Streissguth et al., *Science* 209 [July 18, 1980]: Figure 2, p. 355; copyright 1980 by the American Association for the Advancement of Science.)

mother who smokes has a very small or early baby. It does mean that the risk of such an outcome is higher for mothers who smoke.

The causal mechanism seems to work this way: nicotine constricts the blood vessels, which reduces blood flow to the placenta, in turn reducing nutrition to the fetus. In the long term, such nutritional deprivation seems to increase slightly the risk of learning problems or poor attention span at school age (Naeye & Peters, 1984).

Although research on the effects of smoking is not always easy to interpret, because women who smoke are likely to differ in other ways from those who do not, the moral seems clear: the safest plan is not to smoke during pregnancy. This research also shows a relationship between the "dose" (the amount of nicotine you are taking in) and the severity of consequences for the child. So if you cannot quit entirely, at least cut back.

Drinking.   Recent work on the effects of maternal alcohol ingestion on prenatal and postnatal development also carries a clear message: to be safe, don't drink during pregnancy.

The effects of alcohol on the developing fetus range from mild to severe. At the extreme end of the continuum are children who exhibit a syndrome called **fetal alcohol syndrome (FAS)** (Jones et al., 1973). Mothers of these children are heavy drinkers or alcoholics, and the infants themselves are generally smaller than normal, with smaller brains. They frequently have heart defects, and their faces are distinctively different (as you can see in Figure 2.9). As children, adolescents, and adults, they continue to be shorter than normal, have smaller heads, and score in the IQ range of mild mental retardation. Indeed, FAS is the leading

---

RESEARCH REPORT
Streissguth's Study of Prenatal Alcohol Exposure

The best single study of the consequences of prenatal alcohol exposure has been done by Ann Streissguth and her colleagues (1990; 1989; 1984; 1981; 1980; Olson et al., 1992), who have followed a group of over 500 women and children beginning in early pregnancy. Since the study was begun before there were widespread warnings about the possible impact of alcohol during pregnancy, the sample includes many well-educated, middle-class women with good diets who did not take many other recreational drugs but who did drink alcohol in moderate or even fairly heavy amounts while pregnant—a set of conditions that would be impossible to duplicate today, at least in the United States or other countries in which the risks are well advertised.

Streissguth tested the children repeatedly, beginning immediately after birth, again later in infancy, at age 4, at school age, and again at age 11. She found that the mother's alcohol consumption in pregnancy was associated with sluggishness and weaker sucking in infancy, lower scores on a test of infant intelligence at 8 months, lower IQ at 4 and 7 years, and problems with attention and vigilance at 4, 7, and 11. Teachers also rated the 11-year-olds on overall school performance and on various behavior problems, and on both measures those whose mothers had consumed the most alcohol during pregnancy were rated significantly lower.

Streissguth also was careful to obtain information about other drug use in pregnancy, including smoking, and asked mothers about their diet, their education, and their life habits. She has found that the links between alcohol consumption and poor outcomes for the child hold up even when all these other variables are controlled statistically.

Setting aside those cases in which the child was diagnosed with the full fetal alcohol syndrome, the effects of moderate levels of alcohol use during pregnancy are not large in absolute terms, but they have significant practical consequences. For example, the difference in IQ scores at age 7 between children of abstainers and children of women who drank 1 ounce or more of alcohol per day during their pregnancy was only about 6 points in Streissguth's sample (Streissguth et al., 1990). But this relatively small absolute difference means that three times as many alcohol-exposed children have IQs below 85 than is true among children of abstainers. Alcohol-exposed children are thus greatly overrepresented in special classes in schools and probably also appear in overlarge numbers among high school dropouts and the underemployed in adulthood—although those links remain for longer-term longitudinal studies to confirm.

---

known cause of retardation in the United States, exceeding even Down syndrome (Streissguth et al., 1991).

But the effects of alcohol during pregnancy are not confined to cases in which the mother is clearly an alcoholic or a very heavy drinker. Recent evidence also points to milder effects of moderate or "social" drinking. Children of mothers who drank at this level during pregnancy are more likely to have IQs below 85, and show poorer attention span. I've given some details about one of the best studies in the research report above, so you can get some feeling for how investigators have gone about studying this problem.

We do not yet know if there is any safe level of alcohol consumption during pregnancy, although most of those who work in this field are convinced that there is a linear relationship between the amount of alcohol ingested and the risk for the infant. This means that even at low dosage there is *some* increased risk. Probably it also matters when in the pregnancy the drinking occurs, and it clearly matters how many drinks the mother drinks on any one occasion. Binge drinking has been shown to be significantly riskier than regular smaller doses (Olson et al., 1992a; Streissguth, Barr, & Sampson, 1990). In the face of our remaining ignorance, the *safest* course is not to drink at all.

Cocaine. Significant numbers of pregnant women in the United States (and presumably elsewhere in the world) also take various illegal drugs, most notably cocaine, although it is of course difficult to know exactly how prevalent the problem is, because many women are understandably reluctant to reveal such information to researchers or physicians. The best current estimates are that roughly 3 percent of all babies born in the U.S. have been prenatally exposed to cocaine. The risk is far higher among babies born to poor, inner-city mothers. In these groups, by some estimates, as many as 20 or 30 percent of mothers use cocaine (Hawley & Disney, 1992).

Cocaine appears to cross the placental barrier quite readily, but unlike alcohol, it creates no regular or recognizable syndrome of abnormalities. About a third of all cocaine-exposed babies are born prematurely, and among those born after a normal gestation period, many more are lower than normal in birth weight—a pattern that is very similar to what we see with smoking during pregnancy. In addition, they are three times as likely to have very small head circumferences. Some cocaine-exposed babies also show significant withdrawal symptoms after birth, such as irritability, restlessness, shrill crying, and tremors.

We know much less about the long-term consequences of prenatal cocaine exposure; no groups of such children have been followed much past age 3. Furthermore, it is extremely difficult to tease out the effects of cocaine exposure from the effects of poverty or poor rearing conditions or other co-occurring problems in the child's life. The few bits of information we have suggest that cocaine-exposed babies are more likely to establish an insecure attachment to their mothers, and that they may have greater difficulty with language learning (Hawley & Disney, 1992; Rodning, Beckwith, & Howard, 1991). As with alcohol exposure, we may well find that the effects of cocaine are subtle and long-lasting, but that remains to be shown.

Other Teratogens

There are a great many other teratogens, including excess amounts of vitamin A, methylmercury, and lead, and many drugs or chemicals suspected of being teratogens about which we have insufficient information. These include anticonvulsant medication taken by epileptics, polychlorinated biphenyls (PCBs, compounds widely used in electrical transformers and paint), radiation at high doses, aspirin, some antidepressants, some artificial hormones, and some pesticides (Vorhees & Mollnow, 1987). There is no room for me to go into detail about what we know (or don't know) in each case, but let me say just a word about several of the more practically significant of the items on this list.

Diethylstilbestrol (DES). DES is a synthetic estrogen that at one time was commonly given to pregnant women to prevent miscarriages. The daughters of such women have been found to have higher rates of some kinds of cancers, and as many as 30 percent of the sons have been found to be infertile (Rosenblith & Sims-Knight, 1989).

Aspirin. One of the most widely used drugs, aspirin, is teratogenic in animals when given in high doses. Humans rarely take high enough doses to produce such effects directly, but it turns out that aspirin in moderate amounts can have negative effects on the human fetus if it is ingested along with benzoic acid, a chemical widely used as a food preservative, such as in ketchup. This combination, especially in the first trimester, seems to increase the risk of physical malformations in the embryo/fetus.

Lead. In most industrialized countries, adults are exposed to fairly high dosages of lead, although the introduction of unleaded gasoline has had a significant impact on dosages, as has the elimination of lead-based paint. We have known for some time that high exposure to lead, such as from lead-based paint in old houses, has highly negative consequences, particularly for the child's intellectual development and functioning. But a new set of studies shows that even quite low levels of lead in the blood of newborns or toddlers—levels classified as "safe" by current U.S. federal guidelines and found in children who live in houses without lead-based paint—are associated with slightly lower IQ scores at later ages than we see in children with still lower lead levels (Bellinger et al., 1991; Dietrich et al., 1987). In one longitudinal study, the effects were still detectable at age 10 (Bellinger, Stiles, & Needleman, 1992).

As the study of teratogens expands, psychologists have realized that prenatal development is less insulated, less fully protected than we had first thought. In particular, many chemicals associated with modern industrial societies may have unforeseen effects on the fetus.

▌ Other Influences on Prenatal Development

Diet. Another risk for the fetus is poor maternal nutrition, although it is crucial here to distinguish between chronic *sub*nutrition, and acute *mal*nutrition. When a woman experiences severe malnutrition during pregnancy—such as has happened during wartime in many countries—she has a greatly increased risk of stillbirths, low birth weight, and infant death during the first year of life (Stein et al., 1975). The effects seem to be worse when malnutrition occurs during the last half of the pregnancy, particularly in the final three months. Babies whose mothers suffer severe malnutrition during the final trimester are lighter at birth and have a greatly increased risk of dying during the first year.

The effects of subnutrition or less severe malnutrition, such as the chronic protein-energy malnutrition common in many populations around the world, have been far harder to establish. Babies born into such situations may experience not only prenatal subnutrition, but also mal- or subnutrition after birth and (often) less stimulation in the home. How do we then sort out the effects of the prenatal nutrition? At the moment, most experts in this area have abandoned the previously widely held notion that malnutrition prenatally or postnatally has some *direct* negative effect on the developing brain (Ricciuti, 1993). Instead, what seems to happen is some variation of the interaction pattern I described in Chapter 1 (recall Figure 1.3): malnutrition may make the infant more "vulnerable," perhaps because it makes him less energetic or responsive, or less able to learn from his experiences. In a nonstimulating environment such a vulnerable child is likely to do poorly. But a stimulating environment can overcome the vulnerability.

This pattern is illustrated nicely in the results of a small study by Philip Zeskind and Craig Ramey (1981). They have looked at the outcomes for a small

THE REAL WORLD
Weight Gain and Diet During Pregnancy

Life-styles have been changing; slimness and fitness in women are perhaps more highly valued now than before, especially among younger women of childbearing age. And all women want to give their unborn child the best possible start in the world. So questions about weight gain and diet during pregnancy are of vital concern to many women.

■ WEIGHT GAIN

For many years, physicians thought that the fetus acted as a sort of "parasite" on the mother's body, taking whatever nourishment it needed even at the expense of the mother. Newer research has challenged this assumption, as well as other customs about nutritional needs in pregnancy. We now know that even among obese women, the amount of weight the mother gains is positively correlated with the infant's birth weight. Among women who are underweight at the beginning of their pregnancies, the relationship is even stronger (Seidman, Ever-Hadani, & Gale, 1989). Low weight gain is also associated with higher risk of preterm birth (Abrams et al., 1989).

The old rule of thumb was that a woman should gain 2 pounds per month during the pregnancy. The newer research indicates that this is not nearly enough. The current advice is that a woman who is at her normal weight before pregnancy should gain between 25 and 35 pounds; for those who are underweight before pregnancy or for teen mothers the weight gain should be even larger. Women who gain less than this may have infants who suffer from some fetal malnutrition and who are thus born underweight for their gestational age.

Furthermore, it matters *when* the weight is gained. During the first three months, the woman needs to gain only a minimal amount (2 to 5 pounds). But during the last six months of the pregnancy the woman should be gaining at the rate of about 14 ounces (350 to 400 grams) per week in order to support fetal growth (Pitkin, 1977; Winick, 1980). One practical consequence of this is that a woman who has gained 20 pounds or so during the first four or five months should *not* cut back in order to hold her weight gain to some magic total number. Restricting caloric intake during those final months is exactly the wrong thing to do.

Interestingly, it begins to look as if variations in maternal weight gain during pregnancy may be one contributor to the large difference between blacks and whites in neonatal mortality. The connective chain goes like this: Black women in the United States are, on average, heavier than white women of comparable social class, and more likely to be obese. Because of this, they are more likely to be (badly) advised to restrict their weight gain during pregnancy, which in turn increases the likelihood of low birth weight in the infant (Kempe et al., 1992; Luke & Murtaugh, 1993).

■ A GOOD DIET

Pure poundage is not enough to ensure optimal development for the child. It also matters *what* the mother eats. Caloric requirements go up 10 to 20 percent (perhaps 300 calories a day beyond your maintenance level), but protein needs appear to go up much more markedly. The usual current recommendation is that a pregnant woman of 19 or older needs to take in 1.3 grams of protein per kilogram (2.2 pounds) of her weight. As an example, this would mean that a woman weighing 125 pounds would require about 75 grams of protein per day. For teenagers, the protein requirement is still higher because they are still growing. (Since one egg has about 7 grams of protein, while one cup of cottage cheese has 33 grams, even this heightened requirement is not difficult to meet.) Requirements for most vitamins and minerals also increase during pregnancy. Calcium needs rise 50 percent (from 800 mg to 1200 mg daily), and iron requirements also rise, to perhaps 75 mg daily (Winick, 1980).

Another possible influence on prenatal development is the level of the mother's exercise. What kind of study would you have to do to figure out whether it is okay for pregnant women to maintain high levels of exercise, such as running 30 miles a week?

group of 10 infants, all born to poverty-level mothers, and all extremely thin at birth—usually a sign of prenatal malnutrition. Half of these babies happened to have been assigned randomly to a special enriched day-care program beginning when they were 3 months old. The other five malnourished babies received nutritional supplements but were reared at home in much less stimulating circumstances. Other children in the day-care center had been of normal weight at birth, as were other home-reared children included in the study. Table 2.3 gives the IQ scores of these four groups of children when they were 3 years old. As you can see, the results match Horowitz's model very well. Malnourished infants did well in the stimulating environment of the day-care center but extremely poorly in a less-supportive environment. Well-nourished infants also did better in the day-care environment than at home, but the difference was not nearly so large. Thus malnutrition appeared to create a "vulnerability" that could only be overcome by an enriched environment.

TABLE 2.3 IQ Scores of 3-year-old Children		
	Prenatal Nutritional Status	
Experience After Birth	*Malnourished*	*Well-Nourished*
Enriched day care	96.4	98.1
Home-reared	70.6	84.7

Source: Zeskind & Ramey, 1981, p. 215.

The Mother's Age.   One of the particularly intriguing trends in modern family life in the U.S. and many other industrialized countries is the increasing likelihood that women will postpone their first pregnancy into their late twenties or early thirties. In the United States today, roughly 20 percent of all first births are to women over 30, double the rate in 1970 (Berkowitz et al., 1990; United States Bureau of the Census, 1992). Of course there are many reasons for such decisions, chief among them being the increased need for second incomes in families and the desire of young women to complete job training and early career steps before bearing children. For my purposes in this chapter, though, the key question is the impact of maternal age on the mother's experience of pregnancy and on the developing fetus. And here the recent data paint a somewhat different picture than does older evidence. Current research suggests that mothers over 30 (particularly those over 35), are at increased risk for several kinds of problems, including miscarriage (McFalls, 1990), complications of pregnancy such as high blood pressure or bleeding (Berkowitz et al., 1990), and death during pregnancy or delivery (Buehler et al., 1986).

For example, in one large recent study of nearly 4000 women in New York, all of whom had received adequate prenatal care, Gertrud Berkowitz and her colleagues (1990) found that women 35 and older during their first pregnancies were almost twice as likely as women in their twenties to suffer some pregnancy complication. These effects of age become even greater if the mother has not had adequate prenatal care, or has poor health habits. The negative effects of maternal smoking on birth weight is considerably *greater* among women over 35, for example, than among younger women (Wen et al., 1990).

For infants born to older mothers, the data also point to very slightly increased risk of problems. Older mothers appear to be only slightly more likely to have low-birth-weight infants (Berkowitz et al., 1990; Cnattingius, Berendes, & Forman, 1993), and may well have no heightened risk for bearing a child with birth defects— other than the well-established risk of chromosomal anomalies such as Down syndrome (Baird, Sadovnick, & Yee, 1991). However, researchers in Sweden, where mothers of all ages receive remarkably comprehensive and equal prenatal care, have recently reported higher rates of late-pregnancy miscarriage and heightened infant mortality for infants born to older mothers, especially for first births to mothers over 35 (Cnattingius et al., 1993).

Among teenage mothers, the data are much less clear. Older data pointed to heightened risk of low birth weight and other nonoptimal outcomes among very

Older mothers, like this one, are becoming much more common in the U.S. and in other industrialized countries. Mothers over 30 (especially those over 35) and their infants have *slightly* increased risks of problems during pregnancy and delivery.

young mothers. But newer studies frequently do not show any such effects. Indeed, one very large study of all the consecutive births at one inner-city hospital in Baltimore over a seven-year period indicated that babies born to mothers younger than 18 were *less* likely to have low birth weight than those born to mothers in their twenties (McCarthy & Hardy, 1993). My best reading of the evidence is that to the extent that adolescent childbearing is associated with higher risks to mother or child, those increased risks are more a consequence of inadequate prenatal care than of age per se. Among those teenagers who have decent diets and adequate prenatal care, problems of pregnancy, preterm delivery, or low birth weight are not more common (Strobino, 1987).

Number of Pregnancies. As a general rule, women who have had more than four pregnancies are at greater risk than are women who have had fewer. Their babies are more likely to be stillborn and to be smaller at birth (Kessner, 1973). Eleanor Maccoby and her colleagues (1979) have also found that any child after the first, especially if the pregnancies are closely spaced, has lower levels of hormones in his blood at birth. In particular, firstborn boys in this study had much higher levels of testosterone (the male hormone) at birth than did later-born boys. We don't know yet what the implications of such a difference may be for development, but this study does point to the possibility of some kinds of physical "depletion" in the mother as a result of pregnancy that could affect the physical development of later-born children.

The Mother's Emotional State. Finally, the mother's state of mind during the pregnancy may be significant, although the research findings are decidedly mixed (Istvan, 1986). Results from infrahuman studies are clear: Exposure of the pregnant female to stressors such as heat, light, noise, shock, or crowding significantly increases the risk of low birth weight as well as later problems in the offspring (Schneider, 1992). Studies of humans, however, have not pointed to such a clear conclusion, in part because researchers have not agreed on how one ought to measure such potentially relevant maternal states as anxiety or stress. Many investigators have found no link at all between their measures of the mother's overall life stress and either complications of her pregnancy or problems in the infant. Other investigators have found such links for some groups and not others. For example, Emmy Werner (1986) found that among middle-class women in the Kauai, Hawaii, longitudinal study, those who had negative feelings about their pregnancy, or who were generally anxious or experienced some psychological trauma during the pregnancy, had more birth complications and more infants with low birth weight or poor condition than was true among middle-class women with lower stress or anxiety. But these same patterns did not hold among poor women in this study, many of whom lived in states of chronic stress or disorganization. Thus it may be that long-term, chronic stressors have less impact on a specific pregnancy, while significant *increases* in anxiety or stress during a pregnancy may have more deleterious effects.

Folklore in virtually all cultures certainly points to a causal link between the mother's emotional experiences during her pregnancy and the outcome for the child. But at the moment the best I can do is to say that the hypothesis is still plausible, but not proven. Better epidemiological studies are needed if we are to be able to go further.

Before you read the next section, think about everything you have read so far in this chapter; see if you can figure out what three pieces of advice you would give to a pregnant friend, based on the information you have read. Why those three?

▶ An Overview of Risks and Long-Term Consequences of Prenatal Problems

Every time I write this chapter I am aware that the list of things that can go wrong seems to get longer and longer and scarier and scarier. Physicians, biologists, and psychologists keep learning more about both the major and the subtle effects of prenatal environmental variations, so the number of warnings to pregnant women seems to increase yearly, if not monthly. One of the ironies of this is that too much worry about such potential consequences can make a woman more anxious, and anxiety is on the list of warnings! So before you begin worrying too much, let me try to put this information into perspective.

First, let me say again that *most* pregnancies are normal and largely uneventful, and most babies are healthy and normal at birth.

Second, there are specific preventive steps that any woman can take to reduce the risks for herself and her unborn child. She can be properly immunized; she can quit smoking and drinking; she can watch her diet and make sure her weight gain is sufficient; and she and the child's father can have genetic counseling. In addition, she can get early and regular prenatal care. Many studies show that mothers who receive adequate prenatal care reduce the risks to themselves and their infants. Just one example: Jann Murray and Merton Bernfield (1988), in a study of over 30,000 births, found that the risk of giving birth to a low-birth-weight infant was more than three times as great among women who had received inadequate prenatal care as among those receiving adequate care, and this pattern held among both blacks and whites. Unfortunately, inadequate care remains common in the U.S. In 1988, 21 percent of white mothers and 39 percent of black mothers had no prenatal care in the first trimester; 4.9 percent of whites and 10.5 percent of blacks had either no care at all, or first saw a physician in the seventh month or later (Wegman, 1990). In many inner cities in the U.S., these figures are far higher (Heagarty, 1991).

Given such statistics, it is perhaps not surprising that the U.S. continues to have a relatively high rate of infant mortality. The good news is that this rate has been declining steadily over the past decades, dropping from 20.0 infant deaths per thousand births in 1970 to 9.1 in 1990 (Wegman, 1992). The bad news is that infant mortality is more than twice as high for blacks as for whites (17.7 and 8.2, respectively, in 1988), and that even an overall rate of 9.1 places the U.S. twentieth in the world. Virtually all European countries, where prenatal care is typically free or low-cost and universally available, have lower infant mortality rates, as do Japan (with the lowest rate in the world), Hong Kong, and Singapore.

The black/white difference in infant mortality is so significant a facet of U.S. culture that I need to say a further word about it. This difference has existed at least since record keeping began (in 1915) and has *not* been declining. It is found even when only infants born to college-educated mothers are compared (Schoendorf et al., 1992). Physicians and physiologists do not yet understand all the reasons for this discrepancy, although it is clear that a significantly higher rate of low-birth-weight babies is a major factor (Kempe et al., 1992; Schoendorf et al., 1992). When only normal-weight babies are compared, infant mortality is about the same in the two groups. But saying that only pushes the explanation back one step. We still need to know why blacks in the U.S. have more low-birth-weight babies, and this answer is still unclear.

A third point to be made about prenatal problems is that if something does go wrong, chances are good that the negative consequences to the child will be short-term rather than permanent. And many physical defects can be treated successfully after birth.

Of course some negative outcomes *are* permanent and have long-term consequences for the child. Chromosomal anomalies, including Down syndrome or deviations in sex chromosome patterns, are permanent and nearly always associated with lasting mental retardation or school difficulties (Pennington et al., 1982). Some teratogens also have permanent effects, such as fetal alcohol syndrome or deafness resulting from rubella. And as you'll see in Chapter 3, *very* low-birth-weight infants (those under about 1500 grams about 3½ pounds) have an increased risk of persistent, long-term learning problems or low IQ, regardless of the richness of the environment in which they are reared.

But many of the effects I have talked about in this chapter may be detectable only for the first few years of the child's life, and then only in certain families. The relationship between prenatal problems and long-term outcomes, in fact, generally follows the same pattern I talked about with regard to malnutrition: Low-birth-weight infants, or those with higher lead exposures or other difficulties, are likely to show persisting problems if they are reared in unstimulating or unsupportive environments (Kopp, 1990; Werner, 1986). The same children reared in more rich and varied environments typically catch up to their healthier peers by school age, if not before. So it is not the prenatal problem by itself that is the cause of the later difficulties; it is the combination of a prenatal problem and a relatively poor early environment that seems to produce long-term negative effects. So don't despair when you read the long list of cautions and potential problems. The story isn't as gloomy as it first seems.

▶ Sex Differences in Prenatal Development

Since nearly all prenatal development is controlled by maturational codes that are the same for all members of our species—male and female alike—there aren't very many sex differences in prenatal development. But there are a few, and they set the stage for some of the physical differences we'll see at later ages.

- As I've already pointed out, males secrete testosterone during the early months of gestation, which leads to the "fixing" of the brain so that the proper male hormones are secreted at the right moment later in life. Females do not secrete any equivalent hormone prenatally.
- Females are a bit faster in some aspects of prenatal development, particularly skeletal development. They are about one to two weeks ahead in bone development at birth (Tanner, 1978).
- Despite girls' more rapid development, boys are heavier and longer at birth (Tanner, 1978).
- Males are considerably more vulnerable to all kinds of prenatal problems. Many more boys than girls are conceived— on the order of about 120 to 150 male embryos to every 100 female—but more of the males are spontaneously aborted. At birth, there are only about 105 boys for every 100 girls. Boys are also more likely to experience injuries at birth (perhaps because they are

larger), and they have more congenital malformations (Zaslow & Hayes, 1986). And among those infants who experience severe complications during delivery, boys are more likely to die. For instance, Emmy Werner, in the Kauai longitudinal study, found that more than half of the boy infants experiencing such severe complications died in infancy, compared to less than 20 percent among the girl infants (Werner, 1986).

The striking sex difference in vulnerability is particularly fascinating, especially since it seems to persist. Older boys are more prone to problems as well—a pattern I'll discuss more thoroughly in Chapter 15. The basic genetic difference may well be a contributor. The XX combination affords the girl more protection against the fragile-X syndrome and against nonoptimal genes that may be carried on the X chromosome. For instance, geneticists have found that a gene affecting susceptibility to infectious disease is carried on the X chromosome (Brooks-Gunn & Matthews, 1979). Because boys have only one X chromosome, such a gene is much more likely to be expressed phenotypically in a boy.

Social Class Differences in Prenatal Development

I will be talking much more fully about social class differences in development in Chapter 14, but I cannot leave this chapter without saying a word about the impact of social class on the risks of pregnancy and birth.

The basic sequence of fetal development is clearly no different for children born to poor mothers than for children born to middle-class mothers. But many of the problems that can affect prenatal development negatively are more common among the poor. For example, mothers who have not graduated from high school are about twice as likely as mothers with a college education to have a low-birth-weight infant, or to have an infant stillborn (Kessner, 1973). Poor women are also likely to have their first pregnancy earlier and to have more pregnancies overall, and are less likely to be immunized against such diseases as rubella. They are also less likely to seek prenatal care, or they seek it much later in their pregnancies. Much of this difference could be overcome in the U.S. if we were willing to devote the resources needed to provide good, universal prenatal care. We could significantly reduce not only the rate of infant death but also the rate of physical abnormalities and perhaps even mental retardation. To my mind, this is a goal worth striving for in and of itself. It would also be significantly cheaper for our society, since it costs a great deal less to provide prenatal care than it does to care for a low-birth-weight infant, or a child with significant learning disabilities.

Summary

1. At conception, the 23 chromosomes from the sperm join with 23 from the ovum to make up the set of 46 that will be reproduced in each cell of the new child's body.

2. Each chromosome consists of a long string of deoxyribonucleic acid (DNA), divisible into specific segments, called genes.

3. The child's sex is determined by the twenty-third pair of chromosomes, a pattern of XX for a girl and XY for a boy.

4. Geneticists distinguish between the genotype, which is the pattern of inherited characteristics, and the phenotype, which is the result of the interaction of genotype and environment.

5. During the first days after conception, called the germinal stage of development, the initial cell divides (mitosis), travels down the fallopian tube, and is implanted in the wall of the uterus.

6. The second stage, the period of the embryo, includes the development of the various structures that support fetal development, such as the placenta, as well as primitive forms of all organ systems.

7. The final 30 weeks of gestation, called the fetal period, is devoted primarily to enlargement and refinements in all the organ systems, with neural development in particular occurring relatively late.

8. During the embryonic period, the XY embryo secretes the hormone testosterone, which stimulates the growth of male genitalia and shifts the brain into a "male" pattern. Without that hormone, the embryo develops as a girl, as do normal XX embryos.

9. Normal prenatal development seems heavily determined by maturation—a "road map" contained in the genes. Disruptions in this sequence can occur; the timing of the disruption determines the nature and severity of the effect.

10. Deviations from the normal pattern can be caused at conception by any of a variety of chromosomal anomalies, such as Down syndrome, or by the transmission of genes for specific diseases.

11. Prior to conception, it is possible to test parents for the presence of genes for many inherited diseases. After conception, several diagnostic techniques exist that identify chromosomal anomalies or recessive-gene diseases in the fetus.

12. Some diseases contracted by the mother may affect the child, including rubella, AIDS, CMV, and genital herpes. These may result in disease or physical abnormalities in the child.

13. Alcohol, nicotine, and cocaine all appear to have significantly harmful effects on the developing fetus; the greater the dose, the greater the potential effect appears to be.

14. The mother's diet is also important. If she is severely malnourished there are increased risks of stillbirth, low birth weight, and infant death during the first year of life.

15. Older mothers and very young mothers, along with those who have borne four or more children, also run increased risks, but in many if not most cases these risks are greatly reduced if the mother is in good health and receives adequate prenatal care.

16. Among other teratogens, prenatal lead exposure has been shown to be associated with lower IQs in infancy and early childhood.

17. High levels of anxiety or stress in the mother may also increase the risk of complications of pregnancy or difficulties in the infant, although the research findings here are mixed.

18. Some difficulties in prenatal development can produce permanent disabilities or deformities, such as Down syndrome or deafness from rubella. Other lasting problems, such as learning disabilities, may also be caused by teratogens. But many disorders associated with prenatal problems can be overcome if the child is reared in a supportive and stimulating environment.

19. Sex differences in prenatal development are few in number. Boys are slower to develop, bigger at birth, and more vulnerable to most forms of prenatal stress.

20. Nearly all potential problems of prenatal development are more common among poor women, but these increased risks can be greatly reduced with good diet and adequate prenatal care.

◗ Key Terms

alpha-fetoprotein test (54)

amniocentesis (54)

amnion (46)

autosomes (44)

axon (49)

chorionic villus sampling (54)

chromosome (41)

dendrites (49)

deoxyribonucleic acid (41)

Down syndrome (51)

embryo (46)

fallopian tube (40)

fetal alcohol syndrome (FAS) (58)

fetus (46)

gametes (41)

gene (41)

genotype (41)

glial cells (49)

neuron (49)

ovum (40)

phenotype (45)

placenta (46)

rubella (xx)

sex chromosomes (44)

synapse (50)

ultrasound (54)

uterus (40)

◗ Suggested Readings

The Boston Women's Health Collective. (1992). *The new our bodies, ourselves: A book by and for women*. New York: Simon & Schuster.

This recent revision of a popular book is really focused on the adult female's body, rather than on prenatal development, but it has an excellent discussion of health during pregnancy. This is a strongly feminist book; some of you may not be entirely in sympathy with all of the political views included. But it is nonetheless a very good compact source of information on all facets of pregnancy and childbirth.

Nightingale, E. O., & Goodman, M. (1990). *Before birth: Prenatal testing for genetic disease*. Cambridge, MA: Harvard University Press.

A clearly written small book, addressed to prospective parents who are looking for practical guidance. It includes detailed descriptions of common genetic anomalies and inherited diseases, and of diagnostic procedures. It also discusses ethical questions.

Nilsson, L. A. (1990). *A child is born.* New York: Delacorte Press, Seymour Lawrence.

A remarkable book, full of marvelous photographs of the embryo and fetus. It also has a good basic text describing prenatal development and problems of pregnancy.

Rosenblith, J. F., & Sims-Knight, J. E. (1989). *In the beginning: Development in the first two years of life.* Newbury Park, CA: Sage.

A first-rate text covering prenatal development and infancy. It is an excellent next step in your reading if you are interested in this area.

BIRTH AND THE NEWBORN CHILD

3

Birth

The Stages of Labor
The First Greeting: Parents and Newborns
Birth Choices
Problems at Birth
Assessing the Newborn

Adapting to the Newborn
• **The Real World:** *Postpartum Depression*

The Newborn: What Can He Do?
Reflexes
Perceptual Skills: What the Newborn Sees, Hears, and Feels
Motor Skills: Moving Around
Learning and Habituation
Social Skills

The Daily Life of Infants
Sleeping

Crying
Eating
• **Cultures and Contexts:** *Cultural and Social Class Differences in Patterns of Breast-feeding, and Their Consequences*

Individual Differences Among Babies
Health and Death in the First Year
Variations in Crying Patterns
Temperament
• **Cultures and Contexts:** *Cultural Differences in Infant Temperament*
Sex Differences

Summary

Key Terms

Suggested Readings

Try to imagine that you are a woman nine months pregnant with your first child. The long months of prenatal life are over and the baby is about to be born. If you are like many of today's mothers, you and your partner have explored your options for the location and conditions for your delivery; both of you may have taken prenatal classes; you have tried to prepare yourselves for what the baby will be like and how the advent of this new member of the family will change your life. You are a little apprehensive about the process of delivery, and a bit uncertain about what to expect from the baby and about your own abilities to cope, but you are eager for the whole adventure to begin.

In this chapter I want to try to answer some of the questions that new parents reasonably ask about birth and about newborn babies. Does it make a difference whether the baby is born in a hospital or at home? Does it matter if the father is present or not? What happens if the birth is too early, or if something else goes wrong? I also want to describe the beginnings of the child's independent life so that you can have a clear picture of the starting point for the long developmental

Effacement: cervical thinning

1. Uneffaced cervix

Cervix

2. 50 percent effaced

3. Completely effaced

Dilation: enlargement of the cervical opening

1. Undilated cervix

Cervix

2. Partial dilation (4 cm)

3. Full dilation (10 cm)

Figure 3.1
The process of effacement and dilation during labor. (*Source:* Stenchever, 1978, Figure 5-4, p. 84. Adapted by permission.)

journey. In the past few decades, researchers have discovered that the apparently helpless newborn really has a wide range of quite remarkable abilities. This knowledge has not only changed the information given out to new parents, it has also changed our theories of development.

▶ Birth

The Stages of Labor

Labor progresses through three stages of unequal length.

The First Stage of Labor. Stage 1 covers the period during which two important processes occur: dilation and effacement. The cervix (the opening at the bottom of the uterus) must open up like the lens of a camera (**dilation**) and also flatten out (**effacement**). At the time of actual delivery of the infant, the cervix must normally be dilated to about 10 centimeters (about 4 inches), as you can see in Figure 3.1. This part of labor has been likened to putting on a sweater with a neck that is too tight. You have to pull and stretch the neck of the sweater with your head in order to get it on. Eventually the neck is stretched wide enough so that the widest part of your head can pass through.

A good deal of the effacement may actually occur in the last weeks of the pregnancy, as may some dilation. It is not uncommon for women to begin labor

80 percent effaced and 1 or 2 centimeters dilated. The contractions of the first stage of labor, which are at first widely spaced and later more frequent and rhythmical, serve to complete both processes.

Customarily, stage 1 is itself divided into phases. In the *early* (or *latent*) phase contractions are relatively far apart, and are typically not too uncomfortable. In the *late* phase, which begins when the cervix is about halfway dilated (5 cm) and continues until dilation has reached 8 cm, contractions are closer together and more intense. The last 2 centimeters of dilation are achieved during a period usually called the *transition* phase. It is this period, when contractions are closely spaced and strong, that women typically find the most painful. Fortunately, transition is also ordinarily the shortest phase.

The overall length of the first stage of labor varies widely from one woman to the next. The average duration is roughly 8 hours for women delivering a first infant without anesthesia, with a normal range of 3 to 19 hours (Kilpatrick & Laros, 1989). Women delivering second or later children typically have shorter labors, while those with some form of anesthesia typically have slightly longer labors.

The Second Stage of Labor.   At the end of the transition phase the mother will normally have the urge to help the infant out by "pushing." When the birth attendant (physician or midwife) is sure the cervix is fully dilated, she or he will encourage this pushing, and the second stage of labor—the actual delivery—begins. The baby's head moves past the stretched cervix, into the birth canal, and finally out of the mother's body. Most women find this part of labor markedly less distressing than the transition phase. It typically lasts less than an hour and rarely takes longer than two hours.

Most infants are delivered head first, facing toward the mother's spine. Perhaps 3 percent, however, are oriented differently, either feet first or bottom first (called *breech* presentations). Several decades ago most breech deliveries were accomplished with the aid of medical instruments such as forceps; today nearly four-fifths of breech presentations are delivered by cesarean section (Taffel, Placek, & Liss, 1987)—a procedure I'll discuss more fully in a moment.

The Third Stage of Labor.   Stage 3 is the delivery of the placenta (also called the "afterbirth") and other material from the uterus. You can see all of these steps schematically in Figure 3.2 (p. 75).

The First Greeting: Parents and Newborns

The brief description I've just given does not begin to convey the emotional impact of the experience of childbirth for the mother, or for the father if he is present. For many women there is intense joy as they greet the infant for the first time: laughter, exclamations of delight at the baby's features, first tentative and tender touching. Here's an excerpt from one mother's greeting (Macfarlane, 1977, pp. 64–65):

> She's big, isn't she? What do you reckon? (Doctor makes a comment.) Oh look, she's got hair. It's a girl—you're supposed to be all little. Gosh. Oh, she's lovely. Oh, she's opened her eyes (laughs). Oh lovely (kisses baby).

Most parents are intensely interested in having the baby look at them right away. They are delighted if the baby opens her eyes, and they will try to stimulate her to do so if she doesn't. The parents' first tentative touches also seem to have a

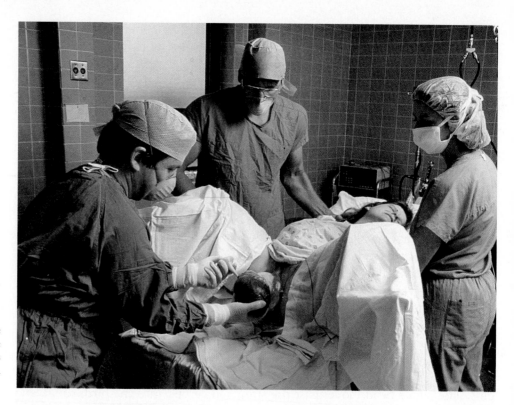

At this point in the delivery, the baby's head is fully out. Notice that the father is present for this delivery, as is now the norm in the United States.

pattern to them: the parent first touches the infant rather gingerly with the tip of a finger and then proceeds gradually to stroking with the full hand (Klaus & Kennell, 1976; Macfarlane, 1977). Whether this same pattern holds in all cultures, I do not know. But the tenderness seen in most of these early encounters is striking.

Birth Choices

Why do you think parents are so interested in having the baby look at them? Do you think this is a universal pattern?

What I am going to say here about birth choices is necessarily specific to options and experiences in industrialized countries. In many other cultures there are no decisions to be made about such questions as where the delivery will occur, whether the father should be present or not, or whether the mother should be given drugs to ease her pain. Custom dictates the answers. But in many Western industrialized countries, patterns and customs in this area continue to change rapidly, which leaves individual parents with decisions to make—decisions that may affect the child's health or the mother's satisfaction with the delivery. Since many of you will face these choices at some point in the future, I want to give you the best current information I have.

Drugs During Delivery.   One key decision concerns the use of drugs during delivery. Three types of drugs are commonly used: (1) *analgesics* (such as the common drug Demerol), which are given during the first stage of labor to reduce pain (all of the analgesics in this group are members of the opium family of drugs); (2) *sedatives* or *tranquilizers* (such as Nembutol, Valium, or Thorazine), given during stage 1 labor to reduce anxiety; and (3) *anesthesia*, given during transition or the second stage of labor to block pain either totally (general anesthesia) or in por-

Uterus Bladder Pubic bone
Birth canal

Rectum Cervix

Before labor begins

Early labor

Transition: just before the baby's head enters the birth canal

The baby's head before crowning

The head crowning

The head emerging

The third stage of labor: the placenta coming loose and about to emerge

The pelvis after the delivery

Figure 3.2
The sequence of steps during delivery is shown clearly in these drawings.

tions of the body (local anesthesia). Of the three, anesthesia is least often used in the United States currently, but the great majority of women receive at least one of these types of drugs (Brackbill, McManus, & Woodward, 1985).

Studying the causal links between such drug use and the baby's later behavior or development has proven to be monumentally difficult. Controlled experiments are obviously not possible, since women cannot be randomly assigned to specific drug regimens. And drugs are given in myriad different combinations. But there are a few reasonably clear conclusions.

First, we know that nearly all drugs given during labor pass through the placenta and enter the fetal bloodstream. Because the newborn lacks the enzymes necessary to break down such drugs quickly, the effect of any drug lasts longer in the baby than it does in the mother. Not surprisingly, then, drugged infants are slightly more sluggish, gain a little less weight, and spend more time sleeping in the first few weeks than do infants of nondrugged moms (Maurer & Maurer, 1988). These differences are quite small but have been observed repeatedly.

Beyond these first few days, however, there are no consistently observed effects from analgesics and tranquilizers, and only a few hints of long-term effects of anesthesia in a few studies (Rosenblith & Sims-Knight, 1989; Sepkoski, 1987). Given such contradictory findings, only one specific piece of advice seems warranted: if you have received medication, you need to bear in mind that your baby is also drugged, and that this will affect her behavior in the first few days. If you allow for this effect, and realize that it will wear off, your long-term relationship with your child is likely to be unaffected.

The Location of Birth: Four Alternatives.   A second choice parents must make is *where* the baby is to be born. Today in the U.S. there are typically four alternatives: (1) a traditional hospital maternity unit; (2) a hospital-based birth center or birthing room, which is located within a hospital but provides a more homelike setting, with labor and delivery both completed in the same room and family members often present throughout; (3) a freestanding birth center, like a hospital birth center except located apart from the hospital, with delivery typically attended by a midwife rather than (or in addition to) a physician; and (4) home delivery.

At the turn of the century, only about 5 percent of babies in the United States were born in hospitals; today the figure is 98.8 percent (Declercq, 1993), with 0.7 percent born at home, and 0.4 percent born in birthing centers—a choice more common among Mexican-American mothers, particularly in Texas. Because home deliveries are so uncommon in the U.S., much of what we know about them comes from research in Europe, where such deliveries are thought to be both more natural and less expensive for the medical care system. In countries where this pattern occurs, home deliveries are encouraged only in uncomplicated pregnancies in which the woman has received good prenatal care. In this group, with a trained birth attendant present at delivery, the rate of delivery complications or infant problems is no higher in home or birth center deliveries than in hospital deliveries (Rooks et al., 1989; Tew, 1985). In contrast, infant mortality rates are significantly higher in *unplanned* home deliveries, in those without trained attendants, or in those in which the mother had experienced some complication of pregnancy (Schramm, Barnes, & Bakewell, 1987).

Incidentally, there is no evidence that babies born at home or in birthing centers are in any way better off in the long run than are babies born in more traditional hospital settings. Assuming appropriate safety precautions, then, the choice should be based on what is most comfortable for the individual woman or couple.

The Presence of Fathers at Delivery.   A third important decision is whether the father should be present at delivery. In the United States today this hardly seems like a "decision." As recently as 1972 only about a quarter of U.S. hospitals permitted the father to be present in the delivery room; by 1980, four-fifths of them did (Parke & Tinsley, 1984), and today the father's presence has become absolutely the norm—an illustration of how a cultural pattern surrounding an event as important as birth can undergo rapid change.

There have been several compelling arguments offered in favor of such a norm: the father's presence may lessen the mother's anxiety and give her psychological support; by coaching her in breathing and other techniques he may help her control her pain; and he may become more strongly attached to the infant by being present at the birth.

The first two of these arguments in favor of the father's presence have been supported by research. When fathers are present, mothers report lower levels of pain and receive less medication (Henneborn & Cogan, 1975). And when the mother has a coach (the father or someone else), the incidence of problems of labor and delivery goes down, as does the duration of labor (Sosa et al., 1980). Furthermore, at least one study shows that women are more likely to report that the birth was a "peak" experience if the father was present (Entwisle & Doering, 1981).

What is far less clear is whether the father's relationship with his infant is affected positively by being present at delivery, or by having an opportunity for early contact with the infant. In the 1970s and 1980s, most parents accepted the statements made by various psychologists and pediatricians that it was essential for the father's bonding with the baby for him to be present at the baby's birth (Greenberg & Morris, 1974; Macfarlane, 1977). In fact it was just such statements that led to the rapid increase in fathers' participation in births in the U.S. and elsewhere. But the evidence has failed to support the early arguments. On the plus side there is some indication that those fathers whose birth experience has been particularly positive show signs of greater attachment to their infant throughout the first year (Peterson, Mehl, & Leiderman, 1979), but this was true whether the father was actually present for the birth or not. Presence at delivery seems to have no magical effect. Thus the father's presence may enhance the marital relationship, but is neither necessary nor sufficient for the father's emerging attachment to his infant (Palkovitz, 1985).

This statement is not in any way intended as an argument against fathers' participation in the delivery process. The fact that the father's presence seems to help the mother control pain, to reduce medication and labor duration, and possibly to enhance the husband-wife relationship all seem to me to be compelling reasons for encouraging fathers to be present. In addition, of course, most fathers report powerful feelings of delight at being present at the birth of their children. Reason enough.

After reading this, which birthing location would you choose, and why?

This couple, like so many today, is taking a prenatal class together. Having the father present at the delivery as coach seems to reduce the mother's pain and even shorten the length of labor.

Had you read or heard before that it is crucial for fathers to be present at their infants' births? Did you believe it? Why? Because it made sense to you, or because the evidence seemed especially good? Will you be more skeptical next time?

Problems at Birth

So far I have been discussing the process of normal, uncomplicated vaginal delivery. But as with prenatal development, there are some things that can alter the normal pattern. The delivery itself may not proceed normally, leading to a surgical delivery through an abdominal incision, called a **cesarean section** (usually abbreviated C-section); the infant may not breathe immediately after birth, or may be born too early, or even too late.

Cesarean Section Delivery. C-section deliveries occur for a variety of reasons, of which the most common is a breech position of the fetus, an active herpes infection, or a mother who has had a previous C-section. In virtually all industrialized countries, the frequency of C-sections rose rapidly in the 1970s and 1980s. This rise was particularly rapid in the U.S., where the rate more than quadrupled between 1970 and 1988, going from 5.5 to 24.7 percent. The rate has now leveled off or even dropped a small amount, amid growing agreement that the current rate is substantially higher than medically necessary. The Centers for Disease Control, in fact, lists the reduction of this rate to something closer to 12 to 15 percent as a health objective for the year 2000 (Centers for Disease Control, 1993).

The rise has had many causes, both in the U.S. and in other countries in which similar increases occurred. Fear of malpractice suits may be one element. But much more of the increase appears to be due to changes in standard medical practice, such as requiring any woman who has had one C-section to have all subsequent deliveries in the same fashion, as well as the widespread use of fetal monitors—equipment that allows the physician to hear the fetal heartbeat, and thus to detect signs of fetal distress. Such signs of distress increasingly have been handled with C-sections, in order to reduce the apparent risk to the infant.

Both these practices have been questioned. For example, there is now good evidence that 50 to 70 percent of all women who have had one C-section could safely deliver subsequent children vaginally (Levano et al., 1986). The number of such women who are encouraged to do so has been increasing of late, but it is still quite low. Similarly, some physicians (Levano et al., 1986) argue that fetal monitoring has led to many unnecessary C-sections, particularly in otherwise low-risk pregnancies.

I do not want to give you the impression that C-sections are never necessary. They clearly are. But there is now virtually universal agreement that the rate has become too high and that it can be considerably reduced without added risk to mothers or infants.

Anoxia: Lack of Oxygen. Another complication that can occur during delivery—and that may in fact be detected by a fetal monitor—is an insufficiency of oxygen for the infant. Such reduced oxygen supply is called **anoxia.** During the period immediately surrounding birth, anoxia may occur because the umbilical circulation system fails to continue the supply of blood oxygen until the baby breathes, or because the umbilical cord has been squeezed in some way during labor or delivery. Perhaps as many as 20 percent of newborns experience some degree of anoxia.

Long-term effects of anoxia have been hard to pin down. Prolonged anoxia is often (but not at all invariably) associated with such major consequences as cerebral palsy or mental retardation. Briefer periods of oxygen deprivation appear to have little long-term effect, but that is still a tentative conclusion.

Low Birth Weight.   In talking about various teratogens I have often mentioned low birth weight as one of the clearest negative outcomes, because babies who weigh too little are at much higher risk for a whole range of other problems, including death during infancy and later learning problems. So it is important to understand as much as we can about the causes and varieties of low birth weight.

Several different labels are used to describe infants with less than optimal weight. All babies below 2500 grams (about 5½ pounds) are described with the most general term of **low birth weight (LBW).** Those below 1500 grams (about 3⅓ pounds) are usually called **very low birth weight.** In 1989, 7.0 percent of all newborns in the U.S. were below 2500 grams—a total of about 45,000 infants each year (United States Bureau of the Census, 1992). Roughly 7800 of those were below 1500 grams. Given what I said in Chapter 2, you will not be surprised to learn that low birth weight is considerably more common among blacks than among either Anglos or Hispanics in the U.S. In 1989, the respective rates were 13.2 percent, 5.7 percent, and 6.2 percent.

There are a variety of reasons for low birth weight, of which the most common is that the infant is born before the full 38 weeks of gestation. Such infants are usually labeled **preterm.** Any birth before 36 weeks of gestation is usually labeled in this way. It is also possible for an infant to have completed the full 38-week gestational period but still weigh less than 2500 grams, or to weigh less than would be expected for the number of weeks of gestation completed, however long that may have been. Such an infant is called **small for date.** Infants in this group appear to have suffered from prenatal malnutrition, such as might occur with constriction of blood flow caused by the mother's smoking, or from other significant problems prenatally. Preterm infants, in contrast, may be early but may have been developing normally in other respects.

All low-birth-weight infants share some characteristics, including markedly lower levels of responsiveness at birth and in the early months of life (Barnard, Bee, & Hammond, 1984). They are also more likely to experience respiratory distress in the early weeks, and may be slower in motor development than their normal-weight peers.

Infant mortality is also correlated with birth weight. About 80 percent of all low-birth-weight infants survive long enough to leave the hospital, but the lower the birth weight the greater the risk of neonatal death. What is surprising is how many of the really tiny babies survive when they have state-of-the-art neonatal care. In hospitals with especially modern and aggressive neonatal intensive care units, as many as half of infants as small as 500 to 1000 grams at birth (1 to 2 pounds) may survive (Astbury et al., 1990).

You might think that all babies this small who do survive will have major developmental problems. But that is not the case. The long-term outcomes depend not only on the quality of care available to the infant, but on just how small the baby was and what kind of family he or she grows up in. Because medical advances in the care of LBW infants have been enormous in the past few decades, the more recently such a baby was born, the better the long-term prognosis seems to be (Kitchen et al., 1991).

If you were given the job of designing a program that would drastically reduce the incidence of low-birth-weight infants, what would you do, given what you now know? Where and how would you target your efforts?

Low-birth-weight infants are kept in special isolettes, like this one, so that the temperature can be controlled. These babies are not only small, they are also more wrinkled and skinny because the layer of fat under the skin has not fully developed.

TABLE 3.1 Two Examples of Long-Term Outcomes for Very Low-Birth-Weight Infants

	Australian Study*	U.S. Study**
Number of babies followed	89	249
Weight at birth	500–999 grams	<1500 grams
Age at testing	8 years	8 years
Percent with severe problems of some type (IQ below 70, deaf, blind, cerebral palsied, etc.)	21.3%	15.7%
Additional percent with significant learning problem or IQ between 70 and 85	19.1%	15.4%

*Victoria Infant Collaborative Study Group, 1991. The study included all surviving children of 500–999 grams born in a single state (Victoria) in Australia between 1979 and 1980. A total of 351 infants were born in that weight range, so only a quarter survived.

**Hack et al., 1991. The study originally included 490 children below 1500 grams born in a single Cleveland, Ohio, hospital between 1977 and 1979. Sixty-four percent survived to age 8.

The great majority of those above 1500 grams who are not small for date catch up to their normal peers within the first few years of life. But those below 1500 grams, especially those below 1000, have significantly higher rates of long-term problems, including neurological impairment, lower IQs, smaller size, and greater problems in school (Collin, Halsey, & Anderson, 1991; Hack et al., 1991; Saigal et al., 1991). You can get a better sense of both the type and incidence of such problems from the data in Table 3.1, which lists the results for two recent studies.

Two points are worth making about the findings from follow-up studies like those shown in the table. First, problems may not show up until school age, when the child is challenged by a new level of cognitive task. Many surviving LBW children who appear to be developing normally at age 2 or 3 later show significant problems in school. Second, even in the extremely low-birth-weight group, the majority of children seem to be fine. So it is not the case that *all* LBW children are *somewhat* affected, but rather that *some* LBW children are significantly affected while others develop normally. Unfortunately, physicians and researchers have not yet found reliable ways to predict which babies are likely to have later difficulties, which means that parents of LBW infants may be left in suspense for many years.

One piece of good news is that we do now know something about treatments that seem to improve the long-term chances of good functioning for LBW infants. Babies provided with special kinds of rhythmic stimulation while still in the hospital, such as water beds, rocking beds, heartbeat sounds, or body massage, are more alert, gain weight faster, and may even have higher IQs later than preterm babies receiving more typical hospital care (Barnard & Bee, 1983;

Scafidi et al., 1990). And when special supports are provided to such infants and to their families—helping the mothers to learn better skills for interaction with their babies and providing stimulating day care for the infants directly—the infants have a better chance of developing normally (Brooks-Gunn et al., 1993b; Spiker, Ferguson, & Brooks-Gunn, 1993).

Assessing the Newborn

It has become customary in most hospitals to evaluate an infant's status immediately after birth, and then again five minutes later, to detect any problems that may require special care. By far the most frequently used assessment system is something called an **Apgar score,** developed by a physician, Virginia Apgar (1953). The newborn is given a score of 0, 1, or 2 on each of five criteria, listed in Table 3.2. The maximum score of 10 is fairly unusual immediately after birth, because most infants are still somewhat blue in the fingers and toes at that stage. At the five-minute assessment, however, 85 to 90 percent of infants are scored as 9 or 10, meaning that they are getting off to a good start (National Center for Health Statistics, 1984). Any score of 7 or better indicates that the baby is in no danger. A score of 4, 5, or 6 usually means that the baby needs help establishing normal breathing patterns; a score of 3 or below indicates a baby in critical condition, although babies with such low Apgar scores can and do often survive.

Scores in the range of 5 to 8, like low birth weight and most other types of initial vulnerability, are associated with long-term risk primarily when the infant grows up in nonoptimal circumstances. In stimulating and supportive environments, most children with low Apgar scores appear to develop normally (Breitmayer & Ramey, 1986).

TABLE 3.2   Evaluation Method for Apgar Scoring

	Score Assigned		
Aspect of Infant Observed	**0**	**1**	**2**
Heart rate	Absent	<100/min.	>100/min.
Respiratory rate	No breathing	Weak cry and shallow breathing	Good strong cry and regular breathing
Muscle tone	Flaccid	Some flexion of extremities	Well flexed
Response to stimulation of feet	None	Some motion	Cry
Color	Blue, pale	Body pink, extremities blue	Completely pink

Source: Francis, Self, & Horowitz, 1987, pp. 731–732.

◗ Adapting to the Newborn

The baby is born and Mom, Dad, and infant return home and must now adapt to one another and to the massive changes in their lives occasioned by this new member of the family. For most adults, the role of parent brings profound satisfaction, a greater sense of purpose and self-worth, and a feeling of being grown-up. It may also bring a sense of shared joy between husband and wife (Umberson & Gove, 1989). In one large study in the U.S., for example, 80 percent of the parents sampled said their lives had been changed for the better by the arrival of children (Hoffman & Manis, 1978). But it is also true that the birth of the first child signals a whole series of changes in parents' lives, and not all these changes are without strain.

In particular, marital satisfaction typically goes down in the first months and years after the first child is born (Rollins & Feldman, 1970). Individuals and couples report a sense of strain made up partly of fatigue, partly of a feeling that there is too much to cope with, anxiety about not knowing how best to care for the child, and a strong sense of loss of time and intimacy in the marriage relationship itself (Feldman, 1987). In longitudinal studies in which couples have been observed or interviewed during pregnancy and then again in the months after the first child's birth, spouses typically report fewer expressions of love, fewer positive actions designed to maintain or support the relationship, and more expressions of ambivalence after the child's birth than before (Belsky, Lang, & Rovine, 1985). Such strains and reduced satisfaction are less noticeable when the child was planned rather than unplanned and among those couples whose marriage was strong and stable before the birth of the child. But virtually all couples experience some strain.

◗ The Newborn: What Can He Do?

Who is this small stranger who brings both joy and strain? What qualities and skills does the newborn bring to this new interactive process? He cries, breathes, looks around a bit. But what else can he do in the early hours and days? On what skills does the infant build?

Reflexes

Infants are born with a large collection of **reflexes,** which are automatic physical responses triggered involuntarily by a specific stimulus. Many of these reflexes are still present in adults, so you should be familiar with them, such as the knee jerk the doctor tests for, or an automatic eye blink when a puff of air hits your eye.

The newborn's reflexes can be roughly grouped into two categories. First, there are many *adaptive reflexes* that help the baby survive in the world into which he is born. Sucking and swallowing reflexes are prominent in this category. So is the rooting reflex—the automatic turn of the head toward any touch on the cheek, a reflex that helps the baby get the nipple into his mouth during nursing. These reflexes are no longer present in older children or adults, but are clearly highly adaptive for the newborn.

Other adaptive reflexes persist over the whole life span, including a withdrawal reaction from a painful stimulus, the opening and closing of the pupil of

THE REAL WORLD
Postpartum Depression

An added difficulty for many women after the birth of a child is a period of depressed mood, often called the "maternity blues" or "postpartum blues." Estimates vary, but Western studies suggest that between half and three-quarters of all women go through a brief period in which they find themselves crying often and feeling unexpectedly low in mood (Hopkins, Marcus, & Campbell, 1984). Most women pass through this depression in a few days and then return to a more positive and more stable mood state. But approximately 10 percent of women appear to experience a longer-lasting and more severe postpartum mood disturbance, commonly called a **postpartum depression** (Campbell et al., 1992).

Clinicians use the term *depression* or the phrase *clinical depression* to describe more than just the blues, although sadness or persisting low mood is one of the critical ingredients. To be diagnosed as suffering from a clinical depression, including postpartum depression, a person must also show some other symptoms, such as poor appetite, sleep disturbances (inability to sleep, or excessive sleep), loss of pleasure in everyday activities, feelings of worthlessness, complaints of diminished ability to think or concentrate, or recurrent thoughts of death or suicide. An individual must show at least half of these symptoms to be diagnosed as clinically depressed.

You can see from this description that such a depressive episode is not a trivial experience. So the fact that as many as 1 woman out of every 10 experiences such feelings after the birth of a child is striking. Fortunately, postpartum depression is normally shorter than other forms of clinical depression. A duration of six to eight weeks seems to be typical, after which the woman gradually recovers her normal mood (Hopkins et al., 1984), although for perhaps 1 or 2 percent of women the depression persists for a year or longer.

Such depressions seem to be more common in women who did not plan their pregnancy, who were high in anxiety during the pregnancy, or whose partner is not supportive of them or is displeased with the arrival of the child (Campbell et al., 1992; O'Hara et al., 1992). They are also more likely to occur in any woman who has experienced high levels of life changes during the pregnancy and immediately after the birth— changes such as moving, death of someone close, loss of a job, or the like. Interestingly, though, postpartum depression does not seem to be more common after a first child than after later children, although a woman who experienced such a depression after her first child is more likely to have a repeat episode after later births (Hopkins et al., 1984).

Understandably, mothers who are in the midst of a significant postpartum depression interact differently with their infants than do mothers whose mood is more normal. For example, Alison Fleming and her colleagues (1988) found that depressed mothers stroked and touched their infants with affection less frequently in the first three months after delivery than did nondepressed mothers. However, these differences did *not* persist after the mother's depression lifted; at 16 months, Fleming could find no differences in mother-child interaction between the mothers who had been depressed and those who had not.

I think it is quite common in our society to pass off a woman's postpartum depression as if it were a minor event, "just the blues." And of course for many women, it is. But for a minority the arrival of a child ushers in a much more significant depressive episode, requiring at the very least a sympathetic and supportive environment, if not clinical intervention.

---

the eye to variations in brightness, and many others. Finally, there are some reflexes that were adaptive in evolutionary history and that are still present in newborn humans, even though they are no longer helpful. The grasping reflex is one clear example. If you place your finger across a newborn baby's palm, he will reflexively close his fist tightly around your finger. If you do this with both palms, the baby's grasp is strong enough so that you can lift him up by his hands in this way. This reflex is also seen in monkeys and apes, for whom it is highly useful, since the infant must be able to cling to the mother's body while she moves about, or to a tree branch or vine. Most observers assume that this reflex in humans is merely one residual from our evolutionary past.

A second category includes the *primitive reflexes*, so called because they are controlled by the more primitive parts of the brain, the medulla and the midbrain, both of which are close to being fully developed at birth. For example, if you make a loud noise or startle a baby in some other way, you'll see her throw her

What would be different
about development, and
about adult–baby interactions,
if babies were born *without*
any reflexes, but instead had
to learn every behavior?

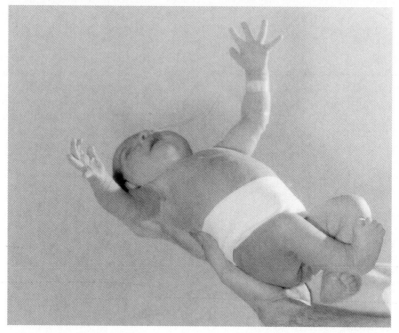

Figure 3.3
These two photos show the Moro reflex very well. In the photo above, the baby is fairly relaxed,
but when the adult suddenly drops the baby (and catches him again), the baby throws his arms out
and arches his back (below). This reflex is present for about the first six months.

arms outward and arch her back, a pattern that is part of the *Moro* or *startle* reflex. Stroke the bottom of her foot and she will splay out her toes and then curl them in, called the *Babinsky* reflex.

By about 6 months of age, when the portion of the brain governing such complex activities as perception, body movement, thinking, and language has developed more fully, these primitive reflexes begin to disappear, as if superseded by the more complex brain functions. When such reflexes persist past this age, it may signal the existence of some kind of neurological problem. The Babinsky, in particular, is used as a diagnostic tool by neurologists if they suspect the existence of some dysfunction in a child or adult.

These two categories of reflexes obviously overlap. Many adaptive reflexes—including the sucking and rooting reflexes—begin to fade late in the first year of life, indicating that they are controlled by the more primitive parts of the brain. But I think it is still helpful to distinguish between those reflexes that continue to have daily usefulness for the baby, and those that are more purely reflections of the status of the nervous system, without other adaptive functions.

Newborns are pretty near-sighted, but they can focus very well at a distance of about 8 to 10 inches—just about the distance between this baby's eyes and her mother's face while she nurses.

Perceptual Skills: What the Newborn Sees, Hears, and Feels

I'll be describing the infant's perceptual skills in detail in Chapter 5, and do not want to steal all that thunder. So let me merely summarize very briefly:

- The newborn can focus both eyes on the same spot, with 8 inches being roughly the best focal distance. Within a few weeks the baby can at least roughly follow a moving object with his eyes, and he can discriminate Mom's face from other faces almost immediately.
- He can easily hear sounds within the pitch and loudness ranges of the human voice; he can roughly locate objects by their sounds, and can discriminate some individual voices, particularly the mother's voice.
- He can taste the four basic tastes (sweet, sour, bitter, and salty) and can identify familiar body odors. From birth, he can recognize his mother by her smell.

Brief as this summary is, several points nonetheless stand out. First of all, newborns' perceptual skills are a great deal better than most parents believe—better than most psychologists or physicians believed until a few years ago. The better our research techniques have become, the more we have understood just how skillful the new baby is.

Even more striking is how well adapted the baby's perceptual skills are for the interactions he will have with the people in his world. He hears best in the range of the human voice; he can discriminate his mother (or other regular caregiver) from others on the basis of smell, sight, or sound almost immediately; the distance at which he can focus his eyes best, about 8 inches, is roughly the distance between the infant's eyes and the mother's face during nursing.

You'll see in Chapter 5 that there is a long way to go in the development of sophisticated perceptual abilities. But the newborn begins life able to make key discriminations and to locate objects through various perceptual cues.

Calves, foals, lambs, and newborns of virtually all mammals other than humans can stand and walk within a few hours of birth. Can you think of any useful evolutionary function for the greater motor helplessness of the human newborn?

Motor Skills: Moving Around

In contrast, the motor skills of the newborn are not very impressive. She can't hold up her head; she can't coordinate her looking and her reaching yet; she can't

Young Lucy was 5 months old when this photo was taken, showing her "airplaning." By this age, you can see that she is able to hold not just her head but part of her chest off the ground—a big advance over the motor skills we see in newborns.

roll over or sit up. These skills emerge only gradually in the early weeks. By 1 month, the baby can hold her chin up off the floor or mattress. By 2 months, she is beginning to swipe at objects near her with her hands.

One of the striking features of young babies' movements is how repetitively they perform their limited range of skills. They kick, rock, wave, bounce, bang, rub, scratch, or sway repeatedly and rhythmically. These repeated patterns become particularly prominent at about 6 or 7 months of age, although you can see some such behavior even in the first weeks, particularly in finger movements and leg kicking (Thelen, 1981). These movements do not seem to be totally voluntary or coordinated, but they also do not appear to be random. For instance, Esther Thelen has observed that kicking movements peak just before the baby begins to crawl, as if the rhythmic kicking were a part of the preparation for crawling. Thelen's work has helped us see the patterns and order in the apparently random movements of the young infant. But even this understanding does not alter the fact that, by contrast with perceptual abilities, the baby's initial motor abilities are quite limited.

Learning and Habituation

It seems obvious that maturation must play a vital role in these early developmental processes. The body systems and parts of the nervous system required for many perceptual skills are largely complete at birth, while those needed for motor control are not.

But is maturation the only process involved? Can a newborn also learn from her experiences? This question has intrigued researchers for decades, for both theoretical and practical reasons. From a theoretical perspective the question is obviously crucial for understanding the relative influences of nature and nurture. From a practical point of view, the same question is also important, because the answer affects the sort of advice parents may be given about appropriate toys or stimulation for their child. For example, if a child's perceptual abilities develop largely through maturation rather than learning, then it doesn't make much sense to buy expensive mobiles to hang above the baby's crib. But if learning is possible from the earliest days of life, then various kinds of enrichment make much more sense.

What does the evidence tell us?

Classical Conditioning.   The bulk of the research suggests that the newborn can be classically conditioned, although it is difficult. By 3 or 4 weeks of age classical conditioning is quite easy to demonstrate in an infant. In particular, this means that the conditioned emotional responses I talked about in Chapter 1 may begin to develop as early as the first weeks of life. Thus the mere presence of Mom or Dad or other favored person may trigger the sense of "feeling good," a pattern that may contribute to what we see as the child's attachment to the parent. Similarly, a child might develop various classically conditioned negative emotional responses that may be part of what we see as temperament.

Operant Conditioning.   Newborns also clearly learn by operant conditioning. Both the sucking response and head turning have been successfully increased by the use of reinforcements such as sweet-tasting liquids or the sound of the mother's voice or heartbeat (Moon & Fifer, 1990). At the least, the fact that conditioning of this kind can take place means that whatever neurological "wiring" is needed for learning to occur is present at birth. Results like this also tell us something about the sorts of reinforcements that are effective with very young children; the fact that the mother's voice is an effective reinforcer is surely highly significant for the whole process of mother-infant interaction.

Schematic Learning.   The fact that babies can recognize voices and heartbeats in the first days of life is also important because it suggests that another kind of learning is going on as well. This third type of learning, sometimes referred to as *schematic learning*, draws both its name and many of its conceptual roots from Piaget's theory. The basic idea is that from the beginning the baby organizes her experiences into expectancies, into "known" combinations. These expectancies, often called *schemas*, are built up over many exposures to particular experiences, but thereafter help the baby to distinguish between the familiar and the unfamiliar. Carolyn Rovee-Collier (1986) has suggested that we might think of classical conditioning in infants as being a variety of schematic learning. When a baby begins to move her head as if to search for the nipple when she hears her mother's footsteps coming into the room, this is not just some kind of automatic classical conditioning, but the beginning of the development of expectancies. From the earliest weeks, the baby seems to begin to map links between events in her world—between the sound of her mother's footsteps and the feeling of being picked up, between the touch of the breast and the feeling of a full stomach. Thus early classical conditioning may be the beginnings of the process of cognitive development.

If you know that babies can see and respond to objects, you're much more likely to buy mobiles to hang over the crib, as 3-month-old Shina-Mira's parents have done.

Habituation.   A related concept is that of **habituation.** Habituation is the automatic reduction in the strength or vigor of a response to a repeated stimulus. An example would probably help: Suppose you live on a fairly noisy street. The sound of cars going by is repeated over and over during each day. But after a while, you not only don't react to the sound, you quite literally *do not perceive it as being as loud*. The ability to do this—to dampen down the intensity of a physical response to some repeated stimulus—is obviously vital in our everyday lives. If we reacted constantly to every sight and sound and smell that came along, we'd spend all our time responding to these repeated events and not have energy or attention left over for things that are new and deserve attention.

The ability to *dishabituate* is equally important. When there is some change in a habituated stimulus, such as a sudden, extra-loud screech of tires on the busy street by your house, you again respond fully. Thus the reemergence of the original response strength is a sign that the perceiver—infant or child or adult—notices some significant change.

It is very clear that a newborn is able both to habituate and to dishabituate (Lipsitt, 1982). She will stop looking at something you keep putting in front of her face; she will stop showing a startle reaction (Moro reflex) to loud sounds after the first few presentations, but will again show a startle response if the sound is changed. Such habituation itself is not a voluntary process; it is automatic. But in order for it to work, the newborn must be equipped with the capacity to "recognize" familiar experiences. That is, she must develop schemas of some kind.

The existence of these processes in the newborn has an added benefit for researchers: it has enabled them to figure out what an infant responds to as "the same" or "different." If a baby is habituated to some stimulus, such as a sound or a particular picture, the experimenter can then present slight variations on the original stimulus to see the point at which dishabituation occurs. In this way, researchers have begun to get a picture of how the newborn baby or young infant experiences the world around her—a point I'll come back to in Chapter 5.

Social Skills

All of the skills of the newborn I have described so far are important for the baby's comfort and survival. But human newborns, unlike those in many other species, are a very long way from being independent. If they are to survive, someone must provide consistent care over an extended period. So the infant's capacity to entice others into the caregiving role is critical. It is here that the "social" skills of infants come into play.

When you think about a newborn baby, you probably don't think of him as particularly social. He doesn't talk. He doesn't flirt. He smiles, but not often during the first weeks. Normal newborns nonetheless have a collection of behaviors that are remarkably effective for attracting and keeping the attention of adults. The reverse is also true, as I pointed out in talking about the baby's perceptual abilities: adult faces and voices are remarkably effective for attracting and keeping the baby's attention, too. It would seem from all this that the adult and the baby are programmed from the beginning to join in a crucial social "dance," one which forms the root of the developing relationship between parent and child and that is critical for the formation of the parent's bond to the child.

The baby's repertoire of social behaviors is quite limited, but these few behaviors appear to be very effective in eliciting care. He cries when he needs something, which ordinarily brings someone to him to provide care. And then he responds to that care by being soothed, which is very reinforcing to the caregivers. He adjusts his body to yours when you pick him up; after the first few weeks, he gets quite good at meeting your eyes in a mutual gaze, or smiling—both of which are very powerful "hooks" for the adult's continued attention.

One other thing the baby does from the beginning which seems to be critical for any social interaction is to take turns. As adults, we take turns all the time, most clearly in conversations and eye contacts. In fact, it's very difficult to have any kind of social encounter with someone who does *not* take turns. Kenneth Kaye (1982) argues that the beginnings of this "turn taking" can be seen in very young infants in their eating patterns. As early as the first days of life, the baby sucks in a "burst-pause" pattern. He sucks for a while, pauses, sucks for a while, pauses, and so on. Mothers enter into this "conversation" too, often by jiggling the baby during the pauses. The eventual sequence looks something like this: suck, pause, jiggle, pause, suck, pause, jiggle, pause. The rhythm of the interaction is really very much like a conversation and seems to underlie many of the social encounters among people of all ages. To be sure, we cannot be certain whether this conversational quality of very early interaction occurs because the adult figures out the baby's natural rhythm and adapts her own responses to the baby's timing, or whether there is some mutual adaptation going on. Nonetheless

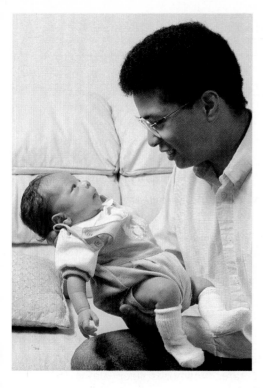

Newborn babies, like this 4-week-old, are very skilled at attracting and keeping the attention of adults. This Dad seems clearly captured!

it is extremely intriguing that we can see this apparent turn taking in an infant 1 day old.

▶ The Daily Life of Infants

Parents are obviously interested in the various skills and capacities of the newborn infant. They are delighted with his smiles and with each new ability as it emerges. But for most parents, the real questions are more practical: What is it like to live with a newborn? How is the infant's day organized? What sort of natural rhythms occur in the daily cycles? What can you expect from the baby, as you struggle to adapt to and care for this new person in your life?

Researchers who have studied newborns have described five different states of sleep and wakefulness in infants, referred to as **states of consciousness,** which I've summarized in Table 3.3 (p. 90). Of these states, the least common in the newborn are the two awake states. At first, babies are awake and not fussing only about two to three hours each day.

The five main states tend to occur in cycles, just as your own states occur in a daily rhythm. Most infants move through the states from deep sleep to lighter sleep to fussing and hunger and then to a brief period of alert wakefulness, after which they become drowsy and drop back into deep sleep. This cycle then repeats itself roughly every two hours: sleep, cry, eat, look; sleep, cry, eat, look. Because the first three parts of this repeating pattern—sleeping, crying, and eating—are so crucial for parents, let me say just a word more about each.

TABLE 3.3 The Basic States of Infant Sleep and Wakefulness

State of Consciousness	Characteristics
Deep sleep	Eyes closed, regular breathing, no movement except occasional startles
Active sleep	Eyes closed, irregular breathing, small twitches, no gross body movement
Quiet awake	Eyes open, no major body movement, regular breathing
Active awake	Eyes open, with movements of the head, limbs, and trunk; irregular breathing
Crying and fussing	Eyes may be partly or entirely closed, vigorous diffuse movement, with crying or fussing sounds

Sources: Based on the work of Prechtl & Beintema, 1964; Hutt, Lenard, & Prechtl, 1969; Parmelee, Wenner, & Schulz, 1964.

Sleeping

The child's sleep periods are important to parents because they provide breaks in what may otherwise seem like constant care. Newborns sleep about 15 to 16 hours each day, with little day-night rhythm (circadian rhythm); they sleep about equal amounts at any given time of day. By 6 or 8 weeks of age, the total amount of sleep per day has dropped slightly, and we see the first signs of circadian rhythms—at least among infants in Western countries, where regular sleep/wake cycles are more highly valued. Babies begin to string two or three 2-hour cycles together without coming to full wakefulness, at which point we say that the baby can "sleep through the night" (Bamford et al., 1990). By 6 months, babies are still sleeping a bit over 14 hours per day, but the regularity and predictability of the baby's sleep is still more noticeable—at least in Western samples. Not only do most 6-month-olds have clear nighttime sleep patterns, they also begin to nap during the day at more predictable times.

I've given you the average figures, but of course babies vary a lot in their sleep patterns. Of the 6-week-old babies in one recent study, there was one who slept only 8.8 hours per day (now there must be one tired set of parents!) and another who slept nearly 22 hours (Bamford et al., 1990). And some babies, even in Western cultures, do not develop a long nighttime sleep period until late in the first year of life.

All these aspects of the baby's sleep pattern have implications for the emerging parent-infant interaction. Psychologists have also been interested in sleep patterns because marked irregularity of sleep patterns may be a symptom of some disorder or problem. Some babies born to mothers who used cocaine during pregnancy have difficulty establishing a regular pattern of sleeping and waking. Brain-damaged infants often have the same kind of difficulties, so any time an infant fails to develop clear sleep/waking regularity, it *may* be a sign of trouble.

Crying

Newborns actually cry less of the time than you might think. One researcher, studying normal newborns, found that the figure ranged from 2 to 11 percent of the time (Korner et al., 1981). Crying seems to increase over the first six weeks of life, and then decreases. Initially infants cry most in the evening, and then shift their crying more toward times just before feedings.

The basic function of the child's cry, obviously, is to signal need. Because babies can't move *to* someone to get taken care of, they have to *bring* someone to them, and crying is the main way they have to attract attention. In fact, infants have a whole repertoire of cry sounds, with different cries for pain or anger or hunger. The basic cry, which often signals hunger, is usually a rhythmical pattern: cry, silence, breath, cry, silence, breath, with a kind of whistling sound often accompanying the in-breath. An anger cry is typically louder and more intense, and the pain cry normally has a very abrupt onset—unlike the more basic kinds of cries, which usually begin with whimpering or moaning. However, not all infants cry in precisely the same way, so each parent must learn the specific sounds of his or her own baby (Wiesenfeld, Malatesta, & DeLoach, 1981).

One of the enduring practical questions for parents about a baby's crying is how they should respond to it. If they pick up the baby right away, every time he cries, will that simply reinforce the baby's crying, so that he will cry more? Or will such an immediate response reassure the child, building the child's expectation that the world is a safe and reliable place?

Ten years ago I was confident that I knew the answer to this question, namely, always to respond immediately. Early studies showed no sign that such immediate responding increased the child's crying, and there was a lot of evidence that predictable responding was one ingredient in development of a secure attachment to the parent. More recent studies, though, make the answer less

It turns out that mothers are better at discriminating among the various meanings of their baby's cries than are fathers. Is this just because mothers spend more time with their babies? How could you design a study that would let you test this possibility?

Figure 3.4
What to do?

clear-cut. It now looks as if the parents' response may need to depend on the type of crying the child is doing. Intense crying, such as when the infant is hurt or significantly distressed—very hungry, very wet and uncomfortable, or the like—should be responded to immediately. But whimpering and milder crying, such as what a baby may do when she is put down for a nap, is another matter. When a parent responds immediately to all these milder cries, babies seem to learn to cry more often (Hubbard & van IJzendoorn, 1987). Thus both reassurance and reinforcement seem to be involved, and it takes real sensitivity on the part of the parent to sort it out.

Eating

Eating is not a "state," but it is certainly something that newborn babies do frequently! Given the normal two-hour cycle of a newborn baby's day, the infant may eat as many as 10 times a day. By 1 month the average number is down to about five and a half feedings, with a very gradual decline from that number over the first year (Barnard & Eyres, 1979). Both breast-fed and bottle-fed babies eat at about the same frequency, but these two forms of feeding do differ in other important ways.

Breast- Versus Bottle-Feeding.   After several decades of extensive research in many countries, physicians and epidemiologists have reached clear agreement that breast-feeding is substantially nutritionally superior to bottle-feeding. Breast milk provides important antibodies for the infant against many kinds of diseases, especially gastrointestinal and upper respiratory infections (Cunningham, Jelliffe, & Jelliffe, 1991). Human breast milk also appears to promote the growth of nerves and intestinal tract (Carter, 1988), and may stimulate better immune system function over the long term.

Those women who find breast-feeding logistically difficult because of work or other demands may take some comfort from the fact that the research indicates that babies derive some protection from as little as one breast-feeding per day. There is also comfort in the observation that the *social* interactions between mother and child seem to suffer no ill effects from bottle-feeding. Bottle-fed babies are held and cuddled in the same ways as are breast-fed babies, and their mothers appear to be just as sensitive and responsive to their babies as are mothers of breast-fed infants (Field, 1977).

I do not want this set of statements to provoke intense guilt in those of you who find that you are physically or otherwise unable to breast-feed. Babies can and do thrive on formula. But it is clear that *if* you have a choice, babies will derive real benefits from breast-feeding.

What specific changes in policies or practices do you think would increase the rate of breast-feeding in the United States (or in your own country)?

▶ Individual Differences Among Babies

Most of my emphasis in the past few pages has been on the ways in which infants are alike. Barring some kind of physical damage, all babies have similar sensory equipment at birth and can experience the same kinds of happenings around them. They all sleep, eat, and cry. But babies also differ in important ways—in health, in temperament, even in their patterns of crying.

CULTURES AND CONTEXTS
Cultural and Social Class Differences in Patterns of Breast-feeding, and Their Consequences

If you look at the incidence of breast-feeding in countries around the world over the past 40 or 50 years, you'll find some very curious patterns. In the 1950s and 1960s, breast-feeding declined dramatically in most Western countries, including the United States. By 1971, only 25 percent of U.S. women breast-fed even for a few weeks. At the same time, breast-feeding continued to be the normative method of infant feeding in non-Western countries, including virtually all Third World countries (World Health Organization, 1981).

In the decades since, these two trends have reversed. Breast-feeding has risen sharply in most industrialized countries as evidence of its importance has come to light; by 1984, 60 percent of U.S. women breast-fed for at least a few weeks (Ryan et al., 1991). In the same years, however, rates and durations of breast-feeding began to drop in many Third World and developing countries.

One contributor to the decline of breast-feeding in less-industrialized countries appears to have been the marketing of infant formula. Manufacturers of formula often gave free samples or free feeding bottles to new mothers and assured women that formula is as good or better for babies, while frequently failing to provide adequate instruction on how formula should be used. Some women, knowing no better and faced with extreme economic hardship, have diluted their infant's formula with water in order to make it stretch further. Sterilization procedures were also not well explained; for many women, proper sterilization was simply not feasible. Worldwide, the concern aroused by this change in normal feeding practices was sufficient to cause the World Health Organization to issue an "International Code of Marketing of Breast-milk Substitutes" in 1981. Marketing practices have since been modified. Yet the decline in breast-feeding has continued (Stewart et al., 1991).

Such a decline is cause for real concern, because bottle-fed babies in developing or Third World countries are at far higher risk of serious disease or death. In Bangladesh, for example, the risk of death from diarrhea is three times higher among bottle-fed than among breast-fed babies; in Brazil, the risk of death from various kinds of infections ranges from 2½ to 14 times higher among the bottle-fed. In all these studies, the risk associated with bottle-feeding is far higher where the sanitary conditions are poorest (Cunningham et al., 1991). Breast-feeding is thus better for two reasons: it provides the baby with needed antibodies against infection, and it is likely to expose the baby to less infection in the first place.

■ PATTERNS IN THE U.S.
In view of such findings, it is disturbing to find that in the United States the trend line is again downward. Between 1984 and 1989 the percentage of women beginning breast-feeding dropped from 60 to 52 percent (Ryan et al., 1991). At both time points, it was the same subgroups that were more likely to breast-feed: older, well-educated, or higher-income mothers. Whites are also more likely than either blacks or Hispanics to breast-feed. In 1989, the respective rates in the first weeks of the baby's life were 58 percent, 23 percent, and 48 percent (Ryan et al., 1991). In all three groups, however, better-educated mothers are more likely to breast-feed, while the less-educated and the poor are least likely to do so (MacGowan et al., 1991). This pattern is of special concern because rates of mortality and illness are already higher among infants born to poor mothers.

A mother's work status also makes some difference in her decision about breast- or bottle-feeding, but it is *not* the deciding factor in many cases. The majority of women who do *not* work also do not breast-feed, while many working women find creative ways to combine employment and breast-feeding (Ryan et al., 1991). If we had societal supports for such a combination, it could be made still easier.

Overall, it is clear that there is still a large public health task remaining, not only in the United States but around the world, to educate women still further about the importance of breast-feeding and to create the cultural and practical supports needed to make breast-feeding easier.

Health and Death in the First Year
Virtually all babies get sick, most of them repeatedly. In the United States, the average baby has seven respiratory illnesses in the first year of life. (That's a lot of nosewipes!) Interestingly, there is now a whole series of studies showing that the incidence of such illnesses is higher among babies in day care than among those reared entirely at home, presumably because babies in group care settings are exposed to a wider range of germs and viruses (Hurwitz et al., 1991). In general, the more different people a baby is exposed to, the more often she is likely to be sick (Wald, Guerra, & Byers, 1991). But this is not the unmitigated negative that it

may appear to be. Children reared entirely at home, with low exposure to others, have very high rates of illness at later ages when they first attend school. Attendance at day care simply means that the baby is exposed earlier to the various microorganisms that cause upper respiratory infections.

Infant Mortality and Sudden Infant Death Syndrome. For a small minority of babies, though, the issue is not a few sniffles, but the possibility of death. I mentioned in the last chapter that 9.1 babies out of every 1000 in the U.S. die in the first year. Most of these deaths occur in the first month of life and are directly linked either to congenital anomalies or to low birth weight. Only about 3.5 deaths per 1000 occur in the remainder of the first year, and nearly half of those are cases of **sudden infant death syndrome (SIDS),** in which an apparently healthy infant dies suddenly and unexpectedly. In 1988 about 5500 babies in the United States died of SIDS (Wegman, 1991). SIDS is certainly not unique to the U.S. It occurs worldwide, although for unexplained reasons, the rate varies quite a lot from country to country. SIDS rates are particularly high, for example, in Australia and New Zealand, and particularly low in Japan and Sweden (Hoffman & Hillman, 1992).

Physicians have not yet uncovered the basic cause of these deaths. But we do know a lot more now about the groups that are at higher risk: babies with low birth weight, males, those with young mothers, and those whose mothers smoked during pregnancy or after birth. SIDS is also more common in the wintertime, and appears to be somewhat more common among babies who sleep on their stomachs (Dwyer & Ponsonby, 1992; Hoffman & Hillman, 1992). The growing evidence on the role of sleeping position has persuaded pediatricians in some countries to change their standard advice to hospitals and families about the best sleeping position for babies. In Norway, for example, when hospitals switched the standard baby sleeping position from side to stomach in the early 1970s, the rate of SIDS rose; when the standard position was switched back in 1989, the rate of SIDS dropped dramatically in the next year (Markestad, 1992). Still, sleeping position cannot be the full explanation, since of course *most* babies who sleep on their stomachs do not die of SIDS.

The link between SIDS and maternal (or paternal) smoking is also becoming clearer and clearer: Babies whose mothers smoked during their pregnancy, or who are exposed to smoke in the months after birth, are about four times as likely to die of SIDS as are babies with no smoking exposure (Mitchell et al., 1993; Schoendorf & Kiely, 1992). One more powerful reason not to smoke. . . .

Variations in Crying Patterns

A far less lethal variation among babies is in the pattern or quality of their crying. Fifteen to 20 percent of infants develop a pattern called *colic,* which involves daily, intense bouts of crying, totaling three or more hours a day. The crying is generally worst in late afternoon or early evening (a particularly inopportune time, of course, since it is usually when the parents are tired and needing time with one another, too). Colic typically appears at about 2 weeks of age and then disappears spontaneously at 3 or 4 months of age. Neither psychologists nor physicians know why colic begins, or why it stops without any intervention. It is a difficult pattern to live with, but the good news is that it *does* go away.

The gratingness of a child's cry also varies from one child to the next and may even be predictive of the child's later intellectual functioning. A number of interesting recent studies have shown that babies with some kind of physical problem—small-for-date babies, preterm infants, babies who experienced complications at delivery—have more piercing, grating, unpleasant cries than do physically normal infants (Lester, 1987; Lester & Dreher, 1989). Among such babies, the quality of the cry is also significantly correlated with IQ and other cognitive measures at age 2 (Huntington, Hans, & Zeskind, 1990). Eventually, it may be possible for physicians to use the presence of such a grating or piercing cry as a signal that there may be some underlying physical problem with the infant.

Temperament

Babies also vary in the way they react to new things, in their typical moods, in their rate of activity, in their preference for social interactions or solitude, in the regularity of their daily rhythms, and in many other ways. These variations usually go by the name *temperament*. I'll be talking about temperament at greater length in Chapter 9, but because the concept will come up often as we go along, it is important at this early stage to introduce some related concepts and terms.

Psychologists who have been interested in these differences have proposed several different ways of describing the key dimensions of temperament. Buss and Plomin (1984; 1986) propose three dimensions: emotionality, activity, and sociability. Rothbart (1989a) proposes two dimensions, while Thomas and Chess (1977) describe nine dimensions, which they organize into three types: the easy child, the difficult child, and the slow-to-warm-up child.

It is not yet clear whether one of these views, or some other, will eventually carry the theoretical day. Thus far, the Thomas and Chess formulation has been the most influential, so let me describe their three basic types for you.

The Easy Child.   Easy children approach new events positively. They try new foods without much fuss, for example. They are also regular in biological functioning, with good sleeping and eating cycles, are usually happy, and adjust easily to change.

The Difficult Child.   By contrast, the difficult child is less regular in body functioning and is slow to develop regular sleeping and eating cycles. These children react vigorously and negatively to new things, are more irritable, and cry more. Their cries also have a more "spoiled," grating sound than do the cries of "easy" babies (Boukydis & Burgess, 1982). Thomas and Chess point out, however, that once the difficult baby has adapted to something new, he is often quite happy about it, even though the adaptation process itself is very difficult.

The Slow-to-warm-up Child.   Children in this group are not as negative in responding to new things or new people as is the difficult child. They show instead a kind of passive resistance. Instead of spitting out new food violently and crying, the slow-to-warm-up child may let the food drool out and may resist mildly any attempt to feed her more of the same. These infants show few intense reactions, either positive or negative, although once they have adapted to something new, their reaction is usually fairly positive.

Interestingly, there is some evidence that these temperamental features occur in differing frequency in different cultures—a set of findings I've explored in the

Young Genevieve is clearly delighted to have figured out how to pull herself up to a standing position. If her disposition is typically this sunny and accepting of new experiences, we would say she has an easy temperament.

CULTURES AND CONTEXTS
Cultural Differences in Infant Temperament

Daniel Freedman (1979) has observed newborn babies from four different cultures: Caucasian, Chinese, Navaho, and Japanese. Of the four, he found that the Caucasian babies were the most active and irritable and the hardest to console (the most "difficult" in Thomas and Chess's terms). Both the Chinese and the Navaho infants were relatively placid, while the Japanese infants responded vigorously but were easier to quiet than the Caucasian infants.

One specific illustration: When Freedman tested each baby for the Moro reflex he found that the Caucasian babies showed the typical pattern in which they reflexively extended both arms, cried vigorously and persistently, and moved their bodies in an agitated way. Navaho babies, on the other hand, showed quite a different pattern. Instead of thrusting their limbs outward they retracted their arms and legs, rarely cried, and showed little or very brief agitation.

Since such differences are visible in newborns, they cannot be the result of systematic shaping by the parents. But the parents, too, bring their temperament and their cultural training to the interaction, which may tend to strengthen or perpetuate such temperamental differences. For instance, Freedman and other researchers have observed that both Japanese and Chinese mothers talk much less to their infants than do Caucasian mothers. These differences in mothers' behavior were present from their first encounters with their infants after delivery, so the pattern is not a response to the baby's quieter behavior. But such similarity of temperamental pattern between mother and child is likely to strengthen the pattern in the child, which would tend to make the cultural differences larger over time.

One of the key points from this research is that our notions of what is "normal" behavior for an infant may be strongly influenced by our own cultural patterns and assumptions. More research like Freedman's is needed for us to describe and understand the range of variations that exists among babies.

---

cultures and contexts discussion above. And in every culture some kind of temperamental variations can be seen in very young infants, and are at least somewhat persistent throughout childhood.

No psychologist studying temperament suggests that such individual differences are absolutely fixed at birth. Any inborn temperamental differences are shaped, strengthened, bent, or counteracted by the child's relationships and experiences. What we do know is that infants enter the world with somewhat different repertoires or patterns of behavior, and that those differences affect not only the experiences the infant may choose, but also help to shape the emerging pattern of interaction that develops between infant and parents. For example, toddlers and preschoolers with difficult temperaments are more often criticized or physically punished by their parents than are easy children, presumably because the child's behavior *is* more troublesome (Bates, 1989; Rutter, 1978a). But once established, such a pattern of criticism and punishment itself is likely to have additional consequences for the child.

Nonetheless, not all parents of difficult children respond in this way. A skilled parent, especially a parent who correctly perceives that the child's "difficultness" is a temperamental quality and not a result of the child's willfulness or the parent's ineptness, can avoid some of the pitfalls, and can handle the difficult child more adeptly.

Sex Differences

Finally, as I did in the last chapter, let me add at least a brief word about sex differences. Most of us, when we hear about a new baby's birth, immediately ask: "Is it a boy or a girl?" So this is clearly a highly salient issue for almost all of us. Given that preoccupation with gender, it may surprise you to know that there are remarkably few sex differences among young infants. As was true at birth, girls continue to be a bit ahead in some aspects of physical maturity, and boys continue to be more vulnerable. For example, more boys die during the first year of life. Male infants also have more muscle tissue than do girls, and they seem to be slightly more physically active (Eaton & Enns, 1986). But boys and girls do not seem to differ on the temperamental dimensions Thomas and Chess have described: boys are not more often "difficult" in temperament, and girls are not more often "easy," even though that is what our stereotypes might lead us to expect. What dominates the system in these early months is "babyness" and not "boyness" or "girlness."

▶ Summary

1. The normal birth process has three parts: dilation, delivery, and placental delivery.

2. The first "acquaintance" process after delivery may be an especially important one for parents. Most parents show an intense interest in the baby's features, especially the eyes.

3. Most drugs given to the mother during delivery pass through to the infant's bloodstream. They have short-term effects on infant responsiveness and on feeding patterns, but long-term effects are not yet well understood.

4. Home deliveries in uncomplicated pregnancies can be as safe as hospital deliveries.

5. The presence of the father during delivery appears to help reduce the mother's discomfort, but appears not to be necessary for the establishment of the father's bond to the infant.

6. More than one-fifth of all deliveries in the U.S. today are by abdominal incision, called cesarean section, because of indications of fetal distress or other specific problems.

7. Several types of problems may occur at birth, including reduced oxygen supply (anoxia) to the infant, or low birth weight.

8. Low-birth-weight infants have higher risk of death during the first year of life, but if they survive, most catch up to full-size peers by school age. Those with birth weights below 1500 grams, or who are very small for date, are more likely to show lasting problems.

9. Most parents experience delight and pleasure at their new role, but there are also strains. The majority of mothers have at least a brief period of "blues"; as many as one-tenth experience a more serious, longer depression. Marital satisfaction also typically declines.

10. The newborn has far more skills than most physicians and psychologists had thought, including excellent reflexes, good perceptual skills, and effective social skills.

11. The important infant reflexes include many crucial adaptive reflexes, such as rooting and sucking.

12. Perceptual skills include focusing both eyes, tracking slowly moving objects, discrimination of the mother by smell, sight and sound, and general responsiveness to smells, tastes, and touch.

13. Motor skills, in contrast, are only rudimentary at birth.

14. Social skills, while rudimentary, are sufficient to bring people close for care and to keep them close for social interactions. The baby can meet a gaze and smile within the first month of life.

15. Newborns can learn from the first days of life, and can habituate to repeated stimulation.

16. Cycles of sleeping, waking, crying, and eating are present from the beginning. Newborns sleep 16 to 18 hours per day, and eat roughly 10 times.

17. Breast-feeding has clear benefits to the baby, providing antibodies against diseases and reducing the risk of disease.

18. Other than death caused by low birth weight or congenital anomalies, sudden infant death syndrome is the most common cause of death in the first year. The risk of SIDS is higher in black infants, those with young mothers, or those whose mothers smoked. The cause is not yet understood.

19. Babies differ from one another on several dimensions, including vigor of response, general activity rate, restlessness, irritability, and cuddliness. These temperamental dimensions, which Thomas and Chess have grouped into "difficult," "easy," and "slow-to-warm-up" types, appear to be at least somewhat stable.

20. Male and female babies differ at birth on a few dimensions. Girls are more mature physically. Boys are more active, have more muscle tissue, and are more vulnerable to stress. No sex differences are found, however, on temperamental dimensions such as cuddliness or sootheability.

▶ Key Terms

anoxia (78)

Apgar score (81)

cesarean section (78)

dilation (72)

effacement (72)

habituation (87)

low birth weight (LBW) (79)

postpartum depression (83)

preterm infant (79)

reflexes (82)

small-for-date infant (79)

states of consciousness (89)

sudden infant death syndrome (SIDS) (94)

very low-birth-weight infants (79)

▶ Suggested Readings

Field, T. (1990). *Infancy*. Cambridge, MA: Harvard University Press.

Another of the fine small books published by Harvard University Press. Field reviews what we know about infancy in an engaging and clear style.

Leach, P. (1983). *Babyhood* (2nd ed., rev.). New York: Knopf.

A detailed look at the first two years of life, written for a lay audience, but based very thoroughly on research. Very readable and practical.

Maurer, D., & Maurer, C. (1988). *The world of the newborn*. New York: Basic Books.

Another excellent description of the newborn written for the lay reader.

Osofsky, J. D. (Ed.). (1987). *Handbook of infant development* (2nd ed.). New York: Wiley-Inter-science.

The material in this splendid collection of papers is considerably more technical than what you will find in either Leach or Maurer & Maurer. But if you are interested in some specific aspect of infant development, there is no better source for a comprehensive review.

PHYSICAL DEVELOPMENT

4

Four Reasons for Studying Physical Development

Basic Sequences and Common Patterns
  Size and Shape
  Bones
  Muscles
  Fat
  Other Body Changes
  Development of the Nervous System
  Hormones

Development of Sexual Maturity
  Sexual Development in Girls
  Sexual Development in Boys

Using the Body: The Effects of Physical Changes on Behavior
  Motor Development in the Early Years
  • *The Real World:* Sports for Children
  Adolescent Sexuality and Pregnancy
  • *The Real World:* Which Teenage Girls Get Pregnant?

Big or Fast Versus Slow or Small: Some Individual Differences in Physical Development
  Differences in Rate
  Social Class and Racial Differences in Physical Development

Health and Illness in Childhood and Adolescence
  • *Research Report:* An Australian Study Illustrating Sex Differences in Body Image Among Adolescents
  • *The Real World:* How to Get Your Teenager to Stop Smoking, or Not to Start

Determinants of Growth: Explanations of Physical Development
  Maturation
  Heredity
  Environmental Effects

Summary

Key Terms

Suggested Readings

When my daughter (who is now 25) was about 8 ½, a lot of well-rehearsed family routines seemed to unravel. She was crankier than usual, both more assertive and more needful of affection, and alternately compliant and defiant. What on earth was happening? Had I done something dreadfully wrong? Was there something going on at school? I mentioned my problems to several colleagues, many of whom told me their own tales about the special difficulties they had had with their daughters between ages 8 and 9. It finally occurred to all of us that there might be a physical explanation: girls of 8 or 9 are actually beginning to experience the first hormone changes of puberty. Perhaps the inconsistent and uncomfortable behaviors I was seeing were one form of response to the changing hormones in the system.

It may amuse you to think of the clever psychologist missing such an obvious possibility. But in fact developmental psychologists have often placed too little emphasis on physical growth. We describe it briefly and then take it for granted. But I am convinced both by the research literature on the effects of physiological change, and by my observations as a parent, that an understanding of physical development is an absolutely critical first step in understanding children's progress, for at least four reasons.

▶ Four Reasons for Studying Physical Development

The Child's Growth Makes New Behaviors Possible. Specific physical changes are needed before the infant can crawl or walk. Similarly, the development of full reproductive capacity at adolescence is based on a complex sequence of physical changes. Thus nonobvious physical changes are often the necessary underpinning of behavior change.

The flip side of this is that the *lack* of a particular physical development may set limits on the behaviors a child is capable of performing. An infant of 10 months cannot be toilet trained, no matter how hard parents may try, because the anal sphincter muscle is not yet fully mature. Toddlers cannot easily pick up raisins or Cheerios from their high chair trays until the muscles and nerves required for thumb-forefinger opposition have developed. Six-year-olds cannot reliably hit baseballs, or throw basketballs through hoops, no matter how much their parents (or their coaches) may pressure them to do so.

The Child's Growth Determines Experience. A child's range of physical capacities or skills can also have a major indirect effect on cognitive and social development by influencing the variety of experiences she can have. An infant who cannot crawl can only explore things that are brought to her or are within easy reach. When she begins to crawl, her experiences are greatly expanded. Similarly, a child who learns to ride a bike widens her horizons still further, as she explores her neighborhood on her own, perhaps for the first time.

The Child's Growth Affects Others' Responses. New physical skills not only change the child's experiences, they also change the way the people around the child respond to her. For example, parents react quite differently to an infant who can crawl than to one who cannot. They begin to say "no" more often, put things out of reach, or put the baby in a playpen more of the time. Such changes in the pattern of interaction between parent and child may have both immediate and long-term consequences for the child's emotional or mental development.

Adults' expectations for children are also affected by the child's size and shape, attractiveness, or physical skills. Children who are pretty or tall or well coordinated are treated differently from those who are homely or petite or clumsy (Brackbill & Nevill, 1981; Lerner, 1985). A Little League baseball coach may be more supportive of a child with advanced large-muscle coordination (good for home runs), while a classroom teacher may be especially appreciative of children whose small-muscle coordination is superior (good for writing and drawing). As a

This 6-year-old is still unsteady on his bike. But once he masters this new physical skill, his life will change as he ranges more independently.

general rule, the larger or more developed a child, the more "adult" his behavior is expected to be.

Adults and children are also biased in favor of some specific body types. In the terminology introduced by Sheldon many years ago (Sheldon, 1940), the most favored type (in Western cultures, at least) is one that is well muscled and square in build, which Sheldon called *mesomorphic*. *Endomorphic* (rounded) and *ectomorphic* (skinny, tall, bony) body types are less preferred by both children and adults—a pattern of preferences that has been found not only in the U.S. but in samples of Japanese and Mexican children and adults as well (Lerner, 1985, 1987). Thus individual differences in physical patterns, or speed of growth, can have profound effects on children's early experiences.

The Child's Growth Affects Self-concept.   The final reason for us to pay close attention to physical development is that physical characteristics and physical skills (or lack of them) have a significant influence on a child's self-concept. I'll be talking about this topic much more fully in Chapters 9 and 10, but let me only point out here that this is another example of the importance of internal models, a concept I introduced in Chapter 1. A child's body image, which is part of her self-concept, is not simply a direct reflection of observable reality. It is instead an internal model shaped by a variety of things, including direct experience, what the child overhears from others, and the child's ideas about the then-current cultural image of an ideal body (Thomas, 1990b). Like all internal models, the body image, once created, becomes relatively difficult to change. A child's choice of activities, her behavior in social situations, and her sense of self-worth are all likely to be affected throughout childhood and adolescence, perhaps even into adulthood, by the body image formed early in childhood. My own body image, for example, includes a strong element of "gawkiness," since I was always taller than everyone else and saw myself as uncoordinated. Whether that is *objectively* true is less important than the fact that I *believe* it to be true, and base my behavior, my choices, my interpretations of my own behavior, on that belief.

For all of these reasons, I think it is important to begin our exploration of development with a fairly detailed look at physical growth and change.

These Texas first graders are all the same age, but not all the same size. Because he is so much smaller, the little guy on the left in the front row is likely to be treated quite differently from his classmates.

Can you think of ways in which the same process has operated in your own life? Has your self-image been affected by your early growth, or by your physical size or shape?

▶ Basic Sequences and Common Patterns

Size and Shape

The most obvious thing about children's physical development is that kids get bigger as they get older. But even this simple statement may conceal some surprises. The biggest surprise for most people is the fact that at birth an infant is already one-third of his final height; by age 2 he is half as tall as he will be as an adult. Another possible surprise is the fact that growth from birth to maturity is neither continuous nor smooth. Figure 4.1, which marks the growth patterns for height for boys and girls, shows that there are four different phases in this process.

During the first phase, which lasts for about the first two years, the baby gains in height very rapidly, adding 10 to 12 inches in length in the first year and tripling his body weight in the same span. At about age 2, the child settles down to a slower but steady addition of 2 to 3 inches and about 6 pounds per year until adolescence.

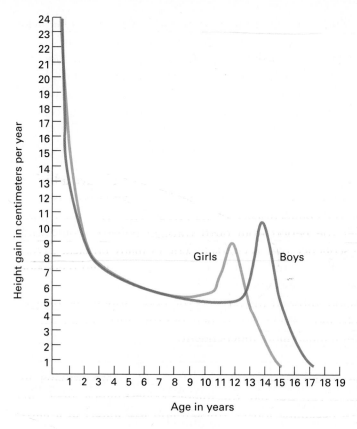

Figure 4.1
These curves show the *gain* in height for each year from birth through adolescence. You can see the several clear phases: very rapid growth in infancy, slower growth in the preschool and elementary school years, a growth spurt at adolescence, and the cessation of growth at adulthood. (*Sources:* Tanner, 1978, p. 14; Malina, 1990.)

The third phase begins with the dramatic adolescent "growth spurt," when the child may add 3 to 6 inches a year for several years, after which the rate of growth again slows until final adult size is reached.

At the same time, the shape and proportions of the child's body are changing. In an adult, the head is about one-eighth or one-tenth of the total height. But the toddler isn't built like that at all. In the 2-year-old, the head is about one-quarter of the total body length.

Individual body parts do not all grow at the same rate, either. This is particularly striking at adolescence. During those years, a teenager's hands and feet grow to full adult size earliest, followed by the arms and legs, with the trunk usually the slowest part to grow. (In fact, a good signal for a parent that puberty is beginning in a child is a rapid increase in shoe size.) Because of this asymmetry in the body parts, we often think of an adolescent as "awkward" or uncoordinated. Interestingly, research does not bear that out. Robert Malina, who has done extensive research on physical development, has found no point in the adolescent growth process at which teenagers become consistently less coordinated or less skillful in physical tasks (Malina, 1990).

Bones

All these visible changes in size and shape are the result of changes on the inside in bones, muscles, and fat. Bones both increase in number and grow harder over the years of childhood.

Number of Bones.   Bones increase in number in the hand, wrist, ankle, and foot. For example, in an adult's wrist there are nine separate bones. In the 1-year-old, there are only three. The remaining six are fully developed by adolescence.

In one part of the body, though, the bones fuse rather than differentiating. The skull of an infant is made up of several bones separated by spaces called **fontanels.** Fontanels allow the head to be compressed without injury during the birth process, and they also give the brain room to grow. The fontanels are filled in by bone by about the end of the first year (Kataria et al., 1988), so that a single connected skull bone is created.

Hardening of Bones.   The infant's bones are also softer and have a higher water content than adults' bones, important properties if the infant's body is to be flexible enough to fit into the cramped space of the uterus. The bones then gradually harden (*ossify*) over the period from birth through puberty. The entire process follows a general sequence that is characteristic of many physical developments in infancy and childhood: it moves from the head downward (**cephalocaudal**) and from the trunk outward (**proximodistal**). For example, bones of the hand and wrist harden before those in the feet. As the bones stiffen, the baby is able to manipulate his body more surely, which increases the range of exploration he can enjoy and makes him much more independent.

Muscles

Unlike bones, which are not all formed at birth, muscle fibers are virtually all present at birth (Tanner, 1978). But like the infant's bones, muscle fibers are initially small and watery, becoming longer, thicker, and less watery at a fairly steady rate throughout childhood. At adolescence, muscles go through a growth spurt, just as height does, so that adolescents become quite a lot stronger in just a few years. Both boys and girls show this increase in muscle tissue and strength, but as you can see in Figure 4.2, the increase is much greater in boys. Among adult men, about 40 percent of total body mass is muscle, compared to only about 24 percent in adult women.

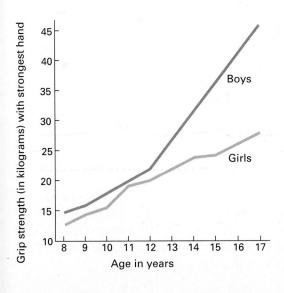

Figure 4.2
Both boys and girls get stronger over the years of childhood and adolescence, but boys gain much more muscle tissue particularly at puberty. (*Source:* Adapted from Montpetit, Montoye, & Laeding, 1967, from Tables 1 and 2, p. 233.)

Differences in hormone patterns at adolescence appear to be major contributors to the sex differences in muscle growth. But there are also some hints that sex differences in exercise patterns or activity may also be involved. For example, boys have comparatively much greater arm strength, but the two sexes are more equal in leg strength (Tanner, Hughes, & Whitehouse, 1981). Such a pattern makes sense if we assume that all teenagers walk and use their legs a similar amount, but that boys use their arm muscles more in various sports activities than girls do. Still, there does seem to be a basic hormonal difference as well, because we know that very fit girls and women are still not as strong as very fit boys and men.

Fat

Another major component of the body is fat, most of which is stored immediately under the skin. This *subcutaneous fat* is first laid down beginning at about 34 weeks prenatally, and has an early peak at about 9 months after birth (the so-called "baby fat"); the thickness of this layer of fat then declines until about age 6 or 7, after which it rises until adolescence.

Once again there is a sex difference in these patterns. From birth, girls have slightly more fat tissue than boys do, and this difference becomes gradually more marked during childhood. At adolescence, the difference grows still further. The size of the change is illustrated nicely in the results of a large study of Canadian teenagers (Smoll & Schutz, 1990). Between seventh and twelfth grades, the percentage of body weight made up of fat rose from 21.8 to 24 percent among girls in this group, but dropped from 16.1 to 14.0 percent among boys. So during and after puberty, proportions of fat rise among girls and decline among boys, while the proportion of weight that is muscle rises in boys and declines in girls.

Of course, as with muscle tissue, this sex difference in fat may be partially a life-style or activity-level effect; girls and women who are extremely athletic, such as long-distance runners or ballet dancers, typically have body fat levels that approximate those of the average boy. But if we compare equally fit boys and girls, boys have lower fat levels.

Other Body Changes

Puberty also brings important changes in other body organs. In particular, the heart and lungs increase considerably in size and the heart rate drops. Both of these changes are more marked for boys than for girls—another of the factors that increases the capacity for sustained effort for boys relative to girls. Before about age 12, boys and girls have similar physical strength, speed, and endurance, although even at these earlier ages, when there is a difference it favors the boys because of their lower levels of body fat. After puberty, boys have a clear advantage in all three (Smoll & Schutz, 1990).

Development of the Nervous System

Growth in height and weight involves changes you can see. Even the changes in muscles, bones, and fat can be detected fairly easily in the child's longer legs, greater strength, or softness or leanness of body. But there are two enormously important types of developmental changes in the body that are not so easy to perceive. The first of these is change in the nervous system.

Suppose you were a member of a local school board, faced with a decision about whether to have teenage boys and girls play on the same competitive teams, such as volleyball, soccer, or baseball. Given what you have read so far, how would you decide the issue, and why?

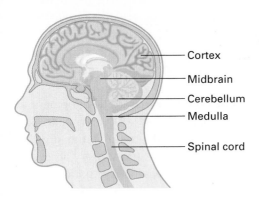

Cortex

Midbrain

Cerebellum

Medulla

Spinal cord

Figure 4.3
The medulla and the midbrain are largely developed at birth. In the first two years after birth it is primarily the cortex that develops, although increases in the dendritic arbor and in synapses also occur throughout the nervous system.

Composition of the Nervous System.   Figure 4.3 shows the main structures of the brain. At birth, as I mentioned briefly in Chapter 3, the **midbrain** and the **medulla** are most fully developed. These two parts, both in the lower part of the skull and connecting to the spinal cord, regulate such basic tasks as attention and habituation, sleeping, waking, elimination, and movement of the head and neck (but not movement of the trunk or limbs)—all tasks a newborn can perform at least moderately well. The least-developed part of the brain at birth is the **cortex,** the convoluted gray matter that wraps around the midbrain and is involved in perception, body movement, and all complex thinking and language.

Recall from Chapter 2 that all of these structures are composed of two basic types of cells, *neurons* and *glial cells*. Virtually all of both types of cells are already present at birth. The developmental process after birth is primarily the creation of synapses, which involves enormous growth of the dendritic arbor as well as of axons and their terminal fibers. Most of that dendritic growth occurs in the cortex, primarily during the first year or two after birth, resulting in a tripling of the overall weight of the brain during those years (Nowakowski, 1987).

This remarkable brain development is not entirely smooth and continuous. Neurophysiologists have found that there is an initial burst of synapse formation, followed by a "pruning" of synapses at about 2 years of age, in which the redundant ones are eliminated and the "wiring diagram" is cleaned up (Greenough, Black, & Wallace, 1987). Taken together, these two developmental patterns mean that the 1-year-old actually has a *denser* set of dendrites and synapses than an adult does—a piece of information that has surprised many psychologists and raised a whole host of interesting questions.

The pruning process is especially fascinating. An example: Early in development each skeletal muscle cell seems to develop synaptic connections with several motor neurons in the spinal cord. But after the pruning process has occurred, each muscle fiber is connected to only one neuron. Some neurophysiologists (Greenough et al., 1987) have suggested that the initial surge of development of the dendritic arbor and synaptic formation follows a built-in pattern; the organism is programmed to create certain kinds of neural connections and does so in abundance, creating redundant pathways. According to this argument, the pruning that then takes place beginning at around 18 months or 2 years is a response to specific experience, resulting in selective retention of the used, or the most efficient, pathways. Putting it briefly, "Experience does not create tracings on a blank tablet; rather experience erases some of them" (Bertenthal & Campos, 1987). Such pruning appears to continue throughout childhood, with perhaps another peak at adolescence, suggesting that there may be a reorganization of pathways at various times in development.

Greenough and his colleagues do not think that all synaptic development is governed by such built-in programming. He suggests that other synapses are formed entirely as a result of specific experience, and go on being created throughout our lives as we learn new skills. But basic motor and sensory processes may initially follow built-in patterns, with pruning then based on experience.

Myelinization.   Another crucial process in neuronal development is the development of sheaths around individual axons, which insulate them from one another and improve the conductivity of the nerve. This sheath is made up of a substance called **myelin;** the process of developing the sheath is called **myelinization.**

The sequence with which nerves are myelinized follows the familiar cephalo-caudal and proximodistal pattern. Thus nerves serving muscle cells in the arms and hands are myelinized earlier than are those serving the lower trunk and the legs. Myelinization is largely complete by age 2, although some continues in the brain well into adolescence.

To understand the importance of myelin, it may help you to know that multiple sclerosis is a disease in which the myelin begins to break down. An individual with this disease gradually loses motor control, with the specific symptoms depending on the portion of the nervous system affected by the disease.

Hormones

A second, less-visible but crucial set of changes over the years of childhood and adolescence is in *hormones*—secretions of the various **endocrine glands** in the body. Hormones govern growth and physical changes in several ways, which I've summarized in Table 4.1.

Of all the endocrine glands, the most critical is the pituitary, since it provides the trigger for release of hormones from other glands. For example, the thyroid gland only secretes thyroxine when it has received a signal to do so in the form of a specific thyroid-stimulating hormone secreted by the pituitary.

Hormones play a role at every stage of physical development, perhaps most strikingly at adolescence, but significantly at earlier stages as well.

Prenatal Hormones.   Thyroid hormone (thyroxine) is present from about the fourth month of gestation, and appears to be involved in stimulating normal brain development. Growth hormone is also produced by the pituitary beginning as early as 10 weeks after conception. Presumably it helps to stimulate the very rapid growth of cells and organs of the body. And as I mentioned in Chapter 2, testosterone is produced prenatally in the testes of the developing male and influences both the development of male genitals and some aspects of brain development.

Hormones Between Birth and Adolescence.   Between birth and adolescence, physical growth is largely governed by thyroid hormone and pituitary growth hormone. Thyroid hormone is secreted in greater quantities for the first

---

Developmental psychologists have been very excited about the discovery of dendritic pruning in the second year of life. Can you see why this might be so interesting? What does it tell us about nature and nurture, and how they interact?

Margin note (handwritten):

Head   trunk
Cephalocaudal

Head, neck, chest, develope
before the muscle and
other develope (inner away)
(middle closes)
Proximal distal

Middle grows faster
than the other
arms develope earlier
than fingers.

TABLE 4.1	**Major Hormones Involved in Physical Growth and Development**	
Gland	Hormone(s) Secreted	Aspects of Growth Influenced
Thyroid	Thyroxine	Normal brain development and overall rate of growth.
Adrenal	Adrenal androgen	Some changes at puberty, particularly the development of secondary sex characteristics in girls.
Testes (in boys)	Testosterone	Crucial in the formation of male genitals prenatally; also triggers the sequence of primary and secondary sex characteristic changes at puberty in the male.
Ovaries (in girls)	Estradiol	Development of the menstrual cycle and breasts in girls but has less to do with other secondary sex characteristics than testosterone does for boys.
Pituitary	Growth hormone, activating hormones	Rate of physical maturation; signals other glands to secrete.

two years of life and then falls to a lower level and remains steady until adolescence (Tanner, 1978), a secretion pattern that obviously matches the pattern of change in height you saw in Figure 4.1.

Secretions from the testes and ovaries, as well as adrenal androgen, remain at extremely low levels until about age 7 or 8, when adrenal androgen begins to be secreted—the first signal of the changes of adolescence (and possibly one of the sources of the changes I observed in my 8-year-old daughter) (Shonkoff, 1984).

Hormones in Adolescence.   The early rise in adrenal androgen is only the first step in a complex sequence of hormone changes at adolescence, which you can see laid out schematically in Figure 4.4.

The timing of these changes varies a lot from one child to the next, but the sequence remains the same. At a signal from the hypothalamus, the pituitary gland begins secreting increased levels of **gonadotropic hormones** (two in males, three in females). These in turn stimulate the development of the glands in the testes and ovaries, which then begin to secrete more hormones, testosterone in boys and a form of **estrogen** called *estradiol* in girls. Over the course of puberty, the levels of testosterone increase 18-fold in boys, while levels of estradiol increase 8-fold in girls (Nottelmann et al., 1987).

At the same time, the pituitary also secretes three other hormones that affect growth and that interact with the specific sex hormones, although as you can see in Figure 4.4, the interaction is a little different for boys and girls. In particular, both the growth spurt and pubic hair development in girls are more influenced by

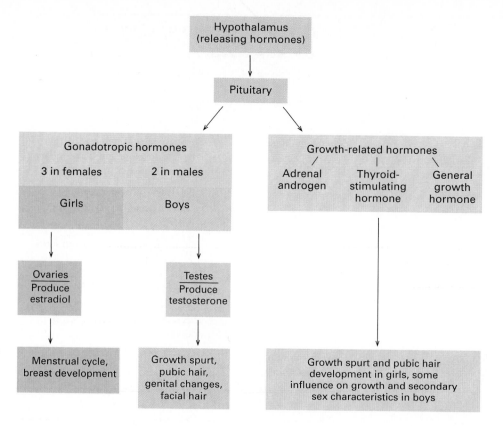

Figure 4.4
The action of the various hormones at puberty is exceedingly complex. This figure oversimplifies the process but gives you some sense of the sequence and the differences between the patterns for boys and girls.

adrenal androgen than is true for boys. Adrenal androgen is chemically very similar to testosterone, so it takes a "male" hormone to produce the growth spurt in girls.

Having said that, I need to add a caution: it is somewhat misleading to talk about "male" and "female" hormones. Both males and females have at least some of each. The difference is essentially in the relative proportion of the two. Within any one gender, these proportions differ as well, so some males have relatively more testosterone or less estrogen, while in others the two may be more balanced. Similarly, some girls may have a pattern of hormones that includes relatively more androgen, while others may have relatively little.

▶ Development of Sexual Maturity

The physical result of the hormonal changes that take place during **puberty** is not only a spurt in height but, more importantly, a set of physical changes that bring about full sexual maturity, including changes in the reproductive systems themselves (called *primary sex characteristics*), such as the testes and penis in the male, and the ovaries, uterus, and vagina in the female, and all those changes in *secondary sex characteristics* that are the more visible signs of puberty, such as breast development, body and facial hair, and lowered voice pitch in boys.

Each of these physical developments occurs in a defined sequence. Following the work of J. M. Tanner (1978), each sequence is customarily divided into five stages, with Stage 1 always representing the preadolescent stage, Stage 2 the first signs of pubertal change, Stages 3 and 4 the intermediate steps, and Stage 5 the

TABLE 4.2 Examples of Tanner's Stages of Pubertal Development

Breast Development	Stage	Male Genital Development
No change except for some elevation of the nipple.	1	Testes, scrotum, and penis are all about the same size and shape as in early childhood.
Breast bud stage: elevation of breast and the nipple as a small mound. Areolar diameter is enlarged over stage 1.	2	Scrotum and testes are slightly enlarged. Skin of the scrotum is reddened and changed in texture but little or no enlargement of the penis.
Breast and areola both enlarged and elevated more than in stage 2 but no separation of their contours.	3	Penis slightly enlarged, at first mainly in length. Testes and scrotum are further enlarged.
Areola and nipple form a secondary mound projecting above the contour of the breast.	4	Penis further enlarged, with growth in breadth and development of glans. Testes and scrotum further enlarged and scrotum skin still darker.
Mature stage. Only the nipple projects, with the areola recessed to the general contour of the breast.	5	Genitalia are adult in size and shape.

Source: Petersen & Taylor, 1980, p. 127.

final adult characteristic. Table 4.2 gives you two examples of these sequences, one for each sex. These stages have proven to be extremely helpful not only for describing the normal progress through puberty, but for assessing the rate of development of individual youngsters.

Sexual Development in Girls

Studies of preteens and teens in both Europe and North America (Malina, 1990) reveal that for girls, the various sequential changes are interlocked in a particular pattern, shown schematically in Figure 4.5. The first steps are typically the early changes in breasts and pubic hair, followed by the peak of the growth spurt. Only then does first menstruation occur, an event called **menarche** (pronounced men-are-kee). Menarche typically occurs two years after the beginning of other visible changes and is succeeded only by the final stages of breast and pubic hair development. Among girls in industrialized countries today, menarche occurs, on average, between age $12\frac{1}{2}$ and $13\frac{1}{2}$, with 95 percent of all girls experiencing this event between the ages of 11 and 15 (Malina, 1990).

Menarche does not signal full sexual maturity. It is possible to conceive shortly after menarche, but irregularity is the norm for some time. In as many as three-quarters of the cycles in the first year, and half the cycles in the second and third years after menarche, no ovum is produced (Vihko & Apter, 1980). Full adult fertility thus develops over a period of years.

The initial irregularity of both ovulation and of the timing of menstrual cycles has some significant practical consequences for sexually active teenagers. For one thing, such irregularity no doubt contributes to the widespread (but false) as-

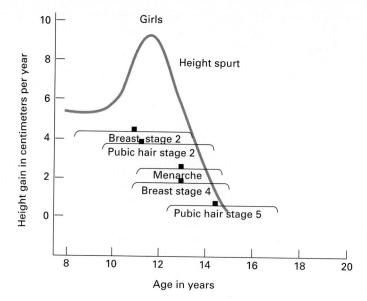

Figure 4.5
The figure shows the normal sequence and timing of pubertal changes for girls. The box on each black line represents the average attainment of that change, while the line indicates the range of normal times. Note the *wide* range of normality for all of these changes. Also note how relatively late in the sequence the growth spurt and menarche occur. (*Sources:* Chumlea, 1982; Garn, 1980; Malina, 1990; Tanner, 1978.)

sumption among early-teenage girls that they cannot get pregnant because they are "too young." At the same time the irregularity makes any form of rhythm contraception unreliable, even among teenagers who have enough basic reproductive knowledge to realize that the time of ovulation is normally the time of greatest fertility—knowledge that is not widespread.

Sexual Development in Boys

In boys, as in girls, the peak of the growth spurt typically comes fairly late in the sequence, as you can see in Figure 4.6. Malina's data suggest that on average a boy completes Stages 2, 3, and 4 of genital development, and Stages 2 and 3 of pubic hair development, before the growth peak is reached (Malina, 1990), with facial hair and the lowering of the voice coming only quite near the end of the sequence. Precisely when in this sequence the boy begins to produce viable sperm is very difficult to determine, although current evidence places this event sometime between ages 12 and 14, usually *before* the boy has reached the peak of the growth spurt (Brooks-Gunn & Reiter, 1990).

Two things are particularly interesting about these sequences. First, if you compare Figures 4.5 and 4.6, you will see that although boys begin the early stages of pubertal change not so much later than girls, girls are about two years ahead of boys in the growth spurt. Most of you remember that period in late elementary school or junior high when all the girls were suddenly taller than the boys. (Do I remember that time! I *towered* over everyone.)

A second intriguing thing is that while the order of development seems to be highly consistent *within* each sequence (such as breast development, or pubic hair development), there is quite a lot of variability *across* sequences. I've given you the normative or average pattern, but individual teenagers often do not follow that normative pattern. For instance, a boy may be in Stage 2 of genital development but already in Stage 5 of pubic hair development; a girl might move

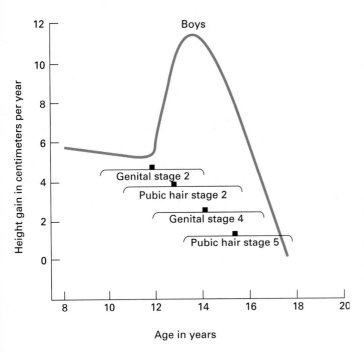

Figure 4.6
The sequence of pubertal changes for boys begins about two years later than does the girls' sequence, but as with girls, the height spurt occurs relatively late in the sequence. (*Sources:* Chumlea, 1982; Malina, 1990; Tanner, 1978.)

through several stages of pubic hair development before the first clear breast changes, or experience menarche much earlier in the sequence than normal. So far physiologists have not figured out why this variation exists or what it might mean, but it is an important point to keep in mind if you are trying to make a prediction about an individual teenager.

▶ Using the Body: The Effects of Physical Changes on Behavior

This brief picture of physical changes in the first 15 years of life should give you some sense of the alterations in muscles, fat, internal organs, and nervous system. But what this description does not convey is the impact of all those changes on the child's behavior. The effects are particularly striking at two time points: (1) in the first two or three years of life, when the baby develops the ability to crawl, walk, and then run, and to pick up and manipulate objects; and (2) at adolescence, when the rapid changes of puberty make mature sexual behavior possible.

Motor Development in the Early Years

Psychologists use the phrase **motor development** to describe the emergence of various abilities to move around and to use the body in skilled ways. It includes various *movement skills*, such as crawling, walking, running, and bike riding, as well as *manipulative skills*, such as grasping or picking up objects, throwing balls, holding a crayon or a pencil, or threading a needle. Nearly all the *basic* skills of both types are complete by about 6 or 7 years of age. After that, change is mostly improvement in performance as the child refines the basic skills and integrates them into more and more complex movement sequences (Malina, 1982). So

6- and 7-year-olds can run, and they can probably dribble a basketball, but they can't yet do both at the same time. Table 4.3 lists some of the key milestones in these emerging abilities.

All these changes, particularly the early ones as the baby gradually shifts from sitting to crawling to walking, are normally a delight for parents to observe and encourage. But they have obvious practical ramifications as well. One obvious example: until a baby is able to crawl or walk, it is not necessary to put dangerous or fragile objects out of reach; when he begins to move around independently, childproofing the house becomes critical. Similarly, the types of toys you would buy or make for a child should clearly be influenced by the child's motor skills. At about 1 year, stacking or nesting toys are likely to be big favorites (and ordinary objects, such as sets of measuring cups, probably work as well as expensive toys). In the second year of life, toys with wheels are very popular, but *push* toys are better than *pull* toys, because the child can see the object while it moves. By about age 2 or 3, the child may for the first time enjoy drawing with *large* crayons or pencils, but cannot yet grasp smaller ones. For 5- and 6-year-olds, though, toys like jacks or marbles make good gifts, because a child this age has the small-muscle coordination to be able to manipulate them.

The emergence of motor skills also has an obvious impact on the timing of children's sports activities—an application I've explored in the real world discus-sion on page 118.

Some steps in motor de-velopment

TABLE 4.3   Sequences of Development of Various Motor Skills

Age	Movement and Manipulative Skills
1 mo.	Lifts head. Holds object if placed in hand.
4–6 mos.	Sits with support. Holds head erect in sitting position. Reaches for and grasps objects.
7–9 mos.	Sits without support. Rolls over from stomach. Stands up using furniture. Transfers objects from one hand to the other.
10–12 mos.	Crawls. Walks grasping furniture. Walks without help (12–13 mos.).
13–18 mos.	Walks backward and sideways. Stacks two blocks. Puts objects into small containers and dumps them.
3–4 yrs.	Walks upstairs one foot per step. Pedals and steers tricycle. Catches large ball. Cuts paper with scissors. Holds pencil between thumb and first two fingers.
7–8 yrs.	Skips freely. Rides two-wheel bicycle. Plays ball games with some skill. Writes individual letters.

Sources: Connolly & Dalgleish, 1989; Capute et al. 1984; The Diagram Group, 1977; Fagard & Jacquet, 1989; Mathew & Cook, 1990; Thomas, 1990a.

Adolescent Sexuality and Pregnancy

At adolescence, the underlying physical changes not only mean that the young person is stronger and faster and better coordinated than before, they also make mature sexual behavior possible. But unlike early motor development, which proceeds in pretty much the same way for all children, sexual behavior involves clear choices for the teenager. Should I or shouldn't I? What do we know about the choices teenagers make about their sexual activity?

As is usually the case, what I can tell you about this is almost entirely specific to the U.S., or to other industrialized countries. It is good to keep in mind that the whole question of adolescent sexuality is a central issue for those of us in such cultures, in large part because we have created such a long delay between physical sexual maturity and social maturity. Young people are physically mature at 13 or 14, but are not financially independent or fully trained until age 20 or later. In cultures in which 12- or 14-year-olds are considered adults, ready to take on adult tasks and responsibilities, to marry and to bear children, adolescent sexuality is handled very differently. In the U.S., where adolescent pregnancy has become extremely common, it is perceived as a significant problem.

Adolescent sexual activity has increased fairly dramatically in the U.S. since the late 1950s (Miller, Christopherson, & King, 1993). In the 1980s, about half of boys and about a quarter of the girls aged 15 to 17 were sexually active. By age 19, over 80 percent of males say they have had at least one experience of intercourse. At every age, there are consistent ethnic differences: Hispanic-American youth are least likely to be sexually active and African-American youth are most likely, with Anglos somewhere in between (Fennelly, 1993). Black adolescents in the U.S. become sexually active about two years earlier than their Anglo or Hispanic peers (Hayes, 1987).

The form and pattern of sexual activity also shows ethnic differences in U.S. groups. Among both Anglos and Hispanics, sexual activity appears to move through a fairly typical sequence over time and within any one dating relationship, from hand-holding to kissing to stroking of breasts or genitals, to intercourse. So intercourse is considerably more likely in couples who are "going steady" and quite unlikely on a first date. Among blacks, at least in the U.S., this sequence does not appear to hold: they are more likely to move directly to intercourse (Miller et al., 1993).

In boys the likelihood of sexual activity is correlated with the amount of testosterone in the blood. Among girls hormones appear to play a smaller role. Girls' *interest* in sexuality is somewhat related to hormones, but the likelihood of intercourse is not (Dyk, 1993). For girls, social influences are far more important ingredients in their decisions about sexuality.

Despite these heightened levels of sexual activity, it is remarkable how little teenagers know about physiology and reproduction. At best, only about half of white and a quarter of black teenagers can describe the time of greatest fertility in the menstrual cycle (Freeman & Rickels, 1993; Morrison, 1985). Many are convinced they cannot get pregnant because they are "too young." Perhaps in part because of such ignorance, contraceptive use is still comparatively low— especially in comparison to most European countries, where teenage sexual behavior is as common but contraceptive information is far more widespread. Both Sweden

THE REAL WORLD
Sports for Children

In the U.S., and increasingly in other industrialized countries, children no longer play much in the street or in backyards; they play on organized teams and groups: soccer teams, Little League baseball, Pee Wee League football, swimming clubs, and the like. Many children begin such programs when they are 6 or 7, often with great enthusiasm. But participation peaks by age 10 or 11, and then declines rapidly. Why?

Kids drop out of such programs because the emphasis on competition and winning is so great (*Harvard Educational Letter,* 1992). Amateur coaches often have no good idea what kinds of motor skills are normal for a 6- or 7-year-old, so when they see a child who does not yet throw a ball skillfully, or who kicks a ball awkwardly, they label this child as clumsy or uncoordinated. From then on, these perfectly normal kids get little playing time or encouragement. Only the stars— children with unusually good or early motor skill development—get maximum attention and exercise.

In fact 6 or 7 is really too early for most children to be playing on full-sized playing fields or in competitive games (Kolata, 1992). It would be far better to wait until age 9 or 10 —if then— for competitive games, and to have kids spend the earlier years learning and perfecting basic skills in activities that are fun regardless of their skill level, and involve as much movement as possible. One expert, Vern Seefeldt, the director of the Institute for the Study of Youth Sports at Michigan State University, says:

Children need to be in situations where their participation and ability to learn skills are maximized. In an adult game, you try to throw the ball so the batter can't hit it or kick the ball where it can't be retrieved. With kids, you need to do just the opposite. (Kolata, 1992, p. 40)

If children begin with organized sports activities as young as 6 or 7, the early experiences should be carefully selected. Soccer or swimming are particularly good, not only because everyone is likely to get at least some aerobic exercise, but also because the basic skills are within the abilities of children of this age. Baseball, in contrast, is *not* a good sport for the average 6- or 7-year-old, because it requires real eye-hand coordination to hit or catch the ball, and most 7-year-olds are not yet proficient at such coordination. By age 10 or so, many children will be ready to play sports such as basketball, but many organized sports, such as tennis, are still difficult for the average child of this age. (Jennifer Capriati, who began her professional tennis career at age 14, is, after all, an *exception,* and not the rule.) Only in adolescence do most young people have the strength and coordination for sports like football.

If you want to encourage your children to be involved in sports, choose carefully. Let the child try several sports to see which one or ones he or she may enjoy, and be sure to select programs in which *all* children are given skill training and encouragement and in which competition is initially deemphasized. And don't push too fast or too hard. If you do, your child is likely to drop out of any type of organized sport by age 10 or 11, saying—as many do —that they feel inadequate, or that it isn't fun anymore.

How many different reasons can you think of why teenagers would *not* use contraceptives? Which of those explanations might account for the lower use of contraception among Hispanic-Americans?

and the Netherlands, for example, have very low teenage birthrates. In both, contraceptive information is widely available and contraceptive use is culturally acceptable (Jones et al., 1986). In the U.S., despite increases in contraceptive use in recent years, less than half of teenage girls use any type of contraceptives the first time they have intercourse, and fewer still regularly use effective methods, such as condoms or the pill (Jorgensen, 1993). Contraceptive use is even less likely among Hispanics than among Anglos (Fennelly, 1993).

Teenage Pregnancy.   Given these facts, we shouldn't be surprised that the rate of teenage pregnancy is high in the U.S.—far higher than in most other industrialized countries (Jones et al., 1986). In the Netherlands, for example, the pregnancy rate for girls between the ages of 15 and 19 is 14 per 1000 girls per year. In the United States it is 96 pregnancies per 1000 girls per year. Sandra Hofferth (1987a) estimates that fully 44 percent of all teenage girls in the U.S. will be pregnant at least once before the age of 20. About half of these pregnancies are carried to term.

Let me try to put these fairly astonishing numbers into some kind of context. Birthrates have actually dropped among the entire U.S. population in the past decades, *including among teenagers*. Indeed the proportion of all births in the United States that were to teenagers has declined steadily since 1975. What has increased steadily since the 1960s is the rate of births to *nonmarried* teens. In 1988, 78 percent of all girls under 18 who gave birth were unmarried; among black girls, the rate was 95 percent (Furstenberg, 1991). Thus it is not that more and more teenagers are bearing children, but that more and more pregnant teenage girls are choosing to rear their children without marrying.

Whether one sees this as a worrisome trend or not depends not only on one's religious or moral beliefs, but also on evidence about the long-term consequences of adolescent childbearing for the adult lives of women. The bulk of that evidence points to negative consequences, although it has been difficult to sort out just what effects are due to early childbearing itself, and which might be due to self-selection or the impact of poverty. Most studies indicate that teenage childbearing—whether married or unmarried—is associated with more children, more closely spaced, fewer years of total education throughout adult life, lower levels of occupational success, lower income in adulthood, and higher likelihood of divorce in adult life. These relationships are found among African-American, Hispanic, and Anglo teens, so these negative outcomes are not just ethnic differences in disguise (Astone, 1993; Freeman & Rickels, 1993; Hofferth, 1987b; Moore et al., 1993).

However, there are some mitigating facts. First of all, more than half of girls who become pregnant before age 18 nonetheless manage to complete high school by the time they are in their early twenties—a fact that runs counter to prevailing stereotypes (Upchurch, 1993). And many of those who struggle economically in their early adult years manage to recover in their thirties and forties, especially if they were able to complete at least high school (Upchurch, 1993; Werner & Smith, 1992). Despite these findings, though, teenage mothers as a group are still disadvantaged. For black inner-city girls in particular, the chances of moving out of poverty in adulthood seem to be far better for those who delay childbearing into their twenties (Freeman & Rickels, 1993). To avoid some of these negative consequences, we may need to take a page or two from pregnancy-prevention expertise developed in many other industrialized countries, especially about appropriate timing and content of sex and/or contraceptive education in the schools.

Teenage sexual activity is not more common in the U.S. than in most Western industrialized countries, but teen pregnancy is. Girls like this one who give birth during their teens are more likely to have problems in adulthood, including lower income, less education, and higher risk of divorce.

▶ Big or Fast Versus Slow or Small: Some Individual Differences in Physical Development

Although virtually all children and teenagers go through the various sequences of physical development in the same order, there are wide individual differences in the *rate* and *timing* of physical changes, as well as in children's physical shape or skills. These differences are interesting in their own right, but they are also im-

---

THE REAL WORLD
Which Teenage Girls Get Pregnant?

Whether a girl becomes pregnant during her teenage years depends on a host of factors, including family background, educational aspirations, timing of sexual activity, and subcultural attitudes. Here are a few of the findings (Hayes, 1987):

- The younger a girl is when she becomes sexually active, the more likely she is to have at least one teen pregnancy.
- Girls who come from poor families, or single-parent families, or those whose parents are relatively uneducated, are more likely to become pregnant.
- Girls whose mothers became sexually active early, and who bore their first child early, are more likely to become pregnant as teens.
- Black and Hispanic teenagers are more likely than are Anglos to become pregnant, in part because blacks are more likely to be sexually active. Hispanics are less likely to be

sexually active, but also less likely to use contraception than are Anglos.

- The better a girl does in school and the stronger her educational aspirations, the more likely she is to use birth control consistently and the less likely she is to get pregnant.
- The more stable and committed the relationship between a teenage girl and her sexual partner, the *less* likely she is to become pregnant.
- Girls who have good communication about contraception with their mothers, and whose mothers support the use of contraception, are less likely to become pregnant.

The riskiest time for pregnancy is in the first year or so after a girl has become sexually active. It is during these early months that girls are least likely to seek out contraceptive information or to use contraception consistently.

---

portant because of the ways in which they can affect a child's self-image, her relationships with her peers, or her general contacts with the world around her.

Differences in Rate

Children vary *widely* in the speed with which they go through all the body and motor changes I have described. Some children walk at 7 or 8 months, others not until 18 months. Some are skillful soccer players at 7 or 8, others not until much later (if at all). These differences are most striking at puberty. Among 12- or 13-year-old girls, for example, there are some who are already at stage 4 or 5 of breast development, and others who are still clearly prepubescent. Some 14-year-old boys are already fully developed, with lowered voices and full beards, while others still have the narrow, slim bodies of children.

As a general rule, a child tends to be consistently early, average, or late in most aspects of physical development. The child who shows slower bone development is also likely to walk later and to have later puberty (Tanner, 1978). Similarly, tall infants tend to be taller teenagers and taller adults. There are exceptions to both of these generalizations, but what Tanner calls the *tempo of growth* is a powerful element in development.

Effects of Differing Rates on Mental Development.   These differences in rate of development appear to have at least some small link to a child's mental development, so that children who are more rapid in physical development are also slightly ahead in mental development (Newcombe & Baenninger, 1989; Tanner, 1978). It is also true that taller children of any given age tend to score higher on IQ tests than do shorter children of the same age (Dornbusch et al., 1987a; Humphreys et al., 1985). The correlations are only in the range of .20 to .30, which is not large. But such a link has been found in studies in a number of countries, including Britain, Sweden, and the U.S.

The possible causes are myriad, including variations in prenatal environment, pre- or postnatal diet, and differences in expectations and opportunities for short versus tall children. Whatever the cause, it is interesting that these differences persist into adulthood. That is, adults who were early developers as children still have a slight intellectual advantage over their slower-developing peers, even though the latter group has caught up in height, brain growth, and physical skill. The most likely explanation is that this carryover into adulthood is a consequence of the psychological effects of earliness or lateness rather than of the physiological effects.

Effects of Differences in Rate on Personality.   Most of the research on the psychological effects of fast or slow growth has focused on only one age period: puberty. What happens to a girl who begins to menstruate at 10, or a boy who does not go through a growth spurt until age 16? Do they turn out differently?

A recent burst of research on this question has led to an interesting and complex hypothesis that once again points to the importance of internal models. The general idea is that each young child or teenager has an internal model about the "normal" or "right" timing for puberty (Faust, 1983; Lerner, 1985; 1987; Petersen, 1987). Each girl has an internal model about the "right age" to develop breasts or begin menstruation; each boy has an internal model or image about when it is right to begin to grow a beard or for his voice to get lower. According to this hypothesis, it is the discrepancy between an adolescent's expectation and what actually happens that determines the psychological effect. Those whose development occurs outside the desired or expected range are likely to think less well of themselves, to be less happy with their bodies and with the process of puberty, perhaps have fewer friends, or experience other signs of distress.

In American culture today, most young people seem to share the expectation that pubertal changes will happen sometime between ages 12 and 14; anything earlier is seen as "too soon," anything later is thought of as late. If you compare these expectations to the actual average timing of pubertal changes, you'll see that such a norm includes girls who are average in development and boys who are *early*. So we should expect these two groups—normal-developing girls and early-developing boys—to have the best psychological functioning. Early-maturing boys may have an added advantage because they are more likely to be of the preferred *mesomorphic* body type, with wide shoulders and a large amount of muscle. Because boys with this body type tend to be good at sports, the early developing boy should be particularly advantaged.

Figure 4.7 shows the specific predictions graphically. Because of the twin advantages of having puberty fall within the "normative" time and having a more mesomorphic body type, early boys should be best-off, followed by average boys and girls. The least well-off should be late-developing boys and early-developing girls, both of whom are "off time."

Research generally confirms these predictions. Girls who are early developers (before 11 or 12 for major body changes) show consistently more negative body images, such as thinking themselves too fat (Petersen, 1987; Simmons, Blyth, & McKinney, 1983; Tobin-Richards, Boxer, & Petersen, 1983). Such girls are also more likely to get into trouble in school and at home (Magnusson, Stattin, & Allen, 1986) and are more likely to be depressed (Rierdan & Koff, 1991; 1993).

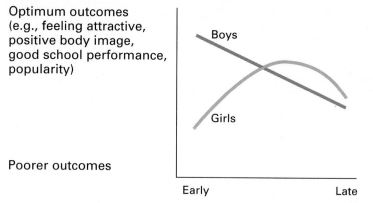

Figure 4.7
According to this model of the effects of early and late puberty, the best position for girls is to be "on time," while the best position for boys is to be "early." For both sexes, however, it is the *perception* of earliness or lateness, and not the actual timing, that is thought to be critical. (*Source:* Adapted from Tobin-Richards et al., 1983, p. 137.)

There are also hints that very late development in girls is also somewhat negative, but the effect of lateness is not so striking for girls as it is for boys.

Among boys, as Figure 4.7 predicts, the relationship is essentially linear. The earlier the boy's development, the more positive his body image, the better he does in school, the less trouble he gets into, and the more friends he has (Duke et al., 1982).

In nearly all of these studies, earliness or lateness has been defined in terms of the actual physical changes. The results are even clearer when researchers have instead asked teenagers about their internal model of earliness or lateness. For example, Rierdan, Koff, and Stubbs (1989) have found that the negativeness of a girl's menarcheal experience was predicted by her *subjective* sense of earliness; those who perceived themselves as early reported a more negative experience. But such a negative experience was *un*related to the actual age of her menarche.

This link between the internal model and the outcome is especially vivid in a study of ballet dancers by Jeanne Brooks-Gunn (1987; Brooks-Gunn & Warren, 1985). She studied 14-to-18-year-old girls, some of whom were serious ballet dancers studying at a national ballet company school. In this group, a very lean, almost prepubescent body is highly desirable. Brooks-Gunn therefore expected that among dancers, those who were very late in pubertal development would actually have a better image of themselves than those who were on time. And that is exactly what she found, as you can see in Figure 4.8. Among nondancers the same age, normal-time menarche was associated with a better body image than late menarche, but exactly the reverse was true for the dancers.

Thus it seems to be the discrepancy or mismatch between the desired or expected pattern and a youngster's actual pattern that is critical, not the absolute age of pubertal development. Because the majority of young people in any given culture share similar expectations, we can see common effects of early or late development. But to predict the effect of early or late development in any individual teenager, we would need to know more about her or his internal model, or the culturally defined models that may be operating.

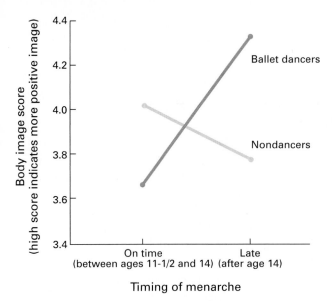

Figure 4.8
Serious ballet dancers clearly prefer to have a very late puberty. In this study, those dancers whose menarche was "on time" by ordinary standards actually had poorer body images than did those who were objectively quite late, while the reverse was true for nondancers. Thus it is perception of timing and not actual timing that is critical. (*Source:* Brooks-Gunn & Warren, 1985, from Table 1, p. 291.)

Social Class and Racial Differences in Physical Development

As a group, poor children grow a bit slower and are a bit shorter than middle-class children, most probably because of dietary differences. Menarcheal age is also about six months later in girls growing up in less-affluent homes than in girls in middle-class homes (Garn, 1980).

Different racial groups, too, show somewhat different rates or patterns of development. Of course in the United States, in which minority racial status and poverty are so often coexisting, some of the racial differences may well be caused by the underlying economic differences. But there appear to be some genuine racial differences as well.

Black infants and children appear to be slightly ahead of white children in some aspects of physical development. In fact, the gestational period for the black fetus seems actually to be slightly shorter than for the white fetus (Smith, 1978). Black babies also show somewhat faster development of motor skills, such as walking, and are slightly taller than their white counterparts, with longer legs, more muscle, and heavier bones (Tanner, 1978). At puberty, black girls have slightly earlier menarche as well (perhaps three months, on average). Thus the tempo of growth appears to be slightly faster in black children than in white.

Asian children also have a relatively rapid tempo of growth but are smaller, with long upper bodies and shorter final height.

▶ Health and Illness in Childhood and Adolescence

The study of both the common patterns and individual differences in normal physical growth forms the core of research on physical development. But for parents, as well as for physicians and for society as a whole, there is another aspect of a child's physical status that is important: her health or illness.

Most kids this age are sick in bed like this about six times a year.

How many different explanations can you think of for such a link between childhood illness and adult health?

Those of us who live in countries with relatively low infant and childhood mortality rates are used to thinking of childhood as a basically healthy time. But in fact, 42 percent of the children in the world are born in countries in which 1 in 5 children dies before age 5 (Wegman, 1992). In contrast, in the United States in 1990, only slightly more than 1 child out of 100 died before age 5. Still, even in such advantaged circumstances, children do get sick; some die.

Health in Early and Middle Childhood. Brief sicknesses, such as colds or viruses (called *acute* illnesses by physicians) are common among young children. I mentioned in Chapter 3 that the average baby has seven or eight respiratory illnesses in the first year. Preschool children have fewer of these acute illnesses, but still perhaps six each year (Parmelee, 1986). In contrast, only roughly 10 percent of children have any kind of chronic illness (an illness lasting six months or longer) during childhood (Starfield & Pless, 1980). The most common types are allergies, asthma, visual and hearing impairments, and diabetes (Starfield, 1991).

One of the most interesting findings on childhood illness is that a pattern of repeated illness in childhood— even just unusually frequent colds—is correlated with higher rates of illness in adolescence and poorer health in adulthood (Power & Peckham, 1990). The correlation is by no means perfect. Many "sickly" children are quite healthy as adults. And of course since we are dealing here with correlational evidence we must be careful about making causal statements. But we can make a *risk* statement: A pattern of frequent or chronic early illness increases the probability of health problems later.

Another danger for children is accidents. In fact, because improvements in health care have enormously reduced the risk of death from infectious diseases, accidents are the major cause of death in the United States for children over the age of 1. Automobile accidents are the most common fatal accident involving children; happily, the rate of such fatalities has dropped noticeably since the advent of laws mandating the use of restraint devices for infants and toddlers traveling in cars (Christophersen, 1989).

Health in Adolescence. Adolescents have fewer colds and flu and other acute illnesses than do infants, toddlers, or school-age children, but they have considerably more accidents and (for males in the United States, at least) are far more likely to die by violence. The three leading causes of death for males between the ages of 15 and 24 are (in order) auto accidents, homicide, and suicide (United States Bureau of the Census, 1992).

More than half of all teenage deaths are due to accidents, and most of these involve cars. Many of the fatal accidents are caused not by poor driving skills, but by risk-taking behaviors like tailgating, speeding, and driving while intoxicated. In about half the cases in which a teenage driver is involved in a fatal auto accident, he or she has a blood alcohol above .10 —the legal limit for intoxication in most states (Millstein & Litt, 1990).

Homicide rates among teens are especially and alarmingly high in American inner cities, where gangs often dominate, where drugs are dealt openly, and where guns are an ordinary part of life. I'll have a whole lot more to say about the effects of this type of concentrated poverty and violence in Chapter 14. For now, I only want to point out that—sadly—such violence has become a major health problem for many teens.

Suicide has also increased among teenagers in the U.S. Rates have tripled since 1960, and now represent about 12 percent of teen deaths. This rise has been particularly noticeable among males. The rate is now nearly 20 deaths per 100,000 among white teenage boys, and roughly half that among black teens (United States Bureau of the Census, 1992). These numbers are not high in absolute terms; auto accidents kill far more teenagers than does suicide. But the trend is disturbing.

Considerably more common, and also increasing, are two eating disorders, bulimia and anorexia nervosa, except in this case it is girls rather than boys who are at greater risk. I want to talk about these disorders at some length, not only because they have become disturbingly common, but because what we are learning about the causes underlines both the impact of cultural values and the importance of the child's internal working models.

Bulimia and Anorexia. Bulimia (sometimes called *bulimia nervosa*) involves an intense concern about weight, combined with binge eating followed by purging, either through self-induced vomiting, excessive use of laxatives, or excessive exercise (Attie, Brooks-Gunn, & Petersen; 1990). Alternating periods of restrained and binge eating are common among individuals in all weight groups. Only when binge eating occurs as often as twice a week and is combined with repeated episodes of some kind of purging is the syndrome properly called bulimia. Bulimics are ordinarily not exceptionally thin, but they are obsessed with their weight, and feel intense shame about their abnormal behavior. Often, they experience significant depression.

The incidence of bulimia appears to have been increasing rather rapidly in recent decades, particularly among white teenage and young adult women. Current estimates vary quite a lot, but everyone agrees that at least 5 percent, and perhaps as many as 18 percent, of teenage girls in the U.S. are bulimic (Millstein & Litt, 1990), with similar rates reported in Australia and England and other Western industrialized countries. In contrast, less than 1 percent of college-age men show this syndrome (Attie et al., 1990; Howat & Saxton, 1988; Johnson et al., 1984; Pyle et al., 1983).

Anorexia nervosa is less common but potentially more deadly. It is characterized by extreme dieting, intense fear of gaining weight, and obsessive exercise. In girls or women, who are by far the most common sufferers, the weight loss eventually produces a cessation of menstruation. Hormone balance is so disturbed that anorexics typically develop thick, soft hair over their bodies. And their body image is so distorted that they can look in the mirror at a skeletally thin body and remain convinced that they are "too fat." Ten to 15 percent of anorexic youth literally starve themselves to death. The incidence of anorexia has been hard to establish; the best current estimate is that it affects between 0.5 and 1 percent of girls or young women in the U.S. (Millstein & Litt, 1990; Rolls, Fedoroff, & Guthrie, 1991), but is considerably more common among subgroups who are under pressure to maintain extreme thinness, such as ballet dancers and high-performance athletes in sports in which thinness is highly valued, such as gymnastics (Stoutjesdyk & Jevne, 1993).

The causes of both disorders are unknown. Some theorists have proposed biological causes, such as some kind of brain dysfunction in the case of bulemics,

---

RESEARCH REPORT
An Australian Study Illustrating Sex Differences in Body Image Among Adolescents

Susan Paxton and her colleagues (1991) have recently reported on a study of Australian high school students that illustrates that the preoccupation with thinness among teenage girls is not restricted to the United States, and shows what that preoccupation can do to girls' body images.

A total of 562 teenagers, in grades 7 through 11, reported on their current weight and height and their judgment of that weight as underweight, good weight, or overweight. They also responded to questions about the effect it might have on their lives if they were thinner, and described their weight control behaviors, including dieting and exercise.

Paxton reports a number of particularly interesting results. First of all, among teenagers who were actually *normal* in weight for their height, 30.1 percent of the girls but only 6.8 percent of the boys described themselves as overweight. Thus the girls *perceive* themselves as too fat when they are actually normal. Furthermore, the majority of girls thought that being thinner would make them happier; a few even thought that being thinner would make them more intelligent. Boys, in contrast, thought that being thinner would actually have some negative effects.

Not surprisingly, these differences in the perception of thinness were reflected in dieting behavior in this sample. Twenty-three percent of the girls reported that they went on a crash diet at least occasionally; 4 percent said they did so once or twice a week. The comparable percentages for boys were 9 and 1 percent, respectively. More girls than boys also reported using diet pills, laxatives, and vomiting, although the rates were low for both sexes. Once again, we see internal models at work.

---

who often show abnormal brain waves. Others argue for a psychoanalytic explanation, such as a fear of growing up in the case of anorexic patients. My own view is that the most promising explanation lies in the discrepancy between the young person's internal image of what kind or shape of body is desired, and her (or his) perception of her own body. Both syndromes seem to be increasing in frequency because of the currently intense emphasis in many Western countries on a very slender, almost prepubescent body shape as the ideal. From very early in life, girls, much more than boys, are taught both explicitly and implicitly that it matters if they are pretty or attractive, and that thinness is one of the critical variables in attractiveness. Current research, for example, shows that roughly three-quarters of teenage girls have dieted or are dieting, while boys rarely do so (Leon et al., 1989).

Those girls who most fully accept and internalize this model of beauty are most prone to develop bulimia or anorexia. For example, Ruth Striegel-Moore and her colleagues (1986) have found that bulimic girls and women are more likely than are nonbulimics to agree with statements like "attractiveness increases the likelihood of professional success."

Both bulimia and anorexia seem to develop in adolescence, and not before that, precisely because one of the effects of puberty is to increase the amount of fat in the girl's body. This is particularly true of early-developing girls, who characteristically acquire and retain higher fat levels than do later-maturing girls. Thus an early-developing girl who deeply believes that thinness is essential for beauty, and that beauty is essential for happiness, especially if she sees her own body as failing to meet her internalized standard, seems at particularly high risk for developing bulimia or anorexia (Attie & Brooks-Gunn, 1989; Rolls et al., 1991; Striegel-Moore et al., 1986).

Health Habits. Over the long run, the most important aspect of children's health may not be their current health, but the health habits they establish. Do they regularly eat high-fat diets, with lots of junk food? Do they smoke and drink? Researchers are finding that the sedentary, high-calorie life-style of American

If you had the power to change our culture in such a way that the rate of bulimia and anorexia would go way down, what changes would you want to make? Why and how?

THE REAL WORLD
How to Get Your Teenager to Stop Smoking, or Not to Start

Nearly half of eighth graders think there is no great risk to smoking a pack or two of cigarettes a day. By senior year, only about 30 percent still believe this, but by then many have a well-established smoking habit, difficult to break. It may seem from this that the right strategy with a young teen is to keep on talking about the long-term consequences of smoking. But it turns out that such an argument doesn't have much impact, at least not in isolation. Several other strategies are much more successful.

Stop Smoking Yourself.
If you yourself are a smoker, the first step is for you to quit. It does no good to tell your child that he or she should do what you say and not what you do. Modeling does not work like that. Kids copy what you do.

Emphasize the Bad Breath.
Tell them about all the negative *social* consequences of smoking. Their breath will smell bad, their teeth will turn yellow, their hair and clothes will smell like smoke all the time, and their ability to do well in athletics may be impaired. Tell them that teenagers themselves say that they find smokers less attractive. And tell teenage girls that smoking will not help them lose weight—a major reason for smoking for nearly all teenage girls—at least not enough to counterbalance the social costs. All of these messages are more effective if they come from other teenagers rather than from Mom and Dad, so if you can lobby the local high school to organize systematic programs, with teens as models, that is even better.

Focus on the Manipulation.
Remind your child that the cigarette companies are trying to manipulate them through advertising. You may want to get them to look at specific ads, and talk about the particular forms of manipulation involved. Because teenagers hate to be manipulated (by you or anyone else), this may be a successful argument.

Lobby the Schools.
If the school your child attends has a designated smoking area, try to persuade the school board to abolish it and simply forbid smoking in any part of the school. In schools that allow smoking, 25 percent more of the students become smokers than is true in schools that forbid it on the grounds.

Pay Attention to Your Child's Friends.
Teenagers whose friends smoke are more likely to take up the habit. You need to start paying attention to this *very* early— certainly by junior high school, when you may still have enough influence over the child's choice of friends to help steer the child toward a different crowd of kids.

Do Not Call Smoking an "Adult Choice."
Many tobacco company programs ostensibly aimed at reducing teenage smoking tell teenagers that they are too young to smoke. But because teenagers want to do anything defined as "adult," this message may encourage smoking rather than the reverse. Instead, tell teenagers that they are old enough to know better; they are old enough to decide *not* to smoke.

---

youngsters is not only contributing to current physical problems, but may also create significantly higher risk of later disease. By some reports 40 percent of adolescents have at least one risk factor associated with heart disease—high cholesterol, overweight, or high blood pressure (*Harvard Educational Letter,* 1987). Significant numbers of teens also smoke and drink—both habits with long-term health implications.

Roughly a quarter of American teens smoke at least occasionally. The good news is that the number of teens who smoke has been declining steadily in the past decades. The bad news is that 30 percent of high school seniors in the late 1980s smoked at least occasionally, and 12 percent smoked at least half a pack a day. Occasional alcohol use is roughly twice as common, and 15 percent of high school seniors are estimated to be heavy drinkers— defined as five or more drinks on three or more occasions in a two-week period (Kazdin, 1993).

Attempts to alter these patterns have been only partially successful, although there are a few things that seem to make a difference—some of which I've explored in the real world discussion above.

▶ Determinants of Growth: Explanations of Physical Development

In what I have said so far, I have mostly been dealing with description, with answering "what" questions. But "why" questions are equally important. Why does physical development occur as it does, and what can affect it?

Maturation

Maturational sequences certainly seem to be part of the explanation, especially for such central patterns as neuronal changes and changes in muscles, bones, and fat. In all these areas, while the *rate* of development varies from one child to the next, the *sequence* is virtually the same for all children, even those with marked physical or mental handicaps. Whenever we find such robust sequences, maturation of some kind seems an obvious explanation.

But Esther Thelen, one of the leading experts on motor development, points out that most of us have an overly simplistic view of the whole idea of maturation (Lockman & Thelen, 1993; Thelen, 1989; 1992). There is no "crawling gene" or "walking gene" that somehow "unfolds" in a sequence. Instead, she argues that some new movement or motor skill is a "final common pathway," a result of a complex system of forces operating together, including cognition, perception, and motivation, as well as underlying physical changes.

For example, for the 12-month-old to be able to walk requires not only the growth of leg muscles, but also abdominal muscles, a change in center of gravity downward from the head, and development of visual skills, among many other ingredients (Thelen, 1984). Using a spoon to feed oneself requires development of muscles in the hand and wrist, bone development in the wrist, eye-hand coordination skills that allow one to readjust the aim of the spoon as one moves it toward one's mouth, and coordination of all of these with properly timed mouth opening (Connolly & Dalgleish, 1989).

Obviously Thelen and her followers are not denying the fundamental significance of the maturation of nerves and muscles. But they are saying that the concept of maturation alone does not *explain* the development of motor skills. In addition, of course, we should not forget the other elements in the explanatory equation.

Heredity

Our genetic heritage is individual as well as species-specific, so that each of us receives instructions for unique as well as shared growth tendencies. Both size and body shape seem to be heavily influenced by such specific inheritance. Tall parents tend to have tall children; short parents tend to have short children. And there are similarities between parents and children in such things as hip width, arm length, and short or long trunk (some ancestor certainly passed on a gene for long arms to me!).

Rate or tempo of growth, as well as final shape or size, seems to be an inherited pattern as well. Parents who were themselves early developers, as measured by such things as bone hardening or age of menarche, tend to have children who are faster developers too (Garn, 1980).

Environmental Effects

There are potent external influences on physical growth as well. One of the clearest pieces of evidence pointing toward such environmental influences is the observation that children in different birth cohorts grow at different rates, a pattern of findings referred to as **secular trends.** For example, the age of menarche has decreased at the rate of about 4 months per decade over the past 100 years among European populations, shifting from an average age of roughly 17 in 1840 to roughly $12^1/_2$ or 13 today (Roche, 1979). Over the same decades, average final height and weight have increased, not only among European populations but among the Japanese as well.

What could account for such changes over time? The most obvious possibility is that there have been changes in diet and life-style.

Diet. Differences in diet not only may help to explain secular trends, they also contribute to the individual differences we see in rates of physical development in any one cohort. Most generally, we know that poorly nourished children grow more slowly, and then don't end up as large (Malina, 1982). If their diet later improves, such children may show some catch-up in height or growth rate, but they are typically shorter and slower than their peers. In addition, of course, malnourished or undernourished children have less energy, which in turn can affect the nature of the interactions the child has with both the objects and the people around him. For example, in a recent study of schoolchildren in Kenya, Michael Espinosa and his colleagues (1992) observed that on the playground, undernourished kids were more solitary and less active than their well-nourished peers. The children in this study were not severely malnourished; they were taking in about 1500 calories per day. This is enough to sustain the child, but not enough to provide the energy needed for play, or perhaps for concentration in school over long periods.

Prenatal Environmental Influences. Prenatal environments can also have long-term effects on a child's physical development. One example is the impact of prenatal exposure to alcohol. Streissguth and her colleagues, whose work I described in Chapter 2, have found that 4-year-olds whose mothers drank while pregnant, compared to those whose mothers did not drink or drank less, had poorer balance and poorer fine motor skills, such as hand steadiness or the ability to tap rapidly with a finger (Barr et al., 1990). Caffeine ingestion and high use of aspirin during the pregnancy were also related to poorer fine motor skills among the 4-year-olds.

Practice. Both diet and prenatal exposures of various kinds are environmental variations that are external to the child, that happen to the child. But we can also think of environmental influences on physical development in terms of the child's own practice of various physical activities. Does a baby who spends a lot of time in a toy called an infant walker, which holds up the baby while he moves around, learn independent walking any sooner than a baby who never has that practice? Does a toddler who has a chance to try to climb stairs learn to climb them sooner, or more skillfully, than a toddler who is rarely exposed to stairs? If you go back and look at Aslin's models of the possible role of early experience in Figure 1.1, you'll see that I am asking whether practice has a *facilitative* effect, or even if it operates as what he calls *attunement*. Alternatively, perhaps practice has no effect at all on the emergence of basic skills.

The answer, as usual, is fairly complicated. Two conclusions are reasonably clear. First, the development of such universal, basic skills as crawling or walking requires some minimum amount of practice just to keep the system working as it should—what Aslin calls a *maintenance* effect of environment. Children who are deprived of such normal practice develop motor skills much more slowly, and not in the normal sequence. A classic study by Wayne Dennis (1960) of children raised in Iranian orphanages is a good illustration. The babies in one of the institutions Dennis observed were routinely placed on their backs in cribs with very lumpy mattresses. They had little or no experience at lying or moving on their stomachs as a normal baby would, and even had difficulty rolling over because of the hollows in the mattresses. These babies almost never went through the normal sequence of learning to walk—presumably because they didn't have enough opportunity to practice all the on-the-stomach parts of the skill. They did learn to walk eventually, but they were about a year late.

We also know that the development of really smooth, coordinated skill in virtually all complex motor tasks requires practice. The strength and coordination required to throw a basketball high enough to reach the basket may develop in predictable ways over the early years, provided the environment is sufficiently rich to promote needed maintenance. But to develop the skill needed to get the ball through the hoop with regularity, from different angles and distances, requires endless practice.

Where we are still uncertain is about the role of practice in the acquisition of the basic component skills, such as sitting, walking up stairs, climbing, or catching objects. Early studies seemed to show that extra practice in such basic skills didn't speed up their development at all, perhaps because virtually all children have enough opportunity for minimal practice in their ordinary lives. But some recent studies contradict this conclusion, including one showing that very young

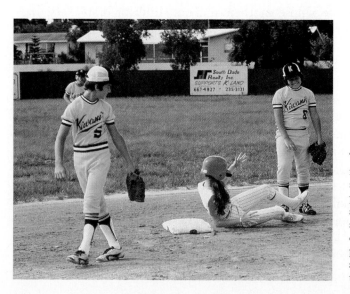

To acquire the basic skills needed to run, even to throw an object like a ball, a child probably doesn't need any special practice. But to be able to run and throw well enough to be a good baseball player requires an enormous amount of very specific practice.

babies who are given more practice sitting are able to sit upright longer than those without such practice (Zelazo et al., 1993). The jury is still out on this one.

As a final point about physical development, let me remind you of something I said at the very beginning of the chapter: The links between experience and physical development operate in both directions. Experience affects the child's skills, but the rate and pattern of the child's physical development also affect his self-image, his personality, his interactions with the world around him. So physical development influences experience as much as the reverse.

▶ Summary

1. It is important to know something about physical growth and development because specific new behaviors are triggered by physical changes, because physical skills affect the kinds of experiences the child can have, and because her feelings about her own body can affect self-concept and personality.
2. Changes in height and weight are rapid during the first two years, then level off to a steady pace until adolescence, when there is a sharp "growth spurt."
3. Bones increase in number, and harden slowly. Muscle tissue increases primarily in density and length of fibers, with a much larger increase at adolescence for boys than for girls.
4. Fat cells are added in the early years, and then again rapidly at adolescence, in this case more for girls than for boys.
5. At birth the medulla and midbrain are most developed; the cortex develops primarily over the first two years. Major neural changes after birth are the growth of dendrites and of synapses, as well as myelinization of axons.
6. Hormones are vital influences throughout growth, particularly during adolescence. The pituitary gland secretes triggering hormones at the beginning of puberty, which stimulate the development of sex hormones, which in turn trigger the development of primary and secondary sex characteristics.
7. Pubertal changes begin as early as 8 or 9 in girls, and continue until the mid-teens. In boys, the changes begin somewhat later, with the growth spurt roughly two years later. In both sexes, the physical changes occur in reliable sequences, starting with changes in secondary sex characteristics, followed by the growth spurt, with reproductive maturity late in the sequence.
8. The collective changes in bone, muscle, fat, and nervous system make possible the emergence of the various motor skills. Most basic motor skills are present by about age 6.
9. At adolescence, pubertal changes make mature sexual behavior possible. Sexual activity among teens has increased in recent decades. Perhaps half of teenage boys and a quarter of teenage girls in the U.S. are sexually active, and 1 in 10 teenage girls becomes pregnant each year.
10. Children differ markedly in the rate with which all these changes take place. In general, rapidly developing children have advantages over slower-developing children in intellectual skill. Personality effects are more complex. In general, children whose physical development is markedly earlier or later than they expect or desire show more negative effects than do those whose development is "on time."

11. Some social class and racial differences can also be detected, with children from poverty-level environments developing more slowly. Both black and Asian children show more rapid tempo of development than do white children.

12. Illness is also a normal part of children's early lives. Young children have brief illnesses six to nine times each year. Chronic illness is less common. Repeated or frequent illness in childhood is associated with poorer health later on.

13. In adolescence, several health problems become more common, including (in the U.S. and Western countries) accidents, suicide, and homicide among males, and eating disorders among females.

14. Eating disorders such as bulimia and anorexia appear to be a response to a major discrepancy between culturally defined body ideals and girls' perceptions of their own bodies.

15. Maturation is a key process underlying physical growth and development, but maturation alone cannot account for the patterns that we see. Some environmental support is required, and specific heredity, prenatal teratogens, and prenatal and postnatal diet affect both the rate and pattern of development in individual children.

16. The role of practice is complex. A minimum amount of practice is required to sustain development of basic physical skills; for more complex skills, specific practice is required for skill acquisition.

▶ Key Terms

anorexia nervosa (125)

bulimia (125)

cephalocaudal (107)

cortex (109)

endocrine glands (110)

estrogen (111)

fontanels (107)

gonadotropic hormones (111)

medulla (109)

menarche (113)

midbrain (109)

motor development (115)

myelin (110)

myelinization (110)

proximodistal (107)

puberty (112)

secular trends (129)

▶ Suggested Readings

The Diagram Group. (1977). *Child's Body*. New York: Paddington Press.

> This nifty book is not new and so may be hard to find, but it is worth the effort. Designed as a parents' manual, it is full of helpful information about physical development, health, and nutrition.

Gullotta, T. P., Adams, G. R., & Montemayor, R. (Eds.). (1993). *Adolescent sexuality*. Newbury Park, CA: Sage.

> A first-rate volume of papers on all aspects of this important subject. Of particular interest are a paper by Dyk reviewing information on physical changes at adolescence, and one by Miller et al. on sexual behavior in adolescents.

Malina, R. M. (1990). Physical growth and performance during the transitional years (9–16). In R. Montemayor, G. R. Adams, & T. P. Gullotta (Eds.), *From childhood to adolescence: A transitional period?* (pp. 41–62). Newbury Park, CA: Sage.

> To some extent Malina has picked up where Tanner has left off, providing us with updated information on normal physical growth. This particular paper focuses on puberty, but it contains references to much of Malina's work on other ages as well.

Tanner, J. M. (1978). *Fetus into man: Physical growth from conception to maturity*. Cambridge, MA: Harvard University Press.

> A detailed but very thorough and remarkably understandable small book that covers all but the most current information about physical growth.

5 PERCEPTUAL DEVELOPMENT

Basic Sensory Skills
Seeing
Hearing
Other Senses

Complex Perceptual Skills: Preferences, Discriminations, and Patterns
Looking
• Research Report: Langlois' Studies of Babies' Preferences for Attractive Faces
Listening
Cross-modal Transfer: Combining Information from Several Senses

Ignoring Perceptual Information: The Perceptual Constancies

The Object Concept
Object Perception

Object Permanence
• Cultures and Contexts: Object Permanence in Zambian Infants

Individual Differences in Perception: Speed and Efficiency

Explanations of Perceptual Development
Nativism Versus Empiricism
An Alternative Theoretical Approach: Eleanor Gibson's Views

Perceptual Development: A Summing-Up

Summary

Key Terms

Suggested Readings

Have you ever seen a baby trying to feed herself something mushy and messy like chocolate pudding? It is a wonderful and fascinating sight—more charming, of course, if someone else has to clean up the child afterward! In the beginning, most babies don't have very good aim, so the chocolate pudding goes in the hair, all over the face, and down the front of the shirt. Most babies are not at all bothered by the mess, and will look at you with delighted grins in the midst of the goo.

In fact, it is no small task for the toddler to get that spoon reliably into her mouth. It obviously involves motor skills, since she has to be able to grasp the spoon and move her hand and arm toward her mouth. But motor skills alone are not enough. She also has to use a wide range of *perceptual* information. She has to see the spoon and/or feel it in her hand, estimate the distance from the mouth and gauge the appropriate trajectory, meanwhile coordinating the visual and kinesthetic information as she goes along, so that she can change her aim if she needs to.

In the last chapter I tried hard to make the case that physical development forms one of the bases for all other aspects of development. We cannot understand the development of the child's thinking, or of her emerging social relationships, without having some understanding of physical development. Here I want to make the same case for perceptual development. Perceptual processes form a part of virtually every task a child must perform, every motor or cognitive skill that is developed. To identify Mom or Dad she has to discriminate among smells, or voices, or faces. To recognize faces, she must pay attention to (and remember) individual features or patterns of features. To learn to talk she must hear differences among sounds, focusing eventually on the repertoire of sounds used in the language spoken around her.

To understand a child's development, then, we have to understand what kinds of sense impressions are possible for her, both at birth and over the years of development. And we have to understand how the child comes to interpret those sense impressions—to discriminate among them, to recognize or understand patterns. In this sense the study of perceptual development forms a kind of bridge between the study of physiological changes, such as the changes in the nervous system I described in the last chapter, and the study of thinking, which I'll be turning to in Chapter 6.

The study of perceptual development has also been significant because it has been a key battleground for the dispute about nature versus nurture, **nativism** versus **empiricism.** How much of our basic perceptual understanding of the world is built in? How much is the product of experience? Because this issue has been so central in studies of perception, the vast majority of the research on perceptual development has focused on the very early months of life, since that is the only time when we can observe the organism when it is relatively uninfluenced by specific experience. The early months are also the time of most rapid change in perceptual skills, and hence a time of greater interest to psychologists trying to understand the processes of development. For both these reasons, most of the information I'll be giving you in this chapter describes perceptual processes in very young infants. But that age limitation makes the issues no less fascinating.

Nearly all of the research I'll be talking about has been done in the past 25 years or so, because it took a while for psychologists to figure out how they could tell just what a newborn or very young baby could see, hear, or discriminate. There are now three widely used methods that allow us to "ask" a baby about what he experiences. In the *preference technique,* devised by Robert Fantz (1956), the baby is simply shown two pictures or two objects, and the researcher keeps track of how long the baby looks at each one. If many infants shown the same pair of pictures consistently look longer at one picture than the other, it not only tells us that babies see some difference between the two, but also may reveal something about the kinds of objects or pictures that capture babies' attention.

Another strategy takes advantage of the processes of *habituation* and *dishabituation* that I described in Chapter 3. You first present the baby with a particular sight or sound over and over until he habituates, that is, until he stops looking at it or showing interest in it. Then you present another sight or sound or object that is slightly different from the original one in some specific way, and watch to see if the baby shows renewed interest (dishabituation). If the baby does show such renewed interest, you know he perceives it as "different" in some way from the original.

Success! The spoon is in the mouth! At 1 year, Genevieve isn't very skillful yet, but she is already able to coordinate the perceptual and motor skills involved in this complex task at least a bit.

The third option is to use the principles of *operant conditioning* I described in Chapter 1. For example, an infant might be trained to turn her head when she hears a particular sound, with the sight of an interesting moving toy as the reinforcement. After the learned response is well established, the experimenter can vary the sound in some systematic way to see whether the baby still turns her head or not.

Research using variations on these three techniques has now yielded a rich array of information about young infants' perceptual capacities. To simplify the descriptive task, let me divide the information into two rough groups, which we might call "basic" and "more complex" skills. The distinction I am using here is similar to the distinction between sensation and perception given in most psychology texts. When we study *sensation*, we are asking just what information the sensory organs receive. Does the structure of the eye permit infants to see color? Is the structure of the ear and of the cortex such that a very young infant can discriminate among different pitches? When we study *perception* we are asking what the individual does with the sensory information, how it is interpreted or combined. So let me begin with the basic sensory capacities present in the newborn or developing over the first years of life.

▶ Basic Sensory Skills

The common theme running through all of what I will say about basic sensory skills is that newborns and young infants have far more sensory capacity than physicians or psychologists thought even as recently as a few decades ago. Perhaps because babies' motor skills are so obviously poor, we assumed that their sensory skills were equally poor. But we were wrong. A newborn does not have all the sensory capacities of a 2-month-old, or a 1-year-old, or an adult. But most of the basic skills are in place in at least rudimentary form.

Seeing

There are a great many basic visual skills, but let me focus on three that seem especially important: acuity, tracking moving objects, and color vision.

Acuity.   **Acuity** refers to how well or how clearly you can perceive something. When you apply for a driver's license and take the eye test that involves reading the letters on one line of a large chart, you're being tested for visual acuity. The usual standard for visual acuity in adults is "20/20" vision. This means that you can see and identify something that is 20 feet away that the average person can also see at 20 feet. A person with 20/100 vision, in contrast, has to be as close as 20 feet to see something that the ordinary person can see at 100 feet. In other words, the higher the second number, the poorer the person's visual acuity.

Until 25 or 30 years ago, many medical texts stated that the newborn infant was blind. Now we know that the newborn has quite poor visual acuity but is quite definitely not blind. Findings from research using a variety of different techniques have converged on a remarkably unanimous conclusion that at birth the infant's acuity is in the range of 20/200 to 20/400 and reaches roughly adult levels (20/20) by about one year of life (Haith, 1990).

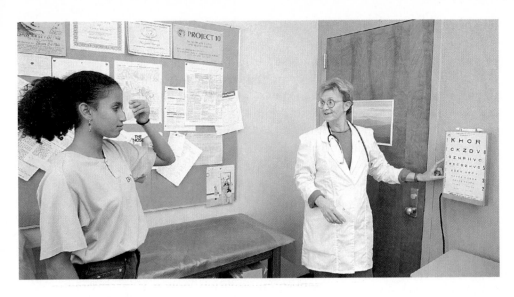

Eye tests like this one are measures of visual acuity.

The fact that the newborn sees so poorly is not so negative a thing as it might seem at first. Of course it does mean that a baby doesn't see faraway things very clearly; he probably can't see well enough to distinguish two people standing nearby. But he sees quite well close up, which is all that is necessary for most encounters with the people who care for him or with objects immediately at hand, such as breast, bottle, or mobiles hanging above his crib.

Locating Objects in the Visual Field.   When our young chocolate pudding eater tries to get the spoon in her mouth, one of the things she needs to do is keep her eyes on her hand or the spoon as she moves it toward herself. This process of following a moving object with your eyes is called **tracking,** and you do it every day in a variety of situations. You track the movement of other cars when you are driving; you track as you watch a friend walk toward you across the room; a baseball outfielder tracks the flight of the ball so that he can catch it. Because a newborn infant can't yet move independently, a lot of her experiences with objects are with things that move toward her or away from her. If she is to have any success in recognizing objects, she has to be able to keep her eyes on them as they move; she must be able to track.

Studies by Richard Aslin (1987a) and others show that tracking is initially fairly inefficient but improves quite rapidly. Infants younger than 2 months show some tracking for brief periods if the target is moving very slowly. But somewhere around 6 to 10 weeks there is a shift, and babies' tracking becomes skillful rather quickly. You can see the change very graphically in Figure 5.1, taken from a study by Aslin.

Color Vision.   The tale I can tell about color vision is similar. Researchers in this field (Bornstein, 1988; Teller & Bornstein, 1987) have established that the types of cells in the eye (cones) necessary for perceiving red and green are clearly present by 1 month, perhaps at birth; those required for perceiving blue

Can you think of other examples of tracking in your everyday life, or examples of professions in which the ability to track well would be especially important?

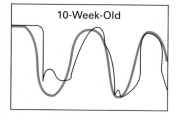

Figure 5.1
The blue line in each figure shows the trajectory of the moving line that each baby tried to follow with its eyes in Aslin's experiment. The black line represents one baby's eye movements. In the upper figure, a 6-week-old more-or-less followed the line, but not smoothly. By 10 weeks the same baby's tracking skill was remarkably smooth and accurate (lower figure). (*Source:* Aslin, 1987a, p. 87. Adapted by permission.)

Why is it important for an infant to be able to identify the direction of some sound? If a baby did not have this ability, how else would he be different?

are probably present by then as well. Thus infants can and do see and discriminate among various colors.

Taken together, these findings certainly do not support the notion that an infant is blind at birth! While it is true that the infant's acuity is initially poor, it improves rapidly, and other visual capacities are remarkably well developed early on. There are also some interesting hints here that there may be some kind of shift of gears at roughly 2 months, since a number of skills (such as smooth pursuit) improve incrementally at about that age. Whether such a change is the result of such neurological changes as the rapid proliferation of synapses and the growth of dendrites, or of changes in the eye itself, or perhaps of the child's experience, we don't yet know.

Hearing

Acuity. Although children's hearing improves up to adolescence, newborns' auditory acuity is actually better than their visual acuity. Current research evidence suggests that within the general range of pitch and loudness of the human voice, newborns hear nearly as well as adults do. They have somewhat more difficulty with high-pitched sounds; such a sound needs to be louder before the newborn can hear it than is true for older children or adults (Werner & Gillenwater, 1990).

Detecting Locations. Another basic auditory skill that exists at birth but improves with age is the ability to determine the location of a sound. You can tell roughly where a sound is coming from in large part because your two ears are separated from one another, so that the sound arrives at one ear slightly before the other. If the sound comes from a source equidistant from the two ears (the "midline"), then the sound arrives at the same time to the two ears. We know that newborns can judge at least the general direction from which a sound has come because they will turn their heads in roughly the right direction. But finer-grained location of sounds is not well developed at birth. For example, Barbara Morrongiello has observed babies' reactions to sounds played at the midline, and then sounds coming from varying degrees away from the midline. Among infants 2 months old it takes a shift of about 27 degrees off of midline before the baby shows a changed response; among 6-month-olds only a 12-degree shift is needed, while by 18 months discrimination of a 4-degree shift is possible—nearly at the skill level seen in adults (Morrongiello, 1988; Morrongiello, Fenwick, & Chance, 1990).

Other Senses

Smelling and Tasting. The senses of smell and taste have been studied much less, but we do have some basic knowledge. As with adults, the two senses are intricately related—that is, if you cannot smell for some reason (like when you have a cold), your taste sensitivity is also significantly reduced. Taste is detected by the taste buds on the tongue, which register four basic tastes: sweet, sour, bitter, and salty. Smell is registered in the mucous membranes of the nose, and has nearly unlimited variations.

Newborns appear to respond differentially to all four of the basic flavors (Crook, 1987). Some of the clearest demonstrations of this come from an elegantly simple set of studies by Jacob Steiner (Ganchrow, Steiner, & Daher, 1983;

NORMAL   SWEET   SOUR   BITTER

Figure 5.2
These are three of the babies Steiner observed in his experiments on taste responses of newborns. The left-hand column shows each baby's normal expression; the remaining columns show the change in expression when they were given sweet, sour, and bitter tastes. What is striking is how similar the expressions are for each taste. (*Source:* J. E. Steiner, 1979. Human facial expressions in response to taste and smell stimulation. In H. W. Reese & L. P. Lipsett [Eds.], *Advances in child development and behavior*, Vol. 13, Figure 1, p. 269. New York: Academic Press.)

Steiner, 1979). Newborn infants who had never been fed were photographed before and after flavored water was put into their mouths. By varying the flavor, Steiner could determine whether the babies reacted differently to different tastes. As you can see in Figure 5.2, babies responded quite differently to sweet, sour, and bitter flavors.

Babies as young as a week old can also tell the difference between such complex smells as personal body odors. Specifically, they can discriminate between their mother's and other women's smells, although this seems to be true only for babies who are being breast-fed, and who thus spend quite a lot of time with their noses against the mother's bare skin (Cernoch & Porter, 1985).

Senses of Touch and Motion.   The infant's senses of touch and motion may well be the best developed of all. Certainly they are sufficiently well developed to get the baby fed. If you think back to the list of reflexes in the newborn I gave you in Chapter 3, you'll realize that the rooting reflex relies on a touch stimulus to the cheek, and the sucking reflex relies on touch in the mouth. Babies appear to be especially sensitive to touches on the mouth, the face, the hands, the soles of the feet, and the abdomen, with less sensitivity in other parts of the body (Reisman, 1987).

I am aware that all of what I have said about these sensory abilities is fairly dry and technical. The important point for you to remember is that, as Reisman puts it, "we think of infants as helpless but they are born with some exquisitely tuned sensory abilities" (1987, p. 265). Studies of more complex perceptual skills make the abilities of very young infants seem even more remarkable.

▶ Complex Perceptual Skills: Preferences, Discriminations, and Patterns

Let's begin, as we did before, with vision.

Looking

Depth Perception. One of the complex skills that has been most studied is depth perception. You need this ability anytime you reach for something, or figure out whether you have room to make a left turn before an oncoming car gets to you. In these cases and many, many others, you need to judge distance or depth, just as our young pudding eater needs to do when she aims her spoon toward the bowl of pudding.

It is possible to judge depth using any (or all) of three rather different kinds of information. First, *binocular* cues involve both of your eyes, each of which receives a slightly different visual image of an object; the closer the object is, the more different these two views are. In addition, of course, information from the muscles of the eyes also tells you something about how far away an object may be. Second, *pictorial* information, also sometimes called *monocular* cues, requires input from only one eye. For example, when one object is partially in front of another one, you know that the partially hidden object is farther away—a cue called *interposition*. The relative size of two similar objects, such as telephone poles, or two people you see in the distance, may also indicate that the smaller-appearing one is farther away. Linear perspective (like railroad lines that seem to get closer together as they are farther away) is another monocular cue. Third, *kinetic* cues come from either your own motion or the motion of some object: if you move your head, objects near you seem to move more than objects farther away (a phenomenon called *motion parallax*). Similarly, if you see some object moving, such as a person walking across a street or a train moving along a track, closer objects appear to move over larger distances in a given space of time.

How early can an infant judge depth, and which of these cues does he use? This is still a hot area of research, so the answer I can give you is not final. The best conclusion at the moment seems to be that kinetic information is used first, perhaps by about 3 months of age; binocular cues are used beginning at roughly 4 months; and pictorial (monocular) cues are used last, perhaps at 5 to 7 months (Aslin, 1987b; Aslin & Smith, 1988; Bornstein, 1992).

I don't have enough room to talk about the research on each of these three types of cues, so let me concentrate on the most extensive and most fascinating line of research, which has involved the use of kinetic cues. In a remarkably clever early study, Eleanor Gibson and Richard Walk (1960) devised an apparatus called a *visual cliff*. You can see from the picture in Figure 5.3 that it consists of a large glass table with a sort of runway in the middle. On one side of the runway there is a checkerboard pattern immediately below the glass; on the other side—the "cliff" side—the checkerboard is several feet below the glass. The baby could judge depth here by several means, but it is primarily kinetic information that is useful, since the baby in motion would see the nearer surface move more than the farther surface. If a baby has no depth perception, she should be equally willing to crawl on either side of the runway, but if she can judge depth, she should be reluctant to crawl out on the "cliff" side.

Think of three or four other everyday situations in which the ability to judge depth is critical.

One of the many skills young Andrea has to have to reach for and grasp her toy is the ability to judge depth. How far away is the toy? Is it near enough for her to reach with her hand?

Since an infant had to be able to crawl in order to be tested in the Gibson and Walk procedure, the original subjects were all at least 6 months old . Most of these infants did *not* crawl out on the cliff side, but were quite willing to crawl out on the shallow side. In other words, 6-month-old babies have depth perception.

But what about younger infants? The traditional visual cliff procedure can't give us the answer, since the baby must be able to crawl in order to "tell us" whether he can judge depth. With younger babies, researchers have studied kinetic cues by watching babies react to apparently looming objects. Most often the baby observes a film of an object moving toward him, apparently on a collision course. If the infant has some depth perception, he should flinch, or move to one side, or blink, as the object appears to come very close. Such flinching has been consistently observed in 3-month-olds (Yonas & Owsley, 1987). Most experts now agree that this is about the lowest age limit of depth perception.

What Babies Look At.   Even though a baby cannot judge depth right away, her behavior is governed by visual information from the very first minutes of life. We know that from the beginning, babies look at the world around them in a nonrandom way. In Marshall Haith's phrase (1980), there are "rules babies look by." Furthermore, those rules seem to change with age.

In the first two months, a baby's visual attention is focused on *where* objects are in his world (Bronson, 1991). He scans the world around him—not very smoothly or skillfully, to be sure, but nonetheless regularly, even in the dark. This general scanning continues until he comes to a sharp light/dark contrast, which typically signals the edge of some object. Once he finds such an edge, the baby stops searching and moves his eyes back and forth across and around the edge. Thus the initial rules seem to be: scan till you find an edge and then examine the edge. Motion also captures a baby's attention at this same age, so he will look at things that move as well as things with large light/dark contrast.

These rules seem to change at about 2 months, perhaps because the cortex has then developed more fully, or perhaps because of experience, or both. Whatever the cause, at about this time the baby's attention seems to shift from *where* an object is to *what* an object is. Put another way, the baby seems to move from a strategy designed primarily to *find things* to a strategy designed primarily to *identify* things. Babies this age begin to scan rapidly across an entire figure, rather than getting stuck on edges. As a result, they spend more time looking at the internal features of some object or array of objects, and are thus better able to identify the objects.

What is amazing about this shift is the degree of detail infants now seem to be able to take in and respond to. They notice whether two pictures are placed horizontally or vertically, they can tell the difference between pictures with two things in them and pictures with three things in them, and they clearly notice patterns, even such apparently abstract patterns as "big-thing-over-small-thing."

In one experiment using a habituation procedure, Albert and Rose Caron (1981) chose stimuli like those in Figure 5.4. The babies were first shown a series of pictures, like those on the left in Figure 5.4, that shared some particular relationship. The example I've shown in the figure is "small over big." After the baby stopped being interested in these training pictures (that is, after he habituated), the Carons showed him another figure (the "test stimulus") that either followed

Figure 5.3
In this "visual cliff" apparatus, like the one used by Gibson and Walk, Mom tries to entice her baby out onto the "cliff" side. But because the infant can perceive depth, he thinks he will fall if he comes toward her, so he stays put, looking concerned.

Training stimuli

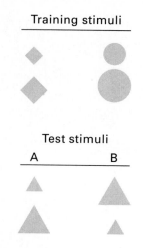

Test stimuli

A   B

Figure 5.4
In the Carons' study, the researchers first habituated each baby to the training stimuli (all "small over large" in this case), then showed each baby two test stimuli: one that had the same pattern (A), and one that had a different pattern (B). Four-month-old babies showed renewed interest in the B stimulus, but not in the A stimulus, showing that they pay attention to the pattern and not just to specific stimuli. (*Source:* Caron & Caron, 1981, p. 227. Adapted by permission.)

Does this mean that researchers ought to believe mothers and fathers more often, when they describe their infants and what the babies can do? How should scientists weigh anecdotal evidence against research evidence?

the same pattern or followed some other pattern, such as those you can see on the right-hand side of Figure 5.4. If the baby had really habituated to the *pattern* of the original pictures (small over large) he should show little interest in stimuli like the A test stimulus (ho hum, same old boring small-over-large thing), but should show renewed interest in the B test stimulus (hey, here's something new!). Caron and Caron found that 3- and 4-month-old children did precisely that. So even at this early age, babies find and pay attention to patterns, and not just to specific stimuli.

Faces: An Example of Responding to a Complex Pattern.   From the beginning of this new era of research on infant perception, researchers have been especially interested in babies' perception of faces, not only because of the obvious relevance for parent-infant relationships, but because of the possibility that there might be a built-in preference for faces or facelike arrangements—a variant of the now-familiar nativism/empiricism issue. After 30 years of research, we do not have all the answers. In fact, there are new surprises in the research all the time. Here is a sample of what we think we know at this point.

First, there is little indication that faces are uniquely interesting to infants, which fails to support one of the early assumptions of many nativists. That is, babies do not systematically choose to look at faces rather than at other complex pictures.

On the other hand, among faces, babies clearly prefer some to others. They prefer *attractive* faces—an intriguing result that I've discussed in the research report on page 143—and it now looks as if they prefer their *mother's* face from the earliest hours of life, a finding that has greatly surprised psychologists, although it may not surprise you.

For years I have been telling my friends and relatives that there was clear research showing that babies can't recognize their mother's face until at least 1 or 2 months of age, but that they can recognize the mother by sound or smell immediately. None of my friends or relatives believed me; they all said, "I don't care what the research says; I know my baby could recognize my face right away." Well, it looks like they were right and the older research (and I) was wrong.

There are several new studies that show this, but the clearest and cleanest is one by Gail Walton (Walton, Bower, & Bower, 1992). She videotaped the faces of 12 mothers of newborns, and then matched each of these faces with the face of another woman whose hair color, eye color, complexion, and hair style were the same as the mom's. Each baby was then tested with both pictures in a modification of the preference technique. These babies, who were only a day or two old at the time of the testing, clearly preferred to look at their mom. Walton also has some preliminary information that babies do *not* discriminate, or do not prefer, their father's face as early as this.

This is a fascinating result. Clearly the baby has to *learn* the mother's features in those first hours after birth. But how is this possible? Is there some kind of imprinting going on here to the first face the baby sees after it is born? If so, then the process should be affected by birth practices, or by the amount of contact the baby had had with various individuals. As is often the case, this one study seems to settle one question but raise many more.

RESEARCH REPORT
Langlois' Studies of Babies' Preferences for Attractive Faces

Of all the current research on infant perception that seems to point toward the conclusion that there are many more built-in abilities and preferences than we had supposed, the most surprising and intriguing to me have been Judith Langlois' studies of infant preferences for attractive faces. Langlois has found that babies as young as 2 months old will look longer at a face that adults judge to be attractive than at one adults judge to be less attractive.

In the first study in this series, Langlois and her colleagues (1987) tested 2-to-3-month-olds and 6-to-8-month-olds. Each baby, while seated on Mom's lap, was shown pairs of color slides of 16 adult Caucasian women, half rated by adult judges as attractive, half rated as unattractive. On each trial, the baby saw two slides simultaneously shown on a screen in front of him/her, with each face approximately life-size, while the experimenter peeked through a hole in the screen to count the number of seconds the baby looked at each picture. Each baby saw some attractive/attractive pairs, some unattractive/unattractive pairs, and some mixed pairs.

The crucial trials are obviously those in which there was one attractive and one unattractive face. The results, which are on the left side of the table below, show that even the 2-to-3-month olds preferred to look at the attractive faces.

One of the nice features of this study is that they used a variety of attractive and unattractive faces, which makes the conclu-

sion clearer. But because they used only Caucasian females, that leaves open the generality of the result. In a still-newer study (Langlois et al., 1991), Langlois used the same procedure but showed some 6-month-old infants pictures of (1) both unattractive and attractive men and women, or (2) attractive and unattractive black women's faces, or (3) baby faces varying in attractiveness, all with neutral expressions. You can see the results on the right half of the table below. Once again the results are consistent: in every case babies look significantly longer at the attractive than the unattractive faces.

In another exploration of this same issue, Langlois, Roggman, and Rieser-Danner (1990) observed 1-year-old babies interacting with an adult wearing either an attractive or an unattractive mask. They found that the toddlers showed more positive affective tone, less withdrawal, and more play involvement with the stranger in the attractive mask. These 1-year-olds also played more with an attractive than an unattractive doll.

It is hard to imagine what sort of learning experiences could account for such a preference in a 2-month-old. Instead, these findings raise the possibility that there is some inborn template for the "correct" or "most desired" shape and configuration for members of our species, and that we simply prefer those who match this template better. If that's true, what kind of consequences might it have for child and adult development, especially the development of the less attractive baby, child, or adult?

Average Looking Time					
	2–3 month olds	**6–8 month olds**	**Male and female**	**Black women**	**Baby faces**
Attractive faces	9.22*	7.24*	7.82*	7.05*	7.16*
Unattractive faces	8.01	6.59	7.57	6.52	6.62

*Contrast between attractive and unattractive faces is statistically significant.

Sources: Langlois et al., 1987, from Table 1, p. 365; Langlois et al., 1991, Table 1, p. 81.

Beyond the question of preference, there is also the issue of just what it is that babies are looking at when they scan a face. Before about 2 months of age, babies seem to look mostly at the edges of the face (the hairline and the chin); after 2 months they seem to look more at the internal features, particularly the eyes—yet another example of the basic shift in rules at 2 months that I already described.

Once babies begin to look at these internal facial features, they also begin to pay attention to emotional expressions and rather quickly learn to tell the differ-

A baby this age can already discriminate his Mom's face from the face of another woman; he can also recognize his Mom's voice and smell.

ence among several common expressions: by 6 or 7 months, babies can discriminate between happy, surprised, and fearful faces (Nelson, 1987). By roughly 10 months, infants can "read" these emotional cues well enough to use Mom's or Dad's expression to judge the fearfulness or safety of some new situation or toy—a process referred to as *social referencing* (Hirshberg & Svejda, 1990). So if the mother takes a 10-month-old to the doctor's office, the baby will check out her expression. If she expresses some concern or fear, the baby is more likely to cry than if Mom's expression had been more neutral or happy; if the mother looks pleased and encouraging when she takes the child to a new playmate's house, the child notes that expression and is more likely to explore freely.

Listening

When we turn from looking to listening we find similarly intriguing indications that very young infants not only make remarkably fine discriminations among individual sounds, but also pay attention to patterns.

Discriminating Speech Sounds. One of the central questions has to do with how early a baby can make discriminations among different speech sounds. This has obvious relevance for the beginnings of language, since a baby cannot learn language until he can hear the individual sounds as distinct. But perception researchers have also been interested in this question because the answers may tell us some very interesting things about what may be built into the neurological system. Much of this research is quite technical, but I will do my best to try to convey to you why psychologists have found the results so remarkable.

For starters, researchers established that as early as 1 month, babies can discriminate between speech sounds like *pa* and *ba* (Trehub & Rabinovitch, 1972). Studies using conditioned head-turning responses have shown that by perhaps 6 months of age, they can discriminate between two-syllable "words" like *bada* and *baga* and can even respond to a syllable which is hidden inside a string of other syllables, like ti*bati* or ko*bako* (Fernald & Kuhl, 1987; Goodsitt et al., 1984; Morse & Cowan, 1982). Even more remarkable, it doesn't even seem to matter what voice quality the sound is said in. By 2 or 3 months of age, babies respond to individual sounds as the same whether they are spoken by male or female voices, or a child's voice (Marean, Werner, & Kuhl, 1992).

That's already pretty impressive evidence that infants listen to quite fine variations in speech sounds, not just at the beginnings of words but in other vocal positions as well. But that is not the end of the story. It also turns out that infants can accurately discriminate among sound contrasts that appear in *any* language, not just sounds that they are actually hearing in the language being spoken around them. Babies in an English-speaking environment can discriminate pairs of sounds that occur in Hindi (a language of India) but not in English; babies in Spanish-speaking environments can discriminate pairs of sounds that are relevant in English but not in Spanish. Japanese babies can discriminate between the *l* and *r* sounds that occur in English but not in Japanese. But by one year of life, this ability has faded, although it does not disappear altogether. Adults can learn to "hear" such sound variations if they work very hard at it, such as when trying to learn to speak a foreign language without an accent. But the infant appears to hear all these distinctions naturally.

An unusually complete study by Janet Werker and Richard Tees (1984) illustrates the point. Combining cross-sectional and longitudinal designs, they first

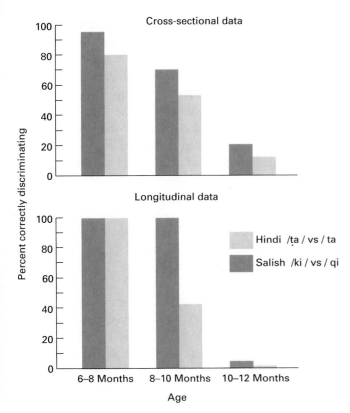

Cross-sectional data

Longitudinal data

Percent correctly discriminating

Hindi /ṭa / vs / ta

Salish /ki / vs / qi

6–8 Months   8–10 Months   10–12 Months

Age

Figure 5.5
In these studies, babies growing up in English-speaking
environments were tested for
their ability to make two discriminations: between two
speech sounds that are used
differently in Hindi but that
are treated as the same in
English, and between a pair
of sounds used differently in
Salish but treated as the same
in English. The upper part
of the figure shows a cross-
sectional comparison, with
12 babies tested at each age.
The lower part of the figure
shows what happened to the
discrimination ability of six
babies studied longitudinally.
You can see that virtually all
the babies could make these
discriminations at 8 months,
but that this ability rapidly
disappeared. (*Source:* Werker
& Tees, 1984, Figure 4,
p. 61. Adapted by permis-
sion.)

studied separate groups of 6-to-8-month-old, 8-to-10-month-old, and 10-to-12-
month-old babies being raised in English-speaking homes. Each baby was tested
on three sound pairs: one heard in English (*ba* versus *da*); one from a North
American Indian language, Salish (*ki* versus *qi*); and one from Hindi, a language
from the Indian subcontinent (*ṭa* versus *ta*). You can see in Figure 5.5 that the 6
to 8-month-old English-environment babies could easily hear and respond to
both the Hindi and Salish contrasts, but very few of the 10 to 12-month-olds
could do so. When Werker and Tees later retested some of the 6-month-olds at 9
and 12 months, they found that these babies had *lost* the ability to make these
discriminations. In separate tests, Werker and Tees also tested Hindi- and Salish-
environment infants, and found that 12-month-old Hindi infants could easily
discriminate the Hindi contrast, and Salish toddlers could still hear the Salish
contrast.

It seems to me that these findings are consistent with what we now know
about the pattern of rapid, apparently preprogrammed, growth of synapses in the
early months of life, followed by synaptic pruning. Many connections are initially
created, permitting discriminations along all possible sound continua. But only
those pathways that are actually used in the language the child hears are retained.

Discriminating Individual Voices.   Newborns also seem to be able to discriminate between individual voices. DeCasper and Fifer (1980) have found that
newborns can tell their mother's voice from another female voice (but not their
father's voice from another male voice) and prefer the mother's. This is easier to
account for than is the newborn's preferences for the mother's face, since the baby
could learn the sound of the mother's voice while still *in utero*. But it is still a
striking finding.

By 6 months, babies even know which voice is supposed to go with which face. If you put an infant of this age in a situation where she can see both her father and mother and can hear a tape-recorded voice of one of them, she will look toward the parent whose voice she hears (Spelke & Owsley, 1979).

Other Sound Patterns. As was true with studies of looking, there is also evidence that infants pay attention to *patterns* of sounds from the very beginning. One particularly striking demonstration of this comes from another study by De-Casper (DeCasper & Spence, 1986). He had pregnant women read a particular children's story (such as Dr. Seuss's *The Cat in the Hat*) out loud each day for the final six weeks of the pregnancy. After the infants were born, he played recordings of the mother reading this same story, or another previously unheard story, to see which the infant preferred. The newborns clearly preferred the sound of the story they had heard *in utero*. Not only does this study demonstrate that key features of the auditory system are well developed some weeks before birth, but shows that even before birth, infants are paying attention to and discriminating among complex patterns of sounds.

Further evidence for the same point comes from the observation that babies as young as 6 months listen to melodies and recognize the patterns. Sandra Trehub and her colleagues (Trehub, Bull, & Thorpe, 1984; Trehub, Thorpe, & Morrongiello, 1985) trained 6-month-old babies to turn their heads toward a loudspeaker for a particular six-tone melody, and then tested the babies with melodies that varied in a number of ways. Babies continued to turn their heads to new melodies if the melody had the same contour (notes going up and down in the same sequence) and were in approximately the same range. They responded to them as different if the contour changed, or if the notes were much higher or much lower. Thus, as is true with patterns of looking, within the first few months of life babies appear to pay attention to and respond to pattern and not just the specific sounds. Whether such pattern perception skills are built into the neurological system as it develops, or whether they are the result of the child's learning after birth, is still a matter of fairly hot debate. But the fact that such skills are present very early in life is no longer in dispute.

Cross-modal Transfer: Combining Information from Several Senses

I have been talking about each sense separately, as if we experience the world through only one sense at a time. But think about the way you receive and use perceptual information; you rarely have information from only one sense at a time. Ordinarily you have *both* sound and sight, or touch and sight, or still more complex combinations of smell, sight, touch, and sound. Psychologists have been interested in knowing how early an infant can combine such information. For example, how early does an infant figure out which mouth movements go with which sounds? How early can a baby recognize by feel a toy he has only seen before? The latter skill is normally called **cross-modal** (or intermodal) **transfer.**

Piaget believed that integration of information from several senses, or cross-modal transfer, was simply not possible until quite late in the first year of life, after the infant had accumulated many experiences with specific objects and how they simultaneously looked, sounded, and felt. Other theorists, including James and Eleanor Gibson, have argued that some intermodal coordination of percep-

---

What might be some practical implications of the fact that fetuses can hear clearly enough to distinguish the particular pattern of a story read to them *in utero*?

tual information is built in from birth. The baby then builds on that inborn set of skills with specific experience with objects. Research favors the Gibsonian view: empirical findings show that cross-modal transfer is possible as early as 1 month and becomes common by 6 months (Rose & Ruff, 1987).

For example, if you attach a nubby or a smooth sphere to a pacifier and give one or the other to each of several babies to suck, you can test for cross-modal transfer using Fantz's preference technique: you show the babies pictures of the two spheres to see if infants look longer at one than at the other. When Meltzoff and Borton (1979) did this , they found that 1-month-old babies preferred to look at the picture of the object they had sucked on earlier. Other investigators have not always found such transfer in infants as young as 1 month, so the phenomenon is not robust at this age. But the very fact that it can be demonstrated at all is significant.

Intersensory integration and transfer are more consistently found in older children, not only between touch and sight, but between other modalities such as sound and sight. For instance, in several delightfully clever experiments, Elizabeth Spelke (1979) showed that 4-month-old infants can connect sound rhythms with movement . She showed babies two films simultaneously, one showing a toy kangaroo bouncing up and down, the other a donkey bouncing up and down, with one of the animals bouncing at a faster rate. Out of a speaker located between the two films the infant heard a tape recording of a rhythmic bouncing sound that matched one of the two rates. In this situation, babies spent more time watching the film that had the rhythm matching the sound they were hearing, a result I find remarkable.

In the same vein, researchers have shown that 4-to-5-month-old babies will look longer at a face of a person mouthing a vowel they are hearing over a loudspeaker than at the face of a person mouthing another vowel (Kuhl & Meltzoff, 1984; Walton & Bower, 1993). Even more remarkable is a study in which 7-month-olds saw pairs of faces displaying happy and angry expressions, while listening to words spoken either in a happy or angry voice. The babies looked longer at the face that matched the *emotion* in the speaking voice—a finding that suggests remarkable sophistication of intermodal transfer in these young infants (Soken & Pick, 1992).

Even if 3-month-old Nellie does not look at this toy while she is chewing on it, she is nonetheless learning something about how it *ought* to look, just based on how it feels in her mouth and in her hands—an example of cross-modal transfer.

All of this burgeoning (and I think fascinating) research on combining of information from several senses has raised some interesting theoretical issues. For one thing it is now perfectly clear that one does not need language to transfer information from one mode to another. And the fact that at least some transfer is possible within the first few weeks of life certainly points rather strongly to the possibility that *some* connections may be built in, although experience with specific objects and combinations clearly make a difference as well. So this body of information enriches but does not settle the nativism/empiricism debate.

▶ Ignoring Perceptual Information: The Perceptual Constancies

All of what I have said so far has been aimed at persuading you that babies are remarkably skillful, from early in life, in making perceptual discriminations of various kinds. But there is another, very different, kind of perceptual skill the infant must also acquire—the ability to *ignore* some kinds of perceptual data. Specifically, the child must acquire a set of rules we call **perceptual constancies.**

When you see someone walking away from you, the image of the person on your retina actually becomes smaller. But you don't see the person getting smaller. You see him as the same size but moving farther away. When you do this, you are demonstrating **size constancy;** you are able to see the size as constant even though the retinal image has changed.

Other constancies include the ability to recognize that shapes of objects are the same even though you are looking at them from different angles, called (logically enough) **shape constancy,** and the ability to recognize that colors are constant even though the amount of light or shadow on them changes, called **color constancy.**

Taken together, the several specific constancies add up to the larger concept of **object constancy,** which is the recognition that objects remain the same even when the sensory information you have about them has changed in some ways. Babies begin to show signs of these constancies at 3 or 4 months of age, and become more skilled over the first several years (Dannemiller, 1989; Granrud, 1986). Let me use shape constancy as an illustration.

Shape constancy has perhaps the most obvious day-to-day relevance for the baby. She has to realize that her bottle is still her bottle even though it is turned slightly and thus presents a different shape; she has to figure out that her toys are the same when they are in different positions. The beginnings of this understanding seem to be present by about 2 or 3 months of age (Cook & Birch, 1984). The classic study was done by Thomas Bower (1966), who first trained 2-month-old babies to turn their heads when they saw a particular rectangle. He then showed them tilted or slightly turned images of the same rectangle to see if the babies would respond to these as "the same," even though the retinal image cast by these tilted rectangles was actually a trapezoid and not a rectangle at all. Two-month-olds did indeed continue to turn their heads to these tilted and turned rectangles, showing that they have some shape constancy.

One of the ironies about perceptual development is that at a later age, when learning to read, a child has to *unlearn* some of these shape constancies. Pairs of letters like *b* and *d*, *p* and *q*, or *p* and *b* are the same shape, except with the direction reversed or one upside down. So in order to learn to read (at least the Latin alphabet) the child must now learn to pay attention to something she has learned to ignore—namely, the rotation of the letter in space.

Of course there is a good deal more to learning to read than simply ignoring shape constancy (and I'll have more to say about it in Chapter 8, when I talk about language development). But we do know that among 5-year-olds, those who have difficulty discriminating between mirror images of shapes also have more difficulty learning to read (Casey, 1986).

▶ The Object Concept

Grasping the various object constancies is only part of a larger task facing the child: figuring out the nature of objects themselves. First of all, an infant must somehow learn to treat some combinations of stimuli as "objects" and others not, a process usually referred to now as *object perception.* For example, if a baby sees a heap of blocks on a carpet, does she "know" that each block is a separate object? Does she treat the carpet as an object as well? What makes an object an object? A still more sophisticated aspect of the infant's emerging concept of objects is the understanding that objects continue to exist even when they are out of view. I know that my computer is still sitting here even when I am not in the room. Does a baby know that Mom continues to exist when she leaves the room, or that her bottle still exists when she drops it over the edge of the crib? Such an understanding is usually referred to as **object permanence.**

Object Perception

The most thorough and clever work on object perception in infants has been done by Elizabeth Spelke and her colleagues (Spelke, 1982; 1985; Spelke, von Hofsten, & Kestenbaum, 1989). Spelke believes that babies are born with certain built-in assumptions about the nature of objects. One of these is the assumption that when two surfaces are connected to one another they belong to the same object, which Spelke calls the *connected surface principle*. To study this, Spelke (1982) first habituated some 3-month-old babies to a series of displays of two objects and other babies to one-object displays. Then the babies were shown two objects touching each other, such as two square blocks placed next to each other so that they created a rectangle. Under these conditions the babies who had been habituated to two-object displays showed renewed interest, clearly indicating that they "saw" this as different, presumably as a single object. Babies who had seen the one-object displays during habituation showed no renewed interest. Spelke has also shown that babies as young as 2 and 3 months old are remarkably aware of what kinds of movements objects are capable of, even when the objects are out of sight. They expect objects to continue to move on their initial trajectory, and they show surprise if the object's movement violates this expectancy. They also seem to have some awareness that solid objects cannot pass through other solid objects.

In one experiment, Spelke (1991) used the procedure shown schematically in the upper part of Figure 5.6. Two-month-old babies were repeatedly shown a series of events like that in the "familiarization" section of the figure: A ball starting on the left-hand side was rolled to the right and disappeared behind a screen. The screen was then taken away and the baby could see that the ball was stopped against the wall on the right. After the baby got bored looking at this sequence (habituated), he or she was tested with two variations, one "consistent" and one "inconsistent." In the consistent variation, a second wall was placed behind the screen and the sequence run as before, except now when the screen was removed, the ball could be seen resting up against the nearer wall. In the inconsistent variation, the ball was surreptitiously placed on the *far* side of the new wall. When the screen was removed the ball was visible in this presumably impossible place. Babies in this experiment were quite uninterested in the consistent condition, but showed sharply renewed interest in the inconsistent condition, as you can see in the lower part of Figure 5.6, which shows the actual results of this experiment.

Spelke is not suggesting that all of the child's knowledge of objects is built in; she is suggesting that *some* rules are built in and that others are learned through experience. Whether she is correct in this theoretical position remains to be seen, but for now her research results are impressive and provocative.

I find it astonishing that a 2-month-old baby can have enough understanding of the physical world to "know" in some fashion that it is unexpected for the ball to be on the other side of the middle wall in this experiment. Are you also astonished by this result?

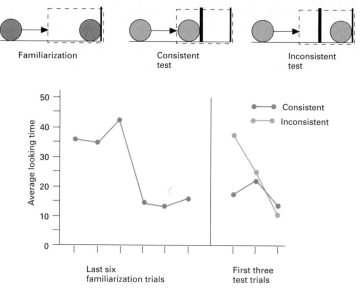

Figure 5.6
The top part of the figure shows a schematic version of the three conditions Spelke used. The bottom half shows the actual results. You can see that the babies stopped looking at the ball and screen after a number of familiarization trials, but showed renewed interest in the inconsistent version—a sign that the babies saw this as somehow different or surprising. The very fact that the babies found the inconsistent trial surprising is itself evidence that infants as young as 2 months have far more knowledge of objects and their behavior than most of us had thought. (*Source:* Spelke, 1991, Figures 5.3 and 5.4. Adapted by permission.)

Late in the first year of life, babies all over the world show the same kind of delight in the game of peekaboo as 9-month-old Jesse shows here. The pleasure appears to come from knowing that the face or person still exists when it is covered up. When the face reappears, this confirms the baby's expectancy and he is delighted.

Object Permanence

The study of object perception is a rather new area of research. In contrast, object permanence has been extensively explored, in large part because this particular understanding was strongly emphasized in Piaget's theory of infant development. According to his observations, replicated frequently by later researchers, there is a series of steps in the child's emerging understanding of object permanence.

The first sign that the baby is developing object permanence comes at about 2 months of age. Suppose you show a toy to a child of this age, then put a screen in front of the toy and remove the toy. When you then remove the screen, the baby shows some indication of surprise, as if she knew that something should still be there (Gratch, 1979; Piaget, 1954). The child thus seems to have a rudimentary schema or expectation about the permanence of an object. But infants of this age show no signs of searching for a toy they may have dropped over the edge of the crib or that has disappeared beneath a blanket or behind a screen.

Six- or 8-month-old babies, however, *will* look over the edge of the crib for the dropped toys, or for food that was spilled. (In fact, babies of this age may drive their parents nuts playing "dropsy" in the high chair.) Infants this age will also search for partially hidden objects. If you put a favorite toy under a cloth but leave part of it sticking out, the infant will reach for the toy, which suggests that in some sense the infant "recognizes" that the whole object is there even though she can see only part of it. But if you cover the toy completely with the cloth or put it behind a screen, the infant will stop looking at it and will not reach for it, even if she has seen you put the cloth over it. You can see an example of just this stage in Figure 5.7.

This changes again somewhere between 8 and 12 months; infants this age will reach for or search for a toy that has been covered completely by a cloth or hidden by a screen (Dunst, Brooks, & Doxsey, 1982). Thus by 12 months, most infants appear to grasp the basic fact that objects continue to exist even when they are no longer visible.

Object constancy has intrigued researchers and theorists in part because it forms one kind of bridge between studies of perception and early cognitive development. Many have also been struck by a possible link between the emergence of object constancy and the infant's earliest attachment. It seems reasonable to assume that some kind of object permanence is required before the baby can become attached to an individual person, such as his mother or father. Since we know that clear single attachments don't appear much before 5 months, right about the time that the baby is showing signs of object permanence, the connection seems very reasonable. Interestingly, and surprisingly to a lot of us, most direct tests of this hypothesis have not shown much sign of such a causal link. Still, the problem may be with our research techniques rather than the hypothesis. As John Flavell (1985) says,

> How ever could a child persistently yearn and search for a specific other person if the child were still cognitively incapable of mentally representing that person in the person's absence? p. 135)

I find Flavell's logic persuasive, but as usual we will have to wait for further research evidence to be sure.

Figure 5.7
This photos show very graphically the response of a 6- or 7-month-old infant in an object permanence test. The baby stops reaching for or searching for the toy when it is hidden from him. An older baby would keep searching or push the screen aside to reach for the toy.

CULTURES AND CONTEXTS
Object Permanence in Zambian Infants

Piaget believed that the emergence of the child's understanding of object permanence followed a universal sequence. One way to test this assumption, of course, is to observe or test children in non-Western societies, particularly infants or children whose early experiences are different from what we see in the U.S. or Europe. Susan Goldberg's longitudinal study of 38 Zambian infants (1972) gives us one such cross-cultural look.

Goldberg's two years of observations in Zambia made clear that the typical experience of a Zambian baby was quite different in a number of respects from that of most Western infants. From shortly after birth, Zambian babies are carried about in a sling on their mother's back. They spend very little time on the floor or in any position in which they have much chance of independent movement until they are able to sit up at about 6 months. At that point they are usually placed on a mat in the yard of the house. From this vantage the baby can watch all the activity around the house and in the neighborhood, but he has few objects to play with. Goldberg reports that the Zambian mothers did not see it as their task to provide play objects for their infants, nor to structure the child's play in any way. And in fact Goldberg says she rarely saw the babies playing with objects, even those that might have been available in the yards.

Yet despite this very limited experience manipulating objects, tests of object permanence showed that the Zambian babies were *ahead* of the American averages on a measure of the object con-

cept at 6 months of age. At 9 and 12 months of age, this pattern was reversed, and the Zambian babies were slightly behind the U.S. norms, but Goldberg believes this difference is due not to any cognitive failure but to the fact that at these ages the Zambian babies were quite unresponsive and passive toward objects, and thus very difficult to test. One possible explanation of this is that in Zambian culture, at least as Goldberg observed it, obedience is a highly valued quality in a child. The baby is trained from very early on to be particularly obedient to prohibitions of various kinds. When the baby plays with some object that he is forbidden to touch, the object is taken away. Perhaps, then, the infant learns that when an object is removed, it means "don't play with that" and he makes no further move to reach for the toy during the object permanence test. This does not necessarily mean that the baby has not understood these later stages of object permanence; it could also mean that our traditional ways of measuring this understanding would need to be modified for these children.

Goldberg's observations thus illustrate both the robustness of some basic developmental patterns *and* the impact of culture on the ways those patterns are displayed by children. Babies in Zambia appear to develop the early steps of the understanding of object permanence even though they have little chance to manipulate objects. But their response to objects is also affected by their training and experience.

▶ Individual Differences in Perception: Speed and Efficiency

I pointed out in the last chapter that the shared patterns of physical development are extremely robust. Virtually the same sequences are seen in all children. The same is clearly true for many of the patterns of perceptual development I've been describing here. But as with physical development, there are nonetheless some individual variations in the process, of which the most interesting are the indications that babies may differ in the efficiency with which they are able to deal with perceptual information.

The most extensive body of research has dealt with variations in "recognition memory" among infants—the ability to recognize that one has seen or experienced some object or person before. We can measure this with a standard habituation test. That is, we can count how many repeated exposures it takes before a baby stops responding with interest to some stimulus. The speed with which such habituation takes place may tell us something about the efficiency of the perceptual/cognitive system and its neurological underpinnings. And if such efficiency lies behind some of the characteristics we normally call "intelligence," then it is possible that individual differences in rate of habituation in the early months of life may predict later intelligence test scores.

That is exactly what researchers have found in studies over the past 15 years. The rate of habituation babies show at 4 or 6 months of age is correlated positively with IQ and language development at 3 or 4 years of age or older; slower habituation is associated with lower IQ and poorer language (McCall & Carriger, 1993). The average correlation is in the range of .45 to .50. This is not an enormous correlation, but it is remarkably high, given the difficulties involved in measuring habituation rate in babies.

Certainly these correlations do not prove that intelligence, as we measure it on an IQ test, is *only* a reflection of some kind of "speed of basic processing." But results like these certainly underline the potential importance of individual differences in perceptual efficiency in early infancy.

❱ Explanations of Perceptual Development

I pointed out at the beginning of this chapter that the study of perception, more than perhaps any other topic in developmental psychology except perhaps intelligence, has been dominated by questions of nature versus nurture, nativism versus empiricism. Certainly there are now other theoretical approaches or issues to choose from, but given the importance of the historical argument between the nativists and the empiricists, it's worthwhile to take a look at just where we stand on this question in our current understanding of perceptual development.

Nativism Versus Empiricism

Arguments for Nativism.   It is certainly not hard to find strong arguments for a nativist position on perceptual development. As researchers have become more and more clever in devising ways to test infants' perceptual skills, they have found more and more skills already present in newborns or very young infants: newborns have good auditory acuity, poor but adequate visual acuity, excellent tactual and taste perception. They have at least some color vision, and have at least rudimentary ability to locate the source of sounds around them.

More important, babies do not have to be taught what to look at. There are "rules" for looking, listening, and touching that can be detected at birth. As Kagan puts it: "Nature has apparently equipped the newborn with an initial bias in the processing of experience. He does not, as the nineteenth-century empiricists believed, have to learn what he should examine" (Kagan, 1971, p. 60). Furthermore, studies like Spelke's work on babies' object understanding points to the strong possibility that other "assumptions" or biases about the way the world is organized may also be built in.

The fact that the "rules" seem to change with age can also be explained in nativist terms, since we know that the nervous system is undergoing rapid maturation during the early months of life, much of it apparently in an automatic way, as synapses are formed rapidly. Furthermore, these "rule changes" seem to occur in bursts. One such set of changes seems to occur at about 2 months, when infants appear to shift away from fixation on contours or edges and toward more detailed analysis of objects or figures. At about the same age the baby becomes able to track objects smoothly. Another shift seems to occur at about 3 or 4 months, when we see a whole host of discrimination skills for the first time, including

What do you think this finding—that babies who habituate faster later have higher IQs—means in practical terms? Could it mean that babies who have had more stimulation in the early months develop more quickly? Could it mean that what we measure with IQ is really all just wiring? What other possibilities can you think of?

depth perception based on kinetic cues, and consistent evidence of cross-modal transfer, especially coordination of auditory and visual information.

Of course it is possible that this apparent pileup of changes at 4 months reflects the accidental fact that many researchers have chosen to study babies of this age rather than younger babies, so we simply know a great deal more about 4-month-olds. But why do researchers choose this age to study? A major reason is that babies this age are significantly easier to test—perhaps because there has now been some underlying maturational shift that makes them more attentive, more able to focus, more stable in state.

Finally, we can find support for a nativist position in comparisons of the perceptual development of babies born *after* the normal gestational period versus those born preterm or at term. In one such study, Yonas (1981) compared the response of two groups of 6-week-old babies: normal-term babies, and a group of babies born 3 to 4 weeks late (postterm). Both sets of infants were tested for depth perception using the method of looming objects. Yonas found that the postterm infants showed more consistent reactions to the looming objects even though both groups had had precisely the same number of weeks of experience with objects since birth. Thus it looks as if it is maturational age, and not experience, that matters in this case, which strengthens a nativist or biological position.

Arguments for Empiricism.   On the other side of the ledger, however, is a great deal of evidence from research with other species that some *minimum level* of experience is necessary to support the development of the perceptual systems—the pattern of environmental effect Aslin calls *maintenance*. For example, animals deprived of light show deterioration of the whole visual system and a consequent decrease in perceptual abilities (Hubel & Weisel, 1963).

It is also possible to find support for the negative version of Aslin's facilitation effect: infants lacking sufficient perceptual stimulation may develop more slowly. Wayne Dennis's study of orphanage babies in Iran, which I described in Chapter 4, illustrates this possibility. The infants who didn't have a chance to look at things, to explore objects with hands and eyes and tongue, and who were deprived of the opportunity to move around freely, were retarded in the development of both perceptual and motor skills.

Attunement, too, may occur. Evidence from studies of other species suggests that those who are completely deprived of visual experiences in the early months of life never develop the same degree of depth perception as do those with full visual experience (Gottlieb, 1976).

The relationship between the built-in process and the role of the environment is a little like the difference between computer hardware and software. The perceptual hardware—specific neural pathways, rules for examining the world, a bias toward searching for patterns, and the like—may be preprogrammed. But the software—the specific program that governs the child's response to a particular real environment—depends on specific experience. A child is *able* to make visual discriminations between people or objects within the first few days or weeks of life. That's built into the hardware. But the specific discriminations she learns, and the number of separate objects she learns to recognize, will depend on her experience. She is initially able to discriminate all the sound contrasts that exist in any spoken language, but the specific sound contrasts she eventually focuses on and the actual language she learns is dependent on the language she hears. The basic system is thus adapted to the specific environment in which the child finds herself. A perfect example of this, of course, is the newborn's ability to discriminate her mother's face from that of a very similar woman's face. Such discrimination *must* be the result of experience, yet the capacity to do so must be built in.

Thus, as is true of virtually all dichotomous theoretical disputes, both sides are correct. Both nature and nurture are involved. No doubt this particular dichotomy will continue to be part of the theoretical vocabulary in studies of perception for a long time to come. But in the past decade or so, theorists have begun to move away from the either/or, yes/no approach to studying perception in young infants and have begun to ask a different set of questions: What are the dimensions of *change* in perceptual skills or preferences with age? What are the roles of context and specific experience in those changes? How are the basic sensory skills, and the basic perceptual discrimination abilities, combined into higher-order perceptual skills, such as judging "objectness" or patterns of sounds or sights? Eleanor Gibson has been one of the key figures in this newer view, so let me sample some of her ideas very briefly, to give you some of the flavor.

An Alternative Theoretical Approach: Eleanor Gibson's Views

Setting aside the nativism/empiricism issue, Gibson turns instead to a search for systematic patterns or dimensions of change in perceptual skills or strategies. She identifies a number of such dimensions (Gibson, 1969; Gibson & Spelke, 1983), four of which are particularly interesting for this discussion.

Purposefulness of Perceptual Activity.   Even as recently as a decade ago, many psychologists thought that the young infant was "captured" by stimulation—that the baby was a relatively passive recipient of stimulation. William James proposed a version of this view over a hundred years ago when he suggested that for the baby, the world was a "blooming, buzzing confusion." Now we know that even the newborn explores the world around herself in an apparently nonrandom way, using some rules, some strategies. Nonetheless, as the child gets older, her rules become more flexibly applied, more intentional, more adapted to the setting.

For example, Brian Vandenberg (1984) gave children aged 4 through 12 years a series of toys to play with, including many novel toys. The younger children tended to have their attention "captured" by one particular toy and to stay with that toy for most of the session. The older children typically looked at and explored all the toys first and then went back to the ones of special interest. Thus as the child gets older, he not only explores more systematically, he does so more intentionally, less controlled by some dominant stimulus.

Awareness of the Meaning of Perceptual Information.   If you see a ball that reflects back the light, you would guess that the ball would feel smooth; you also recognize that round things of a certain size can be held easily in the hand, and thrown. Gibson calls these qualities of objects *affordances*: an object affords the opportunity for certain actions. With development, the infant and the child gradually learn the links between how objects appear and what those objects can do or be used for.

Do you think there might be some individual differences here, too? That is, at any age might there be some children who would be more likely to have their attention captured by something, and others who would scan carefully first? Would such a difference be important in a classroom?

This little guy has clearly learned one of the "affordances" of a bucket: it can carry things.

By school age, children have become considerably less distractible, which is a good thing, because most classrooms are full of noises and activity.

What has been striking in the recent research is the demonstration that almost from the first day of life, babies do pay attention to some such affordances. They notice the underlying pattern, the *information* given in some object or stimulus (Pick, 1986). Over the years of toddlerhood and early childhood they discover more subtle, more complex, or more superordinate meanings or affordances. This development is especially hastened when the baby is able to move more freely on his own, since that enables him to explore objects in new ways.

Degree of Differentiation. Gibson suggests that initially the baby focuses on fairly big chunks or prominent features. With development, the child focuses on more and more detail, on finer gradations, on more difficult discriminations. Newborns pay attention to only a few features, such as the edges of things or movement; older babies attend to many more properties of objects, including their texture, color, shape, density, flexibility, and the like. In each of these areas, the child's discriminations become still more subtle in the preschool and later years—although there are interesting exceptions here, such as the *loss* of discriminability of speech sounds not heard in the child's language environment.

Ignoring the Irrelevant. The fourth dimension Gibson suggests is a gradually improving ability to ignore the irrelevant. This ability is obviously part of what is needed for the child to acquire the various perceptual constancies. But more generally, the child becomes slowly more efficient at focusing on the essentials in some situation, and ignoring everything else. If you're taking an exam, you have to be able to focus your attention on the questions and on your thinking, and not be distracted by the snuffling of the person next to you, or the discomfort of the seat, or even your own anxiety. Similarly, a child in a noisy classroom must learn to focus his attention on the teacher's voice and ignore the voices of the children around him. Children become steadily better at identifying what is irrelevant, and then ignoring it. In one study, for example, Higgins and Turnure (1984) gave preschoolers, second graders, and sixth graders easy and difficult learning tasks to do, with music playing in the background. Preschoolers were much more disrupted by the sound than were older children. In fact the sixth graders actually performed better when there was music playing, as if the distractor forced them to focus their attention more fully on the task.

This sample of Gibson's ideas does not begin to convey the richness of her thinking or the extent of her influence on current researchers, such as Elizabeth Spelke. Whether Gibson's views will form the framework for a dominant future theory of perceptual development is not yet clear. But she has at least helped to turn the field away from a preoccupation with answering questions about whether newborns can do X or Y toward what may be a much more fruitful search for underlying patterns of change or continuity.

❱ Perceptual Development: A Summing-Up

The research on perceptual development in the early years of life has called into question a whole series of previously cherished beliefs about infants and their abilities. Despite their many limitations, infants seem to approach and respond to the world around them in a much more organized and sophisticated way than most psychologists thought 20 or 30 years ago. And the fact that babies respond

Bower, T. G. R. (1989). *The rational infant*. New York: Freeman.

This is the most recent description and theory about infant perception from one of the major researchers and theorists in this area.

Haith, M. M. (1990). Progress in the understanding of sensory and perceptual processes in early infancy. *Merrill-Palmer Quarterly, 36*, 1–26.

In this relatively brief paper Haith looks back on the last 25 years of research on perceptual development. He comments not only on the knowledge gained but on the processes by which scientific progress has been made and the tasks still facing the field. Very interesting reading.

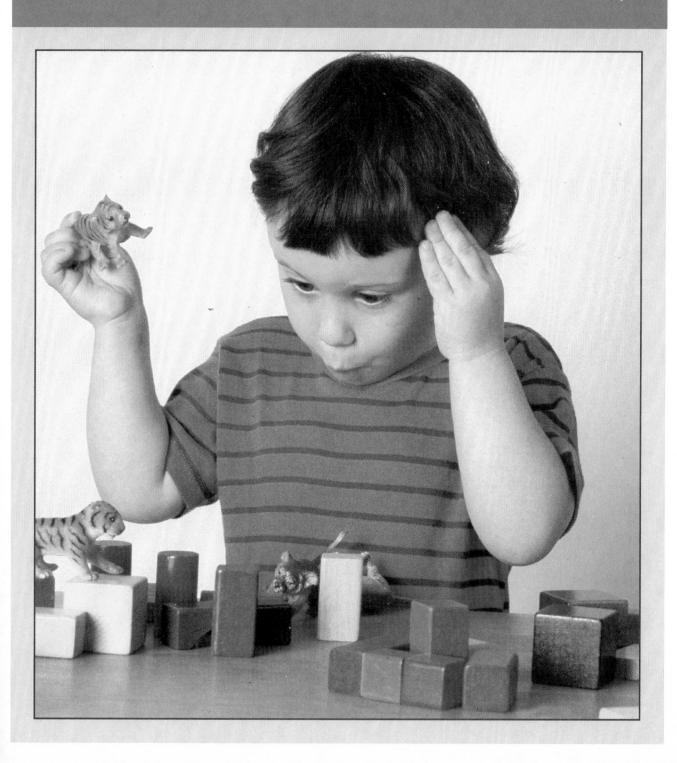

COGNITIVE DEVELOPMENT I: COGNITIVE POWER

6

Three Views of Intelligence

Measuring Intellectual Power: IQ Tests and Other Measures
The First IQ Tests
Modern IQ Tests
Achievement Tests
• *The Real World:* *Performance Tests: A New Way to Measure School Achievement*

Stability and Predictive Value of IQ Tests
Stability of Test Scores
What IQ Tests Predict
Limitations of Traditional IQ Tests

An Alternative View: Sternberg's Triarchic Theory of Intelligence

Explaining Differences in IQ
Evidence for the Importance of Heredity
Evidence for the Importance of Environment
Specific Family Characteristics and IQ

• *Cultures and Contexts:* *Maternal "Responsiveness" in Different Cultures*
School Experience and Special Interventions

Interaction of Heredity and Environment

Group Differences in IQ: Race and Sex Differences
Racial Differences in IQ
• *Cultures and Contexts in the Real World:* *IQ Testing of Blacks in the Schools*
• *Cultures and Contexts:* *How Asian Teachers Teach Math and Science So Effectively*
Sex Differences in IQ

The Measurement of Intelligence: A Last Look

Summary

Key Terms

Suggested Readings

Last year my husband and I lived in Germany for eight months. Because he was born in Germany, and has many relatives there who speak no English, it seemed like a good idea for me to learn enough German to be able to speak to his family. So I took intensive German classes, and struggled to learn new vocabulary and complex grammar. The whole process turned out to be a lot harder than I had expected, but it certainly gave me a chance to observe the ways I go about learning, remembering, and using new information. I had, throughout, an almost physical sense of my brain at work, struggling to create order and sense out of a bombardment of new information. (Periodically my brain would simply go on strike, and refuse to take in anything more—a sensation I suspect most of you have had at one time or another.)

In our everyday lives, each of us faces myriad tasks that call for the same kinds of skills I had to use in learning a new language. We study for exams, try to remember what to buy at the grocery store, balance the checkbook, remember phone numbers, use a map. Not all of us do these things equally well or equally quickly. But all of us perform such activities every day of our lives.

These activities are all part of what we normally describe as *cognitive functioning* or "intelligence." What I will be exploring in this and the next chapter is how we have all acquired the ability to do all these things. One-year-olds cannot use maps or balance a checkbook. How do they come to be able to do so? And how do we explain the fact that not all children learn these things at the same rate, or become as skilled?

Answering questions like these has been complicated by the fact that there are three distinctly different views of cognition or intelligence, each of which has led to a separate body of research and commentary. Blending the three turns out to be a tricky task—one that I don't want to attempt until I have first presented each view separately.

▶ Three Views of Intelligence

Historically, the first approach to studying cognitive development or intelligence was focused on individual differences. People clearly differ in their intellectual skill, their ability to remember lists for the grocery store, the speed with which they solve problems or learn new words, their ability to analyze complex situations. When we say someone is "bright" or "very intelligent," it is just such skills we mean, and our label is based on the assumption that we can rank-order people in their degree of "brightness." It was precisely this assumption that led to the development of intelligence tests, which were designed simply to give us a way of measuring such individual differences in intellectual *power*.

This "power" definition of intelligence, also referred to as a *psychometric* approach, held sway for many years. But it has one great weakness: it does not deal with the fact that intelligence develops. As children grow, their thinking becomes more and more abstract and complex. If you give a 5-year-old a mental list of things to remember to buy at the grocery store she will have trouble remembering more than a few items. She is also very unlikely to use good strategies to aid her memory, such as rehearsing the list, or organizing the items into groups. An 8-year-old would remember more things, and probably would rehearse the list under his breath, or in his head, as he was walking to the store.

The fact that intelligence develops in this way forms the foundation of the second great tradition in the study of cognitive development, the *cognitive developmental* approach of Jean Piaget and his many followers. Piaget's focus was on the development of cognitive *structures* rather than on intellectual power, on patterns of development that are *common* to all children rather than on individual differences.

Is this what you mean when you say someone is "bright" or "intelligent"? What else do you mean by these terms?

These two traditions have lived side by side for several decades, rather like not-very-friendly neighbors who smile vaguely at one another when they meet but never get together for coffee. In the past few years, though, the two have developed a mutual friend—a third view, called the *information processing approach,* that at least partially integrates the first two. Proponents of this third view argue that what is needed is an understanding of the *underlying processes* or strategies that make up all cognitive activity. Joseph Fagan (1992) puts it this way:

> Intelligence is not a faculty or trait of the mind. Intelligence is not mental content. Intelligence is processing. *Knowledge is gained as the result of the assimilation,* over time, *of information by the intellectual processes.* (p. 82, emphasis in original)

Researchers in this tradition obviously ask a different kind of question: What are the basic intellectual processes and how should we measure them? One of the strengths of this approach is that once we have identified such basic processes, we can then ask *both* developmental and individual-differences questions: Do these basic processes change with age, and do people differ in their speed or skill in using them? The research on individual differences in infants' speed of habituation or "recognition memory," which I described briefly in Chapter 5, is an example of one body of research that has emerged from this new theoretical model.

Each of these three views tells us something useful and different about intelligence, so we need to look at all three. In other chapters I usually begin by talking about developmental changes and then turn to a discussion of individual differences. But in this case, I will follow the historical pattern and begin in this chapter by describing the oldest of these three traditions—the measurement of individual differences in intellectual skill. In the next chapter I'll talk about Piaget's views of developmental changes in intellectual structure, and about information processing.

Three-year-old Anna is having a fine time figuring out how to lift the spoon with a magnet. How might you describe the "intelligence" of her behavior from each of the three different perspectives?

▶ Measuring Intellectual Power: IQ Tests and Other Measures

Intelligence tests have a certain mystique about them, and most of us have a greatly inflated notion of the permanence or importance of an IQ score. If you are going to acquire a more realistic view, it's important for you to know something about what such tests were designed to do, and something about the beliefs and values of the men and women who devised them.

The First IQ Tests

The first modern intelligence test was published in 1905 by two Frenchmen, Alfred Binet and Theodore Simon. From the beginning, the test was based on the assumption that individuals differed in mental ability. Equally important, the test had a practical purpose, which was to identify those children who would have difficulty in school. For this reason, the tests Binet and Simon devised were school-like tasks, such as measures of vocabulary, comprehension of facts and relationships, and mathematical and verbal reasoning. For example, can the child describe the difference between wood and glass? Can the young child touch his nose, his ear, his head? Can the child tell which of two weights is heavier?

Lewis Terman and his associates at Stanford University (Terman, 1916; Terman & Merrill, 1937) modified and extended many of Binet's original tests when they translated and revised the tests for use in the U.S. The several Terman revisions, called the **Stanford-Binet,** consist of a series of individual tests for children of each age. There are six tests for 4-year-olds, six tests for 5-year-olds, and so on. When a child takes the tests, he is first given the tests for the year below his actual age, then the tests for his own age, moving upward in age until a level is reached at which he fails them all.

Terman initially described a child's performance in terms of a score called an **intelligence quotient,** later shortened to **IQ.** This score was computed by comparing the child's chronological age with his *mental age* (the level of questions he could answer correctly). For example, a child who could solve the problems for a 6-year-old and half of those for a 7-year-old would have a mental age of 6.5. The formula used to calculate the IQ was

$$\text{Mental age}/\text{Chronological age} \times 100 = \text{IQ}$$

This formula results in an IQ above 100 for children whose mental age is higher than their chronological age and an IQ below 100 for children whose mental age is below their chronological age.

This old system for calculating the IQ is not used any longer, even in the modern revisions of the Stanford-Binet. Nowadays IQs from any type of test are calculated by a direct comparison of a child's performance with those of a large group of other children his own age. But an IQ of 100 is still average, and higher and lower scores still mean above- and below-average performance. The majority of children achieve scores that are right around the average of 100, with a smaller number scoring very high or very low. Figure 6.1 shows the distribution of IQ scores that we would see if we gave the test to thousands of children. You can see that two-thirds of all children will achieve scores between 85 and 115. The groups we refer to as *gifted* or *retarded,* both of which I'll discuss in some detail in Chapter 15, clearly represent only very small fractions of the distribution.

Figure 6.1
The approximate distribution of scores on most modern IQ tests, along with the labels typically used for scores at various levels. The tests are designed so that the average score is 100 and two-thirds of the scores fall between 85 and 115. Because of brain damage and genetic anomalies, there are slightly more low-IQ children than there are very high-IQ children.

Modern IQ Tests

The tests used most frequently by psychologists today are the Revised Stanford-Binet and the Wechsler Intelligence Scale for Children, usually called the **WISC,** which was developed by David Wechsler (1974). The most current revision is called the WISC-III. On the WISC, each child is tested with 10 different types of problems, each ranging from very easy to very hard. The 10 tests are divided into two subgroups, one calling strongly on verbal skills (e.g., vocabulary, describing similarities between objects, general information) and the other involving less-verbal types of thinking, called collectively *performance* tests, such as arranging pictures in an order that tells a story, or copying a pattern using a set of colored blocks. Many psychologists find this distinction between verbal and performance tests helpful, because significant unevenness in a child's test skill may indicate particular kinds of learning problems.

This second grader is working on one of the subtests of the WISC, in which he must use a set of blocks to try to copy the design shown in the book.

Infant Tests.   Neither the Binet nor the WISC can be used with infants much younger than about 3. Infants and toddlers don't talk well, if at all, and the usual childhood tests rely heavily on language. So how do we measure "intelligence" in an infant? This becomes an important question if we want to be able to identify, during infancy, those children who are not developing normally, or if we want to predict later intelligence or school performance.

Most "infant IQ tests," such as the **Bayley Scales of Infant Development** (Bayley, 1969), were constructed rather like IQ tests for older children in that they included series of items of increasing difficulty. But instead of testing school-like skills—skills an infant does not yet have—the items measure primarily sensory and motor skills, such as reaching for a dangling ring (an item for a typical 3-month-old), putting cubes in a cup on request (9 months), or building a tower of three cubes (17 months). Some more clearly cognitive items are also included, such as uncovering a toy hidden by a cloth, an item used with 8-month-old infants to measure an aspect of object permanence.

Tests like the Bayley have proven to be helpful in identifying infants and toddlers who are not developing normally. They are far less useful in predicting later IQ as measured by the Binet or the WISC—a point I will return to shortly. Whether newer tests, like the 1993 revision of the Bayley, will prove to be more predictive of later IQ remains to be seen. But on the whole it looks as if what is being measured on typical infant tests is not the same as what is tapped by the common childhood or adult intelligence tests (Colombo, 1993).

Achievement Tests

Another kind of test of intellectual skill with which you are probably more personally familiar is the **achievement test,** which nearly all of you have taken in elementary and high school. Achievement tests are designed to test *specific* information learned in school, using items like those in Table 6.1 (p. 168). The child taking an achievement test doesn't end up with an IQ score, but his performance is still compared to that of other children in the same grade across the country.

In the United States, virtually all fourth graders—like these in Austin, Texas—are given achievement tests, so as to allow schools to compare their students' performance against national norms.

How are these tests different from IQ tests? IQ tests are intended to tell us something about how well a child *can* think and learn, while an achievement test tells us something about what a child *has* learned. Or, to put it another way, the designers of IQ tests thought they were measuring the child's basic capacity, her underlying **competence,** while an achievement test is intended to measure what

---

TABLE 6.1   Some Sample Items from a Fourth-Grade Achievement Test

Vocabulary

jolly old man

1. angry
2. fat
3. merry
4. sorry

Language expression

Who wants ___ books?

1. that
2. these
3. them
4. this

Mathematics

What does the "3" in 13 stand for?

1. 3 ones
2. 13 ones
3. 3 tens
4. 13 tens

Reference skills

Which of these words would be first in ABC order?

1. pair
2. point
3. paint
4. polish

Spelling

Jason took the *cleanest* glass.

right ___   wrong ___

Mathematics computation

79	149	62
+14	−87	×3

Source: From Comprehensive Tests of Basic Skills, Form S. Reprinted by permission of the publisher, CTB/McGraw-Hill, Del Monte Research Park, Monterey, CA 93940. Copyright © 1973 by McGraw-Hill, Inc. All rights reserved. Printed in the USA.

---

the child has actually learned (her **performance**). This is an important distinction. Each of us presumably has some upper limit of ability—what we could do under ideal conditions, when we are maximally motivated, well, and rested. But since everyday conditions are rarely ideal we typically perform below our hypothetical ability.

In fact, it is not possible to measure competence. We can never be sure that we are assessing any ability under the best of all possible circumstances. We *always* measure performance. The authors of the famous IQ tests believed that by standardizing the procedures for administering and scoring the tests they could come close to measuring competence. Certainly it is good practice to design the best possible test and to administer it carefully. But it is important to understand that no test really measures "underlying" competence, only performance when the test is taken.

James, who is just 17 months old, would clearly pass the 17-month item on the Bayley Scales of Infant Development that calls for the child to build a tower of three blocks.

If you follow this logic to the end, you realize that all IQ tests are really achievement tests. The difference between tests called IQ tests and those called achievement tests is really a matter of degree. IQ tests include items that are designed to tap fairly fundamental intellectual processes like comparison or analysis; the achievement tests call for specific information the child has learned in school or elsewhere. College entrance tests, like the Scholastic Aptitude Tests (SATs, which many of you have taken recently) fall somewhere in between. They are designed to measure basic "developed abilities," such as the ability to reason with words, rather than just specific knowledge. All three types of tests, though, measure aspects of a child or young person's performance and not competence.

▌ Stability and Predictive Value of IQ Tests

For most psychologists, the critical question about IQ tests is not whether they measure intellectual competence, but whether the scores are stable, and whether they predict anything interesting or useful. Many of you will recognize these as issues of the *reliability* and *validity* of the tests.

Stability of Test Scores

One of the bits of folklore about IQ tests is that a particular IQ score is something you "have," like blue eyes or red hair—that a child who achieves a score of, say, 115 at 3 years of age will continue to score in about the same range at age 6 or 12 or 20. This is less true than you probably think.

First of all, as I pointed out earlier, scores on infant IQ tests like the Bayley are not strongly related to later IQs. The typical correlation between a 12-month

THE REAL WORLD
Performance Tests: A New Way to Measure School Achievement

Traditional achievement tests, like IQ tests, are designed to show how well a given child, or a classroom of children, performs against some average or norm. Hence both achievement and IQ tests are sometimes referred to as *norm-referenced*. In both cases the norm is the performance of the average child of a given age. An alternative way to think about testing is to define some criterion, some absolute standard that you think all children should meet, and compare each child's performance to that criterion. Many educators today are advocating exactly such *criterion-referenced* tests. Collectively such tests have come to be called **performance tests.**

For example, suppose that one of the goals of an educational system is that each student be able to write clearly and persuasively, using complete sentences and correct grammar. Such a skill can only be assessed with a test that actually asks the students to write something. Then each student's writing can be evaluated against some absolute standard as acceptable or not acceptable. Similarly, a performance test in science or mathematics might involve an actual science experiment. Children would complete the experiment on their own, and describe and explain the results in writing.

An example would probably help. In one reading/writing test devised as part of the Maryland School Performance Assessment Program, eighth graders are asked to read and write about the intense cold of the winter in the Yukon Territory of Canada. They read a story by Jack London called "To Build a Fire," about a man who dies of the cold. Later they also read a brief excerpt entitled "Hypothermia: Causes, Effects, Prevention." Over several days, the students answer questions in test booklets about these readings, discuss some of the material in class, and at the end must write a piece giving advice to a group of friends about what they would need to do to stay safe on a winter hiking trip, or a story or play or poem expressing their feelings about extreme states, or a speech intended to persuade people not to travel in the Yukon (Mitchell, 1992).

Here's another example, this time from a mathematics performance test for junior high school students:

> *Five students have test scores of 62, 75, 80, 86, and 92. Find the average score. How much is the average score increased if each student's score is increased by 1, 5, 8, or X points? Write a statement about how much the average score is increased if each individual score is increased X points,* and write an argument to convince another student that the statement is true. (Mitchell, 1992, p. 67)

The students' performance on both the writing and mathematics tests are normally scored (by experts, usually on a statewide basis) on a four-point or six-point scale, with the top one or two points reserved for those performances that meet the criterion, and lower scores for unacceptably poor responses. Thus the issue is not whether the students in some class or school do better or worse than other children, but whether each one individually meets some absolute standard.

Tests like these are now in use in a number of states in the United States, as well as in England and Wales, where many of the performance tests of science and mathematics were first devised. They are more complicated (and more expensive) to administer and score than are norm-referenced achievement tests, but they are growing in popularity not only because they assess the actual behaviors or skills educators are interested in, but also because the very existence of such tests shapes the way in which reading, writing, science, and mathematics are taught in the classroom. Just as teachers who know their students will be tested with standard achievement tests inevitably "teach to the test," so teachers who know their students will be tested with performance tests of reading, writing, math, or science must change the way they teach these subjects to be sure that their students acquire the needed reasoning and communication skills. Since these are precisely the skills that most educators believe should be taught in schools, performance tests may prove to be a vehicle for educational reform.

Bayley mental test score and a 4-year-old Binet IQ is only about .20 to .30 (Mc-Call, 1979)—significant, but not robust. Newer tests of infant intelligence, such as those based on habituation rates or other basic processes, may ultimately prove to be more helpful predictors (Colombo, 1993). But at the moment, there is no widely used method of reliably predicting which 1-year-olds will later have high or low IQ scores.

Beginning at about age 3, consistency in IQ test performance on tests like the Binet or WISC increases markedly. If two tests are given a few months or a few years apart, the scores are likely to be very similar. The correlations between adjacent-year IQ scores in middle childhood, for example, are typically in the range of .80 (Honzik, 1986). This high level of predictability, however, masks an interesting fact: most children show quite wide fluctuations in their scores. Robert McCall and his colleagues (1973), for example, looked at the test scores of a group of 80 children who had been given IQ tests at regular intervals from the time they were 2½ until they were 17. The *average* difference between the highest and the lowest score achieved by each child in this group was 28 points, and one child in seven showed a shift of more than 40 points. You can see several examples in Figure 6.2.

Such wide fluctuations are more common in young children. The general rule of thumb is that the older the child the more stable the IQ score becomes. Older children may show some fluctuation in scores in response to major stresses such as parental divorce, or changing schools, or the birth of a sibling, but by age 10 or so, IQ scores are normally highly stable.

What IQ Tests Predict

What do these stable scores predict? In the case of IQ tests, following in Binet's footsteps, psychologists have most often looked at predictions of school perfor-

Given the degree of variability I have described, does it make sense to select children for special classes, such as classes for the gifted, on the basis of a single test score? How else could you go about it?

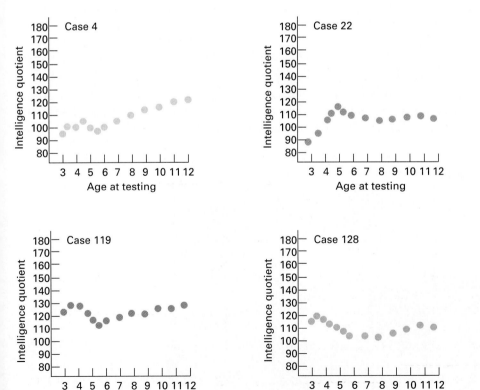

Figure 6.2
The IQ scores of these four children, who were tested repeatedly from early childhood through adolescence, illustrate some of the kinds of changes in IQ scores that can occur over time. (*Source:* Sontag, Baker, & Nelson, 1958, Appendix, pp. 58, 61, 77, 79. Copyright by The Society for Research in Child Development, Inc. Excerpted by permission.)

mance. The research findings on this point are quite consistent: The correlation between a child's test score and her grades in school or performance on other school tests is about .60 (Carver, 1990; Sattler, 1988). This is a strong, but by no means perfect, correlation. It tells us that on the whole, children with top IQ scores will also be among the high achievers in school, and those who score low will be among the low achievers. Still, some children with high IQ scores don't shine in school while some lower-IQ children do.

IQ scores also predict future grades as well as current grades. Preschool children with high IQ scores will tend to do better when they enter school than those with lower scores; elementary-school-age children with higher IQs later do better in high school as well.

It is important to point out that this relationship holds *within* each social class and racial group in the United States. Among the poor, among African-Americans and Hispanics, those with higher IQs are most likely to get good grades, complete high school, and go on to college (Brody, 1992). So this link between IQ and educational achievement is not produced simply by the fact that middle-class kids have both higher IQs and better chances to go on to college.

The fact that these predictions hold for children reared in poverty as well as for children from more affluent families has led a number of theorists to argue that intelligence adds to the child's *resilience*—a concept I talked about in Chapter 1 (Garmezy & Masten, 1991). Numerous studies now show that poor children, be they white, Hispanic, African-American, or other minority group, are far more likely to develop the kind of self-confidence and personal competence it takes to move out of poverty if they have higher IQs (Long & Vaillant, 1984; Luthar & Zigler, 1992; Werner & Smith, 1992). At the other end of the scale, low intelligence is associated with a number of negative long-term outcomes, including adult illiteracy, delinquency in adolescence, and criminal behavior in adulthood (Stattin & Klackenberg-Larsson, 1993). For example, in a 20-year longitudinal study of a group of children born to black teenage mothers in Baltimore, Nazli Baydar (Baydar, Brooks-Gunn, & Furstenberg, 1993) has found that the

How or why do you think a higher IQ makes a child more resilient? For example, in what specific ways might the life of a brighter child living in a slum be different from the life of a less-bright child in the same environment?

Among these high school students, those with higher IQs are not only likely to get better grades, they are more likely to go on to college. Intelligence also adds to the child's resilience—his ability to survive stress, including poverty.

or contextual intelligence may be required as much as or more than the types of skills measured on IQ tests (Sternberg & Wagner, 1993). These are important points to keep in mind as we move on to questions about the origins of individual differences in IQ. What we know about "intelligence" is almost entirely restricted to information about componential intelligence—the kind of intelligence demanded in school. We know almost nothing about the origins or long-term consequences of variations in experiential or contextual intelligence.

Car salesmen, to be successful, probably need a good deal of what Sternberg calls contextual intelligence, or "street smarts."

⟩ Explaining Differences in IQ

You will not be surprised to discover that the arguments about the origins of differences in IQ nearly always boil down to a dispute about nature versus nurture. When Binet and Simon wrote the first IQ test, they did not assume that intelligence as measured on an IQ test was fixed or inborn. But many of the American psychologists who revised and promoted the use of the tests *did* believe that intellectual capacity was inherited and largely fixed at birth. Those who took this view, and those who believed that the environment played a crucial role in shaping a child's intellectual performance, have been arguing for at least 60 years. Let me walk you through some of the major points.

Evidence for the Importance of Heredity

You've already read about some of the evidence for the influence of heredity on IQ. (You may want to go back to the research report on page 7 for a quick review.) You'll recall that identical twins reared together have IQ scores that are highly correlated (.85 on average), while the correlation for same-sex fraternal twins reared together is about .58. The correlation for identical twins reared apart falls somewhere in between (Brody, 1992). This is precisely the pattern of correlations we would expect if there were a strong genetic element at work.

The most common finding in adoption studies is that adopted children's IQs can be predicted better from knowing the IQs or the level of education of their birth parents than from knowing the IQs or education of their adoptive parents (Brody, 1992; Loehlin, Horn, & Willerman, 1989; Phillips & Fulker, 1989; Scarr & Weinberg, 1983). This pattern of findings also supports a genetic explanation.

Evidence for the Importance of Environment

Adoption studies also provide some strong support for an environmental influence on IQ scores, because the actual *level* of IQ scores of adopted children is clearly affected by the environment in which they have grown up. Early studies of adopted children involved mostly children born to poverty-level parents who were adopted into middle-class families. Such children typically have IQs that are 10 to 15 points higher than that of their birth mother (Scarr & Kidd, 1983), suggesting that the effect of the middle-class adoptive family was to raise the child's IQ. But this doesn't tell us whether a *less*-stimulating adoptive family would *lower* the IQ of a child born to average or above-average-IQ parents. That piece of information is now available from a French study by Christiane Capron and Michel Duyme (1989). They identified a group of 38 children, all adopted in infancy, who represent all possible combinations of high and low social class and education in the birth parents and the adoptive parents. Table 6.3 shows the children's

	TABLE 6.3 IQ Scores at Adolescence for Capron and Duyme's Adopted Children		
		Social Class of Adoptive Parents	
Social Class of Adoptive Parents		**High**	**Low**
	High	119.60	107.50
	Low	103.60	92.40

Source: Capron & Duyme (1989), Table 2, p. 553.

IQ scores in adolescence. If you look across both rows, you can see that there is a difference of 11 or 12 points between the IQs of children reared in upper-class homes and those reared in lower-class families, no matter what the social class level or education of the birth parents. At the same time, the data also show a genetic effect, because the children *born to* upper-class parents have higher IQs than do those from lower-class families, no matter what kind of rearing environment they encountered.

Social Class Differences. This relationship between social class and IQ, so clear in the Capron and Duyme study, is echoed in a great deal of other research: Children from poor or working-class families, or from families in which the parents are relatively uneducated, have lower average IQs than do children from middle-class families. You can see this effect particularly vividly in Figure 6.3, which is based on data from a huge national study of over 50,000 children born in 12 different hospitals around the U.S. between 1959 and 1966 (Broman, Nichols, & Kennedy, 1975). In this figure, in order to make sure that we are not confounding social class and ethnic differences, I have given only the results for white children who were tested with the Stanford-Binet at age 4, a total sample of over 11,800 children. As you can see in the figure, the average IQ of the children rises as the family social class rises, and as the mother's education rises.

These differences are *not* found on standardized tests of infant IQ such as the Bayley (Golden & Birns, 1983). But after age $2^{1}/_{2}$ or 3, social class differences appear to widen steadily with age (Farran, Haskins, & Gallagher, 1980), producing what is sometimes called a **cumulative deficit.** The differences are especially large on *verbal* tests (Jordan, Huttenlocher, & Levine, 1992).

Genetic differences could obviously be contributing to the pattern in Figure 6.3, since brighter parents presumably have more education and earn more money, and also pass on their "bright" genes to their children. The results could also be due to differences in prenatal risks, diet, or general health. In addition, there are also real differences in the ways infants and children are treated in these two groups of families that are independently important in cognitive development. It is these differences in early experiences that have been the focus of most of the research on environmental effects on IQ.

Specific Family Characteristics and IQ

When we watch the ways individual families interact with their infants or young children, and then follow the children over time to see which ones later have

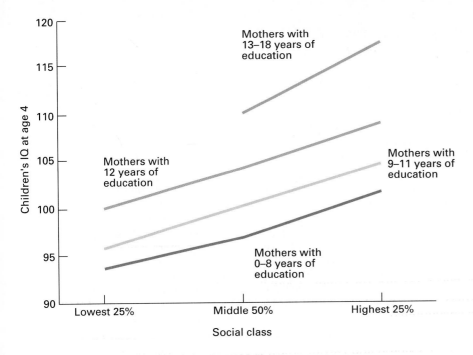

Figure 6.3
Each line represents the IQ scores for 4-year-old white children whose mothers had a particular level of education, and who lived in each of three different social class environments. Clearly, both the mother's education and her social class are related to the child's IQ. (*Source:* Broman, Nichols, & Kennedy, 1975, p. 47.)

high or low IQs, we can begin to get some sense of the kinds of specific family interactions that foster higher scores. At least five dimensions of family interaction or stimulation seem to make a difference. Parents of higher-IQ children tend to do the following:

1. They provide an *interesting and complex physical environment* for the child, including play materials that are appropriate for the child's age and developmental level (Bradley et al., 1989).
2. They are *emotionally responsive* to and *involved* with their child. They respond warmly and contingently to the child's behavior, smiling when the child smiles, talking when the child speaks, answering the child's questions, and in myriad ways responding to the child's cues (Barnard et al., 1989; Bradley & Caldwell, 1984; Lewis, 1993).
3. They *talk to their child*, using language that is descriptively rich and accurate (Sigman et al., 1988).
4. They *avoid excessive restrictiveness*, punitiveness, or control, instead giving the child room to explore, even opportunities to make mistakes (Bradley et al., 1989; Olson, Bates, & Kaskie, 1992b).
5. They *expect* their child to do well and to develop rapidly. They emphasize and press for school achievement (Entwisle & Alexander, 1990).

You may have figured out that there is a methodological problem in research of this type. Because parents provide *both* the genes and the environment, we can't be sure that these environmental characteristics are really causally important. Perhaps these are simply the environmental features provided by brighter parents, and it is the genes and not the environment that cause the higher IQs in

This kind of rich, complex, stimulating environment is consistently linked to higher IQs in children.

CULTURES AND CONTEXTS
Maternal "Responsiveness" in Different Cultures

Many studies in the U.S. and other Western countries have pointed to the central importance of parental *responsiveness* for the child's intellectual and social development. Babies whose mothers and fathers respond to their sounds by talking to the infant, who smile when the baby smiles, who pick up on the baby's other signals, later turn out to have higher IQs, better language, and more secure attachments.

Since this aspect of the parent-infant interaction appears to be so significant, it seems especially important for us to discover if the same relationship holds in other cultures and contexts. Amy Richman and her colleagues (Richman, Miller, & LeVine, 1992) have taken a first step toward answering this question with two studies in other cultures. They compared responsiveness among American and Kenyan mothers, and they observed the responsiveness of Mexican mothers who varied in level of education.

In the Kenyan/American comparison, Richman observed marked differences in the ways mothers responded to their babies. When the Kenyan babies vocalized, cried, or looked at the mother, their mothers were most likely to pick them up and hold them. Mothers in Boston were far more likely to talk to or look at their babies in response to the same baby signals.

There are profound cultural differences at work here. The Kenyan mothers, all from the Gusii tribe, said that they thought it was ridiculous to talk to a baby before the baby is capable of speech. This culture also has different social conventions about eye contact during speech: mutual gaze is much less common than in the U.S. and other Western cultures. Thus the ways the mothers behave with their babies is entirely consistent with cultural beliefs and interaction patterns.

It is also important to note that the two groups did not differ in their absolute amount of responsiveness. Thus both groups of mothers are "responsive" to their babies. But they respond in very different ways. The Gusii mothers "show a pattern of responsiveness that is strikingly designed to reduce distress and maintain calm in the infant during the 1st year of life" (p. 620). In contrast, the responsiveness of the Boston mothers seems designed to stimulate the baby and encourage further interaction.

The Mexican mothers, as a group, showed yet another pattern. They were most likely to look at the baby when the infant vocalized or looked at them, and less likely to pick the baby up than were the Gusii mothers. But they responded to the baby's signals with speech about as often as the Boston mothers did. What is especially interesting here is that Richman found that the amount of formal education the Mexican mothers had received was related to their pattern of responsiveness. The more formal education they had (and the maximum was only about eight or nine years), the more their pattern of responsiveness was like the Boston mothers'. Studies in the U.S. also show that the mother's education is linked in this same way to her manner of interacting with her baby. This does not mean that the Gusii mothers behave as they do because they have little formal education. We don't know if that is the case, and we do know that there are other cultural values and beliefs among the Gusii that contribute to the pattern of responsiveness these mothers show. But the results from the Mexican women show at least that the link between education and patterns of responsiveness is not unique to U.S. samples.

What Richman's study does not tell us is whether these varying styles of responsiveness have differential effects on the child's cognitive development. That piece of the puzzle will have to await further cross-cultural research.

their children. The way around this problem is to look at the link between environmental features and IQ in adopted children. Fortunately we have a few studies of this type, and they point to the same critical environmental features. That is, among adoptive families, those that behave in the ways listed above have adopted children who score higher on IQ tests (Plomin, Loehlin, & DeFries, 1985).

Differences in Environments Within Families.   Within families, there are also differences in the experiences of individual children that affect IQ. Being the oldest of a large family, for example, is a very different experience from being the youngest or being in the middle; being the only girl in a family of boys is different from being a girl with only sisters. Psychologists are just beginning to study these within-family variables. Thus far, we have been looking mostly at fairly obvious differences, like how many children there are in a family, or the child's position within the family, both of which seem to be at least slightly related to the child's IQ. On average, the more children there are in the family, the lower the average IQ of the children. And on average, firstborn children have the highest IQs, with average IQs declining steadily as you go down the birth order (Zajonc, 1983; Zajonc & Marcus, 1975). Children who are born very close together also have slightly lower IQs on average than do those born further apart (Storfer, 1990). One fairly typical set of data is in Figure 6.4, based on scores of nearly 800,000 students who took the National Merit Scholarship examination in 1965, with the scores converted to the equivalent of IQ scores.

Please notice that the differences shown in this figure are not huge. Yet this pattern has been observed repeatedly, in European samples as well as those in the U.S., and leaves us with a puzzle. Why would such a pattern occur? Robert Zajonc's hypothesis is that the birth of each succeeding child "dilutes" the intellectual climate of the home. The oldest child initially interacts only with his parents and thus has a maximally complex and enriching environment. Second- or later-born children, in contrast, experience a lower average intellectual level in the family simply because they interact with both other children and adults. A later-born child *may* have an advantage if the children are very widely spaced, since then he is interacting entirely with others who are intellectually advanced, including both parents and much older siblings.

This hypothesis has prompted a good deal of debate and criticism (Rogers, 1984); most researchers have concluded that it is probably not the right way to conceptualize what is going on, because the data do not always fit the predictions. But no one has yet offered a better explanation. To solve this puzzle, we will need to know a good deal more about the actual experiences of children in different birth-order positions, and in large versus small families.

School Experience and Special Interventions

Home environments and family interactions are not the only source of environmental influence. Many young children also spend a very large amount of time in group care settings, including day care, special programs like Head Start, or regu-

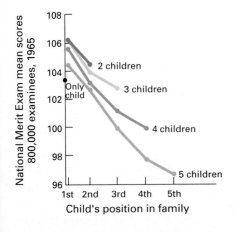

Figure 6.4
These data from the 1965 National Merit Scholarship Qualifying Test show the commonly found relationship between test scores and family size and birth order. Within each family size, the average score is highest for the firstborn and declines with each position in the birth order sequence. (*Sources:* Data from Breland, 1974, recalculated by Storfer, 1990, Table 7, p. 32.)

lar preschools. How much effect do these environments have on the child's intellectual performance?

On a theoretical level, this question is of interest because it may tell us something about early experience in general, and about the resilience of children. Are the effects of an initially impoverished environment permanent, or can they be offset by an enriched experience, such as a special preschool? At a practical level, programs like Head Start are based squarely on the assumption that it *is* possible to modify the trajectory of a child's intellectual development, especially if you intervene early.

Attempts to test this assumption have led to a messy body of research. In particular, children are rarely assigned randomly to Head Start or non–Head Start groups, which makes interpretation difficult. Still, there is some agreement on the effects. Children enrolled in Head Start or other enriched preschool programs, compared to similar children without such preschool, normally show a gain of about 10 IQ points during the year of the Head Start experience. This IQ gain typically fades and then disappears within the first few years of elementary school (McKey et al., 1985), but there is nonetheless a clear residual effect. Children with Head Start or other enriched preschool experience are less likely to be placed in special education classes, somewhat less likely to repeat a grade, and somewhat more likely to graduate from high school (Darlington, 1991; Haskins, 1989). So although the children with preschool experience do not typically *test* much higher (and do *not* differ in IQ), they *function* better in school.

Children in Head Start programs or other enriched preschools don't have higher IQs later, but they are less likely to repeat a grade or to be assigned to special education classes.

Even larger and more lasting effects are found when the special program is begun in infancy. The best-designed and most meticulously reported of the infancy interventions has been carried out by Craig Ramey and his colleagues at North Carolina (Ramey, 1993; Ramey & Campbell, 1987; Ramey & Haskins, 1981a; 1981b; Ramey, Lee, & Burchinal, 1989; Ramey, Yeates, & Short, 1984). Infants from poverty-level families, whose mothers had low IQs, were randomly assigned either to a special day-care program, eight hours a day, five days a week, or to a control group, which received nutritional supplements and medical care but no special enriched day care. The special care program, which began when the infants were 6 to 12 weeks of age and lasted until they began kindergarten, involved very much the kinds of "optimum" stimulation I just described.

The average IQ scores of the children at various ages are shown in Figure 6.5. You can see that the IQs of the children who had been enrolled in the special program were higher at every age, although the scores for both groups declined in the elementary school years. What is perhaps more important is the observation that fully 44 percent of the control group children had IQ scores classified as borderline or retarded (scores below 85), compared to only 12.8 percent of the children who had been in the special program. In addition, the enriched day-care group had significantly higher scores on both reading and mathematics tests at age 12, and were only half as likely to have repeated a grade (Ramey, 1992; 1993).

Ramey found additional insights in the varying experience of the control group children. Some of them had been reared primarily at home, but others had spent periods of time in other types of day care or preschool programs. When he compared the IQ scores of these two groups with those in the special intervention

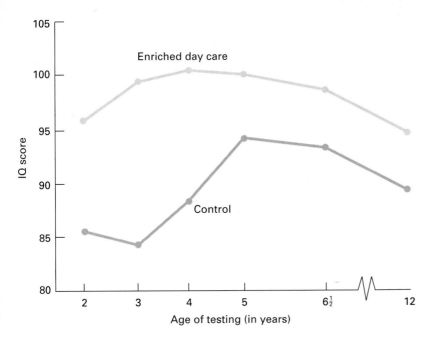

Figure 6.5
In the Ramey study, children were randomly assigned to an experimental group with special day care, or to a control group. At kindergarten, both groups entered public school. The difference in IQ between the experimental and control groups remained statistically significant even at age 12, seven years after the intervention ended. (*Source:* Ramey & Campbell, 1987, Figure 3, p. 135, with additional data from Ramey, 1993, Figure 2, p. 29.)

program he found a consistent rank order: children in the special program were highest, followed by those who had had some kind of day-care experience, with those reared wholly at home the lowest. The IQs at age 4 for these three groups were 101.1, 94.0, and 84.2, respectively (Burchinal, Lee, & Ramey, 1989). So the length and quality of the intervention appeared to be directly related to the size of the effect.

These results do *not* mean that all mental retardation could be "cured" by providing children with heavy doses of special education in infancy. What they do show is that the intellectual power (componential intelligence, at least) of those children who begin life with few advantages can be significantly increased if richer stimulation is provided.

Considering the results of Ramey's study, would you be in favor of providing such enriched day care to all infants from high-risk or poverty-level families? What are the arguments, pro and con?

▶ Interaction of Heredity and Environment

When we put together all the information about the role of heredity and environment in influencing IQ, it is clear that both factors are highly significant. Studies around the world consistently yield estimates that roughly half of the variation in IQ within the population is due to heredity (Plomin, 1989; Plomin & Rende, 1991). The remaining half is clearly due to environment or to interactions between environment and heredity.

One useful way to conceptualize this interaction is with the concept of *reaction range*. The basic idea is that genes establish some range of possible reactions, upper and lower boundaries of functioning. Where a child's IQ score will fall within those boundaries will be determined by environment. Richard Weinberg (1989) estimates that the reaction range for IQ is about 20 to 25 points. That is, given some specific genetic heritage, each child's actual IQ test performance may vary as much as 20 or 25 points, depending on the richness or poverty of the environment in which he grows up. When we change the child's environment for the better, the child moves closer to the upper end of his reaction range. When we change the environment for the worse, the child's effective intellectual performance falls toward the lower end of his reaction range. Thus even though intelligence as measured on an IQ test is highly heritable, the absolute score within the reaction range is determined by environment.

We could also think about the interaction between heredity and environment in terms rather like Horowitz's model (recall Figure 1.3), or using Aslin's concept of maintenance. Some theorists (Turkheimer & Gottesman, 1991) have argued that *within the normal range of environments,* IQ scores may be largely a function of heredity, not because environment is unimportant, but simply because most environments are sufficiently rich to support or maintain normal intellectual development. It is only when environmental quality falls below some crucial threshold that it has a major effect on the level of measured IQ, such as might be true for children reared in an orphanage or in a severely impoverished environment. This view does not necessarily contradict the concept of reaction range. Rather, the argument is that the lower end of any given child's reaction range is likely to be manifested only if the child is reared in an environment that falls below the critical threshold. If we think about it in this way, then it makes sense that special education programs like Ramey's would be effective for children from poverty-level environments, since the program brings the child's experience up into the sufficiently supportive range and thus adequately supports normal intellectual development. The same program provided to a child from a more supportive family environment, however, should have little or no effect on IQ—which is essentially what researchers have found.

▶ Group Differences in IQ: Race and Sex Differences

So far I have sidestepped two difficult issues, namely racial and sex differences in IQ or cognitive power. Because these issues have powerful personal and political ramifications and can easily be blown out of proportion, I do not want to place too much emphasis on either topic. But you need to see what we know, what we don't know, and how we are trying to explain both kinds of differences.

Racial Differences in IQ

A number of different racial differences in intellectual performance have been found, including consistently higher performance on achievement tests—particularly math and science tests—by Chinese and Japanese children (Stevenson et al., 1990; Sue & Okazaki, 1990). But the basic finding that has given researchers and theorists the most difficulty is that in the United States, black children consistently score lower than white children on measures of IQ. This difference, which is on the order of 12 IQ points, is *not* found on infant tests of intelligence, or on measures of infant habituation rate (Fagan & Singer, 1983), but becomes apparent by the time children are 2 or 3 years old (Brody, 1992).

Some scientists have argued that these findings reflect basic genetic differences between the races (Jensen, 1980). Other scientists, even granting that IQ is highly heritable, point out that the 12-point difference falls well within the presumed reaction range of IQ. They emphasize that there are sufficiently large differences in the environments in which black and white children are typically reared to account for the average difference in score (Brody, 1992).

Some of the most convincing research supporting the latter view comes from Sandra Scarr and her colleagues (Scarr & Kidd, 1983; Weinberg, Scarr, & Waldman, 1992). For example, she has found that black children adopted at an early age into white middle-class families, and thus reared in the majority environment, scored only slightly less well on IQ tests than did white children adopted into the same families. In another study of adopted black children, Moore (1986) found that those who had been reared in white families not only had higher IQ scores than those adopted into black families (117 versus 103), they also approached the IQ-testing situation quite differently. They stayed more focused on the task, and were more likely to try some task even if they didn't think they could do it. Black children adopted into middle-class black families did not show this pattern of persistence and effort. They asked for help more often, and gave up more easily when faced with a difficult task. When Moore then observed each adoptive mother teaching her child several tasks, he could see parallel differences. The white mothers were more encouraging and less likely to give the child the answer than were the black mothers.

Findings like these persuade me that the IQ difference we see is primarily a reflection of the fact that the tests, and the schools, are designed by the majority culture to promote a particular form of intellectual activity (Sternberg's componential intelligence), and that many black or other minority families rear their children in ways that do not promote or emphasize this particular set of skills. In fact Sternberg has recently argued that in some black subcultures it is contextual intelligence that is particularly emphasized and trained (Sternberg & Suben, 1986).

In a similar vein, Harold Stevenson has argued that the differences between Asian and American children in performance on mathematics achievement tests result not from genetic differences in capacity, but from differences in cultural emphasis on the importance of academic achievement, number of hours spent on homework, and differences in the quality of the math instruction in the schools (Stevenson & Lee, 1990; Stigler, Lee, & Stevenson, 1987)—a possibility I've explored in the cultures and contexts box on page 185.

The fact that we may be able to account for such racial differences in IQ or achievement test performance by appealing to the concept of reaction range and to cultural or subcultural variations does not make the differences disappear, nor does it make them trivial. But perhaps it puts such findings into a less explosive framework.

Some psychologists have argued that IQ tests and achievement tests are biased against blacks and other minority group members. What kind of research results would demonstrate such bias? What kind would argue against it?

Sex Differences in IQ

In contrast, comparisons of total IQ test scores for boys and girls do *not* reveal consistent differences. It is only when we break down the total score into several

CULTURES AND CONTEXTS
IQ Testing of Blacks in the Schools

One of the primary uses for IQ tests in schools has been to identify children with special needs, so that they can be placed in appropriate special classes. Children whose speed of learning seems to be much faster or slower than normal may be given an IQ test to see if they might be retarded or gifted. The test score is then used along with other data, such as teacher comments and recommendations, to decide if the child should be in a special class.

This use of IQ tests has been the center of a great deal of controversy, largely because when the tests are used in this way, proportionately many more African-American children end up being classified as slow or retarded than is true for whites. Many parents, educators, and psychologists have argued that such a pattern of results occurs because the tests are culturally biased. The tests may contain items that are not equally accessible to blacks and whites. Taking such tests and doing well may also require certain test-taking skills, motivations, or attitudes less common among African-American children.

Assertions of such bias have led to careful reexamination of individual test items, and all obvious types of bias have been eliminated from recent revisions. Despite this, proportionately more black than white children continue to be diagnosed as retarded or slow. This fact has led to a number of lawsuits, including *Larry P. v. Riles,* in which a group of parents of black children sued the California school system for bias in labeling a disproportionately large number of black children as retarded and assigning them to special classes. The parents argued that there was no underlying difference in *competence* between black and white children, so if the tests showed a difference the tests must clearly be biased. The school system argued that IQ tests don't measure underlying capacity or competence but only a child's existing repertoire of basic intellectual skills. By school age, that repertoire has already been affected by such environmental factors as prenatal care, diet, health, and family stability—all of which tend to be poorer among blacks. Thus the test accurately reflects a child's current abilities and is a proper basis for assigning the child to a special program, even though that child might have far greater underlying capacity or competence which could have been expressed under more ideal life circumstances.

The judge in the *Larry P. v. Riles* case ruled in favor of the parents and prohibited the use of standardized IQ test scores for placement in special classes in California. Other legal decisions have gone the other way (Elliott, 1988), so the legal question is not settled, although there are now many places in the U.S. in which the use of IQ tests for diagnosis and placement of black or other minority children is forbidden. One unintended consequence of this is that since placement decisions must still be made, they are now being made on the basis of evidence that may be even more culturally biased, such as less-standardized tests and teacher evaluations.

I have no quick or easy solution to this dilemma. It is certainly true that schools in the United States reflect the dominant middle-class white culture, with all its values and assumptions. But it is also true that succeeding in these schools is essential if the child is to acquire the basic skills needed to cope with the complexities of life in an industrialized country. For a host of reasons, including poorer prenatal care, greater poverty, and different familial patterns, more African-American children appear to *need* special classes in order to acquire the skills they lack. Yet I am well aware that there is a self-fulfilling prophecy about placing a child in a special class. Expectations are typically lower in such classes, so the children—who were already learning more slowly—are challenged still less and so proceed even more slowly. Yet to offer no special help to children who come to school lacking the skills needed to succeed there seems equally unacceptable to me. What do you think?

---

separate skills that some patterns of sex differences emerge. On average, studies in the U.S. show girls are slightly better on verbal tasks and at arithmetic computation, and that boys are slightly better at numerical reasoning. For example, on the math portion of the Scholastic Aptitude Tests (SATs), the average score for boys is consistently higher than the average score for girls. Many of these differences have been getting smaller in recent years, although this is not true for the SAT mathematics score difference, which has persisted over the past three decades among students in the U.S. (Brody, 1992; Byrnes & Takahira, 1993; Jacklin, 1989).

Two other differences are also still found regularly. First, among children who test as gifted in mathematics, boys are considerably more common (Benbow, 1988; Lubinski & Benbow, 1992). And on tests of spatial visualization, like the

CULTURES AND CONTEXTS
How Asian Teachers Teach Math and Science So Effectively

The *way* school is taught also may make a huge difference. A striking example comes from James Stigler and Harold Stevenson's (1991) comparisons of mathematics and science teaching in Asia and America . They have observed in 120 classrooms in Japan, Taiwan, and the United States, and are convinced that Asian teachers have devised a particularly effective mode of teaching these subjects.

Japanese and Chinese teachers approach mathematics and science by crafting a series of "master lessons," each organized around a single theme or idea. These lessons are like good stories, with a beginning, a middle, and an end. They frequently begin with a problem posed for the students. Here is one example from a fifth-grade class in Japan:

> *The teacher walks in carrying a large paper bag full of clinking glass. . . . She begins to pull items out of the bag, placing them, one-by-one, on her desk. She removes a pitcher and a vase. A beer bottle evokes laughter and surprise. She soon has six containers lined up on her desk. . . . The teacher, looking thoughtfully at the containers, poses a question: "I wonder which one would hold the most water?" . . . the teacher calls on different students to give their guesses: "the pitcher," . . . "the teapot." The teacher stands aside and ponders: "Some of you said one thing, others said something different. . . . How can we know who is correct?" (Stigler & Stevenson, 1991, p. 14)*

The lesson continues as the students agree on a plan for determining which will hold the most. Frequently, in such lessons, students are divided into small groups, each with a task, which they then report back to the class as a whole. At the end of the lesson, the teacher reviews the original problem and what they have learned. In this particular case, the children have not only learned something about measurement but about the process of hypothesis testing.

In United States classrooms, in contrast, it is extremely uncommon for a teacher to spend 30 or 60 minutes on a single coherent math or science lesson involving the whole class of children and a single topic. Instead, they shift often from one topic to another during a single math or science "lesson." They might do a brief bit on addition, then talk about measurement, then about telling time, and back to addition. Asian teachers shift *activities* in order to provide variety, such as shifting from lecture format to small-group discussions; American teachers shift *topics* for the same apparent purpose.

Stigler and Stevenson also found striking differences in the amount of time teachers actually spend leading instruction for the whole class. In the United States classrooms they observed, this occurred only 49 percent of the time; group instruction occurred 74 percent of the time in Japan and 91 percent in Taiwan.

Stigler and Stevenson point out that there is nothing in the Asian type of teaching that is new to Western teachers. American educators frequently recommend precisely such techniques. "What the Japanese and Chinese examples demonstrate so compellingly is that when widely implemented, such practices can produce extraordinary outcomes" (p. 45).

---

ones illustrated in Figure 6.6, boys have higher average scores. On measures of mental rotation (illustrated by item *c* in the figure) the sex difference is quite large.

I want to point out that even on tests of mental rotation, the two distributions overlap. That is, there are many girls and women who are good at this type of task, and many boys and men who are not. But this sex difference may have real consequences for some aspects of advanced mathematics and science, where the ability to do mental spatial manipulations is often important. The fact that girls score lower on such tests does not mean that no women are qualified for occupations that demand such skill; it does mean that fewer girls or young women will be able to pass the entrance requirements for such jobs.

As with total IQ scores, there are probably both environmental and biological forces at work in creating these patterns. Biological influences have been most often argued in the case of sex differences in spatial abilities, where there may be both genetic differences and—more speculatively— differences in brain functioning resulting from prenatal variations in hormones (Newcombe & Baenninger, 1989).

Figure 6.6
Three illustrations of spatial ability tests: (a) *Spatial visualization*. The figure at the top represents a square piece of paper being folded. A hole is punched through all the thicknesses of the folded paper. Which figure shows what the paper looks like when it is unfolded? (b) *Spatial orientation*. Compare the three cubes on the right with the one on the left. No letter appears on more than one face of a given cube. Which of the three cubes on the right could be a different view of the cube on the left? (c) *Mental rotation*. In each pair, can the three-dimensional objects be made congruent by rotation? (*Source:* Halpern, 1992, Figure 3.1, p. 50, and Figure 3.2, p. 52.)

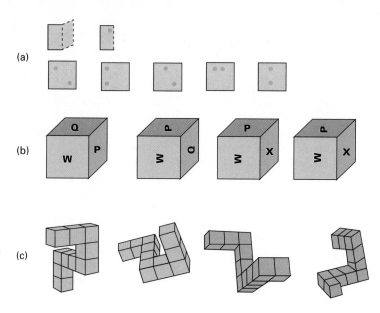

As you can see, a lot of effort has been spent trying to discover or explain possible sex differences in mathematical ability. What are the practical implications either way?

In contrast, environmental explanations have been prominent in discussions of the sex differences in mathematical or verbal reasoning. Especially in the case of mathematics there is considerable evidence that girls' and boys' skills are systematically shaped by a series of environmental factors:

- Boys take more math courses than girls do. When the amount of math exposure is held constant, the sex difference becomes much smaller.
- Parental attitudes about mathematics are markedly different for boys and girls. Parents are more likely to attribute a daughter's success in mathematics to effort or good teaching; poor performance by a girl is attributed to lack of ability. In contrast, parents attribute a boy's success to ability and his failure to lack of application (Holloway & Hess, 1985; Parsons, Adler, & Daczala, 1982).
- Girls and boys have different experiences in math classes. In elementary school, teachers pay more attention to boys during math instruction (and more attention to girls during reading instruction), and in high school, math teachers direct more of their questions and comments to boys, even when girls are outspoken in class.

The cumulative effect of these differences in expectation and treatment show up in high school, when sex differences on standardized math tests usually become evident. In part, then, the sex differences in math achievement test scores appear to be perpetuated by subtle family and school influences on children's attitudes. Whether these differences can explain the greater percentage of boys than girls who show real giftedness in mathematics is not so clear—an issue that continues to be debated rather heatedly.

▶ The Measurement of Intelligence: A Last Look

One of the questions that students often ask at about this point is whether, given the factors that can affect a test score, it is worth bothering with IQ tests at all. I think that these tests do assess some important aspects of children's intellectual performance and that they can be helpful in identifying children who may have difficulties in school. But it is worth emphasizing again that they do *not* measure a lot of other things we may be interested in, including all the facets of intelligence Sternberg describes. An IQ test is a specialized tool, and like many such tools, it has a fairly narrow range of appropriate use. I don't want to throw out this tool, but you have to keep its limitations very firmly in mind when you use it. You also have to keep in mind that the study of IQ is only one facet of the study of cognitive development. In the next chapter we'll look at the equally significant changes with age in children's understanding of the world around them.

▶ Summary

1. When we study the development of "intelligence," we need to distinguish between measures of intellectual power and measures of intellectual structure. IQ tests tap individual differences in intellectual power.

2. The most commonly used individually administered tests are the Stanford-Binet and the Wechsler Intelligence Scales for Children (WISC).

3. All current IQ tests compare a child's performance to that of others her or his age. Scores above 100 represent better-than-average performance; scores below 100 represent poorer-than-average performance.

4. Both IQ tests and school achievement tests measure a child's performance, not capacity or underlying competence. Achievement tests, however, test much more specific school-related information than do IQ tests.

5. Performance tests, which compare a student's performance against some specific criterion, such as the ability to write clearly, have become more common lately.

6. IQ scores are quite stable from one testing to the next, and this becomes more and more true the older the child gets. But individual children's scores still may fluctuate 20 or 30 points or more over the course of childhood.

7. IQ test scores are quite good predictors of school performance and years of education, and are moderately good predictors of later job performance.

8. IQ tests do not measure many other facets of intellectual functioning in which we might be interested, including what Sternberg calls experiential and contextual intelligence.

9. Studies of identical twins and of adopted children show clearly that there is at least some genetic influence on measured IQ. Most psychologists agree that approximately half of the variation in individual IQs may be attributed to heredity.

10. The remaining half is attributed to environmental variation: Poor children consistently test lower than do children from middle-class families; children

whose families provide appropriate play materials and encourage the child's intellectual development test higher on IQ tests.

11. Environmental influence is also shown by increases in test performance among children who have been in special, enriched preschool or infant day-care programs.

12. The interaction of heredity and environment can be understood with the concept of reaction range: heredity determines some range of potential; environment determines the level of performance within that range.

13. A consistent difference of about 12 points on IQ tests is found between white and black children. It seems most likely that this difference is due to environmental and cultural differences between the two groups, such as differences in health and prenatal care, and in the type of intellectual skills trained and emphasized at home.

14. Males and females do not differ on total IQ test scores, but do differ in some subskills. The largest differences are on measures of spatial reasoning, on which males are consistently better.

▌ Key Terms

achievement test (167)

Bayley Scales of Infant Development (167)

competence (167)

componential intelligence (173)

contextual intelligence (174)

cumulative deficit (176)

experiential intelligence (173)

intelligence quotient (IQ) (166)

performance (168)

performance tests (170)

Stanford-Binet (166)

triarchic theory of intelligence (173)

WISC (167)

▌ Suggested Readings

Brody, N. (1992). *Intelligence* (2nd ed.). San Diego, CA: Academic Press.

Dense and detailed, but the best current source I know of for further information about all aspects of this subject.

Elliott, R. (1988). Tests, abilities, race, and conflict. *Intelligence, 12,* 333–350.

An especially clear and fascinating discussion of the several lawsuits about the use of IQ tests in the schools.

Gallagher, J. J., & Ramey, C. T. (1987). *The malleability of children*. Baltimore: Paul H. Brookes Publishing Co.

If you are interested in the subject of the impact of special programs on IQ, this is a reasonably recent and readable source. Included are papers by several of the researchers involved in major intervention studies (including Ramey), as well as reviews of this research by other key figures.

7

COGNITIVE DEVELOPMENT II: STRUCTURE AND PROCESS

Piaget's Basic Ideas

The Processes of Adaptation
The Four Stages
• *The Real World:* Young Children's Play
• *Research Report:* An Illustration of Classification Ability
Lasting Influences from Piaget's Ideas

Cognitive Development in Infancy

Imitation
Memory in Infancy

Cognitive Development in the Preschool Period

Perspective Taking
Appearance and Reality
• *Cultures and Contexts:* Understanding of Appearance and Reality in Other Cultures
Theories of Mind
Other Aspects of Preschool Thought: Conservation and Classification
Overview of the Preschool Child's Thinking

Cognitive Development in the School-Age Child

Direct Tests of Piaget's Ideas

New Themes: Memory and Strategy Development
• *The Real World:* Memory and the Child as Witness
Expertise
Overview of the Thinking of the Schoolchild

Cognitive Development in Adolescence

Why Doesn't Every Teenager Use Formal Logic?

Preliminary Conclusions and Questions

Information Processing in Children

Developmental Approaches to Information Processing
Individual Differences in Information Processing

Putting the Three Approaches Together

Summary

Key Terms

Suggested Readings

Imagine the following scene: Your 5-year-old, John, and your 8-year-old, Anne, come into the kitchen after playing outside, both asking for juice. With both children watching, you take two identical small cans of juice from the refrigerator and pour them into two nonidentical glasses. One glass is narrower than the other, so the juice rises higher in that glass. The 5-year-old, having been given the fatter glass, complains, "Anne got more than I did!" To which Anne replies (with the wonderful grace of the 8-year-old to her sibling), "I did not, you dummy. We both got the same amount. The two cans were just alike." To restore family harmony, you get out another glass identical to Anne's, and pour John's juice into this new glass. The level of the liquid is now the same and John is satisfied.

If this were an item on an IQ test, we'd say that Anne was "right" and John was "wrong." But such an emphasis on rightness or wrongness misses an essential point about this interchange: there seems also to be a *developmental* change, a shift in the way the child sees or understands the world and the relationships of objects. John is not being pigheaded or "dumb." He is merely operating with a different kind of reasoning than Anne's. In a year or two, John will sound like Anne does now.

If we are to understand how children think, we need to understand such changes in the *form* or *structure* of their thinking as well as differences in *power*. How do children come to understand the world around them? What kind of logic do they use, and how does it change over time?

These were precisely the kinds of questions that Jean Piaget asked in his many years of research on children's thinking. Despite the fact that many aspects of his theory have been called into question by later research, his theory set the agenda for most research in this area for the past 30 years, and it still serves as a kind of scaffolding for much of our thinking about thinking. So let me begin by giving you a fairly detailed description of Piaget's original ideas before going on to talk about more current research and theory, including information processing.

▶ Piaget's Basic Ideas

I mentioned in Chapter 1 that Piaget began with the observation that children seem to follow very regular sequences in their development of certain ideas, certain understandings. They make the same kinds of mistakes at similar ages, and seem to arrive at similar solutions. Where could such shared mistakes come from? More broadly, how does a child's knowledge of the world develop?

In answering this question, Piaget's most central assumption was that the child is an active participant in the development of knowledge, *constructing* his own understanding. This idea, perhaps more than any other, has influenced the thinking of all those who have followed Piaget. The modern metaphor is that of the child as a "little scientist," engaged in active exploration, seeking understanding and knowledge.

In constructing such an understanding, Piaget thought that the child tries to *adapt* to the world around himself in ever more satisfactory ways. In Piaget's theory, this process of adaptation is in turn made up of several vital subprocesses.

The Processes of Adaptation

Schemes.   A pivotal concept—and one of the hardest to grasp—is that of a **scheme** (sometimes written as *schema*). This term is often used as roughly analogous to the word *concept* or *mental category* or *complex of ideas*. But Piaget used it even more broadly than that. He saw knowledge as being more than just passive mental categories, but as *actions*, either mental or physical, and each of these actions is what he means by a scheme. So a scheme is not really a category, but the *action of categorizing* in some particular fashion. Some purely physical or sensory actions are also schemes. If you pick up and look at a ball, you are using

The metaphor of the child as a "little scientist," constructing her understanding of the world, comes directly from Piaget's theory.

your "looking scheme," your "picking-up scheme," and your "holding scheme." Piaget proposed that each baby begins life with a small repertoire of such simple sensory or motor schemes, such as looking, tasting, touching, hearing, reaching. For the baby, an object *is* a thing that tastes a certain way, or feels a certain way when it is touched, or has a particular color. Later, the toddler and child develops more clearly mental schemes as well, such as categorizing or comparing one object to another. Over development, the child gradually adds extremely complex mental schemes, such as deductive analysis, or systematic reasoning. According to Piaget, the shift from the simple sensorimotor schemes of infancy to the increasingly complex mental schemes of later childhood is achieved through the operation of three basic processes: **assimilation** and **accommodation** and **equilibration.**

Assimilation. Assimilation is the process of *taking in*, of absorbing some event or experience to some scheme. When a baby looks at and then reaches for a mobile above his crib, Piaget would say that the baby has assimilated the mobile to the looking and reaching schemes; when an older child sees a dog and labels it "dog," she is assimilating that animal to her dog category or scheme. When you read this paragraph you are assimilating the information, hooking the concept onto whatever other concepts (schemes) you have that may be similar.

The key here is that assimilation is an *active* process. For one thing, there is selectivity in the information we assimilate. When I was struggling to learn German last year and listened to my instructor speak, I could only assimilate a portion of what she said—the parts for which I already had schemes—and could only imitate or use the parts that I had assimilated. In addition, the very act of assimilating changes the information that is assimilated, because each assimilated event or experience takes on some of the characteristics of the scheme to which it was assimilated. If I label your new sweater as green (that is, if I assimilate it to my green scheme) even though it is really chartreuse or some other more unusual color, I will remember it as more green and less yellow than it really is.

Accommodation. The complementary process is accommodation, which involves *changing the scheme* as a result of the new information you have taken in by assimilation. As I assimilated new German words and grammar, I gradually changed (accommodated) my concepts and categories, so that now I had mental categories for several forms of past tense instead of only one, or mental groupings of words with a given prefix. The baby who sees and grasps a square object for the first time will accommodate her grasping scheme, so that next time she reaches for an object of that shape her hand will be more appropriately bent to grasp it. Thus in Piaget's theory, the process of accommodation is the key to developmental change. Through accommodation, we reorganize our thoughts, improve our skills, change our strategies.

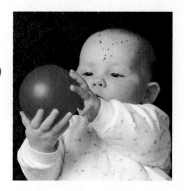

Piaget would say that baby Eleanor is assimilating this ball to her looking and grasping schemes. As she adapts her way of holding, she is also accommodating.

Equilibration.   The third aspect of adaptation is equilibration. Piaget assumed that in the process of adaptation, the child is always striving for coherence, to stay "in balance," to have an understanding of the world that makes overall sense. This is not unlike what a scientist does when she develops a theory about some body of information (and hence the metaphor of the child as a "little scientist"). The scientist wants to have a theory that will make sense out of every observation, that has internal coherence. When new research findings come along, she assimilates them to the existing theory; if they don't fit perfectly, she might simply set aside the deviant data, or she may make minor modifications in her theory. But if enough nonconfirming evidence accumulates, the scientist may have to throw out her theory altogether and start over, or may need to change some basic theoretical assumptions, either of which would be a form of equilibration.

Piaget thought that a child operated in a similar way, creating coherent, more-or-less internally consistent models or theories. But since the infant starts with a very limited repertoire of schemes, the early "theories" or structures the child creates are simply not going to hold up. So Piaget thought the child then made a series of more major changes in the internal structure.

Piaget saw three particularly significant reorganization or equilibration points, each ushering in a new stage of development. The first is at roughly 18 months, when the toddler shifts from the dominance of simple sensory and motor schemes to the use of the first symbols. The second is at roughly ages 5 to 7, when the child adds a whole new set of powerful schemes Piaget calls **operations.** These are far more abstract and general mental actions, such as mental addition or subtraction. The third major equilibration is at adolescence, when the child figures out how to "operate on" ideas as well as events or objects. These three major equilibrations create four stages:

The **sensorimotor** stage, from birth to 18 months

The **preoperational** stage, from 18 months to about age 6

The **concrete operational** stage, from 6 to about 12

The **formal operational** stage, from age 12 onward

The Four Stages

Sensorimotor Stage.   According to Piaget, during this stage the infant (1) responds to the world almost entirely through sensory and motor schemes, (2) functions in the immediate present, responding to whatever stimuli present themselves, (3) does not plan or intend, and (4) has no internal representation of objects—mental pictures, or words, that stand for objects and that can be manipulated mentally. Piaget thought that such internal representations did not develop until about 18 to 24 months.

John Flavell (1985) summarizes all this very nicely:

[The infant] exhibits a wholly practical, perceiving-and-doing, action-bound kind of intellectual functioning; she does not exhibit the more contemplative, reflective, symbol-manipulating kind we usually think of in connection with cognition. The infant "knows" in the sense of recognizing or anticipating familiar, recurring objects and happenings, and "thinks" in the sense of behaving toward them with mouth, hand, eye, and other sensory-motor instruments in predictable, organized, and often adaptive ways. . . . It is the kind of noncontemplative intelligence that your dog relies on to make its way in the world. (p. 13)

Piaget proposed that the infant moved through a series of substages, gradually building toward the development of internal representation at about 18 months. Only then, he thought, can the child both form and manipulate mental images and use symbols. That is, he can have images or words or actions *stand for* something else, a shift that Flavell rightly describes as "radically, drastically, qualitatively different" (Flavell, 1985, p. 82) from what came before. And it is precisely this shift that Piaget saw as the beginning point of the next stage.

Preoperational Stage.   During the years from 2 to 6, Piaget saw the evidence of symbol use in many aspects of the child's behavior. Children this age begin to pretend in their play, for example (a development I've talked about in the real world box on p. 196). At age 2 or 3 or 4 a broom may become a horsie, or a block may become a train. We can also see such symbol use in the emergence of language at about the same time (which I'll describe in the next chapter). And we see the child's improving ability to manipulate these symbols internally in such things as her ability to search more systematically for lost or hidden objects.

Beyond the accomplishment of symbol use, Piaget focused mostly on all the things the preschool age child still *cannot* do, which gives an oddly negative tone to his description of this period. Even the term he used to describe this stage conveys some of this tone: it is *preoperational*.

For example, Piaget described the preoperational child as one who looks at things entirely from his own perspective, his own frame of reference, a characteristic Piaget called **egocentrism** (Piaget, 1954). The child is not being selfish; rather she simply thinks (assumes) that everyone sees the world as she does.

Figure 7.1 is a photo of a classic experiment illustrating this kind of egocentrism. The child is shown a three-dimensional scene with mountains of different sizes and colors. From a set of drawings, he picks out the one that shows the scene the way he sees it. Most preschoolers can do this without much difficulty. Then the examiner asks the child to pick out the drawing that shows how someone *else* sees the scene, such as the little clay man, or the examiner. At this point preschool children have difficulty. Most often they again pick the drawing that shows their *own* view of the mountains (Flavell et al., 1981; Gzesh & Surber, 1985). In Piaget's view, for the child to be able to succeed at this task he must "decenter"—he must shift from using himself as the only frame of reference. Piaget thought that preschool children had not yet achieved this.

He also pointed out that the preschool-age child was captured by the appearance of objects—a theme that still dominates the research on children of this age. In Piaget's work, this theme is evident in some of the most famous of his studies, those on **conservation.**

It was a problem of conservation that confronted Anne and John and their juice glasses; to understand that both glasses of juice held the same amount, John

Think back to everything I said about perceptual skills in infancy in Chapter 5. Does Flavell's description of the sensorimotor infant match what you already know?

Can you think of any examples of egocentrism in your own behavior? What about buying someone else the gift you were hoping to receive yourself? Other examples?

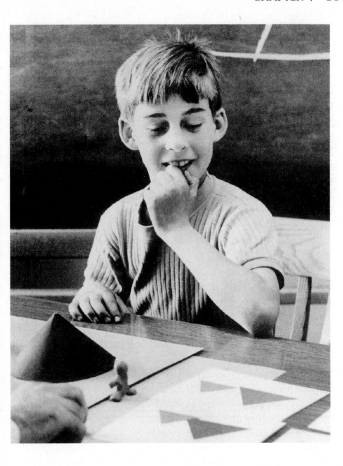

Figure 7.1
One of the types of experimental arrangements used to study egocentrism in children.

would have to ignore the *appearance* of difference, and understand that the amount of juice is "conserved"—remains the same— despite variations in the shape of the container. This is an example of conservation of quantity, one of six different conservations Piaget studied—listed in Table 7.1. In every case, his measurement technique involved first showing the child two equal sets of objects, getting the child to agree they were equal in some key respect such as weight or quantity or length or number, and then shifting or deforming one of the objects and asking the child if they were still equal. Children rarely show any of these forms of conservation before age 5, which Piaget took to be a sign that they were still captured by the appearance of change, and did not focus on the underlying unchanging aspect.

Notice that the understanding of conservation is part of a chain of development that begins with the various object constancies and object permanence in infancy. The sensorimotor infant eventually figures out that objects remain the same even though they appear to change in some respects, and he understands that objects continue to exist even when they are out of sight. Now in the preschool years, he must come to understand that there are other, more abstract, aspects of objects that also remain constant, despite apparent changes, such as their mass or weight.

A third limitation Piaget saw in the preoperational child's thinking was in her ability to classify—to put things together that go together. His observations

THE REAL WORLD
Young Children's Play

If you watch young children during their unstructured time you'll see them building towers out of blocks, talking to or feeding their dolls, making "tea" with the tea set, racing toy trucks across the floor, dressing up in grown-up clothes. They are, in a word, *playing*. This is not trivial or empty activity; it is the stuff on which much of cognitive development seems to be built.

The form of this play changes in very obvious ways during the years from 1 to 6, following a sequence that matches Piaget's stages rather well (Rubin, Fein, & Vandenberg, 1983).

Sensorimotor Play
The child of 12 months or so spends most of her playtime exploring and manipulating objects using all the sensorimotor schemes in her repertoire. She puts things in her mouth, shakes them, moves them along the floor.

Constructive Play
Such exploratory play with objects does continue past 12 months, especially with some totally new object, but by age 2 or so children begin to use objects to build or construct things— creating a block tower, putting together a puzzle, making something out of clay or with Tinkertoys. Such "constructive" play makes up nearly half of the play of children aged 3 to 6 (Rubin et al., 1983).

First Pretend Play
Pretend play also begins at about the same time. The first sign of such pretending is usually something like a child using a toy spoon to "feed" himself, or a toy comb to comb his hair. The toys are still used for their actual or typical purposes (spoon for feeding), and the actions are still oriented to the *self,* but there is pretending involved. Between 15 and 21 months, there is a shift: the recipient of the pretend action now becomes another person or a toy, most often a doll. The child is still using objects for their usual purposes (such as drinking from a cup), but now she is using the toy cup with a doll instead of herself. Dolls are especially good toys for this kind of pretending, because it is not a very large leap from doing things to yourself to doing things with a doll. So children feed dolls imaginary food, comb their hair, soothe them.

Substitute Pretend Play
Between 2 and 3 years of age children begin to use objects to stand for something altogether different. They may comb the doll's hair with a baby bottle while saying that it is a comb, or use a broom to be a horsie, or make "trucks" out of blocks. By age 4 or 5, children spend as much as 20 percent of their playtime in this new, complicated kind of pretending (Field, De Stefano, & Koewler, 1982a).

Sociodramatic Play
Somewhere in the preschool years children also begin to play parts or take roles. This is really still a form of pretending, except that now several children create a mutual pretense. They play "daddy and mommy," "cowboys and Indians," "doctor and patient," and the like. At first children simply take up these roles; later they name the roles to one another, and may give each other explicit instructions about the right way to pretend a particular role. You can begin to see this form of play in some 2-year-olds; by age 4 virtually all children engage in some play of this type (Howes & Matheson, 1992). Interestingly, at about the same ages a great many children seem to create imaginary companions (Taylor, Cartwright, & Carlson, 1993a). For many years psychologists believed that the existence of such an imaginary companion was a sign of disturbance in a child; now it is clear that such a creation is a normal part of the development of pretense in many children.

Children clearly get great delight out of all of these often-elaborate fantasies. Equally important, by playing roles, pretending to be someone else, they also become more and more aware of how things may look or feel to someone else, and their egocentric approach to the world declines.

Constructive play.

First pretend play.

Conservation	Typical Measure
TABLE 7.1 Different Types of Conservation Studied by Piaget	
Number	Two rows with equal numbers of pennies or buttons are laid out parallel to one another with the items matching. Then one row is stretched out longer or squeezed together, or rearranged in some other way, and the child is asked, "Are there the same number?"
Length	Two pencils of identical length are laid one above the other so that they match perfectly. Then one is displaced to the right or left so that one pencil's point sticks out further than the other, and the child is asked if they are now the same length.
Quantity	Two equal beakers are filled with equal amounts of water. One is then poured into a differently shaped glass (tall and thin or short and squat), and the child is asked if there is still the same amount to drink in each.
Substance or Mass	Two equal balls of clay are shown to the child. One is then squished into another shape, such as a sausage or a pancake. The child is asked if there is now the same amount of clay in each.
Weight	Two equal balls of clay are weighed on a balance scale so that the child sees that they weigh the same. One is then deformed into another shape, and the child is asked if they still weigh the same or "have the same amount of weight."
Volume	Two balls of clay are placed in two equal beakers of water so that the child sees that they each displace the same amount of water. Then one ball is deformed, and the child is asked if they will still "take up the same amount of space."

led him to believe that only at about age 4 does a child begin to group objects consistently into categories or classes, at first using only one dimension (e.g., shape, such as round things versus square things) and later two or more dimensions at once (e.g., size *and* shape: small round things versus small square things and large round things versus large square things).

Concrete Operations Stage.   The next great leap forward, according to Piaget, comes somewhere between ages 5 and 7, when the child discovers a set of immensely powerful, abstract general "rules" or "strategies" for examining and interacting with the world, which Piaget calls *concrete operations*. The term *operation* refers specifically to powerful, *internal* schemes such as reversibility, addition, subtraction, multiplication, division, and serial ordering. The child now understands the *rule* that adding to something makes it more, and subtracting makes it less, which means that she can now understand the principle of conservation. She understands that objects can belong to more than one category at once and that categories have logical relationships, which is a great advance over the simple classifications of the preoperational period. The 7-year-old not only can group

---

RESEARCH REPORT
An Illustration of Classification Ability

A good way to illustrate the shift in the child's ability to use classification skills is with the game of twenty questions. In one of my favorite older studies, Frederic Mosher and Joan Hornsby (1966) showed children aged 6 to 11 a set of 42 pictures of animals, people, toys, machines, and the like. The experimenter said he was thinking of one of the pictures, and the child was to figure out which one by asking questions that could be answered "yes" or "no."

There are several ways to figure out which questions to ask. You could simply start at one end of a row of pictures and ask "Is it this one?" about each one in turn until you hit on the right one, or you could point to them in some random order. Mosher and Hornsby called such strategies "hypothesis scanning." A second way is to classify the pictures mentally into a hierarchy of groups, and then ask first about the highest level in your hierarchy—a strategy that requires understanding the principle which Piaget called *class inclusion,* namely that lower classes are included in higher-order classes, as dogs are included in the class of mammals, and mammals are included in the class of animals. In the case of Mosher and Hornsby's photos, you might start, for example, by asking "Is it a toy?" If the answer is yes, you might then ask about the subcategories: "Is it a red toy?" Mosher and Hornsby called this second strategy "constraint seeking."

In their study, 6-year-olds almost never used a constraint (classification) strategy. They relied essentially on guessing. But by age 8, about 60 percent of children's questions reflected a constraint strategy and by age 11 it was nearly 80 percent. Findings like these supported Piaget's description of the concrete operational period.

---

critters into classes of cats and dogs, she also understands that both cats and dogs are *included in* the class of animals.

Piaget also proposed that during this third stage the child develops the ability to use **inductive logic.** He can go from his own experience to a general principle. For example, he can go from the observation that when you add another toy to a set and then count the set, it has one more than it did before, to a general principle that adding to something always makes it more.

Elementary-school children are pretty good observational scientists, and will enjoy cataloging, counting species of trees or birds, or figuring out the nesting habits of guinea pigs. But they are not yet good at **deductive logic,** which requires starting with a general principle and then predicting some outcome or observation, like going from a theory to a hypothesis. Suppose, for example, that I asked you to think of all the ways human relationships would be different if women were physically as strong as men. Coming up with answers requires deductive and not inductive logic, and it is hard because you must imagine things that you have not experienced. The concrete operations child is good at dealing with things he knows or can see and manipulate; he does not do well with manipulating ideas or possibilities. Piaget thought that deductive reasoning did not develop until the period of formal operations in junior high or high school.

An important practical application of this difference in the child's logic is that elementary-school children ought to be able to learn science (and other subjects) more easily if the material is presented "concretely," with plenty of opportunity for hands-on experience and inductive experimentation. They ought to learn less well when scientific concepts or theories are presented in a deductive fashion, which is precisely what research on science instruction has shown (Saunders & Shepardson, 1987).

Formal Operational Stage. Piaget proposed a final step of cognitive development, beginning at about age 12 and continuing to emerge through the teenage years. The most important shift is that the teenager is now able to apply

In your everyday life, when do you use inductive logic? When was the last time you think you used deductive logic?

complex mental operations not just to objects or experiences, but to ideas and to thoughts. One of the first steps in this process is for the child to extend her reasoning abilities to objects and situations which she has not seen or experienced firsthand, or that she cannot see or manipulate directly. Instead of thinking only about real things and actual occurrences, she must start to think about possible occurrences. The preschool child plays "dress up" by putting on real clothes. The teenager *thinks* about options and possibilities, imagining herself in different roles, going to college or not going to college, marrying or not marrying, having children or not.

Using formal operational thought the teenager can also search systematically and methodically for the answer to a problem. To study this, Piaget and his colleague Barbel Inhelder (Inhelder & Piaget, 1958) presented adolescents with complex tasks, mostly drawn from the physical sciences. In one of these tasks, the youngsters were given varying lengths of string and a set of objects of various weights that could be tied to the strings to make a swinging pendulum. They were shown how to start the pendulum by pushing the weight with differing amounts of force, and by holding the weight at different heights. The subject had to figure out which one or combination of these four factors (length of string, weight of object, force of push, or height of push) determine the "period" of the pendulum (the amount of time for one swing). (In case you have forgotten your high school physics, the answer is that only the length of the string affects the period of the pendulum.)

If you give this task to a concrete operational child, she will usually try out many different combinations of length and weight and force and height in an inefficient way. She might try a heavy weight on a long string, and then a light weight on a short string. Since both string length and weight have changed, there is no way to draw a clear conclusion about either factor. An adolescent, in contrast, is likely to try a much more organized approach, attempting to vary just one of the four factors at a time.

Finally, Piaget argued that another facet of this shift is the appearance of deductive logic in the child's repertoire of skills. A great deal of the logic of science is of this deductive type. We begin with a theory and propose, "If this theory is correct, then I should observe such and such." In doing this, we are going well beyond our observations. We are conceiving things that we have never seen but that *ought* to be true or observable. We can think of this change as being part of a general "decentering" process that began earlier. The preoperational child gradually moves away from his egocentrism and comes to be able to take the physical perspective of others. During formal operations, the child takes another step by freeing himself even from his reliance upon specific experiences.

Lasting Influences from Piaget's Ideas

As you will soon see, quite a few of the specifics of Piaget's theory have been called into question. He was wrong about the timing of development of many of the cognitive skills he described, and he was probably wrong about the breadth and generality of the stages themselves. Nevertheless, a number of aspects of his theory remain strongly influential, including the following:

Constructivism. The most pervasively influential idea to come from Piaget's theory is that the child is *constructing* his understanding of the world. He

Most students do not encounter a demand for deductive logic until high school science classes, like this chemistry class.

is not passive; he actively seeks to understand. A majority of developmentalists have accepted this proposition as a starting point (Flavell, 1992).

Qualitative Change.   Piaget's emphasis on qualitative change has also been highly significant. The descriptions of and discussions about the nature of the qualitative changes have shifted, as we have learned more about the knowledge and understanding of children of different ages. But virtually all would agree that a 15-year-old approaches problems and tasks in a way that is not just faster but qualitatively different from the way a 3-year-old approaches the same tasks.

Stages.   Piaget's concept of stages has been perhaps the most controversial of his ideas, but has nonetheless had a profound impact, still seen today. He argued that each stage was a coherent whole, that a child was "in" a given stage or another, and that all of the child's thinking was affected by the basic properties of that stage. By the end of this chapter I think I will have persuaded you that this view of stages is not correct, but the idea that there are sequential changes in the *form* of a child's thinking continues to be the basis for an enormous amount of our research and thinking. In addition, the four-part stage division that Piaget described has shaped the very way we talk about childhood—as well as the way we organize our textbooks. We speak of infants, preschoolers, schoolchildren, and adolescents, almost as if these were four different species. In fact I will use his four-stage division of ages/stages as the structure of my description, not only because it is convenient, but because so many researchers—influenced by Piaget— have studied children in only one age period.

Other Specific Concepts and Terms.   Finally, of course, Piaget has left us with a legacy of terminology and concepts that are widely used. These include *scheme* or *schema, assimilation, accommodation, egocentrism, conservation,* and the *object concept.*

All these influences will be apparent in my descriptions of our current understanding of the development of children's thinking. Let us begin with what we now know about cognition in infancy.

▌ Cognitive Development in Infancy

The focus of a great deal of modern research in cognition in infancy has been on showing that Piaget greatly underestimated the cognitive skill of babies. This same point emerged clearly from all the research on infant perception that I described in some detail in Chapter 5, so this is not news to you. But let me give you several further examples.

Imitation

One active area of study has been the ability of an infant to imitate. This is an important issue not only because Piaget proposed a series of quite specific hypotheses about imitation in the early months, but also because it may tell us what and how soon a baby can learn from modeling—a major form of learning proposed by social-cognitive theorists like Bandura.

Piaget thought infants could imitate actions they could see themselves make, such as hand gestures, as early as the first few months of life. But he thought they could *not* imitate other people's facial gestures until late in the first year. This form of imitation seems to require some kind of cross-modal transfer, combining the visual cues from seeing the other's face with the kinesthetic cues from one's own facial movements. Piaget did not think that cross-modal transfer was possible until at least 8 months, so he didn't think this form of imitation could occur until then either. He further argued that imitation of any action that wasn't already in the child's repertoire did not occur until about 1 year, and that *deferred* imitation, in which a child sees some action and then imitates it at a later point, was possible only at the end of the sensorimotor period, since deferred imitation requires some kind of internal representation.

In broad terms Piaget's proposed sequence has been supported. Imitation of someone else's hand movements or their actions with objects seems to improve steadily during the months of infancy, starting at 1 or 2 months of age; imitation of two-part actions develops much later, perhaps at 15 to 18 months (Poulson, Nunes, & Warren, 1989). Yet there are also two important exceptions to this general confirmation of Piaget's theory: infants imitate some facial gestures in the first weeks of life, and deferred imitation seems to occur earlier than Piaget proposed.

Several researchers have found that newborn babies will imitate certain facial gestures, particularly tongue protrusion (Anisfeld, 1991; Field et al., 1982b; Meltzoff & Moore, 1983). This only seems to work if the model sits there with his tongue out looking at the baby for a fairly long period of time, perhaps as long as a minute. But the fact that babies this young imitate at all is striking—although it is entirely consistent with the observations I reported in Chapter 5 that quite young babies are capable of tactual/visual cross-modal transfer.

Studies of deferred imitation are not so strikingly discordant with Piaget's description, but there is at least one study (Meltzoff, 1988) showing that babies as young as 9 months can defer their imitation over as long as 24 hours. By 14 months, toddlers recall others' actions over periods of two days. In one recent study, Elizabeth Hanna and Andrew Meltzoff (1993) trained a 14-month-old to play with five particular toys in distinctive ways, such as collapsing a collapsible cup, or picking up a string of beads and placing it in a cup. Other babies watched these play behaviors in a laboratory setting. Two days later, an adult unfamiliar to the baby went to the child's home, bringing along the set of toys and giving them to the child one at a time, to see if the child would imitate the actions he had seen the other child perform two days earlier. The majority of the 14-month-olds imitated at least two of these behaviors, while a control group who were given the toys but had not seen the model typically did not use the toys in these particular ways.

These findings are significant for several reasons. First, they make it clear that children of this age can and do learn specific behaviors through modeling, even when they have no chance to imitate the behavior immediately. Second, deferred imitation clearly requires that the baby remember what he saw and connect that memory to the object, all of which seems to require internal representation— which Piaget did not think was present this early. The fact that it is present in children as young as 14 months, and that the children were even able to imitate the action when the imitation occurred in a different setting (at home) from the

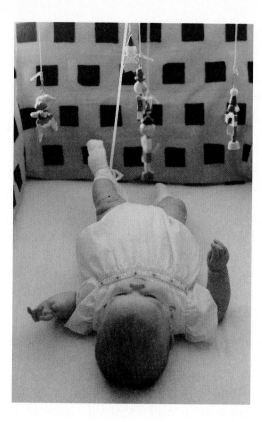

Figure 7.2
This 3-month-old baby in one of Rovee-Collier's memory experiments will quickly learn to kick her foot in order to make the mobile move. And she will remember this connection between kicking and the mobile several days later. (*Source:* Rovee-Collier, 1993, p. 131.)

setting in which the observation occurred (the laboratory), suggests that Piaget was simply wrong about when we are first able to use some kind of internal representation to remember actions and events.

Memory in Infancy

The same point emerges from Carolyn Rovee-Collier's (1993) fascinating studies of memory in very young infants . She has used an ingenious variation of an operant conditioning procedure to demonstrate that babies as young as 3 months of age can remember particular objects and their actions with those objects over periods of as long as a week. And if you "remind" them in between times, they can remember their earlier actions over six weeks.

Rovee-Collier first hangs an attractive mobile over the baby's crib, and watches to see how the baby responds. In particular, she is interested in how often the baby normally kicks her legs while looking at the mobile. Then after three minutes of observation, she attaches a string from the mobile to the baby's leg, as you can see in Figure 7.2, so that each time the baby kicks her leg, the mobile moves. Babies quickly learn to kick repeatedly in order to make this interesting new thing happen. Within three to six minutes, 3-month-olds double or triple their kick rates, showing that learning clearly occurred. She then tests the baby's memory of this learning by coming back some days later, hanging the same mobile over the crib, and counting the rate of the baby's kicks without attaching the string to her foot. If the baby remembers the previous occasion, she should kick at a higher rate than she did when she first saw the mobile, which is precisely what 3-month-old babies do, even after a delay as long as a week.

In some experiments, Rovee-Collier also "reminds" the baby of the original learning by coming back some time after the first training, hanging the mobile over the crib, and tugging on the string herself at the same rate that the baby had learned to kick. So the baby sees the mobile moving in a rhythmic pattern. Then she comes back a third time to check if the baby still kicks at a higher rate when she sees this particular mobile. With the reminder in between, babies as young as 3 months old remember the original learned connection between kicking and the mobile over several weeks.

Why is this so interesting? Primarily because it contradicts Piaget's view of the sensorimotor infant, whom he saw functioning pretty much in the here and now. It shows us, once again, that the young infant is cognitively a whole lot more sophisticated than we had supposed. At the same time, Rovee-Collier's work offers some kind of support for Piaget's views, since she finds that there are systematic gains in the baby's ability to remember over the months of infancy. Two-month-olds can remember their kicking action for only one day, 3-month-olds can remember over a week, and by 6 months the baby can remember over two weeks. Similarly, reminders work better and better as the baby gets older. But all these early infant memories are *strongly* tied to the specific context in which the original experience occurred. Even 6-month-olds do not recognize or remember the mobile if you change the context even slightly, such as hanging a different cloth around the playpen in which the child was originally tested. Thus babies do remember—far more than Piaget believed—but their memories are highly specific. With age, their memories become less and less tied to specific cues or contexts.

Both Meltzoff's studies of imitation and Rovee-Collier's studies of memory raise the more general question of whether infants may be capable of some forms of internal representation well before Piaget thought that they were. The same point arises from much of the research on early perception that I talked about in Chapter 5, including the findings that cross-modal transfer occurs as early as 1 month, and the research on children's responses to patterns like "big over little." All of these accomplishments seem to require that the baby create a fairly complex and abstract mental image. But such findings need not totally refute Piaget. What may develop at 18 or 24 months is the baby's ability to *manipulate* these images in his head, or some greater generality of the images, so that they are less situation-specific. We are left, then, with a picture of an infant who is indeed busily *constructing* schemes, concepts, memories, but one who seems to start out at a far higher level of skill in this process than Piaget had believed (Karmiloff-Smith, 1993).

Rovee-Collier's findings have surprised a lot of developmental psychologists. Do you find the results surprising? Why or why not?

▶ Cognitive Development in the Preschool Period

Much the same picture emerges from the current studies of thinking in the preschool-age child. This is an area of great theoretical and research ferment at the moment, much of it stimulated originally by two of Piaget's observations about children of this age: that their thinking is egocentric, and that they are captured by appearances. From these two starting points has come a rich and intriguing body of evidence suggesting that preschoolers are a great deal less egocentric than Piaget thought, but that they must struggle with the problem of distinguishing between appearance and reality. Many of us have been immensely surprised by the evidence that one of the products of that struggle is the development by age 4 or 5 of a remarkably sophisticated "theory of mind." By that age, amazingly enough, a child seems to realize that other people's actions are governed by what they think and believe, and not by "facts" or "reality."

Perspective Taking

Research on the child's ability to take others' perspectives shows that children as young as 2 and 3 have at least *some* ability to understand that other people see things or experience things differently than they do. For example, children this age will adapt their speech or their play to the demands of their companion. They play differently with older or younger playmates, and talk differently to a younger or a handicapped child (Brownell, 1990; Guralnick & Paul-Brown, 1984).

But such understanding is clearly not perfect at this young age. John Flavell has proposed that there are two levels of such perspective-taking ability. At Level 1, the child knows *that* some other person experiences something differently. At Level 2, the child develops a whole series of complex rules for figuring out precisely *what* the other person sees or experiences (Flavell, 1985; Flavell, Green, & Flavell, 1990). Two- and 3-year-olds have Level 1 knowledge but not Level 2. We begin to see some Level 2 knowledge in 4- and 5-year-olds.

Appearance and Reality

This shift seems to be part of a much broader change in the child's understanding of appearance and reality. Flavell has studied this in a variety of ways such as by showing objects under colored lights to change the apparent color, or putting masks on animals to make them look like another animal. He finds that 2- and 3-year-olds consistently judge things by their appearance; by 5, the child begins to be able to separate the appearance from the underlying reality and knows that some object isn't "really" red, even though it looks red under a red-colored light, or that a cat with a dog mask is still "really" a cat (Flavell, Green, & Flavell, 1989; Flavell et al., 1987).

In the most famous Flavell procedure, the experimenter shows the child a sponge that has been painted to look like a rock. Three-year-olds, faced with this odd object, will either say that the object looks like a sponge and is a sponge, or that it looks like a rock and is a rock. But 4- and 5-year-olds can distinguish the two; they realize that it looks like a rock but *is* a sponge (Flavell, 1986). Thus the older child now understands that the same object can be represented differently, depending on one's point of view.

Using the same type of materials, investigators have also asked if a child can grasp the principle of a *false belief*. After the child has felt the sponge/rock and has answered questions about what it looks like and what it "really" is, you can ask something like this: "John [a playmate of the subject's] hasn't touched this, he hasn't squeezed it. If John just sees it over here like this, what will he think it is?

The 3-year-old on the right is able to adapt her speech and her play to the needs of her blind friend, which is one sign that preschoolers are less egocentric than Piaget thought.

CULTURES AND CONTEXTS
Understanding of Appearance and Reality in Other Cultures

A number of studies from widely differing parts of the globe, and in widely different cultures, suggests that this shift at about age 4 in children's understanding of appearance and reality and of false belief may well be a universal developmental pattern.

Jeremy Avis and Paul Harris (1991) adapted the traditional false belief–testing procedure for use with a pygmy tribe, the Baka, who live in Cameroon. The Baka are a hunter-gatherer people who live together in camps. Each child was tested in his or her own hut, using materials with which they were completely familiar. They watched one adult, named Mopfana (a member of the tribe), put some mango kernels into a bowl. Mopfana then left the hut, and a second adult (also a tribe member) told the child they were going to play a game with Mopfana: they were going to hide the kernels in a cooking pot. Then he asked the child what Mopfana was going to do when he came back. Would he look for the kernels in the bowl, or in the pot? And they asked the child whether Mopfana's heart would feel good or bad before he lifted the lid of the bowl, and after he lifted the lid. Younger children—2-, 3-, and early 4-year-olds—were much more likely to say that Mopfana would look for the seeds in the pot, or to say that he would be sad before he looked in the bowl, while older 4- and 5-year-olds were nearly always right on all three questions.

Similarly, when Flavell used his sponge/rock task with children in mainland China, he found that Chinese 3-year-olds were just as confused about this task as are American or British 3-

year-olds, whereas 5-year-old Chinese children had no difficulty with the problem (Flavell et al., 1983).

Using a somewhat different kind of problem, but one that still touches on the difference between appearance and reality, Paul Harris and his colleagues (Harris, 1989) have asked children in several cultures how characters in a story *really* feel, and what emotion *appears* on their faces. For example:

> *Diana is playing a game with her friend. At the end of the game Diana wins and her friend loses. Diana tries to hide how she feels because otherwise her friend won't play any more. (Harris, 1989, p. 134)*

Four-year-old children in Britain and the United States, faced with such stories, have no trouble saying how the character will really feel, but more trouble saying how the character would look, while by 5 or 6, the child grasps the possible difference. Harris has found that the same age shift occurs in Japan (Gardner et al., 1988), despite the fact that the Japanese culture puts far more emphasis on the disguising of emotions.

In these very different cultures, then, something similar seems to be occurring between age 3 and age 5. In these years, all children seem to understand something general about the difference between appearance and reality, seem to develop a certain type of theory of mind.

Will he think it's a rock or will he think that it's a sponge?" (Gopnik & Astington, 1988, p. 35). By and large, 3-year-olds think that John will believe it is a sponge, while 4- and 5-year-olds realize that because John hasn't felt the sponge, he will have a false belief that it is a rock. Thus the child of 4 or 5 understands that someone else can believe something that isn't true *and will act on that belief.*

Theories of Mind

Evidence like this has led a number of theorists (Astington & Gopnik, 1991; Harris, 1989; Perner, 1991) to propose that the 4- or 5-year-old has developed a new and quite sophisticated **theory of mind.** The child this age has begun to understand that you cannot predict what other people will do solely from observing the situation itself; the other person's desires and beliefs also enter into the equation. So the child develops various theories about other people's ideas, beliefs, and desires, and about how they will affect others' behaviors.

Such a theory of mind does not spring forth full-blown at age 4. Three-year-old children already understand some aspects of the links between people's thinking or feeling and their behavior. They know that a person who wants something will try to get it. They also know that a person will feel sad if she fails and happy if she succeeds (Wellman, 1988), and that she may still want something even if

Consider your own theory of mind. What assumptions do you make about the way other people's behavior is affected by their beliefs, feelings, or ideas? You operate on the basis of such a theory all the time, but can you articulate it?

she can't have it (Lillard & Flavell, 1992). But they do not yet understand the basic principle that each person's actions are based on his own *representation* of reality, and that a person's representation may differ from what is "really" there. People act on the basis of what they believe or feel, even if what they believe is incorrect or what they feel is unexpected or apparently inconsistent in a given situation. Thus a person who feels sad even though she has succeeded at something will act on that sadness, not on the visible success. It is this new aspect of the theory of mind that is clearly absent in the 3-year-old, but that we can see emerging at about 4 or 5.

The theories of mind of the 3- and 4-year-old differ in other ways as well. The 3-year-old seems to assume that everyone knows and experiences the world in the same way he does—a classic form of egocentrism. The 4-year-old seems to understand that there are many worlds, and that other people not only know (or experience) different things, but that it is possible to "know" or believe something that is not true, and to change one's belief. He also understands that he himself may have experienced things differently at different times. He can remember that he used to think something different—that he used to think that the sponge was a rock but no longer believes that— one hint of the development of the ability to be *aware* of what one knows and thinks.

Such an increased awareness of the ways in which thinking operates is also apparent in other areas. For example, between 3 and 5, children figure out that in order to tell if a rock painted like a sponge is really a sponge or a rock, a person would need to touch or hold it. Just looking at it doesn't give you enough information (Flavell, 1993; O'Neill, Astington, & Flavell, 1992). These developments are important because they seem to be the first signs of what psychologists now call **metamemory** and **metacognition**—knowing about the process of memory and the process of thinking.

All of this new work on the child's theory of mind has not only opened up a fascinating new area of research, it has clearly demonstrated that the preschool child is vastly less egocentric than Piaget supposed. By age 4, and in more limited ways at earlier ages, the child has a remarkably sophisticated ability to understand other points of view, and can predict other people's behavior on the basis of deductions about their beliefs or feelings. I don't know about you, but I think this is an amazing—and surprising—achievement.

Other Aspects of Preschool Thought: Conservation and Classification

Other work on this same age period also points to the inescapable conclusion that Piaget badly underestimated the cognitive abilities of the preschool child. For example, studies of classification show that 3- and 4-year-olds are able to classify objects into groups quite readily if you simplify the task or if you make it clear that you want them to use some kind of superordinate category for classifying. For example, Sandra Waxman and Rochel Gelman (1986) told 3- and 4-year-olds that a puppet really liked pictures of food (or animals, or furniture). The children were then given 12 pictures and asked to put the ones the puppet would like in one bin and the ones the puppet would not like in another bin. When they were given the category label in this way, these young children could quite easily classify the pictures into food and nonfood categories, or furniture and nonfurniture categories.

Even at 18 months babies may be capable of some classification. In one study, Alison Gopnik and Andrew Meltzoff (1992) gave toddlers this age sets of objects to play with, such as four different finger rings and four different rocks. The objects were laid out in front of the child in a random array, without any specific instructions except encouragement to the child to handle the objects. Fully half of these young children physically separated the two types of objects into distinct piles or groups.

All in all, this research shows that the basic understanding that things go together in groups is present by at least age 2 (and perhaps earlier). But whether the child can display this understanding will depend on the way you set up the task. Piaget happened to pick a relatively difficult version of the task for his own studies, so he ended up underestimating the child's understanding.

In contrast, studies of conservation have generally confirmed Piaget's basic observations. Although younger children can demonstrate some understanding of conservation if the task is made very simple (Gelman, 1972; Wellman, 1982), most children cannot consistently solve conservation problems until age 5 or 6 or later.

The relatively late development of the child's understanding of conservation makes sense if we think of conservation tasks as a particularly sophisticated form of question about appearance and reality; the amount of juice appears to change, even though in reality it does not. In addition, to grasp the basic principle of conservation the child also has to understand rules about what kinds of manipulations will change quantities (that adding makes something more, for example). But the understanding of the distinction between appearance and reality seems to be a precursor or requirement for conservation tasks.

Overview of the Preschool Child's Thinking

How can we add up the bits and pieces of information about the preschool child's thinking? At the least, we can say that preschool children are capable of forms of logic that Piaget thought impossible at this stage. In particular, by age 4, and certainly by age 5, they not only can take others' perspectives, they understand at least in a preliminary way that other people's behavior rests on inner beliefs and feelings.

One possibility is that Piaget simply got the age wrong, and that the transition he saw at 6 or 7 really happens at around age 4 or 5. Certainly the various understandings that children seem to come to at about that age—about false belief, about appearance and reality, and about other people's physical perspectives—are remarkably stagelike.

Another possibility is that while preschoolers can do some sophisticated-looking things, their understanding remains specific rather than general. It is still tied heavily to specific situations, or can be displayed only with a good deal of support. Studies of both conservation and children's logic show that sophisticated performances can be *elicited* in 2-, 3-, and 4-year-old children, but preschoolers do not typically show such understandings spontaneously. In order for the preschool child to demonstrate these relatively advanced forms of thinking, you have to make the task quite simple, eliminate distractions, or give special clues. The fact that children this age can solve these problems at all is striking, but it is still true that preschool children think differently from older children. The very fact that they can perform certain tasks *only* when the tasks are made very simple or undistracting is evidence for such a difference.

More broadly, preschoolers do not seem to experience the world or think about it with as general a set of rules or principles as we see in older children and thus they do not easily generalize something they have learned in one context to a similar but not identical situation. It is precisely such a switch to general rules that Piaget thought characterized the thinking of the school-age child. So let's see if he was right.

▶ Cognitive Development in the School-Age Child

As was the case for the two age periods we've already explored, research on thinking among school-age children divides fairly neatly into two groups: those directly testing one or another of Piaget's observations, and those that introduce new themes. Let me give you an example of each.

Direct Tests of Piaget's Ideas

Unlike researchers who have studied the first two of Piaget's stages, those who have followed up on Piaget's descriptions of the concrete operational period have generally found that Piaget was right about the ages at which children first show various skills or understandings. A good illustration is a longitudinal study of concrete operations tasks by Carol Tomlinson-Keasey and her colleagues (1979). They followed a group of 38 children from kindergarten through third grade, testing them with five traditional concrete operations tasks each year: conservation of mass, weight, and volume; class inclusion; and hierarchical classification. You can see from Figure 7.3 that the children got better at all five tasks over the three-year period, with two spurts, one between the end of kindergarten and the start of first grade (about the age when Piaget thought that concrete operations really began) and another during second grade. You can also see that the different tasks were not equally easy, even though all of them appear to require similar levels of concrete operational thought. Conservation of mass was easier than conservation of weight, with conservation of volume the hardest of the three. Class inclusion was also generally harder than conservation of mass. In fact, the researchers found that conservation of mass seemed to be a necessary precursor for the development of class inclusion.

Tomlinson-Keasey also found that a child's skill on these tasks, relative to the other children, stayed approximately the same throughout the three years of testing. A 6-year-old who had developed conservation of mass early continued to be ahead of other children later on; a late-developing child went through the same sequence about two years later.

New Themes: Memory and Strategy Development

Some researchers, rather than simply repeating Piaget's tasks, have tried to devise other ways to test the proposition that school-age children approach tasks in ways that are more general, based on broader principles than do younger children. In particular, the notion that older children consciously use strategies for solving

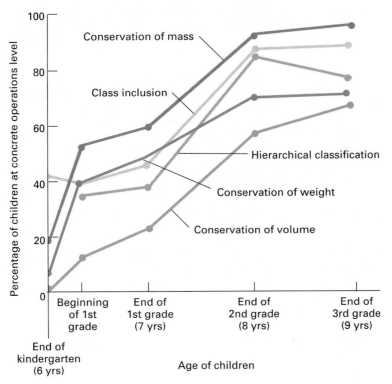

Figure 7.3
These results are from a longitudinal study in which the same children were given a set of concrete operations tasks five different times, beginning in kindergarten and ending in the third grade. (*Source:* Tomlinson-Keasey et al., 1979, adapted from Table 2, p. 1158.)

problems, or for remembering things, has been the basis for a whole new look at cognitive development. Work on memory and memory strategies is a particularly good example.

Rehearsal Strategies. Suppose you're about to go out the door to run some errands. You need to stop at the cleaners, buy some stamps, copy your IRS forms, and buy milk, bread, orange juice, carrots, lettuce, spaghetti, and spaghetti sauce at the grocery store. How do you remember all those things? There are many possible strategies, some of which I have listed (with examples) in Table 7.2. You could rehearse the list, you could organize the route in your mind, you could remember your menu for dinner when you get to the grocery store.

Do children do these things when they try to remember? One classic, early study (Keeney, Cannizzo, & Flavell, 1967) indicated that school-age children did, but younger children did not. Keeney showed children a row of seven cards with pictures on them and told them to try to remember all the pictures in the same order they were laid out. A space helmet, then placed over the child's head, kept the child from seeing the cards but allowed the experimenter to see if the child seemed to be rehearsing the list by muttering under his breath. Children under 5 almost never showed any rehearsal, while 8-to-10-year-old children usually did. Interestingly, when 5-year-olds were *taught* to rehearse, they were able to do so and their memory scores improved. But when these same 5-year-olds were then given a new problem without being reminded to rehearse, they stopped rehearsing. That is, they could use the strategy if they were reminded, but they did not produce it spontaneously—a pattern described as a *production deficiency*.

So how *do* you remember lists of things to buy, or a set of errands you have to run? Do you write them down? What other strategies do you use?

TABLE 7.2   Some Common Information-processing Strategies Involved in Remembering

- **Rehearsal.** Perhaps the most common strategy, which involves either mental or vocal repetition, or repetition of movement (as in learning to dance). May occur in children as young as 2 years under some conditions.

- **Clustering.** Grouping ideas or objects or words into clusters to help you remember them, such as "all animals," or "all the ingredients in the lasagna recipe," or "the chess pieces involved in the move called castling." This is one strategy that clearly benefits from experience with a particular subject or activity, since possible categories are learned, or are discovered in the process of exploring or manipulating a set of material. Primitive chunking occurs in 2-year-olds.

- **Elaboration.** Finding shared meaning or a common referent for two or more things that need to be remembered. The helpful mnemonic for recalling the names of the lines on the musical staff ("Every Good Boy Does Fine") is a kind of elaboration, as is associating the name of a person you have just met with some object or other word. This form of memory aid is not used spontaneously by all individuals, and is not used skillfully until fairly late in development, if then.

- **Systematic searching.** When you try to remember something, you can "scan" the memory for the whole domain in which it might be found. Three- and 4-year-old children can begin to do this to search for actual objects in the real world, but are not good at doing this in memory. So search strategies may be first learned in the external world and then applied to inner searches.

Source: Flavell, 1985.

More recent work suggests that preschool-age children can show some kinds of strategies in their remembering if the task is quite simple, such as the game of hide-and-seek (DeLoache, 1989). In one of DeLoache's research techniques, the child watches the experimenter hide an attractive toy in some obvious place (e.g., behind a couch), and is then told that when a buzzer goes off, she can go and find the toy. While playing with other toys during the four-minute delay interval, 2-year-olds often talked about the toy's hiding place, or pointed to or looked at the hiding place—all of which seem clearly to be early forms of mnemonic strategies.

These results and others like them tell us that there is no magic shift at age 5 or 6 or 7 from nonstrategic to strategic behavior. Primitive strategies are used by children as young as 2, perhaps younger. At the same time, it does appear to be the case that school-age children use strategies far more flexibly and efficiently, and that this becomes more and more true as one moves through the school years. For example, when learning a list of words, 8-year-olds are more likely to practice the words one at a time ("cat, cat, cat"), while still older children practice them in groups ("desk, lawn, sky, shirt, cat"). When the 8-year-olds are tested again a year later, they show signs of a shift toward the more efficient strategy (Guttentag, Ornstein, & Siemens, 1987).

THE REAL WORLD
Memory and the Child as Witness

In England, a 7-year-old was able to provide the police with details of her experience after a sexual assault, and was later able to identify her attacker in a lineup (Davies, 1993). In several famous cases in the United States, children as young as 3 to 5 years old have testified in court about physical or sexual abuse by nursery school teachers, testimony that has sometimes led to convictions. Testimony by children has been increasing in frequency, as courts have relaxed their rules about child witnesses (Penrod, 1993), but it continues to raise a storm of controversy, centering on two main issues: (1) Can young children accurately remember faces or events, and report on their experiences? (2) Are children more suggestible than adults about what they might have seen or experienced? Will they report what they have been told to say, or what they actually saw or felt?

A few answers have begun to emerge from a growing body of research addressing these questions, although in many areas we are a long way from definitive answers. Among other things, there is still a good deal of controversy about whether stress has the effect of improving or worsening children's memory for events—a highly relevant issue, given the fact that most of the events children would be asked to testify about in a court are likely to have been highly stressful. Nonetheless, there are a few things that seem fairly clear.

1. Recall of specific events, or of the faces of people seen at a previous time, does improve with age, but even preschoolers can recall action-related events with considerable accuracy. When experimenters have staged various crises or happenings and later asked children about them, or asked children to identify someone who had been involved in a witnessed event, preschoolers and school-age children can describe what happened, and can pick out a photo of the "culprit" almost as well as adults can. They report less detail than adults do, but they rarely report something that didn't actually occur (Ceci & Bruck, 1993; Davies, 1993). In one real-life study, Steward (1993) asked preschool children to describe their experiences on a recent visit to a medical clinic—visits that had been videotaped at the time. They reported only a quarter of the actual occasions when they had been touched on some part of their body by a medical person, but virtually all (94 percent) of the reports they did give were accurate

2. Younger children, particularly preschoolers, *are* more suggestible than older children or adults. This has usually been studied by showing a film, or telling a story to children and adults. The researchers then ask questions about what the subject saw, and inject some misleading question into the set—a question that assumes something that didn't really happen (e.g., "he was carrying a pipe wrench when he came into the room, wasn't he?"). Some days or weeks later, the subjects are again asked to describe what happened in the film or story. In this way you can check to see whether the inaccurate or misleading suggestion has been absorbed into the story. Young children are more affected than are older children or adults by such misleading suggestions. Of particular importance is the finding that it is possible to mislead young children enough in this way so that they will report inaccurately about physical events, such as having been kissed while being bathed, or having been spanked (Ceci & Bruck, 1993). This is much more true of preschoolers than of school-age children, although no one is quite sure just what mechanism is involved in this age difference.

Thus it *is* possible for an interviewer—psychologist, social worker, attorney, or whoever—to nudge a child's testimony in one direction or another. Adult witnesses are *also* susceptible to suggestions of various kinds. So the difference here is one of degree and not of kind. From the legal point of view, this does not mean that children should not testify; it speaks only to the weight one might give their recollections, and the care that should be used in the framing of questions.

Other Memory Strategies. Other strategies that help improve memory involve putting the items to be learned or remembered into some meaningful organization. When you organize your grocery shopping list in your mind so that all the fruits and vegetables are in one group, and all the canned food in another, you are using this principle, usually called clustering or chunking. George Miller (1956) showed that in active short-term memory, most of us can deal with only seven bits of information at a time, such as a seven-digit phone number. But if each "bit" contains not a single piece of information but a "chunk," such as "vegetables" or "things I need for the macaroni and cheese recipe," then the amount of information you can deal with will increase considerably.

Studies of such clustering or organizing strategies often involve having children or adults learn lists of words that have potential categories built into them.

For example, I might ask you to remember a list of words that includes a mixture of names for furniture, animals, and foods. I let you learn the list any way you wish, but when you then name off the items later, I can check for the kind of organization you used by seeing whether you name the same-category words together.

School-age children do show this kind of internal organization when they recall things, while preschoolers do not. And within the school years, older children use this strategy more and more efficiently, using a few large categories rather than many smaller ones (Bjorklund & Muir, 1988).

In sum, we can see some primitive signs of memory strategies under optimum conditions as early as age 2 or 3, but with increasing age children use more and more powerful ways of helping themselves remember things. In the use of each strategy children also appear to shift from a period in which they don't use it at all, to a period in which they will use it if reminded or taught, to one in which they use it spontaneously. Finally, they use these strategies more and more skillfully, and generalize them to more and more situations. These are obviously changes in the *quality* of the child's strategies as well as the quantity.

Expertise

However, . . . and this is a big however . . . all of these apparent developmental changes may well turn out to be as much a function of expertise as they are of age. Piaget obviously thought that children apply broad forms of logic to all their experiences in any given stage. If that's true, then the amount of specific experience a child has had with some set of material shouldn't make a lot of difference. A child who understands hierarchical classification but who has never seen a picture of a dinosaur ought to be able to create classifications of dinosaurs about as well as could a child who had played a lot with dinosaur models. A child who understands the principle of transitivity (that if A is greater than B, and B is greater than C, then A is greater than C) ought to be able to demonstrate this ability with sets of strange figures as well as she could with a set of toys familiar to her. But in fact that seems not to be the case.

There is now a great deal of research that shows that specific knowledge makes a huge difference. Children and adults who know a lot about some subject or some set of materials (dinosaurs, baseball cards, mathematics, or whatever) not only categorize information in that topic area in more complex and hierarchical ways, they are also better at remembering new information on that topic and better at applying more advanced forms of logic to material in that area. Expertise not only fosters greater speed in performing some well-practiced task, it also changes the way we think about that material and the way we go about solving problems in that domain. Furthermore, such expertise seems to generalize very little to other tasks (Ericsson & Crutcher, 1990).

Much of the most interesting work has been done by Michelene Chi and her various colleagues (Bedard & Chi, 1992; Chi et al., 1989; Chi & Ceci, 1987). In her most famous study (1978) she showed that expert chess players can remember the placement of chess pieces on a board much more quickly and accurately than can novice chess players, *even when the expert chess players are children and the novices are adults.* To paraphrase Flavell (1985), expertise makes any of us look very smart, very cognitively advanced; lack of expertise makes us look very dumb.

These school-age chess players, unless they are rank novices, would remember a series of chess moves or the arrangement of pieces on a chessboard far better than I could, since they have expertise and I do not.

Since young children are novices at almost everything, while older children are more expert at many things, perhaps the apparent age difference in the use of cognitive strategies, such as memory strategies, is just the effect of more specific knowledge, more experience, and *not* the result of stagelike changes in fundamental cognitive structures.

Overview of the Thinking of the Schoolchild

When we look at what we know about the thinking of children between 6 and 12, we find a sort of paradox. On the one hand, Piaget seems to have been more accurate in his descriptions of this period than any other. He did not underestimate the schoolchild's abilities as he had the abilities of infants and preschoolers. Nor did he overestimate them, as he did the skills of the teenager—a point I'll come back to in a moment. What we see in this age period is the emergence, or perhaps the more consistent use, of more complex sorts of analysis and strategy. Children this age, much more than younger children, also know what they know and can reflect on the ways they use to learn or remember things.

All of this sounds very like Piaget's description of this period. Yet it looks very much as if these cognitive skills do not arise at all from the mechanism Piaget suggested, which was some kind of general *equilibration*—a broad reorganization of schemes—at about age 6. The developmental process now appears to be far more gradual, and is affected heavily by the amount of experience the child has in a particular domain. At the same time, it *is* true that the 8-year-old approaches new tasks differently. He is more likely to attempt a more complex strategy, and if that strategy fails, he is more likely to try another one. So although the process may be gradual, there still appears to be genuine qualitative change.

▷ Cognitive Development in Adolescence

Many of the same paradoxes emerge in the research on adolescent thinking. Early research, following Piaget's ideas, did indeed indicate that, as Edith Neimark (1982) put it,

> *An enormous amount of evidence from an assortment of tasks shows that adolescents and adults are capable of feats of reasoning not attained under normal circumstances by [younger] children, and that these abilities develop fairly rapidly during the ages of about 11 to 15.* (p. 493)

Furthermore, many of the qualities of adolescent thought Piaget identified do seem to emerge during this period. Adolescents, much more than school-age children, operate with possibilities in addition to reality, and they are more likely to use deductive logic. As Flavell (1985, p. 98) puts it, the thinking of the school-age child "hugs the ground of . . . empirical reality," while the teenager is more likely to soar into the realm of speculation and possibility. An 8-year-old thinks that "knowing" something is a simple matter of finding out the facts; a teenager is more likely to see knowledge as relative, as less certain (Bartsch, 1993).

Some additional illustrations would probably make the change clearer. In an early cross-sectional study, Susan Martorano (1977) tested 20 girls at each of four grades (sixth, eighth, tenth, and twelfth) on 10 different tasks that require one or more of what Piaget called formal operations skills. Indeed, many of the tasks she used were those Piaget himself had devised. Results from two of these tasks are in

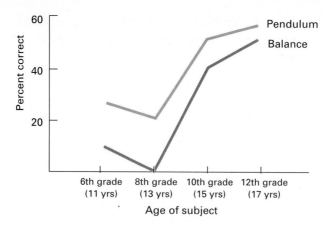

Figure 7.4
These are the results from 2 of the 10 different formal operational tasks used in Martorano's cross-sectional study. (*Source:* Martorano, 1977, p. 670. Copyright by the American Psychological Association.)

Figure 7.4. The pendulum problem is the same one I described earlier; the "balance" problem requires a youngster to predict whether or not two varying weights, hung at varying distances on either side of a scale, will balance. To solve this problem using formal operations, the teenager must consider both weight and distance simultaneously. You can see in the figure that older students generally did better, with the biggest improvement in scores between eighth and tenth grades (between ages 13 and 15).

In a more practical vein, Catherine Lewis (1981) has shown that these new cognitive abilities alter the ways teenagers go about making decisions. Older teenagers are more focused on the future, on possibilities and options, when they consider decisions. Lewis asked eighth-, tenth,- and twelfth-grade students to respond to a set of dilemmas, each of which involved a person facing a difficult decision, such as whether or not to have an operation to remove a facial disfigurement, or how to decide which doctor to trust when the doctors give differing advice. Forty-two percent of the twelfth graders, but only 11 percent of the eighth graders, mentioned future possibilities in their answers to these dilemmas.

In answer to the cosmetic surgery dilemma, for example, a twelfth grader said:

Well, you have to look into the different things . . . that might be more important later on in your life. You should think about, will it have any effect on your future and with, maybe, the people you meet. . . . (Lewis, 1981, p. 541)

An eighth grader, in response to the same dilemma, said:

The different things I would think about in getting the operation is like if the girls turn you down on a date, or the money, or the kids teasing you at school. . . . (Lewis, 1981, p. 542)

The eighth grader, as is characteristic of the school-age child, is focused on the here and now, on concrete things. The teenager is considering things that *might* happen in the future.

But note that even among the twelfth graders in Lewis's study nearly three-fifths did not show this type of future orientation. And take another look at Figure 7.4; only about 50 to 60 percent of twelfth graders solved the two formal operations problems. In Martorano's study, in fact, only 2 of the 20 twelfth-grade subjects used formal operations logic on all 10 problems.

These findings reflect a common pattern in research on adolescent thinking: by no means do all teenagers (or adults) use these more abstract forms of logic

What was the last major decision you had to make? Think for a minute about how you went about it. What factors did you consider? Did you think about future consequences, or only about the here and now?

and thought. Keating (1980) estimates that only about 50 to 60 percent of 18-to-20-year-olds in Western countries seem to use formal operations at all, let alone consistently. In non-Western countries the rates are even lower.

Why Doesn't Every Teenager Use Formal Logic?

Why? There are several possibilities. One is that the usual methods of measuring formal operations are simply extremely difficult or unclear. When the instructions are made clearer, or the subjects are given hints or rules, they can demonstrate some aspects of formal operations (Danner & Day, 1977)—just as preschoolers can display some "concrete operations" skills when tasks are made simpler or clearer.

A related possibility is that expertise is once again the crucial element. That is, most of us have some formal operational ability, but we can only apply it to topics or tasks with which we are familiar. For example, I use formal operations reasoning about psychology because it is an area I know well. But I am a lot less skillful at applying the same kind of reasoning to fixing my car—about which I know next to nothing. Willis Overton and his colleagues (1987) have found considerable support for this possibility in their research. They found that as many as 90 percent of adolescents could solve quite complex logic problems if they were stated using familiar content, while only half could solve the identical logic problem when it was stated in abstract language.

Still a third possibility is that most of our everyday experiences and tasks do not require formal operations. Inductive reasoning or other simpler forms of logic are quite sufficient most of the time. So we get into a cognitive rut, applying our most usual mode of thinking to new problems as well. We can kick our thinking up a notch under some circumstances, especially if someone reminds us that it would be useful to do so, but we simply don't rehearse formal operations very much.

The fact that formal operations thinking is found more often among young people or adults in Western cultures may be interpreted in the same way. Because of the high technology and the complexity of life in industrialized countries, there is simply more demand for formal operational thought in such cultures. By this argument, all nonretarded teenagers and adults are thought to have the *capacity* for formal logic, but only those of us whose lives demand its development will actually acquire it.

Notice that all these explanations undermine the very notion that there is a universal "stage" of thinking in adolescence. Yes, there are more abstract forms of thinking that may develop in adolescence, but they are neither universal nor broadly used by individual teenagers or adults. Whether one develops or uses these forms of logic depends heavily on experience, expertise, and environmental demand.

▶ Preliminary Conclusions and Questions

I have been raising a variety of questions as I have gone along, so you already know that there are many puzzles remaining about cognitive development. To set the stage for a discussion of the third approach, information processing, let me pause for a quick review.

The child comes a long way in only about 15 years. He moves from very rudimentary abilities to represent things to himself with images and words, to classifications, to conservation, to abstract, deductive logic. In broad outline, Piaget's observations about this sequence have been frequently confirmed. Children do clearly change not only in what they know but in the way they approach problems.

But it now seems quite unlikely that this developmental progression involves coherent, general stages of the kind Piaget envisioned. Nor do new cognitive skills emerge full-blown. Rather, they are preceded by more rudimentary or partial versions of the same skills at earlier ages. For example, virtually all the achievements of the concrete operational period are present in at least rudimentary or fragmentary form in the preschool years. This observation undermines the basic notion of a stage as Piaget proposed it.

Most of those who study cognitive development today would thus describe a much more gradual process, characterized by sequences but not by broad stages. This leaves us with at least two major disputes which are far from being resolved. First, as the question is usually put today, is knowledge or cognitive skill totally *domain-specific* or at least partially *domain-general?* If a child learns a new type of logic or a new memory strategy when playing with his favorite dinosaur collection, does this new skill generalize to other tasks, other situations (which would make it domain-general), or does he use this new skill only in the very specific situation in which he first learned it (domain-specific)? Piaget appears to have been wrong about broad general stages, but that still leaves a wide range of possibilities. Development might be *totally* situation(domain)-specific, or it might have at least some generality, with some basic skills or understandings changing with age and being applied across several different domains or tasks. We see some sign of just such a semigeneral, almost stagelike shift in children's theory of mind at about age 4. On the other side of the coin, the research on expertise makes thinking look highly domain-specific.

Second, there is the question of whether cognitive development involves qualitative change or only quantitative change. Do children simply get better or more efficient at basic cognitive processes, or are there new processes, new skills, that emerge gradually over time?

All of these children are intently exploring or experimenting. But do they use the same kinds of logic and strategies as they experiment, or do the older kids approach their play and learning in a different way? This is one of the persisting questions about cognitive development.

The third theoretical approach to the study of intelligence, the information processing approach, has offered new ways to think about and study both of these disputes.

▶ Information Processing in Children

Theorists who study cognitive power ask *how well* a child does intellectual tasks compared to others; those who study structure ask *what type* of logic the child uses in solving problems, and how those structures change with age. The **information processing** theorists ask what the child is *doing* intellectually when faced with a task, what intellectual *processes* she brings to bear, and how those processes might change with age. The information processing approach is not really a theory of cognitive development; it is an approach to studying thinking and remembering—a set of questions, and some methods of analysis.

This third approach has a whole series of theoretical fathers and grandfathers. The direct line of inheritance is from studies of adult intelligence, particularly computer simulations of adult intelligence. In fact the basic metaphor underlying the entire information processing approach has been that of the human mind as computer. Like a computer, we can think of the "hardware" of cognition (the physiology of the brain, the nerves, and connective tissues) and the "software" of cognition (the program that uses the basic hardware). To understand thinking in general, we need to understand the processing capacity of the hardware and just what programs have to be "run" to perform any given task. What inputs (facts or data) are needed, what coding, decoding, remembering, or analyzing is required? To understand cognitive *development*, we need to discover whether there are any changes with age in the basic processing capacity of the system and/or in the nature of the programs used. Do children develop new types of processing (new programs)? Or do they simply learn to use basic programs on new material?

In studies of children's thinking, there are at least two branches to the information processing family tree. On one side is a group of researchers and theorists with a somewhat Piagetian flavor who have given up the notion of stages but are still committed to the notion of qualitatively changing sequences of development (e.g., Siegler, 1981). On the other side are researchers with a strong intellectual-power flavor, who have been trying to identify a set of basic information processing capacities or strategies that may underlie differences in IQ. What is different about what "brighter" people really do when confronted with a problem? These two approaches to the study of information processing are connected, but for the moment let me talk about them somewhat separately.

Developmental Approaches to Information Processing

Changes in Processing Capacity. One obvious place to look for an explanation of developmental changes in cognitive skills is in the hardware itself. Any computer has physical limits to the number of different operations it can perform at one time, or in a given space of time. As the brain and nervous system develop in the early years of life, with synapses formed and then pruned to remove the redundant ones, perhaps the capacity, the speed, or the efficiency of the system increases.

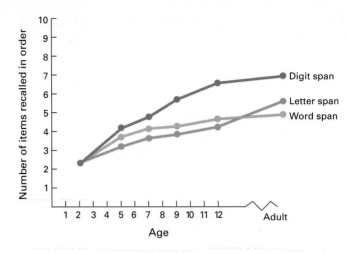

Figure 7.5
Psychologists have tried to measure basic memory capacity by asking subjects to listen to a list of numbers, letters, or words, and then to repeat back the list in order. This figure shows the number of such items that children of various ages are able to remember and report accurately. (*Source:* Dempster, 1981, from Figures 1, 2, and 3, pp. 66, 67, 68.)

One type of evidence that is often mentioned to support the possibility of an age change in processing capacity is the finding that young children are able to remember fewer items in lists of numbers, letters, or words than are older children. You can see the results of one typical study in Figure 7.5.

Such results are consistent with the hypothesis that there is an increase in basic memory capacity with age. But there are a number of plausible competing explanations. For example, younger children clearly have less *experience* with numbers, letters, and words. Perhaps their poorer performance on tests that measure memory span is simply another example of the fact that experts can do things better than novices. In fact, when the degree of experience is better matched, such as by having older children try to remember new letterlike figures, much of the age difference in memory span disappears. Most experts in this area of research now believe that there is probably no basic increase in underlying capacity, but that there may well be improvements in efficiency, which in turn frees up more "memory space" for storage (Schneider & Pressley, 1989).

Processing Efficiency. The best evidence that cognitive processing becomes more efficient is that it gets steadily faster with age. Robert Kail (1991a; 1991b; Kail & Park, 1992) has found virtually the same exponential increase with age in processing speed for a wide variety of tasks, including such perceptual/motor tasks as tapping, simple response time to a stimulus (like pressing a button when you hear a buzzer), and cognitive tasks such as mental addition or subtests from the WISC. He has found virtually identical patterns of speed increases in studies in Korea as well as studies in the United States, which adds a useful bit of cross-cultural validity to the argument.

The most plausible explanation for this common pattern is that there is some fundamental change in the physical system itself that allows greater and greater speed of both response and mental processing. The most likely candidate for such a basic change is the "pruning" of synapses—a process I talked about in Chapter 4 (Hale, Fry, & Jessie, 1993). If pruning begins at about age 2, and then continues steadily throughout childhood, one effect could be to make the "wiring diagram" more efficient and thus faster.

Figure 7.6
This balance scale is similar to what Siegler used in his experiments. (*Source:* From Siegler, 1981, p. 7.)

Use of Strategies.   These increases in capacity or efficiency (speed) are now accepted by most developmentalists as the base upon which cognitive development occurs (Kuhn, 1992). Children also acquire new and qualitatively different strategies, especially in areas in which they have expertise. The existence of these strategies then has the effect of making processing still more efficient, as you have already seen in the research on memory strategies and expertise.

Rules for Problem Solving.   Another area in which information processing researchers have found qualitative progressions is in problem solving. Some of the best-known work in this area has been Robert Siegler's study of the development of *rules* (Siegler, 1976; 1978; 1981). Siegler's approach is a kind of cross between Piagetian theory and information processing. He argues that cognitive development consists in acquiring a set of basic rules, which are then applied to a broader and broader range of problems on the basis of experience. There are no stages, only sequences.

In one test of this approach, Siegler uses a balance scale with a series of pegs on either side of the center, like the one in Figure 7.6. Discs can be placed on these pegs, and the child is asked to predict which way the balance will fall, depending on the location and number of discs (you may recognize this as similar to the task Martorano used in her study of formal operations). A complete solution requires the child to take into account both the number of discs on each side, and the specific location of the discs.

Children do not develop such a complete solution immediately. Instead, Siegler predicts that four rules will develop, in order: Rule I is basically a "preoperational" rule, taking into account only one dimension, the number of weights. Children using this rule will predict that the side with more discs will go down, no matter which peg they are placed on. Rule II is a transitional rule. The child still judges on the basis of number, except when there are the same number of weights on both sides, and in that case takes distance from the fulcrum into account. Rule III is basically a concrete operational rule, since the child tries to take both distance and weight into account simultaneously, except that when the information is conflicting (such as when the side with weights closer to the fulcrum has more weights), the child simply guesses. Rule IV is basically the formal operational rule—the one that Martorano counted as "correct" in her study (recall Figure 7.4). At this point the child/youth figures out the actual formula (distance × weight for each side).

Siegler has found that virtually all children perform on this and similar tasks as if they were following one or another of these rules, and that the rules seem to develop in the given order. Very young children behave as if they don't have a

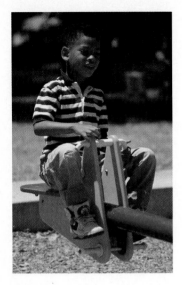

Experience with a teeter-totter may be one source of knowledge about how balance scales work.

Write down three good ways to study. In choosing one of these methods, does it matter what subject you are studying? How do you know all this? Do you think about it consciously when you are starting to study? The fact that you know these things, and can think about them, is evidence that you have metacognition—that you know what you know and how to think.

rule (they guess or behave randomly so far as Siegler can determine); when a rule develops, it is always Rule I that comes first. But progression from one rule to the next is heavily dependent on experience. If children are given practice with the balance scale so that they can make predictions and then check which way the balance actually falls, many show rapid shifts upward in the sequence of rules.

Thus Siegler is attempting to describe a logical sequence children follow, not unlike the basic sequence of stages that Piaget described, but Siegler shows that the specific step in this sequence that we see in a particular child is dependent not so much on age as on the child's specific experience with a given set of material. In Piaget's terminology, this is rather like saying that when accommodation of some scheme occurs, it always occurs in a particular sequence, but the rate with which the child moves through that sequence depends on experience.

Metacognition and Executive Processes. A third area in which information processing researchers have been active is in studying how children come to know what they know. If I gave you a list of things to remember and then asked you later to tell me how you had gone about trying to remember it, you would have little difficulty explaining your mental process. You may even have consciously considered the various alternative strategies and then selected the best one. You could also tell me good ways to study, or which kinds of tasks will be hardest, and why. These are all examples of metamemory or metacognition—knowing about remembering, or knowing about knowing. Such skills are a part of a larger category that information processing theorists refer to as **executive processes:** planning what to do, considering alternative strategies—all similar to what an executive may do.

These skills are of particular interest because there is some suggestion that it may be precisely such metacognitive or executive skills that emerge (gradually) with age. Performance on a whole range of tasks will be better if the child can monitor her own performance, or recognize when a particular strategy is called for and when it is not. I pointed out earlier that 4- and 5-year-old children do show some such monitoring, but it is rarely found earlier than that and it clearly improves fairly rapidly after school age. Such executive skills may well form the foundation of some of the age changes Piaget described.

A Summary of Developmental Changes in Information Processing. If I put together all the bits and pieces of evidence about information processing capacity and skills, I arrive at a set of tentative generalizations:

1. There is probably *not* any increase in the basic processing capacity of the system, but there does seem to be an increase in the efficiency with which the "hardware" is used, which results in steadily greater processing speed.
2. The sheer amount of specific knowledge the child has about any given task increases as the child experiments, explores, studies things in school. This leads to more and more "expert" approaches to remembering and solving problems.
3. Genuinely new strategies are acquired, probably in some kind of order. In particular, the child seems to develop in middle childhood some "executive" or "metacognitive" abilities—she knows that she knows, and can *plan* a strategy for the first time.

4. Existing strategies are applied to more and more different domains, and more and more flexibly. If a child learned to rehearse on one kind of memory problem, the older child is more likely to try it on a new memory task; the younger child (particularly younger than 5 or 6) is not likely to generalize the strategy to the new task—although once again it is true that some transfer is seen in children as young as 2 when the conditions are carefully constructed (Crisafi & Brown, 1986).

5. With increasing age, a wider range of different strategies can be applied to the same problem, so that if the first doesn't work, a back-up or alternative strategy can be used. If you can't find your misplaced keys by retracing your steps, you try a back-up, such as looking in your other purse or the pocket of your jacket, or searching each room of the house in turn. Young children do not do this; school-age children and adolescents do.

Thus some of the changes that Piaget observed and chronicled with such detail and richness seem to be the result simply of increased experience with tasks and problems (a quantitative change, if you will). But there also seems to be a qualitative change in the complexity, generalizability, and flexibility of strategies used by the child.

Individual Differences in Information Processing

While some researchers in the information processing tradition have been asking about developmental changes or sequences, others have been trying to understand individual differences. IQ tests are intended to measure such underlying ability differences by giving people fairly complex cognitive tasks, each of which may require a whole series of more fundamental information processing strategies. Perhaps we could come closer to understanding individual differences in intelligence or intellectual performance if we shifted our attention to those more fundamental processes. Generally the strategy has been to look at the relationship between IQ scores on standard tests and measures of specific information processing. This strategy has yielded a few preliminary connections.

Speed of Information Processing. Since it is becoming clear that increases in speed of processing are one of the underpinnings of age changes in cognitive skills, it makes sense to hypothesize that differences in speed may also underlie individual differences in IQ. A number of different investigators have found just such a link: Subjects with faster reaction times or speed of performance on a variety of simple tasks also have higher IQ scores on standard tests (Vernon, 1987). There are even a number of studies in which speed of processing has been directly linked to central nervous system functioning and to IQ. For example, it is now possible to measure the speed of conduction of impulses along individual nerves, such as nerves in the arm. Philip Vernon (Vernon & Mori, 1992) has found that such a measure correlates about .45 with IQ.

Most of this research has been done with adults, but a link between speed of reaction time and IQ has also been found in a few studies with children (Keating, List, & Merriman, 1985). Furthermore, there are some pretty clear suggestions that such speed-of-processing differences may be built in at birth. The fact that measures of infant habituation and recognition memory are correlated so strongly with later IQ—a finding I talked about in Chapter 5— certainly points to such a conclusion.

Other IQ-Processing Links.   Another research approach has been to compare the information processing strategies used by normal-IQ and retarded children. Two examples:

Judy DeLoache (DeLoache & Brown, 1987) has compared the searching strategies of groups of 2-year-olds who were either developing normally or showed delayed development. When the search task was very simple, such as searching for a toy hidden in some distinctive location in a room, the two groups did not differ in search strategies or skill. But when the experimenter surreptitiously moved the toy before the child was allowed to search, normally developing children were able to search in alternative, plausible places, such as in nearby locations; delayed children simply persisted in looking in the place where they had seen the toy hidden. They either could not change strategies or did not have alternative, more complex strategies in their repertoires.

Other research underlines this difference in the flexibility of strategy use. In several studies, Joseph Campione and Ann Brown (1984; Campione et al., 1985) have found that both retarded and normal-IQ children could learn to solve problems like items (a), (b), and (c) in Figure 7.7, but the retarded children could not transfer this learning to slightly differing problems of the same general type, like item (d) in the figure, while normal-IQ children could. Both sets of studies suggest that flexibility of use of any given strategy may be another key dimension of individual differences in intelligence.

▶ Putting the Three Approaches Together

I hope it is clear by now that the information processing approach offers us some important bridges between the power and structure theories of intelligence in children. It now looks as if there are some basic, inborn strategies (such as noting

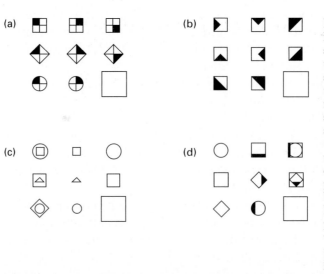

Figure 7.7
For panels (a) through (c) the subject must figure out the "system" in each set and then describe what pattern should go in the empty box in the bottom right-hand corner. Panel (a) shows rotation; panel (b) shows addition of two elements; panel (c) shows subtraction. The figure in panel (d) is harder because the subject must apply *two* principles at once, in this case both addition and rotation rules. Retarded children could do problems like (a), (b), and (c) as well as normal-IQ children, but they did much more poorly on problems like (d). (*Source:* Campione et al., 1985, Figure 1, p. 302, and Figure 4, p. 306.)

differences or similarities), and that these strategies change over the course of the early years of life, with more complex strategies or rules emerging, and old strategies used more flexibly. Plain old experience is also part of the process. The more a child plays with blocks, the better she will be at organizing and classifying blocks; the more a person plays chess, the better he will be at seeing and remembering relationships among pieces on the board. So some of the changes that Piaget thought of as changes in underlying structure are, instead, specific task learning. But there seems to be some structural change as well, such as the emergence of new strategies, particularly metacognitive strategies.

Individual differences in what we normally think of as intelligence can then be conceived of as resulting both from inborn differences in the speed or efficiency of the basic processes (differences in the hardware, perhaps), and from differences in expertise or experience. The child with a slower or less-efficient processing system is going to move through all the various steps and stages more slowly; he will *use* the experience he has less efficiently or effectively, and may never develop as complete a range of strategies as does the initially quicker child. This point is nicely illustrated in a recent study of expertise done in Germany (Schneider & Bjorklund, 1992). School-age children who were very knowledgeable about soccer (experts) had better recall of soccer-related lists than did nonexperts. But high-IQ novices did as well as low-IQ experts on these same tasks. So rich knowledge in some area can compensate somewhat for lower IQ, but it does not create equality. High-IQ experts are still going to be better than medium- or low-IQ experts in any given area.

The information processing approach may also have some real practical applications. The studies of recognition memory in infancy, for example, may give us a way to identify retarded children very early in life, or to sort out from among low-birth-weight infants those that seem at particular risk for later problems. By identifying the key differences between retarded and nonretarded children (or between brighter and less-bright children), we may also be able to identify specific kinds of training that would be useful for a retarded child, or for a child with a learning disability of some type.

I do not want to wax too rhapsodic about the information processing approach. It is well to remember that we do not yet have any tests of information processing ability that could realistically replace the careful use of IQ tests in schools and clinics—although there are a few psychologists who believe that a clinically useful biological measure of IQ will be available within several decades (Matarazzo, 1992). Nor are the sequential theories of information processing development far enough along yet to explain all the differences we see between infants, preschoolers, and older children in performance on various Piagetian tasks. In short, information processing is an important, integrative addition to our understanding of cognitive development, but it does not replace all the other approaches.

▶ Summary

1. The study of cognitive "power" does not tell us what we need to know about the shared changes in the *way* children think about the world around them. Piaget's theory was addressed to this question.

2. Piaget assumed that the child is an active agent in his own development, constructing his own understandings, and adapting to the environment by changing his basic schemes.

3. Schemes and their relationships to one another are changed through the processes of assimilation, accommodation, and equilibration, beginning with primitive schemes at birth and progressing sequentially through several stages.

4. Piaget's first stage is the sensorimotor period, birth to 18 months, during which the baby understands the world in terms of her senses and motor actions.

5. In Piaget's preoperational period, from 18 months to 6 years, the child is able to use symbols to represent objects to himself internally. Piaget saw the child at this age as still egocentric and relatively unskilled.

6. In Piaget's third stage, concrete operations, from age 6 to 12, the child acquires powerful new mental tools, called operations, such as reversibility, addition, subtraction, multiplication, and serial ordering.

7. During the fourth Piagetian stage, formal operations, from age 12 onward, the young person becomes able to manipulate *ideas* as well as objects, approaches problems systematically, and develops the ability to use deductive logic.

8. Post-Piagetian studies of infant cognition show infants to be far more cognitively skilled than Piaget thought. They can imitate from the earliest weeks, and remember events, both of which appear to involve some kind of internal representation.

9. By about age 4, children become significantly less egocentric, can distinguish between appearance and reality in a variety of tasks, and develop a surprisingly sophisticated theory of how minds work. They understand that other people's actions are based on thoughts, feelings, and beliefs, not on "reality."

10. Studies of school-age children confirm many of Piaget's specific observations and also indicate the importance of strategies in children's thinking at these ages. But it is clear that the development of the more complex forms of thought visible at these ages is gradual, not abrupt.

11. Children's cognitive skills are also highly dependent on specific knowledge and expertise.

12. In adolescence, more complex forms of logic and reasoning, similar to what Piaget described, become more prominent, but no more than half of young people display these advanced types of thinking.

13. Collectively these findings make Piaget's strong stage concept untenable, but there is still disagreement about whether the observed changes nonetheless

occur in clusters or groups, and whether the changes are qualitative or quantitative.

14. Information processing theorists ask not about structure, but about the basic processes that make up any cognitive activity, such as decoding, encoding, remembering, planning, or analyzing.

15. Information processing specialists interested in development have asked what ways the basic processes change with age among children. There appear to be clear improvements with age in processing efficiency, perhaps resulting from synaptic pruning.

16. There also appear to be increases with age in the use of various strategies, including memory strategies, and executive processes.

17. Other information processing specialists focus on individual differences in efficiency of basic processes. Higher-IQ individuals, for example, appear to process information more quickly, and apply strategies or knowledge more broadly.

▶ Key Terms

accommodation (192)

assimilation (192)

concrete operations (193)

conservation (194)

deductive logic (198)

egocentrism (194)

equilibration (192)

executive processes (220)

formal operations (193)

inductive logic (198)

information processing (217)

metacognition (206)

metamemory (206)

operation (193)

preoperational stage (193)

scheme (191)

sensorimotor stage (193)

theory of mind (205)

▶ Suggested Readings

Flavell, J. H. (1992). Cognitive development: Past, present, and future. *Developmental Psychology, 28,* 998–1005.

> This brief paper by one of the leading thinkers and researchers in the field of cognitive development gives you a quick tour of what Flavell thinks we now know, don't know, and are still arguing about. Flavell's 1985 book, *Cognitive Development,* cited in the references, is also a wonderful source.

Kuhn, D. (1992). Cognitive development. In M. H. Bornstein & M. E. Lamb (Eds.), *Developmental psychology: An advanced textbook* (3rd ed.). Hillsdale, NJ: Erlbaum.

A first-rate discussion of the strengths and limitations of both Piagetian and information processing approaches.

Schneider, W., & Pressley, M. (1989). *Memory development between 2 and 20*. New York: Springer-Verlag.

An excellent, thorough, up-to-date discussion of all the research on memory in children.

Thomas, R. M. (1990). Basic concepts and applications of Piagetian cognitive development theory. In R. M. Thomas (Ed.), *The encyclopedia of human development and education*. Oxford: Pergamon Press.

This is one of the very best short descriptions of Piaget's theory I have ever read. If you simply need another run at the basic ideas, expressed in someone else's language, this is the place to look.

THE DEVELOPMENT OF LANGUAGE

8

What Is Language Anyway?

Before the First Word: The Prelinguistic Phase
Early Perception of Language
Early Sounds
Early Gestures
• *Research Report:* Early Gestural "Language" in the Children of Deaf Parents

The First Words
The Naming Explosion
• *Cultures and Contexts:* Early Words by Children in Many Cultures
Later Word Learning

Speaking in Sentences: The Development of Grammar
First Sentences: 18 to 27 Months
Grammar Explosion: 27 to 36 Months
Complex Sentences: 30 to 48 Months
• *The Real World:* Bilingual Children

The Development of Word Meaning
Which Comes First, the Meaning or the Word?

Extending the Class
Constraints on Word Learning

Using Language: Communication and Self-Direction

Explaining Language Development
Imitation and Reinforcement
Newer Environmental Theories: Talking to the Child
• *Research Report:* The Importance of Reading to the Child
Innateness Theories
• *Cultures and Contexts:* Universals and Variations in Early Language
Constructivist Theories

Individual Differences in Language Development
Differences in Rate
Differences in Style

An Application of the Basic Knowledge: Learning to Read

Summary

Key Terms

Suggested Readings

A friend of mine listened one morning at breakfast while her 6-year-old and her 3-year-old had the following conversation about the relative dangers of forgetting to feed the goldfish versus overfeeding the goldfish:

6-year-old: It's worse to forget to feed them.
3-year-old: No, it's badder to feed them too much.

6-year-old: You don't say badder, you say worser.
3-year-old: But it's baddest to give them too much food.
6-year-old: No it's not. It's worsest to forget to feed them.

Most of us, listening to children's language like this, are amused and charmed. There is something delightfully creative and unexpected about it all, and yet completely clear. Linguists have also learned an enormous amount about children's language by studying "errors" like *baddest* or *worsest*—just as Piaget learned an enormous amount about the child's thinking by studying children's "wrong" answers. But one of the really remarkable things about language is that children make so few errors of this kind. Out of the enormously complex set of sounds they hear in the language of those around them, children somehow come to be able to speak their native tongue with fluency and accuracy within only a few years. At 6 or 8 months we hear a baby babbling a few sounds; by 18 months the child will probably be using 20 or 30 separate words, and by 3 years children construct long and complex sentences, like those of the 3-year-old in the conversation about the goldfish. Parents usually find this whole sequence fun to listen to, but most of us don't spend a lot of time worrying about just how a child manages all this.

For psychologists and linguists, though, the child's rapid and skillful acquisition of language has remained an enduring puzzle. Is some kind of language-learning faculty built into the organism? Is the child "taught" language in some direct way? Does the child "figure it out" on the basis of what he hears?

In attempting to answer such questions, the vast majority of linguists have looked at changes in both grammar (which the linguists call **syntax**) and word meaning (called **semantics**). Lately there have also been some attempts to explain differences in the rate of language development from one child to the next, and differences in individual children's style of language learning. But before I can explore any of these questions, I need to go back a step.

▶ What Is Language Anyway?

What do we mean by *language?* What are we trying to explain? As most linguists use the term, it has several key features:

1. It is an "arbitrary system of *symbols*" (Brown, 1965, p. 246). Words (or gestures) *stand for* things. But the particular combination of sounds (or gestures) used to stand for some object, event, or relationship varies from one language to another, so the symbols are arbitrary.
2. It is *rule-governed*. Every language has certain rules for stringing together individual symbols, or creating new words, such as the rules for creating superlatives (like *nice, nicer, nicest*) or for past tenses, or for the order of words in sentences.
3. Within those rules, language is *creative*. Speakers of a language combine symbols in new ways to create new meanings. When you talk, you are not restricted to some repertoire of sentences you have heard and learned; you create sentences according to your need at the moment.

Thus language is not just a collection of sounds. Very young babies make several different sounds, but we do not consider that they are using language, since they do not appear to use those sounds to *refer* to things or events (that is, they do not use the sounds as symbols), and they do not combine individual sounds into different orders to create varying meaning. So far as we know, for example, the meaning does not change if a 6-month-old says "kikiki bababa" versus "bababa kikiki."

Some other animals, most notably primates like chimps, and possibly other mammals like dolphins, can also learn to use sound or gestural systems in the symbolic way that we define as language. Chimps, for example, can learn to use sign language or point to sequences of symbols, even creating new combinations of such symbols (Savage-Rumbaugh, 1990). Like human children, chimps also understand a good deal more than they can express, and can accurately follow quite complex verbal requests (Savage-Rumbaugh et al., 1993). But in most cases it takes a good deal of effort to teach them to use expressive language in creative ways. In contrast, as Flavell (1985, p. 248) puts it, "Draconian measures would be needed to *prevent* most children from learning to talk". And as any parent can tell you, once they learn, it is virtually impossible to shut them up!

The developmental process in infants and young children, from prelanguage sounds and gestures to language, follows a remarkably common set of steps.

▶ Before the First Word: The Prelinguistic Phase

Given the definition I've just offered, you may well think that there is little reason for language researchers to study the sounds or gestures of infants. The baby's early sounds are not yet language, so why not start by studying the first obvious words? But investigators have recently discovered that the sounds and gestures that infants make during the **prelinguistic phase** are intimately linked to the emergence of the first words. So let's go back to the beginning.

Chimps like Nim Chimpsky can fairly easily learn signs for individual objects or actions, and can understand and follow quite complex instructions. Here he signs "I see."

Early Perception of Language

Recall from Chapter 5 that babies are born with or very soon develop remarkably good ability to discriminate speech sounds. By 1 or 2 months they pay attention to and can tell the difference between many individual letter sounds; within a few more months they clearly can discriminate among syllables or words. They also have figured out that these speech sounds are matched by the speaker's mouth movements. Researchers have also found that babies in these early months are sensitive to the intonational and stress patterns of the speech they are listening to. For example, Anne Fernald has found that 5-month-olds will smile more when they hear tapes of adults saying something in an approving tone than when they speak in a prohibiting tone, whether the words are in Italian, German, or English (Fernald, 1993). Even more impressive is a study showing that by 9 months of age, babies listening to English prefer to listen to words that have the typical English stress pattern of stressing the first syllable (such as *falter*, *comet*, or *gentle*) rather than those that stress the second syllable (e.g., *comply*, or *assign*) (Jusczyk, Cutler, & Redanz, 1993). Presumably, babies listening to other languages would come to prefer listening to whatever stress pattern was typical of that language. All this research shows that from very early—perhaps from birth—the baby is tuned quite acutely to the language she hears around her.

Early Sounds

This early perceptual skill is not matched right away by much skill in producing sounds. From birth to about 1 month of age, the most common sound an infant makes is a cry, although there are other fussing, gurgling, and satisfied sounds. This sound repertoire expands at about 1 or 2 months, when we begin to hear some laughing and **cooing** vowel sounds, like *uuuuuu*. Sounds like this are usually signals of pleasure in babies, and may show quite a lot of variation in tone, running up and down in volume or pitch.

Consonant sounds appear only at about 6 or 7 months, frequently combined with vowel sounds to make a kind of syllable. Babies this age seem to begin to play with these sounds, often repeating the same sound over and over (such as *babababababa*, or *dahdahdah*). This new sound pattern is called **babbling,** and it makes up about half of babies' noncrying sounds from about 6 to 12 months of age (Mitchell & Kent, 1990).

Any parent can tell you that babbling is a delight to listen to. It also seems to be an important part of the preparation for spoken language. For one thing, we know that infants' babbling gradually acquires some of the intonational pattern of the language they are hearing—a process Elizabeth Bates refers to as "learning the tune before the words" (Bates, O'Connell, & Shore, 1987). At the very least, infants do seem to develop two such "tunes" in their babbling. When they babble with a rising intonation at the end of a string of sounds it seems to signal a desire for a response; a falling intonation requires no response.

A second important thing about babbling is that when babies first start babbling, they typically babble all kinds of sounds, including some that are not part of the language they are hearing. But at about 9 or 10 months, their sound repertoire gradually begins to drift toward the set of sounds they are listening to, with the nonheard sounds dropping out (Oller, 1981)—a pattern that clearly parallels

Why do you suppose babies babble? Do you think it is just the vocal equivalent of rhythmic foot kicking, or can you think of some other purpose it might serve?

RESEARCH REPORT
Early Gestural "Language" in the Children of Deaf Parents

Deaf children of deaf parents are a particularly interesting group to study if we want to understand language development. The children do not hear oral language, but they are exposed to *language*—sign language. Do these children show the same early steps in language development as do hearing children, only using gestural language?

The answer seems to be yes. Deaf children show a kind of "sign babbling" between about 7 and 11 months of age, much as hearing children babble sounds in these same months. Then at 8 or 9 months of age, deaf children begin using simple gestures, such as pointing, which is just about the same time that we see such gestures in hearing babies of hearing parents. At about 12 months of age, deaf babies seem to display their first *referential* signs—that is, signs in which a gesture appears to stand for some object or event, such as signaling that they want a drink by making a motion like a cup being brought to the mouth (Petitto, 1988).

Folven and Bonvillian (1991) have studied an equally interesting group—hearing children of deaf parents. These babies are exposed to sign language from their parents, and to spoken language from their contacts with others in their world, including TV, teachers, other relatives, and playmates. In this small sample of nine babies, the first sign appeared at an average age of 8 months, the first referential sign at 12.6 months, and the first spoken word at 12.2 months. What is striking here is that the first referential signs and the first spoken words appear at such similar times, and that the spoken words appear at such a completely normal time, despite the fact that these children of deaf parents hear comparatively little spoken language.

This marked similarity in the sequence and timing of early language steps in the deaf and the hearing child provides strong support for the argument that the baby is somehow primed to learn "language" in some form, be it spoken or gestural.

---

the findings from the Werker and Tees study I described in Chapter 5 (recall Figure 5.5, p. 145). Findings like these do not tell us that babbling is *necessary* for language development, but they certainly make it look as if babbling is part of a connected developmental process that begins at birth.

Early Gestures

Another part of that connected developmental process may be a kind of gestural language that develops at around 9 or 10 months. At this age we first see babies "demanding" or "asking" for things using gestures or combinations of gestures and sound. A 10-month-old baby who apparently wants you to hand her a favorite toy may stretch and reach for it, opening and closing her hand, making whining sounds or other heartrending noises. There is no mistaking the meaning. At about the same age, babies will enter into those gestural games much loved by parents, like "patty-cake," or "soooo-big," or "wave bye-bye." (Bates, Camaioni, & Volterra, 1975; Bates et al., 1987).

Interestingly, the infant's ability to *understand* the meaning of individual words (which linguists call **receptive language**) also seems to begin at about 9 or 10 months. In one recent study, Elizabeth Bates and her colleagues asked mothers about their 10-month-old babies' understanding of various words (Bates, Bretherton, & Snyder, 1988). On average, the mothers listed 17.9 words understood. By 13 months, that number was up to nearly 50 words. Since infants of 9 to 13 months typically do not speak any individual words, findings like these make it clear that receptive language comes before **expressive language.** Children understand before they can speak.

Adding up these bits of information, we can see that a whole series of changes seem to come together at 9 or 10 months: the beginning of meaningful

What do you think this young fellow is "saying" with his pointing gesture? Before they speak their first words, babies successfully use gestures and body language in consistent ways to communicate meaning.

TABLE 8.1 Brenda's Vocabulary at 14 to 19 Months			
14 Months	**19 Months***		
aw u (I want, I don't want)	baby	nice	boat
nau (no)	bear	orange	bone
d di (daddy, baby)	bed	pencil	checkers
d yu (down, doll)	big	write	corder
nene (liquid food)	blue	paper	cut
e (yes)	Brenda	pen	I do
maem (solid food)	cookie	see	met
ada (another, other)	daddy	shoe	Pogo
	eat	sick	Ralph
	at	swim	you too
	(hor)sie	tape	climb
	mama	walk	jump
	mommy	wowow	

*Brenda did not actually pronounce all these words the way an adult would. I have given the adult version since that is easier to read.

Source: R. Scollon, *Conversations with a one year old.* Honolulu: The University Press of Hawaii, 1976, pp. 47, 57–58.

gestures, the "drift" of babbling toward the heard language sounds, imitative gestural games, and the first comprehension of individual words. It is as if the child now understands something about the process of communication, and is intending to communicate to the adult.

The First Words

Somewhere in the midst of all the babbling, the first words appear, typically at about 12 or 13 months (Capute et al., 1986). The baby's first word is an event that parents eagerly await, but it's fairly easy to miss. A *word*, as linguists usually define it, is any sound or set of sounds that is used consistently to refer to some thing, action, or quality. But it can be *any* sound. It doesn't have to be a sound that matches words the adults are using. Brenda, a little girl studied by Ronald Scollon (1976), used the sound *nene* as one of her first words. It seemed to mean primarily liquid food, since she used it for milk, juice, and bottle. But she also used it to refer to mother and sleep. (You can see some of Brenda's other early words in the left-hand column of Table 8.1.)

Often, a child's earliest words are used only in one or two specific situations, and in the presence of many cues. The child may say "doggie" or "bow-wow" only to such promptings as "How does the doggie go?" or "What's that?" Some linguists

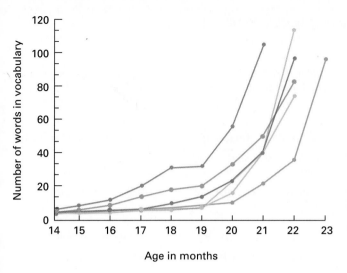

Figure 8.1
Each of the lines in this figure represents the vocabulary growth of one of the children studied by Goldfield and Reznick in their longitudinal study. (*Source:* Goldfield & Reznick, 1990, Figure 3, p. 177.)

describe this period as one in which the child "learns what words do" (Nelson, 1985). The child learns a few words that communicate in particular interactional situations, but has not yet understood that words are *symbolic*—that they refer to objects or events. In this early period children typically learn words very slowly, after many repetitions. It is quite common for children to take 6 months to acquire a vocabulary of 30 words.

The Naming Explosion

Somewhere between 18 and 24 months this pattern shifts, and most children add new words rapidly, as if they had figured out that "things have names." Many toddlers in this phase add 10, 20, or 30 words in a period of weeks. At this point children seem to learn new words with very few repetitions, and they generalize these new words to many more situations.

You can see both aspects of this pattern—the early slow growth, and then the vocabulary spurt—in Figure 8.1, which shows the vocabulary growth curves of six of the subjects studied longitudinally by Goldfield and Reznick (1990). You can also see the change if you go back and look again at Table 8.1, which lists Brenda's vocabulary at both 14 and 19 months.

I should point out that not all children show precisely this pattern. In Goldfield and Reznick's study, for example, 13 out of 24 children showed a vocabulary spurt, while the remaining 11 followed varying growth patterns. A few showed no spurt at all but only gradual acquisition of vocabulary. So we need to be careful here about assuming that the same processes are involved for every child. Still, the most common pattern is like the ones in Figure 8.1.

During the naming explosion, children mostly learn words that are names for things or people, like *ball, car, milk, doggie, he,* or *that.* Verblike words tend to develop later, perhaps because they label *relationships* between objects rather than just a single object (Gleitman & Gleitman, 1992). For example, over half the first 50 words of the eight children Katherine Nelson studied were nounlike words, while only 13 percent were action words (Nelson, 1973). The same pattern has been found in studies of children learning other languages as well, as you can see in the cultures and contexts box on page 234.

CULTURES AND CONTEXTS
Early Words by Children in Many Cultures

Children in every culture studied by linguists have shown the same tendency to learn words for people or things before they learn words for actions or other parts of speech. Here are some (translated) samples from the very early vocabularies of one child from each of four cultures, all studied by Dedre Gentner (1982).

German boy	English girl	Turkish girl	Chinese girl	German boy	English girl	Turkish girl	Chinese girl
Some of the naming words for people or things				Some of the nonnaming words			
Mommy	Mommy	Mama	Momma	cry	run	cry	go
Papa	Daddy	Daddy	Papa	come	all gone	come	come
Gaga	babar	Aba	grandmother	eat	more	put on	pick up
baby	baby	baby	horse	sleep	bye-bye	went pooh	not want
dog	dog	food	chicken	want	want	want	afraid
bird	dolly	apple	uncooked rice	no	no	hello	thank you
cat	kitty	banana	cooked rice				
milk	juice	bread	noodles				
ball	book	ball	flower				
nose	eye	pencil	wall clock				
moon	moon	towel	lamp				
Total percentage of naming words:							
67%	69%	57%	59%				

Isn't it impressive how very similar these early vocabularies are? Of course there are some variations, but all these children had names for Mommy and Daddy, for some other relative, for other live creatures, for food. All but the Chinese child had words for toys or clothes. All four had also learned more naming words than any other type, with very similar proportions. They don't know the *same* words, but the pattern is remarkably similar.

However, just as all children do not show a vocabulary spurt, all children do not follow a noun-before-verb pattern either. Katherine Nelson (1973) first noticed that some toddlers use what she calls an **expressive style.** For them, most early words are linked not to objects but to social relationships. They often learn pronouns (*you, me*) early, and use many more of what Nelson calls "personal-social" words, such as *no, yes, want,* or *please.* Their early vocabulary may also include some multiword strings, like *love you* or *do it* or *go away.* This is in sharp contrast to the children who use what Nelson calls a **referential style,** whose early vocabulary is made up predominantly of nominals.

I'll talk further about such style differences at the end of the chapter. For now I only want to point out that while nounlike terms are the most common early words, they are not the only ones, and some children use them relatively infrequently in the early months.

Later Word Learning

During the preschool years, there is yet another spurt in vocabulary growth, even more astonishing in speed. Children in this age range add as many as 5 to 10 words *a day.* They can accomplish this feat because at this point they seem to pay attention to words in whole groups, such as words that name objects in a single class (such as types of dinosaurs, or kinds of fruit), or words that have similar meanings.

As a personal aside: I was aware of all of these steps in learning German vocabulary last year. Certainly there are many cognates—words that sound the same or similar in English and German—and those I learned quickly. But other types of words I first learned laboriously, one at a time, requiring what seemed endless repetitions. In a second phase that lasted some months, this laborious process got quite a lot faster, but was still not smooth. Finally, toward the end of my eight months, I began to understand and pay attention to such regularities as prefixes and word roots, and suddenly I could learn and remember a dozen words at a time—although even at the end I had roughly the vocabulary of a 4-year-old, or so it seemed!

> If you have learned another language, think about whether your experience matched mine. What about learning something other than language: Do you think that the acquisition of expertise on any kind of intellectual task follows some similar set of steps?

▶ Speaking in Sentences: The Development of Grammar

After the first word, the next big step is when the child begins to string words into sentences, initially using only two words together, then three and four and more. The first two-word sentences usually appear between 18 and 24 months—in fact, you can see two examples in the list of Brenda's 19-month vocabulary in Table 8.1.

Just as the first spoken words are preceded by apparently meaningful gestures, the first two-word sentences have gestural precursors as well. Toddlers often combine a single word with a gesture to create a "two-word meaning" before they actually use two words together in their speech. Elizabeth Bates (Bates et al., 1987) suggests an example: the infant may point to Daddy's shoe and say "Daddy," as if to convey "Daddy's shoe." Or she may say "Cookie!" while simultaneously reaching out her hand and opening and closing her fingers, as if to say "Give cookie!" In both cases a sentencelike meaning is conveyed by the use of gesture and body language combined with a word. Linguists call these word-and-gesture combinations **holophrases,** and they are common in children between 12 and 18 months.

Once the actual speaking of two-word sentences begins, the child moves rapidly through a series of steps or stages, so that within a year or two, most children are able to create quite remarkably complex sentences—as witness the 3-year-old I quoted at the beginning of this chapter.

First Sentences: 18 to 27 Months

The first sentences, which Roger Brown, a famous observer of child language, called Stage I grammar, have several distinguishing features: they are *short*— generally two or three words—and they are *simple*. Nouns, verbs, and adjectives are usually included, but virtually all the purely grammatical markers (which linguists call **inflections**) are missing. At the beginning, for example, children learning English do not normally use the *s* for plurals or put the *ed* ending on verbs to make the past tense, nor do they use the *'s* of the possessive or auxiliary verbs like *am* or *do*. Because only the really critical words are present in these early sentences, Brown (1973; Brown & Bellugi, 1964) describes this as **telegraphic speech.** The child's language sounds rather like what we say when we send a telegram. We keep in all the essential words—usually nouns, verbs, and modifiers—and leave out all the prepositions, auxiliary verbs, and the like.

Interestingly, there is now some dispute among linguists about whether precisely this form of telegraphic speech occurs in children learning all languages. Some research seems to show that what determines the words that children use in their early sentences is the amount of *stress* normally placed on such words when that particular language is spoken. In English (and in many other languages), nouns, verbs, and adjectives are stressed in speech while the inflections are not. But in languages like Turkish, in which inflections are more stressed, children seem to use inflections much earlier (Gleitman & Wanner, 1988). Findings like these certainly raise some interesting questions about the universality of some of the patterns Brown and others have described.

In contrast, there is no dispute about the assertion that even at this earliest stage children create sentences following rules. Not adult rules, to be sure, but rules nonetheless. They focus on certain types of words, and put them together in particular order. They also manage to convey a variety of different meanings with their simple sentences.

For example, young children frequently use a sentence made up of two nouns, such as *Mommy sock* or *sweater chair* (Bloom, 1973). We might conclude from this that a "two-noun" form is a basic grammatical characteristic of early child language. But that misses the complexity. For instance, the child in Bloom's study who said *Mommy sock* said it on two different occasions. The first time was when she picked up her mother's sock and the second was when the mother put the child's own sock on the child's foot. In the first case, *Mommy sock* seems to mean Mommy's sock (a possessive relationship). But in the second instance the child seems to convey "Mommy is putting a sock on me," which is an *agent* (Mommy)–*object* (sock) relationship.

Some other different meanings that children convey with their earliest sentences are listed in Table 8.2. Not all children express all of these relationships or

---

TABLE 8.2   Some of the Different Meanings Children Express in Their Earliest Simple Sentences

Meaning	Examples
Agent-action	Sarah eat; Daddy jump
Action-object	Eat cookie; read book
Possessor–possessed object	Mommy sock; Timothy lunch
Action-location	Come here; play outside
Located object–location	Sweater chair; juice table
Attribute–modified object	Big book; red house
Nomination	That cookie; it dog
Recurrence	More juice; other book

Source: Maratsos, 1983.

TABLE 8.3 Examples of Daniel's Stage I and Stage II Sentences	
Stage I (simple) sentences (age 21 months)	Stage II (more complex) sentences (age 23 months)
A bottle	A little boat
Broke-it	Doggies here
Here (the) bottle	Give you the book
Hi daddy	It's a boy
Horse doggie	It's a robot
Broke it	Little box there
Kitty cat	No book
Poor Daddy	Oh cars
That monkey	That flowers
Want bottle	Where going?

Source: Reprinted by permission of the publisher. D. Ingram, Early patterns of grammatical development, in R. E. Stark (Ed.), *Language behavior in infancy and early childhood*, Tables 6 and 7, pp. 344–345. Copyright© 1981 by Elsevier Science Publishing Co., Inc.

meanings in their early word combinations, and there does not seem to be a fixed order in which these meanings or constructions are acquired, but all children appear to express at least several of these patterns in their earliest, simplest sentences (Maratsos, 1983).

Grammar Explosion: 27 to 36 months

Just as there is a vocabulary explosion following an early, slow beginning, so there is also a grammar explosion following these first simple sentences. Beginning some time in the third year, most children rather quickly add many of the inflections and function words, a process Roger Brown refers to as Stage II grammar. Within a few months, children use plurals, past tenses, auxiliary verbs such as *is* or *does,* prepositions, and the like. They also begin to create negative sentences, and to ask questions with the auxiliary verb in the correct order. You can get a feeling for the sound of the change from Table 8.3, which lists some of the sentences of a little boy named Daniel, recorded by David Ingram (1981). The left-hand column lists some of Daniel's sentences at about 21 months of age, when he was still using the simplest forms; the right-hand column lists some of his sentences only 2½ months later (age 23 to 24 months), when he had shifted into higher gear.

Adding Inflections.   You can get some sense from the table that Daniel did not add all the inflections at once. In this sample, he uses only a few, such as the *s* for plurals, although there is the beginning of a negative construction in "no book" and the beginning of a question form in "where going?" although he does not yet have the auxiliary verb added to the question. Within each language community, children seem to add inflections and more complex word orders in fairly predictable sequences. Among children learning English, Roger Brown (1973) has found that the earliest inflection is most often the *ing* added onto a verb, such as in *I playing*, or *doggie running*. Then come (in order) prepositions like *on* and *in*, the plural *s* on nouns, irregular past tenses (such as *broke* or *ran*), possessives, articles (*a* and *the* in English), the *s* that we add to third person verbs such as *he wants*, regular past tenses like *played* and *wanted*, and the various forms of the auxiliary verb, as in *I am going*.

Questions and Negatives.   There are also predictable sequences in the child's developing use of questions and negatives. In each case, the child seems to go through periods when he creates types of sentences that he has not heard adults use, but that are consistent with the particular set of rules he is using. For example, in the development of questions there is a point at which the child gets a *wh* word (*who, what, when, where, why*) at the front end of a sentence, but doesn't yet have the auxiliary verb put in the right place, for example, *Why it is resting now?* Similarly, in the development of negatives, there is a stage in which the *not* or *n't* or *no* is put in, but the auxiliary verb is omitted, as in *I not crying*, or *there no squirrels*. Then rather rapidly children figure out the correct forms and stop making these "mistakes."

Overregularization.   Another intriguing phenomenon of this second phase of sentence construction that underlines this same apparent rule making of even the earliest sentences is **overregularization** or overgeneralization. This is what the two little girls were doing in the conversation about the goldfish when they created new regularized forms of superlatives (*badder, baddest, worser,* and *worsest*). We can hear the same thing in children's creation of past tenses like *wented* or *goed* or *ated*. Stan Kuczaj (1977; 1978) pointed out that young children initially learn a small number of irregular past tenses and use them correctly for a short time. But then rather suddenly the child seems to discover the rule of adding *ed* and overgeneralizes this rule to all verbs. Then she relearns the exceptions one at a time. Even among preschoolers this type of "error" is not hugely common (only about 2 to 3 percent of all past tenses in English according to one recent study [Marcus et al., 1992]). But these overregularizations stand out because they are so distinctive, and because they illustrate yet again that children create forms that they have not heard but that are logical within their current grammar.

Complex Sentences: 30 to 48 Months

After children have figured out the inflections and basic sentence forms like negation and questions, they soon begin to create remarkably complex sentences, with embedded clauses, tag questions, and sentences combined with conjunctions like *and* and *but*. Here are some examples from de Villiers and de Villiers (1992):

> *I didn't catch it but Teddy did!*
> *I'm gonna sit on the one you're sitting on.*
> *Where did you say you put my doll?*
> *Those are punk rockers, aren't they?*

Past these early stages, children's language continues to develop in various ways. In particular, more complex and difficult sentence forms are added throughout elementary school, and recurrent overregularization errors are eliminated (Bowerman, 1985). For instance, passive forms, like *the food is eaten by the cat*, are not well understood even by 5- and 6-year-olds, and are not used much in spontaneous speech until several years later. But these are refinements. The really giant strides occur between ages 1 and about 4, as the child moves from single words to complex questions, negatives, and commands.

▶ The Development of Word Meaning

To understand language development, it is not enough to know how children learn to string words together to form sentences. We also have to understand how the words in those sentences come to have meaning. Linguists are still searching for good ways to describe (or explain) children's emerging word meaning. So far, several sets of questions have dominated the research.

Which Comes First, the Meaning or the Word?

The most fundamental question is whether the child learns a word to describe a category or class he has *already* created through his manipulations of the world around him, or whether the existence of a word forces the child to create new cognitive categories. This may seem like a highly abstract argument, but it touches on the fundamental issue of the relationship between language and thought. Does the child learn to represent objects to himself *because* he now has language, or does language simply come along at about this point and make the representations easier?

Not surprisingly, the answer seems to be both (Clark, 1983; Cromer, 1991; Greenberg & Kuczaj, 1982). On the cognitive side of the argument are several pieces of evidence I described in Chapter 7, such as the fact that young babies are able to remember and imitate objects and actions over periods of time—long before they have language to assist them.

Further evidence of cognitive primacy comes from the study of the child's use of various prepositions like *in*, *between*, or *in front of*, each of which seems to be used spontaneously in language only after the child has understood the concept (Johnston, 1985).

The naming explosion may also rest on new cognitive understandings, in particular the new ability to categorize things. In several studies, Alison Gopnik and Andrew Meltzoff (1987; 1992) have found that the naming explosion typically occurs just after, or at the same time as, children first show spontaneous categorization of mixed sets of objects. Having discovered "categories," the child may now rapidly learn the names for already-existing categories.

But once the child now understands in some primitive way that names refer to categories, then learning a new name suggests the existence of a new category (Waxman & Hall, 1993), and thus the name affects the child's thinking.

Extending the Class

What kinds of concepts does the child start with? Suppose your 2-year-old, on catching sight of the family tabby, says "See kitty." No doubt you will be pleased that the child has the right word applied to the animal. But this sentence alone doesn't tell you much about the word meaning the child has developed. What does the word *kitty* mean to the child? Does he think it is a name only for that

Children learning English also learn the rules for "tag questions" quite late—those questions we put on the end of a sentence to make it a question, like "isn't it?" or "haven't you?" or "aren't they?" Can you figure out the rule that you use to decide what is the correct tag?

Does this 18-month-old know the word *doll* because she first had a concept of doll and later learned the word, or did she learn the word first and then create a category or concept to go with the word?

THE REAL WORLD
Bilingual Children

What I've said so far about early language development describes what happens when a child learns a *single* language. But what about children who are exposed to two or more languages from the beginning? How confusing is this for a child? And how can parents ease the process? There are at least two important practical questions surrounding the issue of bilingualism:

- Should parents who speak different native languages try to expose their children to both, or will that only confuse the child and make any kind of language learning harder? What's the best way to do this?
- If a child arrives at school age without speaking the dominant language of schooling, what is the best way for the child to acquire that second language?

■ LEARNING TWO LANGUAGES AT THE SAME TIME

Parents should have no fears about exposing their child to two or more languages from the very beginning. Such simultaneous exposure does seem to result in slightly slower early steps in word learning and sentence construction, but bilingual children catch up rapidly.

The best way to help a child to learn two languages fluently is to speak both languages to the child from the beginning, *especially* if the two languages come at the child from different sources. For example, if Mom's native language is English and Dad's is Italian, Mom should speak only English to the infant/toddler and Dad should speak only Italian. (The parents will of course speak to each other in whatever language they have in common.) If both parents speak both languages to the child, or mix them up in their own speech, this is a much more difficult situation for the child and language learning will be delayed (McLaughlin, 1984). It will also work if one language is always spoken at home and the other in a day-care center, or with playmates, or in some other outside situation.

■ BILINGUAL EDUCATION

For many children, the need to be bilingual does not begin in the home, but only at school age. In the United States today, there are 2.5 million school-age children for whom English is not the primary language of the home (Hakuta & Garcia, 1989). Many of those children arrive at school with little or no facility in English. Educators have had to grapple with the task of teaching children a second language at the same time that they are trying to teach them subject matter such as reading and mathematics. The problem for the schools has been to figure out the best way to do this. Should the child be immediately immersed in the new language? Should the child learn basic academic skills in his native language and only later learn English as a second language? Or is there some combination of the two that will work?

The research findings are messy. Still, one thread does run through it all: neither full immersion nor English-as-a-second-language programs are as effective as truly bilingual programs in which the child is given at least some of her basic instruction in subject matter in her native language in the first year or two of school, but is also exposed to the second language in the same classroom (Padilla et al., 1991; Willig, 1985). After several years of such combined instruction, the child then makes a rapid transition to full use of the second language for all instruction. Interestingly, in her analysis of this research, Ann Willig has found that the ideal arrangement is very much like what works best at home with toddlers: if some subjects are always taught in one language, and other subjects in the other language, children learn both most easily. But if each sentence is translated, children do not learn the new language as quickly or as well.

Note, though, that even such ideal bilingual education programs will not be effective for children who come to school without good spoken language in their native tongue. Learning to read, in any language, requires that the child have a fairly extensive awareness of the structure of language—a point I will explore later in this chapter. Any child who lacks such awareness—because she has been exposed to relatively little language, or was not read to or talked to much in infancy and preschool years—will have difficulty learning to read, whether the instruction is given in the native language or in English.

---

particular fuzzy beast? Or does he think it applies to all furry creatures, or all things with four legs, or things with pointed ears, or what?

One way to figure out the kind of class or category the child has created is to see what *other* creatures or things a child also calls a kitty. That is, how is the class *extended* in the child's language? If the child has created a kitty category that is based on furriness, then many dogs and perhaps sheep would also be called kitty. If having a tail is a crucial feature for the child, then some breeds of cat that have no tails might not be called kitty by the child. Or, perhaps the child used the word kitty only for the family cat, or only when petting the cat. This would imply a very narrow category indeed. The general question for researchers has been whether children tend to use words narrowly or broadly, overextending or underextending them.

Our current information tells us that underextension is most common at the earliest stages, particularly before the naming explosion (Harris, 1992)—although even at this early point, overextension also can occur. Once the naming explosion starts, however, overextension seems to be more common. At that stage, we're more likely to hear the word *cat* applied to dogs or guinea pigs than we are to hear it used for just one animal, or for a very small set of animals or objects (Clark, 1983). All children seem to show overextensions, but the particular classes the child creates are unique to each child. One child Eve Clark observed used the word *moon* for cake, round marks on windows, writing on windows and in books, round shapes in books, tooling in leather book covers, round postmarks, and the letter O. Another used the word *ball* to refer not only to toy balls, but also to radishes, and stone spheres at park entrances, while another child used the word *ball* to refer to apples, grapes, eggs, squash, and a bell clapper (Clark, 1975).

Chances are this toddler has a word for *ball*, and chances are also good that he uses the word *ball* to refer to a variety of other round things, which would be an example of overextension.

These overextensions *may* tell us something about the way children think, such as that they have broad classes. But linguists like Clark remind us that part of the child's problem is that he simply doesn't know very many words. A child who wants to call attention to a horse may not know the word *horse*, so may say "dog" instead. Overextensions may thus arise from the child's desire to communicate, and may not tell us that the child fails to make the discriminations involved (Clark, 1977; 1987). As the child learns the separate labels that are applied to the different subtypes of "fuzzy four-legged creatures" the overextension disappears.

Parents may also contribute to a child's overextensions. Carolyn and Cynthia Mervis (1982) found that mothers use labels that they think match the child's categories, rather than using the more precise labels. So they may call leopards and lions "kitty cats," or a toy fire engine a "car." Such a pattern undoubtedly aids communication between mother and child in the early stages of language development, but it also may contribute to what we hear as overextensions in the child's early language.

Constraints on Word Learning

One of the most fundamental questions about word meanings, the subject of hot debate among linguists in recent years, is just how a child figures out which part of some scene a word may refer to. The classic example: A child sees a brown dog running across the grass with a bone in its mouth. An adult points and says "doggie." From such an encounter the toddler is somehow supposed to figure out that *doggie* refers to the animal, and not to running, or bone, or dog-plus-bone, or brownness, or ears, or grass, or any other combination of elements in the whole scene.

Many linguists have proposed that a child could only conceivably cope with this monumentally complex task if he operated with some built-in biases or *constraints* (Markman, 1989; Markman & Hutchinson, 1984; Waxman & Kosowski, 1990; Woodward & Markman, 1991). For example, the child may have a built-in initial assumption that words refer to objects *or* events but not both, or an assumption that words refer to whole objects and not to their parts or attributes.

If Dad says "goose" while he and his toddler are looking at this scene, how does the boy know that "goose" means the animal, and not "white," or "dirt" or "honk honk" or some other feature? In fact, in this case as in most instances, the child first *points* and then the father labels, which greatly simplifies the problem.

Toddlers of 19 to 20 months, for example, already know that if you point at something and give a word, it is the label for that object (Baldwin, 1993), and not a name for some other feature of the scene.

Another possible built-in constraint is the *principle of contrast*, which is the assumption that every word has a different meaning, so if a different word is used, it must refer to some different object or a different aspect of an object (Clark, 1990). For example, in a widely quoted study, Carey and Bartlett (1978) interrupted a play session with 2- and 3-year-old children by pointing to two trays and saying, "Bring me the chromium tray, not the red one, the chromium one." These children already knew the word *red* but did not know the word *chromium*. Nonetheless, most of the children were able to follow the instruction by bringing the nonred tray. Furthermore, a week later about half of the children remembered that the word *chromium* referred to some color, and that the color was "not red." Thus they learned the meaning by contrast.

Many linguists do not accept the idea of built-in constraints. Doubters such as Katherine Nelson (1988) point out that most of the research on language constraints has been done with children who were well past the one-word stage of language. It is possible that such biases, if they exist, are not built in but emerge as the child is learning language. Furthermore, Nelson and others point out that the child rarely encounters a situation in which the adult points vaguely and gives some word. By far the most common scenario is that the parent follows the child's lead, labeling things the child is already playing with or pointing at (Harris, 1992). In fact, children whose parents do more of such responsive, specific labeling seem to learn language somewhat faster (Dunham, Dunham, & Curwin, 1993; Harris, 1992). To the extent that this is true, then the constraints on the process are the child's own conceptual system, and the ability of the adult to interpret the child's meaning, rather than some built-in tendencies within the child.

As these few examples illustrate, the study of the development of word meanings has been much more difficult to conceptualize than has been the develop-

On the basis of this very brief presentation, do you find yourself persuaded by the arguments for built-in constraints, or by the counterarguments?

ment of grammar. Linguists are obviously searching for the rules that govern this process, so that we can understand how and why children use words the way they do. So far, only a few general principles have emerged.

▌ Using Language: Communication and Self-Direction

In the past decade or so, linguists have also turned their attention to a third aspect of children's language, namely the way children learn to *use* speech, either to communicate with others (an aspect of language often called **pragmatics**), or to regulate their own behavior. How early do children know what kind of language to use in specific situations? How early do they learn the "rules" of conversation, such as that you are supposed to take turns?

Language Pragmatics.   Children seem to learn the pragmatics of language at a remarkably early age. For example, children as young as 18 months show adultlike gaze patterns when they are talking with a parent: they look at the person who is talking, look away at the beginning of their own speaking turn, and then look at the listener again when they are signaling that they are about to stop talking (Rutter & Durkin, 1987).

Furthermore, a child as young as 2 years adapts the form of his language to the situation he is in or the person he is talking to —a point I made in the last chapter as well, when talking about children's egocentrism. He might say "gimme" to another toddler as he grabs the other child's glass, but might say "more milk" to an adult (Becker, 1982). Among older children, language is even more clearly adapted to the listener: Four-year-olds use simpler language when they talk to 2-year-olds than when they talk to adults (Tomasello & Mannle, 1985). First graders explain things more fully to a stranger than to a friend (Sonnenschein, 1986), and are more polite to adults and strangers than to peers; both of these trends are still clearer among fourth graders. Thus from very early, probably from the beginning, the child's language is meant to *communicate,* and the child adapts the form of his language in order to achieve better communication.

Language and Self-Control.   Language seems to have another function for the child as well, namely to help control or monitor her own behavior. Such "private speech," which may consist of more fragmentary sentences, muttering, or instructions to the self, is detectable from the earliest use of words and sentences. For example, when 2- or 3-year-olds play by themselves, they give themselves instructions, or stop themselves with words, or describe what they are doing: "No, not there," "I put that there," or "Put it" (Furrow, 1984).

In older children, this self-regulatory use of language is sometimes still apparent, particularly when they are working on hard problems. For example, you may recall from Chapter 7 that Flavell found that elementary-school children muttered to themselves while they were trying to remember lists. Initially, this self-regulatory language is audible; by age 9 or 10 it has largely gone underground (Bivens & Berk, 1990). If we connect this set of findings with the work on information processing I talked about in the last chapter, it begins to sound as if the child uses language audibly to remind himself of some new or complex processing strategy; as the strategy becomes better rehearsed and more flexibly learned, overt language is no longer needed. Such an interpretation is bolstered by the observa-

Do you recognize this pattern? Next time you are in a two-person conversation, monitor yourself and your partner and see if this isn't how it works.

This 3-year-old not only can speak quite fluently, he also knows many of the social rules about how language is used, including rules about who is supposed to look at whom during a conversation.

tion that even adults will use audible language in problem solving when they are faced with especially difficult tasks.

Even this brief foray into the research on the child's use of language points out that a full understanding of language development is going to require understanding of both cognitive development and of the child's social skills and understanding. It reminds us once again that the child is not divided up into tidy packages labeled "physical development" or "social development" or "language development," but is a coherent, integrated system.

▶ Explaining Language Development

If merely describing language development is hard—and it is—explaining it is still harder. Indeed, explaining how a child learns language has proven to be one of the most compelling, and one of the most difficult, challenges within developmental psychology. This may surprise you. I suspect that most of you just take for granted that a child learns to talk by listening to the language she hears. What is magical or complicated about that? Yet the more you think about it, the more amazing and mysterious it becomes. For one thing, as Steven Pinker (1987) points out, there is a veritable chasm between what the child hears as language input, and the language the child must eventually speak. The input consists of some set of sentences spoken to the child, with intonation, stress, and timing. They are spoken in the presence of objects and events, and the words are given in a particular order. All that may be helpful, even essential. But what the child must acquire from such input is nothing less than a set of rules for *creating* sentences. How does the child accomplish this feat? Theories abound. Let me start on the nurture end of the theoretical continuum.

Imitation and Reinforcement

The earliest theories of language were based either on learning theory or on the commonsense idea that language was learned by imitation. Imitation obviously has to play some part, because the child learns the language she hears. Babbling drifts toward the sounds in the heard language; children imitate sentences they hear; they learn to speak with the accent of their parents. And those babies who show the most imitation of actions and gestures are also those who later learn language most quickly (Bates et al., 1982). So the tendency to imitate may be an important ingredient. Still, imitation alone can't explain all of language acquisition because it cannot account for the creative quality of the child's language. In particular, children consistently create types of sentences and forms of words that they have never heard—words like *goed* or *beated* or *worser*.

Reinforcement theories such as Skinner's (1957) fare no better. Skinner argued that parents shape language through systematic reinforcements, gradually rewarding better and better approximations of adult speech. But in fact there is little evidence that parents do anything like this. Instead, parents are remarkably forgiving of all sorts of peculiar constructions and meaning (Brown & Hanlon, 1970; Hirsh-Pasek, Trieman, & Schneiderman, 1984). In addition, children learn many forms of language, such as plurals, with relatively few errors, so some process other than shaping has to be involved.

RESEARCH REPORT
The Importance of Reading to the Child

One intriguing piece of evidence showing the importance of the child's environment in early language learning is a study by G. J. Whitehurst and his colleagues (Whitehurst et al., 1988). They trained some parents to read picture books to their toddlers and to interact with them in a special way during the reading, a pattern called *dialogic* reading. Specifically, they were trained to use questions that could not be answered just by pointing. So a mother reading Winnie the Pooh might say, "There's Eeyore. What's happening to him?" Or the parent might ask, pointing to some object shown in a book, "What's the name of that?" or ask a question about some character in a story, such as "Do you think the kitty will get into trouble?" Other parents were encouraged to read to the child, but were given no special instructions. After a month, the children in the experimental group had shown a larger gain in vocabulary than had the children in the comparison group.

Whitehurst has now replicated this study in Mexico (Valdez-Menchaca & Whitehurst, 1992). One teacher in a day-care center was trained in dialogic reading. She then spent 10 minutes each day reading with each of 10 2-year-olds, all from working-class families. This continued for a period of six to seven weeks. A comparison group of children in the same day-care center spent an equivalent amount of time with the same teacher each day, but were given arts and crafts instruction rather than reading. At the end of the intervention, the children who had been read to had higher vocabulary scores on a variety of standardized tests, and used more complex grammar when talking in a special test conversation with another adult.

The fact that Whitehurst finds the same types of effects in two different cultures, with two different languages, strengthens the argument that richer interactive language between parent and child is one ingredient in fostering the child's language growth.

Newer Environmental Theories: Talking to the Child

Still, it seems obvious that what is said to the child has to play *some* role in the process. At the simplest level, we know that children whose parents talk to them often, read to them regularly, and respond to the child's own verbalizations begin to talk a little sooner. So at least the *rate* of development is affected by the amount of input.

Motherese.   The quality of the parents' language may also be important. In particular, we know that adults talk to children in a special kind of very simple language, often called **motherese.** This simple language is spoken in a higher-pitched voice, and at a slower pace, than is talk between adults. The sentences are short, with simple, concrete vocabulary, and they are grammatically simple. When speaking to children, parents also repeat a lot, with minor variations ("Where is the ball? Can you see the ball? Where is the ball? There is the ball!"). They may also repeat the child's sentence but in a slightly longer, more grammatically correct form—a pattern referred to as an *expansion* or a *recasting*.

Parents don't talk this way to children in order to teach them language. They do so with the hope that they will communicate better. But it may well be very useful, even necessary, for the child's language acquisition. We know, for example, that some kind of higher-pitched, simplified, repetitious language to babies and children occurs in virtually all cultures and language communities, even among deaf parents using sign language to their infants (Masataka, 1992). We also know that babies as young as a few days old can discriminate between motherese and adult-directed speech and *that they prefer to listen to motherese*, whether it is spoken by a female or a male voice (Cooper & Aslin, 1990; Pegg, Werker, & McLoed, 1992). In particular, it seems to be the higher pitch of motherese that babies prefer. Once the child's attention is drawn by this special tone, the very

Imagine yourself talking to an infant you are holding in your arms. Can your hear yourself using "motherese"?

simplicity and repetitiveness of the adult's speech may help the child to pick out repeating grammatical forms.

Children's attention also seems to be drawn to recast sentences. In one recent study, for example, Farrar (1992) found that 2-year-old children were twice or three times as likely to imitate a correct grammatical form after they had heard their mother recast their own sentences than they were when that same correct grammatical form appeared naturally in the mother's conversation. Experimental studies confirm this effect of recastings. Children who are deliberately exposed to higher rates of specific types of recast sentences seem to learn those grammatical forms more quickly (Nelson, 1977).

Sounds good, doesn't it? But there are some holes in this theory. For one thing, while children who hear more expansions learn grammar sooner, children who rarely hear such forms nonetheless acquire a complex grammar, albeit more slowly. And while motherese does seem to occur in the vast majority of cultures and contexts, it does not occur in *all*. For example, Pye (1986) could find no sign of motherese in one Mayan culture, and studies in the United States show it is greatly reduced among depressed mothers (Bettes, 1988). Children of these mothers nonetheless learn language. Thus while motherese may be helpful, it cannot be *necessary* for language.

Innateness Theories

On the other side of the theoretical spectrum we have the innateness theorists, who argue that much of what the child needs for learning language is built into the organism. Early innateness theorists like Noam Chomsky (1965; 1975; 1986; 1988) were especially struck by two phenomena: the extreme complexity of the task the child must accomplish, and the apparent similarities in the steps and stages of children's early language across languages and across children. Newer cross-language comparisons now make it clear that there is more variability than first appeared—a set of findings I've described in the cultures and contexts box on page 247. Nonetheless, innateness theories are alive and well and highly influential.

One particularly influential current innateness theorist is Dan Slobin (1985a; 1985b), who assumes a basic language-making capacity in any child, made up of a set of fundamental *operating principles*. Just as the newborn infant seems to come programmed with "rules to look by," so Slobin is arguing that infants and children are programmed with "rules to listen by."

You've already encountered a good deal of evidence consistent with this proposal in earlier chapters. We know that from earliest infancy, babies focus on individual sounds and on syllables in the stream of sounds they hear, that they pay attention to sound rhythm, and that they prefer speech of a particular pattern, namely motherese. Slobin also proposes that babies are preprogrammed to pay attention to the beginnings and endings of strings of sounds, and to stressed sounds. Together, these operating principles would help to explain some of the features of children's early grammar.

The fact that this model is consistent with the growing information about apparently built-in perceptual skills and processing biases is certainly a strong argument in its favor. But the exploration of this approach is still in its early days, and

CULTURES AND CONTEXTS
Universals and Variations in Early Language

In the early years of research on children's language development, linguists and psychologists were strongly impressed by the apparent similarities across languages in children's early language. You've already seen some of the evidence that supports this impression in an earlier cultures and contexts box (p. 234), illustrating large similarities in early vocabularies. Studies in a wide variety of language communities, including Turkish, Serbo-Croatian, Hungarian, Hebrew, Japanese, a New Guinean language called Kaluli, German, and Italian, have revealed other important similarities in early language:

- The prelinguistic phase seems to be identical in all language communities. All babies coo, then babble; all babies understand language before they can speak it; babies in all cultures begin to use their first words at about 12 months.

- In all language communities studied so far, a one-word phase precedes the two-word phase, with the latter beginning at about 18 months.

- In all languages studied so far, prepositions describing locations are added in essentially the same order. Words for *in, on, under,* and *beside* are learned first. Then the child learns the words *front* and *back* (Slobin, 1985a).

- Children seem to pay more attention to the ends of words than the beginnings, so they learn suffixes before they learn prefixes.

  At the same time, cross-linguistic comparisons show that children's beginning sentences are not nearly so similar as the early innateness theorists had supposed. For example:

- The specific word order that a child uses in early sentences is not the same for all children in all languages. In some languages a noun/verb sequence is fairly common, in others a verb/noun sequence may be heard.

- Particular inflections are learned in highly varying order from one language to another. Japanese children, for example, begin very early to use a special kind of marker, called a *pragmatic* marker, that tells something about the feeling or the context. For instance, in Japanese, the word *yo* is used at the end of a sentence when the speaker is experiencing some resistance from the listener; the word *ne* is used when the speaker expects approval or agreement. Japanese children begin to use these markers very early, much earlier than other inflections appear in most languages.

- Most strikingly, there are languages in which there seems to be no simple two-word sentence stage in which the sentences contain no inflections. Children learning Turkish, for example, use essentially the full set of noun and verb inflections by age 2 and never go through a stage of using uninflected words. Their language is simple but it is rarely ungrammatical from the adult's point of view (Aksu-Koc & Slobin, 1985).

Obviously any theory of language acquisition must account for both the common ground and the wide variations from one language to the next.

---

there are other compelling alternatives. In particular, there are theorists who argue persuasively that what is important is not the built-in biases, but the child's *construction* of language as part of the broader process of cognitive development. In this view, the child is a "little linguist," applying her emerging cognitive understanding to the problem of language, searching for regularities and patterns.

Constructivist Theories
Melissa Bowerman (1985) is the clearest proponent of this view. She puts the proposition this way: "When language starts to come in, it does not introduce new meanings to the child. Rather, it is used to express only those meanings the child has already formulated independently of language" (Bowerman, 1985, p. 372).

If this is true, then we should observe clear links between achievements in language development and the child's broader cognitive development. And, in fact, we do. For example, symbolic play such as drinking from an empty cup, and imitation of sounds and gestures, both appear at about the same time as the child's first words, suggesting some broad "symbolic" understanding that is reflected in a number of behaviors. In children whose language is significantly delayed, both symbolic play and imitation are normally delayed, too (Bates et al., 1987; Snyder, 1978; Ungerer & Sigman, 1984).

A second example occurs later: at about the point at which two-word sentences appear, we can also see children begin to combine several gestures into a sequence in their pretend play, such as pouring imaginary liquid, drinking, then wiping the mouth. Those children who are the first to show this sequencing in their play are also the first to show two- or three-word sentences in their speech (Bates et al., 1987; Brownell, 1988; Shore, 1986).

Obviously, we do not have to choose between Slobin's and Bowerman's approaches. Both may be true. The child may begin with built-in operating principles that aim the child's attention at crucial features of the language input. The child then processes that information according to her initial (perhaps built-in) strategies or schemes. But then she modifies those strategies or rules as she receives new information. The result is a series of rules for understanding and creating language. The strong similarities we see among children in their early language constructions come about both because all children share the same initial processing rules, and because most children are exposed to very similar input from the people around them. But because the input is not identical, because languages differ, language development follows less and less common pathways as the child progresses.

As these brief descriptions of theory make clear, linguists and psychologists who have studied language have made progress. We know a lot more now about how *not* to explain language. But we have not yet cracked the code. The fact that children learn complex and varied use of their native tongue within a few years remains both miraculous and largely mysterious.

▶ Individual Differences in Language Development

The sequences of development of language I have been describing are accurate on the average, but as I have mentioned a few times in passing, there are wide variations in the speed with which children acquire language skill. There also seem to be important style differences.

Differences in Rate

Some children begin using individual words at 8 months, others not until 18 months; some do not use two-word sentences until 3 years or even later. You can see the range of normal variation very clearly in the behavior of the three children Roger Brown studied intensively, Eve, Adam, and Sarah. Figure 8.2 shows the average sentence length (referred to by linguists as the **mean length of utterance,** or MLU) of each of the children at each age. I have drawn a line at the MLU level which normally accompanies a switch from simple, uninflected two-word sentences to more complex forms. You can see that Eve made this transition at about 21 months, while Adam and Sarah passed over this point about a year later.

I should point out that most children who talk late catch up later, and earliness or lateness of complex speech is *not* predictive of later IQ or later reading

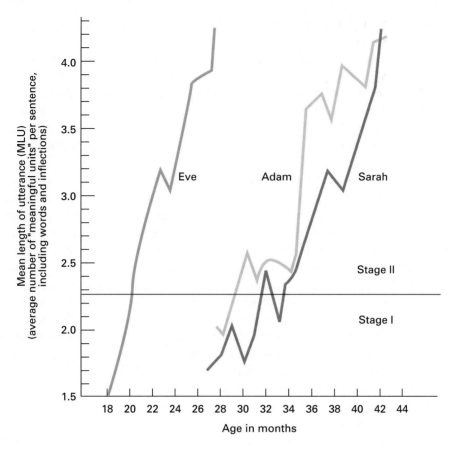

Figure 8.2
Children go through the various steps and stages of language development at markedly different rates, as you can see clearly here. Eve began to use grammatical inflections in her language (noted by the horizontal line across the graph) at about 21 months, while Adam and Sarah were much slower. (*Source:* Brown, 1973, Figure 1, p. 55. Reprinted by permission of the publishers. Copyright 1973 by the president and fellows of Harvard College.)

ability. The exception to this statement is a small group of late talkers who also have poor *receptive* language. This group appears to remain behind in language development, and perhaps in cognitive development more generally (Bates, 1993).

How can we explain these variations in speed of early language development? The alternative possibilities should be familiar by now.

Genetic Explanations.   One possibility is that the rate of language development may be something you inherit—in the same way that intelligence or the rate of physical development may be partially influenced by heredity. Certainly if we assume that some language-processing patterns are built into the brain, it makes sense to think that some children may inherit a more efficient built-in system than others, just as some babies habituate faster to repeated stimuli.

Twin studies and adoption studies designed to test this possibility have yielded the typical mixture of findings. In twin studies, the common finding is that vocabulary size, but *not* grammatical complexity, is more similar in identical than in fraternal twins (Mather & Black, 1984). Adoption studies show that 2-year-olds' language skill can be predicted about equally well from the IQs or language skills of either the natural or the adoptive parents (Hardy-Brown, Plomin, & DeFries, 1981; Plomin & DeFries, 1985). And among adoptive families, those who talked the most and provided the most toys had children whose language was more advanced. What all of this looks like to me is that there are some aspects of language development that are strongly related to the child's overall information processing abilities, such as speed of learning new words and understanding other people's language. Since cognitive abilities have a significant genetic influence, so do these language abilities. But other aspects of language, such as pronunciation and possibly the rate of grammatical development, may be equally influenced by variations in the richness of the child's linguistic environment.

Environmental Explanations.   I have already talked about some such influences. Parents who talk more, who read to the child more and elicit more language from the child, and who respond contingently to the child's language, seem to have children who develop language more rapidly. The fact that this same set of relationships is found in families of *adoptive* children is impressive, since we can be fairly sure that what we are seeing here is not just genetic influence in disguise.

Overall, as with IQ, it seems obvious that both the particular genes the child inherits, and the environment in which the child is growing up, contribute to the rate of language development she will show. I should emphasize once again, though, that although children do differ widely in the timing of their language development, virtually all children progress adequately through the sequence of steps I have been describing. Nearly all children learn to communicate at least adequately; most do so with great skill, regardless of their early rate of progress. One moral for parents is that you should not panic if your child is still using fairly primitive sentences at $2^1/_2$ or even 3—providing, of course, that the child appears to understand what is said to her. Instead of worrying, I would urge you to listen with pleasure to your child's emerging language—to the poetry of it, the wonderfully funny mistakes, the amazingly rapid changes. It is a fascinating process.

Differences in Style

In talking about the child's earliest words, I pointed out that there seem to be two distinct "types" of early vocabulary, which Katherine Nelson originally called "referential" and "expressive" styles. Later researchers have found further signs of such a difference in both grammar and articulation. I have summarized some of the differences in Table 8.4.

Elizabeth Bates and her colleagues (1988; Thal & Bates, 1990) argue that the difference may run fairly deep. Referential-style children are, in some sense, more cognitively oriented children. They are drawn to objects, spend more of their time in solitary play with objects, and interact with other people more often around objects, too. They are much more likely to show a clear spurt in vocabulary development in the early stages, adding a whole lot of object names in a very short space of time, as if they—more than expressive children—had understood the basic principle that things have names. Such children are also advanced in their ability to understand complex adult language.

Expressive-style toddlers, on the other hand, are oriented more toward people, toward social interactions. Their early words and sentences include a lot of "strings" of words that are involved in common interactions with adults. Since

"Where is the fish's eye?" asks Mom. Seventeen-month-old Jesse obviously knows the answer. Moms who talk a lot to their babies, and ask questions in this way, have children who learn to talk sooner.

TABLE 8.4   Some Differences Between Expressive and Referential Children in Early Language

	Expressive	Referential
Early words	Low proportion of nouns and adjectives	High proportion of nouns and adjectives
Vocabulary growth	Slow, gradual; rarely any spurts	Rapid, with clear spurts at one-word stage
Early sentences	May have inflections at Stage I, because of high use of "rote strings" (formulas) inserted into sentences (e.g., "What do you want?")	Few rote strings at Stage I grammar; speech is clearly telegraphic at this stage, with no inflections
Articulation	Less-clear speech	Clearer speech

Source: After Thal & Bates, 1990.

many such strings include grammatical inflections, expressive children's early language often sounds more advanced than that of a referential child. But their vocabularies develop more slowly, with no obvious spurt.

Just how these differences come about is still being hotly debated. It could be that such children are simply matching the quality of the language they are hearing. For example, there are a few hints that firstborn children may be more likely to follow the referential pattern. Perhaps they receive much more intensive language input, with much more emphasis on learning names. Later-borns, who seem to be somewhat more likely to follow an expressive style, may encounter a rather different linguistic environment, with more emphasis on communication. The two styles might also reflect underlying temperamental variations—although the one study I know of that explores this possibility directly has not found such a link (Bates et al., 1988).

Whatever the source, the existence of such large differences in the form or style of early language raises serious questions about the assumption that the early stages of language development are the same for all children, and about virtually all nativist theories of language development. Unless we assume that there are rather radical variations in the input with which the child is working, it is difficult to account for such style differences from a base of common operating principles or other built-in processes. All in all, the literature on style differences in language learning, which seemed like an interesting sidelight when Nelson first described the phenomenon, has turned out to lead to a fascinating set of new questions.

If you had to guess, which of the two styles of early language learning would you bet young Shifra shows?

There are some indications that girls are more likely to follow a referential pattern, while boys may be more often expressive. Can you think of any possible explanations for such a difference?

❱ An Application of the Basic Knowledge: Learning to Read

In Chapter 5, I talked briefly about some of the *perceptual* aspects of learning to read. But of course reading involves language as well. Researchers have found that a child's knowledge of both the sound and the structure of language plays very important roles in early reading.

First of all, knowledge of language structure makes a difference. If you come to a word you don't know as you are reading, it is a great help to have some idea of the *type* of word that could go there, or even some good guesses about which specific words might be likely. Then it is possible to accept or reject those guesses based on the actual letters on the page. Such knowledge helps children as well. In one study, Dale Willows and Ellen Ryan (1986) found that children with higher levels of "grammatical sensitivity" were consistently better readers in first, second, and third grade. This is not just a matter of knowing lots of words—although that helps, too. It is more a matter of being aware of, or knowing, the ways in which sentences are put together.

When the child gets to the point of decoding individual letters, another form of language awareness also seems to be critical, namely awareness of the fact that words are made up of individual sounds, called *phonemes* by linguistics. Hence this type of awareness is called *phonemic awareness*.

Suppose you say to a child, "Tell a word which starts the same as tap" (Maclean, Bryant, & Bradley, 1987). To do this, the child has to be able to identify which sound comes first in the string of sounds that makes that word. He must also be able to recognize this same sound in other words. You can get at this same skill in other ways, such as by asking children to recognize or produce rhyming words, or to say the first sound in a syllable. There is now abundant evidence that children who are more skilled at such tasks at age 3 or 4 or 5 later learn to read much more easily (Adams, 1990; Bryant et al., 1990).

Letter recognition and phonemic awareness also interact with more basic cognitive skills. For instance, Tunmer and his colleagues (1988) have found that the best predictor of reading skill at the end of first grade is the child's letter recognition at the beginning of the year. But among those children who began first grade with poor phonemic awareness or letter recognition, those with good skills on tasks like Piaget's concrete operational problems caught up much more quickly in reading than did children who lagged behind in these basic cognitive skills. Thus good skills in either area—language awareness or logical abilities—can form the foundation for reading, but of the two, language awareness seems to be the more central.

Where does such early language awareness come from? How does it happen that some 5- and 6-year-olds have extensive understanding of the way words are put together, while others have little? The answer seems to be quite simple: exposure and expertise. For a child to learn about letters and sounds, he has to have had a great deal of exposure to language, both written and spoken. Such children are talked to a lot as infants, read to regularly, may have toy letters to play with, are told the sounds that go with each letter, or may be quite specifically taught the alphabet at an early age.

Nursery rhymes are also frequently a significant part of the early experience of good readers. In one study, researchers in England found that children who knew more nursery rhymes at age 3½ later had greater phonemic awareness and learned to read more readily than did those who knew fewer rhymes (Maclean et al., 1987). Because nursery rhyme knowledge was *not* predictive of the child's later mathematical ability in this study, it looks very much as if we are dealing here with a quite specific body of expertise.

Of all the types of early experience that may contribute to such expertise, the most crucial seems to be the experience of being read to, regularly and in a fashion that invites the child's attention and response—a point I made in the research report on reading to children. Families that do not engage in such reading, or do not encourage other prereading experiences, have children who have far more difficulty learning to read once they begin school.

For those lacking such expertise at the start of school, the only solution is to try to build a parallel base of knowledge through many of the same kinds of experiences that more expert readers have had at home. This means that poor readers need a great deal of exposure to sound/letter combinations. But they also need to learn how to recognize patterns of letters in words. One need not—indeed must not— choose between those two hotly contesting educational systems, phonics and "whole word" training. Both are needed.

Chances are that this boy will have an easier time learning to read later because Dad has read to him regularly.

▶ Summary

1. Language can be defined as an arbitrary system of symbols that permits us to say, and to understand, an infinite variety of messages. It is rule-governed and creative.

2. Many of the developments during the "prelinguistic" phase (before the first word) are significant precursors to language. The child discriminates language sounds, babbles sounds that more and more closely approximate the sounds he hears, and uses gestures in communicative ways.

3. At about 1 year of age the earliest words appear. Some of these early words are combined with gestures to convey whole sentences of meaning, a pattern called a holophrase.

4. Vocabulary grows slowly at first, and then usually spurts in a "naming explosion." By 16 to 20 months, most children have a vocabulary of 50 or more words.

5. The first two-word sentences normally appear between 18 and 24 months and are short and grammatically simple, lacking the various grammatical inflections. Many different meanings, such as location, or possession, or agent-object relationships, can nonetheless be conveyed by the child.

6. During a "grammar explosion," the child quite quickly adds the many grammatical inflections, and learns to create questions and negative sentences.

7. By age 3 or 4, most children can construct remarkably complex sentences. Later skills are on the order of refinements, such as learning to understand and use passive sentences.

8. The development of word meanings (semantic development) follows a less-predictable course. Children appear to have many concepts or categories before they have words for them, but learning new words also creates new categories.

9. The earliest words are typically highly specific and context-bound in meaning; later, children typically "overextend" their usage.

10. Many (but not all) linguists believe that in determining word meanings, a child has built-in constraints or biases, such as the assumption that words refer to objects or actions but not both, or the principle of contrast.

11. Children appear to have two uses for language: to communicate, and to direct their own activity. Communication is the dominant use. As early as age 2 children adapt their language to the needs of the listener, and begin to follow culturally specific customs of language usage.

12. Several theories have been offered to explain language development. Two early environmental explanations, based on imitation or reinforcement, have been largely set aside. More recently, emphasis has been placed on the helpful quality of the simpler form of parent-to-child language called motherese, and on the role of expansions and recastings of children's sentences.

13. Innateness theories are also common. They assume the child is born with a set of "operating principles" that focus the child on relevant aspects of language input. Others emphasize the child as a "little linguist," who constructs a language as he constructs all cognitive understandings.

14. Children differ in the rate of development of both vocabulary and grammar, differences explained by both heredity and environmental influences. Despite these variations in rate of early development, however, most children learn to speak skillfully by about age 5 or 6.

15. In the early years of language development, two styles of language can be distinguished, "referential" (focusing on objects and their description) and "expressive" (focusing on words and forms that describe or further social relationships).

16. Research on language can also help to understand the development of reading skill. Metalinguistic awareness of the grammar, semantics, and segmented sounds of language seems to be critical for reading.

▶ Key Terms

babbling (230)	mean length of utterance (248)	receptive language (231)
cooing (230)	motherese (245)	referential style (234)
expressive language (231)	overregularization (238)	semantics (228)
expressive style (234)	pragmatics (243)	syntax (228)
holophrases (235)	prelinguistic phase (229)	telegraphic speech (235)
inflections (235)		

▶ Suggested Readings

de Villiers, P. A., & de Villiers, J. G. (1992). Language development. In M. H. Bornstein & M. E. Lamb (Eds.), *Developmental psychology: An advanced textbook* (3rd ed.) (pp. 337–418). Hillsdale, NJ: Erlbaum.

A remarkably thorough and clear review of this subject, much easier to read than many current discussions or descriptions of language development, and touching on many of the issues I have raised here. Strongly recommended as a next source.

Hakuta, K. (1986). *Mirror of language: The debate on bilingualism*. New York: Basic Books.

An elegant and readable discussion of many of the issues of bilingualism I've discussed in the real world box on page 240.

Harris, M. (1992). *Language experience and early language development: From input to uptake*. Hove, England: Erlbaum.

Margaret Harris is a thoughtful researcher and theorist who argues, in this book, for the importance of the language input for the child's language development. She lays out the alternative theories nicely, and presents a variety of evidence from her own research observations of mothers talking to their infants and toddlers.

Rice, M. L. (1989). Children's language acquisition. *American Psychologist, 44*, 149–156.

A brief, readable review of the current status of our knowledge of language learning.

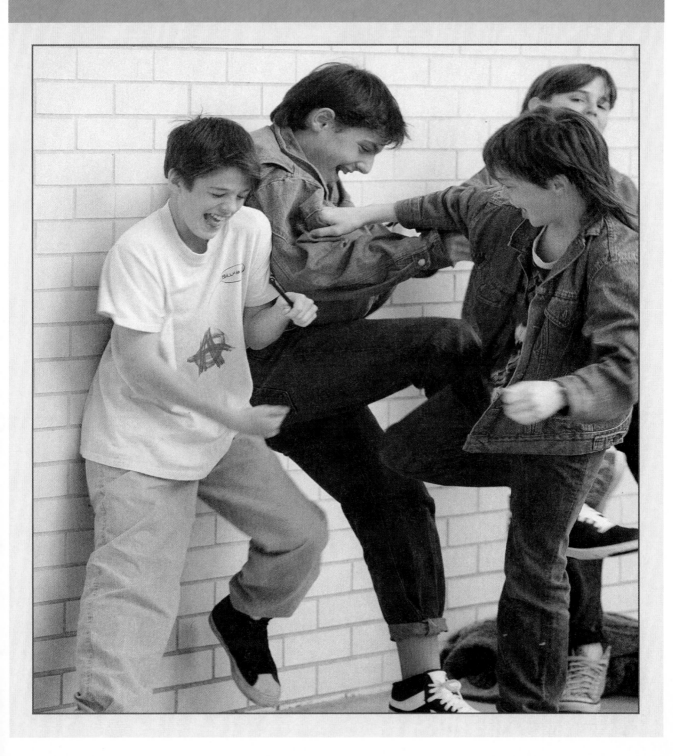

PERSONALITY DEVELOPMENT: ALTERNATIVE VIEWS

9

The Major Alternative Views of Personality

A Biological Approach: Temperament
Basic Propositions
The Evidence
• *Research Report:* The Inheritance of Personality Patterns: Evidence from Adults
• *Research Report:* Temperament and Behavior Problems
Strengths, Weaknesses, and Implications

Learning Approaches to Personality
Basic Propositions
• *The Real World:* Applying Learning Principles at Home
Evidence and Applications
Strengths, Weaknesses, and Implications

Psychoanalytic Approaches to Personality
Basic Propositions
Some Differences Between Freud and Erikson
Freud's Psychosexual Stages
Erikson's Psychosocial Stages
Other Psychoanalytic Views: Bowlby's Model of Attachment
Evidence and Applications
• *The Real World:* The Effects of Divorce: One Test of Psychoanalytic Theory
Strengths, Weaknesses, and Implications

A Tentative Synthesis

Summary

Key Terms

Suggested Readings

Imagine yourself sitting in the back of a day-care center, invisible to the eyes of the children but able to watch a group of 2-year-olds. Since you've just read all about cognitive and language development, your attention may be drawn at first to the ways the children play with toys, or the way they talk to one another and to the teacher. But it won't take you long to notice that cognitive and language skills, however fascinating, are only part of the picture. The other part is the child's emerging *social* skills.

You'll see conflict over toys ("Mine!"), often settled with physical aggression or tears, although signs of helpfulness or altruism are also likely to be visible. You'll see children playing and moving about pretty independently, but you will also see that they still turn to the teacher often for attention and reassurance, or physically cling to her. You'll see boys and girls playing together, but little sign of any real individual friendships.

If you watched the same group of children a few years later, many of these patterns would have changed. By age 5 or 6 we see some friendships formed, but

Each of these elementary-school-age children already has a distinct temperament or personality. Where do the differences come from?

If we wanted to reduce personality to a single measure like an IQ, what might we try to measure? How about "stability" or "maturity" or "healthiness" of personality? Do any of these make sense as a summary statement of personality? Why or why not?

almost entirely between children of the same gender. Clinging and obvious dependence on adults is less in evidence, and disputes are more likely to be dealt with by yelling and name calling than by grabbing or hitting.

All of these are developmental changes, analogous to the changes in cognitive structure I talked about in Chapter 7. At the same time, you cannot watch children for very long without seeing the striking variations in children's approaches to these social tasks. The child who hung about on the edge of the group in nursery school is likely to show something similar in kindergarten; the child who clung more often to the teacher at age 2 or 3 is more likely to be the one who can hardly bear to let go of Mom on the first day of school. The gregarious toddler is probably the one who decides what game they will all play at recess in first grade.

Psychologists normally use the word **personality** to describe these differences in the way children, and adults, go about relating to the people and objects in the world around themselves. Like the concept of intelligence, the concept of personality is designed to describe *enduring individual differences* in behavior. Whether we are gregarious or shy, whether we plunge into new things or hold back, whether we are independent or dependent, whether we are confident or uncertain—all of these (and many more) are usually thought of as elements of personality, presumed to persist over time.

Most theorists and researchers have thought of personality in terms of variations on a set of dimensions, such as aggressiveness or dependency, shyness or gregariousness, securely or insecurely attached, and the like. An individual's personality can then be described as a constellation or profile of those key dimensions.

Just as was true for cognition, we need to understand both the common developmental patterns in children's social development and the individual differences in personality. Why do 5-year-olds normally show signs of individual friendships while 2-year-olds usually do not? What change makes that possible? Why are same-sex play groups much more obvious at school age than among preschoolers? And where do the personality differences come from? How does one child come to be shy and another gregarious? How does one child become a bully, another an accepted and popular friend? How does one child become securely attached, another insecurely attached, and what are the consequences of those variations over the long term?

In this case, however, it is more difficult to keep these two sets of questions tidily separate, in part because in this area there is no single agreed-upon theory of either personality differences or common developmental patterns. Instead, we have several distinct theories, each of which casts the questions differently and each of which has led to quite separate bodies of research. Given that, it makes sense to talk about the theories first, so that you can get some sense of the range of questions that fall under the general label of social and personality development. Then, with the theoretical alternatives as background, I can explore what we know about both basic developmental patterns and individual differences.

▶ The Major Alternative Views of Personality

Three of the four major theoretical orientations I talked about in Chapter 1 are represented among theories of social and personality development: (1) *biological explanations*, focused on possible genetic causes of individual differences in personality, (2) *learning explanations*, also focused on individual differences, but with a very different type of explanatory model, and (3) *psychoanalytically oriented explanations*, designed to describe both developmental change and the origins of individual differences in personality.

▶ A Biological Approach: Temperament

The most clearly biological approach to social and personality development can be found in various theories of temperament. I have talked about this concept in both Chapter 1 and Chapter 3, so it is not new to you. Most theorists conceive of temperament as a *subset* or portion of personality traits, those that have primarily to do with the individual's level of emotional reactivity and with her *style* of interacting with others around her. The term thus describes *how the child* reacts rather than what she can do or why. It includes such qualities as the tendency to approach or draw back from new experiences, or the tendency to be highly physically active or more passive.

The study of temperament has been one of the hottest areas within developmental psychology over the past 10 or 15 years, but we are still in that (exciting) early stage of study in which there is ferment and disagreement. In particular, there is still a lot of dispute about just what aspects of infants' or children's behaviors represent basic temperamental differences. You can get some sense of this dispute by looking at Table 9.1, which lists the dimensions of temperament proposed in three influential current theories. The number of dimensions vary and the labels are different, all of which can lead to a good deal of confusion. But if you look closely you can see that there is some common ground. Both Kagan and Thomas and Chess focus on a child's response to novelty, and Buss and Plomin overlap with Thomas and Chess in their attention to both activity level and emotionality.

Despite these disputes about just how temperament ought to be defined, these theorists nonetheless share a set of basic assumptions, which I can state as a series of propositions—a pattern I will follow with each of the three theoretical approaches I'll talk about in this chapter.

Basic Propositions

Proposition 1: Each individual is born with characteristic patterns of responding to the environment and to other people. The idea here is not so very different from the notion of "inborn biases" or "constraints" I have been talking about in earlier chapters, except that temperament theorists are saying that we each have *individual* as well as shared "behavioral dispositions" to react to stimuli in particular ways. Most temperament theorists assume that these individual patterns have genetic origins, although some also emphasize variations in prenatal environment.

Proposition 2: These behavioral dispositions are rooted in variations in fundamental physiological processes. Many (but not all) temperament theorists take the argument a step further and try to trace differences in behavior to underlying differences in the ways a child's brain, nervous system, or hormone system may work (Gunnar, 1990; Rothbart, 1989b). For example, Jerome Kagan has suggested that differences in what he calls "behavioral inhibition" (and what others might call "shyness") are based on differing thresholds for arousal of those parts of the brain,

TABLE 9.1	Dimensions of Temperament Suggested by Various Theorists	
Thomas and Chess*	**Buss and Plomin**	**Kagan**
Activity level *Rhythmicity* *Approach/withdrawal* *Adaptability to new experience* *Threshold of responsiveness* *Intensity of reaction* *Quality of mood* (+ or −) *Distractibility* *Persistence*	*Activity level:* variations in tempo, in vigor, and in endurance *Emotionality:* variations in the tendency to become distressed or upset easily or intensely (either with fear or anger) *Sociability:* variations in the tendency to seek and be gratified by rewards from social interaction; high level of responsivity toward others	*Inhibition:* degree of approach to or withdrawal from new situations or objects or unfamiliar persons

*Recall from Chapter 3 that Thomas and Chess describe three clusters based on these nine dimensions: the easy child, the difficult child, and the slow-to-warm-up child.

Sources: Thomas & Chess, 1977; Buss, 1989; Kagan, Reznick, & Snidman, 1990.

the amygdala and the hypothalamus, which control responses to uncertainty (Kagan, Reznick, & Snidman, 1990; Kagan, Snidman, & Arcus, 1993). Arousal of these parts of the brain leads to increases in muscle tension and heart rate. Shy or inhibited children are thought to have a *low* threshold for such a reaction. That is, they more readily become tense and alert in the presence of uncertainty, perhaps even interpreting a wider range of situations as uncertain. What we inherit, then, is not "shyness" or some equivalent, but a tendency for the brain to react in particular ways.

Proposition 3: Temperamental dispositions persist through childhood and into adulthood. No theorist is proposing that the initial temperamental dispositions remain unchanged by experience. Temperament thus does not inevitably determine personality. Rather, temperamental variations are the building blocks of personality. They create a kind of "bias" in the system toward particular patterns. Given such a bias, there should be at least *some* stability of temperament over time. Such stability ought to show itself in the form of at least modest correlations between measures of a given temperamental dimension from one age to another.

Proposition 4: Temperamental characteristics affect the way any individual responds to people and things around him, and conversely, affect the way others respond to him. Highly sociable children seek out contact with others; children low on the activity dimension are more likely to choose sedentary activities like puzzles or board games than baseball. At the same time, the sociable child, who may smile more than the detached child, elicits different responses from others. Her parents may smile, pick her up, and talk to her more, simply because she has reinforced their behavior by her positive temperament. The temperamentally "difficult" child may elicit higher rates of criticism or punishment, or receive less praise.

Is this little girl's apparent shyness built in genetically in some fashion? Does the brain of a shy or "behaviorally inhibited" child work differently from that of a less-inhibited child? Jerome Kagan thinks so.

The Evidence

All four of these propositions have been at least partially supported by recent research findings.

Inheritance of Temperament.   The strongest evidence for the genetic basis of both infant temperament and later personality is that identical twins are quite a lot more alike in their temperament than are fraternal twins (Buss & Plomin, 1984; Robinson et al., 1992). This is true in studies of adults, even when the identical twins have been reared apart—a set of findings I have explored in the research report on page 264—and it is true in studies of children and infants over age 1. One fairly typical set of results, in Table 9.2, comes from a study by Buss and Plomin of a total of 228 pairs of identical twins and 172 pairs of fraternal twins whose temperament was rated on Buss and Plomin's three temperament dimensions when they were 5 years old. You can see that the correlations between

TABLE 9.2 Similarity of Identical and Fraternal Twins on Buss and Plomin's Temperament Dimensions		
	Twin correlations	
Temperament scale	Identical	Fraternal
Emotionality	.63	.12
Activity	.62	−.13
Sociability	.53	−.03

Source: Buss & Plomin, 1984, Table 9.2, p. 122.

RESEARCH REPORT
The Inheritance of Personality Patterns: Evidence from Adults

In the past decade, a number of methodologically careful new studies of adult twins have repeatedly demonstrated that identical twins are more like one another than are fraternal twins on a whole host of measures of personality (Loehlin, 1992).

For example, Robert Plomin and his colleagues (1988) have taken advantage of the existence of an amazingly extensive and up-to-date twin registry in Sweden that includes 25,000 pairs of twins born between 1886 and 1958. From this set, they were able to identify 99 pairs of identical twins and 229 pairs of fraternal twins reared apart, and could then compare these with similar groups of twins reared together. On measures of emotionality and activity, identical twins were more similar than fraternal twins, whether they had been reared together or not. The results were less clear for sociability.

A smaller but much more famous study in the United States is the Minnesota Twin Study (Bouchard, 1984; Lykken et al., 1992; Tellegen et al., 1988) —a study that has been the subject of a great many articles in the popular press. These researchers have been particularly interested in identical twins reared apart, frequently arranging for them to meet one another for the first time. On standard personality tests they find the now-familiar pattern: Identical twins are simply much more like one another than are fraternal twins, even when the identical twins did not grow up together. This was true on measures such as positive and negative emotionality (which may be similar to Buss and Plomin's dimension of emotionality), but also on less-obvious measures, such as

a sense of "social potency" or a sense of well-being. Even a measure of "traditionalism"—an affinity for traditional values and a strong allegiance to established authority—shows slightly higher correlations among identical than among fraternal twins.

What has intrigued the popular press much more, though, are the less-precise but far more striking descriptions of the similarities in clothing preferences, interests, posture and body language, speed and tempo of talking, favorite jokes, and hobbies in pairs of identical twins reared apart:

> *One male pair who had never previously met arrived in England sporting identical beards, haircuts, wire-rimmed glasses and shirts. . . . One pair had practically the same items in their toilet cases, including the same brand of cologne and a Swedish brand of toothpaste. . . . [One pair] had the same fears and phobias. Both were afraid of water and had adopted the same coping strategy: backing into the ocean up to their knees. (Holden, 1987, p. 18)*

It is difficult to imagine what sort of genetic process could account for similar preferences in hairstyles or for a particular brand of toothpaste. But we can't merely dismiss the results because they are hard to explain. At the very least, these findings certainly point to strong genetic components in many of the elements of personal style and emotional responsiveness that temperament researchers are trying to identify and track in children.

---

temperament scores of identical twins are consistently high, while those for fraternal twins are essentially zero, indicating a strong genetic effect.

As usual, though, there is some counterevidence. For one thing, results from studies of twins under age 1 show much weaker genetic influence on infant temperament (Gunnar, 1990). Furthermore, among adopted children, the correlations between the temperament of the child and that of the natural parents is not a whole lot higher than the correlation with adoptive parents' temperament (Scarr & Kidd, 1983), which suggests that environment has a role in shaping the child's temperament. Nonetheless, most experts have concluded that there is good evidence for at least some genetic component in our usual measures of temperament.

Physiological Connections. Exploration of links between measures of temperament and measures of specific physiological functions is very new, but the early results are promising. For example, Kagan and his colleagues (1990) have reported correlations in the range of .60 between a measure of behavioral inhibition in children aged 2 to 5 and a series of physiological measures, such as muscle tension, heart rate, dilation of the pupil of the eye, and the chemical composition of both urine and saliva, all of which strongly suggests that temperament is not simply a set of learned habits.

Consistency of Temperament over Time.   Although the research evidence is somewhat mixed, there is growing evidence of consistency in temperamental ratings over rather long periods of infancy and childhood. For example, Australian researchers studying a group of 450 children found that mothers' reports of children's irritability, cooperation/manageability, inflexibility, rhythmicity, persistency, and tendency to approach (rather than avoid) contact were all quite consistent from infancy through age 8. Of these, approach and rhythmicity were the most stable (Pedlow et al., 1993). Thus babies who smile more are friendlier later, and cranky babies tend to be more difficult at school age. Kagan has also found considerable consistency over the same age range in his measure of inhibition, which is based on direct observation of the child's behavior, rather than on the mother's ratings of the child's temperament. He reports that half of babies in his longitudinal study who had shown high levels of crying and motor activity in response to a novel situation when they were 4 months old were still classified as highly inhibited at age 8, while three-fourths of those rated as uninhibited at 4 months remained in that category eight years later (Kagan et al., 1993). There is even some indication of consistency into adulthood. Among the subjects in the sample originally studied by Thomas and Chess and now followed into adulthood, the correlation between one temperament rating made in early adolescence and another in early adulthood was a robust .62 (Korn, 1984). The consistency here is obviously not perfect. In particular, there is less consistency from infancy into toddlerhood than between toddlerhood and later behavior—a pattern reminiscent of what you have already seen for infant IQ scores and later IQ scores. But there is at least some consistency in temperament, even across the "great divide" from infancy to toddlerhood

Temperament and Environment Interactions.   The simplest thing I can say about the research on temperament-environment interactions is that the findings are complex. Buss and Plomin (1984) have proposed that in general, children in the middle range on temperament dimensions typically adapt *to* their environment, while those children whose temperament is extreme—like extremely difficult children—force their environment to adapt to them. Parents of difficult children, for example, adapt to the children's negativity by punishing them more, and providing them with less support and stimulation (Rutter, 1978b) than do parents of more adaptable children (Luster, Boger, & Hannan, 1993; Rutter, 1978b). This pattern may well contribute to the higher rates of significant emotional problems in such children, a set of results I have explored in the research report on page 266.

The finding that difficult babies are more often punished could be interpreted in several ways. How many alternative explanations can you think of?

But this simple statement, while accurate, doesn't convey the additional complexities of the process: The way parents deal with an irritable or difficult child is in turn affected by their own child-rearing skills, the stress they experience, and the amount of social or emotional support they have. For example, Mavis Hetherington (1989) reports that children with difficult temperaments show more problem behavior in response to their parents' divorce, but only if the mother is also depressed and has inadequate social support. In this study, those difficult children whose divorcing mothers were not depressed did not show heightened levels of problems. Thus the child's temperament clearly seems to have an impact, but the effect is not simple or straightforward.

RESEARCH REPORT
Temperament and Behavior Problems

One of the consistent findings in the research on temperament is that children with difficult temperaments are much more likely to show various kinds of emotional disturbance or *behavior problems* than are children with less-extreme temperaments. Included in the category of behavior problems (which I'll be talking about in more detail in Chapter 15, when I discuss abnormal development) are such patterns as overaggressiveness, anxiety, depression, and hyperactivity.

The typical finding is that children who are rated as having aspects of difficult temperament are perhaps twice as likely to show one or another of these behavior problems as are children with less-difficult temperaments (Bates, 1989; Bates, Maslin, & Frankel, 1985; Chess & Thomas, 1984). So babies with more difficult temperaments are more likely to become preschoolers who show some behavior problem, and preschoolers whose temperament is rated as difficult are more likely to have behavior problems at age 10 or 15 or even as adults.

Such findings may sound like a simple restatement of consistency of temperament. Perhaps hyperactivity or aggressiveness or other behavior problems in 5-year-olds or 7-year-olds are simply further manifestations of a basically difficult temperament. But it is not so easy. The majority of children who are rated as showing "difficult" temperament in infancy or the preschool years do *not* develop behavior problems at later ages. They are more *likely* to exhibit such problems, but the relationship is not at all inevitable.

As usual, there is a complex interactive process at work. The key seems to be whether the infant's or child's "difficultness" is acceptable to the parents, or can be managed by the family in some effective way. For example, Fish, Stifter, and Belsky (1991) recently studied the changes and continuities in crying patterns in a small sample of infants. They found that those babies who had cried a great deal as newborns but cried much less at 5 months had mothers who were highly responsive and sensitive to the infant. Babies who cried a lot at both time points had much less responsive mothers. Thus the responsive mother may have reshaped the baby's inborn temperamental behavior. Difficult temperament also seems to increase the risk of behavior problems if there are any other stresses in the family system (such as divorce), or other deficits in the child, such as physical disability or retardation (Chess & Korn, 1980).

Thus difficult temperament does not *cause* later behavior problems. Rather, it creates a *vulnerability* in the child. Such children seem to be less able to deal with major life stresses. But in a supportive, accepting, low-stress environment, many such children move through childhood without displaying any significant behavior problems.

The lesson for parents is not always an easy one. If you are under severe stress, that is precisely the moment when it is hard to provide a maximally supportive, accepting environment for any child, let alone a temperamentally difficult child. But it may still help to keep in mind that a child with a difficult temperament is going to need more attention, more help, more support than will a temperamentally less-volatile child under any kind of stress, such as when the family moves, or when the child changes schools or baby-sitters, or if the family pet dies.

Strengths, Weaknesses, and Implications

There are two great strengths in this approach to the origins of personality. First, it provides a counterweight to what had been the dominant assumptions about the origins of temperament or personality differences. I'm not sure we're looking yet at a real paradigm shift, but the accumulating evidence does make it very difficult to evade the conclusion that here, as in many other areas, there is a good deal more built in than most developmental psychologists had supposed (or felt comfortable assuming) a decade or two ago. The emerging research on the links between behavioral and physiological differences is another important push in the same direction.

Paradoxically, the second strength I see is that this is not a *purely* biological approach; it is an interactionist approach, very much in keeping with much of the current theorizing about development. The child is born with certain behavioral tendencies, but the outcome depends on the transactions between a given child's initial characteristics and the responses of the environment.

On the other side of the ledger I see a number of problems, several of them resulting from the newness of this field of study. First there are still significant problems in measuring temperament. Most current measures of temperament, especially in infants and young children, rely on parents' reports about their own child's behavior or characteristics. Such measures are at least partially suspect because they may reflect the parents' own perceptual biases or temperament as much as they do the child's actual behavior (Power, Gershenhorn, & Stafford, 1990). A second problem arises from the continuing disagreement about just what dimensions we ought to be studying—a disagreement vividly clear in Table 9.1. Because different researchers have used such varying definitions and varying measures, it is often difficult to add up the results of different investigations.

A third drawback for me is that current temperament theories are not fundamentally *developmental* theories. Temperament theories allow for change through the mechanism of interaction with the environment. But they do not tell us whether we might expect systematic age differences in children's responses to new situations or to people; they do not tell us whether the child's emerging cognitive skills have anything to do with changes in the child's temperamental patterns. They do not, in a word, tell us how the *shared* developmental patterns may interact with the inborn individual differences.

None of these problems constitutes a refutation of any of the basic tenets of this theoretical approach. We can simply no longer ignore the importance of genetic differences and basic biology in shaping individual differences in temperament or personality.

This may be just a bad moment for an otherwise sunny-dispositioned child. But if this is a typical reaction, one sign of a "difficult" temperament, this youngster will be at higher risk for a variety of problems.

▶ Learning Approaches to Personality

The emphasis shifts rather dramatically when we look at social learning approaches. Instead of looking at what the child brings to the equation, learning theorists have looked primarily at the reinforcement patterns in the environment as the primary cause of differences in children's patterns of behavior. Of course they do not reject biology. Albert Bandura, arguably the most influential theorist in this group, grants that biological factors such as hormones or inherited propensities (such as temperament, presumably) also affect behavior. But he and others of this persuasion look to the environment as the major source of influence.

These are not new ideas for you. You have already read about the basic concepts in Chapter 1 and encountered a version of such a theory in Skinner's theory of language acquisition. The question here is how to apply this theory specifically to such "personality" characteristics as dependency, nurturance, aggressiveness, activity level, or gregariousness.

There are several distinct schools of thought within the "learning" camp. Some, often called radical behaviorists, argue that only the basic principles of classical and operant conditioning are needed to account for variations in behavior, including personality. Others, like Bandura, emphasize not only observational learning but also important cognitive elements. Both groups would agree with the first two propositions I've listed below; the remaining propositions emerge primarily from Bandura's work.

Basic Propositions

Proposition 1: Behavior is "strengthened" by reinforcement. If this rule applies to all behavior, then it should apply to attachment, shyness, sharing, or competitiveness, too. Children who are reinforced for clinging to their parents, for exam-

THE REAL WORLD
Applying Learning Principles at Home

It is a lot harder than you may think to apply basic learning principles consistently and correctly with children at home or in schools. Virtually all parents do try to reinforce some behaviors in their children by praising them or by giving them attention or treats. And most of us do our best to discourage unpleasant behavior through punishment. But it is easy to misapply the principles, or to create unintended consequences because we have not fully understood all the mechanisms involved.

For example, suppose you have a favorite armchair in your living room that is being systematically ruined by the dirt and pressure of little feet climbing up the back of the chair. You want the children to *stop* climbing up the chair. So you scold them. After a while you may even stoop to nagging. If you are really conscientious and knowledgeable, you may carefully try to time your scolding so that it operates as a negative reinforcer, by stopping your scolding when they stop climbing. But nothing works. They keep on leaving those muddy footprints on your favorite chair. Why? It could be because the children *enjoy* climbing up the chair. So the climbing is intrinsically reinforcing to the children, and that effect is clearly stronger than your negative reinforcement or punishment. One way to deal with this might be to provide something *else* for them to climb on.

Another example: Suppose your 3-year-old son repeatedly demands your attention while you are fixing dinner (a common state of affairs, as any parent of a 3-year-old can tell you). Because you don't want to reinforce this behavior, you ignore him the first six or eight times he says "Mommy" or tugs at your clothes. But after the ninth or tenth repetition, with his voice getting louder and whinier each time, you can't stand it any longer and finally say something like "All right! What do you want?" Since you have ignored most of his demands, you might well be convinced that you have not been reinforcing his demanding behavior. But what you have actually done is to create a partial reinforcement schedule; you have rewarded only every tenth demand or whine. And we know that this pattern of reinforcement helps to create behavior that is *very* hard to extinguish. So your son may continue to be demanding and whining for a very long time, even if you succeed in ignoring this behavior completely.

If such situations are familiar to you, it may pay to keep careful records for a while, keeping track of each incident and your response, and then see if you can figure out which principles are really at work, and how you might change the pattern.

---

ple, should show more clinging than do children who are not reinforced for it. Similarly, a nursery school teacher who pays attention to children only when they get rowdy or aggressive should find that the children get steadily more rowdy and aggressive over the course of weeks or months.

> Can you think of other real-life examples of partial reinforcement in action? What about things you do to please your partner, for which you get a smile only some of the time?

Proposition 2: Behavior that is reinforced on a "partial schedule" should be even stronger and more resistant to extinction than behavior that is consistently reinforced. I talked briefly about this phenomenon in Chapter 1, so you have some idea what is involved. Parents are nearly always inconsistent in their rewards to their children, so most children are on partial schedules of some kind whether the parent intends that or not. That is, they are sometimes reinforced for a particular behavior, but not every time. Because behavior that is rewarded in this way is highly persistent—highly *resistant to extinction*, in the language of learning theory—partial reinforcement patterns are a major factor in the establishment of those distinctive and stable patterns of behavior defined as personality.

Proposition 3: Children learn new behaviors largely through modeling. Bandura has argued that the full range of social behaviors, from competitiveness to nurturance, is learned not just by direct reinforcement, but also by watching others perform those actions. Thus the child who sees her parents taking a casserole next door to the woman who has just been widowed will learn generosity and thoughtful behavior. The child who sees her parents arguing or hitting each other when they are angry will most likely learn violent ways of solving problems.

Children learn from TV, too, and from their peers, their teachers, and their brothers and sisters. A boy growing up in an environment where he observes playmates and older boys hanging around street corners, shoplifting, or stealing hubcaps is going to learn all those behaviors. His continuous exposure to such antisocial models makes it that much harder for his parents to reinforce more constructive behavior.

Learning from modeling is not an entirely automatic process. Bandura points out that what a child (or adult) learns from watching someone else will depend on what she pays attention to, what she is able to remember (both *cognitive* processes), what she is physically able to copy, and what she is motivated to imitate. Because attentional abilities, memory, and other cognitive processes change with age through infancy and childhood, what a baby or child can or will learn from any given modeled event will also change through development (Grusec, 1992).

Proposition 4: Children learn not only overt behavior but also ideas, expectations, internal standards, and self-concepts from reinforcement and modeling. The child learns standards for his own behavior, and expectancies about what he can and cannot do (which Bandura calls *self-efficacy*) from specific reinforcements and from modeling. In this way, the child *internalizes* what he has learned. Once those standards and those expectancies or beliefs are established, they affect the child's behavior in consistent and enduring ways. These beliefs and expectancies form the core of what may be called personality.

Parents are not the only models for social learning.

Suppose you were trying to learn a new sport, such as tennis or soccer, by observing an expert. Can you see how these four principles would affect what you were able to learn from the model?

Evidence and Applications

The Basic Effects of Reinforcement.   There is an *immense* collection of studies supporting the first two propositions. For example, in several studies, experimenters systematically rewarded some children for hitting an inflated rubber clown on the nose. When they later watched the children in a play situation, they found that the children who had been rewarded showed more hitting, scratching, and kicking than did children who hadn't been rewarded for punching the clown (Walters & Brown, 1963). Partial reinforcement in the form of inconsistent behavior from parents also has the expected effect. For example, Sears, Maccoby, and Levin (1977) found that parents who permit fairly high levels of aggression in their children, but occasionally react by punishing it quite severely, have children who are more aggressive than are children whose parents neither permit nor punish aggression.

Both of these principles have been used successfully in therapeutic interventions with families of out-of-control children, such as in Gerald Patterson's studies of aggressive or noncompliant children that I described in Chapter 1. If you go back and look at Figure 1.2 (p. 12) you'll see that the heart of Patterson's model is a link between "poor parental discipline" and resultant conduct problems in the child. He is arguing here that both normal personality patterns and deviant forms of behavior have their roots in daily social exchanges with family members. For example, imagine a child playing in his very messy room. The mother comes into the room and tells the child to clean up his room. The child whines or yells at her that he doesn't want to do it, or won't do it. The mother gives in, and leaves the room, and the child stops whining or shouting.

Patterson analyzes this exchange as a pair of negatively reinforced events. When the mother gives in to the child's defiance, her own behavior (giving in) is negatively reinforced by the ending of the child's whining or yelling. This makes it more likely that she will give in the next time. She has *learned* to back down in order to get the child to shut up. The child has been negatively reinforced for yelling or whining, since the unpleasant event for him (being told to clean his room) stopped as soon as he whined. So he has learned to whine or yell. Imagine such exchanges occurring over and over, and you begin to understand how a family can create a *system* in which an imperious, demanding, noncompliant child rules the roost.

As I pointed out in Chapter 1, Patterson's thinking has moved beyond the simple propositions I have outlined here. Like the current temperament theorists, he emphasizes that what happens in a given family, for a particular child, is a joint product of the child's own temperament or response tendencies, the parents' discipline skills, the parents' personalities, and the social context of the parents' lives. But Patterson is still assuming that basic learning principles can both describe and explain the ways in which the child's behavior pattern (his "personality") is formed or changed. And he has shown that it is possible to *change* the child's typical behavior by helping families learn new and more effective reinforcement and management strategies.

Effects of Modeling. The impact of observational learning has also been demonstrated in literally hundreds of studies (Bandura, 1973; 1977). One interesting—and very practical—sidelight to the process of modeling has been the repeated finding that modeling works better than preaching. So displaying the desired behavior yourself—such as generosity, fairness, or diligent work—works better than simply telling kids that it is good to be generous or fair or hardworking.

For example, in one study, Joan Grusec and her co-workers (1978) had elementary-school children play a miniature bowling game, ostensibly to test the

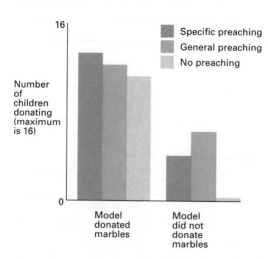

Figure 9.1
These results from Grusec's modeling study illustrate the general finding that modeling is more powerful than preaching in changing children's behavior. (*Source:* Grusec, Saas-Kortsaak, & Simutis, 1978, from Table 1, p. 922.)

game. The children first observed an adult "test" the game, and saw the adult win 20 marbles. Next to the bowling game was a poster that said "Help poor children. Marbles buy gifts." Under the poster was a bowl with some marbles in it. Half the time the adult model donated half his newly won marbles to this bowl; the other half of the time he did not. In addition, the model either "preached" about donating marbles or said nothing. To some of the children he preached in specific terms, saying that the child should donate half his marbles when he played the game, since it would be good to make poor children happy by doing that. To other children, he preached in more general terms, saying that the child should donate half his marbles because it is a good thing to make other people happy by helping them any way one can. The adult model then left the room, and each child had an opportunity to play the bowling game and to decide whether to donate any marbles. You can see in Figure 9.1 how many children in each group (out of a maximum of 16) donated marbles. Clearly, modeling worked better than preaching. And when there is a conflict between what the model says and what the model does—such as when parents smoke but tell their kids that they should not smoke—children generally follow the behavior and not the verbal message. So the old adage "Do what I say and not what I do" doesn't seem to work.

In his explorations of the concept of self-efficacy, Bandura has also shown that changing someone's belief about his ability to do something has a greater impact on his behavior than merely reinforcing him for performing that behavior (Bandura, 1982). There are various ways to produce such a change in belief, such as providing opportunities for a child (or adult) to watch peers succeed at some task at which he typically fails—peers whom he thinks of as like himself in ability. So a child who thinks of himself as unable to hit a baseball might increase his belief in his ability if he could watch other equally inept kids become better hitters. The increase in his own belief (his sense of self-efficacy, in Bandura's terms) will later affect his ability to hit the ball, even without additional practice.

Strengths, Weaknesses, and Implications

Several implications of this overall theoretical approach are worth emphasizing. First of all, unlike temperament theorists, who expect at least a certain amount of consistency of behavior in different situations, learning theorists can handle either consistency or inconsistency in children's behavior. If a child is friendly and smiling both at home and at school, this could be explained by saying that the child was being reinforced for that behavior in both settings rather than by assuming that the child has a "gregarious temperament." But it is equally possible to explain how a child could be the soul of helpfulness at school but never obey his mother at home, or do whatever his father asks but regularly defy his mother. In cases like this, learning theorists merely go searching for the differing patterns of reinforcement in the different settings, or the different expectancies the child may have acquired. Such inconsistencies are more difficult to account for within a narrow biological approach.

A related implication is that learning theorists are supremely optimistic about the possibility of change. Children's behavior can change if the reinforce-

This 7-year-old is happily helping his grandmother fold clothes. But that is no guarantee that he will be equally helpful to his mother—a kind of inconsistency that learning theorists can handle more easily than temperament theorists can.

ment system (or their beliefs about themselves) change, so "problem behavior" can be modified, as Patterson has done with families of aggressive children.

The great strength of this view of social behavior is that it gives an accurate picture of the way in which many behaviors are learned. It is perfectly clear that children do learn through modeling; and it is equally clear that children (and adults) will continue to perform behaviors that "pay off" for them.

The addition of the cognitive elements to Bandura's theory lends further strength, since it offers a beginning integration of learning models and cognitive-developmental approaches. If we were to apply Piaget's language to Bandura's theory we could talk about the acquisition of a "self-scheme"—a concept of one's own capacities, qualities, standards, and experiences. New experiences are then assimilated to that scheme. You will recall from Chapter 7 that one of the characteristics of the process of assimilation as Piaget proposed it is that new experiences or information are modified as they are taken in. In the same way, Bandura is saying that once the child's self-concept is established, it affects what behaviors she chooses to perform, how she reacts to new experiences, whether she persists or gives up on some new task, and the like. If a child believes he is unpopular, for example, then he will not be surprised if others do not choose to sit by him in the lunchroom; if someone does sit next to him, he's likely to explain it to himself in such a way that he retains his central belief, such as "there must have been no place else to sit." In this way the underlying scheme isn't modified (accommodated) very much.

Thus the self-concept, once well formed, serves as a central mediating process leading to stable differences in behavior of the kind we typically call personality. It *can* be modified (accommodated) if the child accumulates enough experience or evidence that doesn't fit with the existing scheme. If the "unpopular" child noticed that classmates regularly chose to sit next to him at lunch even when there were other seats available, he might eventually change his self-scheme, coming to think of himself as "somewhat popular." But since the child (like the adult) will choose activities or situations that fit his self-concept, such as sitting in the corner where no one is likely to see him, he will be partially protected from such "nonconfirming" experiences.

Think for a minute about the ways you choose activities that are consistent with your self-image or self-scheme. What would it take for you to change some of the key portions of your self-scheme?

To be sure, Bandura and Piaget would not agree on how this self-concept or self-scheme develops. Piaget emphasizes internal processes, while Bandura emphasizes reinforcement and modeling as causal factors. But they agree on the impact that such a scheme will have once it has developed.

At the same time, these learning theories have significant weaknesses, particularly the more radical versions. First, from the perspective of many psychologists, there is still too much emphasis placed on what happens *to* the child and not enough on what the child is doing with the information he has. Bandura's theory is much less vulnerable to this charge, but most learning theories of personality are highly mechanistic, and focused on external events. Second, like temperament theories, these are not really *developmental* theories. They can say how a child might acquire a particular behavior pattern or belief, but they do not take into account the underlying developmental changes that are occurring. Given Bandura's emphasis on the cognitive aspects of the modeling process, a genuinely developmental social learning theory could be proposed, although no such theory now exists. Still, despite these limitations, all the theories in this group offer useful descriptions of one source of influence on the child's developing pattern of behavior.

Psychoanalytic Approaches to Personality

Like many temperament theorists, and like social learning theorists of Bandura's stripe, psychoanalytic theorists believe that the interaction between the child's inborn characteristics and the environment plays a central role in shaping differences in personality. But unlike temperament or learning theories, psychoanalytic theories are clearly *developmental* as well, describing systematic changes in children's sense of self, in their needs or drives, and in their relationships with others.

In Chapter 1, I described a number of the key propositions of this approach. Here let me simply summarize Freud's and Erikson's views.

Basic Propositions

Proposition 1: Behavior is governed by unconscious as well as conscious motives and processes. Freud emphasized three sets of instinctual drives: the sexual drive (libido); life-preserving drives, including avoidance of hunger and pain; and aggressive drives. Erikson emphasized a more cognitive process, the drive for identity.

Proposition 2: Personality structure develops over time, as a result of the interaction between the child's inborn drives/needs and the responses of the key people in the child's world. Because the child is often prevented from achieving instant gratification of his various drives, he is forced to develop new skills—planning, talking, delaying, and other cognitive techniques that allow gratification of the basic needs in more indirect ways. Thus the ego is created, and it remains the planning, organizing, thinking part of the personality. The superego, in turn, develops because the parents try to restrain certain kinds of gratification; the child eventually incorporates these parental standards into his own personality.

Proposition 3: Development of personality is fundamentally stagelike, with each stage centered on a particular task or a particular form of basic need. I'll describe both Freud's and Erikson's stages in some detail in a moment. For now, the key point is only that there *are* stages in these theories.

Proposition 4: The specific personality a child develops depends on the degree of success the child has in traversing these various stages. In each stage, the child requires a particular kind of supportive environment for successful resolution of that particular dilemma or for meeting that particular need. A child lacking the needed environment will have a very different personality than one whose environment was partially or wholly adequate. However, while each stage is important, all the psychoanalytic theorists strongly emphasize the crucial significance of the very earliest stages, and focus especially on the adequacy of the relationship between the baby and the central caregiver, usually the mother. This is not quite like saying that infancy is a sensitive period for personality development; rather, Freud and later psychoanalytic theorists argue that the earliest relationship establishes a pattern and sets the child on a particular pathway through the remainder of the stages.

Some Differences Between Freud and Erikson

All four of these general propositions are contained in both Freud's and Erikson's theories, but both the details and the emphases differ in important respects. In Freud's theory, for example, all the cognitive skills develop only because the child needs them to obtain gratification; they have no independent life. In Erikson's theory (and in many other variations of psychoanalytic theory), cognitive skills are part of a set of ego functions that are presumed to develop independently, rather than being entirely in the service of basic gratification.

Basic physical maturation is also more central to Freud's theory than to Erikson's. In Freud's theory, the stages shift from one to the next in part because of maturation of the nervous system. In each stage, the child is attempting to gratify basic physical ("sexual") needs through stimulation of a particular part of the body—that part of the body that is most sensitive at that time. As neurological development proceeds, maximum body sensitivity shifts from the mouth to the anus to the genitals, and this maturational change is part of what drives the stage changes. Erikson granted such physical changes, but placed greater emphasis on shifts in the demands of the social environment. Each stage centers on a specific social conflict, resulting in a psychosocial crisis. For example, stage 4 (industry versus inferiority) begins at about age 6 because that is when the child goes off to school; in a culture in which schooling was delayed, the timing of the developmental task might be delayed as well.

Because of such theoretical differences, Erikson and Freud have described the stages of development rather differently. Because both sets of stages have become part of the vocabulary of developmental psychology, you need to be conversant with both, so let me describe each.

Freud's Psychosexual Stages

Freud proposed five **psychosexual stages,** which I've summarized in Table 9.3.

The Oral Stage: Birth–Year. The mouth, tongue, and lips are the first center of pleasure for the baby, and his earliest attachment is to the one who provides pleasure in the mouth, usually his mother. For normal development the infant requires some optimum amount of oral stimulation—not too much and not too little. If the optimum amount of stimulation is not available, then some libidinal energy may remain attached to (*fixated* on, in Freud's terms) the oral mode of gratification. Such an individual, so Freud thought, will continue to have a strong preference for oral pleasures in later life, as you can see in the right-hand column in Table 9.3.

The Anal Stage: 1–3 Years. As the trunk matures, the baby becomes more and more sensitive in the anal region. At about the same time, her parents begin to place great emphasis on toilet training and show pleasure when she manages to perform in the right place at the right time. These two forces together help to shift the major center of physical/sexual energy from the oral to the anal erogenous zone.

The key to the child's successful completion of this stage (according to Freud) is whether the parents allow the child sufficient anal exploration and pleasure. If toilet training becomes a major battleground, then some fixation of energy at this stage may occur—with the possible adult consequences of excessive orderliness, stinginess, or the opposite.

Freud thought that babies put things into their mouths because that is where they have the most pleasurable sensations. If babies don't get enough oral stimulation, he argued, they may become fixated at the oral stage.

Stage	Age	Erogenous zones	Major developmental task (potential source of conflict)	Some adult characteristics of children who have been "fixated" at this stage according toFreud
			TABLE 9.3 Freud's Stages of Psychosexual Development	
Oral	0–1	Mouth, lips, tongue	Weaning	Oral behavior, such as smoking and overeating; passivity and gullibility.
Anal	2–3	Anus	Toilet training	Orderliness, parsimoniousness, obstinacy, or the opposite (extreme untidiness, for example).
Phallic	4–5	Genitals	Oedipus complex; identification with parent of same sex	Vanity, recklesness, and the opposite.
Latency	6–12	No specific area; sexual energy quiescent	Development of ego defense mechanisms	None: fixation does not normally occur at this stage.
Genital	13–18 and adulthood	Genitals	Mature sexual intimacy	Adults who have successfully integrated earlier stages should emerge from this stage with a more sincere interest in others, realistic enjoyments, mature sexuality.

The Phallic Stage: 3-5 Years.   At about 3 or 4 years of age the genitals increase in sensitivity, ushering in a new stage. One sign of this new sensitivity is that children of both sexes quite naturally begin to masturbate at about this age.

In Freud's view, the most important event that occurs during the phallic stage is the so-called **Oedipus conflict.** He described the sequence of events more fully (and more believably!) for boys, so let me trace that pattern for you.

The theory suggests that first the boy somehow becomes "intuitively aware of his mother as a sex object" (Rappoport, 1972, p. 74). Precisely how this occurs is not completely spelled out, but the important point is that the boy at about age 4 begins to have a sort of sexual attachment to his mother and to regard his father as a sexual rival. His father sleeps with his mother, holds her, and kisses her, and generally has access to her body in a way that the boy does not. The boy also sees

Can you think of any kind of study that would tell us whether Freud was right or not about the Oedipus conflict?

his father as a powerful and threatening figure who has the ultimate power—the power to castrate. The boy is caught between desire for his mother and fear of his father's power.

Most of these feelings and the resultant conflict are unconscious. The boy does not have overt sexual feelings or behavior toward his mother. But unconscious or not, the result of this conflict is anxiety. How can the little boy handle this anxiety? In Freud's view, the boy responds with a defensive process called **identification:** The boy "incorporates" his image of his father, and attempts to match his own behavior to that image. By trying to make himself as like his father as possible, the boy not only reduces the chance of an attack from the father, he also takes on some of the father's power as well. Furthermore, it is the "inner father," with his values and moral judgments, that serves as the core of the child's superego.

A parallel process is supposed to occur in girls. The girl sees her mother as a rival for her father's sexual attentions, and also has some fear of her mother (though less than is true for the boy, since the girl may assume she has already been castrated). In this case, too, identification with the mother is thought to be the "solution" to the girl's anxiety.

The Latency Stage: 5-12 Years.   Freud thought that after the phallic stage there is a sort of resting period before the next major change in the child's sexual development. The child has presumably arrived at some preliminary resolution of the Oedipus conflict, so that there is a kind of calm after the storm. One of the obvious characteristics of this stage is that the identification with the same-sex parent that defined the end of the phallic stage is now extended to others of the same sex. So it is during these years that children's peer interactions are almost exclusively with members of the same sex, and children often have "crushes" on same-sex teachers or other adults.

In elementary school, boys play with boys, girls play with girls. How would Freud explain this?

The Genital Stage: 12-18 and Older.   The further changes in hormones and the genital organs that take place during puberty reawaken the sexual energy of the child. During this period a more mature form of sexual attachment occurs. From the beginning of this period, the child's sexual objects are people of the opposite sex. Freud placed some emphasis on the fact that not everyone works through this period to a point of mature heterosexual love. Some have not had a satisfactory oral period and thus do not have a foundation of basic love relationships. Some have not resolved the Oedipus conflict with a complete or satisfactory identification with the same-sex parent, a failure that may affect their ability to cope with rearoused sexual energies in adolescence.

What we see as the child's "personality," then, is a complex result of all of these processes, depending on the particular stages at which the child may have become fixated, on the particular form of the child's identification with the parents, and on the defense mechanisms that the child adopts.

Erikson's Psychosocial Stages

The same themes occur in Erikson's theory, but the particulars are different. The change in emphasis is noticeable in the name itself; Erikson is talking about **psychosocial stages,** not psycho*sexual* stages. As you can see in Table 9.4, another difference is that Erikson's stages cover the entire life span rather than ending at adolescence.

TABLE 9.4   The Eight Stages of Development Proposed by Erik Erikson

Approximate age	Ego quality to be developed	Some tasks and activities of the stage
0–1	Basic trust versus basic mistrust	Trust in mother or central caregiver and in one's own ability to make things happen. A key element in an early secure attachment.
2–3	Autonomy versus shame, doubt	Walking, grasping, and other physical skills lead to free choice; toilet training occurs; child learns control but may develop shame if not handled properly.
4–5	Initiative versus guilt	Organize activities around some goal; become more assertive and aggressive. Oedipus-like conflict with parent of same sex may lead to guilt.
6–12	Industry versus inferiority	Absorb all of the basic culture skills and norms, including school skills and tool use.
13–18	Identity versus role confusion	Adapt sense of self to physical changes of puberty, make occupational choice, achieve adultlike sexual identity, and search for new values.
19–25	Intimacy versus isolation	Form one or more intimate relationships that go beyond adolescent love; marry and form family groups.
26–40	Generativity versus stagnation	Bear and rear children, focus on occupational achievement or creativity, and train the next generation.
41+	Ego integrity versus despair	Integrate earlier stages and come to terms with basic identity. Accept self.

Basic Trust Versus Basic Mistrust: Birth -1 Year. The first task (or "dilemma" as Erikson sometimes said) occurs during the first year of life, when the child must develop a sense of basic trust in the predictability of the world and in his ability to affect the events around him. Erikson believed that the behavior of the major caregiver (usually the mother) is critical to the child's successful or unsuccessful resolution of this crisis. Children who emerge from the first year with a firm sense of trust are those whose parents are loving and respond predictably and reliably to the child. A child who has developed a sense of trust will go on to other relationships carrying this sense with him; but those infants whose early care has been erratic or harsh may develop *mistrust*; and they too carry this sense with them into later relationships.

Erikson never said, by the way, that the ideal position on any one of the dilemmas is at one extreme pole. In the case of the first stage, for example, there is some risk in being too trusting. The child also needs to develop some healthy mistrust, such as learning to discriminate between dangerous and safe situations.

Autonomy Versus Shame and Doubt: 2-3 Years. Erikson saw the child's greater mobility during the toddler years as forming the basis for the sense of independence or autonomy. But if the child's efforts at independence are not carefully guided by the parents and she experiences repeated failures or ridicule, then the results of all the new opportunities for exploration may be shame and doubt instead of a basic sense of self-control and self-worth. Once again the ideal is not for the child to have *no* shame or doubt; some doubt is needed for the child to understand which behaviors are acceptable and which are not, which are safe and which are dangerous. But the ideal does lie toward the autonomy end of the continuum.

Initiative Versus Guilt: 4-5 Years.   This phase, which is roughly equivalent to Freud's phallic stage, is again ushered in by new skills or abilities in the child. The 4-year-old is able to plan a bit, to take initiative in reaching particular goals. The child tries out these new cognitive skills, attempts to conquer the world around him. He may try to go out into the street on his own; he may take a toy apart, then find he can't put it back together and throw it—parts and all—at his mother. It is a time of vigor, of action and of behaviors that parents may see as aggressive. The risk is that the child may go too far in his forcefulness, or that the parents may restrict and punish too much— either of which can produce guilt. Some guilt is needed, since without it there would be no conscience, no self-control. The ideal interaction between parent and child is certainly not total indulgence. But too much guilt can inhibit the child's creativity and free interactions with others.

If looks could kill! This child is clearly jealous of the new baby and may well be harboring all sorts of angry and aggressive thoughts. A younger child would probably act out those thoughts and feelings directly. But a child of this age, probably in the period Erikson calls *initiative versus guilt*, feels guilty about her feelings and inhibits the angry actions.

Industry (Competence) Versus Inferiority: 6-12 Years.   The beginning of schooling is a major force in ushering in this stage. The child is now faced with the need to win approval through specific competence—through learning to read, do sums, and other school skills. The task of this period is thus simply to develop the repertoire of abilities society demands of the child. If the child is unable to develop the expected skills, he will develop instead a basic sense of inferiority. Yet, some failure is necessary so that the child can develop some humility; as always, balance is at issue. Ideally, the child must have sufficient success to encourage a sense of competence, but should not place so much emphasis on competence that failure is unacceptable or that she becomes a kind of "workaholic."

Identity Versus Role Confusion: 13-18 Years.   The task occurring during puberty is a major one in which the adolescent reexamines his identity and the roles he must occupy. Erikson suggested that two "identities" are involved—a "sexual identity" and an "occupational identity." What should emerge for the adolescent from this period is a reintegrated sense of self, of what one wants to do and be, and of one's appropriate sexual role. The risk is that of confusion, arising from the profusion of roles opening to the child at this age.

Adult Stages.   As you can see in Table 9.4, Erikson proposed three further stages in adulthood: *intimacy versus isolation*, *generativity versus stagnation*, and *ego integrity versus despair*. In early adulthood, successful development requires the ability to set aside the independent identity enough to commit oneself to a truly intimate relationship. In middle adulthood, some form of "generativity" needs to be developed, typically through bearing and rearing children, but also through creative accomplishments, or leaving one's mark upon the world in some other fashion. In late adulthood, the individual needs to create a final, reflective integration, accepting who she is and what she has done with her life. Erikson is one of the few theorists who has proposed such a life-span theory, and it has been one of the great attractions of his approach. For many of us, it is comforting to think that change and growth need not stop at age 18!

Other Psychoanalytic Views: Bowlby's Model of Attachment

Before turning to a review of evidence supporting (or refuting) the psychoanalytic view, I want to reemphasize that Erikson is not the only influential modern theorist whose thinking has been strongly affected by Freud or psychoanalysis. Among those interested particularly in very early child development, John Bowlby's theory of the development of attachment (Bowlby, 1969; 1973; 1980) has had a major impact. He offers an interesting blend of psychoanalytic and biological approaches. Like Freud, Bowlby assumed that the root of human personality lies in the earliest childhood relationships. Significant failure or trauma in those relationships will permanently shape the child's development. Bowlby focused his attention on the child's first attachment to the mother because it is usually the earliest, and is arguably the most central.

To describe how that attachment comes about, Bowlby introduced several concepts from *ethological theory*, which brings evolutionary concepts to bear on the study of behavior. Human evolution, Bowlby suggested, has resulted in the child being born with a repertoire of built-in, instinctive behaviors that elicit caregiving from others—behaviors like crying, smiling, or making eye contact. Similarly, the mother (or other adult) is equipped with various instinctive behaviors toward the infant, such as responding to a cry or speaking in a higher voice. Together these instinctive patterns bring mother and infant together in an intricate chain of stimulus and response that causes the child to form a specific attachment to that one adult—a process I'll be talking about in some detail in Chapter 11.

Although Bowlby's theory is not a full-fledged stage theory of development in the manner of Freud or Erikson, it is nonetheless based on many of the underlying psychoanalytic assumptions. It has also stimulated and profoundly influenced the large body of current research on attachment.

Evidence and Applications

Empirical explorations of Freud's or Erikson's theories are relatively rare, largely because both theories are so general that specific tests are very difficult. For example, to test Freud's notion of fixation we would need much more information about how to determine if a given child is fixated at some stage. What is a sign that a child is fixated at the oral or the anal stage? Should we expect some automatic connection between how early a child is weaned and such ostensibly oral adult behavior as smoking or overeating? When researchers have searched for such direct linkages they have not found them. However, this does not rule out the possibility of a process akin to fixation, albeit perhaps at a subtler level.

Despite these difficulties, researchers have managed to devise tests of some of the basic propositions. Let me mention two bodies of work of this type, studies of the Oedipal period, and studies of the security of attachment.

The Oedipal Period. A 4-year-old boy, after his mother told him that she loved him, said, "And I love you too, and that's why I can't ever marry someone else" (Watson & Getz, 1990a, p. 29). In their studies of Oedipal behavior, Malcolm Watson and Kenneth Getz (1990a; 1990b) have indeed found that children of about 4 or 5 are likely to make comments like this. More precisely, they have found that 4-year-olds, more than any other age group, show more affectionate behavior toward the opposite-sex parent, and more aggressive or antagonistic behavior toward the same-sex parent. You can see the second half of this result in

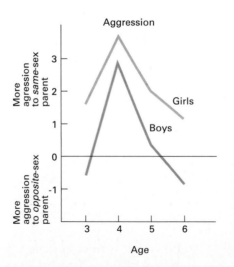

Figure 9.2
The data in this figure are based on the detailed reports of parents on the aggressive behavior of their child toward them. Scores above 0 mean that the child was more aggressive toward the same-sex parent than toward the opposite-sex parent, while scores below 0 mean the reverse. (*Source:* Watson & Getz, 1990b, from Table 3, p. 499.)

THE REAL WORLD
The Effects of Divorce: One Test of Psychoanalytic Theory

Nearly 40 percent of white and 75 percent of black children born in the United States today will experience their parents' divorce by the time they are 16 (Bumpass, 1984). What is the effect on the child of such an experience? I'll talk much more broadly about the effects of divorce in Chapter 13; for now, let me focus on just one issue, because it is a kind of test of psychoanalytic theory. If Freud is correct, the negative impact of divorce should be greatest if the divorce occurred before or during the Oedipal period (ages 3 to 5 approximately), since the Oedipus conflict, and the identification process, require the presence of both parents. Further, if the children live with their mother after a divorce, then the detrimental effect should be much greater for boys than for girls. A girl still has her mother to identify with, so at least her sex-role identification is appropriate. But the boy,

lacking a father, may never go through the identification process properly and may end up with a very confused sex-role orientation and perhaps a weaker superego.

The results of studies of children in divorced families support the second, but not the first, of these hypotheses. Virtually all children show some negative effects of divorce, but for boys the problems are likely to be much greater (Hetherington, 1989; Kline et al., 1989). They are more likely to show behavior problems, or have increased difficulty in school, after a divorce. But it is *not* the case that preschool-age children show more profound or more lasting negative effects than do children of other ages, which calls some of Freud's hypotheses about the Oedipus conflict into question.

Figure 9.2. Whether Freud's explanation of this phenomenon is the correct one remains to be seen, but these results are certainly consistent with his theory.

Security of Attachment. A second research area that has its roots in psychoanalytic theory is the current work on the security or insecurity of children's early attachments. Both Erikson and Freud argue that the quality of the child's first relationship with the central caregiver will shape her relationships with other children, and with other adults at later ages. And of course Bowlby's theory is designed specifically to examine that earliest relationship. I'll be talking a great deal more about early attachments in Chapter 11, but let me give you at least a taste of the research in this area, since it provides a good deal of support for the basic psychoanalytic hypothesis that the quality of the child's earliest relationship affects the whole course of the child's later development. This is particularly clear in the work of Alan Sroufe and his colleagues (1993). In a number of studies, they have first rated children on the security of their attachments to their mothers at about age 1. Later, at preschool, school age, or early adolescence, the same children are observed at school or at special summer camps where they must deal with new relationships or strange adults. The consistent finding from studies like this is that securely attached infants are later more capable, more friendly, more open to new relationships, more skillful with peers. Thus the relationship formed during the earliest stage of psychosocial development seems to create a prototype for later relationships, as Bowlby and Erikson proposed.

Strengths, Weaknesses, and Implications

Psychoanalytic theories like Freud's or Erikson's have several great attractions. First of all, they are *sequential* theories, and there is now increasing evidence (as I've described in earlier chapters) that sequences are built into many of the child's developing skills. Second, they focus our attention on the importance of the child's relationship with the caregivers. More importantly, both these theories

Friendships among teenagers have many causes. But we now have evidence that teens who were securely attached to their mothers as infants form new friendships more easily and quickly than do teens whose earliest attachment was less secure.

suggest that the child's needs or "tasks" change with age, so that the parents must constantly adapt to the changing child. One of the implications of this is that we should not think of "good parenting" as if it were a global quality. Some of us may be very good at meeting the needs of an infant, but quite awful at dealing with teenagers' identity struggles; others of us may have the opposite pattern. The child's eventual personality, and her overall "health," thus depend on the interaction or transaction that develops in the particular family. This is an extremely attractive element of these theories because more and more of the research within developmental psychology is moving us toward just such a transactional conception of the process.

A third strength is that psychoanalytic theory has offered several helpful concepts, such as defense mechanisms and identification, that have been so widely adopted that they have become a part of everyday language as well as theory. These strengths have led to a resurgence of influence of both Erikson's theory and the several second-order or third-order psychoanalytic approaches such as Bowlby's.

The great weakness of all the psychoanalytic approaches is fuzziness. As Jack Block (1987) puts it:

> For all the richness, insight, and seriousness of psychoanalytic theory regarding the understanding of personality functioning, it has also been imprecise, overly facile with supposed explanations, and seemingly inaccessible scientifically.(p. 2)

Identification may be an intriguing theoretical notion, but how are we to measure it? How do we detect the presence of specific defense mechanisms? Without more precise operational definitions, it is impossible to disconfirm the theory. Those areas in which the general concepts of psychoanalytic theory have been fruitfully applied to our understanding of development have nearly always been areas in which other theorists or researchers have offered more precise definitions or clearer methods for measuring some Freudian or Eriksonian construct, such as Bowlby's concept of security of attachment. Psychoanalytic theory may thus sometimes offer a provocative framework for our thinking, but it is not a precise theory of development.

▶ A Tentative Synthesis

I have given you three different views of the origins of those unique, individual patterns of behavior we call personality. Each view can be at least partially supported with research evidence, so it seems impossible to choose one of the three as the "correct" view. But can we combine them in any sensible way? There are those who argue that theories as different as these cannot ever be combined because they make such different assumptions about the child's role in the whole process (Overton & Reese, 1973). I agree in part. I do not think we can simply add up the different sources of influence, and say that personality is merely the sum of inborn temperament, reinforcement patterns, interactions with parents, and some kind of self-scheme.

But more complex combinations may still be fruitful. I have suggested one in Figure 9.3. In this model I am suggesting that the child's inborn temperament is a beginning point—an initial bias in the system. Arrow number 1 shows a *direct re-*

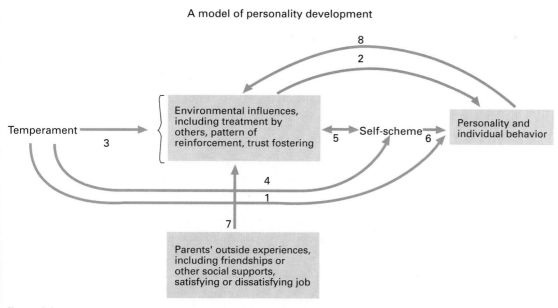

A model of personality development

Figure 9.3
Here is my own proposal for a complex, interactive model describing the formation of individual personality. The effects of inborn temperament and environmental influences do not merely add. Each affects the other, helping to create the child's unique self-scheme, which in turn affects the child's experiences. All of this occurs within the context of the family, which is itself influenced by the parents' own life experiences. What we think of as personality is a complex product of all these forces.

In recent years the concept of "vulnerable" and "invulnerable" children has become prominent in developmental research. How might vulnerability be conceptualized or explained by theorists of each of the several persuasions described in this chapter?

lationship between that inborn temperament and the eventual personality or behavior we see in a child.

I am suggesting a second direct effect in arrow number 2, between the pattern of the child's environment and his eventual behavior. Whether the parents respond reliably and contingently to the infant will affect his trust or the security of his attachment, which will show up in a range of behaviors later; whether the parents reinforce aggressive or friendly behavior will influence the child's future as well.

But most of what happens is much more complicated than that. The way the child is treated is influenced by her temperament (arrow 3), and both the basic temperament and the family environment affect the child's self-scheme—her expectations for others and herself, her beliefs about her own abilities (arrows 4 and 5). This self-scheme or self-concept, in turn, helps to shape the behavior we see, the "personality" of the child.

This system does not exist in a vacuum. In keeping with the ecological approach of Bronfenbrenner and others, arrow 7 suggests that the parents' ability to maintain a loving and supportive relationship with their child is influenced by the parents' own outside experiences—whether they like their jobs, whether they have enough emotional support to help them weather their own crises.

Several elements in this intricate system are nicely illustrated by a study by Susan Crockenberg (1981). She studied a group of 46 mothers and infants over the first year of life. Each child's irritability (an aspect of temperament) was measured when the baby was 5 to 10 days old, and the security of the child's attachment to the mother was measured when the child was 12 months old. We might expect that irritable babies would be more likely to be insecurely attached, merely because they are more difficult to care for. In fact Crockenberg found a small effect of this kind (see Table 9.5). But Crockenberg didn't stop there. She also measured the level of the mother's social support—the degree to which she had family and friends who were sufficiently helpful to assist her in dealing with the strains of a new child or other life changes she might be experiencing. The results of the study show that insecure attachment in the child was most likely when the

---

TABLE 9.5 Influence of Child's Temperament and Mother's Social Support on Child's Secure or Insecure Attachment

Child's irritability	Mother's support	Number of children with secure attachment	Number of children with insecure attachment
High	Low	2	9
High	High	12	1
Low	Low	7	2
Low	High	13	2

Source: Crockenberg, 1981, Table 5, p. 862.

mother had *both* an irritable infant *and* low levels of support. If the baby was irritable but the mother had good support, the child's attachment nearly always developed securely. Only when two difficult conditions occurred together did a poor outcome result for the child.

In a later study, Crockenberg (1987) found that a higher level of anger and noncompliant behavior was common in toddlers who had been irritable as infants *and* whose mothers were angry and punitive toward them. Furthermore, such angry and punitive behavior in the mother was more likely if the mother had experienced rejection in her own childhood, and if she experienced little support from her partner. We are dealing here with a *system* of effects.

Finally, I have included arrow 8 in the diagram to underline the *transactional* elements of the system. Once the child's unique pattern of behaviors and attitudes (personality) is formed, this affects the environment she will encounter, the experiences she will choose, the responses of the people around her, which in turn affect her behavior (Scarr & McCartney, 1983; Sroufe et al., 1993).

No doubt even this fairly complex system underestimates the intricacy of the process of personality development in the child. Most of our research does not yet encompass all the pieces of the puzzle. But the very fact that developmental psychologists are turning toward such complex models seems to me to be a very good thing. Development *is* this complex, and we will not be able to describe it or explain it until we begin to examine and try to measure all these separate forces.

▶ Summary

1. The word *personality* refers to the unique, individual, relatively enduring pattern of relating to others and responding to the world that is characteristic of each individual. *Personality* is a more inclusive term than *temperament*; the latter refers primarily to inborn style of response to the environment.

2. The origins of personality differences have been described in three distinct theoretical approaches: temperament theories (a primarily biological approach), learning theories, and psychoanalytic theories.

3. Temperament theory proposes that each child is born with innately determined patterns or styles of reacting to people and objects. These patterns shape the child's interactions with the world, and affect others' responses to the child.

4. Research supports the proposition that there are reasonably stable differences in temperament among infants and children, at least partially determined by heredity.

5. Traditional learning theorists emphasize the role of basic learning processes, such as reinforcement patterns, in shaping individual behaviors, including patterns of interaction with others.

6. Social learning theorists such as Bandura emphasize, in addition, the role of observational learning, and of the child's learned expectancies, standards, and self-efficacy in creating more enduring patterns of response—all propositions well buttressed by research.

7. Psychoanalytic theorists emphasize the importance of unconscious motives and processes as well as the stagelike emergence of personality. In this approach, the relationship of the child with significant adults, particularly in early infancy, is seen as critical.

8. Freud's psychosexual stages are strongly affected by maturation. Particularly significant is the phallic stage, beginning at about age 4, when the Oedipus conflict is met and mastered through the process of identification.

9. Erikson's psycho*social* stages are influenced both by social demands and by the child's physical and intellectual skills. Each of the major stages has a central task or "crisis," each relating to some aspect of the development of identity.

10. Bowlby's theory of attachment is a particularly influential theory with roots in psychoanalytic thought.

11. Psychoanalytic theory is difficult to test because of its imprecision, but in some areas it has been broadly confirmed, such as in studies of the impact of early attachments on later functioning.

12. Elements of all three views can be combined into an interactionist view of personality development. Temperament may serve as the base from which personality grows by affecting behavior directly, and by affecting the way others respond to the child. Both the temperament and the specific pattern of response from the people in the child's environment affect the child's self-concept or self-scheme, which then helps to create stability in the child's unique pattern of behavior.

▶ Key Terms

identification
(276)

Oedipus conflict
(275)

personality (260)

psychosexual
stages (274)

psychosocial
stages (276)

◗ Suggested Readings

Bates, J. E. (1987). Temperament in infancy. In J. D. Osofsky (Ed.), *Handbook of infant development* (2nd ed.). New York: Wiley-Interscience.

A good basic source on this complex topic.

Erikson, E. H. (1959). *Identity and the life cycle*. New York: Norton (reissued 1980).

The middle section of this book, "Growth and Crises of the Healthy Personality," is the best description I have found of the psychosocial stages of development.

Grusec, J. E. (1992). Social learning theory and developmental psychology: The legacies of Robert Sears and Albert Bandura. *Developmental Psychology, 28*, 776–786.

One of a series of papers to mark the centennial of the American Psychological Association, describing and celebrating the work of key theorists.

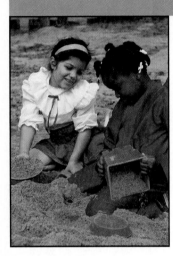

10 THE CONCEPT OF SELF IN CHILDREN

The Concept of Self: Developmental Patterns

The First Step: The Subjective Self
The Second Step: The Objective Self
Self-concept at School Age and Adolescence
Identity in Adolescence
• Cultures and Contexts: Ethnic Identity in Adolescence

Individual Differences in the Self-concept: Self-esteem

Consistency of Self-esteem over Time
Consequences of Variations in Self-esteem
Origins of Differences in Self-esteem

The Self-concept: A Summing-up

The Development of Gender and Sex-Role Concepts

Some Definitions
Developmental Patterns
• Cultures and Contexts: Sex-Role Stereotypes Around the World
Explaining Sex-Role Development
• The Real World: Sex Stereotyping on TV
Individual Differences in Sex-Typing and Sex-Role Stereotypes

Summary

Key Terms

Suggested Readings

Try an experiment for me. Before you read any further, write down 20 answers to the question "Who am I?" Now look at your list and think about what you wrote. My own list includes items like these:

I am a logical, analytic person.

I am lots taller than average and sometimes clumsy.

I am a stubborn, determined person who finishes what she starts.

I am a person with many roles: wife, mother, stepmother, daughter, sister, friend, board member.

I am not a traditionally feminine person.

My list, as yours probably does, includes something about what I look like, something about the roles I occupy, and something about my qualities, attitudes, and beliefs about myself. These are all aspects of my **self-concept;** in Piagetian-style language, my *self-scheme*. For each of us, the self-concept serves as a sort of filter for experience, shaping our choices and affecting our responses to others. Our ideas about our own sex role is a powerful part of that self-concept. Because these beliefs and attitudes about ourselves are so central to our personality and hence to our behavior, it is important for us to try to understand how they develop. So in this chapter I want to explore the origins of both the common developmental pathways and the variations in such concepts from one child to the next.

▶ The Concept of Self: Developmental Patterns

Our thinking about the child's emerging sense of self has been strongly influenced by both Freud and Piaget, each of whom assumed that the baby begins life with *no* sense of separateness. Freud emphasized what he called the *symbiotic* relationship between the mother and young infant in which the two are joined together as if they were one. He believed that the infant does not understand himself to be separate from the mother. Piaget emphasized that the infant's understanding of the basic concept of object permanence was a necessary precursor for the child's attaining *self*-permanence—a sense of himself as a stable, continuing entity. Both of these aspects of early self-development reappear in current descriptions of the emergence of the sense of self. Michael Lewis (1990; 1991; Lewis & Brooks-Gunn, 1979), for example, divides the process into two main steps or tasks.

The First Step: The Subjective Self

Lewis argues that the child's first task is to figure out that he is separate from others and that this separate self endures over time and space. He calls this aspect of the self-concept the **subjective self,** or sometimes the *existential self*, because the key awareness seems to be that "I exist." Agreeing with Freud, Lewis places the beginnings of this understanding in the first two or three months of life. At that time, the baby grasps the basic distinction between self and everything else. In Lewis's view, the roots of this understanding lie in the myriad everyday interactions the baby has with the objects and people in his world. Over the early months, the baby learns that he has effects on things. When he touches the mobile, it moves; when he cries, someone responds; when he smiles, his mother smiles back. By this process the baby separates out self from everything else and a sense of *I* begins.

But it is not until the baby also grasps the concept of object permanence, at about 9 to 12 months, that we can say a subjective self has really emerged. Just as she is figuring out that Mom or Dad continues to exist when out of sight, she is figuring out—at least in some preliminary way—that *she* exists separately and has some permanence.

The Second Step: The Objective Self

This is not the end of the story. It is not enough merely to understand yourself as an agent in the world or a person who has experiences. For a full sense of self, the toddler must also understand herself to be an *object* in the world. Just as a ball has properties—roundness, the ability to roll, a certain feel in the hand—so the "self" also has qualities or properties, such as gender, size, a name, or qualities like shyness or boldness, coordination or clumsiness. It is this *self-awareness* that is the hallmark of the second phase of identity development. Lewis refers to this as the **objective self,** or sometimes the *categorical self*, because once the child achieves self-awareness the process of defining the self involves placing oneself in a whole series of categories.

Studying Self-awareness. It has not been easy to determine just when a child has developed such self-awareness. The most commonly used procedure involves a mirror. First the baby is placed in front of a mirror, just to see how she behaves. Most infants of about 9 to 12 months will look at their own images, make faces, or try to interact with the baby-in-the-mirror in some way. After allowing this free exploration for a time, the experimenter, while pretending to wipe the baby's face with a cloth, puts a spot of rouge on the baby's nose, and then again lets the baby look in the mirror. The crucial test of self-recognition, and thus of awareness of the self, is whether the baby reaches for the spot on her *own* nose, rather than the nose on the face in the mirror.

The results from one of Lewis's studies using this procedure are in Figure 10.1. As you can see, none of the 9-to-12-month-old children in this study touched their noses, but by 21 months, three-quarters of the children showed that level of self-recognition. The figure also shows the rate at which children refer to themselves by name when they are shown a picture of themselves, which is another commonly used measure of self-awareness. You can see that this development occurs at almost exactly the same time as self-recognition in a mirror. Both are present by about the middle of the second year of life, a finding confirmed by other investigators (Bullock & Lütkenhaus, 1990).

We can see signs of this new self-awareness in a whole range of other behavior. It is only at this point in toddlerhood, for example, that we see such self-conscious emotions as embarrassment, pride, or shame, all of which involve some aspect of self-evaluation (Lewis, Allesandri, & Sullivan, 1992). It is also at this point that toddlers begin to insist on doing things for themselves and show a newly proprietary attitude toward toys ("Mine!") or other treasured objects. Looked at this way, much of the legendary "terrible twos" can be understood as an outgrowth of self-awareness.

Having achieved this initial self-awareness, the preschool child begins to define "who I am" by learning about her own qualities and her social roles. The 2-year-old not only knows her own name, she also can probably tell you if she is a

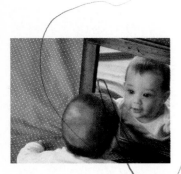

At 4 months, Lucy's pleasure at looking at herself in a mirror comes from the fact that this is an interesting moving object to inspect, not from any understanding that this is *herself* in the mirror.

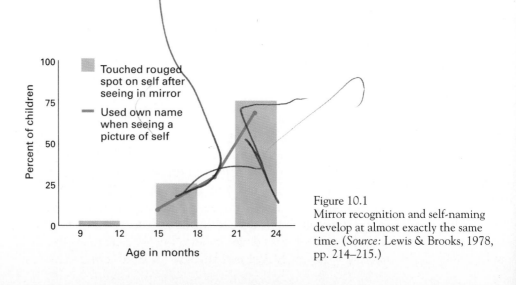

Figure 10.1
Mirror recognition and self-naming develop at almost exactly the same time. (*Source:* Lewis & Brooks, 1978, pp. 214–215.)

girl or a boy, and whether she is big or little. By about age 5 to 7, a child can give you quite a full description of himself on a whole range of dimensions.

At about this same age, toddlers also seem to become aware of themselves as players in the social game. By age 2, the toddler has already learned a variety of social "scripts"—routines of play or interaction with others in her world. Over the preschool years, the toddler learns more about her own roles in these scripts. So she begins to think of herself as a "helper" in some situations, or as "the boss" when she is telling some other child what to do. You have already seen one aspect of this in the emergence of roles in children's sociodramatic play—a pattern I talked about in Chapter 7. As part of the same process, the preschool child also gradually understands her place in the network of family roles. She has sisters, brothers, father, mother, and so on.

These are major advances in the child's understanding. Yet the preschool child's self-concept is still concrete in a number of respects. For one thing, each facet of the self-concept seems to be quite separate, rather like a list: "I'm good at running"; "I don't like to play with dolls"; "I'm a big girl." These separate aspects of the "self-scheme" or internal working model of the self have not yet coalesced into a *global* sense of self-worth (Harter, 1987; 1990; Harter & Pike, 1984). Children this age do not say things like "I am a terrible person," or "I really like myself." Their perceptions of themselves are more tied to specific settings, specific tasks.

The self-perceptions of a preschool-age child are also tied to visible characteristics, such as what he looks like, what or whom he plays with, where he lives, or what he is good or bad at doing, rather than more enduring, inner qualities, such as personality traits or basic abilities. This pattern obviously parallels what we see in cognitive development at the same ages since it is in these same years that children's attention tends to be captured by the external appearance of objects rather than by their enduring properties.

Self-concept at School Age and Adolescence

Over the elementary-school years this concrete self-concept gradually shifts toward a more abstract, more comparative, more generalized self-definition. A 6-year-old might describe herself as "smart" or "dumb"; a 10-year-old is more likely to give a comparative description, such as "smarter than most other kids," or "not as good at baseball as my friends" (Ruble, 1987). At the same time, the child's self-concept also becomes gradually less focused on external characteristics and more on stable, internal qualities. The school-age child also begins to see her own (and other people's) characteristics as relatively stable, and for the first time she develops a global sense of her own self-worth.

A number of these themes are illustrated nicely in an older study by Montemayor and Eisen of self-concepts in 9-to-18-year-olds that used the same "Who am I?" question I asked you to answer at the beginning of this chapter (Montemayor & Eisen, 1977). They found that the younger children in this study were still using mostly surface qualities to describe themselves, such as the description by this 9-year-old:

> My name is Bruce C. I have brown eyes. I have brown hair. I have brown eyebrows. I am nine years old. I LOVE! Sports. I have seven people in my family. I have great! eye site. I have lots! of friends. I live on 1923 Pinecrest Dr. I am going on 10 in September. I'm a

Can you think of some social scripts that a 2- or 3-year-old is likely to learn? What about bedtime rituals? What others?

boy. I have a uncle that is almost 7 feet tall. My school is Pinecrest. My teacher is Mrs. V. I play Hockey! I'm almost the smartest boy in the class. I LOVE! food. I love fresh air. I LOVE school. (Montemayor & Eisen, 1977, pp. 317–318)

In contrast, look at the self-description of this 11-year-old girl in the sixth grade:

My name is A. I'm a human being. I'm a girl. I'm a truthful person. I'm not very pretty. I do so-so in my studies. I'm a very good cellist. I'm a very good pianist. I'm a little bit tall for my age. I like several boys. I like several girls. I'm old-fashioned. I play tennis. I am a very good swimmer. I try to be helpful. I'm always ready to be friends with anybody. Mostly I'm good, but I lose my temper. I'm not well-liked by some girls and boys. I don't know if I'm liked by boys or not. (Montemayor & Eisen, 1977, pp. 317–318)

This girl, like the other youngsters of this age in the Montemayor and Eisen study, not only describes her external qualities, she also emphasizes her beliefs, the quality of her relationships, and general personality traits. Thus as the child moves through the concrete operations period, her self-definition becomes more complex, less tied to external features, more focused on feelings, on ideas.

This trend toward greater abstraction in the self-definition continues during adolescence. Compare the answers of this 17-year-old to the "Who am I?" question with the ones you just read:

I am a human being. I am a girl, I am an individual. I don't know who I am. I am a Pisces. I am a moody person. I am an indecisive person. I am an ambitious person. I am a very curious person. I am not an individual. I am a loner. I am an American (God help me). I am a Democrat. I am a liberal person. I am a radical. I am a conservative. I am a pseudoliberal. I am an atheist. I am not a classifiable person (I.e. I don't want to be). (Montemayor & Eisen, 1977, p. 318)

Obviously this girl's self-concept is even less tied to her physical characteristics or even her abilities than are those of the 11-year-old. She is describing abstract traits or ideology.

You can see the shift I'm describing graphically in Figure 10.2, which is based on the answers of all 262 subjects in the Montemayor and Eisen study. Each of the subjects' answers to the "Who am I?" question was placed in one or more specific categories, such as references to physical properties ("I am tall," "I have blue eyes") or references to ideology ("I am a Democrat," "I believe in God," etc.). As you can see, appearance was still a highly salient dimension in the preteen and early teen years, but became less dominant in late adolescence, at a time when ideology and belief became more salient.

If you asked them to define themselves, these two 16-year-olds would surely give a much more abstract and comparative answer than what you would hear from a 6-year-old.

Identity in Adolescence

This increasing preoccupation with ideology may also be a reflection of the central task of adolescence, as Erikson described it, of *identity versus role confusion*. In Erikson's view, the child's early sense of identity comes partly unglued at puberty with the onset of both rapid body growth and the sexual changes of puberty. He referred to this period as one in which the adolescent mind is in a kind of *moratorium* between childhood and adulthood. The old identity will no longer suffice; a new identity must be forged, one that must serve to place the young person among the myriad roles of adult life— occupational roles, sexual roles, religious roles. Confusion about all these role choices is inevitable. Erikson (1980) put it this way:

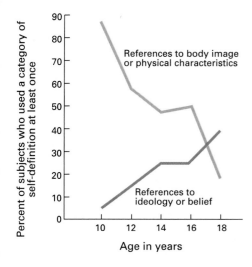

Figure 10.2
As they get older, children and adolescents define themselves less and less by what they look like and more and more by what they believe or feel. (*Source:* Montemayor & Eisen, 1977, from Table 1, p. 316.)

In general it is primarily the inability to settle on an occupational identity which disturbs young people. To keep themselves together they temporarily overidentify, to the point of apparent complete loss of identity, with the heroes of cliques and crowds. . . . They become remarkably clannish, intolerant, and cruel in their exclusion of others who are "different," in skin color or cultural background . . . and often in entirely petty aspects of dress and gesture arbitrarily selected as the signs of an in-grouper or out-grouper. It is important to understand . . . such intolerance as the necessary defense against a sense of identity confusion, which is unavoidable at [this] time of life." (pp. 97–98)

The teenage clique or group thus forms a base of security from which the young person can move toward a unique solution of the identity process. Ultimately, each teenager must achieve an integrated view of himself including his own pattern of beliefs, occupational goals, and relationships.

Nearly all the current work on the formation of adolescent identity has been based on James Marcia's descriptions of *identity statuses* (Marcia, 1966; 1980), which are rooted in Erikson's general conceptions of the adolescent identity process. Following one of Erikson's ideas, Marcia argues that there are two key parts to any adolescent identity formation: a *crisis* and a *commitment*. By a "crisis" Marcia means a period of decision making when old values and old choices are reexamined. This may occur as a sort of upheaval—the classic notion of a crisis—or it may occur gradually. The outcome of the reevaluation is a commitment to some specific role, some particular ideology.

If you put these two elements together, as in Figure 10.3, you can see that four different "identity statuses" are possible.

- **Identity achievement:** The person has been through a crisis and reached a commitment.
- **Moratorium:** A crisis is in progress, but no commitment has yet been made.
- **Foreclosure:** A commitment has been made without the person's having gone through a crisis. No reassessment of old positions has been made. Instead the young person has simply accepted a parentally or culturally defined commitment.
- **Identity diffusion:** The young person is not in the midst of a crisis (although there may have been one in the past) and no commitment has been made. Dif-

Degree of crisis

	High	Low
High	Identity achievement status (crisis is past	Foreclosure status
Low	Moratorium status (in midst of crisis)	Identity diffusion status

Degree of commitment to
a particular role or values

Figure 10.3
The four identity statuses proposed by Marcia, based on Erikson's theory. For a fully achieved identity, the young person must both have examined his or her values or goals and have reached a firm commitment. (*Source:* Marcia, 1980.)

The implication in Marcia's formulation is that the foreclosure status is less developmentally mature—that one must go through a crisis in order to achieve a mature identity. Does this make sense to you?

fusion may represent either an early stage in the process (before a crisis), or a failure to reach a commitment after a crisis.

Whether every young person goes through some kind of identity crisis I cannot tell you, since there have been no longitudinal studies covering all the relevant years. Cross-sectional studies of the years of adolescence and early adulthood, however, suggest that the whole process of identity formation may occur later than Erikson thought, when it occurs at all. In one combined analysis of eight separate cross-sectional studies, Alan Waterman (1985) found that the identity achievement status occurred most often in college, not during the high school years. Among these subjects, the moratorium status was relatively uncommon except in the early years of college. So if most young people are going through an identity crisis, that crisis is fairly late and not lasting terribly long. What's more, about a third of the young people at every age were in the foreclosure status, which may indicate that many young people simply do not go through a crisis at all, but follow well-defined grooves.

It is well to remember that all of the subjects in the studies Waterman analyzed were in college or likely to attend college. It may be that young people who go to work immediately after high school will face the need to form at least an occupational identity earlier than is true for those who go to college. The college years involve a kind of postponement of full adult status, a period in which students are actively encouraged to question, doubt, and try out alternatives. Those who go directly into the working world do not have that luxury and thus must work out some kind of personal identity sooner, a possibility supported by at least some research (Munro & Adams, 1977).

It is also worth pointing out that the whole conception of an adolescent identity crisis has been strongly influenced by current cultural assumptions in Western societies. In such cultures today, full adult status is postponed for almost a decade after puberty. In addition, young people do not normally or necessarily adopt the same roles or occupations as their parents. Indeed, they are encouraged

CULTURES AND CONTEXTS
Ethnic Identity in Adolescence

For minority teenagers, especially those of color in a predominantly white culture, there is another aspect of creating an identity in adolescence: they must also develop an ethnic or racial identity, including self-identification as a member of some specific group and commitment to that group and its values and attitudes, as well as positive (or negative) attitudes about the group.

Jean Phinney (1990; Phinney & Rosenthal, 1992) has proposed that in adolescence, the development of a complete ethnic identity moves through three rough stages. The first stage is an "unexamined ethnic identity," equivalent to what Marcia calls a foreclosed status. For some subgroups in U.S. society, such as African-Americans and Native Americans, this unexamined identity typically includes the negative images and stereotypes common in the wider culture. Indeed, it may be especially at adolescence, with the advent of the cognitive ability to reflect and interpret, that the young person becomes keenly aware of the way in which his own group is perceived by the majority. As Spencer and Dornbusch (1990) put it, "The young African-American may learn as a child that black is beautiful but conclude as an adolescent that white is powerful" (p. 131). The same is doubtless true of other minority groups in the U.S.

Many youngsters in these and other minority groups initially prefer the dominant white culture, or wish they had been born into the majority. An African-American journalist, Sylvester Monroe, who grew up in an urban housing project, clearly describes this initial negative feeling:

> If you were black, you didn't quite measure up. . . . For a black kid there was a certain amount of self-doubt. It came at you indirectly. You didn't see any black people on television, you didn't see any black people doing certain things. . . . You don't think it out but you say, "Well, it must mean that white people are better than we are. Smarter, brighter—whatever." (Spencer & Dornbusch, 1990, pp. 131–132)

Not all minority teenagers arrive at such negative views of their own group. Individual youngsters may have very positive ethnic images if that is the content of the identity conveyed by parents or others around the child. Phinney's point is rather that this initial ethnic identity is not arrived at independently but comes from outside sources.

The second stage is the "ethnic identity search," parallel to the crisis in Marcia's analysis of ego identity. This search is typically triggered by some experience that makes ethnicity salient—perhaps an example of blatant prejudice, or merely the widening experience of high school. At this point the young person begins to compare her own ethnic group with others, to try to arrive at her *own* judgments.

This exploration stage is eventually followed by a resolution of the conflicts and contradictions—analogous to Marcia's status of identity achievement. This is often a difficult process. Some African-American adolescents, for example, who wish to try to compete in and succeed in the dominant culture, may experience ostracism from their black friends, who accuse them of "acting white," and betraying their blackness. Latinos often report similar experiences. Some resolve this by keeping their own ethnic group at arm's length; others deal with it by creating essentially two identities, as expressed by one young Chicano interviewed by Phinney:

> Being invited to someone's house, I have to change my ways of how I act at home, because of culture differences. I would have to follow what they do. . . . I am used to it now, switching off between the two. It is not difficult. (Phinney & Rosenthal, 1992, p. 160)

Some resolve the dilemma by wholeheartedly choosing their own ethnic group's patterns and values, even though that may limit their access to the larger culture.

In both cross-sectional and longitudinal studies, Phinney has found that African-American teens and young adults do indeed move through these steps or stages toward a clear ethnic identity. Furthermore, there is evidence that among black, Asian-American, and Mexican-American teens and college students, those who have reached the second or third stage in this process—those who are searching for or who have reached a clear identity—have higher self-esteem and better psychological adjustment than do those who are still in the "unexamined" stage (Phinney, 1990). In contrast, among Caucasian students, ethnic identity has essentially no relationship to self-esteem or adjustment.

This stagelike model may be a decent beginning description of the process of ethnic identity formation. But let us not lose sight of the fact that the details and the content of the ethnic identity will differ markedly from one subgroup to another. Those groups that encounter more overt prejudice will have a different road to follow than will those who may be more easily assimilated; those whose own ethnic culture espouses values that are close to those of the dominant culture will have less difficulty resolving the contradictions than will those whose family culture is at greater variance with the majority. Whatever the specifics, young people of color and those from clearly defined ethnic groups have an important additional identity task in their adolescent years.

to choose for themselves. In such a cultural system, adolescents are faced with what may be a bewildering array of options, a pattern that might well foster the sort of identity crisis Erikson described.

In the initiation rite of the Kota tribe of the Congo, boys' faces are painted blue to make them appear ghostlike, to symbolize the phantom of their now-departed childhood.

Initiation Rituals.   In many less-industrialized countries, the problem of the change of identity and status at adolescence is handled with initiation rituals, most often at roughly the time of puberty. There is an enormous amount of variability in the content of such rituals, but certain practices are especially common (Cohen, 1964).

One such practice, more common for boys than for girls, is the separation of the child from the family, referred to by anthropologists as *extrusion*. The child may spend the day with his family, but sleep elsewhere, or may live in a separate dwelling with other boys, or with relatives. In traditional Hopi and Navaho cultures, for example, boys typically sleep apart from the family beginning at age 8 or 10. This practice obviously symbolizes the separation of the child from the birth family, marking a coming-of-age. But it also emphasizes that the child "belongs" not just to the family but to the larger group of kin or societal/tribal members.

A second pattern is a ritualized separation of boys and girls around the time of puberty, not only to strengthen incest taboos, but to signify the beginning of the time in life when males and females have quite different life patterns.

The initiation rituals themselves are typically fairly brief, often involving some kind of testing or trial, sometimes with physical mutilation of one sort or another (such as scarring or circumcision), to mark the individual as a member of that tribe or community. During the initiation, the adolescents are also indoctrinated by the elders into customary practices of their culture. They may learn special religious rituals or practices, such as the learning of Hebrew as preparation for the *bar mitzvah* or *bas mitzvah* in the Jewish tradition. They may learn the history and songs of their tribe or people. Often, there is drama and pageantry as part of the entire process. Among the Hopi, for example, both boys and girls go through specific rituals in which they are taught the religious ceremonies of the Katchina cult, and are whipped. After these ceremonies, they may participate fully in the adult religious practices.

In Western industrialized cultures, there are a few pale remnants of such initiation practices remaining, such as boot camp for those who enter the military, or high school graduation ceremonies. But by and large, the shift to adult status is far more protracted and fuzzy, both characteristics that may well contribute to a greater sense of "identity crisis" among teens than is true in other cultures.

▶ Individual Differences in the Self-concept: Self-esteem

So far, I have talked about the self-concept as if there were no values attached to the categories by which we define ourselves. But that's clearly not the case. There is also an evaluative aspect to the self-concept, an aspect you probably noticed in the answers to the "Who am I" question that I have already quoted. The 9-year-old clearly makes a lot of positive statements about himself, while the two older subjects offer more mixed evaluations.

By early elementary-school age, these evaluative judgments coalesce into a *global* self-evaluation. Children at this age readily answer questions about how well they like themselves as people, or how happy they are, or how well they like the way they are leading their lives. This global evaluation of one's own worth is usually referred to as **self-esteem.**

Susan Harter's extremely interesting research on self-esteem suggests that each child's level of self-esteem is a product of two internal assessments or judgments (Harter, 1987; 1990). First, each child experiences some degree of discrepancy between what he would like to be (or thinks he *ought* to be) and what he thinks he is. When that discrepancy is low, the child's self-esteem is generally high. When the discrepancy is high—when the child sees himself as failing to live up to his own goals or values—self-esteem will be much lower.

The standards are not the same for every child. Some value academic skills highly, others value sports skills, or having good friends. The key to self-esteem, Harter proposes, is the amount of discrepancy between what the child desires and what the child thinks he has achieved. Thus a child who values sports prowess but who isn't big enough or coordinated enough to be good at sports will have lower self-esteem than will an equally small or uncoordinated child who does not value sports skill so highly. Similarly, being good at something, like singing, playing chess, or being able to talk to your mother, won't raise a child's self-esteem unless the child values that particular skill.

The second major influence on a child's self-esteem, according to Harter, is the overall sense of support the child feels from the important people around her, particularly parents and peers. Children who feel that other people generally like them the way they are have higher self-esteem scores than do children who report less overall support.

Both these factors are clear in the results of Harter's own research. She asked third, fourth, fifth, and sixth graders how important it was to them to do well in each of five domains, and how well they thought they actually did in each. The total discrepancy between these sets of judgments comprised the discrepancy score. Remember that a high discrepancy score indicates that the child reported that he was *not* doing well in areas that mattered to him. The social support score was based on children's replies to a set of questions about whether they thought others (parents and peers) liked them as they were, treated them as a person, or felt that they were important. Figure 10.4 shows the results for the third and fourth graders; the findings for the fifth and sixth graders are virtually identical, and both sets of results strongly support Harter's hypothesis. Note that a low discrepancy score alone does not protect the child completely from low self-esteem if she lacks sufficient social support. And a loving and accepting family and peer group does not guarantee high self-esteem if the youngster does not feel she is living up to her own standards.

A particularly deadly combination occurs when the child perceives that the parents' support is *contingent* on good performance in some area—getting good grades, making the first-string football team, being popular with other kids. If the child does not measure up to the standard, he experiences both an increased discrepancy between ideal and achievement, and a loss of support from the parents.

Consistency of Self-esteem over Time

How stable are these self-judgments? Is a third grader with low self-esteem doomed to feel less than worthy for the rest of his life? A number of longitudinal studies of elementary-school-age children and teenagers show that global self-esteem is quite stable in the short term, but somewhat less so over periods of several years. The correlation between two self-esteem scores obtained a few months

Whether these girls' self-esteem will be affected by their soccer performance will depend more on whether they value sports prowess than on how successful or unsuccessful they actually are.

Think about the following somewhat paradoxical proposition: if Harter's model is correct, then our self-esteem is most vulnerable in the area in which we may appear (and feel) the most competent. Does this fit with your experience?

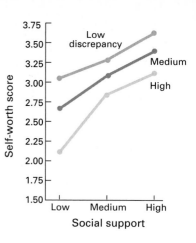

Figure 10.4
For these children in Harter's studies, self-esteem was about equally influenced by the amount of support the child saw herself as receiving from parents and peers, and by the degree of discrepancy between the value the child places on various domains and the skill she sees herself having in each of those domains. (*Source:* Harter, 1987, Figure 9.2, p. 227.)

apart is generally about .60. Over several years, this correlation drops to something more like .40 (Alsaker & Olweus, 1992), a level of consistency that has even been found over periods as long as a decade, from early adolescence into early adulthood (Block & Robins, 1993). So it is true that a child with high self-esteem at age 8 or 9 is more likely to have high self-esteem at age 10 or 11. But it is also true that there is a good deal of variation around that stability. Self-esteem seems to be particularly unstable in the years of early adolescence, around ages 11 and 12. This makes sense in Harter's terms, since these are years when the standards children may set for themselves are likely to change, as they move from elementary school to junior high school and from prepubescence to pubescence (Harter, 1990). In later adolescence, self-esteem appears to become more stable, although still not totally fixed.

Consequences of Variations in Self-esteem
When we look at the consequences of variations in self-esteem, the clearest research finding is that self-esteem is *strongly* negatively correlated with depression in both middle-childhood and adolescence. The lower the self-esteem score, the more depressed the child describes himself to be. The correlations in several of Harter's studies range from −.67 to −.80 —numbers that are quite astonishingly high for research of this type (Harter, 1987; Renouf & Harter, 1990). Bear in mind, though, that this is still correlational evidence. These findings don't prove that there is a causal connection between low self-esteem and depression. They only tell us that the two tend to go together. More persuasive is Harter's finding from her longitudinal studies that when the self-esteem score rises or falls, the depression score drops or rises accordingly.

Origins of Differences in Self-esteem
Where do differences in self-esteem come from? There are at least three sources. First, of course, a child's own direct experience with success or failure in various arenas plays an obvious role. If I take ballet lessons, it will not take me long to figure out whether I am any good at it or not. Comparative information is also involved here, of course. If I see that all the other kids can do things that I cannot

do so easily, or that I find something easy that others struggle with, that adds substantially to my self-knowledge.

Second, the value a child attaches to some skill or quality is obviously affected fairly directly by peers' and parents' attitudes and values. For example, peer (and general cultural) standards for appearance establish benchmarks for all children and teens (which is why the present Western cultural emphasis on extreme thinness in girls has led to so many eating disorders). Similarly, the degree of emphasis parents place on the child's performing well in school is an important element in the child's internal expectations in that area.

Finally, labels and judgments from others play a highly significant role. To a very considerable extent, we come to think of ourselves as others think of us (Cole, 1991). Children who are repeatedly told that they are "pretty" or "smart" or "a good athlete" are likely to have higher self-esteem than are children who are told that they are "dumb" or "clumsy" or a "late bloomer." A child who brings home a report card with Cs and Bs on it, and hears the parent say, "That's fine, honey. We don't expect you to get all As," draws conclusions both about the parents' expectations, and about their judgments of his abilities. From all these sources, the child fashions his ideas (his internal model) about what he should be and what he is.

One of the side effects of this classic American father-son activity is likely to be that the son comes to believe that skill in sports is highly valued by his dad.

▶ The Self-concept: A Summing-up

There are obviously many questions still to be answered. But I want to emphasize once again that a child's self-concept, including her level of self-esteem, appears to be a highly significant mediating concept. Once such a "theory" of the self is well established, once a global judgment of one's self-worth is established, there are reverberations throughout the child's behavior. Among other things, she systematically chooses experiences and environments that are consistent with her beliefs about herself. The child who believes she can't play baseball behaves differently from the child who believes that she can. She is likely to denigrate the importance of sports, or to avoid baseballs, bats, playing fields, and other children who play baseball. If forced to play, she may make self-deprecating remarks like "You know I can't play," or she may play self-defeating games, such as refusing to watch the ball when she swings at it or not running after the ball in right field because she knows she couldn't catch it even if she did get there on time. (If you think all this sounds autobiographical, you're right!)

A child who believes that she can't do long division will behave quite differently in the classroom from the child whose self-concept includes the idea "I am good at math" (or, even more potently, "I am better at math than other kids"). If she believes she is less competent, she may not try to work long division problems on the theory that if you don't try, you can't fail. Or she may try much harder, paying the price in anxiety about failure. At a later age, such a child is much less likely to take further math courses, thus reducing her occupational options.

These beliefs are pervasive, many develop early, and although they are somewhat responsive to changing circumstances, they also act as self-fulfilling prophecies. We need to know a good deal more about the origins of the child's self-definitions if we are to understand how to modify the inaccurate elements.

Can you think of examples of how your own self-concept affects your choices and your behavior?

❱ The Development of Gender and Sex-Role Concepts

A central aspect of the child's self-concept that I have not yet discussed is the gender concept and the accompanying concept of sex roles. How do children come to understand that they are a boy or a girl, and when and how do they learn to identify behaviors and attitudes considered normal and appropriate for their gender in their particular culture? I have saved this set of questions for a separate discussion partly because this has been an area of hot debate and extensive research in the past several decades (so there is a lot to say), and partly because this set of questions has such central personal relevance for so many of us. Women's and men's roles are changing rapidly in most industrialized societies. But our stereotypes about men and women, and our own inner sense of what it means to be "male" or "female" have not always kept pace. If we are to understand ourselves (and rear our children with less confusion, perhaps), we need to know more about the ways in which children learn about gender, and about sex roles.

Some Definitions

Before I can delve into these questions, though, I need to define some terms for you. These words and phrases often get used fuzzily or interchangeably, which only confuses things. I will use these terms and phrases this way:

The **gender concept** is the idea that one is a boy or a girl, and that gender is constant over time.

Sex roles are the set of behaviors, attitudes, rights, duties, and obligations that are part of the "role" of being a boy or a girl, a male or a female in any given culture. All roles have such collections of duties, rights, and expected behaviors. Teachers are supposed to behave in certain ways, as are employees, or mothers, or baseball managers. These are all roles. Sex roles are somewhat broader than most other roles, but they are nonetheless roles. A **sex-role concept** is the set of ideas any one of us has about the specific content of a sex role—what males or females do and are supposed to do.

A **sex-role stereotype** is a narrower set of qualities associated with a given sex role—that set of qualities that defines maleness or femaleness in any given culture. If I asked you to complete the sentence "Men are ————" or "Women are ————," your answer would reflect the cultural sex-role stereotype—a kind of too-broad (and therefore inaccurate) generalization about all men or women. But if I asked you to complete the sentence "Men are supposed to be ————," I would be asking about the culturally defined sex role.

A child's or adult's behavior is said to be **sex-typed** when it matches the stereotype or sex-role expectations for his or her own gender. A girl may know quite well that she is a girl, and be able to describe the sex roles accurately, but still behave in a tomboyish way. We would say that her **sex-role behavior** is less sex-typed than is the behavior of a girl who adopts more traditional play patterns.

If we are going to understand the development of the child's concept of gender, we have to understand all of these elements. How does the child come to know what gender she is? How and when does she develop ideas about sex roles or sex-role stereotyping? And how well and how early do children match their behavior to the sex roles or the stereotypes?

See if you can describe this photo three ways: in terms of sex roles, in terms of sex-role stereotypes, and in terms of sex-typing.

Developmental Patterns

The Development of the Gender Concept.   How soon does a child figure out that she is a girl or he is a boy? It depends on what we mean by "figure out." There seem to be three steps. First, there is **gender identity,** which is simply a child's ability to label his own sex correctly and to identify other people as men or women, boys or girls. By 9 to 12 months, babies already treat male and female faces as if they were different categories (Fagot & Leinbach, 1993). Within the next year, they begin to learn the verbal labels that go with these different categories. By age 2, if you show them a set of pictures of a same-sex child and several opposite-sex children and say "which one is you?" most children can correctly pick out the same-sex picture (Thompson, 1975). By 2½ or 3, most children can correctly label and identify the sex of others as well (point out "which one is a girl" or "which one is a boy" in a set of pictures). Hair length and clothing seem to be especially important cues that children are using for these early discriminations.

Accurate labeling, though, does not signify complete understanding. As is true with all the concepts I talked about in Chapter 7, which show increasing subtlety and complexity over the preschool and early school years, the gender concept undergoes further refinements. The second step is **gender stability,** the understanding that you stay the same gender throughout life. Researchers have measured this by asking children such questions as "When you were a little baby, were you a little girl or a little boy?" or "When you grow up will you be a mommy or a daddy?" Most children understand the stability aspect of gender by about age 4 (Slaby & Frey, 1975).

Finally, there is the development of true **gender constancy,** which is the recognition that someone stays the same gender even though he may appear to change by wearing different clothes or having different hair length. For example, girls don't change into boys by cutting their hair very short or by wearing boys' clothes. It may seem odd that a child who understands that he will stay the same gender throughout life (gender stability) can nonetheless be confused about the effect of changes in dress or appearance on gender. But numerous studies show this sequence, including studies of children growing up in other cultures, such as Kenya, Nepal, Belize, and Samoa (Munroe, Shimmin, & Munroe, 1984).

The underlying logic of this sequence may be a bit clearer if I draw a parallel between gender constancy and the concept of conservation I described in Chapter 7. Conservation of mass or number or weight involves recognition that an object remains the same in some fundamental way even though it changes externally in some fashion. Gender constancy is thus a kind of "conservation of gender," and is not typically understood until about 5 or 6, when the other conservations are first grasped.

The Development of Sex-Role Concepts and Stereotypes.   Obviously, figuring out your gender and understanding that it stays constant is only part of the story. Learning what goes with, or ought to go with, being a boy or a girl is also a vital part of the child's task.

Researchers have studied this in two ways—by asking children what boys and girls (or men and women) like to do and what they are like (which is an inquiry about stereotypes), and by asking children if it is *okay* for boys to play with dolls or girls to climb trees or to do equivalent cross-sex things (an inquiry about roles).

In our society, adults have clear sex-role stereotypes. We think of men as being competent, skillful, assertive, aggressive, and able to get things done. Adults see women as warm and expressive, tactful, quiet, gentle, aware of others' feelings, and lacking in competence, independence, and logic (Broverman et al., 1972; Ruble, 1983; Williams & Best, 1990).

Studies of children show that such stereotyping occurs early. The 3-year-old daughter of a friend announced one day that mommies use the stove and daddies use the grill. Even 2-year-olds already associate certain tasks and possessions with men and women, such as vacuum cleaner and food with women and cars and tools with men. By age 3 or 4, children can assign occupations, toys, and activities to the stereotypic gender. By age 5, children begin to associate certain personality traits with males or females, and such knowledge is well developed by age 8 or 9 (Martin, 1993; Serbin, Powlishta, & Gulko, 1993). The most clearly stereotyped traits are weakness, gentleness, appreciativeness, and softheartedness for women, and aggression, strength, cruelty, and coarseness for males.

Studies of children's ideas about what men and women (or boys and girls) *ought* to be like add an interesting element. A study by William Damon (1977) illustrates the point particularly nicely. He told a story to children aged 4 through 9 about a little boy named George who likes to play with dolls. George's parents tell him that only little girls play with dolls; little boys shouldn't. They buy him some other toys, but still George prefers dolls. The children were then asked a batch of questions about this:

> *Why do people tell George not to play with dolls?*
> *Are they right?*
> *Is there a rule that boys shouldn't play with dolls?*
> *What should George do?*
> *Does George have a right to play with dolls? (p. 242)*

Does this little boy, like the mythical George in Damon's studies, have a right to play with dolls? Four-year-olds and 9-year-olds are likely to think that he does, but many 6-year-olds think it is simply wrong for boys to do girl things, or for girls to do boy things.

Four-year-olds in this study thought it was okay for George to play with dolls. There was no rule against it and he should do it if he wanted to. Six-year-olds, in contrast, thought it was *wrong* for George to play with dolls. By about age 9, children had differentiated between what boys and girls usually do, and what is "wrong." One boy said, for example, that breaking windows was wrong and bad, but that playing with dolls was not bad in the same way: "Breaking windows you're not supposed to do. And if you play with dolls, well you can, but boys usually don't."

What seems to be happening is that the 5- or 6-year-old, having figured out that she is permanently a girl or he is a boy, is searching for a *rule* about how boys and girls behave (Martin & Halverson, 1981). The child picks up information from watching adults, from watching TV, from listening to the labels that are attached to different activities (e.g., "boys don't cry"). Initially they treat these as absolute, moral rules. Later they understand that these are social conventions, at which point sex-role concepts become more flexible, even while the child's understanding of the societal stereotype becomes more and more sharply defined.

CULTURES AND CONTEXTS
Sex-Role Stereotypes Around the World

A child is shown a silhouette of a man, and one of a woman, and told a story: "One of these people is emotional. They cry when something good happens as well as when everything goes wrong. Which person is the emotional person?" Or, "One of these people is always pushing other people around and getting into fights. Which person gets into fights?" (Williams & Best, 1990).

In response to stories like these, third-grade children in the U.S. identify the male figure as aggressive 90 percent of the time, and the female figure as emotional 79 percent of the time. Fourth graders give the stereotyped answer to both stories 100 percent of the time. Are these stereotypes unique to American culture, or does something similar exist in every culture? An amazing cross-cultural study by John Williams and Deborah Best (1990) gives us some answers.

They asked 5- and 8-year-old children in 24 countries these same questions, translated where necessary. Included were countries from every continent, with varying levels of industrialization.

Williams and Best had expected to find some common ground, but as they put it, "We were not prepared, however, for the high degree of pancultural generality that we found" (p. 303). In every country, the children had less-strong sex stereotypes than did adults in that same country, but in every country, the qualities associated with men were stronger and more active than those associated with women, and this was true of young children as well as adults.

Among the children, the characteristics most consistently ascribed to males were aggression, strength, and cruelty, and those most consistently ascribed to females were weakness, gentleness, and appreciativeness. These patterns become stronger with age in all countries, so 8-year-olds gave more stereotypic responses than 5-year-olds. And in virtually all countries, the male stereotype was clearer or more consistent than the female.

There were a few differences, naturally. Children in some countries seem to learn the sex stereotype very early, in others somewhat later. Five-year-olds in Pakistan and New Zealand, for example, already had very clear stereotypes, while those in Brazil and France showed little stereotyping at 5 but clearer stereotyping at 8—a pattern also found among African-Americans. There is also some unique content to sex stereotypes in particular countries. German children, for instance, choose "adventurous," "confident," "jolly," and "steady" as female items, although these are more normally male items in other cultures. Pakistani children identify "emotional" with men; Japanese children associate independence and severity with neither sex. But these are variations on a common theme. In *all* 24 countries, 8-year-olds choose the male figure for stories about aggression, strength, cruelty, coarseness, and loudness, and choose the female figure for stories about weakness. In 23 of 24 countries, 8-year-olds also choose the female story for gentleness, appreciativeness, and softheartedness. Thus not only does every culture appear to have clear sex-role stereotypes, the content of those stereotypes is remarkably similar across cultures.

One of the interesting sidelights in the research on stereotyping is that the male stereotype and sex-role concept seems to develop a bit earlier and to be stronger than the female stereotype or sex-role concept—and this is true in virtually all countries studied. More children agree on what men are or should be like than on what women are or should be. This might happen because children have seen women in more different roles (mother and teacher, for example) than they have seen men. Or it could mean that the female role in our society is more flexible than the male role. At any rate, it is clear that the qualities attributed to the male are more highly *valued* than are the female traits (Broverman et al., 1970). We see it as "good" to be independent, assertive, logical, and strong; it is less good to be warm, quiet, tactful, and gentle. Perhaps girls recognize early that the male role is seen more positively, and aspire to some of the valued male qualities. That would lead to a female role being perceived more broadly. Whatever the reason, it is an interesting finding— one with considerable relevance for understanding adult male and female sex roles and stereotyping.

The Development of Sex-Role Behavior.   The final element in the equation is the actual behavior children show with their own sex, and with the oppo-

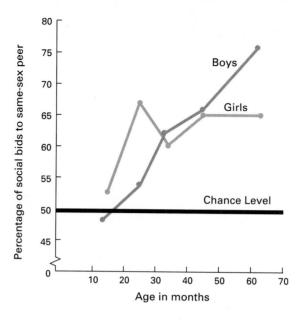

Figure 10.5
Same-sex playmate preference among preschoolers. (*Source:* La Freniere, Strayer, & Gauthier, 1984, Figure 1, p. 1961. Copyright by The Society for Research in Child Development, Inc.)

site sex. The unexpected finding here is that children's *behavior* is sex-typed earlier than are their ideas about sex roles or stereotypes.

By 18 to 24 months, children begin to show some preference for sex-stereotyped toys, such as dolls for girls or trucks or building blocks for boys, which is some months before they can normally identify their own gender (O'Brien, 1992). By age 3, children begin to show a preference for same-sex playmates and are much more sociable with playmates of the same sex—at a time when they do not yet have a concept of gender stability (Maccoby, 1988; 1990; Maccoby & Jacklin, 1987). By school age, peer relationships are almost exclusively same-sex. You can see the early development of this preference in Figure 10.5, which shows the results of a study of preschool play groups. The researchers counted how often children played with same-sex or opposite-sex playmates (La Freniere, Strayer, & Gauthier, 1984). You can see that by age 3, about 60 percent of play groups were same-sex groupings and the rate rose from there.

The other intriguing pattern is that children in early elementary school seem to begin to pay more attention to the behavior of same-sex than opposite-sex adults or playmates, and to play more with new toys that are labeled as being appropriate for their own sex (Bradbard et al., 1986; Ruble, Balaban, & Cooper, 1981). All in all, then, we see many signs that children are both aware of and affected by gender from very early, perhaps by age 1, certainly by age 2. But gender becomes a still more potent force in guiding behavior and attitudes at around age 5 or 6.

How many explanations can you think of for the fact that children begin to prefer to play with same-sex peers as early as age 3?

Explaining Sex-Role Development

Theorists from most of the major traditions have tried their hand at explaining this pattern of development. Freud relied on the concept of identification to explain the child's adoption of appropriate sex-role behavior, but his theory founders on the fact that children begin to show clearly sex-typed behavior long before age 4 or 5, when Freud thought identification occurred.

Social Learning Theory. Social learning theorists, such as Bandura (1977; Mischel, 1966; 1970) have naturally emphasized the role of both direct reinforcement and of modeling in shaping children's sex-role behavior and attitudes. This notion has been far better supported by research. Parents do seem to reinforce sex-typed activities in children as young as 18 months old, not only by buying different kinds of toys for boys and girls, but by responding more positively when their sons play with blocks or trucks, or when their daughters play with dolls (Fagot & Hagan, 1991; Lytton & Romney, 1991). Such differential reinforcement is particularly clear with boys. There is also new evidence suggesting that toddlers whose parents are more consistent in rewarding sex-typed toy choice or play behavior, and whose mothers favor traditional family sex roles, learn accurate gender labels earlier than do toddlers whose parents are less focused on the gender-appropriateness of the child's play (Fagot & Leinbach, 1989; Fagot, Leinbach, & O'Boyle, 1992)—findings clearly consistent with the predictions of social learning theory.

Social learning theorists would argue that little boys prefer to play with trucks because they have been reinforced for such play, as when parents buy them more toys like this. Does this make sense to you?

Interestingly, there is also a fair amount of evidence that differential treatment of sons and daughters is more common among fathers than mothers, and that fathers are particularly likely to be concerned with the appropriate sex-role behavior of their sons (Siegal, 1987). Many fathers seem to be especially uncomfortable with "girlish" behavior in their sons, and are much more likely to show disapproval of such behavior in their sons than they are to disapprove of "tomboyish" behavior in their daughters—which may be one reason that the male stereotype develops earlier and is stronger than is the female stereotype.

Cross-cultural evidence also supports a social learning view. Anthropologist Beatrice Whiting (Whiting & Edwards, 1988), after examining patterns of gender socialization in 11 different cultures, concludes that "we are the company we keep." In most cultures, girls and boys keep different company, beginning quite early, with girls spending more time with women as well as in child-care responsibilities. To the extent that this is true, it would provide each sex with more same-sex than opposite-sex models, and more opportunity for reinforcement of sex-appropriate behavior such as nurturance directed at younger siblings.

Still, helpful as it is, a social learning explanation is probably not sufficient. In particular, there is less differential reinforcement of boy-behavior versus girl-behavior than you'd expect, and probably not enough to account for the very early and robust discrimination children seem to make on the basis of gender. Even children whose parents seem to treat their young sons and daughters in highly similar ways nonetheless learn gender labels and show same-sex playmate choices.

Cognitive-Developmental Theories. A third alternative, based strongly on Piagetian theory, is Lawrence Kohlberg's suggestion that the crucial aspect of the process is the child's understanding of the gender concept (Kohlberg, 1966; Kohlberg & Ullian, 1974). Once the child realizes that he is a boy or she is a girl forever, he or she becomes highly motivated to learn to behave in the way that is expected or appropriate for that gender. Specifically, Kohlberg predicts that we should see systematic same-sex imitation only *after* the child has shown full gender constancy. Most studies designed to test this hypothesis have supported Kohlberg: children do seem to become much more sensitive to same-sex models after they have understood gender constancy (Frey & Ruble, 1992; Ruble et al., 1981). But Kohlberg's theory cannot easily handle the obvious fact that children show clear, differential sex-role behavior, such as toy preferences, long before they have achieved full understanding of the gender concept.

Gender Schema Theory.   The most fruitful current explanation is usually called **gender schema** theory (Martin, 1991; Martin & Halverson, 1981; 1983; Ruble, 1987), a model that has its roots in information processing theories of cognitive development as well as in Kohlberg's theory. Just as the self-concept can be thought of as a "scheme" or "self-theory," so the child's understanding of gender can be seen in the same way. The gender schema begins to develop as soon as the child notices the differences between male and female, knows his own gender, and can label the two groups with some consistency—all of which happens by age 2 or 3. Perhaps because gender is clearly an either/or category, children seem to understand very early that this is a key distinction, so the category serves as a kind of magnet for new information (Maccoby, 1988). In Piaget's terms, once the child has established even a primitive gender scheme, a great many experiences are assimilated to it. Thus as soon as this scheme begins to be formed, children begin to show preference for same-sex playmates or for gender-stereotyped activities (Martin & Little, 1990).

Preschoolers first learn some broad distinctions about what kinds of activities or behavior go with each gender, both by observing other children and through the reinforcements they receive from parents. They also learn a few gender "scripts"—whole sequences of events that normally go with a given gender, such as "fixing dinner," or "building with tools" (Levy & Fivush, 1993)—just as they learn other social scripts at about this age. Then between ages 4 and 6 the child learns a more subtle and complex set of associations for his or her *own* gender— what children of his own gender like and don't like, how they play, how they talk, what kinds of people they associate with. Only at about ages 8 to 10 does the child develop an equivalently complex view of the opposite gender (Martin, Wood, & Little, 1990).

The key difference between this theory and Kohlberg's is that for the initial gender schema to be formed, the child need not understand that gender is permanent. When gender constancy is understood at about 5 or 6, she develops a more elaborated rule or schema of "what people who are like me do," and treats this "rule" the same way she treats other rules — as absolutes. Later, the child's application of the "gender rule" becomes more flexible. She knows, for example, that most boys don't play with dolls, but that they *can* do so if they like.

Many of us, committed to the philosophical goal of equality for women, have taken the rigidity of children's early sex stereotypes as evidence that we have made little progress toward equality ("Mommy, you can't be a psychology doctor, you have to be a psychology nurse"). But gender schema theorists emphasize that such rule learning is absolutely normal, and so is the rigid stereotyping that we see in elementary-school children's ideas about sex roles. Children are searching for

THE REAL WORLD
Sex Stereotyping on TV

In modern cultures, one obvious source for children to acquire information for their sex-role schemas is through TV. From early preschool age, children in the United States spend an average of two to four hours a day in the presence of a TV set that is running. (I put it that way because we don't know how much of the time children actually *watch* the moving image.) Before they begin school, children have already been exposed to thousands of hours of TV; by age 18 the average child has spent more time in front of a TV set than in a classroom (Calvert & Huston, 1987). How are men and women portrayed in all those TV programs and commercials?

Highly stereotypically (Huston, 1983; Huston et al., 1990). Males outnumber females by two to one or three to one on virtually every kind of programming except commercials, but in the latter, the "voice-over" is nearly always male. Women are more often shown at home or in romantic situations; men more often appear in work settings, with cars, or playing sports. Men are shown solving problems, being more active, aggressive, and independent. Women are shown as sex objects, or showing emotions, and are more passive and deferential. Females generally play the "handmaiden" roles—they hand the male character his coat, type his reports, and listen to his troubles.

A continuous exposure to these stereotyped males and females does seem to have at least a small effect on a child's vision of men and women and their roles. In two longitudinal studies, Morgan (1982; 1987) has found that among elementary and high school students, those who watched a lot of TV at the beginning of the study reported more traditional sex-role stereotyping a year later. They were more likely, for example, to think that household chores should be done by women than by men. Even more persuasive is an experiment by Emily Davidson (Davidson, Yasuna, & Tower, 1979), who deliberately exposed some 5- and 6-year-olds to highly sex-stereotyped cartoons. Those who had seen such cartoons, compared to control children who had seen neutral cartoons, later gave more stereotyped answers to questions about the qualities of men and women.

At a more subtle level, Aletha Huston and her colleagues (1984) have found in several studies that toy commercials aimed at boys, and those aimed at girls, are simply designed differently. Boys' commercials are fast, sharp, and loud—lots of quick cuts, loud music, activity. Girls' commercials are gradual, soft, and fuzzy. They have camera fades and dissolves rather than sharp cuts, and use softer background music. Children as young as first grade notice these differences, too. They can watch a commercial of some nonstereotyped toy and tell you whether the *style* of the commercial is suited to a boys' or girls' toy.

TV is clearly not the only source of information children have about sex roles, nor is it likely to be the most crucial source. We know that children growing up without TV nonetheless acquire sex-role stereotypes. Yet TV does have an impact on children's ideas about men and women. Current TV programming appears to foster more stereotyped (and thus inaccurate) sex-role concepts in children than would occur normally.

order, for rules that help to make sense of their experiences. And a rule about "what men do" and "what women do" is a helpful schema for children. Like grammatical rules, children first apply this new rule too rigidly, and then later learn the exceptions. But the rule-learning process seems to be a natural one.

Gender schema theory is surely not the last word. It, too, has limitations. For example, when researchers have measured preschool children's understanding of gender and then looked at how sex-typed their behavior is, they often find only very weak connections (Bussey & Bandura, 1992; Martin, 1993). So 3-year-olds who show the clearest preferences for same-sex playmates are not necessarily the same ones who have the most advanced cognitive understanding of gender. Ultimately, some combination of social learning theory and gender schema theory may be devised that will handle the data better.

Individual Differences in Sex-Typing and Sex-Role Stereotypes

The developmental patterns I have been describing seem to hold for virtually all children. Nonetheless, as usual, we also see quite a lot of variation from child to child in the rigidity of the rule they develop, or in the sex-typing of their behavior.

In our society "tomboys" like this girl are fairly common and largely accepted. But a boy this age who showed "girlish" behavior would experience much more pressure to change, perhaps especially from Dad.

Can you think of any other way to explain the fact that there are more tomboys than there are boys who prefer girls' activities?

As a group, boys usually have stronger (more rigid and more traditional) sex-role stereotypes. Among both boys and girls, however, children whose mothers work outside the home have *less* stereotypic views (more flexible rules) (Powell & Steelman, 1982). Parallel evidence comes from one recent study of children who were cared for in early life by the father instead of the mother. These children, too, later had less-stereotyped views of sex roles (Williams, Radin, & Allegro, 1992). This makes perfectly good sense if the child's sex-role schema is formed primarily (or at least originally) by observing the parents' roles.

Cross-Sex Children. Another group with less-rigid sex stereotypes are children with cross-sex preferences—girls who would rather be boys and boys who would rather be girls (Kuhn, Nash, & Brucken, 1978; Nash, 1975). Having been a tomboy myself, I find such children especially interesting. How does a child come to prefer to be the other sex, or to choose cross-sex playmates or toys?

One possibility is that they are directly trained that way. These children may have been specifically reinforced for aspects of the opposite sex's role. Some girls are given trucks and carpentry tools and taught football by their fathers (or mothers). They may come to wish to be boys. We know that tomboy behavior is more accepted and reinforced than is "girlish" behavior in a boy, so it makes sense from a social learning perspective that there are far more girls who say they would like to be boys than there are boys who say they would rather be girls.

Social learning theory does not fare so well, though, in explaining the results of research by Carl Roberts and his colleagues (1987). They studied a group of boys who showed a strong preference for female toys and playmates from their earliest years of life. When Roberts compared these boys to a group of boys with more typical masculine sex-role behaviors, he found little evidence that the more feminine boys had been specifically reinforced for these behaviors, nor that their fathers were providing models for such behavior. Rather, Roberts found that the feminine boys were more feminine in appearance from earliest babyhood, that they were more often ill or hospitalized early in life, and that they had relatively less contact with both their mothers and fathers on a daily basis, compared to the more masculine boys. This pattern of findings does not fit nicely with a simple social learning explanation.

Alternatively, there might be some biological differences. Roberts and his colleagues' finding that the more behaviorally feminine boys already looked more feminine from earliest infancy is at least consistent with such a possibility, as is their finding that in adulthood, three-quarters of the more feminine boys were homosexual or bisexual. Further evidence for some biological influence on cross-sex behavior comes from studies of girls who have experienced heightened levels of androgen prenatally. (Recall from Chapter 4 that androgen is largely a "male" hormone.) These "androgenized" girls, in comparison to their normal sisters, are later more interested in rough-and-tumble play, more often prefer to play with boys, show less interest in dolls or babies, and have fewer fantasies about being a mother (Meyer-Bahlburg, Ehrhardt, & Feldman, 1986).

Findings like these suggest that actual sex-typing of behavior is affected by prenatal hormones. At the same time, it is also clear that a child's basic gender identity—the gender she thinks of herself as being—is strongly influenced by the label she is given and the treatment she receives from her parents. Children born with ambiguous genitalia, for example, will grow up to think of themselves as being whichever gender they were reared as, even if that gender does not match their genotype (Money, 1987).

Clearly, the gender a child *thinks* he is affects the gender *schema* he develops. The environment is extremely potent. But I think we must keep an open mind about the possible biological origins of some sex-role behaviors. The evidence is not all in yet.

Androgyny.   A very different approach to the study of cross-sex sex-typing has emerged in the past decades in the study of **androgyny.** Until perhaps the early 1970s, psychologists had thought of "masculinity" and "femininity" as opposite ends of the same continuum. A person could be one or the other but couldn't be both. Following the lead of Sandra Bem (1974), and of Janet Spence and Robert Helmreich (1978), psychologists today conceive of masculinity and femininity as two separate dimensions. A person can be high or low on either or both. Thus a person can be both compassionate and independent, both gentle and assertive.

This conceptualization creates four basic "types," as shown in Figure 10.6. The two traditional (strongly sex-typed) sex roles are the masculine and the feminine combinations. The two new "types" that become evident when we think about sex roles in this way are called *androgynous* and *undifferentiated*. Androgynous individuals think of themselves as having both masculine and feminine traits; undifferentiated individuals describe themselves as lacking both—a group that sounds a lot like those with a "diffuse" identity in Marcia's system.

This categorization system says nothing about the accuracy of the child's or the adult's rule or schema about sex roles. A teenage girl, for example, could have a clear notion of the norms for male or female behavior and still perceive *herself* as having some stereotypically masculine qualities. In some sense then, when we

Why should it make such a difference whether we think of masculinity and femininity as two ends of a single continuum, or as two separate dimensions?

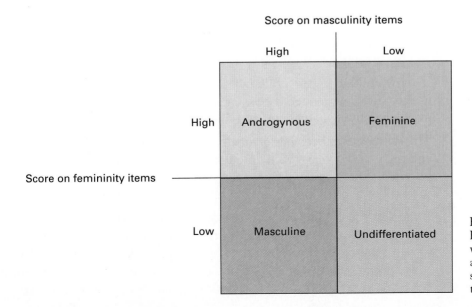

Score on masculinity items

	High	Low
High	Androgynous	Feminine
Low	Masculine	Undifferentiated

Score on femininity items

Figure 10.6
Four sex-role types are created when we think of masculinity and feminity as separate dimensions, rather than as two ends of the same dimension.

study masculinity/femininity/androgyny we are studying the intersection between the self-scheme and the gender scheme.

Perhaps because young children's ideas about sex roles are still quite rigid (or perhaps because we do not yet have good measures of androgyny for young children), there is little sign of androgyny among children younger than 9 or 10. But variations in androgyny, masculinity, and femininity clearly do exist among adolescents.

Several studies show that roughly 25 to 35 percent of high school students in the U.S. describe themselves as androgynous (Lamke, 1982a; Spence & Helmreich, 1978). More girls seem to show this pattern than do boys, and there are more girls in the "masculine" category than there are boys in the "feminine" group —just as there are more tomboys than the opposite. Furthermore, for *both* boys and girls, either a masculine or an androgynous sex-role self-concept is associated with higher self-esteem (Lamke, 1982a; 1982b), doubtless because both boys and girls value many of the qualities that are stereotypically masculine, such as independence and competence. Thus a boy can achieve high self-esteem and success with his peers by adopting a traditionally masculine sex role. For girls, though (at least in this culture), adoption of a traditionally feminine sex role without some balancing "male" characteristics seems to carry a risk of lower self-esteem, and even poorer relationships with peers (Massad, 1981).

Findings like these suggest the possibility that while the creation of rigid rules or schemas for sex roles is a normal— even essential—process in young children, a blurring of those rules may be an important process in adolescence (at least in Western cultures), particularly for girls, for whom a more androgynous self-concept is associated with positive outcomes.

▷ Summary

1. The child's emerging self-concept has several elements, including the awareness of a separate self and the understanding of self-permanence (which may be collectively called the subjective self) and awareness of oneself as an object in the world (the objective self).

2. The subjective self develops in the first year of life; we see real self-awareness and the emergence of the objective self in the second year.

3. In early childhood, the child begins to place herself in basic categories such as age, size, and gender. These early self-definitions appear to be based primarily on physical attributes and things the child can do.

4. The self-concept becomes gradually more abstract in the elementary-school and high school years, including not only actions but also likes and dislikes, beliefs, and more general personality characteristics. Beginning at about age 8 the child also has a global sense of self-worth (self-esteem).

5. At adolescence, there may also be a reevaluation of the self, a process Erikson talks of as the "identity crisis." In theory, adolescents move from a diffuse sense of future occupational or ideological identity, through a period of reevaluation (moratorium), to a commitment to a new self-definition. Whether this occurs to all adolescents or in all cultures is not so clear.

6. Self-concepts also include an evaluative dimension. Self-esteem is shaped both by the degree of discrepancy between a child's goals and his accomplishments, and by the degree of emotional support the child perceives from parents and peers. Children with high self-esteem show lower levels of depression.

7. Gender identity is part of the self-concept. Children generally acquire gender identity (labeling themselves and others correctly) by about age 2 or 3. They develop gender stability (knowing you stay the same gender throughout life) by about 4, and gender constancy (knowing you don't change gender by changing appearance) by about 5 or 6.

8. Children in all cultures studied so far have knowledge of cultural sex-role stereotypes by age 7 or 8; these stereotypes are remarkably similar across cultures.

9. In early elementary school, children create maximally rigid rules about what boys and girls ought to do or are allowed to do. Older children are aware of the social conventions, but do not treat them as incontrovertible rules.

10. Sex-typed behavior is visible from about 18 months of age; children this age begin to show sex-typed toy preferences. By 2½ or 3 they begin to choose same-sex playmates—*before* they have clearly understood gender stability.

11. Theorists of several different traditions have attempted to explain these patterns. Freud's theory, resting on the concept of identification, has little support.

12. Social learning theorists emphasize the role of reinforcement and modeling and argue that children are reinforced for imitating same-sex models. Parents do appear to treat boys and girls in systematically different ways, including punishing boys for girlish behavior, although differential reinforcement appears to be insufficient to account for the degree of early sex-typing.

13. Kohlberg proposes a cognitive-developmental model: children begin to imitate same-sex models only after they have achieved gender constancy. There is some evidence to support this, but the theory does not explain sex-typed behavior at age 2 or 3.

14. Gender schema theory offers a fourth alternative: children begin to acquire a rule about what boys do and what girls do as soon as they figure out the difference, and this schema forms the basis of both stereotyping and sex-typed behavior.

15. More girls than boys show cross-sex preferences in toy choices and behavior. Both environmental and biological elements may play a part in such cross-sex choices.

16. Young people also differ in the extent to which they see themselves as having feminine and/or masculine qualities or traits. Those who describe themselves with both sets of qualities are called androgynous. Girls who describe themselves as androgynous or masculine have somewhat higher self-esteem—at least in U.S. culture.

▶ Key Terms

androgyny (309)

foreclosure (293)

gender concept (300)

gender constancy (301)

gender identity (301)

gender schema (306)

gender stability (301)

identity achievement (293)

identity diffusion (293)

moratorium (293)

objective self (289)

self-concept (288)

self-esteem (296)

sex-role behavior (300)

sex-role concept (300)

sex roles (300)

sex-role stereotypes (300)

sex-typing (300)

subjective self (289)

▶ Suggested Readings

Harter, S. (1987). The determinants and mediational role of global self-worth in children. In N. Eisenberg (Ed.), *Contemporary topics in developmental psychology (pp.219–242)*. New York: Wiley-Interscience.

I think Harter's work is the best being done today on self-esteem. This paper is a very good introduction to her ideas.

O'Brien, M. (1992). Gender identity and sex roles. In V. B. Van Hasselt & M. Hersen (Eds.), *Handbook of social development: A lifespan perspective* (pp. 325–345). New York: Plenum Press.

An excellent, brief, up-to-date presentation of our current basic knowledge on this topic.

THE DEVELOPMENT OF SOCIAL RELATIONSHIPS

11

Attachment Theory: Concepts and Terminology

The Formation of the Parents' Bond to the Child
  The Initial Bond
  Meshing of Attachment Behaviors
  • *The Real World:* Child Abuse and Other Consequences of Failure of Bonding
  Father-Child Bonds

The Attachment Process: Child to Parent
  • *Cultures and Contexts:* Attachment in a Very Different Cultural System
  Attachments in the Preschool and Elementary-School Years
  Parent-Child Relationships at Adolescence
  Attachments to Mothers and Fathers

Individual Differences in the Quality of Infants' Attachments
  Secure and Insecure Attachments

• *Cultures and Contexts:* Secure and Insecure Attachments in Different Cultures

Horizontal Relationships: The Child's Relationships with Other Children
  Developmental Changes in Peer Relationships
  • *The Real World:* Homosexuality Among Adolescents
  Prosocial Behavior and Aggression
  • *The Real World:* Rearing Helpful and Altruistic Children

Individual Differences in Peer Relationships
  Popularity and Rejection
  Sex Differences

Summary

Key Terms

Suggested Readings

At a social gathering several years ago, I watched two young friends, Mark and Marcie, with their 4-month-old son, Alexander. With very little effort, Alexander managed to attract everyone's attention. He looked around him, occasionally gave brief smiles, kicked his feet, shook a rattle, and cried once in a while. Those simple behaviors were enough to have all the adults in the room hovering over him, trying their best to entice a smile. I was not immune to his charms. I trotted out all my playing-with-baby tricks, raising my eyebrows, smiling broadly, calling his name, tickling him a bit on the cheek or on his feet, making clucking noises. My reward was one very small smile and a brief gaze.

Alex's parents, after four months of practice, were a whole lot better than the rest of us at soothing and eliciting responses from him. Either Mom or Dad could get him to smile within just a few seconds; either of them could soothe him quite easily if he cried.

My most immediate reaction to this scene was simple pleasure at seeing loving and attentive parents with their infant. But the psychologist in me was watching too. I could see all of Alex's social skills, his ability to entice. And I could see how much Alex and his parents had already learned about one another, how smoothly they performed a kind of "dance" of interaction. They had *adapted* to one another.

This brief scene focuses our attention on an aspect of development I have largely neglected so far, namely the child's relationships with others—surely a central aspect of any child's (or adult's) life.

Willard Hartup (1989), one of the most astute students of social development, suggests that each child needs experience in two rather different kinds of relationships: *vertical* and *horizontal*. A vertical relationship involves an attachment to someone who has greater social power or knowledge, such as a parent, a teacher, or even an older sibling. Such relationships are complementary rather than reciprocal. The bond may be extremely powerful in both directions, but the actual behaviors the two partners show toward one another are not the same. The child bids for attention, the parent gives nurture, for example. Horizontal relationships, in contrast, are reciprocal and egalitarian. The individuals involved, such as same-age peers, have equal social power and their behavior toward one another comes from the same repertoire.

Hartup's point is that these two kinds of relationships serve different functions for the child, and both are needed for the child to develop effective social skills. Vertical relationships are necessary to provide the child with protection and security. In these relationships the child creates his basic internal working models and learns fundamental social skills. But it is in horizontal relationships— in friendships and in peer groups—that the child practices his social behavior and acquires those social skills that can only be learned in a relationship between equals: cooperation, competition, and intimacy.

These two kinds of relationships clearly affect one another. But because the theory and data tend to be separate, I will necessarily talk about them separately, beginning with the vertical relationships, in particular the core relationship between child and parent.

▶ Attachment Theory: Concepts and Terminology

The strongest theoretical influence in modern-day studies of infant-parent relationships is attachment theory, particularly the work of John Bowlby (1969; 1973; 1980; 1988a; 1988b), whose approach I mentioned in Chapter 9. You'll recall that his thinking has roots in psychoanalytic thought, particularly in the emphasis on the significance of the earliest relationship between mother and child. But he adds important evolutionary and ethological concepts. In his view, "The propensity to make strong emotional bonds to particular individuals [is] a basic component of human nature, already present in germinal form in the neonate" (Bowlby, 1988a, p. 3). Such relationships have *survival* value, because they bring nurturance to the infant. They are built and maintained by an interlocking repertoire of instinctive behaviors that create and sustain proximity between parent and child or between other bonded pairs.

In Bowlby's writings, and in the equally influential writings of Mary Ainsworth (1972; 1982; 1989; Ainsworth et al., 1978), the key concepts are those of an affectional bond, an attachment, and attachment behaviors.

Ainsworth (1989) defines an **affectional bond** as "a relatively long-enduring tie in which the partner is important as a unique individual and is interchangeable with none other. In an affectional bond, there is a desire to maintain closeness to the partner" (p. 711). An **attachment** is a subvariety of emotional bond in which a person's sense of security is bound up in the relationship. When you are attached, you feel (or hope to feel) a special sense of security and comfort in the presence of the other, and you can use the other as a "safe base" from which to explore the rest of the world.

In these terms, the child's relationship with the parent is an attachment, but the parent's relationship with the child is not, since the parent presumably does not feel a greater sense of security in the presence of the infant, or use the infant as a safe base. A relationship with one's adult partner or with a very close friend, however, is likely to be an attachment in the sense in which Ainsworth and Bowlby mean the term.

Since affectional bonds and attachments are internal states, we cannot see them directly. Instead we deduce their existence by observing **attachment behaviors,** which are all those behaviors that allow a child or adult to achieve and retain proximity to someone else to whom he is attached. This could include smiling, making eye contact, calling out to the other person across a room, touching, clinging, crying.

It is important to make clear that there is no one-to-one correspondence between the number of different attachment behaviors a child (or adult) shows on any one occasion and the strength of the underlying attachment. Attachment behaviors are elicited primarily when the individual has need of care or support or comfort. An infant is in such a needy state a good deal of the time; but an older child will be likely to show attachment behaviors only when he is frightened, or tired, or otherwise under stress. It is the *pattern* of these behaviors, not the frequency, that tells us something about the strength or quality of the attachment or the affectional bond.

To understand the early relationship between the parent and the child, we need to look at both sides of the equation—at the development of the parents' bond to the child, and of the child's attachment to the parent.

Think about your own relationships. In Bowlby and Ainsworth's terms, which are attachments and which are affectional bonds?

In this "vertical" social relationship, the son is attached to his dad, but the father's relationship to his son is an "affectional bond" rather than an attachment.

Pick one of your attachment relationships and make a list of all the attachment behaviors you show toward that person. Are any of these the same as the kind of attachment behaviors we see in an infant?

◗ The Formation of the Parents' Bond to the Child

The Initial Bond

If you read the popular press at all, I am sure you have come across articles proclaiming that mothers (or fathers) must have immediate contact with their newborn infant if they are to become properly bonded with the baby. This belief has been based primarily on the work of two pediatricians, Marshall Klaus and John

Kennell (1976), who proposed the hypothesis that the first few hours after an infant's birth is a "critical period" for the mother's development of a bond to her infant. Mothers who are denied early contact, Klaus and Kennell thought, are likely to form weaker bonds and thus be at higher risk for a range of disorders of parenting.

Their proposal was one of many factors leading to significant changes in birth practices, including the now-normal presence of fathers at delivery. I would certainly not want to turn back the clock on such changes. But it now looks as if Klaus and Kennell's hypothesis is probably incorrect. Immediate contact does not appear to be either necessary or sufficient for the formation of a stable, long-term affectional bond between parent and child (Myers, 1987).

A few studies show some short-term beneficial effects of very early contact. In the first few days after delivery, mothers with such contact may show more tender fondling or more gazing at the baby than is true of mothers who first held their babies some hours after birth (Campbell & Taylor, 1980; de Chateau, 1980). But there is little indication of a lasting effect. Two or three months after delivery, mothers who have had immediate contact with their newborns do not smile at them more, or hold them differently than do mothers who had delayed contact.

Only in certain subgroups of mothers, such as first-time mothers, mothers living in poverty, or very young mothers—all groups who are at somewhat higher risk for problems with parenting—are there a few signs that early contact may make a difference. Among such mothers, extended or early contact with the infant in the first days of life seems to help prevent later problems, such as abuse or neglect (O'Connor et al., 1980). But for the majority of mothers, neither early nor extended contact appears to be an essential ingredient in forming a strong affectional bond.

Meshing of Attachment Behaviors

What *is* essential is the opportunity for the parent and infant to develop a mutual, interlocking pattern of attachment behaviors—just what young Alex and his parents had already achieved. The baby signals his needs by crying or smiling; he responds to being held by soothing or snuggling; he looks at the parents when they look at him. The parents, in their turn, enter into this two-person "dance" with their own repertoire of caregiving behaviors. They pick the baby up when he cries, wait for and respond to his signals of hunger or other need, smile at the baby when he smiles, gaze into his eyes when he looks at them. Some researchers and theorists have described this as the development of *synchrony* (Isabella, Belsky, & von Eye, 1989).

One of the most intriguing things about this process is that we all seem to know how to do this particular dance and we do it in very similar ways. In the presence of a young infant most adults will automatically display a distinctive pattern of interactive behaviors, including smiling, raised eyebrows, and very wide-open eyes. And we all seem to use our voices in special ways with babies as well, as you'll remember from the discussion of motherese in Chapter 8. Not only do parents all over the world use the characteristic high-pitched and lilting pattern of motherese, they also use similar intonation patterns. In a study of mother-infant interactions among Chinese, German, and United States mothers, Hanus

Watch yourself next time you interact with a baby. Does your facial expression match the "mock surprise" in the photo? Does your intonation pattern follow the pattern in the Papousek study?

These two moms show almost identical expressions—the classic "mock surprise" expression characteristic of adults when interacting with a baby: raised eyebrows, open mouth, semismile.

and Mechthild Papousek (1991) found that all three groups tended to use a rising voice inflection when they wanted the baby to "take a turn" in the interaction, and a falling intonation when they wanted to soothe the baby.

But while we can perform all these attachment *behaviors* with many infants, we do not form a bond with every baby we coo at in the grocery store. For the adult, the critical ingredient for the formation of a bond seems to be the opportunity to develop real mutuality—to practice the dance until the partners follow one another's lead smoothly and pleasurably. This takes time and many rehearsals, and some parents (and infants) become more skillful at it than others. In general, the smoother and more predictable the process becomes, the more satisfying it seems to be to the parents and the stronger their bond to the infant becomes.

This second step appears to be *far* more important than the initial contact at birth in establishing a strong parental bond to the child. But this second process, too, can fail. I've explored some of the possible reasons for such a failure in the real world box on page 318.

Father-Child Bonds

Most of the research I have talked about so far has involved studies of mothers. Still, many of the same principles seem to hold for fathers as well. The father's bond, like the mother's, seems more dependent on the development of mutuality than on contact immediately after birth. Aiding the development of such mutuality is the fact that fathers seem to have the same repertoire of attachment behaviors as do mothers. In the early weeks of the baby's life, dads touch, talk to, and cuddle their babies in the same ways that mothers do (Parke & Tinsley, 1981).

Past these first weeks of life, however, we see signs of a kind of specialization of parents' behaviors with their infants and toddlers—at least among parents in the industrialized societies in which these observations have been done. Dads spend more time playing with the baby, with more physical roughhousing. Moms spend more time in routine caregiving, and also talk and smile more at the baby

THE REAL WORLD

Child Abuse and Other Consequences of Failure of Bonding

In any given year, about 3 percent of children in the United States suffer from neglect, or from physical or sexual abuse (United States Bureau of the Census, 1992). Most such abuse is inflicted on older children; the average age of children in cases reported to Child Protective Services is 7. But in many cases the origins of later abuse or neglect may lie in a failure of the parent to form a strong affectional bond to the baby in the first months of life. Such a failure can occur if either the baby or the parents lack the skills to enter into the "dance" of interaction fully. Of the two, the more serious problems seem to arise if it is the parent who lacks skills, but problems can also arise when the baby is handicapped in some way, or otherwise lacks the full repertoire of attachment behaviors (van IJzendoorn et al., 1992).

For example, blind babies smile less and do not show mutual gaze, and preterm infants are typically very unresponsive in the early weeks and months (Fraiberg, 1974; 1975). Most parents of handicapped or premature infants form a strong bond to the child despite the baby's problems, but the rate of abuse is higher among preterm than term infants, and higher among families whose babies are sick a lot in the first few months (Sherrod et al., 1984).

On the other side of the interaction, a parent might lack "attachment skill" because she or he did not form a secure attachment with her or his own parents, perhaps because of abuse (Crittenden, Partridge, & Claussen, 1991). The majority of parents who abuse their children were themselves abused as children—although it is important to emphasize that the reverse is not the case: the majority of adults who experienced abuse in childhood manage to break the cycle of violence and refrain from abusing their children (Zigler & Hall, 1989). Those who are unable to break this cycle are typically those who lack other social skills, who have no adequate social supports, or who are living under high levels of stress.

Another serious problem on the parents' side of the equation is depression, which disrupts not only the parents' nurturing behavior, but affects the child's response as well. Babies interacting with depressed mothers, or even with mothers who have been told to look depressed or "blank faced," smile less, show more sad and angry facial expressions, and are more disorganized and distressed (Field et al., 1990; Pickens & Field, 1993). Depressed mothers, for their part, are slower to respond to their infant's signals, and are more negative— even hostile— to their infants (Rutter, 1990). All in all, these relationships appear to lack synchrony. That is, the mother and infant are not "dancing" well together. These deficiencies in the mother's behavior with the infant even persist after the mother is no longer depressed, and they generalize beyond the mother-infant dyad; babies with depressed mothers show similar distressed or nonsynchronous behaviors when they interact with a nondepressed adult (Field et al., 1988).

One common theme in all these findings is that a parent, regardless of depression or history of abuse, is more likely to abuse a child when her current life conditions are highly stressful. So abuse is more likely in families in which there is alcoholism in one parent (Famularo et al., 1986), large families, single-parent households, and families living in poverty or in extremely crowded conditions (Garbarino & Sherman, 1980; Pianta, Egeland, & Erickson, 1989; Sack, Mason, & Higgins, 1985). Even these adverse conditions can be surmounted, though, if the parents have adequate emotional support, either from one another, or from others outside the family.

Brandon's dad, like most fathers, is far more likely to toss the baby in the air or play with him in this vigorous physical way than is his mom.

(Walker et al., 1992). This does not mean that fathers have a weaker affectional bond with the infant; it does mean that the attachment behaviors they show toward the infant are typically somewhat different from those mothers show.

We do not yet know whether such sex differences in parenting behaviors are reflections of culturally based role definitions, or whether they might be instinctive, built-in differences. One crucial test would be to study families in which the father is the primary caregiver to see if the parental behavioral roles are reversed. So far we have only pale imitations of this crucial test—studies in which the father had been a major caregiver for a few months of the child's early life. The three such studies I know of, done in Sweden, the United States, and Australia, have yielded totally contradictory results (Field, 1978; Lamb et al., 1982; Russell, 1982), which leaves the question still open.

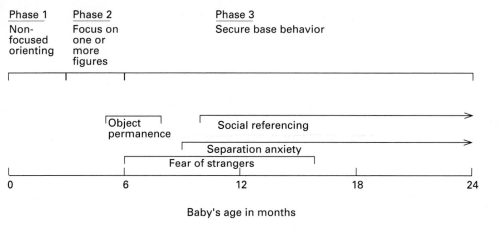

Figure 11.1
This schematic may help you see how the various threads of development of attachment are woven together.

▶ The Attachment Process: Child to Parent

Like the parents' bond to the baby, the baby's attachment emerges gradually. Bowlby (1969) suggested three phases in the development of the infant's attachment, which I've sketched schematically in Figure 11.1.

Phase 1: Nonfocused Orienting and Signaling. Like Piaget, Bowlby thought the baby begins life with a set of innate behavior patterns that orient him toward others and signal his needs. Mary Ainsworth describes these as "proximity promoting" behaviors—they bring people closer. In the newborn's repertoire, these include crying, making eye contact, clinging, cuddling, and responding to caregiving efforts by being soothed. But at first, as Ainsworth (1989) says, "These attachment behaviors are simply emitted, rather than being directed toward any specific person" (p. 710).

At this stage there is little evidence of an attachment. Nonetheless, the roots of attachment are to be found in this phase. The baby is building up expectancies, schemas, the ability to discriminate Mom and Dad from others. The smooth, predictable interactions that strengthen the parents' bond also form the base for the baby's emerging attachment.

Phase 2: Focus on One or More Figure(s). By 3 months of age, the baby begins to aim her attachment behaviors somewhat more narrowly. She may smile more to the people who regularly take care of her, and may not smile readily to a stranger. Yet despite the change, Bowlby and Ainsworth have argued that the infant does not yet have a full-blown attachment. There are still a number of people who are favored with the child's "proximity promoting" behaviors and no one person has yet become the "safe base." Children in this phase show no special anxiety at being separated from their parent, and no fear of strangers.

Phase 3: Secure Base Behavior. Bowlby thought that the baby forms a genuine attachment only at about 6 months of age. At the same time, the dominant mode of the baby's attachment behavior changes. Because the 6-to-7-

month-old begins to be able to move about the world more freely by creeping and crawling, she can move *toward* the caregiver as well as enticing the caregiver to come to her. Her attachment behaviors therefore shift from mostly "come here" signals (proximity promoting) to what Ainsworth calls "proximity seeking," which we might think of as "go there" behaviors. We also see a child of this age using the "most important person" as a safe base from which to explore the world around her— one of the key signs that an attachment exists.

I should note that not all infants have a *single* attachment figure, even at this early point. Some may show strong attachment to both parents, or to a parent and another caregiver, such as a baby-sitter or a grandparent. But even these babies, when under stress, usually show a preference for one of their favored persons over the others.

Once the child has developed a clear attachment, at about 6 to 8 months, several related behaviors also appear. One of these is social referencing, which I talked about in Chapter 5. The 10-month-old begins to check out Mom's or Dad's expression before deciding whether to venture forth into some novel situation. At about the same age, babies also typically show both fear of strangers and separation protest.

Fear of Strangers and Separation Protest. Both these forms of distress are rare before 5 or 6 months, rise in frequency until about 12 to 16 months, and then decline. The research findings are not altogether consistent, but it looks as though fear of strangers normally appears first, while separation anxiety starts a bit later but continues to be visible for a longer period, a pattern I've marked in Figure 11.1.

Such an increase in fear and anxiety has been observed in children from a number of different cultures, and in both home-reared and day-care-reared chil-

---

CULTURES AND CONTEXTS
Attachment in a Very Different Cultural System

Is the sequence of phases Bowlby and Ainsworth describe universal? Do all babies go through this same sequence, no matter what kind of family or culture they live in? Maybe yes, maybe no. Ainsworth herself observed the same basic three phases in forming a clear attachment among children in Uganda, although they showed a more intense fear of strangers than is usually found in American samples. But among the Ganda, as in American and other Western families, the mother is the primary caregiver. What would we find in a culture in which the child's early care is much more communal?

Edward Tronick and his colleagues (Tronick, Morelli, & Ivey, 1992) have studied just such a culture, a pygmy group called the Efe, who forage in the forests of Zaire. They live in small groups of perhaps 20 individuals in camps, each consisting of several extended families, often brothers and their wives.

Infants in these communities are cared for communally in the early months and years of life. They are carried and held by all the adult women, and interact regularly with many different adults. If they have needs, they are tended by whichever adult or older child is nearby; they may even be nursed by women other than the mother, although they normally sleep with the mother.

Tronick and his colleagues report two things of particular interest about early attachment in this group. First, Efe infants seem to use virtually any adult or older child in their world as a safe base, which suggests that there is no single central attachment. But at the same time, beginning at about 6 months, the Efe infants nonetheless seem to insist on being with their mother more and to prefer her over other women, although other women continue to help care for the child.

Thus even in an extremely communal rearing arrangement, there is still some sign of a central attachment, albeit perhaps less dominant. At the same time, it is clear, as Inge Bretherton (1992b) says, that "attachment behavior is never purely instinctive, but is heavily overlain with cultural prescriptions" (p. 150).

dren in the United States, all of which makes it look as if there are some basic cognitive or other age-related developmental timetables underlying this pattern (Kagan, Kearsley, & Zelazo, 1978). But while the general timing of these two phenomena may be common to virtually all children, the intensity of the fearful reaction is not. Children differ widely in how much fear they show toward strangers or toward novel situations. Some of this difference may reflect basic temperamental variations (Berberian & Snyder, 1982). Heightened fearfulness may also be a response to recent upheaval or stress in the child's life, such as a recent move, or a parent's changing jobs. It is also clear that the stranger's behavior makes a considerable difference. When a substitute caregiver is responsive and warm but does not approach too closely, babies show less fear than when the baby-sitter pays little attention to the child or touches the child too soon (Gunnar et al., 1992; Mangelsdorf, 1992). Whatever the origin of such variations in fearfulness, the pattern does eventually disappear in virtually all toddlers, typically by the middle of the second year. And while it is going on, parents can take advantage of the existence of social referencing to try to reduce the child's fear: your child is more likely to accept a stranger if he sees you talking and smiling to the stranger first.

Attachments in the Preschool and Elementary-School Years

By age 2 or 3, most attachment behaviors have become less visible. Children this age are cognitively advanced enough to understand Mom if she explains why she is going away and that she will be back, so their anxiety at separation wanes. They can even use a photograph of their mother as a "safe base" for exploration in a strange situation (Passman & Longeway, 1982), which reflects another cognitive advance. Of course attachment behaviors have not completely disappeared. Two-year-olds still want to sit on Mom's or Dad's lap, they are still likely to seek some closeness or proximity when Mom returns from some absence, but in nonfearful or nonstressful situations the child is able to wander farther and farther from her safe base without apparent distress.

An even broader change occurs at about age 4, when the child's attachment seems to change in quality. Bowlby describes this new stage or level as a *goal-corrected partnership*. Marvin and Greenberg (1982) describe it this way:

> It now becomes possible for children to realize that they share with their mothers a relationship that is not totally dependent on interaction within physical proximity. That is, mother and child can now share a joint goal or plan whether they are together or apart, and the child thus realizes that the relationship continues even when they are separated. (p. 49)

Just as the first attachment probably requires that the baby understand that his mother will continue to exist when she isn't there, so now the preschooler grasps that the *relationship* continues to exist even when the partners are apart. Children this age are much less distressed at separation; but they get upset if they don't know what's happening or haven't shared in the planning (Marvin & Greenberg, 1982).

Once this understanding has been achieved, visible attachment behaviors go underground even more. Among elementary-school children, it is only in stressful situations that we see overt attachment behaviors. And because fewer experiences are new and potentially stressful to the 7- or 8-year-old than to the

Can you think of anything other than the generally lower level of novelty or stress that might account for the elementary-school child's rather sharp drop in overt affection displayed toward parents?

preschooler, we see much less obvious safe base behavior, and less open affection from child to parent in this age group (Maccoby, 1984).

Parent-Child Relationships at Adolescence

In adolescence, the scene shifts somewhat, because teenagers have two, apparently contradictory, tasks in their relationships with their parents: to establish autonomy from the parents, and to maintain their sense of relatedness (attachment) with their parents. We can see both processes at work when we look at teen-parent relationships. The push for autonomy shows itself in increases in conflict between parent and adolescent; the maintenance of connection is seen in the continued strong attachment of child to parent.

Increases in Conflict. The rise in conflict has been documented by a number of researchers, most notably Laurence Steinberg (1988). In the great majority of families, it seems to consist of an increase in mild bickering or conflicts over everyday issues, such as rules and regulations, dress codes, dating, grades, or housekeeping. Teenagers and their parents interrupt each other more often, become more impatient with one another.

This increase in discord is widely found, but we need to be careful not to assume that it signifies a major disruption of the quality of the parent-child relationship. Steinberg estimates that only 5 to 10 percent of the families studied in the United States experience a substantial or pervasive deterioration in the quality of parent-child relationship in these years of early adolescence—a fact that flies in the face of the usual assumption that adolescence is a time of inevitable *Sturm und Drang* (storm and stress).

But if the rise in conflict doesn't signal the relationship is falling apart, what does it mean? Steinberg and others have suggested that the temporary discord, far from being a negative event, may instead be developmentally healthy and necessary—a part of the process of individuation and separation (Hill, 1988; Steinberg, 1988; 1990). Among primates, we see the same kind of increase in conflict, especially between adult males and the newly adolescent males. The young males begin to make competitive gestures, and may be driven off into a brief period of independent life before returning to the troop. Among humans, we have some evidence that the increase in family conflict is linked with the hormonal changes of puberty, rather than age, which would lend further support to the argument that this is a normal and even necessary process.

For example, in a short-term longitudinal study, Steinberg (1988) followed a group of teenagers over a one-year period, assessing their stage of puberty and the quality of their relationship with their parents at the beginning and end of the year. He found that as the pubertal stages began, family closeness declined, parent-child conflict rose, and autonomy in the child went up. Other researchers (Inoff-Germain et al., 1988) have taken this a step further by measuring actual hormone levels and showing links between the rise of the various hormones of puberty and the rise in aloofness toward or conflict with parents. Among girls, conflict seems to rise after menarche (Holmbeck & Hill, 1991).

The pattern of causes is obviously complex. Hormonal changes themselves may be causally linked to increases in assertiveness, perhaps especially among boys. But parents' reactions to pubertal changes may also be highly important

It is a myth that parents and teenagers are constantly in conflict.

parts of the mix. Visible pubertal changes, including menarche, change parents' expectations for the child, and increase their concern about guiding and controlling the adolescent to help her avoid the shoals of too great a level of independence.

In fact, there is good evidence that adolescence may actually be more stressful to *parents* than to the young people themselves (Gecas & Seff, 1990). Almost two-thirds of parents perceive adolescence as the most difficult stage of parenting, because of both loss of control over the adolescent and fear for the adolescent's safety resulting from increased independence.

In the midst of the increased conflict, and perhaps partially as a result of it, the overall level of the teenager's autonomy within the family increases steadily throughout the adolescent years. Parents give the youngster more and more room to make independent choices and to participate in family decision making. Steinberg argues that this "distancing" is an essential part of the adolescent development process.

Attachment to Parents.   Paradoxically, in the midst of the temporarily heightened family conflict and the "distancing," teenagers' underlying emotional attachment to their parents remains strong. Results from a recent study by Mary Levitt and her colleagues (1993) illustrate the point.

Levitt interviewed African-American, Hispanic-American, and Anglo/European-American children aged 7, 10, and 14. Each child was shown a drawing with a set of concentric circles. They were asked to place in the innermost circle the "people who are the most close and important to you—people you love the most and who love you the most." In the second circle, children were asked to place the "people who are not quite as close but who are still important—people you really love or like, but not quite as much as the people in the first circle." The outermost circle contained names of somewhat more distant members of this personal "convoy." For each person listed, the interviewer then asked about the kind of support that person provided.

Levitt found that for all three ethnic groups, at all three ages, parents and other close family were by far the most likely to be placed in the inner circle. Even among 14-year-olds, friends were not often placed in this position. So the parents remain central. At the same time, it is clear from Levitt's results that peers become increasingly important as providers of support, as you can see in

You might find it interesting to complete such a "personal convoy" map for your own relationships. Are your parents in the center circle? Friends? Partner?

Figure 11.2
African-American (Af), Anglo-American (An), and Hispanic-American (Hs) children and teens were asked about the amount and type of support they received from various members of their "social convoy." Note that for teens, friends become more significant sources of support, but parents do not become *less* important. (*Source:* Levitt, Guacci-Franco, & Levitt, 1993, Figure 2, p. 815. Reprinted by permission.)

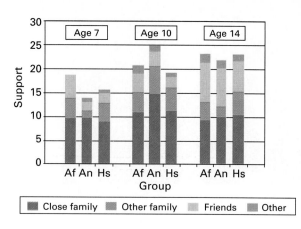

Figure 11.2. This figure shows the total amount of support the children and adolescents described from each source. Friends clearly provided more support among the 14-year-olds than among the younger children, a pattern that is clear for all three ethnic groups. You can also see in the figure that extended family support is more significant for Hispanic-American teens than for Anglos, a pattern that matches other research on Hispanic family patterns, as I have mentioned before.

This basic pattern is confirmed in other research. In general, a teenager's sense of well-being or happiness is more strongly correlated with the quality of his attachment to the parents than to the quality of his attachments to his peers, a pattern found in a study in New Zealand as well as research in the United States (Greenberg, Siegel, & Leitch, 1983; Raja, McGee, & Stanton, 1992). Thus even while the teenager is becoming more autonomous, the parents seem to continue to provide a highly important psychological safe base.

Attachments to Mothers and Fathers

I pointed out earlier that both fathers and mothers appear to form strong bonds to their infants, although their behavior with infants varies somewhat. But what about the child's half of this relationship? Are infants and children equally attached to their fathers and mothers?

In general, yes. From the age of 7 to 8 months, when strong attachments are first seen, infants prefer *either* the father or the mother to a stranger. And when both the father and the mother are available, an infant will smile at or approach either or both, *except* when he is frightened or under stress. When that happens, especially between 8 and 24 months, the child typically turns to the mother rather than the father (Lamb, 1981).

As you might expect, the strength of the child's attachment to the father at this early age seems to be related to the amount of time the dad has spent with the child. Gail Ross (Ross et al., 1975) found she could predict a baby's attachment to the father by knowing how many diapers the dad changed in a typical week. The more diapers, the stronger the attachment! But greatly increased time with the father does not seem to be the only element, since Michael Lamb and his Swedish colleagues have found that infants whose father was the major caregiver for at least a month in the first year of the child's life were nonetheless more strongly attached to their mothers than their fathers (Lamb et al., 1983). For the

If Gail Ross is right, then young Edwin will be likely to form a strong attachment to his dad because his dad changes his diapers.

father to be consistently *preferred* over the mother would probably require essentially full-time paternal care. As this option becomes more common in our society, it will be possible to study such father-child pairs to see if a preference for the father develops.

▶ Individual Differences in the Quality of Infants' Attachments

Go to a day-care center sometime and watch the way the babies or toddlers greet their parents at the end of the day. Some are calmly pleased to see Mom or Dad, running to be hugged, showing a new toy, or smiling when picked up, showing no distress. Others may cry, or cling strongly to the parent. All these babies have moved through the typical sequence from preattachment to attachment, but the *quality* of their attachments differs. In Bowlby's terminology, infants have different **internal working models** of their relationships with parents and key others. This concept introduces a distinctly cognitive flavor to the discussion, very like the concepts of the "self-scheme" or the "gender-schema" I talked about in the last two chapters. This internal working model of attachment relationships includes such elements as the child's confidence (or lack of it) that the attachment figure will be available or reliable, the child's expectation of rebuff or affection, and the child's sense of assurance that the other is really a safe base for exploration.

The internal model begins to be formed late in the child's first year of life and becomes more complex and firmer through the first four or five years. By age 5, most children have clear internal models of the mother (or other caregiver), a self-model, and a model of relationships. Once formed, such models shape and explain experiences and affect memory and attention. We notice and remember experiences that fit our model, and miss or forget experiences that don't match. More importantly, the model affects the child's behavior: The child tends to re-create, in each new relationship, the pattern with which he is familiar. Alan Sroufe (1988) gives a nice example that may make this point clearer:

> What is rejection to one child is benign to another. What is warmth to a second child is confusing or ambiguous to another. For example, a child approaches another and asks to play. Turned down, the child goes off and sulks in a corner. A second child receiving the same negative reaction skips on to another partner and successfully engages him in play. Their experiences of rejection are vastly different. Each receives confirmation of quite different inner working models. (p. 23)

In a sense, these internal models are not unlike the social *scripts* that the preschooler develops in other areas (Bretherton, 1993). They contain expectations for sequences of behavior, rules for behavior with various individuals, and interpretations of others' actions.

If internal working models tend to persist and to affect later relationships, is this the same as saying that the first few years of life are a critical period for the creation of patterns of relationships? How else could we conceptualize it?

Secure and Insecure Attachments

All the theorists in this tradition share the assumption that the first attachment relationship is the most influential ingredient in the creation of the child's working model. Variations in that first attachment relationship are now almost universally described using Mary Ainsworth's category system (Ainsworth et al., 1978; Ainsworth & Wittig, 1969). She distinguishes between **secure attachment**

> **TABLE 11.1 Categorization of Secure and Insecure Attachment in Ainsworth's Strange Situation**
>
> **Securely attached.** Child shows low-to-moderate levels of proximity seeking to mother; does not avoid or resist contact if mother initiates it. When reunited with mother after absence, child greets her positively, or is easily soothed if upset. Clearly prefers mother to stranger.
>
> **Insecurely attached: detached/avoidant.** Child avoids contact with mother, especially at reunion after an absence. Does not resist mother's efforts to make contact, but does not seek much contact. Treats stranger and mother about the same throughout.
>
> **Insecurely attached: resistant/ambivalent.** Greatly upset when separated from mother, but mother cannot successfully comfort child when she returns. Child both seeks and avoids contact, at different times. May show anger toward mother at reunion, and resists both comfort from and contact with stranger.
>
> **Insecurely attached: disorganized/disoriented.** Dazed behavior, confusion, or apprehension. Child may show contradictory behavior patterns simultaneously, such as moving toward mother while keeping gaze averted.
>
> *Sources:* Ainsworth et al., 1978; Main & Solomon, 1990.

and two types of **insecure attachment,** which she has assessed using a procedure called the **Strange Situation.**

The Strange Situation consists of a series of episodes in a laboratory setting, typically used when the child is between 12 and 18 months of age. The child is first with the mother, then with the mother and a stranger, alone with the stranger, completely alone for a few minutes, reunited with the mother, left alone, and then reunited first with the stranger, and then the mother. Ainsworth suggested that children's reactions to this situation could be classified into three types: *securely attached, insecure/avoidant,* and *insecure/ambivalent* (also sometimes called *resistant*). Mary Main (Main & Solomon, 1990) has suggested a fourth group, which she calls *insecure/disorganized/disoriented.* I have listed some of the characteristics of the different types in Table 11.1.

Normally, roughly two-thirds of children are rated as securely attached. The probability that a child will be insecurely attached is much higher among children reared in poverty-level families, in families with a history of abuse, or in families in which the mother is diagnosed as seriously depressed (Cicchetti & Barnett, 1991; Spieker & Booth, 1988). A disorganized/disoriented pattern seems especially likely in families in which the parents had some unresolved trauma in their own childhoods, such as either abuse or their own parents' death (Main & Hesse, 1990).

The category system Ainsworth devised, and the theory that lies behind it, have prompted an enormous amount of research and new theory, much of it fascinating, and much of it with practical ramifications. So let me take some time to explore a few of the issues and implications.

Stability of Attachment Classification.   One of the key questions is whether the quality of the child's attachment is stable over time. Does a child who is securely or insecurely attached to his mother at 12 months still show the same quality of attachment at 24 or 36 months, or at school age? This is a partic-

CULTURES AND CONTEXTS
Secure and Insecure Attachments in Different Cultures

Studies in a variety of countries have pointed to the possibility that secure attachments may be more likely in certain cultures than others. The most thorough analyses have come from a Dutch psychologist, Marinus van IJzendoorn, who has examined the results of 32 separate studies in eight different countries. You can see the percentage of babies classified in each category for each country in the table below (van IJzendoorn & Kroonenberg, 1988).

CROSS-CULTURAL COMPARISONS OF SECURE AND INSECURE ATTACHMENTS

Country	Number of studies	Percentage of each attachment type		
		Secure	Avoidant	Ambivalent
West Germany	3	56.6	35.3	8.1
Great Britain	1	75.0	22.2	2.8
Netherlands	4	67.3	26.3	6.4
Sweden	1	74.5	21.6	3.9
Israel	2	64.4	6.8	28.8
Japan	2	67.7	5.2	27.1
China	1	50.0	25.0	25.0
United States	18	64.8	21.1	14.1
Overall Average		65.0	21.3	13.7

Source: Based on Table 1 of van IJzendoorn & Kroonenberg, 1988, pp. 150–151.

We need to be cautious about overinterpreting the information in this table, because in most cases there are only one or two studies from a given country, normally with quite small samples. The single study from China, for example, included only 36 babies. Still, the findings are thought-provoking.

The most striking thing about these data is actually their consistency. In each of the eight countries, a secure attachment is the most common pattern, found in more than half of all babies studied; in six of the eight, an avoidant pattern is the more common of the two forms of insecure attachment. Only in Israel and Japan is this pattern significantly reversed. How can we explain such differences?

One possibility is that the Strange Situation is simply not an appropriate measure of attachment security in all cultures. For example, because Japanese babies are rarely separated from their mothers in the first year of life, being left totally alone in the midst of the Strange Situation may be far more stressful for them, which might result in more intense, inconsolable crying and hence a classification of ambivalent attachment. The counter argument is that comparisons of toddlers' actual behavior in the Strange Situation suggest few cultural differences in such things as proximity seeking or avoidance of Mom, all of which gives us more confidence that the Strange Situation is tapping similar processes among children in many cultures (Sagi, van IJzendoorn, & Koren-Karie, 1991).

It is also possible that the *meaning* of a "secure" or "avoidant" pattern is different in different cultures, even if the percentages of each category are similar. German researchers, for example, have suggested that an insecure/avoidant classification in their culture may reflect not indifference by mothers, but explicit training toward greater independence in the baby (Grossmann et al., 1985).

On the other hand, research in Israel (Sagi, 1990) shows that the Strange Situation attachment classification predicts the baby's later social skills in much the same way as is found in United States samples, which suggests that the classification system is valid in both cultures.

At the moment, the most plausible hypothesis is that the same factors in mother-infant interaction contribute to secure and insecure attachments in all cultures, and that these patterns reflect similar internal models. But it will take more research like the Israeli work, in which the long-term outcomes of the various categories are studied, before we can be sure if this is correct.

ularly important question for those researchers and therapists who are concerned about the possible permanence of effects of early abuse or neglect or other sources of insecure attachment. Can children recover from such early treatment? And is an initially securely attached child permanently buffered from the effects of later difficult life circumstances?

The answer—as usual!—is yes and no. When the child's family environment or life circumstances are reasonably consistent, the security or insecurity of attachment does remain stable. For example, in a stable, middle-class sample, Mary Main and her colleagues (Main & Cassidy, 1988; Main, Kaplan, & Cassidy, 1985) found strong correlations between ratings of security of attachment at 18 months and at 6 years. But when the child's circumstances change in some major way— such as when she starts going to day care or nursery school, or Grandma comes to live with the family, or the parents divorce or move—the security of the child's attachment may change as well, either from secure to insecure, or the reverse. In poverty-level families, in which instability of circumstances is more common, changes in attachment security are also common.

The very fact that a child's security can change from one time to the next does not refute the notion of attachment as an internal working model. Bowlby suggested that for the first two or three years, the particular pattern of attachment a child shows is in some sense a property of each specific *relationship*. For example, recent studies of toddlers' attachments to mothers and fathers show that about 30 percent of the time the child is securely attached to one parent and insecurely attached to the other, with both possible combinations equally represented (Fox, Kimmerly, & Schafer, 1991). It is the quality of each relationship that determines the child's security in that pair. If that relationship changes markedly, the security of the baby's attachment to that individual may change too. But Bowlby argued that by age 4 or 5, the internal working model becomes more general, more a property of the *child*, more generalized across relationships, and thus more resistant to change. At that point, the child tends to impose it upon new relationships, including relationships with teachers or peers.

Thus a child may "recover" from an initially insecure attachment, or lose a secure one. But consistency over time is more typical, both because children's relationships tend to be reasonably stable for the first few years, and because once the internal model is clearly formed, it tends to perpetuate itself.

Origins of Secure and Insecure Attachments.   Where do these differences come from? For the development of a secure attachment, the common denominators seem to be both acceptance of the infant by the parents and *contingent responsiveness* from the parents to the infant (Isabella, 1993; Pederson et al., 1990). Contingent responsiveness does not just mean that the parents love the baby or take care of the baby well, but rather that in their caregiving and other behavior toward the child they are sensitive to the child's own cues and respond appropriately. They smile when the baby smiles, talk to the baby when he vocalizes, pick him up when he cries, and so on.

In contrast, mothers of babies rated as insecure/avoidant are likely to be "psychologically unavailable" to their infants (to use Alan Sroufe's phrase). Mothers may show such a withdrawn or neglecting pattern for a variety of reasons, but a common ingredient is depression in the mother—a phenomenon I talked about briefly in the real world box on page 318.

Infants rated as insecure/ambivalent are likely to have mothers who are inconsistent in their responses to the infant, rejecting the infant's bids for contact some of the time, responding positively at other times.

Long-Term Consequences of Secure and Insecure Attachments. Ainsworth's classification system has proven to be extremely helpful in predicting a remarkably wide range of other behaviors in children, both as toddlers and in later childhood. Dozens of studies show that children rated as securely attached to their mothers in infancy are later more sociable, more positive in their behavior toward others, including friends and siblings, less clinging and dependent on teachers, less aggressive and disruptive, more empathetic, and more emotionally mature in their approach to school and other nonhome settings (e.g., Frankel & Bates, 1990; Lyons-Ruth, Alpern, & Repacholi, 1993; Youngblade & Belsky, 1992).

Most of this research has been on preschool or early-elementary-school children, so we cannot say with certainty that these early effects persist longer than age 6 or 7. But in the one study I know of in which children with known early attachment histories have been followed as far as preadolescence, the pattern of findings is the same.

Alan Sroufe and his colleagues, in a study I described briefly in Chapter 1, have now followed 47 of the several hundred children in his larger sample up to ages 10 and 11 (Sroufe, 1989; Sroufe, Carlson, & Schulman, 1993; Urban et al., 1991). At that age, the children were observed during a specially designed summer camp. The counselors rated each child on a range of characteristics, and observers noted how often children spent time together or with the counselors. Naturally, neither the counselors nor the observers knew what the children's initial attachment classification had been. The findings are clear: those with histories of secure attachment were rated as more self-confident and as having more social competence. They complied more readily with counselor requests, expressed more positive emotions, and had a greater sense of their ability to accomplish things—something Bandura calls *self-efficacy* and Sroufe calls *agency*. They created more friendships, especially with other securely attached youngsters, and engaged in more complex activities when playing in groups. The majority of those with histories of insecure attachment showed some kind of deviant behavior pattern at age 11, such as isolation from peers, bizarre behavior, passivity, hyperactivity, or aggressiveness. Only a few of the originally securely attached children showed any of these patterns.

I should emphasize again that these 47 children are the only ones yet studied over this length of time, and it is risky to build too tall a theoretical edifice on such a small empirical foundation. But Sroufe's data fit very well with the results from studies of younger children as well as with newer studies that show links between adolescents' *current* attachment status (measured with an interview) and emotional health or effective functioning. Collectively the findings point to potentially long-term consequences of attachment patterns or internal working models of relationships constructed in the first year of life. But fluidity and change also occur, and we need to know much more about the factors that tend to maintain, or alter, the earliest models.

▶ Horizontal Relationships: The Child's Relationships with Other Children

Because most theories of social and personality development have strongly emphasized the centrality of parent-child interactions, until recently most psychologists thought of relationships with peers as much less important. But that view is now changing as it becomes clear that peer relationships play a unique and significant role in a child's development.

Developmental Changes in Peer Relationships

Infants and Preschoolers.   Children first begin to show some positive interest in other infants as early as 6 months of age. If you place two such babies on the floor facing each other, they will touch each other, pull each other's hair, reach for the other's clothing. By 10 months these behaviors are even more evident. Children this age apparently still prefer to play with objects, but will play with each other if no toys are available. By 14 to 18 months, we begin to see two or more children playing together with toys— occasionally cooperating together, but more often simply playing side by side with different toys, a pattern often called *parallel play*. Babies are *interested* in one another. They gaze at other babies, smile, make noises at each other. But it isn't until around 18 months that we begin to see much coordinated play, such as when one toddler chases another, or one imitates the other's action with some toy. At about this same age, babies also begin to show the first signs of playmate preferences as well (Brownell & Brown, 1992), even some signs of individual friendships. For example, Carollee Howes (1983; 1987) noted that children this young showed consistent preferences for one or more playmates over a full-year period in a day-care center. Still, these early peer interactions are still quite primitive. Most of the time, toddlers ignore one another's bids for interaction, and when they play together it is mostly around common toys.

These 2-year-olds are playing next to each other, but they are not playing *with* each other—a pattern sometimes called *parallel play*.

By 3 or 4, children appear to prefer to play with peers rather than alone and their play with one another is much more cooperative and coordinated. We see various forms of group pretend play, much of it already organized along gender lines (Hartup, 1992). And friendships become clearer and somewhat more stable as well. Robert Hinde and his co-workers (1985) defined as friends any pair of children who spent at least a third of their playtime next to one another. By this criterion, only about 20 percent of a group of 3½ year-olds showed signs of a stable friendship; by age 4, half of these same children regularly played this often with one child. To be sure, these early friendships are based more on sheer proximity and shared play interests than is true of friendships among older children, but some kind of consistent preference is already visible at this early age.

School Age.   Peers become even more important among school-age children. The vertical relationships with parents or teachers obviously don't disappear, but playing with other kids is what 7-, 8-, 9-, or 10-year-old children prefer. Such activities—along with watching TV—take up virtually all children's time when they are not in school, eating, or sleeping (Timmer, Eccles, & O'Brien, 1985).

Shared play interests continue to form the major basis of these school-age peer relationships. Furthermore, kids this age *define* play groups in terms of common activities, rather than in terms of common attitudes or values. You can see this pattern in Figure 11.3, which shows the results of a study by Susan O'Brien & Karen Bierman (1988). They asked fifth-, eighth-, and eleventh-grade subjects to tell them about the different groups of kids that hang around together at their school, and then to say how they could tell that a particular bunch was "a group." For the fifth graders, the single best criterion of "a group" was that the kids did things together. For eighth graders, shared attitudes and common appearance became much more important.

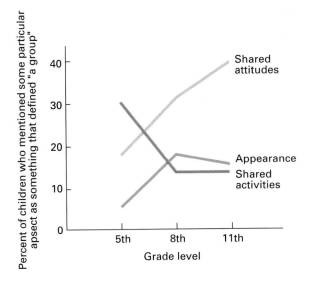

Figure 11.3
O'Brien and Bierman's results illustrate the change between elementary and high school in children's ideas about what defines "a group" of peers. (*Source:* O'Brien & Bierman, 1988, Table 1, p. 1363.)

I'll be talking much more about the child's *understanding* of social relationships and processes in the next chapter, but let me just point out here that this "concreteness" in the elementary-school child's view of peers is entirely consistent with what I've already told you about the character of the self-concept in children this same age, and with some of Piaget's ideas about the thinking of a concrete operational child.

Beyond the centrality of shared activities, the most striking thing about peer group interactions in the elementary-school years is how sex-segregated they are, a pattern that appears to exist in every culture in the world (Harkness & Super, 1985). Boys play with boys, girls play with girls, each in their own areas and at their own kinds of games. There are some ritualized "boundary violations" between these separate territories, such as chasing games (e.g., "You can't catch me, nyah nyah," followed by chasing accompanied by screaming by the girls) (Thorne, 1986). But on the whole, girls and boys actively avoid interacting with one another. Given a forced choice between playing with a child of the opposite gender, or a child of a different race, researchers have found that elementary-school-age children will make the cross-race choice rather than the cross-gender choice (Maccoby & Jacklin, 1987).

Friendships in this age range are naturally also sex-segregated. In one study, parents reported that about a quarter of the friendships of their 5- and 6-year-olds but *none* of the friendships of their 7-and 8-year-olds were cross-sex (Gottman, 1986).

School-age children spend more time with their friends than do preschoolers, and they gradually develop a larger collection of individual friendships. Second graders name about four friends each, while seventh graders name about seven (Reisman & Shorr, 1978). Their behavior within these relationships is quite different than what they display with strangers, but I suspect the differences are not

These 12-year-old pals are likely to have quite a different form of relationship than would same-age boys—less competitive and more compliant with one another.

quite what you would predict: Children are more *polite* to strangers or nonfriends. With chums they are more open with one another, which means not only that they exchange supportive comments, but also that they are more critical toward one another than toward strangers.

There are also intriguing differences in the quality of relationship in boys' and girls' friendships in these years. Waldrop and Halverson (1975) refer to boys' relationships as *extensive* and to girls' relationships as *intensive*; boys' friendship groups are larger and are more accepting of newcomers than are girls'. Boy friends play more outdoors, and roam over a larger area in their play. Girl friends are more likely to play in pairs or in smaller, more exclusive groups, and they spend more playtime indoors or near home or school (Gottman, 1986).

At the level of actual interaction we also see sex differences. Boys' groups and boys' friendships appear to be focused more on competition and dominance than are girls' friendships. In fact, among school-age boys, we see *higher* levels of competition between pairs of friends than between strangers, which is the opposite of what we see among girls. Friendships between girls also include more agreement, more compliance, and more self-disclosure than is true for boys. For example, Leaper (1991) finds that "controlling" speech—a category that includes rejecting comments, ordering, manipulating or challenging, defiance or refutation, or resisting the other's attempt to control—is twice as common in 7- and 8-year-old male friend pairs as among female pairs. Among the 4- and 5-year-olds in this study there were no sex differences in controlling speech.

None of this should obscure the fact that there are great similarities in the interactions of male and female friendship pairs in the years of middle childhood. As one example, collaborative and cooperative exchanges are the most common forms of communication among both boys and girls. Neither should we necessarily conclude that boys' friendships are less important to them than are girls'. Nonetheless, it seems clear that there are differences in form and style that may well have enduring implications for the patterns of friendship over the full life span.

Adolescents. Many of these patterns change at adolescence. Mixed-sex groups begin to appear; conformity to the peer group values and behaviors increases and parents' influence on the child wanes (even while the attachment to the parents remains strong). Teenagers spend more than half their waking hours with other teenagers, and less than 5 percent of their time with either parent. Of the roughly 40 percent of their hours that can be counted as leisure time, they spend two-fifths socializing with friends, most of that time talking (Csikszentmihalyi & Larson, 1984). And these friendships have become increasingly intimate, in the sense that adolescent friends share more and more of their inner feelings and secrets, and are more knowledgeable about each other's feelings. Loyalty and faithfulness become more valued characteristics of friendship.

But beyond these changes in individual relationships, the *function* of the peer group changes in adolescence. In elementary school, peer groups are mostly the setting for mutual play, and for all the learning about relationships and the natural world that is part of such play. But the teenager uses the peer group in another way. He is struggling to make a slow transition from the protected life of the family to the independent life of adulthood, and the peer group becomes the *vehi-*

cle for that transition. As Erikson pointed out, the clannishness and intense conformity to the group is a normal— even an essential—part of the process.

Such conformity seems to peak at about age 13 or 14 (at about the same time that we see a drop in self-esteem, as you'll recall from Chapter 10) and then wanes as the teenager begins to arrive at a sense of identity that is more independent of the peer group. For example, Thomas Berndt (1979) has found that among adolescents, the 12-to-14-year-olds are the most likely to say they would be influenced by their peers to do such mildly antisocial activities as soaping someone's windows on Halloween.

Lest you think that all 13- and 14-year-olds run amok with their peers, I should point out that most experts today have concluded that for the great majority of teenagers, peers have far less influence than we had believed (Berndt, 1992). That is not to say that there is no effect. It takes only a trip to the local high school to see the conformity to specific dress or hair customs to be persuaded of the influence. But let us remember that adolescents *choose* their friends, their crowd. And they are likely to choose to associate with a group that shares their values, attitudes, and behaviors. If the discrepancy between their own ideas and their friends' becomes too great, teens are more likely to move toward a more compatible group of friends than to be persuaded to shift toward the first group's values or behaviors. Furthermore, teenagers report that when explicit peer pressure is exerted, it is more likely to be *against* misconduct than toward it (Brown, Clasen, & Eicher, 1986). Thus while peer influence is stronger in these adolescent years than at other times, for most teens the effect is not enormous.

Can you make any reasonable guesses about what qualities would characterize teenagers who are most and least susceptible to peer pressure? Temperamental qualities? Intellectual skills? Attachment history?

Changes in Peer Group Structure in Adolescence.   The structure of the peer group also changes over the years of adolescence. The now-classic early study is Dunphy's observation of the formation, dissolution, and interaction of teenage groups in a high school in Sydney, Australia, between 1958 and 1960 (Dunphy, 1963). He identified two important subvarieties of groups, using labels that have become widespread in writing on adolescence. The first type, which Dunphy called **cliques,** are made up of four to six young people who appear to be strongly attached to one another. Cliques have strong cohesiveness and high levels of intimate sharing. In the early years of adolescence, these cliques are almost entirely same-sex groups—a residual of the preadolescent pattern. Gradually, however, the cliques combine into larger sets Dunphy called **crowds,** made up of several cliques, some male and some female. Finally, the crowd breaks down again

What stage of teen group formation do you think this represents?

into heterosexual cliques, and finally into loose associations of couples. In Dunphy's study, the period of the fully developed crowd was roughly between ages 13 and 15—the very years when we see the greatest conformity to peer pressure.

Not all current observers of teenage peer groups agree with Dunphy that the crowd is made up simply of a collection of cliques. Bradford Brown (1990), for example, uses the term *crowd* to refer to the "reputation-based" group with which a young person is identified, either by choice or by peer designation. Groups with labels (in the United States, at least) like *jocks, brains, nerds, punks, radicals, normals,* or *populars* are crowds in Brown's sense of the term. Cliques, in contrast, are always groups that the individual teenager chooses. But Brown would agree with Dunphy that in early adolescence, cliques are almost entirely same-sex; by late adolescence they have become mixed in gender.

Within any given school, these various cliques and reputation groups are organized into a clear, widely understood pecking order. Individual cliques may even have specific territory, such as a particular table in the lunchroom where they always sit. Among students in the seventh, eighth, and ninth grades in the United States—the years when cliques are most dominant in the social hierarchy of adolescence—the highest-status cliques/crowds are made up of boys who play sports (often called *jocks*) and girls who are cheerleaders, although there are schools in which more scholastically oriented groups, or those with other shared interests, also have some social standing.

Whatever labels are applied, and whatever specific clique or crowd a teenager may identify with, there is agreement among theorists that the peer group performs the highly important function of helping the teenager make the shift from unisexual to heterosexual social relationships. The 13- or 14-year-old can begin to try out her new relationship skills in the somewhat protected environment of the crowd or clique; only after some confidence is developed do we see the beginnings of dating and later of more committed heterosexual pair relationships, a pattern clear in the data in Table 11.2, which shows the age of the first date in a

TABLE 11.2	Age at First Date Among United States Adolescents (in percentages)	
Age	Males	Females
13 or younger	21.2	8.6
14	17.9	16.2
15	21.2	33.6
16	29.5	29.3
17–18	7.2	10.0

Source: Thornton, 1990,

Table 1, pp. 246–247.

THE REAL WORLD
Homosexuality Among Adolescents

I have talked about the normal sequence of peer relationships in adolescence as moving gradually toward committed heterosexual partnerships. But of course heterosexual experience is not the only kind teenagers may have. Homosexual contact is also fairly common, especially for boys and especially in childhood or early adolescence. Research on homosexuality in teenagers is not abundant, but indicates that perhaps 15 percent of boys and 10 percent of girls have at least one homosexual contact; 2 to 3 percent report continuing homosexual relationships (Dreyer, 1982). Among adults, homosexuality appears to characterize 4 to 6 percent of the population in Western countries (for which we have the best data), although estimates vary widely (Gonsiorek & Weinrich, 1991).

Recent evidence has strengthened the hypothesis that homosexuality may be built in, either genetically or through hormone patterning *in utero.* Most convincing is a recent twin study by Bailey and Pillard (1991). In this sample, when one twin was homosexual the probability that the second twin was also homosexual was 52 percent among identical twins, but only 22 percent among fraternal twins. By comparison, the equivalent "concordance rate" was only 11 percent among pairs of biologically unrelated boys adopted into the same families.

Such biological evidence does not mean that there are no environmental causes of homosexuality. No behavior is entirely controlled by either nature or nurture, as I have said many times.

At the very least, we know that nearly half the identical twins in the Bailey and Pillard study did *not* share the same sexual preferences. Something beyond biology must be at work, although we do not yet know what environmental factors may be involved.

Whatever the cause, homosexual teenagers are a minority. These adolescents face high levels of prejudice and stereotyping, and are at high risk for a variety of problems. In one study, for example, four-fifths of homosexual teens interviewed in Minneapolis had deteriorating school performance, and more than a quarter dropped out of high school (Remafedi, 1987a). They must also cope with the decision about whether to "come out" about their homosexuality. Those who do come out are far more likely to tell peers than parents, although there is a risk attached to the decision to tell peers. In his Minneapolis study, Remafedi found that 41 percent of homosexual male youths had lost a friend over the issue (Remafedi, 1987b), and many experience harassment from peers. Some research suggests that as many as two-thirds of homosexual youth have not told their parents (Rotheram-Borus, Rosario, & Koopman, 1991).

There is obviously much that we do not know about homosexual adolescents. But it is a reasonable hypothesis that the years of adolescence may be particularly stressful for this subgroup. Like ethnic-minority youth, homosexual teens have an additional task facing them in forming a clear identity.

---

large sample of Detroit teenagers (Thornton, 1990). The majority did not begin dating until 15 or 16, which is after the point of maximum dominance of the crowd.

Prosocial Behavior and Aggression

This broad sketch of peer relationships from toddlerhood through adolescence makes clear the various roles that peers play in children's development over these years, and how central such relationships are. What it does not convey is some of the changes in the actual content or quality of children's peer interactions. To fill in some of the gaps, let me say just a word or two about the two ends of the positive/negative continuum, namely prosocial behavior and aggression.

Prosocial Behavior.   This class of behavior is defined by psychologists as "intentional, voluntary behavior intended to benefit another" (Eisenberg, 1992, p. 3). In everyday language, this is essentially what we mean by **altruism,** and it changes with age, just as other aspects of peer behavior change.

We first see such **prosocial behaviors** in children of about 2 or 3—at about the same time that they begin to show real interest in play with other children. They will offer to help another child who is hurt, offer a toy, or try to comfort another person (Marcus, 1986; Zahn-Waxler & Radke-Yarrow, 1982). As I pointed out in Chapter 7, children this young have only a beginning understanding of the fact that others feel differently from themselves, but they obviously understand enough about the emotions of others to respond in supportive and sympathetic ways when they see other children or adults hurt or sad.

Past these early years, there are a number of trends. Older children are more likely to share objects or money with others (such as donating marbles in the game I described in Chapter 9). School-age children and adolescents are also more likely than are preschoolers to provide physical and verbal assistance to someone in need (Eisenberg, 1992). But not all prosocial behaviors show this pattern. Comforting another child, for example, may be more common among preschool and early-elementary-school children than at older ages (Eisenberg, 1988; 1990).

At any age, children vary a lot in the amount of altruistic behavior they show. For those of you interested in knowing more about how helpful or altruistic children come to be that way, I've explored some of the research in the box on page 337.

Aggression.   If you have watched children together, you know that all is not sweetness and light in the land of the young. Children do support and share with their friends, and they do show affectionate and helpful behaviors toward one another, but they also tease, fight, yell, criticize, and argue over objects and territory. Researchers who have studied this more negative side of children's interactions have looked mostly at **aggression,** which we can define as behavior with the apparent intent to injure some other person or object (Feshbach, 1970).

Every child shows at least some aggression, but the form and frequency of aggression change over the years of childhood. When 2- or 3-year-old children are upset or frustrated, they are more likely to throw things or hit each other. As their verbal skills improve, however, there is a shift away from such overt physical aggression toward greater use of verbal aggression, such as taunting or name-calling. In the elementary-school and adolescent years, physical aggression becomes still less common, and children learn the cultural rules about when and how much it is acceptable to display anger or aggression. In most cultures, this means that anger is more and more disguised, and aggression more and more controlled with increasing age (Underwood, Coie, & Herbsman, 1992).

One interesting exception to this general pattern is that in all-boy pairs or groups, at least in United States studies, physical aggression seems to remain both relatively high and constant over the years of childhood (Cairns et al., 1989). Indeed, at every age, boys show more aggression and more assertiveness than do girls, both within friendship pairs and in general. Table 11.3 gives some highly representative data from a very large, careful survey in Canada (Offord, Boyle, & Racine, 1991) in which both parents and teachers completed checklists describing each child's behavior. In the table I've listed only the information provided by teachers, but parent ratings yielded parallel findings. It is clear that boys are described as far more aggressive on nearly any measure.

It seems inescapable that there is at least some biological basis for this sex difference. Similar sex differences occur in all human societies and in all primates, and there appears to be at least some hormonal link to levels of testosterone (Maccoby & Jacklin, 1974). So boys are doubtless more inclined toward aggression from the beginning. But nurture as well as nature is surely involved. You will

THE REAL WORLD
Rearing Helpful and Altruistic Children

If you wish to encourage your own children to be more generous or altruistic, here are some specific things you can do, based on the work of Eisenberg (1992) and others:

1. *Create a loving and warm family climate.* This is especially effective if such warmth is combined with clear explanations.

2. *Explain why and give rules.* Clear rules about what *to* do as well as what *not* to do are important. Explaining the consequences of the child's action in terms of its effects on others is also good; for example: "If you hit Susan it will hurt her." Equally important is stating *positive* rules or guidelines; for example: "It's always good to be helpful to other people," or "We should share what we have with people who don't have so much."

3. *Provide prosocial attributions.* Attribute your child's helpful or altruistic action to the child's own internal character: "You're such a helpful child!" or "You certainly do a lot of nice things for other people." This strategy begins to be effective with children at about age 7 or 8, at about the same time that they are beginning to develop global notions of self-esteem. In this way you may be able to affect the child's self-scheme.

4. *Have children do helpful things.* Children can help cook, take care of pets, make toys to give away, teach younger siblings or tutor in school, and so forth. This can backfire if the coercion required to get the child to do the helpful thing is too strong: the child may now attribute his "good" behavior to the coercion ("Mother made me do it"), rather than to some inner trait of his own ("I am a helpful/kind person"), and no future altruism is fostered.

5. *Model thoughtful and generous behavior.* Stating the rules clearly will do little good if your own behavior does not match what you say!

remember from Chapter 10, for example, that fathers and mothers begin to reinforce sex-stereotyped toy choice and behavior in their children at very early ages, and that this is particularly true of sons.

At the same time, it is also true that the same family forces appear to foster high levels of aggression in both boys and girls. Highly aggressive children—male or female—are most likely to come from families that display inconsistent discipline, rejection of the child, harsh punishment, and lack of parental supervision (Eron, Huesmann, & Zelli, 1991). Thus while the *rate* of aggression differs between the sexes, the family dynamic that contributes to it does not.

TABLE 11.3 Percentage of Boys and Girls Aged 4 to 11 Rated by Their Teachers as Displaying Each Type of Aggressive Behavior		
Behavior	**Boys**	**Girls**
Mean to others	21.8	9.6
Physically attacks people	18.1	4.4
Gets in many fights	30.9	9.8
Destroys own things	10.7	2.1
Destroys others' things	10.6	4.4
Threatens to hurt people	13.1	4.0

Source: Offord, Boyle, & Racine, 1991, from Table 2.3, p. 39.

▶ Individual Differences in Peer Relationships

Collectively children may move toward greater and greater ability to interact effectively with their peers, toward greater altruism and away from overt expression of aggression, toward greater intimacy in their relationships with peers. But there are clearly enormous differences in the degree to which children acquire such skills, or in the degree to which they express themselves with overt aggression. In recent years, the study of such individual differences in social skills and popularity has been one of the hottest topics in all of developmental psychology. Researchers have struggled to understand why some children are rejected by their peers, while others are not.

Popularity and Rejection

Psychologists who study popularity (and unpopularity) in children have recently concluded that it is important to make a distinction between several subgroups of unpopular children. The most frequently studied are those children who are overtly *rejected* by peers. If you ask children to list peers they would *not* like to play with, or if you observe which children are avoided on the playground, you can get a measure of rejection of this type. A second type has come to be called *neglected*. Children in this category are reasonably well liked, but lack individual friends and are rarely chosen as most preferred by their peers. Neglected children have been studied far less than have the rejected, but the preliminary evidence suggests that while neglect is much less stable over time than is rejection, neglected children are nonetheless more prone to depression and loneliness than are accepted children (Cillessen et al., 1992; Rubin et al., 1991).

Where might such differences in popularity or peer acceptance come from?

Qualities of Rejected and Popular Children.   Some of the characteristics that differentiate popular and unpopular children are things outside a child's control. In particular, attractive children and physically larger children are more likely to be popular—perhaps merely a continuation of the preference for attractive faces that Langlois detected in young infants and that I described in Chapter 5. The most crucial ingredient, though, is not how the child looks but how the child behaves.

Popular children behave in positive, supporting, nonpunitive, and nonaggressive ways toward most other children. They explain things, and take their playmates' wishes into consideration. Rejected children are aggressive, disruptive, and uncooperative. To be sure, not all aggressive children are rejected. It is when they *also* lack compensating positive social skills that they are most likely to be overtly rejected by their peers (Black, 1992; Coie & Cillessen, 1993; Denham & Holt, 1993; Newcomb, Bukowski, & Pattee, 1993).

This conclusion emerges from a variety of types of research, including at least a few cross-cultural studies. Aggression and disruptive behavior is linked to rejection and unpopularity among Chinese children as well as American children, for example (Chen, Rubin, & Sun, 1992). Among the best sources of evidence, however, are studies in which groups of previously unacquainted children are brought together to play for some number of hours, over several weeks. At the end of these sessions, the children pick their favorite and least-favorite playmates from among the group. Since the researchers have observed the actual behavior of the

---

Do you think it is a reasonable hypothesis that neglected children are likely to have been insecurely attached as infants? How could you test such a hypothesis?

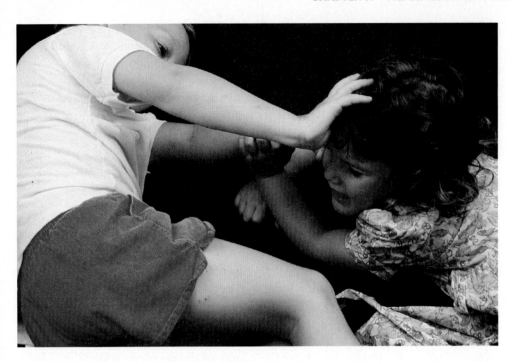

If Christopher is this aggressive with his peers, and not just with his sister (as shown here), he is likely to be rejected by other children, a pattern with potential long-term consequences.

children throughout the sessions, they can link the child's behavior with his or her later popularity. In these studies, children who are most consistently positive and supportive are those who end up being chosen as leaders or as friends. Those who consistently participate in conflicts are more often rejected.

Rejected children also seem to have quite different internal working models of relationships and of aggression from those of popular children. In a whole series of studies, Kenneth Dodge has shown that aggressive/rejected children are much more likely to see aggression as a useful way to solve problems. They are also much more likely to interpret someone else's behavior as hostile or attacking than is true for less-aggressive or more-popular children. Given an ambiguous event, such as being hit in the back with a ball, aggressive or rejected children— especially boys—are much more likely to assume that the ball was thrown on purpose, and to then retaliate. In turn, such retaliation is likely to elicit hostility from others, further confirming their expectation that other people are hostile to them (Dodge et al., 1990; Dodge & Frame, 1982; Quiggle et al., 1992).

This body of research can also be linked to Gerald Patterson's work, whose model I described in Chapter 1 (Figure 1.2, p. 12) and in Chapter 9. Patterson is persuaded that a child's excess aggressiveness can be traced originally to ineffective parental control. But once the child's aggressiveness is well established, the child displays this same behavior with peers, is rejected by those peers, and is then driven more and more toward the only set of peers who will accept him, usually other aggressive or delinquent youngsters.

The seriousness of this set of connected problems is amply demonstrated in a growing body of research showing that rejection by one's peers in elementary school is one of the very few aspects of childhood functioning that consistently predicts behavior problems or emotional disturbances in adolescence and adulthood (Dishion, 1990; Eron, 1987; Farrington, 1991; Serbin et al., 1991).

For example, Janis Kupersmidt and John Coie (1990), in a study of a small group of fifth graders who were followed to the end of high school, report that negative outcomes in high school—including poor school performance, regular truancy, dropping out of school, or juvenile court appearance—were considerably more common among rejected children than among the popular.

In a 22-year longitudinal study, Leonard Eron has found that aggressiveness toward peers (and its accompanying peer rejection) at age 8 was related to various forms of aggressiveness at age 30, including "criminal behavior, number of moving traffic violations, convictions for driving while intoxicated, aggressiveness toward spouses, and how severely the subjects punished their own children" (Eron, 1987, p. 439). There are obviously several ways we could explain such a link between early unpopularity and later behavior problems. Early problems with peers might be merely the most visible reflection of a general maladjustment that later manifests itself as delinquency or emotional disturbance. It could also mean that a failure to develop friendships itself causes problems that later become more general. Or it could signify a seriously warped internal working model of relationships, or all of the above. Whatever the source of the problem, you will be glad to know that not all rejected children remain rejected or develop serious behavior problems or delinquency. The worst long-term prognosis is for those children who are rejected over a period of years; the best is for those who also show some altruistic or prosocial behavior in addition to aggression (Tremblay, 1991).

Sex Differences

As a final word in this long and complex chapter, let me make a couple of additional brief points about a topic I have only touched on as we have gone along, namely sex differences in social behavior. First, in many obvious ways, there are fewer sex differences in children's behavior than our cultural stereotypes might lead us to expect. The most consistent difference is in the area of aggression/dominance/competitiveness, which *is* consistent with gender stereotypes. Boys do indeed show more of all of these behaviors, beginning at an early age. But contrary to most expectations, there is little sign that girls are consistently more nurturant or dependent on others, or more compliant to adults' wishes. Girls are also not more sociable; they do not, for example, have more friends than boys do.

But at a subtler level, we are beginning to understand that there are important differences in the *ways* boys and girls go about interacting with one another. I've already mentioned several of the bits of information that point us toward this conclusion, but let me pull them together for you:

- Pairs of boy friends are *more* competitive with each other than are pairs of strangers.
- Aggression between boys does not decline over the years of elementary school, while aggression between girls, and between boys and girls, does drop.
- Friendships between girls are much more intimate, with much more self-disclosure.

– Boy friends are more likely to gather in large groups than in paired chumships, and the boys are less likely to exchange confidences and more likely to engage in some mutual activity, such as sports.

We also have a variety of indications that the same differences in style of relationship are evident in adults, with adult women continuing to describe more-intimate friendships than do men, and with women continuing to focus their attention in groups or pairs on actions that tend to keep the interaction going. Men are more likely to be task-oriented, women to be relationship-oriented.

Eleanor Maccoby (1990) describes the girls'/women's pattern as an *enabling style*. Enabling includes such behaviors as supporting the partner, expressing agreement, making suggestions. All these behaviors tend to foster a greater equality and intimacy in the relationship and keep the interaction going. In contrast, boys and men are more likely to show what Maccoby calls a *constricting* or *restrictive* style. "A restrictive style is one that tends to derail the interaction—to inhibit the partner or cause the partner to withdraw, thus shortening the interaction or bringing it to an end" (Maccoby, 1990, p. 517). Contradicting, interrupting, boasting, or other forms of self-display are all aspects of this style. Campbell Leaper (1991) labels these two styles *cooperative* and *domineering*, which conveys much the same message. These are subtle but profound differences and we still know little about how they arise in earliest childhood and whether equivalent differences occur across cultures. "If we are to adapt ourselves successfully to the rapid changes in the roles and relationships of the two sexes that are occurring in modern societies" (Maccoby, 1990, p. 519), we obviously need to know a great deal more about these apparently pervasive gender differences.

Do your observations of adult relationships match the distinction Maccoby is making here? What do you think happens when one man and one woman interact in some non-romantic encounter? Is the resulting style some combination of enabling and constricting, or does one style dominate?

▶ Summary

1. Both vertical relationships with adults and horizontal relationships with peers are of central significance in the child's social development. In particular, skills in forming and maintaining reciprocal relationships can only be learned with peers.

2. It is important to distinguish between an affectional bond (an enduring tie to a uniquely viewed partner) and an attachment, which involves the element of security and a safe base.

3. An attachment is deduced from the existence of attachment behaviors.

4. For the parents to form a strong bond to the infant, what is most crucial is the learning and repetition of mutually reinforcing and interlocking attachment behaviors, and not immediate contact at birth.

5. Fathers as well as mothers form strong bonds to their infants, but fathers show more physically playful behaviors with their children than do mothers.

6. Initially the infant shows attachment behaviors toward nearly anyone but no preferential attachment. By 5 to 6 months of age, most infants have formed at least one strong attachment, usually to the major caregiver.

7. Attachment behaviors become less visible during the preschool years except when the child is stressed. By age 4 or 5 the child understands the constancy of the relationship.

8. The basic attachment to the parents remains strong in adolescence, despite an increase in parent-child conflict, the greater independence of the teenager, and the greater impact of the peer group.

9. Children differ in the security of their first attachments, and thus in the internal working model they develop. The secure infant uses the parent as a safe base for exploration and can be readily consoled by the parent.

10. The security of the initial attachment is reasonably stable and is fostered by contingent responsiveness and acceptance by the parent.

11. Securely attached children appear to be more socially skillful, more curious and persistent in approaching new tasks, and more mature.

12. Children's relationships with peers become increasingly significant for their social development past the age of about 2. In elementary school, peer interactions are focused mostly on common activities; in adolescence, peer groups also become the vehicle for the transition from dependence to independence. The peer group is maximally influential at about ages 12 to 14.

13. By age 4 or 5 most children have formed individual friendships, and show preferential positive behavior toward friends. Friendship becomes more common, and more stable, in the elementary-school years, and more intimate in adolescence.

14. Prosocial behavior, such as helpfulness or generosity, is apparent as early as age 2 or 3, and generally increases throughout childhood.

15. Young children also show such negative social patterns as aggressiveness. Physical aggression peaks at 3 or 4, and is replaced more and more by verbal aggression among older children. Boys show more aggressiveness at every age.

16. Popularity among peers, in elementary school or later, is most consistently based on the amount of positive and supportive social behavior shown by a child toward peers.

17. Rejected children are typically those who show heightened levels of aggression toward peers and lack social skills. Such children appear to have different internal working models than do nonrejected children. They are also at much higher risk for later behavior problems such as delinquency.

18. Boys and girls appear to have quite different styles of interacting with one another, with girls' pairs or groups showing a more "enabling" style.

▶ Key Terms

affectional bond (315)

aggression (336)

altruism (335)

attachment (315)

attachment behavior (315)

clique (333)

crowd (333)

insecure attachment (325)

internal working model (325)

prosocial behavior (335)

secure attachment (325)

Strange Situation (325)

▶ Suggested Readings

Bretherton, I. (1992). The origins of attachment theory: John Bowlby and Mary Ainsworth. *Developmental Psychology, 28,* 759–775.

A clear, current, thoughtful review of both Bowlby's and Ainsworth's ideas, including new data from anthropology and other cross-cultural analyses.

Dunn, J. (1993). *Young children's close relationships.* Newbury Park, CA: Sage.

A wonderful small book, written in a clear and engaging style by one of the experts on children's social relationships.

Eisenberg, N. (1992). *The caring child.* Cambridge, MA: Harvard University Press.

A brief, clear, current summary of what we know about the development of prosocial and altruistic behavior.

Hartup, W. W. (1989). Social relationships and their developmental significance. *American Psychologist, 44,* 120–126.

Hartup has always been one of my favorite authors. His style is clear, his ideas interesting. Here he gives a brief review of some of the current work on social interactions.

Lickona, T. (1983). *Raising good children.* Toronto: Bantam Books.

One of the very best "how to" books for parents I have ever seen, with excellent, concrete advice as well as theory. His emphasis is on many of the issues I raised in the real world box on rearing altruistic children.

Tannen, D. (1990). *You just don't understand.* New York: William Morrow.

If you are at all interested in differences between women's and men's conversational and interactive styles, this book is a *must* read. I found it fascinating, and I learned a lot that has been a great help.

12

THINKING ABOUT RELATIONSHIPS: THE DEVELOPMENT OF SOCIAL COGNITION

Some General Principles and Issues
- **The Cognitive Side of Social Cognition**
- **The Social Side of Social Cognition**
  - *Research Report: The Link Between a Child's Popularity and His Ability to Read Others' Intentions or Emotions*

Thinking About Other People: Feelings and Qualities
- **Reading Others' Feelings**
- **Describing Other People**

Thinking About Relationships

Thinking About What People *Ought* to Do
- **Kohlberg's Stages of Moral Development**

Eisenberg's Model of Prosocial Reasoning
Gilligan's Ethic of Caring

Social Cognition and Behavior
- *The Real World: Application of Kohlberg's Theory to Education*

Social Cognition and General Cognitive Development

Summary

Key Terms

Suggested Readings

Think for a minute about the conversations you have with your friends. Haven't you said things like "I thought Jack was my friend, but now it turns out I can't really trust him," or "I've been trying to figure Jane out. Sometimes she's shy and sometimes she's the life of the party," or "Lots of people believe that I'm really the confident person I look like on the outside, but my friends know how insecure I really am"?

All of these statements reflect some aspect of what psychologists have come to call **social cognition**—thinking about people, what they do and should do, how they feel. If you are anything like I am (and I assume you are) then you, too, spend a great deal of time and energy analyzing other people, trying to under-

344

stand, trying to predict what your friends, partner, or co-workers will do. In fact, in our everyday life, knowledge about people and relationships is probably more important than many of the more abstract kinds of knowledge or thinking I talked about in Chapters 6 and 7. Where does such social knowledge come from? How does children's thinking about people, about relationships, about right and wrong, change over time?

These questions are not new in this book. I have touched on many facets of social cognition as I have gone along. The infant's emerging ability to recognize individuals and to use facial expressions and other body cues for social referencing is one kind of social cognition, as is the development of a theory of others' minds. One could also argue that the proposed "internal working model" of attachment is a kind of social cognition, as is the child's self-scheme. What I need to do now is to pull these various threads together, and describe some of the more general ideas about social cognition that have been emerging in the past few years. In the process, I hope to build a few bridges between what have been separate discussions of thinking and social relationships.

▶ Some General Principles and Issues

As you might imagine, researchers and theorists have approached questions about social cognition from two different directions—from studies of cognition, and from studies of social interaction.

The Cognitive Side of Social Cognition

One way to think about social cognition is simply to conceive of it as the application of general cognitive processes or skills to a different topic, in this case people or relationships. In Chapter 7, I talked about all the ways in which children's thinking changes from infancy through adolescence. We might assume that at any given age a child applies these fundamental ways of thinking to her relationships as well as to objects. In this view, the child's understanding of self and others, of social relationships, reflects or is based on her overall level of cognitive development, such as her level of perspective-taking skills (Selman, 1980).

This way of looking at social cognition has a powerful intuitive appeal. After all, as John Flavell (1985) points out , it is the same head doing the thinking when a child works on a conservation problem and when she tries to understand people. Furthermore, as you will see very clearly as we go through the evidence, many of the same principles that seem to apply to general cognitive development hold here as well, such as the following:

- *Outer to inner characteristics.* Younger children pay attention to the surface of things, to what they look like; older children look for principles, for causes.
- *Observation to inference.* Young children base their conclusions initially only on what they can see or feel; later they make inferences about what ought to be, or what might be.
- *Definite to qualified.* Young children's "rules" are very definite and fixed (such as sex-role rules); by adolescence, rules begin to be qualified.
- *Observer's view to general view.* Children also become less "egocentric" with time—less tied to their own individual view, more able to construct a model of some experience or some process that is true for everyone.

All of these dimensions of change describe children's emerging social cognition, just as they describe the development of thinking about objects. But to reduce social cognition merely to such general principles is to ignore some critical differences.

The Social Side of Social Cognition

The most obvious difference is that people, as objects of thought, are simply not the same as rocks or beakers of water or balls of clay. Among many other things, people behave *intentionally*, and they can reveal or conceal information about themselves. In fact, learning to "read" other people is one of the key social-cognitive skills, as is grasping the possibility of concealment or misleading cues and taking this into account. Further, unlike relationships with objects, relationships with people are mutual and reciprocal. Other people talk back, respond to your distress, offer things, get angry.

Children also have to learn special rules that apply to social interactions, such as politeness rules, or rules about when you can and cannot speak, or about power or dominance hierarchies, all forms of social *scripts* (Schank & Abelson, 1977)—a concept I have mentioned several times before. Children presumably learn these scripts from their own experience, developing strong expectations about how people will behave, in what order, in which settings. Furthermore, these scripts probably change with age not just because children's cognitive skills change, but also simply because the rules (scripts) themselves change as children move from one social setting to another. One obvious example is the set of changes that occurs when children start school. The script associated with the role of "student" is simply quite different from the one connected with the role of "little kid." Classrooms are more tightly organized, expectations for obedience are higher, and there are more drills and routines to be learned than was probably true at home or even in nursery school. These changes are bound to affect the child's pattern of thinking.

Most of the research on children's emerging social understanding puts the cognitive horse before the social relationship cart, implying that it is the "understanding" part of the system that is paramount. I will inevitably foster this impression further in this chapter, since most of what I describe will be research on the cognitive "side." But it is important to keep the social side in mind as well.

▶ Thinking About Other People: Feelings and Qualities

One of the child's first social needs is to be able to "read" people—to understand what other people may be feeling or thinking, or what they may be like.

Reading Others' Feelings

Think of sitting in a classroom while the professor hands back the midterm exams. The person on your right, after looking at her exam, raises her head and smiles widely. The person on your left stays hunched over his test and turns down his mouth as he shakes his head a bit. A third person near you breathes a huge sigh and sits in a more relaxed posture, but does not smile. You easily deduce that the first person did well on the test and is happy, that the second person did less well than he expected or hoped, and is distressed, perhaps even feeling guilty, and

Think for a minute about how you tell when someone else is concealing some feeling. What clues do you use? How sure can you be of your interpretation?

RESEARCH REPORT
The Link Between a Child's Popularity and His Ability to Read Others' Intentions or Emotions

The study of children's social cognitions is not just a dry, obscure topic, interesting only for theoretical reasons. It turns out that whether a given child is good or poor at reading cues from others has some fairly direct relevance for the success of the child's social relationships. One good illustration comes from a series of studies by Kenneth Dodge and his colleagues: They have shown that unpopular children are significantly less skilled than are popular children at reading others' intentions.

In one study, Dodge (Dodge, Murphy, & Buchsbaum, 1984) showed kindergarten, second-grade, and fourth-grade children videotapes, each of which showed an interaction in which one child destroyed the toy of a second child. These videos were carefully created so that the destroying child's intent was varied. In some vignettes, the intent was clearly hostile, in others it was accidental, in some it was ambiguous, and in others it was pro social, such as knocking down the playmate's block tower in order to help clean up the room. Dodge found that in each age group, the popular children were better at detecting the actor's intent, with neglected and rejected children least accurate. In particular, neglected and rejected children were more likely to see

hostile intent when it was not present, a pattern that has been found in other studies, especially among rejected children (Dodge & Feldman, 1990).

Of course this study does not tell us what is causing what. Does a child become unpopular because he sees hostility where it didn't exist? Or does he see hostility in ambiguous situations because he has been rejected? Perhaps both, although we have at least some indications that such problems arise earlier in childhood because of harsh discipline from the parents (Strassberg et al., 1992; Weiss et al., 1992). Whatever the origin, it is clear that once such a "hostile attributional bias" has been established, it affects the child's later relationships. For example, when children are placed in new groups to interact with one another, those youngsters who begin such a process with a tendency to attribute hostile intent to others are more likely to be rejected later by their new playmates (Dodge & Feldman, 1990). And when highly aggressive children are given training specifically designed to reduce their hostile attributional bias, their level of aggression declines—an important real-life application (Hudley & Graham, 1993).

---

that the third person is relieved. How did you know that? What clues did you use? Presumably you used three types of information: facial expression, other body language, and the context in which it all occurred. Because you knew that tests were being handed back, you were alert for both happy and sad reactions, and you interpreted the body language accordingly. The same body language in another setting might mean something a bit different.

There is obviously both cognitive skill and social information involved in this whole process. You need to be able to identify various body signals, including facial expressions; you need to understand various kinds of emotions, and know that it is possible for people to feel several emotions at the same time; you need to understand the social context, and you need to have a theory of mind that helps you link the two. In this case, you need the basic understanding that another person will be happy or sad depending on how well he does on some task.

Research on children's understanding of others' emotions suggests that they acquire these various forms of knowledge gradually over the years from about age 1 to adolescence. You already know that by 10 to 12 months, babies can tell the difference between positive and negative facial expressions on others' faces, because at that age they already show *social referencing*. You also know (from Chapter 7) that by age 3, the child has begun to develop a theory of mind that includes the understanding that another person will feel sad if she fails or happy if she succeeds. A year or so later, at about age 4, the child begins to understand that others' behavior is governed by their beliefs and desires. Further, the preschool child begins to figure out that particular emotions occur in situations involving specific

Preschool children would have no difficulty understanding the emotion Laura is expressing here.

relationships between desire and reality. Sadness, for example, normally occurs when someone fails to acquire some desired object, or loses something desired (Harris, 1989).

All of this may make it sound as if 4- and 5-year-olds have already understood everything they need to know about others' emotions. In fact, there is a good deal of more sophisticated knowledge still to come, such as understanding more complex or subtle emotions, and in grasping the fact that a person can have more than one emotion at the same time, even competing emotions.

For example, 4-year-olds can easily recognize facial expressions and situations that convey the emotions happy, sad, mad, loving, and scared. But feelings like pride or shame are understood only in middle childhood (Harter & Whitesell, 1989). Similarly, by age 6, children understand that a person can switch rather rapidly from sadness to happiness if circumstances change, but it is only at about age 10 that children begin to understand that a person can feel opposite feelings (ambivalence) at the same moment (Harter & Whitesell, 1989), and only in adolescence that they realize that a person can feel opposite feelings about the *same* object or event: "I was happy I was joining the new club but also a little worried because I didn't know anyone in it." "I was happy that I got a present but mad that it wasn't exactly what I wanted" (Harter & Whitesell, 1989, p. 86).

Cross-cultural Comparisons.   One might reasonably ask—as with virtually all the developmental sequences I have given you in this book—whether children in every culture learn about emotions in this same way. In this case, we have a bit of evidence.

The Utka, an Inuit band in northern Canada, have two words for fear, distinguishing between fear of physical disaster and fear of being treated badly. In some African languages, there are no separate words for fear and sorrow. Samoans use the same word for love, sympathy, and liking, and Tahitians have no word at all that conveys the notion of guilt. These examples, drawn by James Russell (1989) from the anthropological literature, remind us that we need to be very careful when we talk about the "normal" process of a child learning about emotional expression and emotional meaning. From our English-speaking, Western perspective, emotions like fear or anger seem like "basic" emotions that all infants would understand early and easily. But what would be the developmental sequence for a child growing up in a culture in which fear and sorrow are not distinguished?

At the same time, the work of Paul Ekman (1972; 1973) has given us evidence of a strong cross-cultural similarity in people's facial expressions when conveying certain of these same "basic" emotions, such as fear, happiness, sadness, anger, and disgust. (Figure 12.1 shows two such common expressions.) In all cultures studied so far, adults understand these facial expressions as having the same core meaning. Cultural variations are laid on top of these basic expressive patterns, and cultures have different rules about which emotions may be expressed and which must be masked. But there appears to be some common ground as well. One could argue that infants and toddlers are already quite good at discriminating and understanding these shared patterns. Even 2-year-olds can recognize and categorize happy and sad expressions. The child must then slowly learn all the cultural overlays—the links between emotion and situation that hold in each

Figure 12.1
What emotion is being expressed in each of these photos? If you said happiness and fear, you agree with virtually all observers, in many countries, who have looked at these pictures. (*Source:* Copyright Paul Ekman.)

culture, the specific meanings of emotional language, the scripts that govern the appropriate expression of emotion in a given culture.

The Development of Empathy.   Psychologists have also explored the development of the child's ability to read the emotions and cues of others by studying the development of **empathy.** Empathy involves two aspects, the apprehension of another person's emotional state or condition, and then the matching of that emotional state oneself. The empathizing person experiences the same feeling that he imagines the other to feel, or a congruent feeling. *Sympathy* involves the same apprehension of the other's emotional state, but it is accompanied not by a matching emotion but by a general feeling of sorrow or concern for the other (Eisenberg et al., 1989). Generally speaking, empathy seems to be the earlier response developmentally, and among older children and adults, sympathy often seems to grow out of an initial empathic response.

The most thorough analysis of the development of empathy (and sympathy) has been offered by Martin Hoffman (1982; 1988), who describes four broad steps, which I've summarized in Table 12.1 (p. 350). The first stage, "global empathy," which is visible in infants, seems to be a kind of automatic empathic distress response. Hoffman (1988) says:

> An 11-month-old girl, on seeing a child fall and cry, looked as if she was about to cry herself, and then put her thumb in her mouth and buried her head in her mother's lap, which is what she would do if she herself were hurt. (pp. 509–510)

This changes as early as 12 or 18 months, as soon as the child has a clear understanding of the difference between self and other. The toddler still shows a matching emotion, but understands that the distress is the other person's and not her own. Nonetheless, her solution to the other's distress is still likely to be egocentric, such as offering the distressed person a teddy bear.

Do you cry at weddings and funerals, even when you do not know the people involved really well? Is that a form of empathy?

TABLE 12.1 Stages in the Development of Empathy Proposed by Hoffman

- *Stage 1: Global empathy.* Observed during the first year. If the infant is around someone expressing a strong emotion, he may match that emotion, such as beginning to cry when he hears another infant crying.

- *Stage 2: Egocentric empathy.* Beginning at about 12 to 18 months, when the child has a fairly clear sense of his separate self, children respond to another's distress with some distress of their own, but may attempt to "cure" the other person's problem by offering what they themselves would find most comforting. They may, for example, show sadness when they see another child hurt, and go to get their *own* mother to help.

- *Stage 3: Empathy for another's feelings.* Beginning as young as 2 or 3, and continuing through elementary school, children note others' feelings, partially match those feelings, and respond to others' distress in nonegocentric ways. Over these years, children distinguish a wider and wider (and more subtle) range of emotions.

- *Stage 4: Empathy for another's life condition.* In late childhood or adolescence, some children develop a more generalized notion of others' feelings, and respond not just to the immediate situation, but to the other individual's general situation or plight. So young people at this level may become more distressed over another person's sadness if they know that that sadness is chronic, or if they know that the person's general situation is particularly tragic, than if they see it as a more momentary problem.

Source: Hoffman, 1982; 1988.

Children's empathic responses become more and more subtle over the preschool and elementary-school years, as they become better readers of others' emotions. By middle childhood, many children can even empathize with several different emotions at once, as when they see another child make a mistake and fall during a game. The observing child may see and empathize with both the hurt and the sense of shame or embarrassment, and be aware that the victim may prefer *not* to be helped. In adolescence a still more abstract level emerges, when the child moves beyond the immediate situation and empathizes (or sympathizes) with another person's general plight.

Notice that both the developmental progressions I've been describing—in reading others' emotions and in empathizing with them—reflect several of the general principles I outlined earlier, and parallel the changes Piaget described. In particular, we see a shift from observation to inference: With increasing age, the child's empathic response is less and less guided by just the immediate, observed emotions seen in others, such as facial expressions or body language, and much more by the child's inferences or deductions about the other person's feelings. But this is not a swift change. For example, research in England by Paul Harris and his associates (Harris, Olthof, & Terwogt, 1981) shows that not until adolescence do young people become fully aware that other people may hide their emotions, or act differently from the way that they feel "inside."

Children as young as 2 or 3 show this kind of empathic response to other people's distress or delight.

As you might expect, not all children show equal amounts of such empathic responses. We know little about where such differences may come from, but one clue is that children with histories of secure attachment show more empathic responses than do others (Kestenbaum, Farber, & Sroufe, 1989).

Describing Other People

We can see the same kind of shift from observation to inference in studies of children's descriptions of others, as well as a clear change in focus from outer to internal characteristics. There seem to be at least three steps. Up to perhaps ages 6 to 8, when children are asked to describe others, they focus almost exclusively on external features—what the person looks like, where he lives, what he does. This description by a 7-year-old boy, taken from a study in England by Livesley & Bromley (1973), is typical:

> *He is very tall. He has dark brown hair, he goes to our school. I don't think he has any brothers or sisters. He is in our class. Today he has a dark orange [sweater] and gray trousers and brown shoes. (p. 213)*

When young children do use internal or evaluative terms to describe people, they are likely to use quite global terms, such as "nice" or "mean" or "good" or "bad." Further, young children do not seem to see these qualities as lasting or general traits of the individual, applicable in all situations or over time (Rholes & Ruble, 1984). In other words, the young child has not yet developed a concept we might think of as "conservation of personality."

Then beginning at about age 7 or 8, at just about the same time that children seem to develop a global sense of self-esteem, we see the emergence of similar ideas of global or enduring personality in others. The child begins to focus more on the inner traits or qualities of another person, and to assume that those traits will be visible in many situations (Gnepp & Chilamkurti, 1988). You can see the change in this (widely quoted) description by a nearly-10-year-old:

> *He smells very much and is very nasty. He has no sense of humour and is very dull. He is always fighting and he is cruel. He does silly things and is very stupid. He has brown hair*

Before you read the rest of this section, write down a description of a friend or an acquaintance. Then as you read along, compare your descriptions to the ones children give.

and cruel eyes. He is sulky and 11 years old and has lots of sisters. I think he is the most horrible boy in the class. He has a croaky voice and always chews his pencil and picks his teeth and I think he is disgusting. (Livesley & Bromley, 1973, p. 217)

This description still includes many external, physical features, but goes beyond such concrete, surface qualities to the level of personality traits, such as lack of humor, or cruelty.

In adolescence, young people's descriptions begin to include more comparisons of one trait with another or one person with another, more recognition of inconsistencies and exceptions, more shadings of gray (Shantz, 1983), as in this description by a 15-year-old:

> *Andy is very modest. He is even shyer than I am when near strangers and yet is very talkative with people he knows and likes. He always seems good tempered and I have never seen him in a bad temper. He tends to degrade other people's achievements, and yet never praises his own. He does not seem to voice his opinions to anyone. He easily gets nervous. (Livesley & Bromley, 1973, p. 221)*

I can illustrate these changes less anecdotally with some findings from two studies by Carl Barenboim (1977; 1981). He asked children ranging in age from 6 to 16 to describe three people. Any descriptions that involved comparing a child's behaviors or physical features with another child, or with a norm, he called *behavioral comparisons* (such as "Billy runs a lot faster than Jason," or "She draws the best in our whole class"). Statements that involved some internal personality construct he called *psychological constructs* (such as "Sarah is so kind," or "He's a real stubborn idiot!"), while any that included qualifiers, explanations, exceptions, or mentions of changes in character, he called *organizing relationships* (e.g., "He's only shy around people he doesn't know," or "Usually she's nice to me, but sometimes she can be quite mean"). Figure 12.2 shows the combined findings from the two studies. You can see that behavioral comparisons peaked at around age 8 or 9, psychological statements peaked at about age 14, and organizing relationships did not appear until age 10 and were still increasing at age 16.

I am sure that many of you have noticed the strong resemblance between this series of changes and the development of children's self-descriptions that I outlined in Chapter 10 (Figure 10.2, p. 293). This parallel illustrates yet again that the same underlying cognitive shifts seem to be involved in both understanding of others and understanding of the self.

▌ Thinking About Relationships

When we shift from the child's understanding of individuals to the study of children's understanding of relationships, I can sing many of the same songs again. Basically the same patterns emerge here no matter what type of relationship we study—the relationship with parents, with other authority figures, with groups, or with friends—but I think the richest vein has been in the research on children's understanding of friendships, so let me take that as illustration.

In the last chapter I described the developmental changes in the actual relationships children have with their friends—what they do together, how enduring

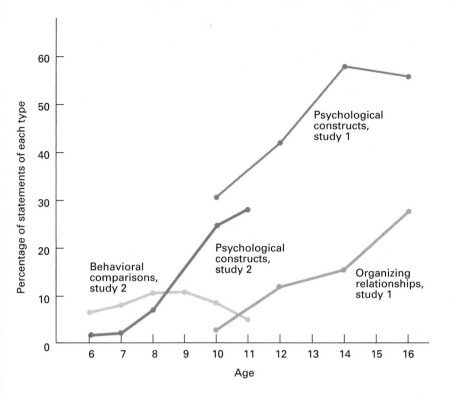

Figure 12.2
Results from Barenboim's two studies of children's descriptions of others. Study 1 involved children aged 10 to 16, study 2 involved children 6 through 11. (*Sources:* Study 1: Barenboim, 1977, Table 1, p. 1471; study 2: Barenboim, 1981, Figure 1, p. 134.)

and intimate their friendships are. Here I want to talk about how the child *understands* the nature of friendship itself.

Among preschool children, friendships seem to be understood mostly in terms of physical characteristics. If you ask a young child how people make friends, the answer is usually that they "play together," or spend time physically near each other (Damon, 1977; 1983; Selman, 1980). Friendship is understood to involve sharing toys, or giving goods to one another.

Selman's research and extensive studies by Thomas Berndt (1983; 1986) show that in elementary school this early view of friendship gives way to one in which the key concept seems to be *reciprocal trust*. Friends are now people who help and trust one another. Since this is also the age at which children's understanding of others becomes less external, more psychological, we shouldn't be surprised that friends are now seen as special people, with particular desired qualities other than mere proximity. In particular, generosity and helpfulness become part of the definition of friendship for many children. Children this age also understand friendship to have a temporal dimension: friends are people with whom one has a history of connection and interaction, rather than someone one has just met or played with once.

Berndt finds a further change at adolescence, as friends come to be seen as people who *understand* one another, who share their innermost thoughts or feelings. Friendships are also seen as more exclusive, more long-term. Friends should comfort one another, be with one another, forgive one another. Friendships at this stage are often intense relationships, with many hours spent on the phone or talking in person, sharing every detail, every thought, every activity.

Damon suggests that still another change takes place for some young people in late adolescence or early adulthood, which is parallel to the shift to more qualified statements Barenboim found in his studies of children's descriptions of others. At this point young people understand that even very close friendships cannot fill every need and that friendships are not static: they change, grow, or dissolve, as each member of the pair changes. A really good friendship, then, is one that *adapts* to these changes. At this age, young people say things about friendship like "trust is the ability to let go as well as to hang on" (Selman, 1980, p. 141).

Let me again make these generalizations concrete with some actual research findings, this time from a cross-sectional study by Brian Bigelow and John La Gaipa (1975). They asked several hundred children in Canada to write an essay about how their expectations of best friends differed from their expectations of other acquaintances. The answers were scored along many dimensions, three of which I have shown in Figure 12.3. You can see that references to "demographic similarity" (e.g., "We live in the same neighborhood") were highest among fourth graders, while mentions of loyalty and commitment were highest among seventh graders. References to intimacy potential (e.g., "I can tell her things about myself I can't tell anyone else") did not appear at all until the seventh grade, and then increased further in eighth grade.

Taking together all of what I have told you so far, it seems clear that the patterns of developmental change in children's understanding of themselves, of others, and of relationships are strikingly similar, shifting in all the ways I listed at the beginning of the chapter: from outer to inner characteristics, from observation to inference, from definite to qualified, from an egocentric to a general view.

▶ Thinking About What People *Ought* to Do

A somewhat different facet of the child's emerging social understanding is her judgment or explanation of other people's *actions*. The aspect of this that has most intrigued developmental psychologists is the child's judgment of the "moral-

How would you define a friend or friendship? What do you expect from a friend that you do not expect from an acquaintance? What do you *give* to a friend that you would not give to an acquaintance? Think about it for a minute.

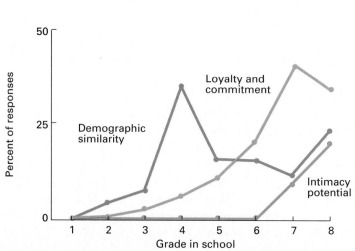

Figure 12.3
Some of the changes in children's ideas about friendship are clear from these findings from Bigelow and La Gaipa's study. (*Source:* Bigelow & La Gaipa, 1975, from Table 1, p. 858.)

ity" of actions. How does a child decide what is good or bad, right or wrong in other people's behavior, and in his own behavior? You make these kind of judgments often in your everyday life. Should you complain about the store clerk who seems to have given you back too little change? Should you turn in a classmate you see cheating on an exam? What about someone who lies in a job interview? Does your judgment change if you know that the person desperately needs the job to support his handicapped child?

Kohlberg's Stages of Moral Development

Piaget was the first to offer a description of the development of moral reasoning (Piaget, 1932), but Lawrence Kohlberg's work has had the most powerful impact (Colby et al., 1983; Kohlberg, 1964; 1976; 1980; 1981). Building on and revising Piaget's ideas, Kohlberg pioneered the practice of assessing moral reasoning by presenting a subject with a series of hypothetical dilemmas in story form, each of which highlighted a specific moral issue, such as the value of human life. One of the most famous is the dilemma of Heinz:

> In Europe, a woman was near death from a special kind of cancer. There was one drug that the doctors thought might save her. It was a form of radium that a druggist in the same town had recently discovered. The drug was expensive to make, but the druggist was charging ten times what the drug cost him to make. He paid $200 for the radium and charged $2000 for a small dose of the drug. The sick woman's husband, Heinz, went to everyone he knew to borrow the money, but he could only get together about $1000 which is half of what it cost. He told the druggist that his wife was dying, and asked him to sell it cheaper or let him pay later. But the druggist said, "No, I discovered the drug and I'm going to make money from it." So Heinz got desperate and broke into the man's store to steal the drug for his wife. (Kohlberg & Elfenbein, 1975, p. 621)

After hearing this story, the child or young person is asked a series of questions, such as whether Heinz should have stolen the drug. What if Heinz didn't love his wife? Would that change anything? What if the person dying was a stranger? Should Heinz steal the drug anyway?

On the basis of answers to dilemmas like this one, Kohlberg concluded that there were three main levels of moral reasoning, with two stages within each level, summarized briefly in Table 12.2.

At Level I, **preconventional morality,** the child's judgments are based on sources of authority who are close by and physically superior to himself—usually the parents. Just as his descriptions of others at this same stage are largely external, so the standards the child uses to judge rightness or wrongness are external rather than internal. In particular, it is the outcome or consequences of his actions that determine the rightness or wrongness of those actions.

In stage 1 of this level—the *punishment and obedience orientation*—the child relies on the physical consequences of some action to decide if it is right or wrong. If he is punished, the behavior was wrong; if he is not punished, it was right. He is obedient to adults because they are bigger and stronger.

In stage 2—*individualism, instrumental purpose, and exchange*—the child begins to do things that are rewarded and avoid things that are punished. (For this reason, the stage is sometimes called a position of "naive hedonism.") If it feels good, or brings pleasant results, it is good. There is some beginning of concern for

---

TABLE 12.2   Kohlberg's Stages of Moral Development

Level I: Preconventional Morality

- *Stage 1: Punishment and obedience orientation.* The child decides what is wrong on the basis of what is punished. Obedience is valued for its own sake, but the child obeys because the adults have superior power.

- *Stage 2: Individualism, instrumental purpose, and exchange.* The child follows rules when it is in his immediate interest. What is good is what brings pleasant results.

Level II: Conventional Morality

- *Stage 3: Mutual interpersonal expectations, relationships, and interpersonal conformity.* Moral actions are those that live up to the expectations of the family or other significant group. "Being good" becomes important for its own sake.

- *Stage 4: Social system and conscience (law and order).* Moral actions are those so defined by larger social groups or the society as a whole. One should fulfill duties one has agreed to and uphold laws except in extreme cases.

Level III: Principled or Postconventional Morality

- *Stage 5: Social contract or utility and individual rights.* Acting so as to achieve the "greatest good for the greatest number." The teenager or adult is aware that most values are relative and laws are changeable, although rules should be upheld in order to preserve the social order. Still, there are some basic nonrelative values, such as the importance of each person's life and liberty.

- *Stage 6: Universal ethical principles.* The adult develops and follows self-chosen ethical principles in determining what is right. These ethical principles are part of an articulated, integrated, carefully thought-out, and consistently followed system of values and principles.

Sources: After Kohlberg, 1976, and Lickona, 1978.

---

other people during this phase, but only if that concern can be expressed as something that benefits the child himself as well. So he can enter into agreements like "If you help me, I'll help you."

As illustration, here are some responses to variations of the Heinz dilemma, drawn from studies of children and teenagers in a number of different cultures, all of which would be rated as stage 2:

> "He should steal the food for his wife because if she dies he'll have to pay for the funeral, and that costs a lot" (Taiwan).
> He should steal the drug because "he should protect the life of his wife so he doesn't have to stay alone in life" (Puerto Rico).
> [Suppose it wasn't his wife who was starving but his best friend. Should he steal the food for his friend?] "Yes, because one day when he is hungry his friend would help" (Turkey). (All quotes from Snarey, 1985, p. 221)

At the next major level, **conventional morality,** there is a shift from judgments based on external consequences and personal gain to judgments based on rules or norms of a group to which the child belongs, whether that group is the family, the peer group, a church, or the nation. What the chosen reference group defines as right or good *is* right or good in the child's view, and the child internalizes these norms to a considerable extent.

Stage 3 (the first stage of level II) is the stage of *mutual interpersonal expectations, relationships, and interpersonal conformity* (sometimes also called the *good boy/nice girl* stage). Children at this stage believe that good behavior is what pleases other people. They value trust, loyalty, respect, gratitude, and maintenance of mutual relationships. Andy, a boy Kohlberg interviewed who was at stage 3, said:

> *I try to do things for my parents, they've always done things for you. I try to do everything my mother says, I try to please her. Like she wants me to be a doctor and I want to, too, and she's helping me get up there. (Kohlberg, 1964, p. 401)*

Another mark of this third stage is that the child begins to make judgments based on intentions as well as on outward behavior. If someone "means well" or "didn't mean to do it," their wrongdoing is seen as less serious than if they did it "on purpose."

Stage 4, the second stage of the conventional level, shows the child turning to larger social groups for her norms. Kohlberg labeled this the stage of *social system and conscience*. It is also sometimes called the *law and order orientation*. People reasoning at this stage focus on doing their duty, respecting authority, following rules and laws. The emphasis is less on what is pleasing to particular people (as in stage 3) and more on adhering to a complex set of regulations. The regulations themselves are not questioned.

The transition to level III, **principled morality** (also called *postconventional morality*), is marked by several changes, the most important of which is a shift in

By this age, the majority of teenagers are using stage 3 moral reasoning: What is good is what family or peers define as good and right.

the source of authority. At level I, children see authority as totally outside themselves; at level II, the judgments or rules of external authority are internalized, but they are not questioned or analyzed; at level III, a new kind of personal authority emerges in which individual choices are made, with individual judgments based on self-chosen principles.

In stage 5 at this level—called the *social contract* orientation by Kohlberg—we see the beginning of such self-chosen principles. Rules, laws, and regulations are still seen as important because they insure fairness. But people operating at this level also see times when the rules, laws, and regulations need to be ignored or changed. Our American system of government is based on moral reasoning of this kind, since we have provisions for changing laws and for allowing personal protests against a given law, such as during the civil rights protests of the 1960s, the Vietnam War protests of the 1960s and 1970s, or the protests against apartheid in the 1980s.

In his original writing about moral development, Kohlberg also included a sixth stage, the *universal ethical principles* orientation. People who reason in this way assume personal responsibility for their own actions on the basis of fundamental and universal principles, such as justice and basic respect for persons. Kohlberg later waffled a good bit on whether such a stage was the logical and necessary end point of the sequence, and on whether people reasoning at such a level actually existed (Kohlberg, 1978; 1984; Kohlberg, Levine, & Hewer, 1983). If they exist at all, it seems likely that such universal ethical principles guide the moral reasoning of only a few very unusual individuals—perhaps those who devote their lives to humanitarian causes, such as Mother Teresa or Gandhi.

In all of this, it is *very* important to understand that what defines the stage or level of a person's moral judgment is not the specific moral choice but the *form of reasoning* used to justify that choice. For example, either the choice that Heinz should steal the drug, or that he should not, could be justified with logic at any given stage. I've already given you some examples of a stage 2 justification for Heinz's stealing the drug; here's a stage 5 justification of the same choice, drawn from a study in India:

> [*What if Heinz was stealing to save the life of his pet animal instead of his wife?*] *If Heinz saves an animal's life his action will be commendable. The right use of the drug is to administer it to the needy. There is some difference, of course—human life is more evolved and hence of greater importance in the scheme of nature—but an animal's life is not altogether bereft of importance.* . . . (Snarey, 1985, p. 223, drawn originally from Vasudev, 1983, p. 7)

If you compare this answer to the ones I quoted before, you can clearly see the difference in the form of reasoning used, even though the action being justified is precisely the same.

Kohlberg argued that this sequence of reasoning is both universal and hierarchically organized, just as Piaget thought his proposed stages of cognitive development were universal and hierarchical. That is, each stage follows and grows from the preceding one and has some internal consistency. Individuals should not move "down" the sequence, but only "upward" along the stages, if they move at

Imagine a society in which everyone handled moral issues at Kohlberg's stage 3. Now think about one in which everyone operated at stage 5. How would these two societies be likely to differ?

Kohlberg thought that there were at least a few people, perhaps like Mother Teresa, whose moral reasoning was based on universal ethical principles.

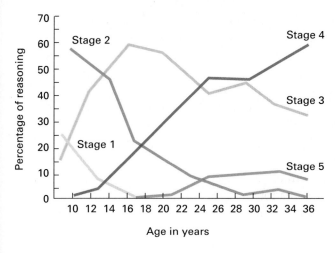

Figure 12.4
These findings are from Colby & Kohlberg's long-term longitudinal study of a group of boys who were asked about Kohlberg's moral dilemmas every few years from age 10 through early adulthood. Note that postconventional or principled reasoning was quite uncommon, even in adulthood. (*Source:* Colby et al., 1983, Figure 1, p. 46. Copyright by The Society for Research in Child Development. Reprinted by permission.)

all. Kohlberg did *not* suggest that all individuals eventually progress through all six stages, nor even that each stage is tied to specific ages. But he insisted that the order is invariant and universal. Let me take a critical look at these claims.

Age and Moral Reasoning.   Kohlberg's own findings, confirmed by many other researchers (Rest, 1983; Walker, de Vries, & Trevethan, 1987), show that preconventional reasoning (stages 1 and 2) is dominant in elementary school, and stage 2 reasoning is still evident among many early adolescents. Conventional reasoning (stages 3 and 4) emerges as important in middle adolescence, and remains the most common form of moral reasoning in adulthood. Postconventional reasoning (stages 5 and 6) is relatively rare, even in adulthood. For example, in one study of men in their 40s and 50s, only 13 percent were rated as using stage 5 moral reasoning (Gibson, 1990).

Let me give you two examples illustrating these overall age trends. The first, shown in Figure 12.4, comes from Kohlberg's own longitudinal study of 58 boys, first interviewed when they were 10, and now followed for more than 20 years (Colby et al., 1983). Table 12.3 shows cross-sectional data from a study by Lawrence Walker and his colleagues (1987). They studied 10 boys and 10 girls at each of four ages, and interviewed the parents of each child as well. Note that Walker scored each response on a 9-point scale rather than just scoring the five main stages. This system, which has become quite common, allows for the fact that many people's reasoning falls between two specific stages.

The results of these two studies are not identical, but there is nonetheless remarkable agreement on the order of emergence of the various stages and on the approximate ages at which they predominate. In both studies, stage 2 reasoning dominates at age 10, and stage 3 reasoning is most common at about age 16.

Sequence of Stages.   The evidence also seems fairly strong that the stages follow one another in the sequence Kohlberg proposed. There have been a number of long-term longitudinal studies of teenagers and young adults, in the United States (Colby et al., 1983), in Israel (Snarey, Reimer, & Kohlberg, 1985), and in Turkey. In each, the changes in subjects' reasoning nearly always occurred in the hypothesized order. Subjects did not skip stages, and only about 5 to 7 percent of

TABLE 12.3		Children and Their Parents Who Show Moral Reasoning at Each of Kohlberg's Stages							
	Stage								
Age	1	1–2	2	2–3	3	3–4	4	4–5	5
6 (1st grade)	10%	70%	15%	5%	—%	—%	—%	—%	—%
9 (4th grade)	—	25	40	35	—	—	—	—	—
12 (7th grade)	—	—	15	60	25	—	—	—	—
15 (10th grade)	—	—	—	40	55	5	—	—	—
Adults (parents with an average age of about 40)	—	—	—	1	15	70	11	3	—

Source: Walker, de Vries, & Trevethan, 1987, Table 1, p. 849.

the time was there any indication of regression (movement down the sequence rather than up). Similarly, when Walker retested the subjects in his study two years later, he found only 6 percent had moved down, mostly only half a stage, while 22 percent had moved up and none had skipped a stage (Walker, 1989). Such a rate of regression is about what you would expect to find, given the fact that the measurements of stage reasoning are not perfect. On the whole, I agree with James Rest (1983) that the evidence is "fairly compelling" that moral judgment changes over time in the sequence Kohlberg describes.

Universality. But is this sequence of stages only a phenomenon of Western culture? Or has Kohlberg uncovered a genuinely universal process? Thus far, variations of Kohlberg's dilemmas have been presented to children or adults in 27 different cultural areas, including both Western and non-Western, industrialized and nonindustrialized (Snarey, 1985).

John Snarey, who has reviewed and analyzed these many studies, notes several things in support of Kohlberg's position: (1) In studies of children, an increase with age in the stage of reasoning used is found consistently; (2) the few longitudinal studies report "strikingly similar findings" (Snarey, 1985, p. 215), with subjects moving upward in the stage sequence with few reversals; (3) cultures differ in the highest level of reasoning observed. In complex urban societies (both Western and non-Western), stage 5 is typically the highest stage observed, while in those cultures Snarey calls "folk" societies, stage 4 is typically the highest. Collectively, this evidence seems to provide quite strong support for the universality of Kohlberg's stage sequence.

Moral Development: A Critique. Kohlberg's theory about the development of moral reasoning has been one of the most provocative theories in all of developmental psychology. There have been over 1000 studies exploring or testing aspects of the theory, and several competing theories have been proposed. The remarkable thing is how well the theory has stood the test of this barrage of research and commentary. There does appear to be a clear set of stages in the development of moral reasoning, and these stages seem to be universal.

Still, the theory has not emerged unscathed. Some psychologists are less impressed than Snarey with the data on universality (Shweder, Mahapatra, & Miller, 1987). Also troubling is the fact that so few teenagers or adults seem to reason at the postconventional level (stages 5 and 6). Shweder points out that the effective range of variation is really only from stage 2 to stage 4, which is not nearly so interesting or impressive as is the full range of stages.

But by far the most vocal critics have been those who have pointed out that Kohlberg is really not talking about all aspects of "moral reasoning." Instead, as Kohlberg himself acknowledged in his later writings (Kohlberg et al., 1983), he is talking about the development of reasoning about *justice and fairness*. But what about moral reasoning about doing good, or reasoning based on some other ethic than justice, such as an ethic based on concern for others or for relationships? Let me take a quick look at two such alternative views.

Eisenberg's Model of Prosocial Reasoning

Most of the moral dilemmas Kohlberg posed for his subjects deal with wrongdoing—with stealing, punishment, disobeying laws. Few tell us anything about the kind of reasoning children use in justifying *prosocial behavior*. I mentioned in Chapter 11 that altruistic behavior is visible in children as young as 2 and 3; but how do children explain and justify such behavior?

Nancy Eisenberg and her colleagues (Eisenberg, 1986; Eisenberg et al., 1987) have explored such questions by proposing dilemmas to children in which self-interest is set against the possibility of helping some other person. One story involves a child walking to a friend's birthday party. On the way, he comes upon another child who has fallen and hurt himself. If the party-bound child stops to help, he will probably miss the cake and ice cream. What should he do?

The earliest type of response to dilemmas like this, characteristic of preschool children, is what Eisenberg calls *hedonistic* reasoning. Children this age are concerned with self-oriented consequences rather than moral considerations. They say things like "I'd help because she'd help me the next time," or "I wouldn't help because I'd miss the party." This approach gradually shifts to one Eisenberg calls *needs-oriented* reasoning, in which the child expresses concern rather directly for the other person's need, even if the other's need conflicts with the child's own wishes or desires. Children operating on this basis say things like "She'd feel better if I helped." At this stage, children do not express principles or indicate any reflectiveness about generalized values; they simply respond to the other's needs.

Still later, typically in adolescence, children say they will do good things because it is expected of them, a pattern highly similar to Kohlberg's stage 3 reasoning, and in late adolescence, some young people give evidence that they have developed clear, internalized values that guide their prosocial behavior: "I'd feel a responsibility to help because of my values," or "If everyone helped, society would be a lot better."

Some sample data from Eisenberg's longitudinal study of a small group of American children, in Figure 12.5, illustrate the shift from hedonistic to needs-oriented reasoning. By early adolescence, hedonistic reasoning has virtually disappeared (the lowest possible score on this scale is 4), while needs-oriented reasoning has become the dominant form. Eisenberg (1986) reports that similar patterns have been found among children in West Germany, Poland, and Italy,

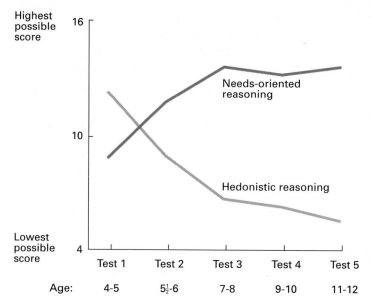

Figure 12.5
Every two years Eisenberg asked the same group of children what a person should do when confronted with each of a series of dilemmas about doing good, such as helping someone who is hurt. She then analyzed their form of reasoning. On each of these measures, the minimum score is 4 and the maximum is 16. (*Source:* Eisenberg et al., 1987, from Table 1, p. 715.)

but that kibbutz-reared Israeli elementary-school children show little needs-oriented reasoning. Instead, they are more likely to reason on the basis of the humanness of recipients and on internalized values and norms, a pattern consistent with the strong emphasis on egalitarianism and communal values in the kibbutzim. These findings point to perhaps a larger role of culture in children's prosocial reasoning than in reasoning about justice, although that is still a highly tentative conclusion.

There are obviously strong parallels between the sequences of changes in prosocial reasoning Eisenberg has described, and Kohlberg's levels and stages of moral reasoning. Children seem to move from a self-centered orientation (what feels good to me is right) to a stance in which social approval guides both reasoning about justice and about doing good. What is right is what other people define as right; one should do good things because others will approve of you if you do. Much later, some young people seem to develop internalized, individualized norms to guide both kinds of reasoning.

Despite these obvious parallels, though, researchers have typically found that children's reasoning about prosocial dilemmas such as Eisenberg's, and their reasoning about Kohlberg's justice or fairness dilemmas are only moderately correlated. The sequences of steps may be similar, but as was true of so many of the developments I talked about in Chapter 7, children seem to move through these sequences at somewhat different speeds.

Eisenberg's research, as well as the work of others in the same vein, helps to broaden Kohlberg's original conception, without changing the fundamental arguments. In contrast, Carol Gilligan has questioned some of the basic tenets of Kohlberg's model.

Gilligan's Ethic of Caring

Carol Gilligan (1982a; 1982b; 1987; Gilligan & Wiggins, 1987) is fundamentally dissatisfied with Kohlberg's focus on justice and fairness as the defining features of moral reasoning. Gilligan argues that there are, in fact, at least two distinct "moral orientations": justice, and care. Each has its own central injunction: not to treat others unfairly (justice), and not to turn away from someone in need (caring). Boys and girls learn both of these injunctions, but Gilligan has hypothesized that girls are more likely to operate from an orientation of caring or connection, while boys are more likely to operate from an orientation of justice or fairness. Because of these differences, they tend to perceive moral dilemmas quite differently.

Given the emerging evidence on sex differences in styles of interaction and in friendship patterns, which I talked about in the last chapter, Gilligan's hypothesis makes some sense. Perhaps girls, focused more on intimacy in their relationships, judge moral dilemmas by different criteria. But in fact, research on moral dilemmas has not shown that boys are more likely to use justice reasoning or that girls more often use care reasoning. Several studies of adults do show such a pattern (Lyons, 1983), but studies of children generally have not (Smetana, Killen, & Turiel, 1991; Walker et al., 1987).

For example, Lawrence Walker (Walker et al., 1987) scored children's answers to moral dilemmas using both Kohlberg's fairness scheme and Gilligan's criteria for a care orientation. He found no sex difference for either hypothetical dilemmas like the Heinz dilemma, or for the real-life dilemmas suggested by the children themselves. Only among adults did Walker find a difference, in the direction that Gilligan would expect.

Gilligan's arguments have often been quoted in the popular press as if they were already proven, when in fact the empirical base is really quite weak. Gilligan herself has done no systematic studies of children's (or adults') care reasoning. Yet despite these weaknesses, I am not ready to discard all of her underlying points, primarily because the questions she is asking seem to me to fit so well with the newer research on sex differences in styles of relationship. The fact that we typically find

Suppose Gilligan is right, and adult women typically reason with an ethic of caring while men reason with an ethic of justice. What do you think would be the implications of such a difference—for male/female relationships, for men and women as political leaders, or in other ways?

Gilligan argues that these young women are much more likely to be using an "ethic of caring" than an "ethic of justice" as a basis for their moral judgments. This *may* be true among adult women; it appears not to be true among children or adolescents.

no differences between boys and girls in their tendencies to use care versus justice orientations does not mean that there are no differences in the assumptions males and females bring to relationships, or to moral judgments. This seems to me to be clearly an area in which we need to learn a great deal more.

▶ Social Cognition and Behavior

In Chapter 11 I talked about children's social behavior; in this chapter I have been talking about children's thinking about relationships. What is the connection between the two? Can we predict a child's behavior, such as his moral choices, his generous behavior, or the quality of his relationships, from knowing the stage or level of his social cognition? Yes and no. Knowing the form or level of a child's reasoning cannot tell us *precisely* what he will do in a real-life situation. But there are nonetheless some important links between thinking and behavior.

Empathic Understanding and Behavior. One possible link is the one between empathy and prosocial behavior. The findings are not completely consistent, but Eisenberg's research shows that more empathic or other-oriented children tend to be more likely to share or help others in real situations (Eisenberg & Mussen, 1989).

Such a connection between empathy and kind behavior is particularly clear in adolescence. For example, Martin Ford (1982) studied the links between teenagers' empathy and their social competence. Ford asked ninth and twelfth graders about six hypothetical situations that would demand real social skill, such as the following:

> One of your school's best teachers has tragically died in an accident. The students in your grade have gotten together and decided to do something for the teacher's family. The class decides that someone should make a personal visit to the teacher's family. This person would bring flowers and try to tell the family how sorry the students were to lose such a good teacher and a good friend. Who in your grade do you think would be a good person to make the visit to the teacher's family?" (Ford, 1982, p. 339)

These situations are hypothetical, but by having students rate *each other*, he could see which teenagers were perceived by their classmates as being particularly skillful or thoughtful in difficult social situations. Ford found that adolescents who were chosen by their peers as being the best in such situations also displayed more empathy and role-taking ability on separate tests.

Friendship Understanding and Friendship Behavior. Similar links appear in studies of relationships. As a general rule, children with more mature reasoning about friendships are less likely to be aggressive with their peers and more likely to show sharing or other helpful behavior toward their friends in actual interactions.

In one study, Lawrence Kurdek and Donna Krile (1982) found that among children in the third through the eighth grades, those with higher scores on a measure of understanding of individuals and friendships were more likely to be involved in mutual friendships than were children with lower scores. Similarly, Selman (1980) compared children's scores on a measure of social reasoning with teachers' ratings of the children's social strengths and weaknesses. He found that children with more mature reasoning were more likely to be described by their teachers as showing higher levels of helpful or other prosocial behaviors.

An intriguing exception to this pattern, however, is the finding I reported in the last chapter, that in friendships between boys, competition and not sharing or not helping is often the dominant pattern. Furthermore, Berndt finds that among boys, the level of competition or cooperation is unrelated to their level of social cognitive reasoning about either friendship or the justification for helpfulness (Berndt, 1983). Thus while there is generally a correlation between the maturity of a child's social reasoning and his friend-making skills, more mature reasoning does not invariably increase the level of helpfulness or cooperation in actual friendship pairs among males. Once again, then, we have evidence that the "relationship rules" are different for boys than for girls, a pattern that I think is both fascinating and important.

Moral Judgment and Behavior.   Kohlberg's theory has sometimes been criticized on the grounds that children's or adults' moral behavior does not always match their reasoning. But Kohlberg never said that there should be a one-to-one correspondence between the two. Reasoning at stage 4 (conventional reasoning) does not mean that you will never cheat, or always be kind to your mother. Still, the form of reasoning a young person typically applies to moral problems should have at least *some* connection with real-life choices. One such connection proposed by Kohlberg is that the higher the level of reasoning a young person shows, the stronger the link to behavior ought to become. Thus young people reasoning at stage 4 or stage 5 should be more likely to follow their own rules or reasoning than should children reasoning at lower levels.

For example, Kohlberg and Candee (1984) studied students involved in the early "Free Speech" movement at Berkeley in the late 1960s (a precursor to the Vietnam War protests). They interviewed and tested the moral judgment levels of a group that had participated at a sit-in in the university administration building, plus a group randomly chosen from the campus population. Of those who thought it was morally right to sit in, nearly three-quarters of those reasoning at stage 4 or 5 actually did sit in, compared to only about a quarter of those reasoning at stage 3. Thus the higher the stage of reasoning, the more consistent the behavior was with the reasoning.

In other research, Kohlberg and others approached the question simply by asking whether there is a link between stage of moral reasoning and the probability of making some "moral choice," such as not cheating. In one study, Kohlberg (1975) found that only 15 percent of students reasoning at the principled level (stage 5) cheated when they were given an opportunity, while 55 percent of conventional-level and 70 percent of preconventional students cheated.

Similarly, Eisenberg has found that certain types of prosocial reasoning are correlated with a child's altruistic behavior. For instance, in a group of 10-year-olds, she found that hedonistic reasoning was negatively correlated with a measure of the child's willingness to donate to UNICEF the nickels they earned for participating in the study (Eisenberg et al., 1987). In addition, there is now strong evidence that delinquents have lower levels of moral reasoning than do

Why do you think it is that among boys, competition is such a strong feature of friendship interactions, no matter what level of reasoning the boys may otherwise have about relationships or morality?

Do you think that a person's stage or level of moral reasoning has any impact on political behavior, such as voting or political party affiliation? Can you generate a hypothesis about such a link and figure out how you might test it?

nondelinquents (Chandler & Moran, 1990; Smetana, 1990), even when the two groups are carefully matched for educational and social class levels. Thus those who actually do break the law also reason at lower levels about moral issues.

Yet despite this abundance of evidence for a link between moral reasoning and behavior, no one has found the correspondence to be perfect. After all, in Kohlberg's studies, 15 percent of the principled moral reasoners did cheat, and a quarter of stage 4 and stage 5 reasoners who thought it morally right to participate in a sit-in did not do so. As Kohlberg (1979) says, "One can reason in terms of principles and not live up to those principles" (p. 672).

What else besides level of reasoning might matter? We don't have all the answers to that question yet, but some influences are clear. First, simple habits are involved. Every day each of us faces small moral situations that we have learned to handle in a completely automatic way. Sometimes these automatic choices may be at a lower level of reasoning than we would use if we sat down and thought about it. For example, I may make the same donation to a particular charity every year without stopping to consider whether I could now afford more, or whether that particular charity is really the place where my money could best be used.

Second, in any given situation, even though you might think it morally right to take some action, you may not see that action as morally *necessary* or obligatory. I might be able to make a good argument for the moral acceptability of a sit-in protest, but still not see it as my *own* duty or responsibility to participate.

Third, the cost to the person of doing something helpful (or refraining from doing something morally "wrong," like cheating) may be an important factor. If helping someone else has little cost in time, money, or effort, then most children and adults will help, regardless of their overall level of social cognitive reasoning. But when there is some cost—such as was the case for the children in Eisenberg's study who were asked if they wanted to donate some of the nickels they earned to help other children—then we find a more consistent correlation between level of reasoning and behavior. This suggests the more general principle that moral reasoning becomes a factor in moral behavior only when there is something about the situation that heightens the sense of moral conflict, such as when there is a cost involved, or when the individual feels personally responsible.

Finally, there are often competing motives or ethics at work as well, such as the pressure of a peer group, or motives for self-protection or self-reward. Gerson and Damon (1978) found this very clearly in a study in which they asked groups of four children to divide up 10 candy bars. The candy was a reward for work the children had done on a project, and some of the group members had worked harder than others. When asked separately about how the candy bars ought to be divided, children usually argued for various kinds of fair arrangements, such as a model in which the child who worked the hardest should get the most. But when faced with the actual distribution of the candy bars, some children gave themselves the most; others went along with a group consensus and divided the candy equally. We might expect that in early adolescence, when the impact of the peer group is particularly strong, this group effect on moral actions might be especially strong, too.

Most children and adults will readily show helpful actions like this if there is little personal cost attached. But if the cost of helping goes up —as when you're in a hurry to get somewhere else— then those with higher levels of moral reasoning are more likely to help.

THE REAL WORLD
Application of Kohlberg's Theory to Education

Kohlberg believed that his theory of the development of moral reasoning had some fairly direct practical implications for education. The question that interested him was whether children or young people can be taught higher stages of moral reasoning, and if so, whether such a change in moral reasoning would change their behavior in school.

We know from early research by Elliot Turiel (1966) that at least under some conditions, exposing young people to moral arguments one step above their own level of reasoning can lead to an increase in their level of moral judgment. Young people who attend college also continue to show increases in moral stage scores, while those who quit school after high school typically show no further increase (Rest & Thoma, 1985), perhaps because college students continue to spend time arguing moral and philosophical issues with one another.

Evidence like this led Kohlberg to argue that it might be possible to raise high school students' level of moral reasoning by introducing classes in which moral dilemmas were discussed, a possibility that has been tested in a variety of schools. On average, programs of this kind succeed in shifting young people's moral reasoning upward about a half a stage (Schaefli, Rest, & Thoma, 1985). The largest effects are generally found in programs lasting more than three or four weeks and are especially clear in programs with college-age students. Among high school students, there is some impact but it is not as large.

An even broader-based educational application, designed to change students' moral behavior as much as their moral reasoning, has been the development of the so-called "just community." These experimental schools, typically set up as a "school within a school," operate as a kind of laboratory for moral education (Higgins, 1991; Higgins, Power, & Kohlberg, 1984; Kohlberg & Higgins, 1987; Power & Reimer, 1978).

Kohlberg insisted that the crucial feature of these just communities must be complete democracy: Each teacher and student has one vote, and community issues and problems must be discussed in open forum. Rules are typically created and discussed at weekly community-wide meetings. In this way, students become *responsible* for the rules, and for one another.

In experimental schools following this model, Kohlberg and his co-workers found that students' level of Kohlbergian moral reasoning shifted upward; so did their reasoning about responsibility and caring. The link between moral reasoning and moral behavior was strengthened as well. For example, stealing and other petty crime virtually disappeared in one school after the students had repeatedly discussed the problem and arrived—painfully—at a solution that emphasized the fact that stealing damaged the whole community, and thus the whole community had to be responsible. After one stealing episode, for instance, the group agreed that if the stolen money had not been returned (anonymously) by a specified date, each community member would be assessed 15 cents to make up the victim's loss (Higgins, 1991).

This effect of just communities makes sense when you think about the factors that seem to affect moral behavior. In these schools, two elements are added that would tend to support more moral behavior: a sense of personal responsibility, and a group norm of higher moral reasoning and caring.

Classes in moral education have not proven to be the "quick fix" that many educators hoped for. The gains in moral reasoning are not huge, and may not be reflected in increases in moral behavior in the school unless there is an effort to alter the overall moral atmosphere of the entire school. But these programs do show that there are provocative and helpful applications of at least some of the abstract developmental theories.

Thus moral *behavior* results from a complex of influences, of which the level of moral reasoning is only one element. Our knowledge about these links is improving, but we badly need to know more, both about group pressure, and about all the other factors that lead each of us to behave in ways that are less thoughtful, considerate, or fair than we "know how" to do. Kohlberg's own fascination with this set of questions, and with the question of how one raises a person's level of moral reasoning, led him and his colleagues to a series of bold attempts to apply the theory to schooling. I've explored some of this research in the real world box above.

▶ Social Cognition and General Cognitive Development

Before I leave this subject, there is one other set of linkages I need to explore, namely the potential connection between the sequences of development of social cognition, such as Kohlberg's stages of moral reasoning, and the broader sequences of cognitive development I described in Chapter 7. Earlier in this chapter I suggested several key dimensions that seem to characterize both sets of changes, such as a shift in focus from outer to inner characteristics. But I need to look at those possible connections more systematically.

We know that IQ is weakly linked to a child's level of social reasoning (Shantz, 1983). The correlations, which are in the range of +.20 to +.40, mean that children with higher IQs typically show slightly more advanced forms of social reasoning than do children of the same age with lower IQs.

Surprisingly, we know much less about any possible connections between overall cognitive *structure* and social-cognitive reasoning. The most concrete proposal was offered by Kohlberg, who hypothesized that the child first moves to a new level of logical thought, then applies this new kind of logic to relationships as well as objects, and only then applies this thinking to moral problems. More specifically, Kohlberg argued that at least some formal operations, and at least some mutual perspective taking in relationships are necessary (but not sufficient) for the emergence of conventional moral reasoning. Full formal operations and still more abstract social understanding may be required for postconventional reasoning.

The research examining such a sequential development is scant, but it supports Kohlberg's hypothesis. Lawrence Walker (1980) found that among a group of fourth to seventh graders he had tested on all three dimensions (concrete and formal operations, social understanding, and moral reasoning), half to two-thirds were reasoning at the same level across the different domains, which makes the whole thing look unexpectedly stagelike. When a child was ahead in one progression, the sequence was always that the child developed logical thinking first, then more advanced social understanding, and then the parallel moral judgments.

This research seems to tell us that there is *some* coherence in a child's or young person's thinking or reasoning about quite different problems. A child who has not yet understood principles of conservation is not likely to understand that another person's behavior may not match his feelings. But once conservation is understood, the child begins to extend this principle to people and to relationships. Similarly, a young person still using concrete operations is unlikely to use postconventional moral reasoning. But the coherence is not automatic. The basic cognitive understanding makes advances in social and moral reasoning *possible* but does not guarantee them. Experience in relationships, and with moral dilemmas, is necessary too.

The moral of this (if you will excuse the pun) is that just because a young person or adult shows signs of formal operations does *not* necessarily mean that the teenager or young adult will show sensitive, empathic, and forgiving attitudes toward friends or family. You may find it helpful to bear this in mind in your own relationships.

Why might it be important, either practically or theoretically, whether there is any link between children's approach to moral dilemmas and their level of Piagetian cognitive reasoning?

▶ Summary

1. Many of the principles of developmental change that describe overall cognitive development also describe the changes in social cognition, including a shift in focus from outer to inner characteristics, from observation to inference, from definite to qualified judgment, and from a particular to a general view.

2. Social cognition differs from other aspects of cognition in that the child must learn that people behave with intention, mask feelings, and operate by special socially defined scripts or rules.

3. Children learn to read others' emotional expressions fairly early, although more complex emotions and emotional blends are learned only later, as are links between situations and emotions.

4. Empathy—being able to match or approximate the emotion of another—is seen in young infants, but becomes less egocentric and more subtle through the preschool and elementary-school years.

5. Children's descriptions of others shift from a focus on external features to a focus on personality traits and to a more qualified, comparative description at adolescence, paralleling the shifts in children's self-descriptions.

6. Children's thinking about their relationships, such as friendships, shows strongly parallel shifts, moving from definitions of friendship as people who share physical space or activities to those emphasizing trust and to those emphasizing intimacy at adolescence.

7. Children's reasoning about what people ought to do, usually called moral reasoning, has been most fully described by Kohlberg.

8. Kohlberg proposed six stages, divided into three levels. The child moves from preconventional morality, dominated by punishment and "what feels good," to conventional morality, dominated by group norms or laws, to postconventional (principled) morality, dominated by social contracts and basic ethical principles.

9. Cross-sectional and longitudinal research shows that the stages occur in subjects from all countries studied, that the stages occur in the order listed, and that the modal level for young adults is conventional morality.

10. Alternative models of moral reasoning include Eisenberg's stages of prosocial reasoning (reasoning about why to do something good), and Gilligan's proposal that there is a parallel ethic of caring.

11. A child's level of social cognition is at least somewhat predictive of the type of social behavior she will show. More empathic teenagers show somewhat higher levels of social skill; children with higher levels of reasoning about friendships have more and more intimate friendships; higher-level moral reasoning is associated with higher likelihood of "moral" behavior or resistance to temptation.

12. Other factors that may influence moral behavior include group pressure, whether the individual sees the moral action as necessary or obligatory, the

cost of some moral action, and the presence of other motivations, such as self-interest.

13. Social-cognitive development is somewhat related to broader sequences of cognitive development. In particular, conventional levels of moral reasoning seem to require (as a necessary, but not sufficient, condition) at least beginning formal operations, as well as fairly advanced reasoning about social relationships.

▶ Key Terms

conventional morality (357)

empathy (349)

preconventional morality (355)

principled morality (357)

social cognition (344)

▶ Suggested Readings

Flavell, J. H. (1985). *Cognitive development* (2nd ed.). Englewood Cliffs, NJ: Prentice-Hall.

I have recommended this excellent text before. In this case, you may want to look at the very good chapter on social cognition.

Hoffman, M. L. (1988). Moral development. In M. H. Bornstein & M. E. Lamb (Eds.), *Developmental psychology: An advanced textbook* (2nd ed.). Hillsdale, NJ: Erlbaum.

Not all psychologists are as persuaded as I am of the general validity of Kohlberg's stage theory. Hoffman is one of the articulate skeptics, so this paper would give you a look at an alternate view.

Kurtines, W. M., & Gewirtz, J. L. (Eds.). (1991). *Handbook of moral behavior and development*. Hillsdale, NJ: Erlbaum.

This is a massive three-volume work, prepared as a commemoration of the work of Lawrence Kohlberg. Volume 1 deals with theory, Volume 2 with research, and Volume 3 with application. If this area intrigues you, there is no more current, complete source.

THE ECOLOGY OF DEVELOPMENT: THE CHILD WITHIN THE FAMILY SYSTEM

13

Theoretical Approaches

Systems Theory
Bronfenbrenner's Ecological Approach

Dimensions of Family Interaction

The Emotional Tone of the Family
• *Research Report:* The Long-term Consequences of Hostility and Abuse
Responsiveness
Methods of Control
• *The Real World:* To Spank or Not to Spank
Communication Patterns

Patterns or Styles of Child Rearing

A Research Example: The Work of Steinberg and Dornbusch
Adding Up What We Know About Parental Style

Other Aspects of Family Dynamics

The Child's Characteristics

• *Cultures and Contexts:*
China's One-Child Policy
Siblings: Treated the Same or Differently?
The Parents' Characteristics
Family Structure: Divorce and Other Variations
• *Cultures and Contexts:* The Benefits of Extended Families
• *The Real World:* Softening the Effects of Divorce

Some Exosystem Effects: The Impact of Parents' Work and Social Support on Family Functioning

The Impact of Parents' Jobs on the Family and the Child
Social Support for Parents

Summary

Key Terms

Suggested Readings

In the midst of a recession, Sam McKenzie's company had to lay off workers, and six months ago Sam, aged 35, lost his job as a machinist. Sam's wife, Edith, still has her job as a clerk in the local grocery store, but Sam's unemployment compensation is running out. Money is tight. Sam has tried hard to persuade himself that these things happen to people, but mostly he blames himself and his lack of education. He also finds it very difficult to have to rely so much on his wife's income, since he thinks it is the man's job to support the family. And he most definitely does not think it is a man's job to get the kids off to school or put the meat loaf in the oven at 5:00 so that dinner will be ready when his wife comes home from work. Over the months, he has become increasingly gloomy and irritable. He drinks more, has trouble sleeping, and has been arguing more with Edith. The kids have also felt the change—not just in the things they can't buy now, but in the whole atmosphere at home. Sam snaps at them often and most of the time is much stricter with them—though there are times, too, when he seems to pay no attention at all. The kids also notice that he hugs them a lot less. David, who is 13, has started yelling back much more frequently than he used to, and has been spending more and more time with his school buddies. Nine-year-old Jennifer has reacted differently: she's become quite withdrawn and depressed, and no longer spends much time with her friends. Both the children have had a lot more colds and other sicknesses than usual, too.

What the McKenzie family has experienced is fairly typical of families when the father loses his job (Crouter & McHale, 1993). It also illustrates two important points—points that I made in a preliminary way in Chapter 1, but that may have gotten a bit lost in all the intervening chapters.

First, to understand the child's development we must go beyond the child himself and whatever intrinsic developmental patterns may exist; we must go beyond the dyad of child and mother, or child and father. We need to look at the whole ecology of development—at the pattern of interaction within the family, and at the influences of the larger culture on that family. David and Jennifer McKenzie have been affected by Sam's job loss both directly and indirectly, and some of those effects may be very long-lasting. Studies by Glen Elder (1974; 1981; 1984), for example, show that some children whose families experienced major financial upheavals during the Great Depression in the 1930s continued to show the emotional scars well into adult life.

Second, the McKenzie story illustrates that there is a *system* of influences at work. Sam's job loss was not just an economic event. It affected Sam's attitudes, his self-esteem, his behavior, and it reverberated through the entire family system, affecting every other person and every relationship.

In this chapter and the next I want to explore this larger psychological and ecological system in which the child's development occurs—the family system, with all that entails, and the larger culture in which the family is embedded. I introduced some of the current thinking about such family and cultural influences in Chapter 1, but let me both refresh your memory and set the stage by delving a bit more deeply into the theoretical issues.

▶ Theoretical Approaches

Thirty years ago, most child development texts and books of advice to parents emphasized the role of the parents in "molding" the child, as if the child were some sort of shapeless block of clay. The parents' task was thought to be to *socialize* the child, to shape the child's behavior so that it fit well into the expectations and rules of society. This clay-molding view has now given way to a far more complex view, most commonly called *systems theory*.

Systems Theory

Systems theorists such as Sameroff (1983) emphasize that any system—biological, economic, psychological—has certain properties. First and foremost, a system has "wholeness and order," which is another way of saying that the whole is greater than the sum of its parts. The whole consists both of parts and their *relationship* to one another. The usual analogy is that of a melody, which is far more than a set of individual notes. It is the relationship of those notes to each other that creates the melody.

A second key feature of a system is that it is *adaptive*, in precisely the same way that Piaget talks about the child's cognitive system being adaptive. When there is a change in any part of the system, or some new element added, the system will "assimilate" if it can, but will "accommodate" if it must. So systems resist change as much as they can by absorbing new data or new parts, but if that doesn't work—as it often doesn't—then the system changes. For example, when a second child is born into a family, the parents may try to keep to their old routines as much as possible, but the presence of this new individual in the family system will inevitably force accommodations as well. And that will be particularly so if the new baby is temperamentally very different from the first child.

Combining these two features of systems, you can see that any change in any one part of a system will affect every other part. Furthermore, there are feedback loops set in motion. In the McKenzie family's experience, for example, Sam's distress led him to be more negative toward Edith, which made their relationship worse. Such a worsening of the marital relationship, along with Sam's own basic distress, led to changes in both parents' behavior toward the children, to which the kids reacted with changes of their own. Once set in motion, the changes in David's and Jennifer's behavior in turn affected Sam and Edith. David has become more defiant, to which Sam responds by becoming even more strict and demanding, which affects David's behavior in still more negative ways.

Although virtually all psychologists would now grant the general validity of such a systems approach, figuring out how to conceptualize the various parts of such systems has been no small task. Urie Bronfenbrenner, who originally coined the phrase *ecology of development* has offered one approach.

Bronfenbrenner's Ecological Approach

Bronfenbrenner (1979; 1989), whose work I talked about briefly in Chapter 1, proposes that we think of the ecological system in which the child develops as having a series of layers or concentric circles. The most central circle, which he calls *microsystems,* includes all those settings in which the child has direct personal experience, such as most centrally the family, but also school, a day-care center, or a job setting where a teenager works.

The next layer, which Bronfenbrenner calls *exosystems,* includes a whole range of system elements that the child does not experience directly, but that influence the child because they affect one of the microsystems, especially the family. The parents' work and workplace is one such element, as is the parents' network of friends.

Finally, there is what Bronfenbrenner calls the *macrosystem,* which describes the larger cultural or subcultural setting in which both the micro- and exosystems

Do you think that entire cultures are systems in this same sense? Suppose all violent TV, all highly aggressive games, and all handguns were banned. How might such a change reverberate through the entire cultural system?

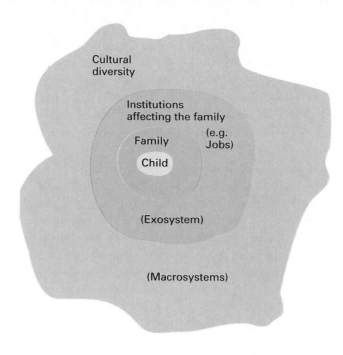

Figure 13.1
A simplified model of the ecology of development, drawing on both Bronfenbrenner's concepts and those of Szapocznik. (*Source:* Szapocznik & Kurtines, 1993, adapted from Figure 3, p. 402.)

are embedded. The poverty or wealth of the family, the neighborhood in which the family lives, the ethnic identity of the family, and the larger culture in which the entire system exists are all parts of this macrosystem.)

Figure 13.1 is a simplified version of this model, drawing both from Bronfenbrenner, and from the work of José Szapocznik (Szapocznik & Kurtines, 1993), who refers to it as a *contextualist paradigm*. The child's development is presumably some highly complex product of whatever qualities he himself brings to the system, plus the interactive effects of all these layers in the system, plus the effects of those microsystems that are not in the figure at all, such as schools, day care, or jobs that may affect the child directly.

You can also see that trying to understand development in this way is *immensely* difficult. It is hard to keep all the elements of the system in mind at once, let alone to try to study all the relevant parts simultaneously. Perhaps frustrated by that difficulty, or perhaps because of the long tradition of examining family and cultural effects in more linear ways, psychologists have continued to design research that explores only small pieces of the total system. Thus much of what we know about family and cultural influences on children is piecemeal rather than systemic. But using the model in Figure 13.1 as a general framework, let us plunge in anyway. We'll begin in this chapter by looking more closely at that most-studied and most obviously influential microsystem, the family. Then in Chapter 14 I'll look at other microsystems affecting the child directly, as well as at the larger cultural influences.

Naturally I have talked about family influences on the child many times already. You have seen how family interaction patterns affect the security of the child's attachment, patterns of aggressiveness, and language and cognitive development. But I have not talked about the family as a system, with all its complexities. To understand how that system works, and how it might affect the child, we need first to have some way of describing the many possible patterns of interaction that can occur in families. Then we have to try to understand the ways in which other factors inside and outside of the family will affect those patterns—factors such as the parents' personalities, the family structure, and the parents' job experiences.

▶ Dimensions of Family Interaction

Those researchers who have focused most directly on the patterns of interaction between parents and children have identified several major dimensions on which families differ and which seem to be significant for the child. These include the emotional tone of the family, the responsiveness of the parent to the child, the manner in which control is exercised, and the quality and amount of communication.

The Emotional Tone of the Family

The first key element for the child seems to be the relative **warmth versus hostility** of the home. "Warmth" has been difficult to define and measure, but intuitively and theoretically it is clear that it is highly important for the child. A warm parent cares about the child, expresses affection, frequently or regularly puts the child's needs first, shows enthusiasm for the child's activities, and responds sensitively and empathically to the child's feelings (Maccoby, 1980). On the other end of the continuum are parents who overtly reject their children—saying and expressing with their behavior that they do not love or want the child.

Such differences have profound effects. Psychologists have found that children in warm and loving families are more securely attached in the first two years of life, have higher self-esteem, are more empathic, more altruistic, more responsive to others' hurts or distress, and have higher measured IQs in preschool and elementary school (Maccoby, 1980; Schaefer, 1989; Simons, Robertson, & Downs, 1989). They are also less likely to show delinquent behavior in adolescence. Several studies show that among children and teens growing up in poor, tough neighborhoods, the lives of those who do *not* become delinquent are distinguished most by a single ingredient: they have experienced high levels of maternal love (Glueck & Glueck, 1972; McCord, McCord, & Zola, 1959).

I suspect that the role of warmth in fostering a secure attachment of the child to the parent is one of the key elements in this picture. You already know from Chapter 11 that securely attached children are more skillful with their peers, more exploratory, more sure of themselves. Warmth also makes children generally more responsive to guidance, so the parents' affection and warmth increase the potency of the things that parents say to their children, and the efficiency of their discipline (MacDonald, 1992).

I am sure it is obvious to all of you that loving a child is a critical ingredient in the child's optimum development. But sometimes it helps to restate the obvious.

Responsiveness

A second key element is **responsiveness** by the parent to the child, a concept you've come across repeatedly in earlier chapters. Responsive parents are those who pick up on the child's signals appropriately, and then react in sensitive ways to the child's needs. Parents who do more of this have youngsters who learn language somewhat more rapidly, who show higher IQ and more speedy cognitive

---

RESEARCH REPORT
The Long-term Consequences of Hostility and Abuse

The other end of the warmth continuum is, of course, hostility, a pattern of parental behavior associated with a whole range of lousy outcomes for children, especially when that hostility takes physical form, as abuse.

Physically abused children are far more likely than are nonabused children to become aggressive or delinquent later in childhood, or to engage in violence as adults (including such behaviors as date rape or spousal abuse). They are more likely to be substance abusers in adolescence and adulthood, to attempt suicide, to have emotional problems such as anxiety or depression or more serious forms of emotional illness, and to have lower IQs and poorer school performance (Malinosky-Rummell & Hansen, 1993).

Sexually abused children also show a wide variety of disturbances, including fears, posttraumatic stress disorder, behavior problems, and poor self-esteem (Kendall-Tackett, Williams, & Finkelhor, 1993). Children who suffer either type of abuse do not typically show *all* these symptoms, but they are far more likely than are their nonabused peers to show some form of significant disturbance. The more lasting and severe the abuse, the greater the likelihood of problems of these types.

The picture is not totally bleak. Some abused children show no measurable symptoms, and when the abuse is stopped, many children show a decline in symptoms of distress, especially when the mother is supportive and protective toward the child. But let us not lose sight of the fact that long-term problems are common among children who experience this degree of hostility or hurt, nor of the fact that our society has not yet found good ways of reducing the incidence of such abuse.

---

development, who are more likely to be securely attached, and who are more compliant with adult requests and more socially competent (Bornstein, 1989).

Methods of Control

It is the nature of children that they will often do things their parents do not want them to do, ask for things they cannot have, or refuse to obey their parents' requests or demands. From early days, parents are inevitably faced with the task of controlling the child's behavior, a process more popularly called *discipline*. Since I have not talked much about this aspect of parent-child interactions, I need to break the subject up into several elements.

One element of control is the *consistency of rules*—simply making it clear to the child what the rules are, what the consequences are of disobeying (or obeying) them, and then enforcing the rules consistently. Some parents are very clear and consistent; others waffle or are fuzzy about what they expect or will tolerate. Studies of families show that parents who are clear and consistent have children who are much less likely to be defiant or noncompliant—a pattern you'll remember from Gerald Patterson's research, which I've mentioned several times (e.g,. Figure 1.2). But such clarity does not produce little robots. Children from families with consistent rules are also more competent and sure of themselves (Baumrind, 1973), and less aggressive (Patterson, 1980).

A related element is the *level of expectations* the parents have for the child's behavior. Is the child expected to show relatively more mature behavior, or does the parent feel it is important not to expect too much, too soon? Studies of such variations show that, within limits, higher expectations seem to be associated with better outcomes. Children whose parents make high demands on them, expecting them to help around the house or to show relatively mature behavior for their age, have higher self-esteem, show more generosity and altruism toward others, and have lower levels of aggression. Obviously this can be carried much too far. It is unrealistic and counterproductive to expect a 2-year-old to set the table for dinner every day or to tie his own shoes. But when parents expect the child to be as independent and helpful as possible for his age, that does seem to foster a sense of competence in the child that carries over into other situations.

Another element of parental control is the degree of **restrictiveness** imposed. This is not the same thing as clear or consistent rule setting. A parent can be relatively low in restrictiveness and still have clear rules. For example, you might have a rule that your 10-year-old can stop off at another child's house after school to play without arranging it ahead of time, but must call you to tell you where he is if he does so. That would be a clear rule, but relatively low restrictiveness. On the other hand, a parent who insists on keeping a child within eyesight at all times, or who puts a toddler in a playpen for most of the day rather than risk having the child pull the drawers open would be considered restrictive.

Restrictive parents also frequently use a distinctive form of language with their children, namely *imperative* sentences, such as "Stop that" or "Come here" or "Do what I tell you." They are less likely to explain the rules to the children, but instead use their own power to control the child.

The other end of the continuum is usually listed as *permissive* parenting, which frequently also includes relatively few rules and few imperatives. Sometimes permissive parenting patterns emerge from a sense of helplessness about controlling the child at all. In other cases permissiveness reflects a specific philosophy of child rearing that emphasizes the child's need for freedom and opportunity to explore.

Evidence on the impact of restrictiveness and permissiveness is mixed. Highly restrictive parents are likely to have quite obedient, unaggressive children. But such children are also likely to be somewhat timid, and may have difficulty establishing close relationships with peers.

Low restrictiveness (permissiveness), on the other hand, is also not a wholly positive strategy. Children with highly permissive parents—who may exert far too little control—are likely to show only moderate independence and to be relatively thoughtless of others. Overall, children seem to respond most positively to clear rules consistently enforced, to realistic demands and expectations, combined with only moderate restrictiveness.

You might think that children reared in permissive families have been specifically encouraged and reinforced for independence and decision making. Can you think of any reason why they would nonetheless show *less* independence and responsibility?

Finally, to understand the process of control we have to understand the role of *punishment*. When a child does something you don't want (like writing on the wall, or hitting her brother, or staying out past a curfew), or fails to do something you do want (like cleaning his room), most parents respond with some kind of punishment, such as withholding privileges or treats, assigning extra chores, sending a child to his room, "grounding," verbal scolding, or spanking. The most controversial of these is spanking. Because of the importance of the question, I have explored the pros and cons of such physical punishment in the real world box on page 380. But I want to make a number of other points about punishment strategies in general.

First, as Gerald Patterson (1975) says, "Punishment 'works.' If you use it properly it will produce rapid changes in the behavior of other people" (p. 19). The operative word here, though, is "properly." The most effective punish-

THE REAL WORLD
To Spank or Not to Spank

The short, emphatic answer to the question "Should I spank my child?" is NO. I am well aware that this is easier to say than to do (and I admit to having applied a hand to my own children's rear ends on one or two occasions, even knowing that it would do little good and some potential damage). But the information we have about the effects of physical punishment, including spanking, seems to me to be so clear that a firm answer to the question is possible.

Note please: I am not talking here about physical abuse, although certainly some parents do abuse their children by spanking excessively with a switch or a brush or other objects. I'm talking about the ordinary kind of spanking—two or three hard swats on the rear—that most people think of as normal and helpful. Even physicians generally approve physical punishment of this kind. In one recent survey of family physicians and pediatricians, roughly two-thirds said they approved of spanking (McCormick, 1992). But in my view they are wrong.

In the short term, spanking a child usually *does* get the child to stop the particular behavior you didn't like, and it seems to have a *temporary* effect of reducing the chance that the child will repeat the bad behavior. Since that's what you wanted, it may seem like a good strategy. But even in the short term there are some negative side effects. The child may have stopped misbehaving, but after a spanking he is likely to be crying, which may be almost as distressing as the original misbehavior. And crying is a behavior that spanking does not decrease: It is virtually impossible to get children to stop crying by spanking them! So you have exchanged one unpleasantness for another, and the second unpleasantness (crying) can't be dealt with by using the same form of punishment.

Another short-term side effect is that *you* are being reinforced for spanking whenever the child stops misbehaving after you spank her. Thus you are being "trained" to use spanking the next time, and a cycle is being built up.

In the longer term, the effects are clearly negative. First, when you spank, the child observes you using physical force or violence as a method of solving problems or getting people to do what you want. You thus serve as a model for a behavior you do *not* want your child to use with others. Second, by repeatedly pairing your presence with the unpleasant or painful event of spanking, you are undermining your own positive value for your child. Over time, this means that you are less able to use *any* kind of reinforcement effectively. Eventually even your praise or affection will be less powerful in influencing your child's behavior. That is a very high price to pay.

Third, there is frequently a strong underlying emotional message that goes with spanking—anger, rejection, irritation, dislike of the child. Even very young children read this emotional message quite clearly (Rohner, Kean, & Cournoyer, 1991). Spanking thus helps to create a family climate of rejection instead of warmth, with all the attendant negative consequences.

Finally, there is research evidence that children who are spanked—just like children who are abused—more often show higher levels of aggression and less popularity with their peers, lower self-esteem, and more emotional instability (Rohner et al., 1991). These are not outcomes parents intend for their children.

I am *not* saying that you should never punish a child. I *am* saying that *physical punishment,* such as spanking, is not a good way to go about it. If you have been brought up in a family in which spanking was the standard method, you may simply not know other ways. If you find yourself in this position, a parenting class— often offered by community colleges or other community organizations—might be of help.

Think about your own upbringing. What types of control strategies did your parents use? What kinds of punishment? How might you want to change these patterns in bringing up your own children?

ments—those that produce long-term changes in the child's behavior without unwanted or negative side effects—are those used *early* in some sequence of misbehavior, with the lowest level of emotion possible, and the mildest level of punishment possible. Taking a desired toy away when the child *first* uses it to hit the furniture (or a sibling), or consistently removing small privileges when a child misbehaves will "work," especially if the parent is also warm, clear about the rules, and consistent. It is far less effective to wait until the screams have reached a piercing level, or until the fourth time a teenager has gone off without telling you where she's going, and then weighing in with yelling, loud comments, and strong punishments.

Second, to a considerable degree, parents get back what they give out in the way of punishment. As I pointed out in Chapter 9, children learn by observation as well as by doing, so they learn the adults' ways of coping with stress and forms of punishment. Yelling at children to stop doing something, for example, may bring a *brief* change in their behavior (which thus reinforces the parent for yelling, by the way). But it also increases the chances that children will yell back on other occasions.

Communication Patterns

Two things about communication within the family seem to make a difference for the child: the amount and richness of language spoken *to* the child, and the amount of conversation and suggestions *from* the child that the parent encourages. Listening is important as well as talking.

When I say "listening," I have in mind more than merely saying "uh-huh" periodically when the child talks. I also mean conveying to the child the sense that what he has to say is *worth* listening to, that he has ideas, that his ideas are important and should be considered in family decisions.

There is much less research on the quality of communication within families than on some of the other dimensions I have been describing, so we are a long way from understanding all of the ramifications. In general, children from families with open communication are seen as more emotionally or socially mature (Baumrind, 1971; Bell & Bell, 1982).

Open communication may also be important for the functioning of the family as a unit. For example, in a study of a national sample of families with adolescents, Howard Barnes and David Olson (1985) measured communication by asking the parents and teenagers to agree or disagree with statements like "It is easy for me to express all my true feelings to my [mother/father/child]." As you can see in Figure 13.2, the researchers found that those families in which parents and child reported good, open communication, compared to those with poorer communication, also described their families as more adaptable in the face of stress or change, and said they were more satisfied with their families.

This dad seems to be willing to listen carefully to his son, even though the boy is angry and accusatory.

▶ Patterns or Styles of Child Rearing

Each of these dimensions of variation among families has a demonstrable effect on the child, but if we are going to try to use a systems theory approach, it is not enough to look at each dimension independently. We also have to think about how they interact with one another to create *styles* or *patterns* of child rearing.

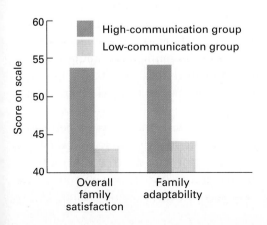

Figure 13.2
Good family communication was associated with both satisfaction and adaptability in this study of over 400 adolescents and their parents. (Sources: Barnes & Olson, 1985, Table 3, page 445.)

	Accepting, responsive	Rejecting, unresponsive
Demanding, controlling	Authoritative, reciprocal	Authoritarian, power-assertive
Undemanding, low in control attempts	Indulgent, permissive	Neglecting, uninvolved

Figure 13.3
Maccoby and Martin expanded on Baumrind's categories in this two-dimensional typology. (*Source:* Adapted from E. E. Maccoby & J. A. Martin, 1983. Socialization in the context of the family: Parent-child interaction. In E. M. Hetherington [Ed.], *Handbook of child psychology*, Figure 2, p. 39. New York: Wiley).

The most influential proposal about such styles has come from Diana Baumrind (1972), who has looked at combinations of four aspects of the dimensions I've just described: (1) warmth or nurturance, (2) level of expectations, which she describes in terms of "maturity demands," (3) the clarity and consistency of rules, and (4) communication between parent and child. Baumrind saw three specific combinations of these characteristics:

- The **permissive style** is high in nurturance, but low in maturity demands, control, and communication.
- The **authoritarian style** is high in control and maturity demands, but low in nurturance and communication.
- The **authoritative style** is high in all four.

Eleanor Maccoby and John Martin (1983) have proposed a variation of Baumrind's category system, shown in Figure 13.3, that I find even more helpful. They emphasize two dimensions, the degree of demand or control on the one hand, and the amount of acceptance/rejection or responsiveness on the other. The intersection of these two dimensions creates four types, three of which correspond fairly closely to Baumrind's authoritarian, authoritative, and permissive types. Maccoby and Martin's fourth type, the neglecting or uninvolved type, was not identified by Baumrind in her early work, although recent research makes it clear that this is an important group to study.

The Authoritarian Type.   Children growing up in authoritarian families—with high levels of demand and control but relatively low levels of warmth or responsiveness—do less well in school, are typically less skilled with peers than are children from other types of families, and have lower self-esteem. Some of these children appear subdued; others may show high aggressiveness or other indications of being out of control. Which of these two outcomes occurs may depend in part on how skillfully the parents use the various disciplinary techniques. Patterson finds that the "out of control" child is most likely to come from a family in which the parents are authoritarian by inclination, but lack the skills to enforce the limits or rules they set.

The Permissive Type.   Children growing up with indulgent or permissive parents, too, show some negative outcomes. They do slightly less well in school in adolescence, are likely to be more aggressive—particularly if the parents are specifically permissive toward aggressiveness—and to be somewhat immature in their behavior with peers and in school. They are less likely to take responsibility, and are less independent.

The Authoritative Type.   The most consistently positive outcomes have been associated with the authoritative pattern, in which the parents are high in both control and warmth, setting clear limits but also responding to the child's individual needs. Children reared in such families typically show higher self-esteem, are more independent but at the same time are more likely to comply with parental requests, and may show more altruistic behavior as well. They are self-confident and achievement-oriented in school and get better grades, and in late adolescence they are more likely to use postconventional moral reasoning (Boyes & Allen, 1993).

The Neglecting Type.   The most consistently negative outcomes are associated with the fourth pattern, the neglecting or uninvolved type. You may remember from the discussion of secure and insecure attachments in Chapter 11 that one of the family characteristics often found in children rated as insecure/avoidant is the "psychological unavailability" of the mother. The mother may be depressed, or may be overwhelmed by other problems in her life and simply not have made any deep emotional connection with the child. Whatever the reason, such children continue to show disturbances in their relationships with peers and with adults for many years. In less-extreme cases the effects are also detectable. In a short-term longitudinal study, Robert Hinde and Joan Stevenson-Hinde (1986) found that children whose mothers were both uninvolved and low in control when the children were $3^1/_2$ showed a somewhat odd combination of friendliness and high levels of hostility with peers eight months later. And at adolescence, youngsters from neglecting families are more impulsive and antisocial and much less achievement-oriented in school (Block, 1971; Pulkkinen, 1982).

A Research Example: The Work of Steinberg and Dornbusch

The best single piece of research demonstrating the effects of these several styles is an extremely large longitudinal study of over 8000 high school students in California and Wisconsin, by Laurence Steinberg and Sanford Dornbusch and their colleagues (Dornbusch et al., 1987b; Lamborn et al., 1991; Steinberg, Elmen, & Mounts, 1989; Steinberg et al., 1992b). They measured three of the four parenting styles (all but the neglecting) by asking the teenagers themselves to complete a questionnaire about their relationship with their parents. Questions reflecting an authoritarian style included one about how often the parents tell the teen not to argue with adults, and another about whether or not the parents say that they are correct and not to be questioned. Students were also asked how their parents would react if they got bad grades, or good grades. An authoritarian response was scored if a student said that his parents would punish him if he got poor grades, and tell him to do better if he got good grades.

If the student reported that hard work was not important to the parents, or that the parents didn't care if the student got bad grades, or that there were no rules about TV watching, or that the parents did not attend school functions or help the student with homework, the family was rated as high in permissiveness. Students whose families were rated as authoritative replied positively to items saying that their parents told the teen to look at both sides of the issues, that the parents sometimes agreed that the teen knew more, that they emphasized joint decision making in the family, and that they praised good grades and offered to help after bad grades, urging the student to try harder.

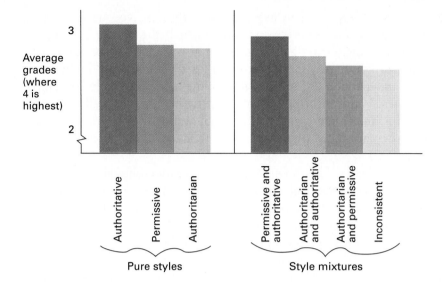

Figure 13.4
School grades as a function of parental style—pure styles or mixtures—in Steinberg and Dornbusch's large study of teenagers. (*Source:* Dornbusch et al., 1987b, from Table 4, p. 1255.)

Notice from the figure that the *worst* grades were for teens from families who were inconsistent—who showed some characteristics of all three family styles. How could you explain this?

Steinberg and Dornbusch then looked at the relationship between these family styles and the teenager's school performance. Figure 13.4 gives one of the main results, the link between family style and school grades. The information about school grades also came from the students, who chose a broad category that best described their grades, such as "mostly A's," or "about half B's and half C's." These category scores were then converted to a scale, with 4 representing the highest category and .5 the lowest, and it is this scale score that is shown in Figure 13.4.

The figure shows the grades not only for the three pure styles, but also for several mixtures of style—a possibility in this case because of the way parental style was measured. It is clear that the pure authoritative style (high scores on authoritative items and low scores on permissive and authoritarian items) is associated with the best grades, with a mixture of authoritative and permissive styles the second best, and either permissive or authoritarian parenting, or a combination of the two, associated with poorer outcomes.

Steinberg and Dornbusch continued their contact with these teenagers over two years, which allowed them to look at possible links between the parents' style at the beginning of the study and the students' *later* school performance. In this longitudinal analysis, they found the same kinds of patterns: those students whose parents were most authoritative at the beginning of the study continued to get better grades and to be more involved in school over the succeeding two years.

But the system is more complex than this makes it sound. It is not just that authoritative parents create a good family climate and thereby support and motivate their child optimally. Authoritative parents also behave differently *toward the school*. They are much more likely to be involved with the school, attending school functions, or talking to teachers, and this involvement seems to play a crucial role in the process. When an otherwise authoritative parent is *not* also more involved with the school, the outcomes for the student are not so clearly positive. Similarly, a teenager whose parent is highly involved with the school but is not authoritative shows less optimal outcomes. It is the combination of authoritativeness and school involvement that is associated with the best results (Steinberg et al., 1992b).

Ethnic Group Differences in Styles. Because the sample in the Steinberg and Dornbusch study is so large, it has been possible for them to look separately at subgroups of African-American, Hispanic-American, and Asian-American youth and their families (Steinberg et al., 1991). In the process, they have uncovered some very interesting patterns that point us both toward common processes and toward unique cultural variations.

Table 13.1 shows the percentages of families from each of the four ethnic groups involved in this study who can be described as authoritative, broken down further by social class and the intactness of the family. The authoritative pattern was most common among white families and least common among Asian-Americans, but in each ethnic group, authoritative parenting was more common among the middle class and (with one exception) more common among intact families than in single-parent or stepparent families.

More important, Steinberg and Dornbusch find that many of the relationships between authoritative parenting and positive outcomes occurred in all ethnic groups. In all four groups, teenagers from authoritative families had more self-reliance, and less delinquency, than did those from nonauthoritative families.

School performance, on the other hand, is *not* linked to authoritative parenting in the same ways in all four groups: good grades are linked to such a parenting style for whites and for Hispanic-Americans, but only very weakly for Asian-Americans or African-Americans. In particular, Asian-Americans as a group do extremely well in school even though their parents are among the least authoritative. Thus styles of parenting *cannot* explain the ethnic group differences in academic achievement.

In an effort to understand these group differences, Steinberg and Dornbusch have looked at a variety of other aspects of the family and cultural systems (Steinberg, Dornbusch, & Brown, 1992a). One key element seems to be the beliefs students and parents have about the importance of education for later success in life.

TABLE 13.1 Ethnic Differences in Authoritative Parenting (in percentages of families)

Ethnic group	Working-class		Middle-class	
	Intact*	Not intact	Intact	Not intact
White	17.2	11.5	25.0	17.6
Black	13.4	12.2	14.0	16.0
Hispanic	10.7	9.8	15.8	12.9
Asian	7.5	6.1	15.6	10.8

*"Intact" means the child is still living with both biological parents; "not intact" may mean either single-parent family, or stepfamily, or any other family configuration other than both natural parents.

Source: Steinberg et al., 1991, from Table 1, p. 25.

All four ethnic groups share a belief that doing well in school will lead to better chances later. But the groups disagree on the consequences of doing poorly in school. Asian students, more than any other group, believe that a good job is unlikely to follow a bad education, while both Hispanics and blacks are more optimistic (or more cavalier) about the risks associated with poor school performance. Perhaps as a result of their greater fear of failure, Asian students spend much more time on homework than do other groups.

Furthermore, Asian-American students (and whites) get very good peer support for academic achievement, while African-American teens get little peer support for such an activity, which undermines the beneficial effects of authoritative parenting. Indeed, interviews with the African-American students in the Steinberg and Dornbusch study suggest that academically oriented African-American youths find it very difficult to find a peer group that will support their academic goals. Those who nonetheless persist in their striving for achievement often resolve the issue by choosing peers primarily from other ethnic groups. Thus the dilemma for African-American students, more than any other subgroup in American culture, seems to involve a choice between doing well in school and being popular.

Taking all of this together, it appears that authoritative parenting is associated with positive psychological outcomes such as higher self-esteem and lower levels of psychological distress in all groups. But academic achievement is a more complex process, involving a heavier dose of peer influence that may either support or override the impact of parental style.

Adding Up What We Know About Parental Style

When we combine the Steinberg/Dornbusch study with all the other evidence about the impact of parental style, several conclusions seem important. First, it seems clear that children are affected by the family "climate" or style. Although we do not have the sort of longitudinal data needed to be sure, I suspect that these effects persist well into adulthood. Second, many of us are accustomed to thinking about family styles as if permissive and authoritarian patterns were the only options. But we now know that many parents are *both* affectionate and firm, and that children respond to this combination in very positive ways.

Finally, even these types do not begin to describe the complexity of the family microsystem or the larger system in which the child is embedded. Both the outcomes for the child, and the styles or types themselves, are also affected by the dominant ethnic culture to which the child is exposed, by peer relationships, and by myriad other factors that we are only beginning to study and understand.

▶ Other Aspects of Family Dynamics

The studies of parental style have been extremely fruitful and fascinating, but there are many other variables involved in the complex process we might call family dynamics. Each child brings her own temperament or other qualities to the mixture; parents bring their own personalities and habits; the relationship between siblings may have a powerful effect, as does clearly the structure of the family itself.

African-American parents like these are often quite authoritative in their parenting style, and typically place a high value on academic excellence. But African-American peer groups devalue or even scorn academic achievement, and thus undermine family effects.

The Child's Characteristics

One of the first things to understand is that the influences in the parent-child system flow both ways. Children influence their parents as well as the other way around. I have already talked about one such influence in Chapter 9, namely the child's temperament. Children with "difficult" temperaments seem to elicit more punishment (especially if the family is under some kind of stress), and may also affect a parent's mood. More generally, such children may have much more difficulty adapting to any change in the family system, such as a family divorce.

The child's temperament can also affect the parents' relationship with each other. For example, one group of researchers (Stoneman, Brody, & Burke, 1989) observed that the parental relationship was most compromised when the firstborn child was a daughter with an "active-emotional" temperament, but the same was not true either for firstborn boys with a similar temperament, or for any later-born children—yet another illustration of the fact that to understand this system we need to look at it in its entirety.

The child's position in the family shows up as an important ingredient in other research as well. Parents generally have higher expectations for maturity in their firstborn, and may well be more responsive, more child-centered with the first child. Firstborns are also punished more, in part because parents are simply less skilled in using noncoercive forms of control with their first child.

The child's age also makes a difference—a point that may seem obvious, but is well worth reemphasizing. As the child develops, very different demands are made on the parents. As any parent can tell you, caring for an infant is a quite different task from caring for a 2-year-old, or a 12-year-old. The areas in which control will be needed change over time, the degree of push for independence changes, the child's intellectual and language abilities change. Parents quite naturally adapt to these changes, altering their own pattern— even perhaps their style—as the child grows older. At the same time, there is an indication that parents show some consistency in their behavior toward children of the same age. That is, parents behave toward the second child when he is 2 as they had toward the first child when she was 2, even though they are now treating the older child as a 4-year-old (Boer, Godhart, & Treffers, 1992). Such a clearly rational set of changes in the parents' behavior over time has the effect of changing the family system over time.

Siblings: Treated the Same or Differently?

Such changes over time may be one contributor to a phenomenon that has been puzzling developmental psychologists more and more in recent years, namely the fact that two children from the same family so often turn out quite differently. I think that until recently, most of us assumed that parental style was rather like the weather in a given location: it affected everyone in the same way. If one child experienced an authoritative style, then such a style must characterize the *family*; all other children in the same household would experience the same style, the same pattern of interaction with parents, and the children would thus turn out similarly—similar skills, similar personalities, similar strengths and weaknesses. But both pieces of this assumption now look wrong. Children growing up in the same family turn out quite differently, and the family system, perhaps even the family style, can be quite different for one child than for another.

CULTURES AND CONTEXTS
China's One-Child Policy

A particularly fascinating cultural experiment regarding family size has been under way in China since 1979, when the government instituted an intense family-planning effort to reduce the normal family size to one child. This was done for economic and political reasons, since China has about 21 percent of the population of the world but only 7 percent of the arable land. The Chinese were facing the prospect that enormous food shortages with attendant social unrest would occur if something was not done about their population explosion. What they did was adopt a one-child policy. At present, this policy is still rigorously followed in urban areas, but in rural areas, families are generally allowed to have two children (Falbo, 1992).

In the early years of the policy, the Chinese themselves had many fears that these only children would become family tyrants,

spoiled by parents and grandparents. But recent studies do not confirm that fear. Toni Falbo (1992; Falbo & Poston, 1993), an American researcher who has been involved in a series of large survey studies of Chinese children, reports that she can find few differences between only and nononly children, either in school performance or in personality. Thus by *Chinese* standards, the one-child policy has been a success. It has not led to a generation of "little emperors" as some had feared, although it is still early to know what effect this policy will have on the society as a whole in the decades to come, when the only children have become adults. A culture made up of only children is likely to differ in a whole variety of ways, many of them unanticipated, from one in which larger families prevail.

Are you and your siblings alike in a lot of ways, or do you have quite different traits, skills, attitudes? Can you trace any of those differences to variations in the way you were treated as children?

Some of the best evidence comes from several studies by Judy Dunn (Dunn & McGuire, 1994) in both England and the United States. She has found that parents may express warmth and pride toward one child and scorn toward another, may be lenient toward one and strict with another. Here's an example from one of Dunn's observations, of 30-month-old Andy and his 14-month-old sister, Susie.

> Andy was a rather timid and sensitive child, cautious, unconfident, and compliant. . . . Susie was a striking contrast—assertive, determined, and a handful for her mother, who was nevertheless delighted by her boisterous daughter. In [one] observation of Andy and his sister, Susie persistently attempted to grab a forbidden object on a high kitchen counter, despite her mother's repeated prohibitions. Finally, she succeeded, and Andy overheard his mother make a warm, affectionate comment on Susie's action: "Susie, you are a determined little devil!" Andy, sadly, commented to his mother, "I'm not a determined little devil!" His mother replied, laughing, "No! What are you? A poor old boy!" (Dunn, 1992, p. 6)

Not only are such episodes common in family interactions, children are highly sensitive to such variations in treatment. Notice how Andy had monitored his mother's interaction with Susie, and then compared himself to his sister. Children this age are already aware of the emotional quality of exchanges between themselves and their parents, as well as the exchanges between their siblings and parents. Dunn finds that those who receive less affection and warmth from their mothers are likely to be more depressed, worried, or anxious than are their siblings. And the more differently the parents treat siblings, the more rivalry and hostility there is likely to be between the brothers and sisters (Brody et al., 1992).

Of course parents treat children differently for many reasons, *including* the child's age. Susie and Andy's mother may have been just as accepting of naughty behavior from Andy when he was a toddler. But Andy does not remember that; what he sees is the contrast between how he and Susie are treated now. Thus even when parents are consistent in the way they respond to each child at a given age, at any moment they are *not* behaving consistently toward all children, and the children notice this and create internal models about the meaning of those differences in treatment.

Parents also respond to temperamental differences in their children, to gender differences, and to variations in the children's skills or talents, all of which creates a unique pattern of interaction for each child. It is becoming increasingly clear that such differences in treatment are an important ingredient in the child's emerging internal model of self, and contribute greatly to variations in behavior between children growing up in the same families.

The Parents' Characteristics

The parents bring their own life histories, their own personalities, into the family dynamic as well. I could spend a whole chapter talking about the parents' half of this equation, but lacking such space, let me give only two brief illustrations.

First, when either parent is significantly depressed it has a profound effect on the entire family system. You already know from Chapter 11 that an insecure attachment is more likely when the mother is depressed. Depressed parents also perceive their children as more difficult and problematic, and are more critical of them, even when objective observers cannot identify any difference in the behavior of such children and the children of nondepressed mothers (Richters & Pellegrini, 1989; Webster-Stratton & Hammond, 1988). Thus the parent's depression changes not only her behavior, but her perception of the child's behavior, both of which alter the family system.

The parent's own internal working model of attachment also seems to have a very strong effect on the family system, and thus on the child. Mary Main and her colleagues have devised an interview that allows them to classify the security or insecurity of the parent's attachment to his or her own parents (Main & Hesse, 1990; Main, Kaplan, & Cassidy, 1985). Using this interview, Main and others have now found that those parents who are themselves securely attached are much more likely to have a child who is also securely attached.

The history and personal qualities the parents bring with them to the family interactive system obviously help to shape the style of parenting they show with their children—whether authoritarian, authoritative, or some other. But they do more than that. They affect the parents' perceptions of the child as well as the parents' behavior, and thus affect the system in myriad subtle ways.

Can you think of other parental qualities, skills, or attributes that might affect the family system?

Family Structure: Divorce and Other Variations

Another obvious aspect of the family system is the particular configuration of people who live together in a given family unit—an aspect usually called *family structure*. I suspect that many of us still harbor the illusion that the most common family structure is a father, a mother, and several children. And no doubt many of us still think that the majority of children spend all of their childhood and adolescence with the same mom and dad. But in the United States today, both those assumptions are wrong.

Sandra Hofferth (1985) has generated some particularly startling estimates, based on a longitudinal study of over 5000 American families who have been followed since 1968. She projects that only 30 percent of white children in the

When we think of "the family," no doubt most of us think of a family like this, with a father and mother and several children. But in fact, in the United States it now is the exception rather than the rule for a child to spend his or her entire childhood and adolescence in such a family system.

United States born in 1980 will still be living with their two natural parents at age 17. For black children, the figure is only 6 percent. Other estimates, based on cross-sectional comparisons, are somewhat more optimistic (Bumpass, 1984; Norton & Glick, 1986). But it would appear that at least 60 percent, and possibly as many as 70 or 80 percent, of children in the United States today are likely to spend at least *some* part of their childhood in a single-parent household, and perhaps 35 percent will spend at least a part of their childhood living with a step-parent.

An equally striking look at the enormous variety of family structures comes from a study of a large sample of children from a poor, black Chicago neighborhood whose family patterns were first observed when they were in first grade in 1967 (Kellam, Ensminger, & Turner, 1977), and then again in 1976, when they were adolescents (Hunter & Ensminger, 1992). Figure 13.5 shows the results for both time points so that you can see the changes that occurred and the enormous variety of family structures that existed. In this sample, the most common stable family structure was a single-parent family. Two-parent families were somewhat less likely to have persisted over the 10 years; 42 percent of those who still lived with both parents in first grade experienced some kind of marital dissolution in the following 10 years—divorce, separation, or death.

Even this remarkably complex picture doesn't convey the whole story, because many of these families had shifted several times during the decade. Divorced mothers, for example, may have had live-in relationships with one or more men before a remarriage, or may have lived for a while with their own parents. All in all, it is clear that the *majority* of children in the United States today experience at least two different family structures, often many more than that in the course of their growing up. This is especially true of African-Americans, but is increasingly true of other ethnic groups in our culture as well.

In other industrialized countries, single-parent families are less common, but they are on the rise everywhere. By the mid-1980s, the proportions ranged from less than 5 percent in Japan, to about 15 percent in Australia, the United King-

If cultures are systems too, then this enormous increase in the number of children experiencing a single-parent family structure has to have some impact on the whole system. What might be the long-term effects of this change?

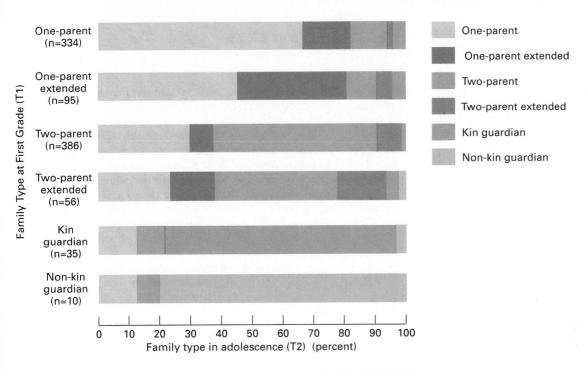

Figure 13.5
This figure is complicated, but it is worth your study. Each row represents a group of black children who had been in a particular form of family in first grade. The divisions on each row then indicate what kind of family structures those children lived in at adolescence. You can also get some sense of the proportions of each type of structure by looking at the number of families of each type at first grade (given as n = xxx along the left). (*Source:* Hunter & Ensminger, 1992, Figure 1, p. 443. Copyright 1992 by the National Council on Family Relations, 3989 Central Ave. NE, Suite 550, Minneapolis, MN 55421. Reprinted by permission.)

dom, and Sweden, to nearly 25 percent in the U.S. (Burns, 1992). Because cultures are complex, knowledge gleaned about the impact of family structure on children's development in one country may not hold elsewhere. But the issue is growing in importance in many parts of the world.

What do we know about the impact on children of being reared in such varied or varying family structures? Not as much as we'd like, but let me explore several issues.

The Impact of Divorce Itself.   Any change in the family structure is accompanied by dislocation and stress. In the case of divorce or separation, when an adult is subtracted from the family, the dislocation seems to be especially severe. In the several years immediately after a divorce, children become more defiant, more negative, more aggressive or depressed or angry. If they are of school age, their school performance typically drops for at least a while (Furstenberg & Cherlin, 1991; Hetherington, 1989; Hetherington & Clingempeel, 1992). There is some disagreement about how long this negative effect may last for the child. Some investigators report lingering effects 5 and 10 years later (Wallerstein, 1984; 1989). Others do not find such lasting effects (Hetherington, 1989), but all agree that in the short term, children are disturbed.

CULTURES AND CONTEXTS
The Benefits of Extended Families

Because single-parent families have become so common in the United States, researchers here tend to develop a kind of tunnel vision when it comes to studies of "family structure." For us, the question nearly always translates to a comparison of single-parent families with two-parent families. But in many parts of the world, the normative form of family life is not the nuclear or two-parent family, but rather an *extended* family, in which several generations live together in the same household. One recent study from the Sudan provides a kind of antidote to our typical cultural myopia.

Al Hassan Al Awad and Edmund Sonuga-Barke (1992) compared the incidence of childhood problems for children who lived in Western-style nuclear families (mother and father only) versus those who lived in traditional extended families, in which three generations lived in the same household. All these families lived in towns near Khartoum (the capital of Sudan), and the two groups were matched for social status and approximate income. The mothers were interviewed about their child's behavior and problems.

The findings are very clear: children reared in extended households were described as better-off than were those living in nuclear households. They had fewer conduct problems, fewer sleep problems, and better self-care, and were less likely to be overly dependent. The best single predictor of these good outcomes was the involvement of the child's grandmother in the child's care, and this was true within the group of nuclear families as well as in the comparison of nuclear and extended families.

How many different explanations for this result can you think of? Should we generalize this finding to Western cultures, and conclude that extended families would typically be better for children? How could you check out such a hypothesis?

Extended families like this one have their own strengths, too often ignored. In the United States, such families are much more common among African-Americans and Hispanic-Americans than among European-Americans.

You'll remember from the real world box on divorce in Chapter 9 that these negative effects seem to be considerably larger for boys than for girls. In adolescence, there are some signs that girls are more disrupted by a divorce than are boys, although this has not been found in every study (Hetherington, 1991a; 1991b; Hetherington & Clingempeel, 1992).

The same sort of disruption occurs in the parents' behavior, too. The adults may show wide mood swings, experience problems at work, or suffer from poor health. Their parenting style also changes, becoming much less authoritative, almost neglectful (Hetherington, 1989). In particular, they do much less well at monitoring their children's behavior and setting clear rules or limits, a pattern that typically persists for several years, even if the mother remarries (Hetherington & Clingempeel, 1992).

In all of this, it is not clear yet just what the causal agent is, because there are so many changes that happen at the same time when a couple divorces: the loss of one member of the family system, a rise in conflict between the parents, economic hardship (especially for the single mother, in most cases), and other stressful life changes. The disruption in the children's behavior, and in the adults' behavior, seems to result from some combination of these factors, although of them all, open conflict between the parents may well be the most critical (Amato, 1993).

Interestingly, it appears that many of these negative effects for both the adult and the children are mitigated when the mother has another adult in the home—her own mother, a friend, a live-in boyfriend (Dornbusch et al., 1985; Kellam et al., 1977)—which suggests that a two-adult system in a family may simply be more stable, or easier to manage.

Stepparent Families.   However—and this is an important however—there are various indications that this buffering effect of a second adult in the home may *not* extend to stepparent family structures (mother-stepfather, or father-stepmother). For example, Dornbusch, in the same large study I've been describing, finds that stepparent families show higher levels of authoritarian and lower levels of authoritative child-rearing styles (Dornbusch et al., 1987b), and the children have lower school grades and higher rates of delinquency than do children in two-natural-parent families. Mavis Hetherington, one of the key researchers in this field, has found something similar in a major study comparing intact, single-mother, and mother-stepfather families, all with adolescent children (Hetherington & Clingempeel, 1992). The stepfathers in this study were consistently less likely to be authoritative than were nondivorced fathers. Indeed, stepfathers were typically disengaged from the child-rearing role, with little involvement or rapport with their stepchildren. These patterns persisted even several years after the remarriage, suggesting that the process of adaptation in these families is extremely difficult. For remarried families with younger children, the process appears to be somewhat easier, although just why that should be so is not yet clear (Hetherington, 1989).

The literature on stepparent families also contains a curious finding, now replicated several times: In remarried families, the closer the parents' own relationship is, the *more* problems the children display (Brand, Clingempeel, & Bowen-Woodward, 1988; Hetherington, 1989). This seems to be especially true in the years immediately following the remarriage, and in cases in which the mother and children lived alone for some years. What is striking about this finding is that in studies of nondivorced families, just the opposite is typically found. That is, the closer the parents' relationship, the better off the children are.

One can perhaps make sense of this finding within a systems perspective by assuming that after the original divorce, the children not only were given more independence, they also took on various family roles from which they were displaced when the new stepfather appeared on the scene. And the closer the relationship of the mother and stepfather, the more displaced the children feel. However we explain it, this finding illustrates how enormously complex the family system is. We simply cannot assume that something like high marital satisfaction is going to have precisely the same effect on every family. The effect will vary as a

Can you think of any other explanation(s) for this odd finding?

Stepfamily structures like this one are extremely complex, full of strains and difficulties not found in original families.

function of the family's history, the age of the children, the specific style of child rearing, and many other factors.

At the same time, dimensions of family style seem to have very much the *same* effect on children, regardless of the structure of the family. In particular, authoritative child rearing is linked to low levels of disturbed behaviors and higher levels of psychological adjustment in the child, whether the child is growing up with a single mother, with a mother and stepfather, with two natural parents, or in any other family structure. Similarly, anytime the relationship between the two adults in the family system weakens in some fashion, as when the husband and wife are experiencing stress or heightened conflict, behavior standards for children decline, and this is true whether the couple divorces or not (Goldberg, 1990). So some basic psychological "rules" about family dynamics and their effects seem to apply very widely, while others may be specific to particular family structures.

Legal and Living Arrangements.   Are there any "rules" or guidelines to tell us whether one form of legal or living arrangement after a divorce is better for children than others? Until fairly recently in the United States, custody was virtually always given to mothers. In the last decade or so, more fathers have asked for and been given custody, and a growing number of divorcing parents arrange for joint custody and/or shared living arrangements in which children spend part of each week or month with each parent. There also seems to be a growing tendency for divorced fathers to maintain close contact with their children, even when the children live full-time with the mother. In one recent study in California that followed a group of over 1000 divorcing families over a $3^1/_2$ year period, only 14 percent of children who lived with their mother after the divorce had not seen their father within the past year, and roughly 40 percent had regular overnight visits with him (Maccoby & Mnookin, 1992).

But whether any of these variations in custody or visitation after a divorce have any long-term effect on the child's functioning is not so clear. It doesn't seem to matter whether teenagers live with the same-sex parent or the opposite-sex parent (Downey & Powell, 1993); it doesn't seem to make much difference whether children live with their father or their mother (Buchanan, Maccoby, &

Dornbusch, 1992), although those living in dual arrangements may be *slightly* better off. It isn't even clear whether maintaining contact or closeness with the non-custodial parent is critical for the child's continuing emotional balance or health (Furstenberg & Cherlin, 1991). What seems to matter for the child is the quality of the monitoring the parents are able to maintain, and the emotional closeness the child has with the custodial parent—both points I have made in the real world box on softening the effects of divorce (see p. 396). Thus, as has been true of much of what I have said about family dynamics, it is the *process* that is the most critical, not the structure itself.

◗ Some Exosystem Effects: The Impact of Parents' Work and Social Support on Family Functioning

The family process is itself affected by a wide range of experiences in the *parents'* lives—experiences that occur outside the family's interactions, but that nonetheless affect those interactions. The two examples I want to talk about are the parents' jobs and their network of social support.

The Impact of Parents' Jobs on the Family and the Child

There is an odd quirk in the existing research on the effects of parents' work on children: nearly all of the research on mothers' employment compares mothers who work with those who do not, while nearly all of the work on the impact of fathers' employment focuses on fathers who have *lost* their jobs. We have no research on mothers who lose their jobs, nor any comparing stay-at-home fathers with employed fathers. Given our cultural history, I suppose this pattern of research makes some sense, although it certainly leaves some significant gaps in our knowledge. Fortunately, a new body of work is beginning to emerge that asks a very different kind of question, about the impact of the *quality* of the parents' work experience on family life.

Mothers' Employment.   How is life different for children whose mothers work, compared to those whose mothers stay home? Do these two groups of children differ in any systematic way? These questions are obviously not entirely separable from all the issues about day care I'll be talking about in the next chapter, since it is precisely because the mother is working that most children are in alternate care. But the question is also relevant when we look at families with school-age children, where the impact of the mother's work is not so totally confounded with the effects of the child's alternative care.

The cumulative findings from the hundreds of studies of maternal employment are now fairly clear: For children past infancy, in this culture at this time in history, maternal employment has a generally positive effect, although the results are slightly different for boys than for girls. Girls whose mothers work are more independent, have more egalitarian sex-role concepts, and admire their mothers more than do girls whose mothers do not work. Boys whose mothers work also have more egalitarian sex-role concepts, but some early studies showed that boys of working mothers had somewhat lower academic achievement than did boys whose mothers stayed home. More recent studies, however, have not replicated this finding *except* in cases in which the mother works more than 40 hours a week (Hoffman, 1989).

In the United States today, roughly 60 percent of women with children under age 3 and three-quarters of those with school-age or adolescent children work at least part-time. In general, the effects seem to be beneficial for the children.

THE REAL WORLD
Softening the Effects of Divorce

Given the rate of divorce in our culture, a significant percentage of you reading these words will go through a divorce when you have children still living at home. There is no way to eliminate all the disruptive effects of such an event on your children, but here are some specific things you can do that are likely to soften or shorten the effects:

1. Try to keep the number of separate changes the child has to cope with to a minimum. If at all possible, keep the children in the same school, the same home, the same day-care setting, and so on.

2. Maintain your own network of support, and use that network liberally. Stay in touch with friends, seek out others in the same situation, join a support group. In whatever way you can, nurture yourself and your own needs (Hetherington & Camera, 1984).

3. Help your children stay in touch with the noncustodial parent. If you are the noncustodial parent, maintain as much contact as possible with your child(ren), calling regularly, seeing them regularly, attending school functions, and so forth. I should tell you that the evidence on this point is actually quite mixed; some studies show no positive benefit to the child of continued regular contact with the noncustodial parent (Emery,

1988). The difficulty in interpreting these results is that contact with the noncustodial parent is often confounded with the quality of the relationship between the now-divorced parents, which leads to the next point.

4. If you and your ex-spouse continue to have conflict, try very hard not to fight in front of the children. Conflict between the spouses itself seems not to be inevitably detrimental; it is the conflict that the child actually sees and hears that adds to the child's level of stress and disruption (Emery, 1988). If such conflict is low, then increased contact with the noncustodial parent seems most likely to be beneficial to the child.

5. Whatever else you do, do not use the child as a go-between or talk disparagingly about your ex-spouse to your child. Children who feel caught in the middle between the two parents are more likely to show various kinds of negative symptoms, such as depression or behavior problems (Buchanan, Maccoby, & Dornbusch, 1991).

In the midst of your own emotional upheaval from a divorce, these are not easy prescriptions to follow. But if you are able to do so, your children will suffer less.

Most researchers in this area assume, as I do, that it is not the mother's job per se that produces these effects, but rather that her employment alters the family system in at least two ways:

First, having a job may affect the mother's own view of herself, by increasing her self-esteem or her morale, and thereby changing the way she relates to the rest of the family. For example, a woman who begins working generally acquires more power in the spousal relationship, in part because she now has demonstrable earning power, and because she may feel more independent (Spitze, 1988). Such power or self-esteem also spills over into her interaction with her children, perhaps especially with a daughter. For example, Bronfenbrenner finds that working mothers give more positive descriptions of their young daughters than do nonworking mothers, which may help to account for the more positive outcomes for daughters associated with maternal employment (Bronfenbrenner et al., 1984).

Second, the mother's employment forces changes in daily routines and in interaction patterns simply because she is not at home for as many hours. Fathers in dual-worker families spend somewhat more time in child care and household tasks than do fathers with homemaker wives, although it is still true that working mothers do far more of this work than do fathers (Shelton, 1990). This change in the division of labor may then have an effect on the quality of the parents' interaction with children, as well as altering the role models each parent provides for the child.

These effects of employment on the woman and on her family are not automatic or uniform. The mother's attitude toward her work is an important intervening variable. Numerous studies show that the most negative outcomes are found among children in two subgroups: those with mothers who would prefer to work but are staying at home, and those with mothers who dislike their jobs or are unwilling workers (DeMeis, Hock, & McBride, 1986; Lerner & Galambos, 1986). The most positive outcomes occur when the mother wants to work, and works at a job she likes. In such families, the mother's style of child rearing is more likely to be authoritative (Greenberger & Goldberg, 1989).

Fathers' Employment or Unemployment.   I have already touched on the effects of a father's job loss when I talked about the McKenzie family at the beginning of this chapter. The results of many studies show a very clear pattern. When a man loses his job, it puts enormous strain on his marriage so that marital conflict rises and both parents show more symptoms of depression. As a result—just as we see in divorcing families—both become less-skillful parents, monitoring less well, being less consistent, less affectionate. The children respond to this deterioration in their parents' behavior in the same way children do during a divorce: they show a variety of symptoms, including sometimes depression, or aggression or delinquency. Often their school performance declines (Conger et al., 1992; Flanagan & Eccles, 1993). The negative pattern can be softened if the unemployed father receives enough emotional support from his wife, and is generally cured when the father again finds work. But the whole sequence illustrates nicely how an event outside the family affects the child through the impact on the parents' behavior toward one another and toward the child.

The newer studies that examine the effects of the quality of the parents' work point to a similar conclusion. One particularly interesting finding comes from the work of Melvin Kohn and Carmi Schooler (Kohn, 1980; Kohn & Schooler, 1983). They have found that men (or women) whose jobs require higher levels of self-direction and autonomy show increases in intellectual flexibility. Routine, highly supervised jobs lead to decreases in intellectual flexibility. Such routine jobs also seem to spill over into family life; over time, men who work at such jobs come to place greater emphasis on obedience from their children than is true for men in more intellectually flexible jobs. Thus the character of the job the man does affects his way of thinking, particularly his thinking about authority, and he applies that thinking to his interactions with his children.

Other research suggests that some specific jobs are quite likely to have negative spillover into family life. Both police work and military positions, for example, have been found to be linked with higher rates of abuse or family violence or disruption (Hoffman, 1984). Men with particularly demanding jobs, too, may have less time to spend with their families, which will again alter the interaction patterns.

I hope that these few bits illustrate that the kinds of questions psychologists are now asking about parents' employment have become much more subtle, much more oriented to a systems approach. But these questions are also much tougher to answer than the simpler ones we started with.

In December of 1991, these General Motors workers had just heard that the company would be laying off 74,000 employees over the next few years. Those who actually lost their jobs are likely to have experienced significant family upheaval.

Social Support for Parents

A second aspect of the parents' life that affects the family microsystem is the quality of the parents' network of relationships, and their satisfaction with the social support they receive from that network. The general point is fairly easy to state: Parents who have access to adequate emotional and physical support—from each other, or from friends and family—are able to respond to their children more warmly, more consistently, and with better control (Crnic et al., 1983; Taylor, Casten, & Flickinger, 1993b). Their children, in turn, look better on a variety of measures (Melson, Ladd, & Hsu, 1993).

The effect of social support on parents is particularly evident when they are experiencing stress of some kind, such as job loss, chronic poverty, teenage childbirth, a temperamentally difficult or handicapped infant, divorce, or even just fatigue. You may recall the discussion in Chapter 9 of a study by Susan Crockenberg (1981) that illustrates the point nicely. She found that temperamentally irritable infants were very likely to end up with an insecure attachment to their mothers only when the mother *lacked* adequate social support. When the mother felt that she had enough support, similarly irritable children were later securely attached. There are many other examples of this "buffering effect" of social support:

- New mothers who lack good social and emotional support are more likely to suffer from postpartum depression than are those with adequate support (Cutrona & Troutman, 1986).
- Divorced parents who have help and emotional support from friends or family members are much more able to maintain a stable and affectionate environment for their children than are those who grapple with the problem in isolation (Hetherington, 1989).
- Among African-American single mothers, those who have enough aid and emotional support from kin show a more authoritative style of parenting than do single mothers lacking such aid (Taylor et al., 1993b).

As a general rule, social support seems to allow parents to mobilize the best parenting skills they may have in their repertoire. Of course not all "help" from families or friends feels like support (I'm sure you have all been given unwanted advice from your parents or in-laws or friends). The key is not the objective amount of contact or advice received, but the parent's *satisfaction* with the level and quality of the support he or she is experiencing. The moral seems to be that at those times of greatest difficulty or stress—when a new child is born, when a child presents special difficulties, when the family moves or experiences major changes—you most need the emotional and physical support of others. But if you wait until that difficult moment to look around and see who is there to help, you may not find what you need. Social networks must be developed and nurtured over time. But they certainly seem to pay dividends for parents, and thus for children.

▶ Summary

1. To understand children's development we must move beyond examination of the child alone, or the mother-child pair. We must examine the total ecological system.

2. A system is understood as being more than the sum of its parts. It is also adaptive to change, and any change in any one part of the system affects every other part.

3. Bronfenbrenner conceives of the child's ecological system as composed of three types of elements: microsystems, such as the family or the school, in which the child is directly involved; exosystems, such as the parent's job, which affect the child indirectly by influencing some aspect of a microsystem; and macrosystems, such as the ethnic subculture, or the broader society or culture in which the family exists.

4. Within the family microsystem, several dimensions of parental behavior toward children seem to be particularly significant, including the emotional tone of the family, the method of maintaining control, and the patterns of communication.

5. Families that provide high levels of warmth and affection, compared to those that are more cold or rejecting, have children with more secure attachments and better peer relationships.

6. Families that have clear rules and standards, and relatively high levels of expectation or maturity demands, and that enforce those rules and expectations consistently, have children with the greatest self-esteem and the greatest competence across a broad range of situations.

7. Children who are talked to frequently, in complex sentences, and who are listened to in turn, not only develop language more rapidly, they also have more-positive and less-conflicted relationships with their parents.

8. These elements of parental behavior occur in combinations or styles of child rearing. Four such styles, suggested by several theorists, are authoritative, authoritarian, permissive, and neglecting.

9. The authoritative style is high in nurturance, control, communication, and maturity demands; the authoritarian is high in control and maturity demands but low in warmth and communication; the permissive style is high in warmth and low in communication, control, and maturity demands; the neglecting style is low on all dimensions.

10. The authoritative style appears to be the most generally effective for producing confident, competent, independent, and affectionate children. The most negative outcomes are found in neglecting families.

11. Research by Steinberg and Dornbusch suggests that there are some ethnic differences in the ways in which family styles affect children. In particular, Asian-American children do generally very well in school despite low rates of authoritative parenting. Family belief systems and peer culture also appear to play a role.

12. The family system is also affected by the child's characteristics, such as temperament, age, gender, and position in the family.

13. Siblings growing up in the "same" family nonetheless often turn out very differently. New research suggests that parents often behave quite differently toward each child.

14. Parental characteristics that affect the family system include depression, and the parent's own internal working model of attachment.

15. The structure of the family also has an impact on family functioning, which in turn affects children's behavior. The majority of children born in the United States today will spend at least a portion of their childhood in one-parent families.

16. Changes in family structure are likely to produce short-term disruption (often including an increase in authoritarian or neglecting child-rearing style) before the system adapts to a new form.

17. Stepparent families, particularly those containing adolescents, are relatively slow to adapt, and often continue to show nonauthoritative parenting for long periods.

18. Variations in custody arrangements after divorce appear to have less direct connection to good or poor outcomes than might be expected. What matters is the process of family interaction, far more than the structure.

19. A mother's employment affects the family system by changing the mother's self-image, increasing her power, and altering the distribution of labor. The effects on the children are generally positive, especially for girls.

20. Loss of job by a father disrupts the family system, decreasing authoritative child rearing, reducing marital satisfaction. Children often show disrupted behavior. The character of a man's job also has an effect on his family interactions.

21. The impact of family change or stress is mitigated by the availability of a sufficient amount of social support from the parents' social network.

▶ Key Terms

authoritarian parental style (382)	permissive parental style (382)	restrictiveness (379)
authoritative parental style (382)	responsiveness (377)	warmth versus hostility (377)

▶ Suggested Readings

Boer, F., & Dunn, J. (Eds.). (1992). *Children's sibling relationships: Developmental and clinical issues.* Hillsdale, NJ: Erlbaum.

A first-rate collection of papers on a subject that is of growing interest to many psychologists. Each paper is relatively brief and reviews the available literature on one aspect of sibling relationships.

Cherlin, A. J. (1992). *Marriage, divorce, remarriage.* Cambridge, MA: Harvard University Press.

An excellent, current review of all aspects of family formation, dissolution, and structural variations. It includes a long discussion of the impact of both race and poverty on the various trends.

Furstenberg, F. F., Jr., & Cherlin, A. J. (1991). *Divided families: What happens to children when parents part*. Cambridge, MA: Harvard University Press.

A relatively brief, current review of this important subject, aimed at lay readers and decision makers rather than at other psychologists. The focus is on the impact of divorce on children.

Maccoby, E. E., & Mnookin, R. H. (1992). *Dividing the child: Social and legal dilemmas of custody*. Cambridge, MA: Harvard University Press.

A well-written, interesting report of a large study of over 1000 divorcing families in California. Maccoby is a psychologist and Mnookin an attorney; their focus in this book is mostly on the parents' decisions about custody and visitation, and about changes over time in the family system.

Pence, A. R. (Ed.). (1988). *Ecological research with children and families: From concepts to methodology*. New York: Teachers College Press.

This volume contains a whole series of papers dealing with various aspects of Bronfenbrenner's ecological approach, both the theory itself and specific studies done to explore parts of the theory.

The Child's Experience of Day Care

Who Is Taking Care of the Children?

Effects of Day Care on Cognitive Development

Effects of Day Care on Personality

Effects of Day Care on Children's Attachment to Parents
• Soap Box: The Need for a Family Policy in the United States

The Impact of Schools

School and Self-Judgments
School Quality

Joining the Work World: The Impact of Jobs on Teenagers

Causal Effects or Self-selection?

The Impact of the Mass Media
• Research Report: Family Viewing Patterns

Positive Educational Effects of TV
Negative Effects of TV on Cognitive Skills
Television and Aggression

Macrosystem Effects: The Impact of the Larger Culture

Economic Variations: Social Class and Poverty

• Soap Box: Children in Danger
Ethnicity
The Culture as a Whole

Summary

Key Terms

Suggested Readings

The ecological approach to studying the family's influence on the child's development has brought us many new insights. But of course we cannot stop at the edges of the family. We also have to look at the other institutions that affect the child directly, including day-care or preschool settings, schools, jobs, and the mass media, especially TV. And as a final step, we need to try to understand the ways in which all of these institutions are embedded in still broader subcultural and cultural contexts. It is a tall order, but let us plunge in, beginning with day-care and school experiences.

▶ The Child's Experience of Day Care

In virtually every industrialized country in the world, women have gone into the workforce in great numbers in the past two decades. In the United States the change has been particularly rapid and massive: in 1972, only 24 percent of women with children under age 1 were in the labor force; by 1991 the *majority* of such women were working outside the home at least part-time, a rate that appears to be higher than for any other country in the world (Cherlin, 1992a). It is now typical for infants as well as school-age children to spend a significant amount of time being cared for by someone other than a parent. Similar but less-massive changes have occurred in other countries, but in the discussion to follow I'm going to be talking almost exclusively about day care as it exists in the United States.

What effect does such nonparental care have on infants and young children? As you can easily imagine, this is *not* a simple question to answer, for a whole host of reasons:

- There is an enormous variety of different care arrangements all lumped under the general title of "day care."
- Children enter these care arrangements at different ages, and remain in them for varying lengths of time. Some children have the same alternate caregiver over many years; others shift often from one care setting to another.
- Day care varies hugely in quality.
- Families who place their children in day care are undoubtedly different in a whole host of ways from those who care for their children primarily at home. How can we be sure that effects attributed to day care are not the result of family differences instead?

Most of the research we have to draw on does not really take these complexities into account. Typically, researchers have compared children "in day care" with those "reared at home," and assumed that any differences between the two groups were attributable to the day-care experience. Recent studies are often better, but we are still a long way from having clear or good answers to even the most basic questions about the impact of day care on children's development. Nonetheless, because the question is so critical, you need to be aware of what we know, as well as what we do not yet know.

Who Is Taking Care of the Children?

Let me begin at the descriptive level. Just who is taking care of all those children while their parents work? In some countries, such as France or Belgium, child care is organized and subsidized by the government and free to all parents. At the other end of the continuum lies the United States, where we have no national standards for care and only minimum government subsidies, primarily in the form of income tax credits for the poor, and support for the Head Start program for 3- and 4-year-olds. In our culture, each family must make its own arrangements as best it can.

Figure 14.1 shows the solutions parents have found. The figure includes data for all children under age 5 in the United States in 1988 whose mothers were employed at least part-time outside the home. The most common pattern is obviously for a child to be cared for in another person's home, most often by another

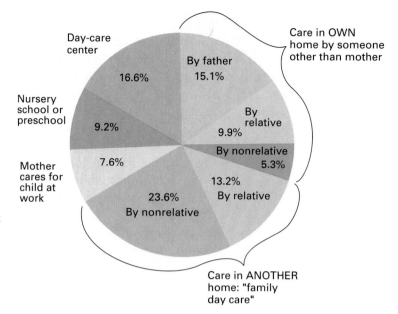

Figure 14.1
Child-care arrangements for children 5 and under in the United States in 1988. The most common arrangement is what is usually called *family day care*, that is, care in someone else's home. (*Source:* United States Bureau of the Census, 1992, Table 600.)

mother who takes in a few children for care—a pattern usually called **family day care.** Care in the child's own home by someone other than a parent is next most common, with day-care *centers* actually the least common. This pattern varies somewhat by age. Among 3- and 4-year-olds, center care is the most frequent choice; for infants under 1 year of age, care by a relative and family day care are much more common (Hayes, Palmer, & Zaslow, 1990).

High-quality care is possible in any of these settings, although they do differ from one another in systematic ways. For example, center care typically provides the most cognitive enrichment, while family day-care homes typically provide the least; both center care and family day care give the child an opportunity to play with same-age peers, while at-home care does not (Clarke-Stewart, 1987). Such variations make it very difficult to talk about global effects of day care, because the systems are quite different. Furthermore, the bulk of the research evidence is based on studies of children in center care, and we cannot be sure that these findings will generalize to children in family day care or with at-home care by someone other than a parent.

Effects of Day Care on Cognitive Development

Early research suggested that day care of any variety has little effect of any kind on the cognitive development of children from advantaged families, while children from disadvantaged families often show some cognitive gains (Scarr & Eisenberg, 1993). When the child care is highly cognitively enriched, the effect is especially clear, as in the Ramey programs I talked about in Chapter 6 (see Figure 6.5).

Several recent studies, however, suggest that this apparently clear conclusion requires some qualification. On the positive side, a study in Sweden, where day care is typically of very high quality, suggests that even middle-class children may

The majority of children in the U.S. have at least some experience with nonparental care, although group care like this day-care center is not the most common form.

benefit intellectually from day care, especially when they begin in such care in infancy. Andersson (1992) found that among a large group of 13-year-olds, those who had spent the most time in day-care centers had better school performance throughout elementary school compared to those totally home-reared, or those with only minimal day-care experience.

On the other side, there is a very good, large, new study in the United States (Baydar & Brooks-Gunn, 1991) that suggests exactly the opposite: that white middle-class children who enter child care in the first year of life, compared to those reared at home, do *less* well on cognitive tests at age 3 or 4. Baydar and Brooks-Gunn studied 1181 3- and 4-year-olds, all children of a nationally representative sample of young adults who have participated in a large longitudinal study called the National Longitudinal Study of Youth. In this sample, the researchers were able to compare children who had entered day care at various ages with those who had been cared for largely or entirely by parents. They found that among the white children—but *not* among the black children—those who began some kind of alternative care in the first year of life had the lowest vocabulary scores later in preschool, whether they were from advantaged or poverty-level families. The most negative effects were found for white children who began day care between 3 months and 9 months of age, and no negative effects were found for those who entered day care after age 1.

It is not clear how we can reconcile these discrepant findings. Perhaps the quality of care is crucial, especially when the child is under age 1. We do know that most alternative care is not highly cognitively enriched, and this may be especially important early on. Consistency of care—present in Sweden, but perhaps not available to many in the United States—may also be critical. Or perhaps white mothers who return to work soon after their child's birth are different in systematic ways from those who do not—ways that would contribute to the differences in later IQ measures. At this point, we cannot settle the question.

Of all these possible explanations of the discrepant findings, which one(s) do you think are most likely to be correct?

Effects of Day Care on Personality

Findings on the impact of day care on children's personalities are even more varied. A number of investigators have found that children in day care are more sociable, more popular, and have better peer-play skills than do those reared primarily at home. Andersson (1989; 1992) found this in his longitudinal study in Sweden, as have researchers in the United States (Scarr & Eisenberg, 1993). In general, this positive effect seems to be larger for children who enter day care in infancy as opposed to later—precisely the opposite of the Baydar findings for cognitive effects. However, the positive effect of day care on sociability and peer skills seems to hold only for *good-quality* care (Field, 1991; Howes, 1990).

On the negative side of the ledger is the fairly common finding that children who have been in day care, compared to those reared by parents at home, are more aggressive with peers and less compliant with teachers and parents at later ages (Belsky & Eggebeen, 1991; Haskins, 1985). Not everyone reports such an effect, and the level of aggressiveness described by most authors is not extreme. But the very fact that *some* day-care experiences are linked to increased aggressiveness and noncompliance has raised a cautionary note.

But how should we interpret these findings? By some measures day-care children seem to be *more* socially competent; by other measures, they seem less so. One possibility is that teachers in many day-care centers, in an effort to encourage children to be independent, have also inadvertently reinforced aggressiveness and excessive assertiveness. Maybe. In one day-care center whose children had shown heightened aggressiveness, the center staff deliberately altered their program to emphasize positive social skills. After this change, the heightened aggressiveness disappeared (Finkelstein, 1982).

Alternatively, some have interpreted the aggressiveness as a sign that children in day care learn to think for themselves more, are more independent and assertive (Clarke-Stewart, 1990; 1992). Others argue that the key may be the quality of the day care, not day care itself, as indicated by the very positive outcomes Field observed for children who had been in stable, good-quality care. Still others, such as Jay Belsky—a psychologist who has generally taken the most pessimistic view of all the findings on day care— conclude that these hints of behavioral maladjustment among children in day care should be taken very seriously (Belsky, 1990; 1992) and reflect more basic difficulties in the child, such as problems with attachment.

Effects of Day Care on Children's Attachment to Parents

The hottest debate concerns just this question of attachment. Specifically, can an infant or toddler develop a secure attachment to her mother or father if she is repeatedly separated from them? We know that the majority of infants develop secure attachments to their fathers, even though the father typically goes away every day to work, so it is clear that such regular separations do not *preclude* secure attachment. Still, perhaps separation from both parents on a daily basis might adversely affect the security of the child's attachment.

We can narrow the window of uncertainty a good deal if we consider the child's age at the time she or he first enters day care. All parties to the current dispute agree that children who enter day care after the first year of life show *no* consistent loss of security of attachment to their parents. Where there is disagreement is about those infants who enter day care before 12 months of age.

Until about a decade ago, most psychologists reading the relevant research had concluded that there was no negative effect of infant day care. But then Belsky, in a series of papers and in testimony before a congressional committee, sounded an alarm (Belsky, 1985; 1987; 1990; 1992; Belsky & Rovine, 1988). Combining data from several studies, he concluded that there was a heightened risk of an insecure attachment among infants who enter day care before their first birthday. Controversy erupted. Since that time, a number of other researchers have analyzed the combined results from larger numbers of studies and confirmed Belsky's original conclusion.

Summing across the findings from 13 different studies involving 897 infants, Michael Lamb (Lamb, Sternberg, & Prodromidis, 1992) finds that 35 percent of infants who had experienced at least 5 hours per week of nonmaternal care were insecurely attached, compared to 29 percent of the infants with exclusively nonmaternal care. He also found that the risk of an insecure attachment did *not* rise as the number of hours of the mother's employment increased. That is, babies whose mothers worked 40 hours a week, or 20 hours a week, were not more likely to be insecurely attached than those whose mothers worked 5 hours a week.

This is clearly not a huge difference, although it is statistically significant. The present controversy swirls around how to interpret or explain this difference.

Belsky has his supporters. Alan Sroufe, one of the major figures in studies of early attachment, points out that we know that security of attachment is fostered both by the child's sense of the responsiveness of care, and by the opportunity for parent and child to fine-tune their interactive dance. Both of these may be disrupted by placing the child in day care, although clearly in the majority of cases, parents find ways to counteract such disruptions, because the majority of children in day care are nonetheless securely attached (Sroufe, 1990).

On the other side of the argument are ranged a group of researchers who either don't believe that there is a serious problem to be dealt with, or argue that there are so many confounding variables that it is impossible to draw any clear conclusion. For one thing, there is a serious problem of self-selection involved in any comparison of day-care and parent-reared infants. Mothers who work are different in other ways from mothers who do not. More are single mothers, more prefer to work, or find child care onerous. So how can we be sure that any heightened probability of insecure attachment is due to the day-care experience, and not to other experiences?

There may also be a problem with using the Strange Situation as a measure of attachment security for day-care children. To assess security, the child must be at least mildly stressed— otherwise we simply don't see enough attachment behaviors to make a judgment. A child in day care, who is used to repeated separations from Mom, may simply not experience the episodes of the Strange Situation as stressful, and thus may show behavior that looks like avoidance but is really an indication of relative comfort in the situation (Clarke-Stewart, 1990).

For these and other reasons, Alison Clarke-Stewart (1990) concludes that "at the present time . . . it is not appropriate to interpret the difference, as Belsky ap-

Only when babies enter day care before age 1, as some of these youngsters seem to have done, is there a slightly increased likelihood of an insecure attachment. There is still a major dispute about how to interpret this finding.

What other differences might you expect between working and nonworking mothers of infants? How might those differences affect the likelihood that a child would be securely or insecurely attached?

SOAP BOX

The Need for a Family Policy in the United States

In a recent paper, Louise Silverstein (1991) makes a number of compelling points:

In 1990, fewer than 7% of American families reflected the two-parent model of husband as breadwinner and mother as homemaker (Braverman, 1989). Thus, the question of whether mothers should work is essentially irrelevant to modern family life. Mothers do work, and "child care is now as essential to family life as the automobile and the refrigerator" (Scarr et al., 1990, p. 26). (p. 1028)

However, the United States remains the only one of 75 industrialized nations that does not have a government-sponsored family policy that provides some form of paid maternity benefits, parental leave, and subsidized child care. (p. 1025)

Silverstein's central argument is that psychologists have contributed to this lack of official support for the modern family by continuing to focus so much research attention on the question of the potential ill effects of mothers' employment, or of day care.

Instead, she argues, we must devote our research attention to the "negative consequences of the lack of affordable, government-subsidized, high-quality programs" (p. 1030).

A panel convened by the National Academy of Sciences to study child care in the United States echoes these concerns. Their basic conclusions include the following:

1. Existing child care services in the United States are inadequate to meet current and likely future needs of children, parents, and society as a whole. . . . The general accessibility of high-quality, affordable child care has immediate and long-term implications for the health and well-being of children, parents, and society as a whole. . . .

2. Of greatest concern is the large number of children who are presently cared for in settings that do not protect their health and safety and do not provide appropriate developmental stimulation. (Hayes et al., 1990, p. xii)

Assuming that these statements are accurate, what do you think we ought to do about it? What new policies or programs would we need?

---

pears to, as suggesting that these children are emotionally insecure" (p. 69). Others have concluded that there may indeed be a link between some aspect of day care and security of attachment, but that we simply don't yet know what the link might be (Lamb et al., 1992).

One can also argue that Belsky is asking the wrong question. For the vast majority of families, the question is not "Should I put my child in day care?" but rather "Given that I have to work to help support my family, how do I find good-quality, affordable care for my child?"

We do know that the quality of the child's care makes a difference. Indeed, most of the positive outcomes of day care I have been describing are found *only* in good-quality programs, while inconsistent care, or poor-quality custodial care, can be actively detrimental to the child. In Table 14.1 I've listed the characteristics of good-quality programs, a list that might serve as a starting point in your evaluation of alternatives if and when you face this choice with your own children.

▶ The Impact of Schools

Another vitally important "microsystem," one experienced by virtually all children in every culture, is school. School begins at age 5 or 6 or 7, and in industrialized countries, typically continues through age 16 or older. During these 10 or more years, the child learns an enormous number of facts and develops new and much more complex forms of thinking, many of which I talked about in Chapter 7. In fact, we have good evidence from studies in many different countries—Mex-

---

TABLE 14.1 Ideal Characteristics of a Day-Care Setting

- **A low teacher/child ratio:** For children younger than 2, the ratio should be no higher than 1:4; for 2-to-3-year-olds, ratios between 1:4 and 1:10 appear to be okay.

- **A small group size.** The smaller the number of children cared for together—whether in one room in a day-care center or in a home—the better for the child. For infants, a maximum of 6 to 8 per group appears best; for 1-to-2-year-olds, between 6 and 12 per group; for older children, groups as large as 15 or 20 appear to be okay.

- **A stable relationship with a single caregiver.**

- **A clean, colorful space, adapted to child play.** Lots of expensive toys are not critical, but there must be a variety of activities that children will find engaging, organized in a way that encourages play.

- **A daily plan with at least some structure, some specific teaching, some supervised activities.** Too much regimentation is not ideal, but children are better off with *some* structure.

- **A caregiver with some knowledge of child development.**

- **A caregiver who is positive, involved, and responsive to the child, not merely custodial.**

Sources: Clarke-Stewart, 1992; Howes, Phillips, & Whitebook, 1992; Scarr & Eisenberg, 1993.

---

ico, Peru, Colombia, Liberia, Zambia, Nigeria, Uganda, Hong Kong, and others—that school experiences are *causally* linked to the emergence of such advanced cognitive skills (Stevenson & Chen, 1989; Stevenson et al., 1991). Children who do not attend schools not only do not learn many complex concepts and strategies, they are also not as good at generalizing a learned concept or principle to some new setting. So attending school helps children learn to think—precisely what it is intended to do.

But this is quite obviously not the only effect that school experience has on the child. During those 10 or 12 formative years, children hone their social skills in the context of peer contacts and establish crucial beliefs and attitudes about their own abilities, a central part of the self-scheme. These beliefs and attitudes then shape or limit the choices they will make later in childhood and adulthood.

School and Self-Judgments

Kindergarten and first-grade children seem to judge themselves and their abilities mostly on direct experience of their own success or failure. They pay relatively little attention to how well others do at a particular task; in fact the great majority will confidently tell you that they are the smartest kid in their class. But by third grade or so, children begin to compare themselves with others, and judge themselves accordingly. They notice whether their classmates finished a test sooner than they did, or whether someone else got a better grade or more corrections on his spelling paper. Teachers' behavior shows a similar change: In the first few grades, teachers emphasize effort and work habits. Gradually they begin to use more comparative judgments. By junior high, children are being compared not only to each other but to fixed standards, other schools, or national norms (Stipek, 1992).

The beliefs about their own abilities that students develop through this process are usually quite accurate. Students who consistently do well in comparison to others come to believe that they are academically competent. Further, and perhaps more important, they come to believe that they are in control of academic outcomes. Interestingly, this seems to be less true of girls than of boys, at least in American culture. On average, girls get better school grades than boys do, but they have lower perceptions of their own ability. When they do well, they are more likely to attribute it to hard work rather than ability; when they do poorly, they see it as their own fault (Stipek & Gralinski, 1991).

Of course some of these attitudes and beliefs come from home rather than or as well as from the school. You may recall from Chapter 6 that some evidence shows parents attribute a daughter's good performance in math to hard work, but a son's good math grades to ability. Such differences may well be sustained or extended by experiences in school. Teachers convey their beliefs about a student's ability in a variety of ways, many of them quite subtle, and this information seems to become increasingly salient to children over time. By seventh or eighth grade, certainly, most students have very well established ideas about their own skills and their ability to control the events around themselves.

In adolescence, these attitudes and beliefs begin to have very concrete and long-term effects. Students who believe they can do well are more likely to choose classes that prepare them for college. Students who do not believe they can do well make quite different choices, or may drop out of school altogether. Let me say just a few words about these two ends of the achievement continuum.

Achievers. You'll remember from Chapter 6 that the best single predictor of a student's academic performance in high school is IQ, and that this is true for every ethnic and social class group in American society. Both adolescent IQ and school grades also predict adult job success to at least some degree (Barrett & Depinet, 1991). A myriad of studies of military jobs, for example, show correlations in the range of .45 to .55 between scores on IQ-like tests and the recruits' later

These sixth graders in a Japanese school, like schoolchildren everywhere, make judgments about their own abilities and potentials on the basis of their school successes and failures.

proficiency and success at a wide range of jobs (Hunter & Hunter, 1984; Ree & Earles, 1992). Outside of the military, the same general relationship holds, although education plays a key intervening role. Students with higher IQs or better grades in high school tend to go on to more years of additional education, and this is as true among children reared in poverty as it is among the middle class (Barrett & Depinet, 1991). Those extra years of education, in turn, have a powerful effect on the career path a young person enters in early adulthood (Featherman, 1980; Rosenbaum, 1984).

These relationships exist not just because brighter kids have an easier time with schoolwork, but also because the cumulative effect of success over many years of schooling fosters a greater sense of self-efficacy in these intellectually more able students. Those who achieve, especially those who achieve despite poverty backgrounds or other daunting obstacles, also are more likely to have parents who have high aspirations for them (Brooks-Gunn, Guo, & Furstenberg, 1993a), or an authoritative family style, so there is—as always—an interaction between the effect of the family and the effect of the school.

You are surely an achiever, or you would not be reading this book. Does the profile of the achiever fit you?

Underachievers.   The power of beliefs is particularly clear in the case of "underachievers," those students whose school performance is well below the level that would be predicted by their IQ or other test scores. These young people come from families at every economic level, and from every ethnic group. But what they have in common, among other things, is a lower level of self-esteem than those of apparently equal ability who perform well in school (McCall, Evahn, & Kratzer, 1992). That is, they do not *believe* they can do well, even when their test scores indicate that they could. Underachievers also have lower aspirations and goals, and when they reach early adulthood, they are less likely to go on to more schooling or to find a job that is commensurate with their ability. One large study of nearly 6000 youths by Robert McCall and his colleagues (1992) shows that by their late twenties, underachievers were earning less money and had jobs of lower status than did young people who had worked up to their abilities in school.

Dropouts.   About 15 percent of students who enter high school in the United States fail to graduate. Boys are more likely to drop out than are girls, and among ethnic groups, Asian-Americans have the lowest dropout rates (less than 5 percent), with Native Americans the highest (23 percent). Whites (12 percent), African-Americans (17 percent), and Hispanics (19 percent) fall in between.

In the case of dropouts, social class is a far better predictor than is ethnicity. Kids growing up in poor families are considerably more likely to drop out of high school than are those from more economically advantaged families. When you hold social class constant there are essentially no differences in dropout rates among blacks, whites, and Hispanics (Entwisle, 1990). But because minority youth in the United States are so much more likely to come from poor families, or from families that do not provide psychological support for academic achievement, they are also more likely to drop out of school. Among those whose peer group also puts less value on achievement, as is true of many black and Hispanic teen groups in the United States, the risk of dropping out is even stronger (Takei & Dubas, 1993).

Teenagers who drop out of school list many reasons for such a decision, including not liking school, poor grades, being suspended, or needing to find work to support a family. Girls who drop out most often do so because they plan to marry, or are pregnant, or feel that school is simply not for them (Center for Educational Statistics, 1987). Lists of reasons like this, though, don't begin to capture the multifaceted nature of the decision to drop out. It is too simple, for example, to say that girls drop out because they are pregnant; some get pregnant because they are not interested in school and feel that they are ready for adult life. Low self-esteem or a low sense of self-efficacy, perhaps fostered by years of low achievement, also undoubtedly plays some role, just as it does among underachievers. In recent years, during economic hard times, many teenagers have also come to the conclusion that a high school diploma won't buy them much in the job world—not a totally unreasonable view, given the poor job prospects for many high school graduates in many parts of the country (and the world) today (Rosenbaum, 1991).

Yet in the long term, teens who use such a rationale for dropping out of high school are wrong. Unemployment is higher among high school dropouts than in any other education group, and dropouts who find jobs earn lower wages than do those with a high school diploma. The difference between these two groups is not as large as it once was; a man or woman with a high school diploma can no longer count on finding good-paying, skilled industrial jobs as was the case several decades ago. But a high school education still offers some advantage. Those who drop out enter a very different—and far less optimal—life trajectory.

School Quality

A very different set of questions about school experience has to do with variations in the quality of the schools themselves. Real estate agents have always touted a "good school district" as a reason for settling in one town or neighborhood rather than another. Now we have research to show that the real estate agents were right: specific characteristics of schools, and teachers, do affect children's development.

Researchers interested in possible effects of good and poor schools have most often approached the problem by identifying unusually "effective" or "successful" schools (Good & Weinstein, 1986; Rutter, 1983). In this research, an effective school is defined as one in which pupils show one or more of the following characteristics at higher rates than you would predict, knowing the kind of families or neighborhoods the pupils come from: high scores on standardized tests, good school attendance, low rates of disruptive classroom behavior or delinquency, a high rate of later college attendance, or high self-esteem. Some schools seem to achieve such good outcomes consistently, year after year, so the effect is not just chance variation. When these successful schools are compared to others in similar neighborhoods that have less-impressive track records, certain common themes emerge, summarized in Table 14.2.

What strikes me when I read this list is how much effective schools sound like authoritative parenting. There are clear goals and rules, good control, good communication, and high nurturance. The same seems to be true of effective teachers: it is the "authoritative" teachers whose pupils do best academically. Such teachers have clear goals, clear rules, effective management strategies, and personal and warm relationships with their pupils (Linney & Seidman, 1989).

TABLE 14.2 Characteristics of Unusually Effective Schools

- **Qualities of pupils.** A *mixture* of backgrounds or abilities but with a reasonably large concentration of pupils who come to school with good academic skills. When too many children have poor skills, it is more difficult for the rest of the things on this list to occur.

- **Goals of the school.** Effective schools have a strong emphasis on academic excellence, with high standards and high expectations, clearly stated by the administration and shared by the staff.

- **Organization of classrooms.** Classes are focused on specific academic learning. Daily activities are structured, with a high percentage of time in actual group instruction.

- **Homework.** Homework is assigned regularly, graded quickly.

- **Discipline.** Most discipline is handled within the classroom, with relatively little fallback to "sending the child to the principal." In really effective schools, not much class time is actually spent in discipline, because these teachers have very good control of the class. They intervene early in potentially difficult situations rather than imposing heavy discipline after the fact.

- **Praise.** Pupils receive high doses of praise for good performance, or for meeting stated expectations.

- **Teacher experience.** Teacher *education* is not related to effectiveness of schools, but teacher *experience* is, presumably because it takes time to learn effective class management and instruction strategies.

- **Building surroundings.** Age or general appearance of the school building is not critical, but maintenance of good order, cleanliness, and attractiveness does have an effect.

- **School leadership.** Effective schools have strong leaders, and those leaders state their goals clearly and often.

- **Responsibilities for children.** In effective schools, children are more likely to be given real responsibilities—in individual classrooms and in the school as a whole.

- **Size.** As a general rule, smaller schools are more effective, in part because in such schools children feel more involved and are given more responsibility. This effect is particularly clear in studies of high schools.

Sources: Linney & Seidman, 1989; Rutter, 1983.

But as with any system, the quality of the whole is more than the sum of the qualities of the teachers or classrooms. Each school also has an overall climate or ethos that makes a difference for the youngsters. The most positive school climate occurs when the principal provides clear and strong leadership, when there are widely shared goals, dedication to effective teaching, and concrete assistance provided for such teaching. In such schools, pupils and parents are respected, and there is usually a high rate of parent participation in school activities. If you are making a decision about a city, or a neighborhood, in which to rear your children, these are the qualities to look for.

▶ Joining the Work World: The Impact of Jobs on Teenagers

In earlier historical eras (and in many cultures around the world today), teenagers were already considered adults and fulfilled normal adult work responsibilities. They worked in the mines, in the fields, herding animals, fishing. Child labor laws changed this picture drastically in the nineteenth century in most industrialized countries. Today, adolescents are in school for many hours each day and are not available for adult work—although the typical school year, with a long summer vacation, was intended quite explicitly to allow young people to join in the labor of farming and harvest during the growing season.

Yet increasingly, adolescents have jobs. Beginning in about 1950 in the United States, teenage employment rates have risen quite steadily. Today, roughly three-fifths of all high school juniors have some kind of formal part-time job during at least part of the school year, and the great majority of students have had at least some work experience before they graduate (Bachman & Schulenberg, 1993; Greenberger & Steinberg, 1986).

For some, such work is an economic necessity. Others work in order to support their favorite hobbies or habits—to earn the money to buy a stereo, perhaps a car, or to go out for pizza with their friends. Parents are frequently very supportive of such work on the grounds that it "builds character," and teaches young people about "real life." Here's one parental voice:

> *Let's face it . . . some time in life, someone is going to tell you what to do. . . . I think work is the only place to learn to deal with it. . . . Parents can give you a little discipline, but it isn't accepted. . . . You can't learn that in school, because there is another so-called tyrant, the teacher. But then they get . . . a boss, and you get out there and learn it. (Greenberger & Steinberg, 1986, p. 39)*

But are parents right about such beneficial effects of work? Does it really teach responsibility and reliability? Quite the contrary. Results of several decades of research—at least for teenagers in the United States, for whom we have data—suggest that the more hours adolescents work, the more *negative* the consequences are.

In the largest single study, Jerald Bachman and John Schulenberg (1993) accumulated information from over 70,000 students, seniors in the graduating classes of 1985 through 1989. Subjects were drawn each year from both private and public schools in every state in the country. Roughly four-fifths of the students—both males and females—worked at least a few hours per week, most of them for pay. Nearly half of the boys (46.5 percent) and more than a third of the girls (38.4 percent) worked more than 20 hours per week.

Bachman and Schulenberg found that for both males and females, the more hours a student worked, the more he or she used drugs (alcohol, cigarettes, marijuana, cocaine), the more aggression he or she showed toward peers, the more ar-

Most part-time teen jobs are low-skill and low-paying, like this one. Such jobs do not appear to build character, but rather to have negative effects.

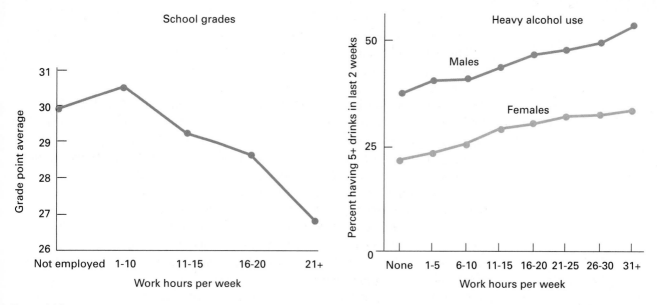

Figure 14.2
The data on the left come from Steinberg and Dornbusch's study; the data on the right come from Bachman and Schulenberg. (*Sources:* Steinberg & Dornbusch, 1991, upper section of Figure 1, p. 308; Bachman & Schulenberg, 1993, upper right section of Figure 1, p. 226.)

guments he or she had with parents, the less sleep he or she got, the less often he or she ate breakfast, the less exercise he or she had, and the less satisfied he or she was with life. An impressive list of negatives, isn't it?

Bachman and Schulenberg do not report on a link between school grades and outside employment, but that information can be gleaned from the same Steinberg and Dornbusch study of Wisconsin and California teens I talked about at some length in the last chapter (Steinberg and Dornbusch, 1991; Steinberg, Fegley, & Dornbusch, 1993). In this case, they have employment information from 5300 ninth to twelfth graders, data collected in 1987 and 1988.

Figure 14.2 shows two of the many results from these two studies, to give you some sense of the magnitude of the effects. It shows the relationship between work and school grades from the Steinberg and Dornbusch study, and the link between heavy alcohol use and work from the Bachman and Schulenberg study. I should note, by the way, that Steinberg and Dornbusch found essentially the same pattern of results for all the ethnic groups in their study, and for students from every economic level. So this is a widespread and significant effect.

In light of your own experience and the results of these studies, would you want your own children to work when they are teenagers?

Causal Effect, or Self-selection?

At this point, some of you are undoubtedly thinking that results like those in Figure 14.2 may not mean that working during the high school years *causes* bad effects. Instead, they may reflect self-selection: those students who are least interested in school, who already hang out with others who smoke or drink more, may be the same ones who choose to work more. Steinberg and his colleagues (1993) were able to check this possibility by looking at a subset of their sample over time. They found that those who later worked 20 hours a week had indeed been less involved with or committed to school in earlier years, which illustrates the effect of self-selection. But after they began working, these same students became even more withdrawn from school, and showed increases in both drug use and delinquency, and *lower* self-reliance than they had shown before they began work.

These are not comforting findings. It is difficult to escape the conclusion that teenage employment distracts young people from academic tasks. What is more, there appear to be few, if any, compensations: teens with jobs do not show higher self-reliance or self-esteem, as many theorists and policy planners had supposed. They also seem to learn some less-than-ideal lessons about the "real world," because they typically work in low-paying, repetitive, often meaningless jobs in which authority is arbitrary and unethical practices, such as stealing from your employer, are common (Greenberger & Steinberg, 1986).

The one area in which we do see some positive benefit from adolescent employment is in prospects for future jobs, and in later wages. For example, high school seniors who have had part-time jobs are more likely to report that they have full-time work lined up after their graduation. And those who see their jobs as providing skills that will be useful in the future seem to get some benefits and to be troubled by fewer negative side effects (Mortimer et al., 1992). But this minor benefit was seen primarily for those whose teenage employment was in skilled areas, such as skilled trades, factories, or health care. Students who have worked only in fast-food restaurants, or in retail sales, baby-sitting, or the like do not seem to have any leg up on future employment.

All of this does not mean that no teenager should ever work. There are obviously situations that will demand such employment, and certain types of skill training that may offer an important counterweight to the potential negative effects. But findings like these certainly should make parents pause before they (we) encourage teenagers to work on the grounds that it will build character.

▶ The Impact of the Mass Media

Still a fourth direct influence on children, particularly in industrialized countries, is the mass media, particularly television. Ninety-eight percent of American homes have a television set, which young children (between 2 and 11) watch an average of 28 hours a week. Adolescents watch about 23 hours a week (American Psychological Association, 1993). Indeed, "by the time American children are 18 years old, they have spent more time watching television than in any other activity except sleep" (Huston et al., 1990). High levels of viewing are more common among African-American children than among whites or Hispanics, and more common in families in which the parents are less well educated (Anderson et al., 1986).

Viewing rates are not as high in most other countries, but TV ownership is above 50 percent of households in most of Eastern and Western Europe and in Latin America, so this is not an exclusively American phenomenon (Comstock, 1991).

Just what are children seeing during all of those hours? Preschoolers see many programs designed specifically to be educational or informative, such as "Sesame Street" or "Mister Rogers' Neighborhood." As they get older, however, children increasingly watch cartoons, comedies, and adult-entertainment programs (Huston et al., 1990).

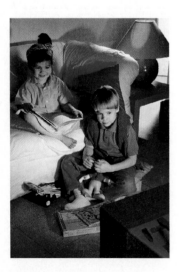

In the United States, children the age of these two watch an average of four hours of TV every day. Amazing.

RESEARCH REPORT
Family Viewing Patterns

Statements about the average number of hours of children's viewing disguise very large variations among families, not only in viewing patterns but also in attitudes about television. To a considerable extent, parents control their children's TV through explicit rules and through attitudes—an example of the way in which broad cultural forces interact with individual family styles. Nearly half of families have consistent rules about what type or which specific programs a child may view; about 40 percent restrict the number of hours a child can watch, while another 40 percent encourage the child's viewing at least some of the time (Comstock, 1991).

Michelle St. Peters (St. Peters et al., 1991), in one recent study, found that she could classify families into one of four types on the basis of the degree of regulation and degree of encouragement of TV viewing parents imposed. *Laissez-faire* parents had few regulations but did not specifically encourage viewing. *Restrictive* parents had high regulations and gave little encouragement, while *promotive* parents had few regulations and high levels of encouragement for TV viewing. *Selective* parents had high regulations but encouraged some specific types of viewing.

In a two-year longitudinal study of 5-year-olds and their parents, St. Peters found that children in restrictive families watched the least TV (11.9 hours per week). When they watched, it was most likely to be entertainment or educational programs aimed specifically at children (such as "Sesame Street," "Mr. Rogers' Neighborhood," or Walt Disney). The heaviest viewers were children with parents classed as promotive, who watched an average of 21.1 hours per week. They watched not only children's programs but also adult comedy, drama, game shows, and action adventure. In laissez-faire families, children watched an intermediate number of hours (16.7), mostly devoted to child entertainment and comedy, a pattern similar to what appeared in the selective families, although the latter group watched more informative programs directed at children than did laissez-faire children.

The key point here is that families create the conditions for children's viewing, and thus for what children learn from TV. Not only do parents establish a degree of regulation, they may also watch with the child and interpret what the child sees. A family that wishes to do so can take advantage of the beneficial things TV has to offer and minimize exposure to programs with aggressive, violent, or sexist content. The difficulty for many families, however, is that such a planned approach to TV may mean that the parents will have to give up their own favorite programs.

I can give you only a few tidbits from the vast amount of research designed to detect any effects such viewing may have on children, and on adults. Still, a taste is better than no meal at all.

Positive Educational Effects of TV

Programs specifically designed to be educational, or to teach children positive values, do indeed have demonstrable effects. This is particularly clear among preschoolers, for whom most such programming is designed. Children who watch "Sesame Street" more regularly, for example, develop larger vocabularies than do children who do not watch or watch less often (Rice et al., 1990), and those who watch programs that emphasize sharing, kindness, and helpfulness, such as "Mister Rogers' Neighborhood," or "Sesame Street," or even "Lassie," show more kind and helpful behavior (Murray, 1980).

Negative Effects of TV on Cognitive Skills

In elementary school and high school, however, there is evidence that higher levels of TV viewing are associated with *lower* scores on achievement tests, including measures of such basic skills as reading, arithmetic, and writing. This is particularly clear in the results of an enormous study in California that included over 500,000 sixth and twelfth graders (California Assessment Program, 1980). In this very large sample, the more hours the students watched TV, the lower their scores

How many different explanations can you think of for the relationship between amount of TV watching and school performance? What kind of data would you need to check the plausibility of each of your explanations?

on standardized tests. This relationship was actually *stronger* among children from well-educated families, so this result is not an artifact of the fact that working-class or low-education families watch more TV. However, among children with limited English fluency, high levels of viewing were associated with somewhat higher school achievement. Thus television can help to teach children things they did not already know (including language), but among children with basic skills at the start of school, TV viewing time appears to have a negative effect on school performance.

Television and Aggression

By far the largest body of research has focused on the potential impact of TV on children's aggressiveness. On American television, the level of violence has remained high over the past two decades (despite many congressional investigations and cries of alarm). In prime-time programs, a violent act occurs 5 or 6 times per hour; on Saturday morning cartoons, the rate is 20 to 25 times per hour. MTV, available in roughly 60 percent of homes in the U.S., has far higher rates of violence than prime-time commercial shows.

Observers also agree that the "good guys" are just as likely to be violent as the "bad guys," and that violence on most TV programs is rewarded; people who are violent get what they want. In fact, violence is usually portrayed as a successful way of solving problems. Furthermore, the consequences of violence—pain, blood, and damage—are seldom shown, so the child is protected from seeing the painful and negative consequences of aggression, and thus receives an unrealistic portrayal of those consequences.

Does the viewing of such a barrage of violence *cause* higher rates of aggression or violence in children? Demonstrating such a causal link is rather like demonstrating a causal link between smoking and lung cancer. Unequivocal findings would require an experimental design—a strategy ruled out for obvious ethical reasons. One cannot assign some people randomly to smoke for 30 years, nor assign some children to watch years of violent TV while others watch none. But we now have three types of research evidence that all point strongly toward the existence of a causal link.

Some short-term experiments have been done in which one group of children is exposed to a few episodes of moderately aggressive TV while others watch neutral programs. These studies generally show a short-term increase in aggression among those who watched the aggressive programs. A second type of research relies on correlational evidence, which, as always, leaves us with a problem of interpretation. For example, children who already behave aggressively may *choose* to watch more TV and more violent TV. And families in which TV is watched a great deal may also be more likely to use patterns of discipline that will foster aggressiveness in the child. Nonetheless, good correlational studies also suggest a causal connection. One research example will make the point clear.

In his 22-year longitudinal study of aggressiveness from age 8 to age 30, Leonard Eron (1987) has found that the best predictor of a young man's aggressiveness at age 19 was the violence of television programs he watched when he was 8. Twelve years later, when the men were 30, Eron found that the seriousness of criminal behavior was strongly related to the frequency of TV viewing at age 8,

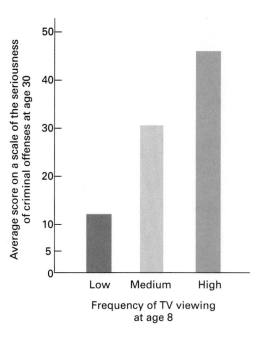

Figure 14.3
These data from Leonard Eron's 22-year longitudinal study show the relationships between the amount of TV a group of boys watched when they were 8 and the average severity of criminal offenses they had committed by the age of 30. (*Source:* Eron, 1987, Figure 3, p. 440.)

as you can see in Figure 14.3. The pattern is the same for women, by the way, but the level of criminal offenses is far lower, just as the level of aggression is lower among girls in childhood.

Eron also found that at age 8, boys who watched a lot of violent television were already more highly aggressive with their peers, indicating that aggressive boys choose to watch more violent TV. However, among the already-aggressive 8-year-olds, those who watched the most TV were more delinquent or aggressive as teenagers and as adults (Eron, 1987; Huesmann, Lagerspetz, & Eron, 1984). Shorter-term longitudinal studies in Poland, Finland, Israel, and Australia show similar links between TV viewing and aggression among children in each case (Eron, Huesmann, & Zelli, 1991), which further strengthens the point. Evidence like this suggests that the causality runs both ways: "Aggressive children prefer violent television, and the violence on television causes them to be more aggressive" (Eron, 1987, p. 438).

The newest type of evidence, perhaps the most persuasive of all, comes from epidemiology. Brandon Centerwall (1989; 1992) proposed that if we think of societal violence as an epidemic disease, we could use exactly the same strategy to study it that an epidemiologist would use in trying to trace the causal factors in any other epidemic. In his study, Centerwall looked at the homicide rate in Canada, and among whites in both the United States and South Africa, as a function of the time since television was introduced into each country.

TV was introduced in both the United States and Canada in about 1950, in South Africa about 25 years later. In each of these three countries, the homicide rate began to rise *rapidly* 10 to 15 years after TV viewing became widespread. That is, as soon as the first generation of children who had grown up watching

Figure 14.4
Centerwall looked at societal violence as if it were a disease, and asked what relationship the introduction of TV in each culture had to the rate of such violence. (*Source:* Centerwall, 1989, combined from Figure 1, p. 6, and Figure 2, p. 7. Adapted by permission of Academic Press, Inc.)

TV became adults, homicide rates soared. Figure 14.4 shows the results for both Canada and the United States.

Taking all three types of evidence together, the conclusion seems inescapable that "viewing violence increases violence" (American Psychological Association, 1993, p. 33). It also leads to emotional desensitization toward violence, and to a belief that aggression is a good way to solve problems. Violent television is clearly not the only nor even the major cause of aggressiveness among children or adults. But it is a significant influence, both individually and at the broader cultural level.

For parents, the clear message from all the research is that television is an educational medium. Children learn from what they watch—vocabulary words, helpful behaviors, and aggressive behaviors and attitudes. The overall content of television—violence and all—may indeed reflect general cultural values. But an individual family can pick and choose among the various cultural messages by controlling what the child watches on TV.

Given what you have just read, would you restrict your child's TV watching, and if so, in what way? Would you be willing to give up having a television altogether if you thought that was necessary for your child's optimum development?

▶ Macrosystem Effects: The Impact of the Larger Culture

Finally, we come explicitly to the question of contexts and cultures. Each family, and thus each child, is embedded in a series of overlapping contexts, each of which affects the way the family itself interacts, and each of which affects all other parts of the system. These contexts include the overall economic position of the family, the ethnic group to which the family belongs, and the larger culture in which all of this exists. These days one should probably also think about the global culture, because the global marketplace affects job opportunities and standards of living in individual countries. But that is a level of complexity I cannot yet begin to grasp.

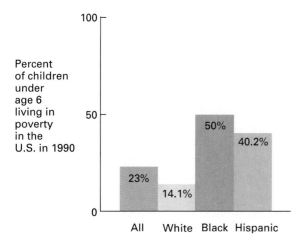

Percent of children under age 6 living in poverty in the U.S. in 1990

Figure 14.5
The percentage of children under age 6 living in poverty in the United States. (*Source:* United States Bureau of the Census, 1992, Table 719, p. 457.)

Economic Variations: Social Class and Poverty

Every society is made up of social layers, usually called **social classes,** with each layer having a different degree of access to goods or status. In Western societies, the social class of a given family is most often defined in terms of the income and education of the adults in that family. In the United States, three social classes are usually identified: middle-class, working-class, and poverty-level families. Members of each of these groups or social layers tend to share certain values or styles of interaction (Luster, Rhoades, & Haas, 1989), with the largest differences found between families living in poverty and those in higher social class groups. For children, it is clear that the disadvantages of poverty are enormous.

Figure 14.5 shows the percentages of young children of different ethnic groups in the United States who live below the poverty line— defined in 1990 as an income for a family of four of $13,359 per year or less. *More children in the United States live in poverty than in any other industrialized country in the world.* And in this country, poverty is a far more common experience for minority children and youth, especially if they live with a single mother. Roughly 70 percent of black and Hispanic children reared by single mothers live in poverty.

Furthermore, when minority families are poor, they stay poor longer. Vonnie McLloyd (1993) notes that two-fifths of black children, but only 6 percent of white, grow up in families that are poor for as long as 5 to 6 years. Half of white children grow up in families that are never poor and never live in a poor neighborhood, while this is true for only 5 percent of blacks. Thus even those black families that do not fall below the poverty line at any one moment are likely to have fallen below it at some time, and/or spend some time living in a poor neighborhood.

The Effects of Poverty on Families and Children.   Among many other things, poverty reduces options for parents. They cannot afford prenatal care, so their children are more likely to be born with some sort of disability. When the mother works, she has fewer choices of affordable child care. Such children spend more time in poor-quality care, and they shift more from one care arrangement to another. Poor families are also larger (Broman, Nichols, & Kennedy, 1975), with children more closely spaced, and they live in smaller and less-adequate housing. The total environment is more chaotic, more highly stressed, with fewer resources.

Mothers and fathers living in poverty also treat their children quite differently than do mothers and fathers in working-class or middle-class families in the United States. They talk to them less, provide fewer age-appropriate toys, spend less time with them in intellectually stimulating activities, and are stricter and more physical in their discipline, explaining things less often and less fully (Farran, Haskins, & Gallagher, 1980). They are more likely to be either neglecting or authoritarian, and less likely to be authoritative (Dornbusch et al., 1987b).

Some of this pattern of parental behavior is undoubtedly a response to the extraordinary stresses and special demands of the poverty environment (among other things, obedience may be quite simply more necessary in some poverty environments); some of the pattern may also be straightforward modeling of the way these same parents were brought up in their own childhood; some may be a product of ignorance of children's needs. Poor parents with relatively more education, for example, typically talk to their children more, are more responsive, and provide more intellectual stimulation than do equally poor parents with lower levels of education (Kelley, Sanches-Hucles, & Walker, 1993). But whatever the cause, children reared in poverty not only experience different physical conditions but quite different interactions with their parents.

Not surprisingly, such children turn out differently, as I have pointed out repeatedly in earlier chapters. Children from poverty environments have higher rates of birth defects and early disabilities; they recover less well from early problems; they are more often ill and malnourished throughout their childhood years. Typically, they also have lower IQs and move through the sequences of cognitive development described by Piaget more slowly. The more years they have lived in poverty, the larger the observed IQ decrement, even when family structure and the mother's level of education are taken into account (Duncan, 1993). They do less well in school, and are less likely to go on to college (Patterson, Kupersmidt, & Vaden, 1990). Such children, in turn, are more likely to be poor as adults, thus continuing the cycle through another generation.

The Special Case of Inner-City Poverty. All of these effects are probably much worse for children growing up in poverty-ravaged urban areas. They are exposed to street gangs and street violence, to drug pushers, to overcrowded homes and abuse. Whole communities have become like war zones.

In the United States, almost 13 million children live in such urban poverty (Garbarino, Kostelny, & Dubrow, 1991). More than one and a half million of these live in public housing developments, including some with the highest crime rates in the country. A recent survey in Chicago (Kotulak, 1990) revealed that nearly 40 percent of elementary-school and high school students in the inner city had witnessed a shooting, a third had seen a stabbing. Guns are common in schools as well as on the streets. I was stunned to read that in a study in Seattle, Washington (a city with a rate of urban poverty well below that of Chicago, New York, or Los Angeles), investigators found that 11.4 percent of the teen males re-

When you look at scenes of urban poverty like this, you can see why some refer to them as "war zones."

ported owning a handgun. A third of these gun owners had fired at someone (Callahan & Rivara, 1992).

In the early years of childhood, when youngsters spend most of their time with a parent or other caregiver, or with siblings, it may be possible for parents to protect them from some of the dangers inherent in such poverty environments. But in middle childhood, when children pass through the streets to travel to and from school and to play with their peers, they experience the impact of urban poverty and decay far more keenly. Many show all the symptoms of post-traumatic stress disorder (Garbarino et al., 1992), including sleep disturbances, irritability, inability to concentrate, angry outbursts, and hypervigilance. Many experience flashbacks or intrusive memories of traumatic events. And because they are likely to have missed out on many of the forms of intellectual stimulation and consistent family support that would allow them to succeed in school, they have high rates of problems and academic failures. Less than half of urban poor children graduate from high school (Garbarino et al., 1991). The reasons for such school failures are complex, as I have already pointed out, but there is little doubt that the chronic stress experienced by poor children is one highly significant component.

The Role of Stress and Protective Factors.   Arnold Sameroff and his colleagues have argued that the effects of various different kinds of stresses accumulate. A child may be able to handle one or two, but as the stresses and risks accumulate, the probability that a child will thrive intellectually, emotionally, or socially declines steadily (Sameroff et al., 1987). For a child growing up in poverty, perhaps especially urban poverty, the chances of experiencing multiple separate types of stress are very high indeed.

At the same time, studies of resilient and vulnerable children (Easterbrooks, Davidson, & Chazan, 1993; Garmezy & Masten, 1991; Masten, Best, & Garmezy,

Are you also shocked by such statistics? What do you think we ought to do about it?

SOAP BOX
Children in Danger

I cannot leave the subject of urban poverty—so common now in America—without getting up on my soap box one more time by quoting some of James Garbarino's eloquent words:

What is truly needed in America's urban war zones is restoration of a safe environment where children can have a childhood, and where parents can exert less energy on

protecting children from random gunfire and more on helping children to grow. No one can eliminate all risk from the lives of families. But America does have the resources to make a real childhood a real possibility even for the children of the urban poor. But sometimes the war close to home is the most difficult to see. (Garbarino et al., 1991, p. 148)

1990) suggest that there are certain characteristics or circumstances that may help to protect some children from the detrimental effects of repeated stresses and upheavals, including the following:

- High IQ in the child
- Competent adult parenting, such as an authoritative style
- Effective schools
- A secure initial attachment of the child to the parent

For example, in a major longitudinal study in Kauai, Hawaii, Emmy Werner (Werner, Bierman, & French, 1971; Werner & Smith, 1982) has found that a subset of those children reared in poverty nonetheless became competent, able, autonomous adults. The families of these resilient children were clearly more authoritative, more cohesive, and more loving than were the equivalently poor families whose children had worse outcomes. Similarly, studies of boys reared in high-crime inner-city neighborhoods show that high intelligence and at least a minimum level of family cohesion are key ingredients affecting a boy's chance of creating a successful adult life pattern (Long & Vaillant, 1984; McCord, 1982). Boys reared in poverty-level families in which there was alcoholism, parents with strong antisocial tendencies, or low IQ were simply less likely to develop the competence needed to raise themselves out of their difficult circumstances.

Thus the outcome depends on some joint effect of the number of stresses the child must cope with, and the range of competencies or advantages the child brings to the situation. Poverty does not guarantee bad outcomes, but it stacks the deck against most children.

Ethnicity

In the United States, social class and ethnic group membership are strongly linked to one another, because poverty status is so much more common among some ethnic groups than others. But if we are to gain an understanding of children's development, we need to understand the separate effects of ethnic group membership. What difference does it make to a child to grow up in a Hispanic family, as opposed to an Asian, Native American, white, or black family? In what ways do the varying values and attitudes, or the varying patterns of child rearing, alter outcomes for the child? We have touched on these questions throughout the book, but let's take one final look at what we know about ethnic effects, using the several major ethnic groups in the United States as illustration.

First, though, we need a better definition of ethnicity than I have given so far. Porter and Washington (1993) define it this way:

*An **ethnic group** is a subgroup whose members are perceived by themselves and others to have a common origin and culture, and shared activities in which the common origin or culture is an essential ingredient. (p. 140, emphasis added)*

Note that race and ethnicity are not the same. *Ethnicity* refers primarily to social and cultural characteristics, while *race* normally designates a group with specific physical characteristics. Thus Hispanic-, African-, and Asian-Americans may be viewed as both ethnic and racial categories, while Polish-Americans or Italian-Americans would be regarded only as ethnic groups.

These Irish-Americans marching in a St. Patrick's Day parade would fit the definition of an ethnic group, but are not a race.

African-Americans. African-Americans, the largest ethnic minority group in the United States, including roughly 12 percent of the total population, have a culture that has been shaped by their African heritage, their experience of slavery, and a continuing experience of discrimination and segregation. The central values of this ethnic culture include the following (American Psychological Association, 1993, p. 38):

- Communalism, as opposed to individualism
- A strong religious or spiritual orientation
- An emphasis on the importance of children for family continuity
- Harmony and a sense of connection with nature
- Role flexibility

These values, especially the emphasis on communalism and the importance of children, have contributed to a pattern of family structures that is quite different from what exists within European-American culture. European-Americans think of "the family" as (normatively) a father, mother, and several children. But within the African-American culture, "family" has a much broader definition, including many variations of extended family structures. Martin and Martin (1978), in their book *The Black Extended Family*, define it this way:

a multigenerational, interdependent kinship system which is welded together by a sense of obligation to relatives; is organized around a dominant figure; extends across geographic boundaries to connect family units to an extended family network; and has a built in mutual aid system for the welfare of its members and the maintenance of the family as a whole. (p. 1)

Thus the key is not just that three or more generations often live in the same household, but also that contact with nonresident kin is also frequent and integral to the functioning of the family unit. When asked, African-Americans overwhelmingly report a strong sense of family solidarity (Hatchett & Jackson, 1993; Wilson, 1986; 1989).

Within this subculture, marriage does not play the dominant role in family formation that it does among European-Americans. Far fewer black adults marry, they are less likely to be satisfied with their marriages, and divorce is more common (Broman, 1993). One result is that a much larger percentage of black children are born to or reared by unmarried mothers. But because of the cultural emphasis on the importance of children and on communalism, these single mothers occupy a different niche within the African-American culture than in the majority culture in the United States. European-American single mothers are more

Black families see children as essential for family continuity, and emphasize communalism more than individualism. Such cultural values are expressed in a myriad of subtle ways.

likely to receive financial help from their parents; African-American single mothers are more likely to live in an extended family with their own mother or grandmother (Wilson, 1986).

These extended family structures allow individuals to combine their economic resources, and they provide social and emotional support to the members of the household. I mentioned in the last chapter that the presence of the grandmother seems to provide especially helpful support for the young single mother; black children in such three-generation families do better in school and show fewer behavior problems than do black children reared in single-mother households. There is also some evidence that the presence of the grandmother increases the chance that an infant will develop a secure rather than an insecure attachment (Egeland & Sroufe, 1981). Thus the extended family not only has a cultural history, it also seems to be a successful adaptive strategy for many black families.

Religion also appears to play a special, positive role within the African-American community. The church is a place for participation and belonging, a structure in which prestige and status can be conferred on those who take on specific roles. For black children, participation in church activities seems to be a plus as well; a few studies suggest that those who are active in a church are more likely to be successful in other arenas, such as school or on the job (Lee, 1985).

The culture of African-American families is also profoundly shaped by the persistence of prejudice and discriminatory housing practices, the difficulty in finding good jobs, the (often accurate) perception that hard work will not necessarily yield good results. In many inner cities, the combined effect of these forces has been to create a subculture in which illegal activity or idleness becomes the norm for African-American teenagers, especially teenage boys (Spencer & Dornbusch, 1990). And among adult black men, "economic marginality" appears to be a significant precursor to divorce or family strain—a pattern that is not unique to the black subculture, but that is particularly relevant for this group precisely because job opportunities are more limited.

Because so many black families and children live in or near poverty, it is very difficult to sort out which patterns are due to economic conditions and which to distinctive African-American cultural processes. The two obviously interact, and are further embedded within the larger culture in which prejudice and discrimination against blacks are still a part of everyday life.

Hispanic-Americans.   The same is true of Hispanic-Americans, for whom poverty is also endemic. The term *Hispanic* actually covers a wide range of separate groups, all with some historical link to Spain, but which often differ significantly from one another in values and cultural traditions. Of the 22 million Hispanic-Americans in 1990 (9 percent of the total U.S. population), 13 million were Mexican-Americans (also called Chicanos), nearly 3 million were Puerto Ricans about a million were Cubans and the rest were from other countries (United States Bureau of the Census, 1992). Within this diverse group, Puerto Ricans have the highest poverty rates, and have a divorce rate comparable to that of African-Americans. Both Chicanos and Cubans have divorce rates more like the dominant Anglo (European-American) culture.

All of these subgroups, however, share a number of cultural values, including the following (American Psychological Association, 1993, p. 38):

- Preference for group participation (allocentrism)
- Strong commitment to and adherence to family (familism)
- Avoidance of personal conflict (*simpatía*)
- Respect for and deference to authority (*respeto*)

In addition, of course, there is also the common thread of the Spanish language. The great majority of Hispanics in the United States today are either monolingual in Spanish, or bilingual. Because of rapid recent immigration, more than half of Hispanic-American school-age children have only limited English proficiency; among those children and adults who are second- or third-generation Americans, there is generally a shift toward English as the dominant language, but many if not most continue to speak Spanish in the home (Chapa & Valencia, 1993; Grenier, 1985). In many communities there are also Spanish-language newspapers and radio and TV stations, as well as neighborhoods in which Spanish is the dominant tongue.

The significance of family life within the Hispanic culture is hard to exaggerate. The nuclear family is the core of this kin system, although contact with extended family members, and with "fictive kin," is frequent. Fictive kin, who are also a common part of the extended family system within African-American families, might include a child's godparents, or other friends of the real parents who

This Hispanic family has obviously assimilated some of the larger American culture: they are celebrating Thanksgiving. At the same time, they have doubtless retained many features of Hispanic culture, including the centrality of family loyalty.

Are there any "fictive kin" in your own family network? What is their role within the family?

take on a long-term connection with the family and with each child (Keefe & Padilla, 1987).

In general, Hispanics see frequent contacts with kin not only as enjoyable, but also as vital signs of the closeness of kin relationships. It is not enough to write or talk on the phone; to maintain close ties you need to see and touch your relatives and friends. Among Hispanics, an individual's self-esteem may also be more strongly related to the valuation given by the kin group. William Madsen (1969) describes the difference this way:

> When an Anglo fails, he thinks first of how this failure will affect him and his status in society. When a Chicano fails, his first evaluation of the failure is in terms of what it will do to his family and how it will affect his relationship to other family members. (p. 224)

There is some indication that this pattern is stronger in first-generation immigrants, who rely almost exclusively on family members for emotional support and problem solving. Second-generation immigrants seem to have more extensive nonkin networks. But in both generations, the extended family clearly plays a more central role in the daily life of Hispanics than it does in the Anglo culture.

This emphasis on the central role of the family is reflected in the values taught to children. In Chicano parlance, the relevant set of values is called *bien educado*, and includes politeness, respect, loyalty, and attachment to the extended family and cooperation with others. Hispanic mothers emphasize the importance of a child showing proper demeanor in public; Anglo mothers, in contrast, are more likely to value individual autonomy in their child (Harwood, 1992).

These values are taught in the home through all the mechanisms I have described throughout the book: modeling, direct reinforcement, and style of family interaction. A number of studies suggest that the more fully the parents identify with their Hispanic ethnic heritage, the more likely it is that the child will show these valued qualities, such as concern for others (Knight, Cota, & Bernal, 1993).

These values often conflict with the strong individualism and competitiveness of the dominant Anglo culture. Where the values of the minority and majority cultures overlap is in the value placed on education. Hispanic parents, like both African-American and Anglo parents, place a strong value on doing well in school. Yet Hispanic youth are even more likely to drop out of school or to get poor grades in school than are African-American teens (Spencer & Dornbusch, 1990). This pattern has been difficult to explain. It is certainly linked partially to poverty, perhaps also to persisting language difficulties. It may also arise in part from the emphasis on deference and respect that are part of *bien educado*, because such an emphasis means that Hispanic parents are quite likely to show an authoritarian rearing style. We know that such a rearing style is associated with poorer school performance, so it may be that the very aspect of Hispanic culture that is one of its greatest strengths may also contribute to less-optimal school outcomes for children—at least within the larger Anglo cultural system.

Asian-Americans. But wait a minute. That can't be all the explanation either, because Asian-American families *also* place great stress on obedience to family, on respect for elders, on family honor. Their family style is rarely authoritative, yet Asian-American children do extremely well in school—in American schools as well as in Asian schools. Where do the differences lie?

If you look at a list of key values of Asian-American culture, you can see that some of the ingredients are similar, but the whole is distinct. These values include the following (American Psychological Association, 1993, p. 39):

- Pacifism, self-discipline, and self-control—all values linked to Confucianism, and so common for those Asian groups with a strong Confucian heritage (Chinese, Korean, Vietnamese, and Japanese)
- An emphasis on hierarchy and respect in social systems and personal relationships (parents are superior to children; men are superior to women)
- Strong family links; young people are expected to obey elders
- A strong belief that each person controls his or her own destiny
- A powerful work ethic and belief in the importance of achievement

Asian-American families resemble Hispanic families in some respects. They often include three generations in the same household; they are generally hierarchically organized with the father as the clear head, with a strong emphasis on the interdependence of family members. But there are important differences as well, among the most important being the attitude toward achievement. Asian-American families expect their children to work very hard to achieve (Harrison et al., 1990; Stevenson, 1988), and they believe in *effort* as one of the primary roads to success. In contrast, in the broader American culture, *ability* rather than hard work is seen as the key to success. This difference is not trivial. If you believe in ability as the key ingredient, then there is not much point in pressing for greater effort, and you will accept mediocre performance from your child. But an Asian parent, believing in the centrality of effort, takes a very different attitude toward both success and failure. He takes success more or less for granted, but responds to failure by insisting on more effort. As a result of these different belief systems, Asian-American parents spend more time tutoring their children, and have higher standards for the child's achievement. They are also less likely to be satisfied with the schools, believing that the schools, too, can always do better.

Given all these differences, we shouldn't be surprised that Asian-American children as a group do achieve at higher levels in schools (Slaughter-Defoe et al., 1990; Stevenson, 1988), just as Asian children from Japan, China, Taiwan, and Korea regularly outperform American children and teenagers on standardized tests of math and science. Asian-Americans have the highest rate of high school completion and the highest rate of college completion of any group in the United States, including Anglos.

Asian families are also more stable, more upwardly mobile, less likely to be poor than other groups. Eighty percent of Asian families involve a married couple, compared to 65 percent among Hispanics, and 47 percent among African-Americans. A corollary is that single parenthood is relatively uncommon among Asian-Americans. Collectively, all of these factors mean that Asian-Americans are least likely to live in poverty of any of the minority groups I have described here.

Think about your own beliefs for a moment. Do you think of effort or ability as the most significant element in an individual's success? Has your belief about this affected your own choices or behavior at any point in your life?

Asian-American parents typically place great emphasis on the importance of hard work to reach academic goals. And they back this up by supervising their children's homework.

Ethnicity in Perspective.   What conclusions can we draw about the role of ethnicity in children's development from these three brief (and necessarily simplistic) sketches? Sadly, not many. Most research has involved comparisons of each ethnic group with children or families in the Anglo culture; until recently, most of this research assumed that the Anglo culture was right or best, and all other variations were inferior. That assumption has faded, but we rarely have information about all these groups at the same time, and even less often have data about whether the same *processes* operate in each subgroup. What we are left with is a kind of snapshot of each group, without being able to tell which characteristics are the most crucial, which attitudes or values the most significant.

For example, if we look for reasons for good or poor school performance in different subcultural experiences, what conclusions can we draw? Bilingualism cannot be the sole answer, because both Asian-Americans and Hispanics are typically bilingual; child-rearing style cannot be the sole answer because Asian-American parents are most likely to be authoritarian, yet their children do well in school. Doubtless it is the *pattern* of values and parental behavior that is crucial, and not any one variable operating at once. Cultures and subcultures are incredibly complex systems, and their effects come from the combination and not merely from the adding up of a set of separate variables. In addition, of course, because we are talking about subcultures here, there is also the issue of how each culture, each set of values, combines or conflicts with the values of the majority culture. For a child growing up with a foot in each culture, these are highly important issues.

> Imagine a largish group of European-Americans set down in the midst of some quite different culture, such as perhaps China or Japan. What cultural conflicts would the children of this subgroup be likely to experience?

The Culture as a Whole

The culture as a whole is also a system, made up of values, assumptions, and beliefs, a political and an economic system, a pattern of personal relationships, and so forth. Each piece of that system affects all the other parts; changing one part changes the whole. The wide cultural consequences of the rapid increase of women in the labor force is a very good example. It has led, among many other things, to a huge new demand for day care (with consequent changes in children's lives), to changes in male-female relationships, to new political alignments, and to shifts in patterns of interactions within families, which in turn affect children in still other ways.

Throughout the book, I have pointed to a variety of patterns or sequences of children's development that seem to occur regardless of cultural context. The stages of moral judgment, the early stages of language development, the creation of internal models of attachment, physical maturation, the development of a theory of mind—all of these and many other patterns appear to be universal aspects of development.

But examples of cultural differences are also easy to come by. At the most visible and measurable level are variations in children's specific beliefs, the social scripts that they learn, and the pattern of family and kin relationships they experience.

An interesting example comes from the work of Giyoo Hatano and his colleagues (1993), who compared beliefs about the nature of plants and animals among Japanese, Israeli, and American kindergarten, second-grade, and fourth-grade children. Piaget noted, and others have confirmed, that children typically begin with the idea of *animism*, in which they attribute not only life but also feelings and self-awareness to inanimate objects, to plants, and to animals. Later they differentiate among these several facets of life and understand that plants are alive but have no self-awareness. Hatano's study confirms the broad features of this shift: younger children in all three cultures had much stronger beliefs in animism. But Hatano also found differences in the developmental pattern, depending on the specific cultural beliefs about life.

Japanese culture includes the belief that plants are much like humans; in the Buddhist system, even a blade of grass is thought to have a mind. In contrast, in Israeli culture, plants are put into a quite different category from animals and humans. When children in these two countries, along with U.S. children, were asked if a tree or a tulip were alive, 91 percent of the Japanese but only 60 percent of the Israeli fourth graders said that it was. In contrast, a fifth of Japanese fourth graders still attributed sensory properties to plants, saying that a tree or a tulip could feel that it is cold, or could feel pain if it is hit with a stick. Overall, because of their stronger distinction between plants and animals, Israeli children were much slower than either Japanese or American children to come to the understanding that people, animals, and plants are all alive. This study thus illustrates both an underlying developmental pattern that seems to be shared across cultures (or at least across these three cultures), but also cultural variations on that basic pattern.

It is not hard to generate similar examples. Cultures may vary in the proportion of securely and insecurely attached children because of variations in their typical child-rearing styles or beliefs, even while the *process* by which a child becomes securely or insecurely attached is much the same from one culture to another; adolescents in all cultures need to change their identity to at least some extent in order to move into the adult world, but cultures that provide initiation rituals at puberty may make the process much simpler and less confusing.

Certainly we need to know a great deal more about how such cultural variations affect development. But as I pointed out in Chapter 1, we also have to ask a more subtle set of questions. In particular, we need to know whether the *relationship* between environmental events or child characteristics and some outcome for the child is the same in every culture. Is authoritative child rearing optimal in all cultures, or are there settings in which some other style is better to prepare children for adult life? Are aggressive children unpopular in every culture, or are there some settings in which this quality would be highly valued? Indeed, is unpopularity in childhood a major risk factor for adult dysfunction in every culture?

As yet we do not have answers, although researchers are beginning to ask the questions. Steinberg and Dornbusch, for example, asked whether authoritative parental style had the same effects in each of several ethnic groups in the United States. They found that it did not; this finding forces us to reexamine our assumptions about the way parental style operates to affect children's development.

It is extremely difficult to conceptualize the developmental process as part of a complex system, and even harder to design research that allows us to look at all the pieces of the puzzle at the same time. But it is precisely that kind of research we need if we are to be able to understand the full impact of the ecology of the child's development, including cultural and subcultural influences.

▶ Summary

1. Children's development is influenced by institutions beyond the family that affect them directly, including day care, school, jobs, and television. Development is also affected by the subculture and culture in which the child grows up.

2. The majority of children in the United States now spend some part of their infancy or preschool years in some form of nonparental care. The most common form of such care is "family day care."

3. The impact of day care on cognitive development is somewhat unclear, although good-quality day care appears to provide some cognitive benefit to children from poor families. There is a similar dispute about the impact on personality. Some studies show children in day care to be more aggressive; others show them to be more socially skillful.

4. Numerous studies show a small difference in security of attachment between children in day care and those reared at home. Interpreting this difference has proven difficult and contentious.

5. The quality of care appears to be a highly significant element. Good-quality care involves small groups of children, in clean spaces designed for children's play, with responsive caregivers trained in child development.

6. One of the main effects of school experience is to shape a child's sense of self-efficacy. By adolescence, children have a clearly developed idea of their comparative skills and abilities. These beliefs are a significant element in decisions about high school completion or dropping out.

7. Unusually effective schools have features much like an authoritative parenting style: clear rules and control, high expectations, good communication, and high nurturance.

8. The majority of teenagers in the United States hold down part-time jobs. The more hours a student works, the lower his school grades, the more drugs or alcohol he uses, and the more aggression he shows.

9. The average American child watches four hours of television per day. Preschoolers can learn vocabulary, politeness, or other skills. Among school children, the more TV watched, the lower the school grades.

10. Experts agree that watching violence on TV also increases the level of personal aggression or violence shown by a child, and later in adulthood.

11. Children growing up in poverty, perhaps especially urban poverty, are markedly disadvantaged in many ways, including lower access to medical care, and exposure to multiple stresses. They do more poorly in school, and drop out of school at far higher rates.

12. Some protective factors, including a secure attachment, higher IQ, authoritative parenting, and effective schools, can counterbalance poverty effects for some children.

13. The African-American subculture includes a strong emphasis on extended family households and contact, and on religion, but a weaker emphasis on

marriage as the vehicle for household formation. Because a large fraction of African-Americans live in poverty, it is difficult to sort out the separate effects of ethnic culture and poverty.

14. Hispanic-Americans, too, place great emphasis on family ties, on family honor and solidarity, heightened by the use of a shared language. Kin contact is frequent and central to daily life. Values taught to children include politeness, respect, and loyalty, an emphasis somewhat at odds with the individualism of the larger society.

15. Asian-Americans also emphasize respect and loyalty to family, but stress the central importance of effort (rather than inherent ability) as the path to achievement. Asian-American families are more stable, with lower divorce rates and fewer single-parent families; their children achieve in school at a higher rate than any other ethnic group.

16. As yet we know far too little about the ways in which these varying mixtures of values and family patterns interact to affect children's development.

17. When we compare whole cultures, our ignorance also exceeds our knowledge. Some patterns of development appear to be independent of culture, such as perhaps moral judgment reasoning. Others are affected by cultural variation, but the basic processes of such influence appear to be the same across cultures, such as perhaps the fostering of a secure attachment.

18. Finally, there are some aspects of development in which both the observed pattern of development and the process by which it occurs vary as a function of cultural or subcultural patterns.

▶ Key Terms

ethnic group
(425)

social class (421)

family day care
(404)

▶ Suggested Readings

Booth, A. (Ed.). (1992). *Child care in the 1990s: Trends and consequences*. Hillsdale, NJ: Erlbaum.

>   If you want to get the day-care debate from the horses' mouths, this is an excellent source. It includes a summary of the effects of day care on children by Alison Clarke-Stewart, along with a reply by Belsky and others. If nothing else, this book will persuade you that academic arguments are not always dry and dull; there is plenty of heat here!

Garbarino, J., Dubrow, N., Kostelny, K., & Pardo, C. (1992). *Children in danger: Coping with the consequences of community violence*. San Francisco: Jossey-Bass.

>   A striking, frightening book about children growing up in "war zones," including urban poverty in the United States, as well as in literal war zones in other countries.

McAdoo, H. P. (Ed.). (1993). *Family ethnicity: Strength in diversity*. Newbury Park, CA: Sage.

>   A very helpful collection of papers describing the family life and experiences of African-Americans, Hispanic-Americans, Native Americans, Asian-Americans, and Muslims

ATYPICAL DEVELOPMENT

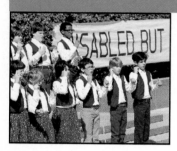

How Common Are Such Problems?
- **Cultures and Contexts:** *Problem Behaviors Among Children in Kenya and Thailand*

Developmental Psychopathology: A New Approach

The Psychopathologies of Childhood

Externalizing Problems
Internalizing Problems: The Example of Depression
- **The Real World:** *Adolescent Suicide and Its Prevention*
Vulnerability and Resilience
Developmental Psychopathology: A Reprise

Intellectually Atypical Development

Mental Retardation
Learning Disorders

Giftedness

Physically Atypical Development

The Deaf Child
The Blind Child
- **Research Report:** *Basic Attachments Between Blind Babies and Their Mothers*

Sex Differences in Atypical Development

The Impact of an Atypical Child on the Family

A Final Point

Summary

Key Terms

Suggested Readings

When Jeffrey was 4, he couldn't walk or talk and spent most of his time in a crib. His parents fed him pureed baby food through a bottle. After six years with a loving foster family, at age 10 Jeffrey is now in a special class in a regular elementary school and is learning to print and read.

Nine-year-old Archie seemed "different from other children even when he started school." Often he was "disoriented" or "distractible." Although he scored in the normal range on an IQ test, he had great difficulty learning to read. Even after several years of special tutoring he could read only by sounding out the words each time; he didn't recognize even familiar words by sight (Cole & Traupmann, 1981).

Janice's parents are worried about her. Right about the time that she turned 13 she seemed to change in quite disturbing ways. She's lost weight, even though she's growing fast; she doesn't seem to call up her friends anymore, and is listless and gloomy. This has been going on for about six months now, and her parents think this is just not normal; they're going to talk to the school counselor about her, and will consider family therapy if it will help.

Each of these children is "atypical" in some way. In each, the developmental processes I have been describing in the past 13 chapters haven't quite worked in the normal way. Jeffrey is a Down syndrome child, and is mentally retarded. Archie has some kind of learning disability, while Janice shows many signs of a clinical depression.

▶ How Common Are Such Problems?

How common are such problems? Given the critical practical relevance of this question, you'd think that psychologists and epidemiologists would long ago have come to some agreement. But we haven't, in large part because the line between typical and atypical is very much a matter of degree rather than of kind. *Most children show at least some kinds of "problem behavior" at one time or another.* For example, parents in the United States report that 10 to 20 percent of 7-year-olds still wet their beds at least occasionally; 30 percent have nightmares; 20 percent bite their fingernails; 10 percent suck their thumbs; and 10 percent swear enough for it to be considered a problem. Another 30 percent or so have temper tantrums (Achenbach & Edelbrock, 1981). Problems like these, especially if they last only a few months, should more properly be considered part of "normal" development. Usually we label a child's development "atypical" or deviant only if a problem persists for six months or longer, or if the problem is at the extreme end of the continuum for that behavior.

When we count only such extreme or persisting problems, the incidence is much lower—although nonetheless higher than most of you will have guessed. Table 15.1 gives some current estimates for each of a series of deviant patterns. Some of these numbers are based on extensive data and are widely accepted, such as the 3.5 percent rate of mental retardation. Others are still in some dispute, such as the rate of depression in adolescence. Where the findings are not in agreement, I have given the range of current estimates.

We might also want to combine all these individual rates in some way, to give us some idea of the total percentage of children with one kind or problem or another. Unfortunately, this is not a simple matter of addition, since there is a good deal of overlap in the various categories. For example, many children with serious learning disabilities also show an attention deficit disorder or conduct disorders. Still, even if we allow for some overlap, the totals are astonishing: between 14 and 20 percent of children and teenagers show at least *some* form of significant psychopathology (Brandenburg, Friedman, & Silver, 1990). If we add in cognitive disorders, the total is at least 20 percent. That is, at least one in five, and maybe as many as one in four children will show at least one form of deviant or abnormal behavior, *at some time in their early years*. The majority of these children will require some form of special help in school, in a child guidance clinic, or the equivalent. When you think of these figures in terms of the demands this places on the school system and on other social agencies, the prospect is somewhat staggering.

Do you think that such high rates of problems would be found in every culture? Why or why not?

TABLE 15.1   Estimated Incidence of Various Types of Atypical Development in the United States and Other Developed Countries

Type of problem	Percentage of children 0–18 with that problem
Psychopathologies	
Externalizing problems:	
(1) Attention deficit disorder (hyperactivity)	3 to 5%
(2) Conduct disorders	5 to 7%
(3) Arrested by police (delinquency)	3%
Internalizing problems:	
(1) Significant anxiety and fear	2.5%
(2) Serious or severe depression	
Elementary-school-age children	0.015%
Adolescents	3 to 8%
Psychoses (the most severe pathologies)	0.08%
Intellectually atypical development	
IQ below 70 (mentally retarded)	3.5%
Speech and language problems, including delayed language, articulation problems, and stuttering	3.5%
Serious learning disability	4.0%
Physical problems	
Autism	0.04%
Significant hearing impairment	0.5%
All other problems, including blindness, cerebral palsy, epilepsy, etc.	0.2%

Sources: Barkley, 1990; Brandenburg et al., 1990; Broman et al.,1987; Cantwell, 1990; Chalfant, 1989; Kopp & Kaler, 1989; Rutter, 1989; Rutter & Garmezy 1983; Tuna, 1989.

If we are going to meet those needs, we must obviously understand the origins of such atypical patterns. In this chapter I can give you only a glimpse of our current knowledge, but I can at least alert you to the issues and remaining questions about the most common forms of deviance.

▶ Developmental Psychopathology: A New Approach

Our knowledge about the dynamics of deviant development in general, and psychopathology in particular, has been enormously enhanced in the past few years

---

CULTURES AND CONTEXTS
Problem Behaviors Among Children in Kenya and Thailand

There is now a growing body of information showing links between particular cultural values and the type of emotional or behavioral problem children may show. In one recent study, John Weisz and his colleagues (1993) compared the incidence of externalizing and internalizing problems among teenagers in a rural Kenyan group, the Embu, and a rural Thailand group with the rates among rural black and white youth in the United States. Both the Thai and Embu cultures place great emphasis on obedience and politeness, a pattern of cultural values that appears to be linked to higher rates of "overcontrolled" or internalizing problems, such as shyness, fearfulness, or depression. In contrast, the United States culture, with its greater emphasis on individual freedom, appears to foster higher rates of "undercontrolled" or externalizing problems, such as fighting, showing off, or hyperactivity.

In each of the three cultures, parents were asked a series of questions about specific behaviors or symptoms their child showed. Weisz found that the Embu teens had the highest rates of internalizing and the lowest rate of externalizing problems, while American white teens had the highest rates of undercontrol, followed by African-American teens. Interestingly, the Thai group showed low rates of both types of problems, although other studies in Thailand have shown high levels of overcontrol problems in this culture.

The fact that the Embu and Thai patterns are not the same certainly reminds us yet again that cultural effects are not going to be so simple as a difference between an emphasis on obedience or on personal freedom. But the results also remind us that the pattern of frequencies of various types of problems that we note in U.S. populations are at least in part a product of our culture.

---

by the emergence of a new theoretical and empirical approach, called **developmental psychopathology,** pioneered by such researchers as Norman Garmezy, Michael Rutter, Dante Cicchetti, Alan Sroufe, and others (Cicchetti, 1989; Rutter & Garmezy, 1983). These theorists have emphasized several key points:

First, normal and abnormal development both emerge from the same basic processes. To understand either we must understand both and how they interact with one another. The task of a developmental psychopathologist is to uncover those basic processes—both to see how they work "correctly" in the case of normal development, and to identify the *developmental deviations* and their causes (Sroufe, 1989). Alan Sroufe's studies of the consequences of secure or insecure attachment, which I discussed in Chapter 11, are good examples of research based on such assumptions.

Second, the approach is *developmental*. Theorists in this new tradition are interested in the *pathways* leading to both deviant and normal development, from earliest infancy, through childhood, and into adult life. What are the sequences of experiences that lead to increased risk of depression in adolescence? What is the pathway leading to antisocial behavior, or to peer rejection? And what are the factors that may inhibit or exacerbate an early deviation, or may turn an initially normal developmental trajectory into a deviant pattern?

One of the potentially exacerbating factors may be the underlying developmental pathway itself. Each age has special tasks and special stresses that interact with the child's ongoing patterns and internal models to produce either normal or deviant behavior. For example, there is growing evidence that rates of depression among young people rise markedly at adolescence. A developmental psychopathologist would ask what is unique about adolescence that would contribute to such heightened depression rates.

He or she would also want to know what special qualities or early experiences a child may bring to the experience of puberty that might increase or decrease her risk of developing a pathological pattern such as depression. One of the unexpected results of many recent studies of children thought to be "at risk" for particular kinds of problems, such as children reared by depressed parents, or children in divorcing families, or abused children, has been that some children seem to be unexpectedly resilient in the face of what appear to be disturbing circumstances. The obverse has also been found repeatedly: some children seem to be unexpectedly vulnerable, despite what appear to be supportive life circumstances. Developmental psychopathologists such as Rutter and Garmezy have not only taken the lead in studying resilient children, they have insisted that these "exceptions" to the general rules offer us crucial information about the basic processes of both normal and abnormal development.

There is now a growing body of research cast in this framework that can help us examine the origins and manifestations of the array of psychopathologies.

The Psychopathologies of Childhood

The most helpful way to organize the many types of psychopathologies, in my view, is to divide the set into two large categories: **externalizing problems** (also described as *disturbances of conduct*), such as hyperactivity, excessive aggressiveness or defiance, and delinquency, in which the deviance is directed outward; and **internalizing problems** (also called *emotional disturbances*), such as depression, anxiety, or eating disorders, in which the deviance is largely internal to the individual.

Externalizing Problems

Conduct Disorders. One of the most obvious types of externalizing problems is what we might call in layperson's terms *delinquency* or *antisocial behavior*. In the most recent revision of the American Psychiatric Association's *Diagnostic and Statistical Manual of Mental Disorders* (called DSM-III-R), this is labeled a **conduct disorder,** and includes high levels of aggression, argumentativeness, bullying, disobedience, irritability, and threatening and loud behavior.

It has been clear for a long while that there are a number of subvarieties of conduct problems. In the last few years, developmental psychopathologists have struggled to find improved ways to characterize those variations. Achenbach (1993) argues for two subtypes: *aggressive behavior*, which includes arguing, being mean to others, destruction of objects, fighting, attacking, showing off, sudden mood changes, temper tantrums, loudness, and the like, and *delinquent behavior*, which includes specific lawbreaking such as setting fires and stealing, but also a lack of guilt, lying, running away from home, swearing and obscenity, and use of alcohol and drugs.

In contrast, Hinshaw (Hinshaw, Lahey, & Hart, 1993) argues that the crucial issue is when the deviant behavior began. *Childhood-onset conduct disorders* are more serious, with high levels of aggression, and are far more likely to persist to adult criminality; *adolescent-onset* problems appear to be milder, more transitory, more a function of hanging about with bad companions than a deeply ingrained behavior problem.

Why does it matter what kind of category system we use, or how good it is?

These two category systems overlap a good deal. The cluster of problems Achenbach calls aggressive behavior typically begins early and is much more persistent, and thus fits within Hinshaw's childhood-onset group, while delinquent behavior most often begins in adolescence and is less persisting and serious. But the fit between the two taxonomies is not perfect. In particular, many children with early-onset conduct problems show both aggressive and delinquent behaviors. But both of these category systems may turn out to be helpful in aiming researchers toward clearer questions about the origins of the various types of conduct disorders.

The developmental pathway for early-onset conduct disorders is one you are familiar with by now from all I have said about Patterson's research on aggressive children. In early life, these are children who throw tantrums and defy parents; indeed they may well have insecure attachments as well (Greenberg, Speltz, & DeKlyen, 1993). Once the defiance appears, if the parents are not up to the task of controlling the child, the child's behavior worsens to overt aggression toward others, who then reject the child, which aggravates the problem, pushing the seriously aggressive child in the direction of other children with similar problems, who form the only peer group. By adolescence, these youngsters are firmly established in antisocial behavior, and in adulthood they are highly likely to continue with aggression, crime, or—at the least—a chaotic life.

The degree of continuity of this form of deviant behavior is quite striking. The correlation between aggression in childhood and in adulthood averages .60 to .70—very high for data of this kind—and is replicated in studies in both England and the United States (Farrington, 1991). One example, which you may remember from Chapters 11 and 14, is Leonard Eron's longitudinal study of aggressive boys. Those who were most aggressive at age 8 were much more likely to show antisocial or damaging aggressive behaviors as adults than were those who had been less aggressive at age 8 (Eron, 1987).

There is also some indication that the early-onset/aggressive syndrome has a much stronger genetic component than is true for the later-onset/delinquent pattern (Achenbach, 1993). Thus the preschooler who already shows defiant and oppositional behavior as well as aggressiveness may have strong inborn propensities for such behavior. But if Patterson is correct—and I think he is—then whether that propensity will develop into a full-fledged, persisting conduct disorder will depend on the unfolding sequence of events, including the parents' ability to handle the child's early defiance.

Incidentally, although aggressive behavior as well as conduct disorders of all types are far more common among boys than among girls, the pattern does also occur in some girls. And they, like equivalent boys, have a poor prognosis for adult normality (Zoccolillo, 1993). There are also girls who show adolescent-onset delinquent behaviors, including alcohol and drug use and lawbreaking. So although the incidence is lower, it is important to remember that conduct disorders are not a uniquely male problem.

Attention Deficit Hyperactivity Disorder.   A second important category of externalizing psychopathology has been given a rather long-winded name in DSM-III: **attention deficit hyperactivity disorder (ADD).** The briefer and more

We can't tell from one picture whether these preschool boys are consistently aggressive or defiant. But we know that those who do show high levels of such behavior at this early age are far more likely to have long-term problems than are those who only develop conduct disorders/delinquency at later ages.

What kind of social policy implications (if any) do you see in the fact that early-onset conduct disorders are most likely to persist to adult criminality or violence?

TABLE 15.2 Diagnostic Criteria for Attention Deficit Hyperactivity Disorder

---

The onset of the problem must be before age 7, and the disturbance must last at least six months, during which at least eight of the following are present:

1. Often fidgets with hands or feet or squirms in seat (in adolescents, this may be limited to subjective feelings of restlessness)
2. Has difficulty remaining seated when required to do so
3. Is easily distracted by extraneous stimuli
4. Has difficulty awaiting turn in game or group situations
5. Often blurts out answers to questions before they have been completed
6. Has difficulty following through on instructions from others (not due to oppositional behavior or failure of comprehension), for example, fails to finish chores
7. Has difficulty sustaining attention in tasks or play activities
8. Often shifts from one uncompleted activity to another
9. Has difficulty playing quietly
10. Often talks excessively
11. Often interrupts or intrudes on others, for example, butts into other children's games
12. Often does not seem to listen to what is being said to him or her
13. Often loses things necessary for tasks or activities at school or at home (e.g., toys, pencils, books, assignments)
14. Often engages in physically dangerous activities without considering possible consequences (not for purpose of thrill-seeking), for example, runs into street without looking

---

Source: Diagnostic and statistical manual for mental disorders (3rd ed., rev.), 1987. Washington, DC: American Psychiatric Association, pp. 53–54. Copyright © 1987 by the American Psychiatric Association.

---

common name is simply **hyperactivity.** A glance at the diagnostic criteria, which I've listed in Table 15.2, will tell you quickly that the hallmarks of this disorder are physical restlessness and problems with attention—precisely as the label implies (Barkley, 1990).

But the list in Table 15.2 cannot really convey the quality of behavior of such children. Their interactions with their peers are so distinctively different that novice observers need to watch videotapes for only a few minutes before they can reliably distinguish between a child diagnosed as hyperactive and a normally behaving child—even when the hyperactive child displays no aggression and the sound is turned off (Henker & Whalen, 1989). The body language is different, the level of activity is different, and the child's social behavior is often inappropriate. About half of such children also show conduct disorders, and most do poorly in school.

By definition, this is an early developing disorder. It is also a persistent problem in the majority of such children, lasting well into adulthood for at least half of those diagnosed as having this disorder (Henker & Whalen, 1989). But the severity of the long-term problem seems to be strongly influenced by whether or not the child also develops a conduct disorder. It is the combination of hyperac-

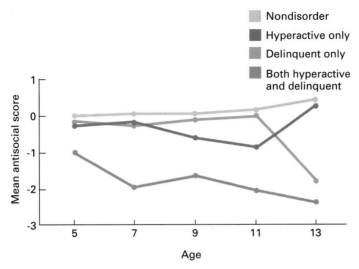

Nondisorder
Hyperactive only
Delinquent only
Both hyperactive and delinquent

Figure 15.1
The boys in Moffitt's study had been studied every two years from the time they were 5. When they were 13, they were assigned to one of four hyperactivity/delinquency categories, and then Moffitt backtracked from that age. You can see that those who were *both* delinquent and hyperactive at 13 had shown markedly higher rates of antisocial behavior from the time they were 5, while those who were only hyperactive at 13 had been much less socially deviant at earlier ages. (*Source:* Moffitt, 1990, Figure 1, p. 899.)

tivity and aggressiveness or delinquency that is especially deadly (Barkley et al., 1990). You can see one facet of this effect in the results of a recent longitudinal study by Terrie Moffitt (1990) of a group of 434 boys in New Zealand, including all boys born in a particular town over a one-year period. When the boys were 13 they were classed in one of four groups based on the presence or absence of two factors: attention deficit disorder and delinquency. Moffitt then traced backward for each of these groups, looking at scores at earlier ages on measures of antisocial behavior, intelligence, and family adversity. You can see the results for antisocial behavior in Figure 15.1.

It is clear that the boys who, as adolescents, showed *both* hyperactivity and delinquency had been the most antisocial at every earlier age. Hyperactivity that was not accompanied by antisocial behavior at early ages was also not linked to delinquency at 13. Other research tells us that this same group of hyperactive *and* delinquent boys are also the most likely to have continued serious problems in adulthood, including criminal behavior.

Where might hyperactivity come from? Because the pattern begins so early and has such a strong physical component, most clinicians have assumed that this problem has some kind of biological origin. Surprisingly, early research failed to confirm such a biological hypothesis. There is no sign of any overt brain damage, and typical neurological tests do not reveal any underlying physical problem. But in the past few years, three converging lines of evidence have provided support for the biological hypothesis.

First, physicians and psychologists have known for some time that a biological *treatment* is very often effective in reducing or eliminating the deviant behavior. Many (but not all) hyperactive children treated with a stimulant medication (most commonly Ritalin) show decreases in demanding, disruptive, and noncompliant behaviors, and more attentiveness in the classroom (Henker & Whalen, 1989). Second, there is accumulating evidence that a pattern of hyperactivity is inherited, at least in certain families. About a quarter of the parents of hyperactive children themselves have a history of hyperactivity (Biederman et al., 1990). Studies of twins also show a genetic contribution. Among identical twins, if one is diagnosed as hyperactive the other is highly likely to have the same diagnosis; among fraternal twins this "concordance rate" is much lower (Deutsch & Kinsbourne, 1990).

Finally, newer methods of assessing brain function have begun to reveal differences between the brains of hyperactive and nonhyperactive individuals. In one widely publicized study, Alan Zametkin and his colleagues (1990) used positron-emission tomography (PET) scans to examine the glucose (sugar) metabolism in the brains of the hyperactive and normal adults. All the hyperactive adults reported that they had also been hyperactive as children, and all had at least one offspring with the same diagnosis. Each subject was injected with a concentrated dose of glucose, and then repeated PET scans were done to look at how the brain metabolized the sugar. Zametkin found that the hyperactive adults had significantly slower brain metabolism of the glucose, and this was especially so in the portions of the brain that are known to be involved in attentiveness and the ability to inhibit inappropriate responses. Results like this may represent a real breakthrough, not only in helping us to understand the origins of hyperactivity, but conceivably in devising better treatments. At the very least, they greatly strengthen the argument that this disorder has biological origins.

But being more sure about the origins does not settle all the important questions. From the point of view of developmental psychopathology we also need to understand how such an initially deviant biological pattern affects the child's interactions with parents and peers to produce the common combination of hyperactivity and antisocial behavior. For many hyperactive children, the pathway is very like the one Patterson has described for defiant or aggressive children. These kids are just plain hard to raise. And those parents whose child management skills are not up to the task of dealing with the hyperactive toddler's typically higher rates of noncompliance, or those who face major family stresses that prevent them from maintaining good child-care routines, may find that the child's behavior becomes more and more disruptive, which in turn affects the child's emerging social skills adversely. By school age, parent-child conflict is high, as is child-peer conflict. Poor school performance makes it worse by lowering the child's self-esteem. Such children are then on a pathway that is highly likely to lead to continued problems in adolescence and adulthood (Campbell, 1990). In Moffitt's New Zealand study, for example, those boys who eventually showed the combination of hyperactivity and delinquency came from families with much higher levels of stress and fewer resources. The hyperactive boys who did not develop the accompanying antisocial behavior came from families with lower than average levels of stress and more resources.

Internalizing Problems: The Example of Depression

A different set of antecedents, and a different pathway, is found among children who show internalizing forms of disturbance. The particular form of deviance that has been most often addressed within the framework of developmental psychopathology has been **depression,** so let me use that as an example.

For many years, psychiatrists took the position that significant depression could not occur in children or adolescents. But there is now abundant evidence that depression is actually quite common in adolescence, and occurs at least occasionally among younger children. Both Thomas Achenbach and Michael Rutter, in separate large studies, have found that approximately 10 percent of preadolescent children, and 40 percent of adolescents, are described by parents or teachers as appearing miserable, unhappy, sad, or depressed (Achenbach & Edelbrock, 1981; Rutter, Tizard, & Whitmore, 1981). When teenagers themselves are asked about their state of mind, a third describe at least moderate levels of depressed mood (Petersen et al., 1993).

When depressive episodes last six months or longer and are accompanied by other symptoms such as disturbances of sleeping and eating, and difficulty concentrating, they are usually referred to as *clinical depression* or a *depressive disorder*. Recent epidemiological studies tell us that such severe forms of depression are relatively rare in preadolescents, but are quite surprisingly common among adolescents. Estimates range fairly widely, as you have already seen in Table 15.1, but the most comprehensive studies suggest that at least 3 percent and perhaps as many as 8 percent of teenagers can be diagnosed as clinically depressed at any one time. And perhaps twice that many will experience a serious depression at some time in their adolescent years (Compas, Ey, & Grant, 1993; Petersen et al., 1993).

We can't know for sure what has caused this teenager's dejected look, but we do know that depressed mood and significant clinical depressions are considerably more common in the adolescent years than most psychiatrists or psychologists once thought.

Interestingly, among preadolescents, boys are about as likely as girls to be unhappy or depressed; among teenagers (as among adults) girls more often report high or chronic levels of depression, a sex difference that has been found in a number of industrialized countries, and among African-Americans, Hispanic-Americans, and Anglo-Americans (Petersen et al., 1993; Roberts & Sobhan, 1992).

Although teenagers and preadolescents who describe themselves as depressed do not invariably display all the symptoms of a full-blown clinical depression as seen in adulthood, depressed youngsters do show the same kind of hormonal and other endocrine changes during their depressed episodes as are observed in depressed adults, so we know that depression in children is a real and potentially serious clinical state, not just a "normal" or transitory unhappiness.

The search for the developmental pathways leading to later depression begins with the clear finding that children growing up with depressed parents are much more likely than are those growing up with nondepressed parents to develop depression themselves (Downey & Coyne, 1990). Of course this could indicate a genetic factor at work here, a possibility supported by at least a few studies of twins and adopted children (Petersen et al., 1993). Or we could understand this link between parental and child depression in terms of the changes in the parent-child interaction that are caused by the parent's depression.

I have mentioned several times that depressed mothers are much more likely than are nondepressed mothers to have children who are insecurely attached. In particular, their behavior with their child is so nonresponsive that it seems to foster in the child a kind of helpless resignation. Such a sense of helplessness has been found to be strongly related to depression in both adults and adolescents (Dodge, 1990).

Of course not all children of depressed parents are themselves depressed. About 60 percent show no abnormality at all. Whether a child moves along a

---

THE REAL WORLD
Adolescent Suicide and Its Prevention

One possible accompaniment of depression is suicide. Suicide is very uncommon in children before adolescence. Even among children between 10 and 14, less than 1 child in 100,000 in the United States commits suicide each year. But among those between 15 and 19, the rate is considerably higher, and rising, as I pointed out in Chapter 4.

The likelihood of suicide is about four times as high among adolescent boys as among girls, and nearly twice as high among whites as among nonwhites *except* for Native American youth, who attempt and commit suicide at higher rates than any other group (Blum et al., 1992). The rate among Native Americans is 26.3 per 100,000 per year, compared to about 20 per 100,000 among white teen males.

In contrast, suicide *attempts* are estimated to be three times more common in girls than in boys (Garland & Zigler, 1993). Girls, more often than boys, use less-"successful" methods, such as self-poisoning. In one study in England, for example, the rate of hospital admissions for self-poisoning among girls rose from 4 per 10,000 among 12-year-olds to over 50 per 10,000 at age 16. Among boys, the rate at age 16 was one-fifth that level (Hawton & Goldacre, 1982).

It is obviously very difficult to uncover the contributing factors in successful or completed suicides, because the crucial individual is no longer available to be interviewed. Researchers and clinicians are forced to rely on secondhand reports by parents or others about the mental state of the suicide before the act—reports that are bound to be at least partially invalid, because in many cases the parents or friends had no suspicion that a suicide attempt was imminent. Nonetheless, it does seem clear that some kind of significant psychopathology is virtually a universal ingredient, including but not restricted to depression. Behavior problems such as aggression are also common in the histories of completed suicides, as is a family history of psychiatric disorder or suicide, or a pattern of drug or alcohol abuse (Garland & Zigler, 1993).

But these factors alone are not enough to explain suicidal behavior. After all, many teenagers (or adults) display one or more of these risk factors, and very few actually commit suicide. David Shaffer and his colleagues, in their analysis of the problem of suicide prevention (Shaffer et al., 1988), suggest at least three other elements that seem to be involved:

1. Some triggering stressful event. Studies of suicides suggest that among adolescents, this triggering event is often a disciplinary crisis with the parents, or some rejection or humiliation, such as breaking up with a girlfriend or boyfriend, or failure in some valued activity.

2. Some altered mental state, which might be an attitude of hopelessness, or reduced inhibitions from alcohol consumption, or rage (Swedo et al., 1991). Among girls, in particular, the sense of hopelessness seems to be common: a feeling that the world is against them *and they can't do anything about it.*

3. There must be an opportunity—a loaded gun available in the house, a bottle of sleeping pills in the parents' medicine cabinet, or the like.

Attempts to prevent teen suicide have not been notably successful. Despite the fact that most suicides and suicide attempters have displayed significantly deviant behavior for some period of time before the event, most do not find their way to mental health clinics or other professionals, and increasing the availability of such clinics has not proven effective in reducing suicide rates.

Other prevention efforts have focused on education, such as providing information to all high school students about risk factors in the hope that students might recognize a problem in a friend. Special training in coping abilities has also been offered, so that teenagers might be able to find some nonlethal solution to their problems. Unfortunately, most such programs appear to be ineffective in changing student attitudes or knowledge (Shaffer et al., 1991).

These discouraging results are not likely to change until we know a great deal more about the developmental pathways that lead to this particular form of psychopathology. What makes one teenager particularly vulnerable and another able to resist the temptation? What combination of stressful circumstances is most likely to trigger a suicide attempt, and how do those stressful circumstances interact with the teenager's personal resources? Only when we can answer questions of this kind will we be on the road to understanding teenage suicide.

---

pathway toward depression or not seems to be a function of a whole series of protective or disruptive factors (Billings & Moos, 1985):

- If the parent's depression is short-lived, or is medically treated so that the symptoms are less severe, the child has a much better chance of avoiding depression herself.

- The more other forms of stress the family experiences in addition to one parent's depression, such as an illness, family arguments, work stress, loss of income, job loss, or marital separation, the more likely the child is to show depressive symptoms.
- The more emotional and logistical support the family receives from others, the less likely the child is to show depressive symptoms.

This set of findings obviously fits nicely into the systems theory framework I described in Chapters 13 and 14: The family system can buffer the child from the effects of a parent's depression far more effectively if there are adequate social supports and not too many other stresses. But when stresses accumulate, the effect is magnified.

In fact, this detrimental role of stress is just as clear among children whose parent or parents are not depressed. A similar effect results from any combination of stresses, such as the parents' divorce, or the death of a parent or another loved person, or the father's loss of job, a move, changing schools, or whatever (Compas et al., 1993). Indeed the role of such individual life stresses may help to explain the sex differences in depression among adolescents. Anne Petersen (Petersen, Sarigiani, & Kennedy, 1991) has recently proposed that girls typically experience more challenges or stresses during adolescence than do boys. In particular, she argues that girls are more likely to encounter simultaneous stressful experiences in adolescence, such as pubertal changes combined with a shift in schools. In her own longitudinal study, Petersen finds that when such synchronous stresses are taken into account, the sex difference in adolescent depression disappears. That is, in this study, depression was *not* more common among girls than among boys when both groups had encountered equal levels of life stress or simultaneous stressful experiences.

Yet another possible causal factor in adolescent depression is social isolation from peers in early elementary school (Hymel et al., 1990). You'll remember from Chapter 11 that peer *rejection* is associated with externalizing problems (aggression); but *isolation* from peers is linked with depression. Yet another possible pathway is through lowered self-esteem—a connection you encountered in Chapter 10. Susan Harter's studies tell us that a young person who feels she (or he) does not measure up to her own standards is much more likely to show symptoms of a clinical depression. The fact that depression increases markedly in adolescence makes good sense from this point of view. We know that in adolescence, children are much more likely to define themselves and others in *comparative* terms—to judge against some standard, or to see themselves as "less than" or "more than" some other person. We also know that at adolescence, appearance becomes highly salient, and that a great many teenagers are convinced that they do not live up to the culturally defined appearance standards. Self-esteem thus drops in early adolescence, and depression rises.

Harter's work is certainly helpful here, but it does not answer all our questions about why depression rises so markedly at adolescence. Nor does it tell us why some teenagers are likely to see themselves as inadequate, or to respond to such a sense of inadequacy with depression, while others do not. We obviously need to know a good deal more about the pathways that lead a child to be vulnerable to such stresses at puberty or at any other point in life.

Can you think of any other reasons why girls (in Western cultures at least) would have higher rates of depression than boys?

Do you recall having been significantly depressed during adolescence? If so, do any of these explanations or causal factors fit your own experience?

Vulnerability and Resilience

This question of vulnerability or resilience has been a persistent theme among developmental psychopathologists. The research findings suggest that the same kinds of protective factors I listed in Chapter 14, when I talked about children growing up in poverty, play a role for children experiencing other kinds of stresses as well. Children who are securely attached to someone (whether it be a parent or someone else), who have good cognitive skills and sufficient social skills to make connections with peers, are better able to weather the stresses they encounter.

For example, in her studies of resilience among school-age children, Ann Masten (1989) has found that when children have experienced a year with high levels of life stresses, those with higher IQs are much less likely to respond to that stress by becoming disruptive. Masten speculates that this may be due to the fact that such children, who have a history of successful problem solving, have a stronger sense of self-efficacy, which may help to make them more resistant to frustration.

On the other side of the coin are the vulnerable children, who are far more likely to show some kind of significant psychopathology in the face of stress. Some kinds of vulnerabilities are inborn: physical abnormalities, prenatal trauma or preterm birth, prenatal malnutrition, or exposure to disease *in utero*. A tendency toward "difficult" temperament, which also seems to be inborn, is another significant vulnerability, not only because by definition such children have greater difficulty adapting to new experiences, but because their difficult temperament can easily affect the relationships they develop with their parents or other caregivers. Horowitz's model (Figure 1.3), which I have referred to repeatedly, suggests that such initial vulnerabilities greatly increase the likelihood that the child will develop some later problem. Only optimal rearing conditions can protect such children adequately.

Other vulnerabilities emerge during infancy or early childhood. An insecure early attachment, and the internal working model that accompanies it, seems to make a child more vulnerable to stress at later ages, particularly to stresses that involve losses or severe strains on key relationships. And any combination of circumstances that results in a high rate of aggressive or disruptive behavior with peers makes a child more vulnerable to a whole variety of stresses in the elementary-school and high school years (Masten, 1989).

All in all, it seems very helpful to think of each child as possessing some inborn *vulnerabilities*, some *protective factors* such as a secure attachment or a middle-class family, and some *resources*, such as higher IQ, an array of friends, or good peer interaction skills. How any given child will react to stressful life circumstances or to normal developmental passages like school entry or adolescence will depend on the relative weight of these three elements— *and* on how many separate stresses the child must face at the same time. Any child, no matter how basically resilient, is more likely to show at least a short-term behavior problem when multiple stresses pile up at the same moment.

How would you describe your own vulnerabilities, protective factors, and resources?

Developmental Psychopathology: A Reprise

I think that even this brief foray into research on psychopathology makes clear that a developmental framework is the only one that is going to yield real understanding of the emergence of deviant behavior. Even for a disorder such as hyperactivity, which appears to be rooted in an inborn biological dysfunction, the severity and persistence of the disorder can be best understood in terms of the child's cumulative patterns of interaction and the child's own internal models of relationships. Ultimately, studies within this emerging tradition of developmental psychopathology may end up telling us as much about normal development as about the emergence of pathology.

▶ Intellectually Atypical Development

If you go back and look at Table 15.1 you'll see that the various forms of intellectually atypical development rank right up there with the various psychopathologies in frequency of occurrence among children. Roughly 1 in 10 children shows at least some form of intellectual abnormality.

Whether a child will show a behavior problem at a stressful time like moving will depend in part on whether he faces several other stresses or life changes at the same time—such as perhaps his parents' divorce.

Mental Retardation

Definitions and Labels.   Of all the atypical children listed in Table 15.1, probably those studied most thoroughly are those labeled **mentally retarded.** Not too many decades ago, when mental ability was thought of as a fixed trait, mental subnormality was considered a kind of incurable disease. Labels like "idiot" or "feeble-minded" were used. But this older view has changed a great deal. Not only have the old negative labels been changed, but the basic assumptions about the nature of retardation have changed, too.

Mental retardation is now (correctly, I think) viewed as a *symptom* rather than as a disease. And like any symptom, it can change. A child's life circumstances or his health may change, and his IQ score may go up or down as a result. Remember from Chapter 6 that *many* children's IQ test scores vary as much as 30 points over the childhood years. Of course many children with low IQ scores will continue to function at a low level throughout life. But it is important for educators and parents to understand that a single low IQ score need not invariably mean that the child will function at that level forever. For many children, improvement is possible.

The Assessment of Retardation.   A child is normally designated as retarded if he tests below an IQ of 70, *and* has significant problems in **adaptive behavior**—such as an inability to dress or eat alone, or a problem getting along with others or adjusting to the demands of a regular school classroom. As Thomas Achenbach (1982) says, "Children doing well in school are unlikely to be considered retarded no matter what their IQ scores" (p. 214).

Low IQ scores are customarily divided up into several ranges, with different labels attached to each, as you can see in Table 15.3. I've given both the labels used by psychologists, and those that may be more common in the school system. (There are no school system labels for children with IQs below about 35 because schools very rarely deal with children functioning at this level.)

The farther down the IQ scale you go, the fewer children there are. More than 80 percent of all children with IQs below 70 are in the "mild" range; only about 2 percent of the low-IQ youngsters (perhaps 3500 children in the U.S.) are profoundly retarded (Broman et al., 1987).

TABLE 15.3   IQ Scores and Labels for Children Classed as Retarded

Approximate IQ score range	Label used by psychologists	Label used in schools
68–83	Borderline retarded	(No special label)
52–67	Mildly retarded	Educable mentally retarded (EMR)
36–51	Moderately retarded	Trainable mentally retarded
19–35	Severely retarded	(No special label)
Below 19	Profoundly retarded	(No special label)

Cognitive Functioning in Retarded Children.   In recent years there has been a great deal of fascinating research on thinking and information processing in retarded children, much of it by Ann Brown, Joseph Campione, and their colleagues (Campione, Brown, & Ferrara, 1982; DeLoache & Brown, 1987). As you may recall from Chapter 7, this research has been a significant ingredient in the emerging information processing approach to studying cognitive development in children. Brown and Campione find that retarded children have these characteristics:

1. They think and react more slowly.
2. They require much more complete and repeated instruction to learn new information or a new strategy (compared to normal-IQ children, who may discover a strategy for themselves, or profit from incomplete instruction).
3. They do not generalize or transfer something they have learned in one situation to a new problem or task. They thus appear to lack those "executive" functions that enable older, higher-IQ children (or adults) to compare a new problem to familiar ones, or to scan through a repertoire of strategies until they find one that works.

On simple tasks, retarded children learn in ways and at rates that are similar to those of younger normal-IQ children. The more significant deficit lies in higher-order processing. These children *can* learn, but they do so more slowly and require far more exhaustive and task-specific instruction.

Causes of Retardation.   About 15 to 25 percent of mentally retarded children have some identifiable physical problem (Broman et al., 1987). **Chromosomal anomalies** such as Down syndrome or the Fragile X syndrome are one major culprit. As Scarr and Kidd (1983) put it, "Having too much or too little [genetic material] will affect intelligence, always for the worse" (p. 380). A child may also inherit a specific disease or **inborn error of metabolism** which can cause retardation if not treated. The best-known such inherited metabolism error is phenylketonuria (PKU), which I described in Chapter 2 (Table 2.2).

Still a third physical cause of retardation is **brain damage,** which can result from a large number of causes, including prenatal maternal diseases like syphilis or cytomegalovirus, malnutrition, or alcoholism. Brain damage may also occur during birth or by some accident after birth (e.g., auto accidents, or falling out of a treehouse on your head).

The remaining three-quarters of retarded children show no signs of any brain damage or other physical disorder. In almost all cases, such children come from families in which the parents have low IQs, or where there is serious family disorganization, mental illness in the parents, or emotional or cognitive deprivation in the home. Often both genetic and environmental influences operate simultaneously.

Large-scale studies have now shown quite conclusively that these several causes of retardation are not distributed evenly across the range of low IQ scores. The lower the IQ, the higher the likelihood that there is some physical cause. This is especially clear from the results of the Collaborative Perinatal Project, which involved nearly 40,000 American children studied from before birth to age 7—the same study from which I drew the findings I showed in Figure 6.3. In this sample, 71.7 percent of white and 53.9 percent of black children with IQs below 50 had some kind of major disorder of the central nervous system. In contrast, among those with IQs between 50 and 70, only 13.9 percent of whites and 6.3 percent of blacks had any identifiable physical abnormality (Broman et al., 1987).

You can see this difference even more vividly in another set of data from the same study. It happened that in a fair number of cases the sample included several children from the same family. So Broman and her colleagues were able to look at the IQs of the *siblings* of retarded children. The results for white children are in Figure 15.2.

The siblings of those with IQs below 50 had normal IQs; none were retarded. But the siblings of the mildly retarded were themselves fairly likely to be mildly retarded as well, a pattern that suggests quite different causes in the two groups. Among black children, whose family circumstances are more likely to be impoverished, the results are less clear. Siblings in both groups are about equally likely to be retarded themselves. But the findings as a whole strongly support the con-

About 15 percent of mentally retarded children have clear physical abnormalities, such as Down syndrome.

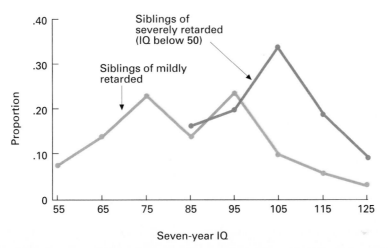

Figure 15.2
These data suggest that there are really two quite different kinds of retarded individuals: those whose retardation is caused by physical abnormalities, who usually have IQs below 50 and have normal-IQ siblings, and those whose retardation is cultural-familial in origin, usually with IQs in the mildly retarded range. The siblings of the latter group are *also* more likely to be retarded. (*Source:* Broman et al., 1987, Figure 10-1, p. 269.)

clusion that there are really two distinct types of retardation, each with its own set of causes.

One implication of this conclusion is that interventions like the enriched day care and preschool Ramey devised (recall Figure 6.5) are more likely to be effective in preventing or ameliorating milder retardation that has familial-cultural causes. This is not to say that we should ignore environmental enrichment or specific early training for children with physically caused retardation. Greater breadth of experience would enrich their lives and may help to bring their level of functioning closer to the top end of their "reaction range." But even massive early interventions are not going to make most brain-damaged or genetically anomalous children intellectually normal, although they can help the child to function much more independently (Spiker, 1990).

Learning Disorders

Definitions and Labels. Some children with normal IQs and essentially good adaptive functioning nonetheless have difficulty learning to read, or write, or do arithmetic. The typical label for this problem is **learning disability (LD)** although you will also hear terms like *dyslexia* (literally "nonreading") or *minimal brain damage.* The official definition of this problem includes the presumption that the difficulty arises from some kind of central nervous system dysfunction or damage.

How *many* such children there are, and how they should be characterized, is still a matter of considerable dispute. Sylvia Farnham-Diggory (1992), one of the leading experts in the field, argues that up to 80 percent of all children classified by school systems as learning-disabled are misclassified. She claims that only about 5 out of every 1000 children are genuinely learning-disabled. The remainder who are so classified are more appropriately called slow learners, or they suffer from some other difficulty, perhaps a temporary emotional distress, poor teaching, or whatever.

Practically speaking, however, the term is used very broadly within school systems (at least within the United States) to label a grab bag of children who have unexpected or otherwise unexplainable difficulty with schoolwork, particularly reading. In 1985–1986, 4.7 percent of all children in the U.S. were so labeled (Farnham-Diggory, 1992).

There are good reasons why schools identify so many children as learning-disabled. For one thing, the diagnostic problem is extremely difficult. The designation of a learning disability is basically a *residual* diagnosis. It is the label normally applied to a child who does not learn some school task, who is *not* generally retarded, and does *not* show persistent or obvious emotional disturbance or a hearing or vision problem. Thus we can say what learning disability is *not*; what we cannot say is what it *is.*

The identification problem is complicated still further by the fact that among children identified as LD, the specific form of the problem varies widely, with some displaying difficulties in reading only, some having trouble with reading and spelling (such as the boy whose writing sample is shown in Figure 15.3), and others having more difficulty with arithmetic.

Furthermore, school districts receive federal funds to pay for special education for children identified as learning-disabled, but do *not* receive such funds for

Figure 15.3
This is part of a story written by
13-year-old-Luke, who has a significant and persisting learning
disability. The little numbers
next to some of the words are
Luke's word counts. They show
that despite his severe writing
handicap, his counting abilities
were intact. (*Source:* Farnham-
Diggory, 1992, p 61. Reprinted
by permission of the President
and Fellows of Harvard College.)

One day me and my brith wit out hunting The sar kie BiT we cume not Fied The sarking use we drup in a Theocatei bit we cume not Fied

education of children labeled as "slow learners." Thus there is a strong financial incentive to label almost any kind of delayed or slow learning a "learning disability."

For all of these reasons, I cannot give you any kind of precise estimate of the frequency of the problem, although I am inclined to believe Farnham-Diggory's 5 out of 1000.

The Nature of the Problem.   Given such problems with definition, we shouldn't be surprised that the search for causes has been fraught with difficulties. As Farnham-Diggory (1986) says, "We are trying to find out what's wrong with children whom we won't be able to accurately identify until after we know what's wrong with them" (p. 153).

The most central problem has been with the basic assumption that learning disability has a neurological basis. The problem is that children so labeled (like hyperactive children) rarely show any signs of major brain damage on any standard tests—perhaps because many children are mislabeled, or perhaps because the brain dysfunction is more subtle than what can be measured with standard tests.

The most promising current view is that a large number of small abnormalities develop during prenatal life, each involving some irregularity of neuron arrangement, or clumps of immature brain cells, or scar or congenital tumors, or the like. The growing brain compensates for these problems by "rewiring" around the problem areas. These rewirings, in turn, may slightly scramble normal information processing procedures, just enough to make reading or calculation or some other specific task very difficult (Farnham-Diggory, 1992).

Another explanation of the problem, one you may recall from Chapter 8, is that reading disability may reflect a more general problem with language. There is now abundant evidence that children with reading problems are likely to have one or both of two kinds of language problems: (1) relative lack of awareness of the individual sounds in words ("phonemic awareness"), and (2) relative lack of knowledge of the semantic and grammatical structure of language (Siegel, 1993; Stanovich, 1993; Vellutino, 1987). Further, researchers have shown that providing training in hearing individual sounds improves the reading skills of poor readers. Findings like these have been very helpful in devising remedial programs for children with reading disabilities. But they do not tell us why a child might have such language deficits in the first place. The problem may lie in brain dysfunction, or it

Can you think of any way out of this dilemma? Should schools be given additional funds for those labeled as "slow learners" too? What might be the effects of such a policy?

School can surely be a discouraging and frustrating place for a child with a learning disability.

may well be that children whose reading problem has such an origin are among the 80 percent Farnham-Diggory says are misclassified. They do indeed have a reading problem, but they may not have a neurological problem underlying it.

I want to emphasize that the continuing confusion and disagreement about identification and explanation of learning disability occurs despite thousands of research studies and a great deal of theorizing by thoughtful and capable people. Not surprisingly, the uncertainty at the theoretical level is reflected in confusion at the practical level. Children are labeled "learning disabled" and assigned to special classes, but whether the child will be helped by a particular type of intervention program will depend on whether that specific program is (1) any good, and (2) happens to match his or her type of disability or problem. Remediation does seem to be possible, but it is *not* simple, and a program that works well for one child may not work at all for another. Of course this is not good news for parents whose child may be having difficulty with some aspect of schooling, whose only recourse is trial and error and eternal vigilance. But it reflects the disordered state of our knowledge.

Giftedness

For parents whose children lie at the other end of the intellectual continuum, the gifted, the problem is almost as tough. Finding good programs for such children is a continuing dilemma. Let me give you an extreme example, a child named Michael described by Halbert Robinson (1981):

> When Michael was 2 years and 3 months old, the family visited our laboratory. At that time, they described a youngster who had begun speaking at age 5 months and by 6 months had exhibited a vocabulary of more than 50 words. He started to read English when he was 13 months old. In our laboratory he spoke five languages and could read in three of them. He understood addition, subtraction, multiplication, division, and square root, and he was fascinated by a broad range of scientific constructs. He loved to make puns, frequently bilingual ones." (p. 63)

Michael's IQ on the Stanford-Binet was in excess of 180 at age 2; two years later, when Michael was 4¹/₂ he performed on the test like a 12-year-old, and was listed as having an IQ beyond 220.

Definitions and Labels.   We can certainly all agree that Michael should be labeled as **gifted.** But defining the term precisely is more difficult (Sternberg & Davidson, 1986). Giftedness includes those with exceptional specific talents, such as musical or artistic skills, or specific mathematical or spatial ability, as well as those with very high IQs. This broadening of the definition of giftedness has been widely accepted among theorists, who agree that there are many kinds of exceptional ability, each of which may reflect unusual speed or efficiency with one or another type of cognitive function.

Within school systems, however, giftedness is still typically defined entirely by IQ test scores, such as all scores above 130 or 140. Robinson suggested that it may be useful to divide the group of high-IQ children into two sets, the "garden variety gifted," with high IQs (perhaps 130 to 150) but without extraordinary ability in any one area, and the "highly gifted" (like Michael) with extremely high IQ scores and/or remarkable skill in one or more areas. These two groups of children may have quite different experiences at home and in school.

Cognitive and Social Functioning in Gifted Children. Just as retarded children show slower and less-efficient information processing, the gifted show extremely rapid and flexible strategies. They learn quickly and transfer that learning broadly (Sternberg & Davidson, 1985). Further, they seem to have unusually good *metacognitive* skills: they know what they know and what they don't know, and they make good use of cognitive plans (Jackson & Butterfield, 1986).

Whether such advanced intellectual abilities transfer to *social* situations is not so well established. Many parents are concerned about placing their gifted child in a higher grade because of fears that the child will not be able to cope socially; others have assumed that rapid development in one area should be linked to rapid development in all areas.

One famous and remarkable early study of gifted children, by Lewis Terman, pointed to the latter conclusion. Terman selected about 1500 children with high IQs from the California school system in the 1920s. These children—now adults in their sixties, seventies, and even eighties—have been followed regularly throughout their lives (Sears & Barbee, 1977; Terman, 1925; Terman & Oden, 1947; 1959). Terman found that the gifted children he studied were better-off than their less-gifted classmates in many ways other than school performance. They were healthier; they were interested in many things such as hobbies and games; and they were successful in later life. Both the boys and the girls in this study went on to complete many more years of education than was typical of children of their era and had successful careers as adults.

Elizabeth Lovance of Hartland, Wisconsin, on the right, skipped several grades and graduated from high school at age 14. She said of her experience of being accelerated through school: "I would have had a mental breakdown if I had remained where I was."

More recent research has painted a somewhat less uniformly rosy picture. On the plus side are studies that show that the self-esteem of gifted children is as high or higher than that of less-bright children, and that they have essentially the same risks of depression or other psychopathology as do those with average IQs. Furthermore, good social development seems to be just as likely for gifted children who have been accelerated through school as for those who have been kept with their age-mates but provided with "enrichment" programs (Janos & Robinson, 1985; Robinson & Janos, 1986).

Such optimism about the social robustness of gifted children may have to be tempered somewhat, however, in the case of the highly gifted subgroup, such as those with IQs above 180. These children are *so* different from their peers that they are likely to be seen as strange or disturbing. And these highly gifted children do show higher rates of emotional problems than do non-gifted children (Janos & Robinson, 1985).

Also on the negative side of the ledger is the fact that many gifted children are so bored by school that they drop out, often because their school district does not allow acceleration in grade, or has no special programs for the gifted. One observer (Fetterman, 1990) estimates that as many as *30 percent* of all school dropouts would test as gifted. Given the fact that there is little sign of social maladjustment associated with grade skipping, it seems to make very good sense to

Are you persuaded by my arguments in favor of encouraging grade skipping by gifted children? If you were a parent of a gifted child, what kind of data would you want to have to help make a decision on this question?

encourage accelerated schooling, if only to help ward off terminal boredom for the gifted child.

▌ Physically Atypical Development

The last group of children I want to talk about, albeit briefly, are those with some clear physical problem, such as blindness or deafness. Such children experience very substantial difficulties in everyday living; most require special schooling or special facilities in school.

The Deaf Child

Most children with hearing loss can function adequately with the assistance of a hearing aid. In fact, many physicians are now fitting **hearing-impaired** children with hearing aids during infancy rather than waiting until the child is of preschool age. The situation is quite different, though, for the profoundly deaf child— one whose hearing loss is so severe that even with mechanical assistance his comprehension of sound, especially language, is significantly reduced. Here are a few facts about this group:

1. The vast majority of deaf children (about 90 percent) are born to *hearing* parents and thus grow up in a world dominated by spoken language.
2. Most profoundly deaf children have major deficits in both spoken and written language. They have difficulty speaking, most do not lipread well, and most read at only the most basic level (Schlesinger & Meadow, 1972).
3. Among the deaf, those with deaf parents usually do as well or *better* on measures of written and spoken language than do those with hearing parents (Liben, 1978).

It is this last fact that is the most surprising and which raises key practical and theoretical questions. Why would children raised by deaf parents have a better prognosis? Schlesinger and Meadow argue that the major reason is that these children are learning a language—in this case sign language—at the normal time. Deaf parents use sign language with each other and with their children, so the children learn that language. But a deaf child of hearing parents, unless the parents learn to sign, will learn no language. Such children do develop their own gestures, even stringing two gestures together into a kind of simple sentence. But beyond this level, the child needs language input. If the emphasis is placed exclusively on *oral* language, the deaf child has much more difficulty developing either speech or reading than if the child is taught sign language, lipreading, and oral language at the same time (Greenberg, Calderon, & Kusche, 1984; Moores, 1985). Some children with good combined training can function in a normal school environment, but even with good early training, most deaf children require special schooling.

This hearing mother has learned to use sign language so that she can communicate with her deaf child.

The Blind Child

If I had asked you, before you read this chapter, to tell me which would be worse, to have been blind or deaf from birth, most of you would have said it would be far worse to be blind. Yet from the point of view of the child's ability to function in

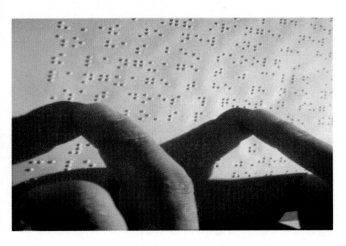

With the advent of small audiotape machines and books-on-tape, braille is not taught or learned by the blind as often as before. But signs in braille are still used in a variety of public places, such as elevators.

most normal settings, including school, blindness is a smaller handicap. The blind child can learn to read (with braille), can talk with others, can listen to tapes and to a teacher, and so on. Because of this greater academic potential, and because of the enormous role of language in forming and maintaining social relationships, there are more options open to the blind child or adult than to the deaf.

Still, there are obviously important limitations for the blind, and important potential pitfalls. One of these lies in the earliest relationship with the parent, which I've discussed in the research report on page 456. Later relationships may be impaired for the same reasons.

The long-term consequences of either deafness or blindness seem to depend in part on how early intervention is begun. Early intervention that involves the family seems especially helpful, which is precisely what we should expect from the perspective of developmental psychopathology. If family interventions, such as Fraiberg suggests, can help families to form secure attachments and to establish more optimum patterns of interaction, then some of the second- and third-order effects of the child's physical problem may be avoided.

▶ Sex Differences in Atypical Development

One of the most fascinating facts about atypical development is that virtually all forms of disorder are more common in boys than in girls. (The major exception is depression, which, as I've already mentioned, is more common among adolescent girls and women.) I've put some of the comparisons in Table 15.4 (p. 457), but even this list does not convey the extent of the difference. With very few exceptions, studies of the impact of environmental stresses show that boys are more adversely affected. This is true in studies of divorce, parental discord, parental mental illness, parental job loss, and many others. In these situations boys are more likely to show disturbed behavior, or a decline in school performance, or some other indication of a problem (Zaslow & Hayes, 1986).

RESEARCH REPORT
Basic Attachments Between Blind Babies and Their Mothers

In Chapter 11, I briefly mentioned Selma Fraiberg's work with blind infants as part of the discussion of the parent's attachment to the child. Because Fraiberg's work is so fascinating, I want to expand on the point.

Fraiberg (1974; 1975; 1977) found that blind babies begin to smile at about the same age as sighted babies (about 4 weeks) but that they smile less often. And at about 2 months, when the sighted baby begins to smile regularly at the sight of the parent's face, the blind baby's smiles become less and less frequent. The blind infant's smile is also less intense, more fleeting.

The other thing blind babies don't do is enter into mutual gaze. They don't look right at their parents, and everything we know about parents' responses to their babies underlines the importance of mutual gaze for the parents' feeling of attachment to the baby. Furthermore, the facial expressions of the blind infant are muted and sober. Many observers, including parents, conclude that the baby is depressed or indifferent. The combination of these circumstances often leaves the parents feeling as if the baby has rejected them.

Fraiberg found that most of the mothers of the blind babies in her studies gradually withdrew from their infants. They provided the needed physical care, but they stopped playing with the baby, and gave up trying to elicit smiles or other social interactions. They often said they didn't "love" this baby.

Fortunately, it's possible to solve this particular problem. Fraiberg found that these mothers could be helped to form a strong bond with their infant if they could be shown how to "read" the baby's other signals. The blind child's face may be sober and relatively expressionless, but her hands and body move a lot and express a great deal. When the child *stops* moving when you come into the room, this means she is listening to your footsteps. Or she may move her hands when she hears your voice rather than smiling as a sighted child would do.

When parents of blind children learn to respond to these alternative "attachment behaviors" in their babies, then the mutuality of the relationship can be reestablished. And when this happens, and the parents are able to provide more varied stimulation, blind children develop more normal behavior in other ways. In particular, they don't show the "blindisms" so often observed in blind youngsters, such as rocking, sucking, head banging, and other repetitive actions.

Here then is a clear example of how psychological research can lead to very practical applications with families.

How are we to explain differences like this? One possibility is that the double X chromosome gives the girl protection from any form of inherited disorder or anomaly. Girls are obviously less likely to inherit any recessive disease that is carried on the sex chromosomes. We also have some hints that there may be a gene on the X chromosome that affects the individual's ability to respond effectively to stress. Since girls have two X chromosomes they are less likely to suffer from any disorder in that gene. If this explanation is valid, then the appropriate conclusion is not that *all* boys are more vulnerable, but that *more* boys than girls have some minor neurological dysfunction, or high vulnerability to stressors of various kinds.

Two other physiological factors may also be important, each potentially explaining one or two of the differences listed in Table 15.4. First, hormonal differences may be important contributors. Since it is possible to construct a persuasive argument for the role of male hormone in aggressive behavior, it is not a very great leap to the hypothesis that the higher incidence of conduct disorders among boys may also be related in some way to hormone variations. A second possible physiological contributor is the comparative level of physical maturity of boys and girls. Because girls of any age are more physically mature than are boys of the same age, they may have more resources with which to meet various

TABLE 15.4 Sex Differences in the Incidence of Atypical Development	
Type of problem	**Approximate ratio of males to females**
Psychopathologies	
Attention deficit hyperactivity disorder	2:1
Conduct disorders including delinquency	5:1
Anxiety and depression: preadolescence	1:1
Anxiety and depression: adolescence	1:2
Estimated number of all children with all diagnoses seen in psychiatric clinics	2:1
Intellectual atypical development	
Mental retardation	3:2
Learning disabilities	3:2
Physical problems	
Blindness or significant visual problems	1:1
Hearing impairment	5:4
Autism	3:1

Sources: Achenbach, 1982; Anthony, 1970; Eme, 1979; Rutter, 1989; Rutter & Garmezy, 1983; Zoccolillo, 1993.

problems. For example, researchers have frequently observed that infant boys are more irritable and less able to achieve physical or emotional equilibrium after being upset than are infant girls (Haviland & Malatesta, 1981). Since such fussiness is also common in *younger* babies, the problem may not be maleness, but immaturity.

Experiences after birth may also contribute to the differing rates of deviance. One hypothesis is that adults are simply more tolerant of disruptive or difficult behavior in boys than in girls. By this argument, boys and girls initially respond similarly to stressful situations, but boys learn early that various forms of acting out, tantrums, or defiance are tolerated or not punished severely. Girls learn to inhibit these responses—perhaps even to internalize them—because adults respond quite differently to them. There is not a great deal of research that tests such a hypothesis, but there are at least fragments of support (Eme, 1979). Cross-cultural studies of cultures in which *both* boys and girls are discouraged from behaving aggressively or assertively would provide very useful data to test such an explanation.

Whatever the explanation—and none of the existing explanations seems very satisfactory to me—it is nonetheless extremely interesting that girls do seem to be less vulnerable, less likely to show virtually any type of atypical development.

Can you think of any other explanations?

▶ The Impact of an Atypical Child on the Family

How does a family deal with an atypical child? In some instances of course, deficiencies or inadequacies in the family are part of the *cause* of the child's atypical development. But whether the original cause lies in the family or not, once a child does show some form of deviant development the family is inevitably affected, often adversely.

Grief.   One of the first reactions is often a form of grief, almost as if the child had died. This reaction makes sense if you think about the fact that the *fantasy* "perfect child" did die or was never born. The parents grieve for the child-that-never-will-be, as expressed poignantly by one parent:

> *I wept for the perfect baby I had lost, for the sunsets he would never see, for the 4-year-old who would never be able to play outside unsupervised. (Featherstone, 1980, p. 26)*

As with other forms of grief, denial, depression, and anger are all natural elements. For many parents, there is also some guilt (e.g., "If only I hadn't had those drinks at that party while I was pregnant").

In some cases this process may result in an emotional rejection of the infant, aggravated by the difficulty many atypical infants have in entering fully into the mutually adaptive parent-child process. Such rejection seems to be particularly common when the marital relationship is conflicted, or when the family lacks adequate social support (Howard, 1978)—a pattern that makes good sense if we think of the family unit as a system rather than merely as a set of dyadic interactions.

Adaptation by the Family.   Once the initial shock and grief are dealt with as well as they can be, the family must work toward an ongoing adaptive system with the atypical child. There are often massive financial burdens; there are problems of finding appropriate schooling; there are endless daily adjustments to the child's special needs.

> *I look at the people down the street. Their kids are 15 and 18 and now they can just get in the car and take off when they want to . . . and then I think, "When will that happen for us? We'll always have to be thinking of Christopher. . . . We'll never have that freedom." (Featherstone, 1980, p. 17)*

The system that evolves most often leaves the mother primarily in charge of the atypical child; with physically handicapped children especially, fathers seem quite often to withdraw from interaction with or care of the child (Bristol, Gallagher, & Schopler, 1988). This is not a general withdrawal of the father from the family system, since such fathers continue to be involved with their other children. But the father's selective withdrawal leaves the mother with added burdens. One predictable response, among both mothers and fathers, is depression. Parents of atypical children are also more likely to have low self-esteem, and to have lower feelings of personal competence (Howard, 1978). Where the marital relationship was poor before the birth of the atypical child, the presence of the handicapped child in the family system seems to increase the likelihood of further discord. However, there is no consistent indication that having an atypical child results in an average increase in marital disharmony or risk of divorce (Longo & Bond, 1984).

The fact that many (even most) parents manage to adapt effectively to the presence of an atypical child is testimony to the devotion and immense effort expended. But there is no evading the fact that rearing such a child is very hard work, and that it strains the family system in ways that rearing a normal child does not.

▶ A Final Point

As a final point, I think it is crucial for me to state clearly what has been only implicit throughout this chapter: children whose development is atypical in some respect are much more *like* normally developing children in other respects than they are unlike them. Blind and deaf and retarded children all form attachments in much the same way that physically and mentally normal children do (Lederberg & Mobley, 1990); children with conduct disorders go through the same sequences of cognitive development that more adjusted children show. It is very easy, when dealing with an atypical child, to be overwhelmed by the sense of differentness. But as Sroufe and Rutter and all the other developmental psychopathologists are beginning to say so persuasively, the same basic processes are involved.

▶ Summary

1. Approximately 20 percent of all children in the United States will need some form of special assistance because of atypical development at some time in childhood or adolescence.

2. Studies of psychopathology are more and more being cast in a *developmental* framework, with emphasis on the complex pathways that lead to deviance or normality. Such a framework also emphasizes the importance of the child's own resilience or vulnerability to stresses.

3. Psychopathologies can be divided into two groups: externalizing and internalizing.

4. One type of externalizing problem is conduct disorders, including patterns of both excess aggressiveness and delinquency. Conduct disorders can also be divided into early- and late-onset problems. The former are more serious and persistent.

5. Early-onset conduct disorders appear to have a genetic component, and to be exacerbated by poor family interactions, and subsequent poor peer relations.

6. Attention deficit hyperactivity disorder is another type of externalizing problem, beginning in early childhood and typically persisting. The problems encountered by such children are much more acute if they also display conduct disorders.

7. Hyperactivity appears to have an initial biological cause, but deviant patterns are aggravated or ameliorated by subsequent experience.

8. Depression is one form of internalizing problem, relatively uncommon in childhood but common in adolescence. Depressed youngsters are more likely

to have a family history of parental depression, or to have developed low self-esteem or have a history of being ignored by peers.

9. Family stress, or stress experienced directly by the child, especially multiple simultaneous stresses, exacerbate any existing or underlying tendency toward pathology.

10. Children with inborn vulnerabilities (difficult temperament or physical problems), few protective factors, and few resources, are more likely to respond to stressful circumstances with pathology.

11. Children with mental retardation, normally defined as IQ below 70 combined with significant problems of adaptation, show slower development and more immature or less-efficient forms of information processing strategies.

12. Two groups of retarded can be identified: those with clear physical abnormalities, overrepresented among the severely retarded, and those without physical abnormalities but with low-IQ parents and/or deprived environments, who are overrepresented among the mildly retarded.

13. Roughly 4 percent of the school population in the United States are labeled as learning-disabled. There is still considerable dispute about how to identify genuine learning disability, and many may be misclassified.

14. Learning disability may be caused by small anomalies in brain function; alternatively, they may reflect broader language or cognitive deficits, or both.

15. *Gifted* is a term applied to children with very high IQs or to those with unusual creativity or special skill. Their information processing is unusually flexible and generalized. Socially they appear to be well-adjusted, except for the small group of unusually highly gifted students.

16. Deaf children do best when they can develop a language (in this case signing) at the normal language-learning age.

17. Blind children may have difficulty with early relationships because their interpersonal signals are quite different. However, they adapt much more readily to school than do the deaf.

18. Boys show almost all forms of atypical development more often than girls do. This may reflect genetic differences, hormone differences, or differences in cultural expectations.

19. Families with atypical children experience chronically heightened stress and demands for adaptation. This is frequently accompanied by depression or other disturbance in the parents.

▶ Key Terms

adaptive behavior (447)

attention deficit hyperactivity disorder (ADD) (439)

brain damage (448)

chromosomal anomalies (448)

conduct disorder (438)

depression (442)

developmental psychopathology (437)

externalizing problems (438)

gifted (452)

hearing-impaired (454)

hyperactivity (440)

inborn errors of metabolism (448)

internalizing problems (438)

learning disability (450)

mentally retarded (447)

▶ Suggested Readings

Farnham-Diggory, S. (1992). *The learning-disabled child*. Cambridge, MA: Harvard University Press.

> This revision of an excellent book will give you an up-to-date source, pitched at the level of the lay reader.

Lewis, M., & Miller, S. M. (Eds.). (1990). *Handbook of developmental psychopathology*. New York: Plenum Press.

> This book was very definitely written for fellow professionals, so it is often very dense and technical. But if you are interested in any aspect of psychopathology, this is absolutely the most current and valuable source.

Petersen, A. C., Compas, B. C., Brooks-Gunn, J., Stemmler, M., Ey, S., & Grant, K. E. (1993). Depression in adolescence. *American Psychologist, 48*, 155–168.

> A brief, fairly dense review of the most current information on this important subject.

16

PUTTING IT ALL TOGETHER: THE DEVELOPING CHILD

Transitions, Consolidations, and Systems

Age Periods in Perspective
From Birth to 18 Months
The Preschool Years: From 18 Months to 6 Years
The Elementary-School Years: From 6 to 12
Adolescence: From 12 to 20

Returning to Some Basic Questions
What Are the Major Influences on Development?

Does Timing Matter?
What Is the Nature of Developmental Change?

Individual Differences

A Final Point: The Joy of Development

Summary

Key Terms

Suggested Readings

I remember the sense of unfairness I had in a world history class in high school when, after I had carefully learned all the kings of England in order, and all the kings of France in order, I was asked on a test to say who had been king of France at the same time when Henry VIII had ruled England. I hadn't the foggiest idea; we had never studied it that way.

You may have something of the same feeling about the developing child. For example, you know a good deal about the sequence of development of language, and about the sequential changes in cognitive functioning and in attachments, but you probably have not hooked these different developmental sequences to one another very well. If I asked you now what was happening at the same time that the child first used two-word sentences, you would probably have a difficult time answering. So what I want to do in this brief chapter is to put the child back together a bit by looking at the things that are happening at the same time.

I also want to take another look at some of the key questions I raised in Chapter 1: What are the major influences on development? Does the timing of experience matter? What is the nature of developmental change? Are there stages or sequences? And how best can we understand individual differences in development?

Think about it. What else is going on when the child first uses two-word sentences?

▶ Transitions, Consolidations, and Systems

I see the process of development as being made up of a series of alternating periods of rapid growth (accompanied by disruption or disequilibrium) and periods of relative calm or consolidation. Change is obviously going on all the time, from conception to death. But I am persuaded that there are particular times when the changes pile up, or when one highly significant change occurs. This might be a major physiological development like puberty, or a highly significant cognitive change, such as the beginning of symbol usage at about 18 months, or some other major shift.

When such a significant change occurs, it has two related effects. First, in systems theory terms, any one change inevitably affects the entire system. So a rapid increase of skill in one area, like language, demands adaptation in all parts of the developing system. Because the child can now talk, her social interactions change, her thinking changes, no doubt even her nervous system changes, as new synapses are created and redundant old ones are pruned. Similarly, the child's early attachment may affect her cognitive development by altering the way she approaches new situations; the hormonal changes of puberty affect parent-child relations.

Second, when the system changes in such a major way, the child sometimes seems to come "unglued" for a while. The old patterns of relationships, of thinking, of talking, don't work very well any more and it takes a while to work out new patterns. Erikson frequently uses the word *dilemma* to label such periods of semiupheaval. Klaus Riegel (1975) once suggested the phrase *developmental leaps*, which conveys nicely the sense of excitement and blooming opportunity that often accompany these pivotal periods. I'm going to use the more pedestrian term *transition* to describe the times of change or upheaval, and the term *consolidation* to describe the in-between times, when change is more gradual. Collectively, these concepts may help us examine what is happening during each of the major age periods.

▶ Age Periods in Perspective

From Birth to 18 Months

Figure 16.1 shows the various changes during the first 18 months of life. The rows of the figure roughly correspond to the chapters of this book; what we need to do now is read up and down the figure rather than just across the rows.

The overriding impression one gets of the newborn infant— despite her remarkable skills and capacities—is that she is very much on automatic pilot. There seem to be built-in rules or schemas that govern the way the infant looks, listens, explores the world, and relates to others.

One of the really remarkable things about these rules, as I pointed out in Chapters 3 and 5, is how well designed they are to lead both the child and the caregivers into the "dance" of interaction and attachment. Think of an infant being breast-fed. The baby has the needed rooting, sucking, and swallowing reflexes to take in the milk; in this position, the mother's face is at just about the optimum distance from the baby's eyes for the infant's best focusing; the mother's

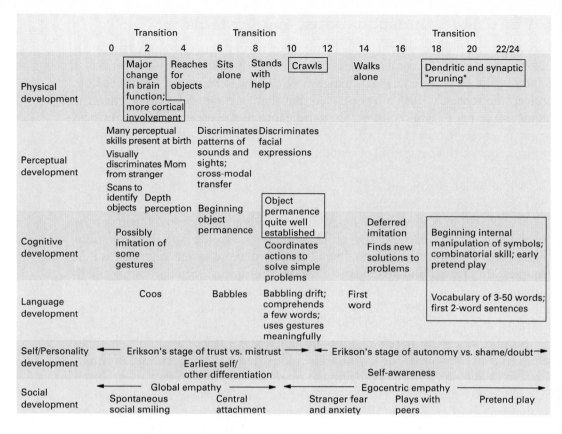

Figure 16.1
This brief summary chart shows some of the simultaneous developments during infancy. I have outlined the several developmental changes that seem to me to be pivotal at each of several ages.

facial features, particularly her eyes and mouth, are just the sort of visual stimuli that the baby is most likely to look at; the baby is particularly sensitive to the range of sounds of the human voice, particularly the upper register, so the higher-pitched, lilting voice most mothers use is easily heard by the infant; and during breast-feeding the release of a hormone called *cortisol* in the mother has the effect of relaxing her and making her more alert to the baby's signals. Both the adult and the infant are thus primed to interact with one another.

Sometime around 6 to 8 weeks, however, there are several changes in the system. Both because of the child's early explorations, and because of simple physical maturation, the child's actions and perceptual examinations of the world seem to switch into a different gear, one controlled much more by the cortex and less by the primitive portions of the brain. The child now looks at objects differently, apparently trying to identify *what* an object is rather than merely *where* it is; at this age she also smiles more, sleeps through the night (at least in Western cultures), and generally becomes a more responsive creature.

Because of these changes in the baby, and also because it takes most mothers six to eight weeks to recover physically from the delivery (and for the mother and father jointly to begin to adjust to the immense change in their routine), there are big changes in mother-infant interaction patterns as well at this time. The need for routine caretaking continues, of course (ah, the joys of diapers!), but as the child stays awake for longer periods, and smiles and makes eye contact more, exchanges between parent and child become more playful and smoother-paced.

Once this transition has occurred there seems to be a brief period of consolidation lasting perhaps six months. Of course change continues during this consolidation period. There are gradual neurological changes, with the motor and perceptual areas of the cortex continuing to develop. The child's perceptual skills also show rapid change in these months, with depth perception, clear cross-modal transfer, and identification of patterns of sounds and sights all emerging. The child is also exploring the world around him in an active way, which seems essential for the development of the object concept and other changes in cognitive skill. But a series of changes between about 7 and 9 months creates a new disequilibrium, a new transition: (1) the baby forms a strong central attachment, followed a few months later by separation anxiety and fear of strangers; (2) the infant begins to move around independently (albeit very slowly and haltingly at first); (3) communication between infant and parents changes substantially, as the baby begins to use meaningful gestures and to comprehend individual words; (4) object permanence is grasped at a new level—the baby now understands that objects and people can continue to exist even when they are out of sight. At the very least, these changes profoundly alter the parent-child interactive system, requiring the establishment of a new equilibrium, a new consolidation, a new system.

Eight-month-old Brandon can not only crawl, he undoubtedly also has a firm attachment to either or both parents, can perhaps understand a few words, and has a beginning understanding of object permanence. All these more-or-less simultaneous changes alter the system profoundly.

This new system seems to endure with only minor adjustments until 18 or 20 months of age, at which point the child's language and cognitive development appear to take another major leap forward—a set of changes I'll describe shortly.

Possible Causal Links.   Looking at simultaneous developments in various subperiods is helpful for grasping the totality of development, but doesn't provide an understanding of the system of interactions or the causal connections between the various changes. So let me speculate a bit about some possible causal links.

For the transition at 2 months, the key causal event seems to be a set of physiological changes in the nervous system, although we are still a long way from describing those changes in detail, or connecting such neurological changes to observed changes in the baby's behavior.

The transition at roughly 8 months is more difficult to explain. We do not know whether the confluence of these several changes is merely accidental—a series of separate lines of development that happen to come together at roughly this age— or whether there are one or two key underlying changes that are causally involved in all. We know that dendritic and synaptic development and myelinization of nerves are all still occurring rapidly at this age and are obviously implicated in many of the changes we see at this transition. But neurological changes are continuous; no one has yet identified a special set of neurological changes that occurs at about 8 months that would account for something like the shift in prelanguage skills.

Another candidate for a key change at 8 months is the development of object permanence, which may rest on basic neurological change but which is also a product of eight months of assimilation of and accommodation to basic experience. Once achieved, however, such an understanding may have a variety of repercussions, including stimulating the development of a basic attachment—although as I pointed out in Chapter 5, the research examining such a link directly has not provided strong support for this hypothesis.

We might also turn this hypothesis on its head and argue that the attachment may cause, or at least affect, the child's cognitive development. For example, there is a growing body of evidence showing that securely attached toddlers explore more freely, persist longer in their play, and develop the object concept more rapidly (Bates et al., 1982), perhaps because they are simply more comfortable exploring the world around them from the safe base of their secure persons. Alternatively, it may be that the sort of parent-child interaction that fosters a secure attachment is *also* optimal for fostering language and cognitive skill. In particular, *contingent responsiveness* from the parent seems to be a positive ingredient in the emergence not only of a secure attachment but of more rapid cognitive growth.

What's your best guess here? Which of these alternatives seems most persuasive to you?

These speculations about causal links between parallel changes may give you some sense of the issues with which physiologists and psychologists are now grappling, but don't let them obscure the basic point: Whatever causes this set of changes, once they have occurred the system is remarkably different than it was even a few months before. The baby now participates more actively with her environment and with the people around her. Inevitably, this enriches and widens the range of her experience, and demands new types of behaviors from her caregivers.

The Preschool Years: From 18 Months to 6 Years

The most striking thing about the transition at 18 to 24 months (which is clear in both Figure 16.1 and figure 16.2) is the beginning of the use of symbols by the child, in language and in thinking. This fundamental shift is reflected in many different aspects of the child's life. We see it in language, in the child's approach to cognitive tasks, and in play, where the child now pretends, having an object *stand for* something else. We also see the impact of symbol use in the emergence of self-awareness, and in changes in the child's attachment behaviors. When language is rudimentary and the child's locomotion is poor, then clinging, touching, holding, and crying are just about the only stress-related attachment behaviors available to the child. But as language becomes more skillful, and as the child is able to think about her parents when they are not there (to represent them symbolically), her behavior changes. The attachment may be no less strong, but it can be maintained at greater physical distance.

Off into the world he goes! This quality of independence and individuality is both one of the most charming and most difficult aspects of the preschool period.

At this same age, as I pointed out briefly in Chapter 8, the child also shows a rapid and broad emergence of *combinatorial skills* (Brownell, 1986; Brownell & Carriger, 1990). At about the time that the child first strings two words together into a sentence we also first see strings of two pretend actions in the child's play, and the first turn taking and cooperation in their interactions with other children. Interestingly, studies of mentally retarded children tell us that *mental age* rather than chronological age is the critical predictor of these changes (Siebert, Hogan, & Mundy, 1986). When the child reaches the mental age of about 20 months, all of these combinatorial skills emerge in rapid order.

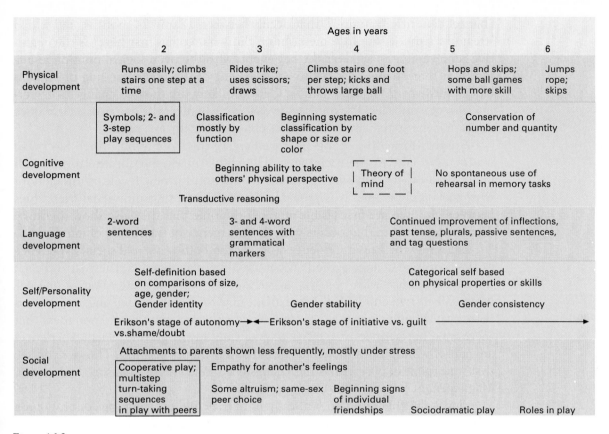

Figure 16.2
A brief summary of parallel developments during the preschool years.

In the beginning, these newfound skills and new independence are not accompanied by much impulse control. Two-year-olds are pretty good at doing; they are lousy at *not* doing. They see something, they go after it; when they want something, they want it NOW! If frustrated, they wail, or scream, or shout (isn't language wonderful?). A large part of the conflict parents experience with children at this age—famous as the "terrible twos"—comes about because the parent *must* limit the child, not only for the child's own survival, but to help teach the child impulse control (Escalona, 1981).

The preschool years also stand out as the period in which the seeds are sown for the child's—and perhaps the adult's—social skills and personality. The attachment process in infancy continues to be formative because it helps to shape the internal working model of social relationships the child creates. But in the years from 2 to 6, this early model is revised, consolidated, and established more firmly. The resultant interactive patterns tend to persist into elementary school and beyond. The 3-, 4-, or 5-year-old who develops the ability to share, to read others' cues well, to respond positively to others, and to control aggression and impulsiveness, is likely to be a socially successful, popular 8-year-old. In contrast, the noncompliant, hostile preschooler is far more likely to become an unpopular, aggressive schoolchild (Campbell et al., 1991; Patterson, Capaldi, & Bank, 1991).

Possible Causal Links.   What is causing this intricate and wide-ranging set of changes? One possibly crucial causal factor is the important neurological

If a parent of a 2-year-old complained to you about the "terrible twoness" of his child, what comments might you make? How could you explain the child's behavior to the parent in a way that might make it easier to deal with?

change, dendritic "pruning," that occurs between 12 and 24 months, and which streamlines the wiring in some fashion. But what comes first here? Is the cognitive achievement of symbols the key event, with the neurological pruning resulting from that change? Or is the achievement of the understanding of symbols based on the neurological changes? Or, most likely, are the two changes interacting with one another? We don't know yet, but whatever the cause, it is clear once again that the system and all its facets change radically as a result.

Another formative change is the emerging theory of mind, which has broad effects, especially in the social area. The child's newfound abilities to read and understand others' behaviors form the foundation for new levels of interactions with peers and parents. It is probably not accidental that individual friendships between children are first visible at about the time that they also show the sharp drop in egocentrism that occurs with the emergence of the theory of mind.

But surely the causal influences (again) run both ways, and social experience causes cognitive change as well. When children play together, they expand each other's experience with objects, suggesting new ways of pretending to one another. When two children disagree about how to explain something, or insist on their own different views, such experience enhances the child's awareness that there *are* other perspectives, other ways of thinking or playing. Such experiences are part of what pushes the child toward a new theory of mind. Thus we can see that time spent in play with other youngsters is much more than social (Bearison, Magzamen, & Filardo, 1986).

Play with other children is also a part of the child's developing concept of sex roles. Noticing whether other people are boys or girls, and what toys boys and girls play with, is itself the first step in the long chain of sex-role learning.

All in all, the sense one gets of this period is that the child is making a slow but immensely important shift from dependent baby to independent child. This shift is made possible by physical change, by language, by many and varied play encounters with other children, by new abilities to control impulses. At the same time (and from some of the same causes) the child's thinking is *decentering*, becoming less egocentric, and less tied to the outside appearances of things.

The Elementary-School Years: From 6 to 12

Figure 16.3 summarizes the changes and continuities of middle childhood. You can see from the figure that there are many gradual changes: greater and greater physical skill, less and less reliance on appearance and more and more attention to underlying qualities and attributes, greater and greater role of peers.

The one period in which there seems to be a more rapid change is right at the beginning of middle childhood, at the point of transition from the preschooler to the schoolchild. Some kind of a shift at this age has been noted in a great many cultures. There seems to be widespread recognition that a 6-year-old is somehow qualitatively different from a 5-year-old: more responsible, more able to understand complex ideas. Among the Kipsigis of Kenya, for example, the age of 6 is said to be the first point at which the child has *ng'omnotet,* translated as *intelligence* (Harkness & Super, 1985). The fact that schooling begins at this age seems to reflect an implicit or explicit recognition of this fundamental shift.

Psychologists who have studied development across this transition have pointed to a whole series of changes.

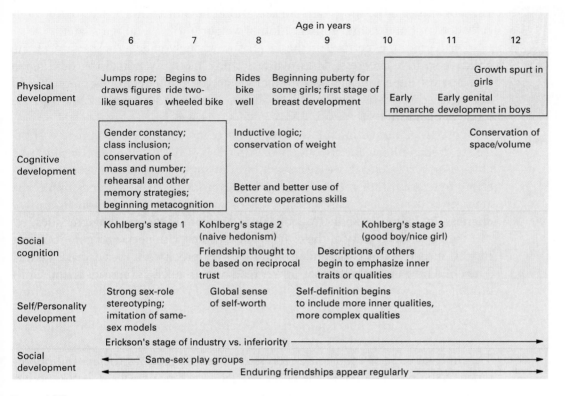

Figure 16.3
A summary of parallel changes during the elementary-school years.

- Cognitively, there is a shift to what Piaget calls concrete operational thinking. The child now understands conservation problems, seriation, and class inclusion. More generally, the child seems to pay less attention to surface properties of objects and more to underlying continuities and patterns. We see this not only in children's understanding of physical objects but in their understanding of others, of relationships, and of themselves. In studies of information processing, we see a parallel rapid increase in the child's use of executive strategies.
- In the self-concept, we first see a global judgment of self-worth at about age 7 or 8.
- In peer relationships, gender segregation becomes virtually complete by age 6 or 7, especially in individual friendships.

The apparent confluence of these changes is impressive, and seems to provide some support for the existence of a Piaget-like stage. On the surface, at least, there seems to be some kind of change in the basic structure of the child's thinking that is reflected in all aspects of the child's functioning. But impressive as these changes are, it is not so clear that what is going on here is a rapid, pervasive, structural change to a whole new way of thinking and relating. Children don't make this shift all at once in every area of their thinking or relationships. For example, while the shift from a concrete to a more abstract self-concept may become noticeable at 6 or 7, it occurs quite gradually and is still going on at 11 and

These boys are typical of children their age in every part of the world: they play almost exclusively with same-sex peers.

As a way to grasp the importance of social contacts, try to imagine a child who grew up without ever playing with another child. How would such a child be different? What kind of adult would he or she become?

12. Similarly, a child may grasp conservation of quantity at age 5 or 6, but typically does not understand conservation of weight until several years later.

Furthermore, expertise, or the lack of it, strongly affects the pattern of the child's cognitive progress. Thus, while I think most psychologists would agree that a set of important changes normally emerges at about this age, most would also agree that there is no rapid or abrupt reorganization of the child's whole mode of operating.

Possible Causal Links.   In trying to account for the developmental shifts we see during middle childhood, my bias in the past has been to see the cognitive changes as most central, the necessary but not sufficient condition for the alterations in relationships and in the self-scheme during this period. For example, the emergence of a global sense of self-worth seems to rest on important cognitive changes, including an ability to look beyond or behind surface characteristics.

Similarly, the quality of the child's relationships with peers and parents seems to rest, in part, on a basic understanding of reciprocity and perspective taking. The child now understands that others read him as much as he reads them. Children of 7 or 8 will now say of their friends that they "trust each other," something you would be very unlikely to hear from a 5-year-old.

Such a cognitive bias dominated theories and research on middle childhood for many decades, largely as a result of the powerful influence of Piaget's theory. This imbalance has begun to be redressed in recent years, as the central importance of the peer group and the child's social experience has been better understood. There are two aspects to this revision of thinking. First, we have reawakened to the (obvious) fact that a great deal of the experience on which the child's cognitive progress is based occurs in social interactions, particularly in play with other children. Second, we have realized that social relationships make a unique set of demands, both cognitive and interactive. Unlike relationships with objects, relationships with people are mutual and reciprocal. Other people talk back, respond to your distress, offer things, get angry. There are social and cognitive lessons that can *only* be learned in human interaction.

Just what role physical change plays in this collection of developments I do not know. Clearly there *are* physical changes going on. Girls, in particular, are going through the first steps of puberty during elementary school. But no research I know of hooks the first row in Figure 16.3 with any of the other rows. We know that bigger, more coordinated, early developing children are likely to have slightly faster cognitive development and be somewhat more popular with peers, but not much else. Obviously this is an area in which we need far more knowledge.

Adolescence: From 12 to 20

Early adolescence is, almost by definition, a time of transition, a time in which there is significant change in virtually every aspect of the child's functioning. Late adolescence is more a time of consolidation, when the young person establishes a cohesive new identity, with clearer goals and role commitments. Norma Haan (1981), borrowing Piaget's concepts, suggests that early adolescence is a time dominated by assimilation, while late adolescence is primarily a time of accommodation.

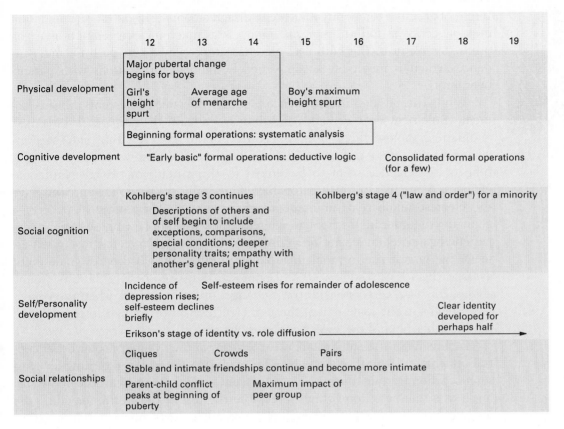

Figure 16.4
A brief summary of parallel developments during adolescence.

The 12- or 13-year-old is assimilating an enormous amount of new physical, social, and intellectual experiences. While all this absorption is going on, but before it is digested, the young person is in a more or less perpetual state of disequilibrium. Old patterns, old schemes no longer work very well, but new ones have not been established. It is during this early period that the peer group is so centrally important. Ultimately, the 16- or 17- or 18-year-old begins to make the needed accommodations, pulls the threads together, and establishes a new identity, new patterns of social relationships, new goals and roles.

Early Adolescence.   In some ways the early years of adolescence have a lot in common with the early years of toddlerhood. Two-year-olds are famous for their negativism and for their constant push for more independence. At the same time they are struggling to learn a vast array of new skills. Teenagers show many of these same qualities, albeit at much more abstract levels. Many of them go through a period of negativism, particularly with parents, right at the beginning of the pubertal changes. And many of the conflicts with parents center on issues of independence—they want to come and go when they please, listen to the music they prefer at maximum volume, and wear the clothing and hair styles that are currently "in."

It is easy to overstate the depth or breadth of the conflict between young teenagers and their parents. For the great majority of teenagers, there is no major

Independence in a new form.

turmoil but only a temporary increase in disagreements or disputes. The depiction of adolescence as full of *Sturm und Drang* is as much an exaggeration as is the phrase *terrible twos*. But both ages are characterized by a new push for independence, which is inevitably accompanied by more confrontations with parents over limits.

While this push for independence is going on, young adolescents are also facing a whole new set of demands and skills to be learned—new social skills, new and more complex school tasks, a need to form an adult identity. The sharp increases in the rate of depression and the drop in self-esteem we see at the beginning of adolescence seem to be linked to this surplus of new demands and changes. A number of investigators have found that those adolescents who have the greatest number of simultaneous changes at the beginning of puberty—changing to junior high school, moving to a new town or new house, perhaps experiencing a parental separation or divorce—also show the greatest loss in self-esteem, the largest rise in problem behavior, and the biggest drop in grade point average (Eccles & Midgley, 1990; Simmons, Burgeson, & Reef, 1988). Young adolescents who can cope with these changes one at a time, as when the youngster remains in the same school through eighth or ninth grade before shifting to senior high school, show fewer symptoms of stress.

Facing major stressful demands, the 2-year-old uses Mom (or some other central attachment figure) as a safe base for exploring the world, returning for reassurance when fearful. Young adolescents seem to do the same with the family, using it as a safe base from which to explore the rest of the world, including the world of peer relationships. Parents of young adolescents must try to find a difficult balance between providing the needed security, often in the form of clear rules and limits, and still allowing independence—just as the parent of a 2-year-old must walk the fine line between allowing exploration and keeping the child safe. Among teenagers, as among toddlers, the most confident and successful are those whose families manage this balancing act well.

Still a third way in which theorists have likened the young teenager to the 2-year-old is in egocentrism. David Elkind (1967) suggested some years ago that there is a rise in egocentrism in adolescence. This new egocentrism, according to Elkind, has two facets: (1) the belief that "others in our immediate vicinity are as concerned with our thoughts and behavior as we ourselves are" (Elkind & Bowen, 1979, p. 38), which Elkind describes as having an *imaginary audience*; and (2) the possession of a *personal fable*, a tendency to consider their own ideas and feelings unique and singularly important. This is typically accompanied by a sense of invulnerability—a feeling that may lie behind the adolescent's apparent attraction to high-risk behavior, such as unprotected sex, drugs, drinking, high-speed driving, and the like.

Elkind's own research (Elkind & Bowen, 1979) shows that the preoccupation with others' views of the self (imaginary audience behavior) peaks at about ages 13 to 14. Teenagers this age are most likely to say that if they went to a party where they did not know most of the kids, they would wonder *a lot* about what the other kids were thinking of them. They also report that they worry a lot when someone is watching them work, and feel desperately embarrassed if they discover a grease spot on their clothes, or have newly erupted pimples. Of course younger children and adults may also worry about these things, but they seem to be much less disturbed or immobilized by these worries than are 13- and 14-year-olds. You'll recall that this is the same age at which teens seem to be most susceptible to peer pressure, and the peak age for the type of peer group Dunphy calls the crowd.

Drawing a parallel between the early adolescent and the toddler also makes sense in that both age groups face the task of establishing a separate identity. The toddler must separate herself from the symbiotic relationship with Mom or central caregiver. She must figure out not only that she is separate but that she has abilities and qualities. Physical maturation also allows her new levels of independent exploration. The young adolescent must separate himself from his family, and from his identity as a child, and begin to form a new identity as an adult.

Late Adolescence.   To carry the basic analogy further, late adolescence is more like the preschool years. Major changes have been weathered, and a new balance has been achieved. The physical upheavals of puberty are mostly complete, the family system has changed to allow more independence and freedom, and the beginnings of a new identity have been created. This period is not without its strains. For most young people, a clear identity is not achieved until college age, if then, so the identity process continues. And the task of forming emotionally intimate sexual or presexual partnerships is a key task of late adolescence. Nonetheless, I think Haan is correct that this later period is more one of accommodation than assimilation. At the very least we know that it is accompanied by rising levels of self-esteem, and declining levels of family confrontation or conflict.

Possible Causal Links.   How might all these simultaneous changes be connected to one another? There has been a good deal of interest in this set of questions in recent years, but we are still a long way from clear answers.

The obvious place to begin is with the role of puberty itself. Puberty not only defines the beginning of early adolescence, it clearly affects all other facets of the young person's development, either directly or indirectly.

Direct effects might be seen in several ways. Most clearly, the surges of pubertal hormones stimulate sexual interest while they also trigger body changes that make adult sexuality and fertility possible. These changes seem inescapably causally linked to the gradual shift from same-sex peer groupings to heterosexual crowds and finally to heterosexual pair relationships.

Hormone changes may also be directly implicated in the increases in confrontation or conflict between parents and children, and the rise in various kinds of aggressive or delinquent behavior. Steinberg's research suggests such a direct link because he finds pubertal stage and not age to be the critical variable in predicting the level of adolescent-parent conflict. Other investigators have found that in girls, the rise in estradiol at the beginning of puberty is associated with increases in verbal aggression and a loss of impulse control, while in boys, increases in testosterone are correlated with increases in irritability and impatience (Paikoff & Brooks-Gunn, 1990). But there are also many studies in which no such connection is found, which has led most theorists to conclude that the connections between pubertal hormones and changes in adolescent social behavior are considerably more complicated than we had first imagined.

Does the comparison of early adolescence and toddlerhood make sense to you? If it is a valid comparison, then does that suggest that development is somehow like a spiral, returning to the same issues repeatedly, but at levels of ever-greater complexity?

By late adolescence, the form of peer interaction has changed radically.

One of the complications is that the physical changes of puberty have highly significant indirect effects as well. When the child's body grows and becomes more like that of an adult, the parents begin to treat the child differently and the child begins to see himself as a soon-to-be-adult. Both of these changes may be linked to the brief rise in parent-adolescent confrontation, and may help to trigger some of the searching self-examinations that are part of this period of life.

Physiological changes may also play some role in the shift to formal operations. There is some indication, for example, that a second major synaptic and dendritic "pruning" occurs at adolescence. At the same time, any link between formal operational thinking and pubertal change cannot be inevitable, because we know that all adolescents experience puberty but not all make the transition to formal operations. The best guess at the moment is that neurological or hormonal changes at adolescence may be *necessary* for further cognitive gains but they cannot be *sufficient* conditions for such developments.

An equally attractive possibility is that cognitive changes are the most central. The cognitive shift from concrete to formal operations obviously does not cause pubertal changes, but cognitive development may be central to many of the other changes we see at adolescence, including changes in the self-concept, the process of identity formation, increases in level of moral reasoning, and changes in peer relationship.

There is ample evidence, for example, that the greater abstractness of the child's self-concept and of his descriptions of others are intimately connected to the broader changes in cognitive functioning (Harter, 1990). You will also remember from Chapter 12 that the shift in the child's thinking from concrete operations to at least beginning formal operations seems to be a necessary precondition for the emergence of more advanced forms of social cognition and moral judgment. Finally, some ability to use formal operations may also be necessary but not sufficient for the formation of a clear identity. One of the characteristics of formal operations thinking is the ability to imagine possibilities that you have never experienced and to manipulate ideas in your head. These new skills may help to foster the broad questioning of old ways, old values, old patterns that is a central part of the identity formation process. For example, several studies show that among high school and college students, those in Marcia's identity achievement or moratorium statuses are much more likely also to be using formal operations reasoning than are those in the diffusion or foreclosure statuses (Leadbeater & Dionne, 1981; Rowe & Marcia, 1980). In Rowe and Marcia's study, the *only* individuals who showed full identity achievement were those who were also using full formal operations. But the converse was not true. That is, there were a number of subjects who used formal operations who had not yet established a clear identity. Thus formal operations thinking may *enable* the young person to rethink many aspects of his life, but it does not guarantee that he will do so.

All in all, we are left with the impression that both the physical changes of puberty and the potential cognitive changes of formal operations are central to the phenomena of adolescence, but the connections between them, and their impact on social behavior, remain unclear.

▶ Returning to Some Basic Questions

With this brief overview in mind, let me now go back to some of the questions I raised in Chapter 1 and see if the answers can be made any clearer.

What Are the Major Influences on Development?

In Chapter 1 and throughout the book I have contrasted nature and nurture, nativism and empiricism, as basic explanations of developmental patterns. In every instance I have also said that the real answer lies in the interaction between the two. By now I hope it is this interactive message that you will take away with you. I can perhaps make the point clearest by going back to Aslin's five models of environmental/internal influences on development I showed in Figure 1.1. You'll recall that he is proposing one purely physical model (which he calls maturation) in which some particular development would occur regardless of environmental input, and one purely environmental pattern (which he calls induction) in which some development is entirely a function of experience. These two "pure" alternatives make logical sense, but in fact, probably neither of them actually occurs at all. *All* of development is a product of various forms of interaction between internal and external influences.

Even in those areas of development that appear to be the most clearly biologically determined or influenced, such as physical development or early perceptual development, normal development can occur *only* if the child is growing in an environment that falls within the range of adequate or sufficient environments. The fact that the vast majority of environments fall within that range in no way reduces the crucial importance of the environment. John Flavell (1985) puts it this way: "Environmental elements do not become any less essential to a particular form of development just because they are virtually certain to be available for its use" (p. 284).

Similarly, even those aspects of development that seem most obviously to be a product of environment, such as the quality of the child's first attachment, rest on a physiological substrate and on instinctive patterns of attachment behaviors. The fact that all intact children possess that substrate and those instincts makes them no less essential for development.

At the same time, it is not enough merely to say that all development is a product of interaction of nature and nurture. We need to be able to specify much more clearly just how that interaction operates. Aslin's models illustrate three of the many alternatives, but in most cases what we see is doubtless a subtle combination of many interactive patterns.

Furthermore, the form and extent of the interaction may well vary as a function of the aspect of development we are talking about. It may help to think of different facets of development along a continuum, with those most fully internally programmed on one end, and those most externally influenced on the other.

Physical development defines one end of this continuum, since it is very strongly shaped by internal forces. *Given the minimum necessary environment, maturational timetables are extremely powerful and robust, particularly during

The fact that virtually all babies have some chance to hold and examine objects does not mean that such experience is unimportant in the child's emerging perceptual or motor skills. Most (if not all) so-called maturational sequences require particular kinds of environmental inputs if they are to occur at all.

infancy and adolescence. Next along the continuum is probably language (although some experts will argue with this conclusion, given the possible dependency of language development upon prior cognitive developments). Language seems to emerge with only minimal environmental support—though here, too, the environment must fall within some acceptable range. At the very least, the child must hear language spoken (or see it signed). Still, specific features of the environment seem to matter a bit more here than is true for physical development. For example, parents who respond contingently to their children's vocalizations seem to be able to speed up the process, an example of what Aslin calls facilitation.

Cognitive development falls somewhere in the middle of the continuum. Clearly there are powerful internal forces at work. Let me quote John Flavell (1985) once again:

> There is an impetus to childhood cognitive growth that is not ultimately explainable by this environmental push or that experiential shove. (p. 283)

Whether the impressive regularity of the sequences of cognitive development arises from built-in processes like assimilation and accommodation, or whether there are physiological changes in information processing capacity, or some combination of the two, we don't yet know. But it is clear that this engine is moving along a shared track. At the same time, we know that the specific qualities of the environment affect both cognitive power and structure. Children with varied and age-appropriate toys, with encouragement for exploration and achievement, with parents who are responsive to the child's overtures, show faster cognitive development and higher eventual IQ scores—not just facilitation in Aslin's models, but actual attunement.

Social and emotional development lie at the other end of the continuum, where the impact of the environment seems to be the greatest, although even here there are obviously genetic factors at work. Temperament may well be inborn, and attachment behaviors may be instinctive; both of these inborn factors certainly shape the child's earliest encounters with others. But the balance of nature/nurture seems to lean more toward nurture in this area. In particular, the security of the child's attachment, and the quality of the child's relationships with others outside of the family, seem to be powerfully affected by the specific quality of the interactions within the family.

Even this fairly complex analysis, however, only begins to scratch the surface. For one thing, many of the statements I have just made need to be modified in terms of *when* a particular environmental event takes place.

Does Timing Matter?

You've encountered many variations of the timing hypothesis through the chapters of this book, but the most pervasive question has been whether the early years of life are a critical or sensitive period, establishing many of the trajectories of the child's later development. To borrow an analogy from Clarke (1968; Clarke & Clarke, 1976): When we construct a house, does the shape of the foundation determine the final structure partially or completely, or can many final structures be built on the original foundation? Are any flaws or weaknesses in the original foundation permanent, or can they be corrected later, after the house is completed?

There are arguments on both sides. Some, such as Sandra Scarr, point to the fact that virtually all children successfully complete the sensorimotor period; and even mild and moderately retarded children achieve some form of what Piaget called concrete operations. The term that has been widely used to describe such developmental patterns is **canalization,** a notion borrowed from an embryologist named Waddington (1957). He suggested that we think of development metaphorically as a marble rolling down a gully on a hillside. Where the gully is narrow and deep, development is said to be "highly canalized." The marble will roll down that gully with little deviation. Other aspects of development, in contrast, might be better depicted with much flatter or wider gullies, with many side branches. Thus Scarr and others argue that in the early years of life, development is highly canalized, with strong "self-righting" tendencies. If deflected, the baby rapidly returns to the bottom of the gully and proceeds along the normal track. Such self-righting is illustrated, for example, by the large percentage of low-birth-weight or other initially vulnerable babies who nonetheless catch up to their normal-birth peers in physical and cognitive development by the time they are 2 or 3.

On the other side of the argument are the obvious cases in which an early experience has been highly formative. Some prenatal influences are permanent; some effects of early cognitive impoverishment, malnutrition, or abuse may also be long-lasting.

Thus the early years of life seem to be a sensitive period for some kinds of development and at the same time seem to be highly canalized. There are at least two different resolutions of this apparent paradox. First, if we think of such canalization not just as a product of powerful built-in programming, but as the result of such programming *occurring in a sufficiently supportive environment,* much of the apparent dispute disappears (Scarr-Salapatek, 1976; Turkheimer & Gottesman, 1991). It is only when a child's particular environment falls outside of the range of sufficiently supportive environments that we see a so-called environmental effect, such as a child reared in an extremely impoverished orphanage setting, or a child who is regularly physically abused. In these conditions, environmental effects can be strongly negative and long-lasting. The earlier such a deviation occurs, the more pervasive the effects seem to be. In this way of looking at critical periods versus canalization, infancy may be less *frequently* pivotal in the pattern of the child's development than are more minor deviations in toddlerhood or the preschool years. But *if* the deviations in infancy are extreme enough to deflect the infant from the normal developmental path—as in the case of severe abuse or malnutrition—the effect is larger than at any other age.

Robert Cairns (1991) offers a second resolution to the apparent dispute between infancy as a critical period and infancy as highly canalized, when he points out that in any given period, some facets of development may be highly canalized while other facets may be strongly responsive to environmental variation. In infancy, for example, physical, perceptual, and perhaps linguistic development may be strongly canalized, but the development of attachments and of internal working models of attachment are clearly affected by the specific experiences the child

If infancy is a critical period for some aspects of personality development, then these little guys' characters are already well formed. Whether this is true or not remains one of the most crucial theoretical and practical issues in developmental psychology.

Does either of these resolutions of the paradox persuade you? If not, why not?

has within the family. Indeed, I would argue that all internal working models— of attachment, of gender identity and self-concept, of peer relations—are likely to be more powerfully affected by early than by later experiences, simply because the model, once formed, affects and filters all later experience.

A particularly nice example of this kind of early effect comes from one of Alan Sroufe's studies of the long-term consequences of attachment security. He and his colleagues (Sroufe, Egeland, & Kreutzer, 1990) compared two groups of elementary-school children. One group had had a good adaptation in infancy, with a secure attachment, but for various reasons had not functioned well in the preschool years. The second group had shown poor adaptation at both ages. When these two groups of children were assessed at elementary-school age, Sroufe found that those who had had a good early start "rebounded" better. They had better emotional health and peer competence at school age than did those who had had a poor adaptation in infancy, even though both groups had functioned poorly as preschoolers. The infancy experience is not totally formative; the child's current circumstances also have a major impact. But at least in this domain, early experience leaves a lingering trace.

Timing and internal models interact in yet another way when we look at the effect of earliness or lateness of some experience such as puberty. What matters in this case seems not to be the actual timing, but the child's interpretation of that timing, the child's internal model.

Still a third way to think about timing is to emphasize the importance of specific psychological tasks at different ages. Erikson's theory, for example, emphasizes each of a series of psychological dilemmas. Any experience that affects the way a child resolves a particular task will be formative at that time; at an earlier or later time the same experience might have much less effect. Alan Sroufe and Michael Rutter (1984) have offered a broader list of age-graded tasks, given in Table 16.1. In this way of looking at things, the child is seen as *focusing* on different aspects of the environment at different times. Thus during the period from 1 to $2\frac{1}{2}$, when the child is focused on mastery of the object world, the quality and range of inanimate experiences the child has access to may be of special importance.

Overall, I do not think that any specific age is "critical" for all aspects of development; I do think that for any aspect of development, some ages are more central than others, and that during those times, patterns are set which affect later experience. As Alan Sroufe (1983) says, "Development is hierarchical; it is not a blackboard to be erased and written upon again. Even when children change rather markedly, the shadows of the earlier adaptation remain" (pp. 73–74).

What Is the Nature of Developmental Change?

My bias has no doubt been apparent all through the book, so you can predict my conclusion that developmental change is more qualitative than quantitative. Certainly the child acquires more vocabulary words, more information processing strategies. But these are used in different ways by older children than by younger ones. Further, it seems clear that these qualitative changes occur in sequences. Such sequences are apparent in physical development, in cognitive development, in social and moral development.

TABLE 16.1	Tasks or Issues in Each of Several Age Periods, as Proposed by Sroufe and Rutter
Age in years	**Issues or tasks**
0–1	Biological regulation; harmonious dyadic interaction; formation of an effective attachment relationship
1–2½	Exploration, experimentation, and mastery of the object world (caregiver as secure base); individuation and autonomy; responding to external control of impulses
3–5	Flexible self-control; self-reliance; initiative; identification and gender concept; establishing effective peer contacts (empathy)
6–12	Social understanding (equity, fairness); gender constancy; same-sex chumships; sense of "industry" (competence); school adjustment
13+	"Formal operations" (flexible perspective taking; "as if" thinking); loyal friendships (same-sex); beginning heterosexual relationships; emancipation; identity

Source: Sroufe & Rutter, 1984, adapted from Sroufe, 1979.

Stages.   Whether it is meaningful to speak of stages, however, is still an open question. Some hierarchically organized stages have certainly been observed, Kohlberg's stages of moral reasoning being the most obvious example. And there are certainly examples of apparently stagelike changes across domains, such as what happens at about 18 to 24 months, when the child seems to discover the ability to combine symbols and we see new behavior in language, in thinking, and in play with other children. But the majority of the evidence has not supported the notion of pervasive changes in structure. More commonly, each new skill, each new understanding, seems to be acquired in a fairly narrow area first, and is only later generalized more fully. In fact, one of the things that differentiates the gifted or higher-IQ child from the lower-IQ or retarded child is how quickly and broadly the child generalizes some new concept or strategy to new instances.

Despite this nonstagelike quality of most developmental change, it is still true that if you compare the patterns of relationship, of thinking, of problem solving of two children of widely differing ages—say, a 5-year-old and an 11-year-old—they will differ in almost every respect. So there is certainly orderliness in the sequences, and some linkages between them, but probably not major stages quite like those Piaget proposed.

Continuities.   In the midst of all of this change, all these sequences, all the new forms of relating and thinking, there is also continuity. Each child carries forward some core of individuality. The notion of temperament certainly implies such a core, as does the concept of an internal working model. Alan Sroufe once again offers an elegant way of thinking about this central core. Continuity in development, he says, "takes the form of coherence across transformations" (Sroufe,1983, p. 51). Thus specific behavior we see in the child may change; the clinging toddler may not be a clinging 9-year-old. But the underlying attachment model or the temperament that led to the clinging will still be at least partially present, manifesting itself in new ways. In particular, it has become increasingly clear that some *mal*adaptations persist over time, as seen in the consistency of high levels of aggression or tantrum behavior, and in the persistence of some of the maladaptive social interactions that flow from insecure attachments. Our task as psychologists is to understand both coherence or consistency, and the underlying patterns of development or transformation.

◗ Individual Differences

The whole issue of individual continuities emphasizes the fact that development is individual as well as collective. I have talked about individual differences in virtually every chapter, so you know that both inborn differences and emergent or environmentally produced differences are present among children in every aspect of development. All of this is familiar stuff by now and bears little repeating. But I want to try to tie together many of the threads I have been weaving in this chapter by returning to a dimension of individual differences I have talked about several times, namely vulnerability and resilience.

I think it is useful to define these concepts somewhat differently than usual, in terms of the *range of environments which will be sufficiently supportive for optimal development*. By this definition, a vulnerable infant is one with a narrow range of potentially supportive environments. For such a child, only the most stimulating, the most responsive, the most adaptive environment will do. When the child's environment falls outside of that range, the probability of a poor outcome is greatly increased. A resilient child, in contrast, is one for whom any of a very wide range of environments will support optimum development. A resilient child may thus be more strongly canalized, a vulnerable child less so.

Some kinds of vulnerabilities are inborn, such as genetic abnormalities, or prenatal trauma or stress, or preterm birth, or malnutrition. Any such child will thrive only in a highly supportive environment. You've encountered this pattern again and again through the chapters of this book.

- Low-birth-weight infants typically have normal IQs if they are reared in middle-class homes, but have a high risk of serious retardation if they are reared in poverty (Werner, 1986).
- Prenatally malnourished infants, or those with other complications during pregnancy or delivery, look normal if reared in highly stimulating special preschools, but have significantly lower IQs if reared at home by low-education mothers (Breitmayer & Ramey, 1986; Zeskind & Ramey, 1981).
- Children born with cytomegalovirus are much more likely to have learning problems in school if they are reared in poverty-level environments than if they are reared in middle-class families (Hanshaw et al., 1976).

So far that's fairly straightforward. But let me propose a further, more speculative, theoretical step: I think that "vulnerability" in this sense does not remain constant throughout life. A more general proposition, which I suggest as a working hypothesis, is that each time the child's environment falls outside of the range of acceptably supporting environments *for that child* (that is, each time there is a mismatch between the child's needs and what is available), the child becomes *more vulnerable*, while each period during which the child's needs are met makes the child more resilient. For example, I would predict that a temperamentally difficult child whose family environment was nonetheless sufficient to foster a secure attachment will become more resilient, more able to handle the next set of tasks, while a temperamentally easy child who nonetheless developed an insecure attachment would become more vulnerable to later stress or environmental insufficiency.

Furthermore, the qualities of the environment that are critical for a child's optimum development no doubt change as the child passes from one age to another. Responsive and warm interactions with parents seem particularly central in the period from perhaps 6 months to 18 months; richness of cognitive stimulation seems particularly central between perhaps 1 year and 4 years; opportunity for practicing social skills with peers may be especially central at a later age. Thus as the tasks change with age, the optimum environment will change also. Among other things, this means that the same family may be very good with a child of one age, and not so good with a child of another age.

Most generally, this model leads to the conclusion that even the most "vulnerable" child can show improvement if her environment improves markedly. Because some congenitally vulnerable children do not encounter sufficiently supportive environments, their vulnerability will continue to increase. In this way, early problems will often persist. But at the same time, improvement is possible, even likely. *Most* children manage to survive and thrive, despite stresses and vulnerabilities. As Emmy Werner (1986) puts it, "We could not help being deeply impressed by the resilience of most children and youth and their capacity for positive change and personal growth" (p. 5).

> What I am suggesting is that resilience or vulnerability is a little like a bank account. Vulnerable children start out with little in the account, while resilient children have a lot. Experience then adds to or subtracts from the account. Does this make sense to you? Can you think of any other implications of this concept than those I have suggested here?

▶ A Final Point: The Joy of Development

On a similarly optimistic note, I want to end both this chapter and the book by pointing out that in the midst of all the "crises" and "transitions" and "vulnerabilities" there is a special *joyous* quality to development. When a child masters a new skill, she is not just pleased, she is delighted and will repeat that new skill at length, quite obviously getting vast satisfaction from it. A 5-year-old I once knew learned to draw stars and drew them on everything in sight, including paper, walls, clothes, and napkins. It was so much *fun* to draw stars. A 10-year-old who learns to do cartwheels will delightedly display this new talent to anyone who will watch and will practice endlessly.

The same joyous quality can be part of the family's development as well. Confronting and moving successfully through one of the periodic (and inevitable) upheavals in family life can be immensely pleasing. Watching your child progress, liking your child, enjoying walking or talking together, are all deeply satisfying parts of rearing children. When parents cry at their son's or daughter's high school graduation or wedding, it is not merely sentiment. It is an expression of that sense of love, pride, and wonderment that you have gotten this far.

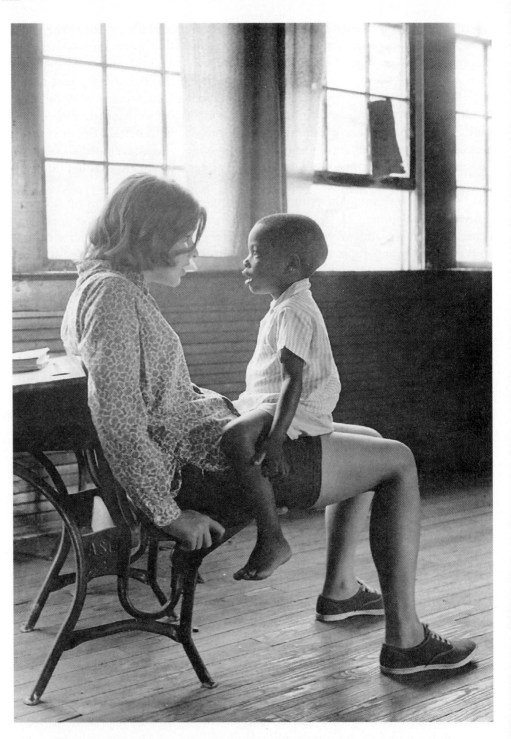

I have used this photo at the end of every edition of this book because it speaks to me so eloquently of the quality of joy, of discovery, that is so much a part of development.

⟩ **Summary**

1. The child's development may be thought of as a series of alternating periods of transition and consolidation. The transitions occur when there are individual major changes, or pileups of smaller changes.

2. To understand development we must understand the system, not just the individual parts. A change in any part of the system affects all the other facets.

3. Within infancy, there appear to be at least two transition periods, one at about 2 months, and the other at roughly 8 months.

4. The 2-month transition seems particularly influenced by neurological change; the one at 8 months has many threads and we do not yet know the causal links between them.

5. The transition at 18 months is marked by the remarkable emergence of symbolic activity, evidenced in language, in thinking, in play. A general combinatorial ability also appears at about this time, with a more sophisticated theory of mind several years later.

6. These cognitive accomplishments combine with major new motor skills to allow the child significantly greater independence, which in turn fosters further cognitive growth.

7. The transition at ages 5 to 7 is marked both by the beginning emergence of still more-powerful cognitive skills, and by the beginning of school. A general "decentering" is manifested in children's relationships with their peers as well as in their thinking.

8. The transition at adolescence is triggered primarily by the physical changes of puberty, but is accompanied by still further cognitive changes, major alterations in patterns of peer interaction, increases in family disruption, and increases in depression.

9. A shift toward formal operations at adolescence may be one contributor to a rise in self-questioning; pubertal changes may have both direct and indirect effects on the other developments of this period.

10. All facets of development are the product of some combination or interaction of internal and external influences.

11. Nonetheless, the various facets of development can be arrayed along a continuum from those most affected by internal influences to those most affected by external influences, in the following order: physical development, language, cognition, and social/personality development.

12. Paradoxically, development in the early years of life appears to be both highly canalized and (at extremes of environment) highly sensitive to environmental variation.

13. The early years of life may also be especially important for all children because internal working models are established in that period.

14. Each age period can also be thought of as having a set of central tasks; experiences that are especially important for the successful completion of those tasks will thus be "critical" for that age.

15. Development seems clearly to be made up of a large number of widely shared (if not universal) sequences. But whether there are broad, structurally different stages is less clear.

16. The dimension of vulnerability/resilience is one way to think about individual differences. The dimension may be defined in terms of the range of environments which will support optimal development for a particular child. A large range implies resilience; a narrow range defines vulnerability.

17. Vulnerability may be increased or decreased over time, depending on the adequacy or inadequacy of environments at each of a series of points in development. Children may thus recover from, or surmount, even very poor starts.

18. For both the child and the parent, development is full of joy as well as travail.

▶ Key Terms

canalization (477)

▶ Suggested Readings

Many of the books I have suggested in earlier chapters are relevant here as well, including both the Rosenblith and Sims-Knight (1989) and Osofsky (1987) books on infancy, and Flavell's book on cognitive development (1985), which includes an elegant discussion of many of the basic issues I have been talking about in this chapter. Let me also suggest several other books that give the flavor of particular ages.

Collins, W. A. (Ed.). (1984). *Development during middle childhood: The years from six to twelve.* Washington, DC: National Academy Press.

This collection of papers touches on all facets of school-age children: biology, cognition, self-understanding, family and peer relationships, school, and atypical development. An excellent source of information about this often-neglected age period.

Feldman, S. S., & Elliott, G. R. (Eds.). (1990). *At the threshold: The developing adolescent.* Cambridge, MA: Harvard University Press.

An especially good and helpful collection of papers on adolescence—an age period that has been "discovered" by psychologists in the past decade.

GLOSSARY

accommodation   That part of the adaptation process by which a person modifies existing schemes to fit new experiences, or creates new schemes when old ones no longer handle the data.

achievement test   A test usually given in schools, designed to assess a child's learning of specific material taught in school, such as spelling or arithmetic computation.

acuity   Sharpness of perceptual ability—how well or clearly one can see or hear or use other senses.

adaptive behavior   An aspect of a child's functioning often considered in diagnosing mental retardation. Can the child adapt to the tasks of everyday life?

affectional bond   A "relatively long-enduring tie in which the partner is important as a unique individual and is interchangeable with none other."

aggression   Behavior with the apparent intent to injure some other person or object.

alpha-fetoprotein test   A prenatal diagnostic test frequently used to screen for the risk of neural tube defects.

altruism   Giving or sharing objects, time, or goods with others, with no obvious self-gain.

amniocentesis   A medical test for genetic abnormalities in the embryo/fetus that may be done at about 15 weeks of gestation.

amnion   The sac or bag, filled with liquid, in which the embryo/fetus floats during prenatal life.

androgyny   A self-concept including, and behavior expressing, high levels of both masculine and feminine qualities.

anorexia nervosa   A disorder characterized by extreme dieting, intense fear of gaining weight, and distorted body image.

anoxia   A shortage of oxygen. If it is prolonged, it can result in brain damage. This is one of the potential risks at birth.

Apgar score   An assessment of the newborn completed by the physician or midwife at one minute and again at five minutes after birth, assessing five characteristics: heart rate, respiratory rate, muscle tone, response to stimulation, and color.

assimilation   That part of the adaptation process that involves the "taking in" of new experiences or information into existing schemes. Experience is not taken in "as is," however, but is modified (or interpreted) somewhat so as to fit the preexisting schemes.

attachment   The positive affective bond between one person and another, such as that of the child for the parent.

attachment behavior   The collection of (probably) instinctive behaviors of one person toward another that bring about or maintain proximity and caregiving, such as the smile of the young infant; behaviors that reflect an attachment.

attention deficit hyperactivity disorder (ADD)   The technical term for what is more normally called hyperactivity, characterized by short attention span, distractibility, and heightened levels of physical activity.

authoritarian parental style   One of the three styles described by Baumrind, characterized by high levels of control and maturity demands and low levels of nurturance and communication.

authoritative parental style   One of the three styles described by Baumrind, characterized by high levels of control, nurturance, maturity demands, and communication.

autosomes   The 22 pairs of chromosomes in which both members of the pair are the same shape and carry parallel information.

axon   The long appendagelike part of a neuron; the terminal fibers of the axon serve as transmitters in the synaptic connection with the dendrites of other neurons.

babbling   The vocalizing, often repetitive, of consonant-vowel combinations by an infant, typically beginning at about 6 months of age.

Bayley Scales of Infant Development   The best-known and most widely used test of infant "intelligence."

behavior genetics   The study of the genetic basis of behavior, such as intelligence or personality.

brain damage   Some injury to the brain, either during prenatal development or later, that results in improper functioning of the brain.

bulimia   A pattern of intense concern about weight, combined with binge eating followed by purging, either through self-induced vomiting, excessive use of laxatives, or excessive exercise.

canalization   Term used to describe the degree to which development may be shaped by underlying maturational forces (as opposed to environment) during some period in the life span.

cephalocaudal   From the head downward. Describes one recurrent pattern of physical development in infancy.

cesarean section   Delivery of the child through an incision in the mother's abdomen.

chorionic villus sampling   A technique for prenatal genetic diagnosis involving taking a sample of cells from the placenta. Can be performed earlier in the pregnancy than amniocentesis.

chromosomal anomalies   Variations in the number or configuration of the normal set of 23 pairs of chromosomes, almost always resulting in physical or mental abnormalities in the affected child. Down sydrome is an example of a chromosomal anomaly.

chromosome The structure in each cell in the body that contains genetic information. Each chromosome is made up of many genes.

classical conditioning One of three major types of learning. An automatic unconditioned response such as an emotion or a reflex comes to be triggered by a new cue, called the conditioned stimulus (CS), after the CS has been paired several times with the original unconditioned stimulus.

clique A group of six to eight friends with strong affiliation bonds and high levels of group solidarity and loyalty.

cohort A group of persons of approximately the same age who have shared similar major life experiences, such as cultural training, economic conditions, or type of education.

color constancy The ability to see the color of an object as remaining the same despite changes in illumination or shadow. One of the basic perceptual constancies that make up "object constancy."

competence The behavior of a person as it would be under ideal or perfect circumstances. It is not possible to measure competence directly.

componential intelligence One of three types of intelligence in Sternberg's triarchic theory of intelligence; that type of intelligence typically measured on IQ tests, including analytic thinking, remembering facts, and organizing information.

concrete operations The stage of development between ages 6 and 12 proposed by Piaget, in which mental operations such as subtraction, reversibility, and multiple classification are acquired.

conditioned stimulus In classical conditioning, the stimulus that, after being paired a number of times with an unconditioned stimulus, comes to trigger the unconditioned response.

conduct disorder Diagnostic term for a pattern of behavior involving high levels of aggressive, antisocial, or delinquent behavior.

conservation The concept that objects remain the same in fundamental ways, such as weight or number, even when there are external changes in shape or arrangement. Typically understood by children after age 5.

contextual intelligence One of three types of intelligence in Sternberg's triarchic theory of intelligence; often also called "street smarts," this type of intelligence includes skills in adapting to an environment, and in adapting an environment to one's own needs.

control group The group of subjects in an experiment that receives either no special treatment or some neutral treatment.

conventional morality The second level of moral judgment proposed by Kohlberg, in which the person's judgments are dominated by considerations of group values and laws.

cooing An early stage during the prelinguistic period, from about 1 to 4 months of age, when vowel sounds are repeated, particularly the *uuu* sound.

correlation A statistic used to describe the degree or strength of a relationship between two variables. It can range from +1.00 to -1.00. The closer it is to 1.00 the stronger the relationship being described.

cortex The convoluted gray portion of the brain which governs most complex thought, language, and memory, among other functions.

critical period A period of time during development when the organism is especially responsive to and learns from a specific type of stimulation. The same stimulation at other points in development has little or no effect.

cross-cultural research Research involving comparisons of several cultures or subcultures.

cross-modal transfer The ability to coordinate information from two senses, or to transfer information gained through one sense to another sense at a later time; for example, identifying visually something you had previously explored only tactually.

cross-sectional study A study in which different groups of individuals of different ages are all studied at the same time.

crowd A larger and looser group of friends than a clique, with perhaps 20 members; normally made up of several cliques joined together.

culture A system of meanings and customs, shared by some identifiable group or subgroup, and transmitted from one generation of that group to the next.

cumulative deficit Any difference between groups in IQ (or achievement test) scores that becomes larger over time.

deductive logic Reasoning from the general to the particular, from a rule to an expected instance, or from a theory to a hypothesis. Characteristic of formal operational thought.

dendrites The branchlike parts of a neuron which serve as the receptors in synaptic connections with the axons of other neurons.

deoxyribonucleic acid Called DNA for short, this is the chemical of which genes are composed.

dependent variable The variable in an experiment which is expected to show the impact of manipulations of the independent variable.

depression A combination of sad mood, sleep and eating disturbances, and difficulty concentrating. When all these symptoms are present it is usually called *clinical depression*.

developmental psychopathology A relatively new approach to the study of deviance that emphasizes that normal and abnormal development have common roots, and that pathology can arise from many different pathways or systems.

dilation The first stage of childbirth, when the cervix opens sufficiently to allow the infant's head to pass into the birth canal.

Down syndrome A genetic anomaly in which every cell contains three copies of chromosome 21 rather than two. Children born with this genetic pattern are usually mentally retarded and have characteristic physical features.

effacement The flattening of the cervix which, along with dilation, allows the delivery of the infant.

ego In Freudian theory, that portion of the personality that organizes, plans, and keeps the person in touch with reality. Language and thought are both ego functions.

egocentrism A cognitive state in which the individual (typically a child) sees the world only from his own perspective, without awareness that there are other perspectives.

embryo The name given to the organism during the period of prenatal development from about two to eight weeks after conception, beginning with implantation of the blastocyst into the uterine wall.

empathy As defined by Hoffman, it is "a vicarious affective response that does not necessarily match another's affective state but is more appropriate to the other's situation than to one's own" (Hoffman, 1984, p. 285).

empiricism   Opposite of *nativism*. The theoretical point of view that all perceptual skill arises from experience.

endocrine glands   These glands, including the adrenals, the thyroid, the pituitary, the testes, and the ovaries, secrete hormones governing overall physical growth and sexual maturing.

equilibration   The third part of the adaptation process, as proposed by Piaget, involving a periodic restructuring of schemes into new structures.

estrogen   The female sex hormone secreted by the ovaries.

ethnic group   "A subgroup whose members are perceived by themselves and others to have a common origin and culture, and shared activities in which the common origin or culture is an essential ingredient" (Porter & Washington, 1993, p. 140).

executive processes   Proposed subset of information processes involving organizing and planning strategies. Similar in meaning to metacognition.

experiential intelligence   One of three types of intelligence described by Sternberg in his triarchic theory of intelligence; includes creativity, insight, and seeing new relationships among experiences.

experiment   A research strategy in which subjects are assigned randomly to groups which are then provided with experiences that vary along some key dimension.

experimental group   The group (or groups) of subjects in an experiment that is given some special treatment intended to produce some specific consequence.

expressive language   The term used to describe the child's skill in speaking and communicating orally.

expressive style   One of two styles of early language proposed by Nelson, characterized by low rates of nounlike terms, and high use of personal-social words and phrases.

externalizing problems   Category of psychopathologies that includes any deviant behavior primarily directed away from the individual, such as conduct disorders or hyperactivity.

fallopian tube   The tube down which the ovum travels to the uterus and in which conception usually occurs.

family day care   Nonparental care in which the child is cared for in someone else's home, usually with a small group of other children.

fetal alcohol syndrome (FAS)   A pattern of physical and mental abnormalities, including mental retardation and minor physical anomalies, found often in children born to alcoholic mothers.

fetus   The name given to the developing organism from about eight weeks after conception until birth.

fontanels   The "soft spots" in the skull present at birth. These disappear when the several bones of the skull grow together.

foreclosure   One of four identity statuses proposed by Marcia, involving an ideological or occupational commitment without having gone through a reevaluation.

formal operations   Piaget's name for the fourth and final major stage of cognitive development, occurring during adolescence, when the child becomes able to manipulate and organize ideas as well as objects.

gametes   Sperm and ova. These cells, unlike all other cells of the body, contain only 23 chromosomes rather than 23 pairs.

gender concept   The understanding of one's own gender, including the permanence and constancy of gender.

gender constancy   The final step in developing a gender concept, in which the child understands that gender doesn't change even though there are external changes in things like clothing or hair length.

gender identity   The first step in gender concept development, in which the child labels herself correctly and categorizes others correctly as male or female.

gender schema   A fundamental schema created by children beginning at age 18 months or younger by which the child categorizes people, objects, activities, and qualities by gender.

gender stability   The second step in gender concept development, in which the child understands that a person's gender continues to be stable throughout the lifetime.

gene   A uniquely coded segment of DNA in a chromosome which affects one or more specific body processes or developments.

genotype   The pattern of characteristics and developmental sequences mapped in the genes of any specific individual. Will be modified by individual experience into the phenotype.

gifted   Normally defined in terms of very high IQ (above 140 or 150), but may also be defined in terms of remarkable skill in one or more specific areas, such as mathematics or memory.

glial cells   One of two major classes of cells making up the nervous system, glial cells provide the firmness and structure, the "glue" to hold the system together.

gonadotropic hormones   Hormones produced in the pituitary gland which stimulate the sex organs to develop.

habituation   An automatic decrease in the intensity of a response to a repeated stimulus, which enables the child or adult to ignore the familiar and focus attention on the novel.

hearing-impaired   The phrase currently used in place of "hard of hearing" to describe children or adults with significant hearing loss.

holophrases   The expression of a whole idea in a single word. Characteristic of the child's language from about 12 to 18 months.

hyperactivity   The common term for attention deficit hyperactivity disorder.

id   In Freudian theory, the first, primitive portion of the personality; the storehouse of basic energy, continually pushing for immediate gratification.

identification   The process of taking into oneself ("incorporating") the qualities and ideas of another person, which Freud thought was the result of the Oedipus conflict at ages 3 to 5. The child attempts to make himself or herself like the parent of the same sex.

identity achievement   One of four identity statuses proposed by Marcia, involving the successful resolution of an identity "crisis," resulting in a new commitment.

identity diffusion   One of four identity statuses proposed by Marcia, involving neither a current reevaluation nor a firm personal commitment.

inborn errors of metabolism   Inherited patterns of physical dysfunction in which the infant or child fails to metabolize one or more amino acids in the normal fashion. Phenylketonuria is the best-known such error.

independent variable A condition or event that an experimenter varies in some systematic way in order to observe the impact of that variation on the subjects' behavior.

inductive logic Reasoning from the particular to the general, from experience to broad rules. Characteristic of concrete operational thinking.

inflections The grammatical "markers" such as plurals, possessives, past tenses, and the equivalent.

information processing Phrase used to refer to a new, third approach to the study of intellectual development that focuses on changes with age, and individual differences, in fundamental intellectual skills.

insecure attachment Includes both ambivalent and avoidant patterns of attachment in children; the child does not use the parent as a safe base and is not readily consoled by the parent if upset.

intelligence quotient (IQ) Originally defined in terms of a child's mental age and chronological age, IQs are now computed by comparing a child's performance with that of other children of the same chronological age.

internalizing problems A category of psychopathologies in which the deviant behavior is directed inward, including anxiety and depression.

internal working model of social relationships. Cognitive construction, for which the earliest relationships may form the template, of the workings of relationships; for example, expectations of support or affection, trustworthiness, and so on.

intrinsic reinforcements Those inner sources of pleasure, pride, or satisfaction that serve to increase the likelihood that an individual will repeat the behavior that led to the feeling.

learning disability (LD) Term broadly used to describe any child with an unexpected or unexplained problem in learning to read, spell, or calculate. More precisely used to refer to a subgroup of such children who have some neurological dysfunction.

libido The term used by Freud to describe the pool of sexual energy in each individual.

longitudinal study A research design in which the same subjects are observed or assessed repeatedly over a period of months or years.

low birth weight (LBW) The phrase now used (in place of the word *premature*) to describe infants whose weight is below the optimum range at birth. Includes infants born too early (preterm or short-gestation infants) and those who are "small for date."

maturation The sequential unfolding of physical characteristics, governed by instructions contained in the genetic code and shared by all members of the species.

mean length of utterance Usually abbreviated MLU; the average number of meaningful units in a sentence. Each basic word is one meaningful unit, as is each inflection, such as the *s* for plural or the *ed* for a past tense.

medulla A portion of the brain that lies immediately above the spinal cord; largely developed at birth.

menarche Onset of menstruation in girls.

mentally retarded Those children who show a pattern of low IQ, poor adaptive behavior, and poor information processing skill.

metacognition General and rather loosely used term describing an individual's knowledge of his own thinking processes. Knowing what you know, and how you go about learning or remembering.

metamemory A subcategory of metacognition; knowledge about your own memory processes.

midbrain A section of the brain lying above the medulla and below the cortex that regulates attention, sleeping, waking, and other "automatic" functions. Largely developed at birth.

modeling A term used by Bandura and others to describe observational learning.

moratorium One of four identity statuses proposed by Marcia, involving an ongoing reexamination but without a new commitment as yet.

motherese The word linguists often use to describe the particular pattern of speech by adults to young children. The sentences are shorter, simpler, repetitive, and higher-pitched.

motor development Growth and change in ability to do physical activities, such as walking, running, or riding a bike.

myelin Material making up a sheath that develops around most axons. This sheath is not completely developed at birth.

myelinization The process by which myelin is added.

nativism Opposite of *empiricism* . The view that perceptual skills are inborn and do not require experience to develop.

negative reinforcement The strengthening of a behavior that occurs because of the removal or cessation of an unpleasant stimulus.

neuron The second major class of cells in the nervous system, neurons are responsible for transmission and reception of nerve impulses.

object constancy The general phrase describing the ability to see objects as remaining the same despite changes in retinal image.

objective self Second step in the development of the self-concept; awareness of the self as an object with properties.

object permanence Part of the object concept. The recognition that an object continues to exist even when it is temporarily out of sight.

observational learning Learning of motor skills, attitudes, or other behaviors through observing someone else perform them.

Oedipus conflict The pattern of events Freud believed occurred between ages 3 and 5 when the child experiences a "sexual" desire for the parent of the opposite sex; the resulting fear of possible reprisal from the parent of the same sex is resolved when the child "identifies" with the parent of the same sex.

operant conditioning One of the three major types of learning in which the probability of a person performing some behavior is affected by positive or negative reinforcements.

operation Term used by Piaget for complex, internal, abstract, reversible schemes, first seen at about age 6.

overregularization The tendency on the part of children to make the language regular, such as using past tenses like "beated" or "goed."

ovum The gamete produced by a woman, which, if fertilized by a sperm from the male, forms the basis for the developing organism.

partial reinforcement Reinforcement of behavior on some schedule less frequent than every occasion.

perceptual constancies A collection of constancies, including shape, size, and color.

performance   The behavior shown by a person under actual circumstances. Even when we are interested in competence, all we can ever measure is performance.

performance tests   A new category of criterion-referenced tests used in some school systems today, in which students are required to demonstrate some actual skills, such as writing, performing experiments, or mathematical reasoning.

permissive parental style   One of the three styles described by Baumrind, characterized by high levels of nurturance and low levels of control, maturity demands, and communication.

personality   The collection of individual, relatively enduring patterns of reacting to and interacting with others that distinguishes each child or adult.

phenotype   The expression of a particular set of genetic information in a specific environment; the observable result of the joint operation of genetic and environmental influences.

placenta   An organ that develops during gestation between the fetus and the wall of the uterus. The placenta filters nutrients from the mother's blood, acting as liver, lungs, and kidneys for the fetus.

positive reinforcement   Strengthening of a behavior by the presentation of some pleasurable or positive stimulus.

postpartum depression   A severe form of the common experience of postpartum blues. Affecting perhaps 10 percent of women, this form of clinical depression typically lasts six to eight weeks.

pragmatics   The rules for the use of language in communicative interaction, such as the rules for taking turns, the style of speech appropriate for varying listeners, and the equivalent.

preconventional morality   The first level of morality proposed by Kohlberg, in which moral judgments are dominated by consideration of what will be punished and what feels good.

prelinguistic phase   The period before the child speaks his first words.

preoperational stage   Piaget's term for the second major stage of cognitive development, from age 2 to age 6, marked at the beginning by the ability to use symbols, and by the development of basic classification and logical abilities.

preterm infant   Descriptive phrase now widely used to label infants born before 37 weeks of gestational age.

principled morality   The third level of morality proposed by Kohlberg, in which considerations of justice, individual rights, and contracts dominate moral judgment.

prosocial behavior   See *altruism*.

proximodistal   From the center outward. With *cephalocaudal*, describes the pattern of many physical changes in infancy.

psychosexual stages   The stages of personality development suggested by Freud, including the oral, anal, phallic, latency, and genital stages.

psychosocial stages   The stages of personality development suggested by Erikson, including trust, autonomy, initiative, industry, identity, intimacy, generativity, and ego integrity.

puberty   The collection of hormonal and physical changes at adolescence that brings about sexual maturity.

punishment   Unpleasant consequences, administered after some undesired behavior by a child or adult, with the intent of extinguishing the behavior.

receptive language   Term used to describe the child's ability to understand (receive) language, as contrasted to his ability to express language.

referential style   Second style of early language proposed by Nelson, characterized by emphasis on objects and their naming and description.

reflexes   Automatic body reactions to specific stimulation, such as the knee jerk or the Moro reflex. Many reflexes remain among adults, but the newborn also has some "primitive" reflexes that disappear as the cortex is fully developed.

responsiveness   An aspect of parent-child interaction. A responsive parent is sensitive to the child's cues and reacts appropriately, following the child's lead.

restrictiveness   Term used to describe a particular pattern of parental control, involving limitation of the child's movements or options, such as the use of playpens or harnesses in a young child, or strict rules about play areas or free choices in an older child.

rubella   A form of measles that, if contracted during the first three months of a pregnancy, may have severe effects on the developing baby.

scheme   Piaget's word for the basic actions of knowing, including both physical actions (sensorimotor schemes, such as looking or reaching) and mental actions, such as classifying or comparing or reversing. An experience is assimilated to a scheme, and the scheme is modified or created through accommodation.

secular trends   Patterns of change over several cohorts in such things as the timing of menarche or height or weight.

secure attachment   Demonstrated by the child's ability to use the parent as a safe base and to be consoled after separation, when fearful, or when otherwise stressed.

self-concept   The broad idea of "who I am," including the existential self and the categorical self.

self-esteem   A global judgment of self-worth; how well you like who you perceive yourself to be.

semantics   The rules for conveying meaning in language.

sensitive period   Similar to a critical period except broader and less specific. A time in development when a particular type of stimulation is particularly important or effective.

sensorimotor stage   Piaget's term for the first major stage of cognitive development, from birth to about 18 months, when the child moves from reflexive to voluntary action.

sequential designs   A family of research designs which involves multiple cross-sectional or multiple longitudinal studies, or a combination of the two.

sex chromosomes   The X and Y chromosomes, which determine the sex of the child. In humans, XX is the female pattern, XY the male pattern.

sex-role behavior   The performance of behavior that matches the culturally defined sex role, such as choosing "sex-appropriate" toys, or playing with same-sex children.

sex-role concept   The understanding of what males and females do and are "supposed to do."

sex roles   The set of behaviors, attitudes, rights, duties, and obligations that are part of the "role" of being a boy or a girl, a male or a female in any given culture.

sex role stereotypes   The overextension, or too-rigid definition, of sex roles or sex-role behavior.

sex-typing   See *sex-role behavior*.

shape constancy   The ability to see an object's shape as remaining the same despite changes in the shape of the retinal image. A basic perceptual constancy.

size constancy   The ability to see an object's size as remaining the same despite changes in the size of the retinal image. A key element in this constancy is the ability to judge depth.

small-for-date infant   An infant who weighs less than is normal for the number of weeks of gestation completed.

social class   Widely used term to describe broad variations in economic and social positions within any given society. Four broad groups are most often described: upper class, middle class, working class, and lower class (also called poverty level). For an individual family, the designation is based on the occupations and education of the adults in the household.

social cognition   Term used to describe an area of research and theory focused on the child's *understanding* of social relationships.

Stanford-Binet   The best-known American intelligence test. It was written by Louis Terman and his associates on the basis of the first tests by Binet and Simon.

states of consciousness   Five main sleep/wake states that have been identified in infants, from deep sleep to active awake.

Strange Situation   A series of episodes used by Mary Ainsworth and others in studies of attachment. The child is observed with the mother, with a stranger, left alone, and when reunited with stranger and mother.

subjective self   The first step in the development of the self-concept; the initial awareness that "I exist" separate from others.

sudden infant death syndrome (SIDS)   Unexpected death of an infant who otherwise appears healthy. Also called crib death. Cause is unknown.

superego   In Freudian theory, the "conscience" part of personality, which develops as a result of the identification process. The superego contains the parental and societal values and attitudes incorporated by the child.

synapse   The point of communication between the axon of one neuron and the dendrites of another, where nerve impulses are passed from one neuron to another, or from a neuron to some other type of cell, such as a muscle cell.

syntax   The rules for forming sentences; also called grammar.

telegraphic speech   A characteristic of early child sentences in which everything but the crucial words is omitted, as if for a telegram.

teratogen   Any outside agent, such as a disease or a chemical, whose presence significantly increases the risk of deviations or abnormalities in prenatal development.

theory of mind   The theory a child or adult has about the way his own and other people's minds work, and how others are affected by their beliefs and feelings. By 4 or 5, children have a well-developed theory of mind.

tracking   Also called smooth pursuit. The smooth movements of the eye used to follow the track of some moving object.

triarchic theory of intelligence   A theory advanced by Sternberg, proposing the existence of three types of intelligence: the componential, the contextual, and the experiential.

ultrasound   A form of prenatal diagnosis in which high-frequency sound waves are used to provide a picture of the moving fetus. Can be used to detect multiple pregnancies, gestational age, and many physical deformities, such as neural tube defects.

unconditioned response   In classical conditioning this is the basic unlearned response that is triggered by the unconditioned stimulus.

unconditioned stimulus   In classical conditioning this is the cue or signal that automatically triggers (without learning) the unconditioned response.

uterus   The female organ in which the blastocyst implants itself and within which the embryo/fetus develops. (Popularly referred to as the womb.)

very low-birth-weight infants   Phrase now commonly used to describe infants who weigh 1500 grams ($3^1/2$ lbs) or less at birth.

warmth versus hostility   The key dimension of emotional tone used to describe family interactions.

WISC   The Wechsler Intelligence Scale for Children, the most current revision of which is called the WISC-III. Another well-known American IQ test which includes both verbal and performance (less verbal) subtests.

REFERENCES

Abrams, B., Newman, V., Key, T., & Parker, J. (1989). Maternal weight gain and preterm delivery. *Obstetrics and Gynecology, 74,* 577–584.

Achenbach, T. M. (1982). *Developmental psychopathology* (2nd ed.). New York: Wiley.

Achenbach, T. M. (1993). Taxonomy and comorbidity of conduct problems: Evidence from empirically based approaches. *Development and Psychopathology, 5,* 51–64.

Achenbach, T. M., & Edelbrock, C. S. (1981). Behavioral problems and competencies reported by parents of normal and disturbed children aged 4 through 16. *Monographs of the Society for Research in Child Development, 46*(1, Whole No. 188).

Adams, M. J. (1990). *Beginning to read: Thinking and learning about print.* Cambridge, MA: MIT Press.

Adler, A. (1948). *Studies in analytical psychology.* New York: Norton.

Ainsworth, M. D. S. (1972). Attachment and dependency: A comparison. In J. L. Gewirtz (Ed.), *Attachment and dependency* (pp. 97–138). Washington, DC: V. H. Winston.

Ainsworth, M. D. S. (1982). Attachment: Retrospect and prospect. In C. M. Parkes & J. Stevenson-Hinde (Eds.), *The place of attachment in human behavior* (pp. 3–30). New York: Basic Books.

Ainsworth, M. D. S. (1989). Attachments beyond infancy. *American Psychologist, 44,* 709–716.

Ainsworth, M. D. S., Blehar, M., Waters, E., & Wall, S. (1978). *Patterns of attachment.* Hillsdale, NJ: Erlbaum.

Ainsworth, M. D. S., & Wittig, B. A. (1969). Attachment and exploratory behavior of one-year-olds in a strange situation. In B. M. Foss (Ed.), *Determinants of infant behavior* (Vol. 4, pp. 113–136). London: Methuen.

Aksu-Koc, A. A., & Slobin, D. I. (1985). The acquisition of Turkish. In D. I. Slobin (Ed.), *The crosslinguistic study of language acquisition: Vol. 1. The data* (pp. 839–878). Hillsdale, NJ: Erlbaum.

Al Awad, A. M. E. L., & Sonuga-Barke, E. J. S. (1992). Childhood problems in a Sudanese city: A comparison of extended and nuclear families. *Child Development, 63,* 906–914.

Alsaker, F. D., & Olweus, D. (1992). Stability of global self-evaluations in early adolescence: A cohort longitudinal study. *Journal of Research on Adolescence, 2,* 123–145.

Amato, P. R. (1993). Children's adjustment to divorce: Theories, hypotheses, and empirical support. *Journal of Marriage and the Family, 55,* 23–38.

American Psychological Association. (1993). *Violence and youth: Psychology's response: Vol. 1. Summary report of the American Psychological Association Commission on violence and youth.* Washington, DC: American Psychological Association.

Anderson, D. R., Lorch, E. P., Field, D. E., Collins, P. A., & Nathan, J. G. (1986). Television viewing at home: Age trends in visual attention and time with TV. *Child Development, 57,* 1024–1033.

Andersson, B. (1989). Effects of public day-care: A longitudinal study. *Child Development, 60,* 857–886.

Andersson, B. (1992). Effects of day-care on cognitive and socioemotional competence of thirteen-year-old Swedish school children. *Child Development, 63,* 20–36.

Anisfeld, M. (1991). Neonatal imitation. *Developmental Review, 11,* 60–97.

Anthony, E. J. (1970). The behavior disorders of childhood. In P. H. Mussen (Ed.), *Carmichael's manual of child psychology* (Vol. 2, 3rd ed.) (pp. 667–764). New York: Wiley.

Apgar, V. A. (1953). A proposal for a new method of evaluation of the newborn infant. *Current Research in Anesthesia and Analgesia, 32,* 260–267.

Aslin, R. N. (1981a). Experiential influences and sensitive periods in perceptual development: A unified model. In R. N. Aslin, J. R. Alberts, & M. R. Petersen (Eds.), *Development of perception: Psychobiological perspectives: Vol. 2. The visual system* (pp. 45–93). New York: Academic Press.

Aslin, R. N. (1981b). Development of smooth pursuit in human infants. In D. F. Fisher, R. A. Monty, & J. W. Senders (Eds.), *Eye movements: Cognition and visual perception* (pp. 31–51). Hillsdale, NJ: Erlbaum.

Aslin, R. N. (1987a). Motor aspects of visual development in infancy. In P. Salapatek & L. Cohen (Eds.), *Handbook of in* fant perception, Vol. 1. From sensation to perception (pp. 43–113). Orlando, FL: Academic Press.

Aslin, R. N. (1987b). Visual and auditory development in infancy. In J. D. Osofsky (Ed.), *Handbook of infant development* (2nd ed.) (pp. 5–97). New York: Wiley-Interscience.

Aslin, R. N., & Smith, L. B. (1988). Perceptual development. *Annual Review of Psychology, 39,* 435–473.

Astbury, J., Orgill, A. A., Bajuk, B., & Yu, V. Y. H. (1990). Neurodevelopmental outcome, growth and health of extremely low-birthweight survivors: How soon can we tell? *Developmental Medicine and Child Neurology, 32,* 582–589.

Astington, J. W., & Gopnik, A. (1991). Theoretical explanations of children's understanding of the mind. In G. E. Butterworth, P. L. Harris, A. M. Leslie, & H. M. Wellman (Eds.), *Perspectives on the child's theory of mind* (pp. 7–31). New York: Oxford University Press.

Astone, N. M. (1993). Are adolescent mothers just single mothers? *Journal of Research on Adolescence, 3,* 353–371.

Attie, I., & Brooks-Gunn, J. (1989). Development of eating problems in adolescent girls: A longitudinal study. *Developmental Psychology, 25,* 70–79.

Attie, I., Brooks-Gunn, J., & Petersen, A. (1990). A developmental perspective on eating disorders and eating problems. In M. Lewis & S. M. Miller (Eds.), *Handbook of developmental psychopathology* (pp. 409–420). New York: Plenum Press.

Avis, J., & Harris, P. L. (1991). Belief-desire reasoning among Baka children: Evidence for a universal conception of mind. *Child Development, 62,* 460–467.

Bachman, J. G., & Schulenberg, J. (1993). How part-time work intensity relates to drug use, problem behavior, time use, and satisfaction among high school seniors: Are these consequences or merely correlates? *Developmental Psychology, 29,* 220–235.

Bailey, J. M., & Pillard, R. C. (1991). A genetic study of male sexual orientation. *Archives of General Psychiatry, 48,* 1089–1096.

Baird, P. A., Sadovnick, A. D., & Yee, I. M. L. (1991). Maternal age and birth defects: A population study. *The Lancet, 337,* 527–530.

Baldwin, D. A. (1993). Early referential understanding: Infants' ability to recognize referential acts for what they are. *Developmental Psychology, 29,* 832–843.

Bamford, F. N., Bannister, R. P., Benjamin, C. M., Hillier, V. F., Ward, B. S., & Moore, W. M. O. (1990). Sleep in the first year of life. *Developmental Medicine and Child Neurology, 32,* 718–724.

Bandura, A. (1973). *Aggression: A social learning analysis.* Englewood Cliffs, NJ: Prentice-Hall.

Bandura, A. (1977). *Social learning theory.* Englewood Cliffs, NJ: Prentice-Hall.

Bandura, A. (1982). The self and mechanisms of agency. In J. Suls (Ed.), *Psychological perspectives on the self* (pp. 3–40). Hillsdale, NJ: Erlbaum.

Bandura, A. (1986). *Social foundations of thought and action: A social cognitive theory.* Englewood Cliffs, NJ: Prentice-Hall.

Bandura, A. (1989). Social cognitive theory. *Annals of Child Development, 6,* 1–60.

Barenboim, C. (1977). Developmental changes in the interpersonal cognitive system from middle childhood to adolescence. *Child Development, 48,* 1467–1474.

Barenboim, C. (1981). The development of person perception in childhood and adolescence: From behavioral comparisons to psychological constructs to psychological comparisons. *Child Development, 52,* 129–144.

Barkley, R. A. (1990). Attention deficit disorders: History, definition, and diagnosis. In M. Lewis & S. M. Miller (Eds.), *Handbook of developmental psychopathology* (pp. 65–76). New York: Plenum Press.

Barkley, R. A., Fischer, M., Edelbrock, C. S., & Smallish, L. (1990). The adolescent outcome of hyperactive children diagnosed by research criteria: I. An 8-year prospective follow-up study. *Journal of the American Academy of Child and Adolescent Psychiatry, 29,* 546–557.

Barnard, K. E., & Bee, H. L. (1983). The impact of temporally patterned stimulation on the development of preterm infants. *Child Development, 54,* 1156–1167.

Barnard, K. E., Bee, H. L., & Hammond, M. A. (1984). Developmental changes in maternal interactions with term and preterm infants. *Infant Behavior and Development, 7,* 101–113.

Barnard, K. E., & Eyres, S. J. (1979). *Child health assessment: Part 2. The first year of life* (DHEW Publication No. HRA 79-25). Washington, DC: U.S. Government Printing Office.

Barnard, K. E., Hammond, M. A., Booth, C. L., Bee, H. L., Mitchell, S. K., & Spieker, S. J. (1989). Measurement and meaning of parent-child interaction. In J. J. Morrison, C. Lord, & D. P. Keating (Eds.), *Applied developmental psychology* (Vol. 3, pp. 40–81). San Diego: Academic Press.

Barnes, H. L., & Olson, D. H. (1985). Parent-adolescent communication and the circumplex model. *Child Development, 56,* 438–447.

Barr, H. M., Streissguth, A. P., Darby, B. L., & Sampson, P. D. (1990). Prenatal exposure to alcohol, caffeine, tobacco, and aspirin: Effects on fine and gross motor performance in 4-year-old children. *Developmental Psychology, 26,* 339–348.

Barrett, G. V., & Depinet, R. L. (1991). A reconsideration of testing for competence rather than for intelligence. *American Psychologist, 46,* 1012–1024.

Bartsch, K. (1993). Adolescents' theoretical thinking. In R. M. Lerner (Ed.), *Early adolescence: Perspectives on research, pol-*

icy, and intervention (pp. 143–157). Hillsdale, NJ: Erlbaum.

Bates, E. (1993). Commentary: Comprehension and production in early language development. *Monographs of the Society for Research in Child Development, 58*(3–4, Serial No. 233), 222–242.

Bates, E., Bretherton, I., Beeghly-Smith, M., & McNew, S. (1982). Social bases of language development: A reassessment. In H. W. Reese & L. P. Lipsitt (Eds.), *Advances in child development and behavior* (Vol. 16, pp. 8–68). New York: Academic Press.

Bates, E., Bretherton, I., & Snyder, L. (1988). *From first words to grammar: Individual differences and dissociable mechanisms.* Cambridge: Cambridge University Press.

Bates, E., Camaioni, L., & Volterra, V. (1975). The acquisition of performatives prior to speech. *Merrill-Palmer Quarterly, 21,* 205–226.

Bates, E., O'Connell, B., & Shore, C. (1987). Language and communication in infancy. In J. D. Osofsky (Ed.), *Handbook of infant development* (2nd ed.) (p. 149–203). New York: Wiley-Interscience.

Bates, J. E. (1987). Temperament in infancy. In J. D. Osofsky (Ed.), *Handbook of infant development* (2nd ed.) (pp. 1101–1149). New York: Wiley-Interscience.

Bates, J. E. (1989). Applications of temperament concepts. In G. A. Kohnstamm, J. E. Bates, & M. K. Rothbart (Eds.), *Temperament in childhood* (pp. 321–356). Chichester, England: Wiley.

Bates, J. E., Maslin, C. A., & Frankel, K. A. (1985). Attachment security, mother-child interaction, and temperament as predictors of behavior problem ratings at age three years. In I. Bretherton & E. Waters (Eds.), Growing points of attachment theory and research. *Monographs of the Society for Research in Child Development, 50*(1–2, Serial No. 209), 167–193.

Baumrind, D. (1971). Current patterns of parental authority. *Developmental Psychology Monograph, 4*(1, Part 2).

Baumrind, D. (1972). Socialization and instrumental competence in young children. In W. W. Hartup (Ed.), *The young child: Reviews of research* (Vol. 2, pp. 202–224). Washington, DC: National Association for the Education of Young Children.

Baumrind, D. (1973). The development of instrumental competence through socialization. In A. D. Pick (Ed.), *Minnesota symposium on child psychology* (Vol. 7, pp. 3–46). Minneapolis: University of Minnesota Press.

Baydar, N., & Brooks-Gunn, J. (1991). Effects of maternal employment and child-care arrangements on preschoolers' cognitive and behavioral outcomes: Evidence from the children of the National Longitudinal Survey of Youth. *Developmental Psychology, 27,* 932–945.

Baydar, N., Brooks-Gunn, J., & Furstenberg, F. F. (1993). Early warning signs of functional illiteracy: Predictors in childhood and adolescence. *Child Development, 64,* 815–829.

Bayley, N. (1969). *Bayley scales of infant development.* New York: Psychological Corporation.

Bearison, D. J., Magzamen, S., & Filardo, E. K. (1986). Sociocognitive conflict and cognitive growth in young children. *Merrill-Palmer Quarterly, 32,* 51–72.

Becker, J. A. (1982). Children's strategic use of requests to mark and manipulate social status. In S. A. Kuczaj II (Ed.), *Language development: Vol. 2. Language, thought, and culture* (pp. 1–36). Hillsdale, NJ: Erlbaum.

Bedard, J., & Chi, M. T. H. (1992). Expertise. *Current Directions in Psychological Science, 1,* 135–139.

Bell, L. G., & Bell, D. C. (1982). Family climate and the role of the female adolescent: Determinants of adolescent functioning. *Family Relations, 31,* 519–527.

Bellinger, D., Sloman, J., Leviton, A., Rabinowitz, M., Needleman, H. L., & Waternaux, C. (1991). Low-level lead exposure and children's cognitive function in the preschool years. *Pediatrics, 87,* 219–227.

Bellinger, D. C., Stiles, K. M., & Needleman, H. L. (1992). Low-level lead exposure, intelligence and academic achievement: A long-term follow-up study. *Pediatrics, 90,* 855–861.

Belsky, J. (1985). Prepared statement on the effects of day care. In Select Committee on Children, Youth, and Families, House of Representatives, 98th Congress, Second Session, *Improving child care services: What can be done?* Washington, DC: U.S. Government Printing Office.

Belsky, J. (1987). *Science, social policy and day care: A personal odyssey.* Paper presented at the biennial meetings of the Society for Research in Child Development, Baltimore, April.

Belsky, J. (1990). The "effects" of infant day care reconsidered. In N. Fox & G. G. Fein (Eds.), *Infant day care: The current debate* (pp. 3–40). Norwood, NJ: Ablex.

Belsky, J. (1992). Consequences of child care for children's development: A deconstructionist view. In A. Booth (Ed.), *Child care in the 1990s: Trends and consequences* (pp. 83–94). Hillsdale, NJ: Erlbaum.

Belsky, J., & Eggebeen, D. (1991). Early and extensive maternal employment and young children's socioemotional development: Children of the National Longitudinal Survey of Youth. *Journal of Marriage and the Family, 53,* 1083–1110.

Belsky, J., Lang, M. E., & Rovine, M. (1985). Stability and change in marriage across the transition to parenthood: A second study. *Journal of Marriage and the Family, 47,* 855–865.

Belsky, J., & Rovine, M. (1988). Nonmaternal care in the first year of life and the security of infant-parent attachment. *Child Development, 59,* 157–167.

Bem, S. L. (1974). The measurement of psychological androgyny. *Journal of Consulting and Clinical Psychology, 42*, 155–162.

Benbow, C. P. (1988). Sex differences in mathematical reasoning ability in intellectually talented preadolescents: Their nature, effects, and possible causes. *Behavioral and Brain Sciences, 11*, 169–232.

Berberian, K. E., & Snyder, S. S. (1982). The relationship of temperament and stranger reaction for younger and older infants. *Merrill-Palmer Quarterly, 28*, 79–94.

Berch, D. B., & Bender, B. G. (1987). Margins of sexuality. *Psychology Today, 21*(12), 54–57.

Berg, J. M. (1974). Aetiological aspects of mental subnormality. In A. M. Clarke & A. D. B. Clarke (Eds.), *Mental deficiency: The changing outlook* (3rd ed.) (pp. 82–117). New York: Free Press.

Berkowitz, G. S., Skovron, M. L., Lapinski, R. H., & Berkowitz, R. L. (1990). Delayed childbearing and the outcome of pregnancy. *New England Journal of Medicine, 322*, 659–664.

Berndt, T. J. (1979). Developmental changes in conformity to peers and parents. *Developmental Psychology, 15*, 608–616.

Berndt, T. J. (1983). Social cognition, social behavior, and children's friendships. In E. T. Higgins, D. N. Ruble, & W. W. Hartup (Eds.), *Social cognition and social development: A sociocultural perspective* (pp. 158–192). Cambridge: Cambridge University Press.

Berndt, T. J. (1986). Children's comments about their friendships. In M. Perlmutter (Ed.), Cognitive perspectives on children's social and behavioral development. *Minnesota symposia on child psychology* (Vol. 18, pp. 189–212). Hillsdale, NJ: Erlbaum.

Berndt, T. J. (1992). Friendship and friends' influence in adolescence. *Current Directions in Psychological Science, 1*, 156–159.

Bertenthal, B. I., & Campos, J. J. (1987). New directions in the study of early experience. *Child Development, 58*, 560–567.

Betancourt, H., & Lopez, S. R. (1993). The study of culture, ethnicity, and race in American psychology. *American Psychologist, 48*, 629–637.

Bettes, B. A. (1988). Maternal depression and motherese: Temporal and intonational features. *Child Development, 59*, 1089–1096.

Biederman, J., Faraone, S., Keenan, K., Knee, D., & Tsuang, M. (1990). Family-genetic and psychosocial risk factors in DSM-III attention deficit disorder. *Journal of the American Academy of Child and Adolescent Psychiatry, 29*, 526–533.

Bigelow, B. J., & La Gaipa, J. J. (1975). Children's written descriptions of friendships: A multidimensional analysis. *Developmental Psychology, 11*, 857–858.

Billings, A. G., & Moos, R. H. (1985). Children of parents with unipolar depression: A controlled 1-year follow-up. *Journal of Abnormal Child Psychology, 14*, 149–166.

Bivens, J. A., & Berk, L. E. (1990). A longitudinal study of the development of elementary school children's private speech. *Merrill-Palmer Quarterly, 36*, 443–463.

Bjorklund, D. F., & Muir, J. E. (1988). Remembering on their own: Children's development of free recall memory. In R. Vasta (Ed.), *Annals of child development* (Vol. 5, pp. 79–124). Greenwich, CT: JAI Press.

Black, B. (1992). Negotiating social pretend play: Communication differences related to social status and sex. *Merrill-Palmer Quarterly, 38*, 212–232.

Blackman, J. A. (1990). Update on AIDS, CMV, and herpes in young children: Health, developmental, and educational issues. In M. Wolraich & D. K. Routh (Eds.), *Advances in developmental and behavioral pediatrics* (Vol. 9, pp. 33–58). London: Jessica Kingsley Publishers.

Block, J. (1971). *Lives through time.* Berkeley, CA: Bancroft.

Block, J. (1987). *Longitudinal antecedents of ego-control and ego-resiliency in late adolescence.* Paper presented at the biennial meetings of the Society for Research in Child Development, Baltimore, April.

Block, J., & Robins, R. W. (1993). A longitudinal study of consistency and change in self-esteem from early adolescence to early adulthood. *Child Development, 64*, 909–923.

Bloom, L. (1973). *One word at a time.* The Hague: Mouton.

Blum, R. W., Harmon, B., Harris, L., Bergeisen, L., & Resnick, M. D. (1992). American Indian–Alaska Native youth health. *Journal of the American Medical Association, 267*, 1637–1644.

Boer, F., & Dunn, J. (Eds.). (1992). *Children's sibling relationships: Developmental and clinical issues.* Hillsdale, NJ: Erlbaum.

Boer, F., Godhart, A. W., & Treffers, P. D. A. (1992). Siblings and their parents. In F. Boer & J. Dunn (Eds.), *Children's sibling relationships: Developmental and clinical issues* (pp. 41–54). Hillsdale, NJ: Erlbaum.

Booth, A. (Ed.). (1992). *Child care in the 1990s: Trends and consequences.* Hillsdale, NJ: Erlbaum.

Bornstein, M. H. (1987). Sensitive periods in development: Definition, existence, utility, and meaning. In M. H. Bornstein (Ed.), *Sensitive periods in development: Interdisciplinary perspectives* (pp. 3–18). Hillsdale, NJ: Erlbaum.

Bornstein, M. H. (1988). Perceptual development across the life cycle. In M. H. Bornstein & M. E. Lamb (Eds.), *Developmental psychology: An advanced textbook* (2nd ed.). Hillsdale, NJ: Erlbaum.

Bornstein, M. H. (1989). Maternal responsiveness: Characteristics and consequences. *New Directions for Child Development, 43*.

Bornstein, M. H. (1991). *Cultural approaches to parenting.* Hillsdale, NJ: Erlbaum.

Bornstein, M. H. (1992). Perception across the life span. In M. H. Bornstein & M. E. Lamb (Eds.), *Developmental psy-*

chology: An advanced textbook (3rd ed.) (pp. 155–210). Hillsdale, NJ: Erlbaum.

Bornstein, M. H., Tal, J., & Tamis-LeMonda, C. S. (1991). Parenting in cross-cultural perspective: The United States, France, and Japan. In M. H. Bornstein (Ed.), *Cultural approaches to parenting* (pp. 69–90). Hillsdale, NJ: Erlbaum.

Bornstein, M. H., Tamis-LeMonda, C. S., Tal, J., Ludemann, P., Toda, S., Rahn, C. W., Pecheux, M., Azuma, H., & Vardi, D. (1992). Maternal responsiveness to infants in three societies: The United States, France, and Japan. *Child Development, 63,* 808–821.

The Boston Women's Health Collective. (1992). *The new our bodies, ourselves: A book by and for women.* New York: Simon & Schuster.

Bouchard, T. J., Jr. (1984). Twins reared apart and together: What they tell us about human diversity. In S. Fox (Ed.), *The chemical and biological bases of individuality.* New York: Plenum Press.

Bouchard, T. J. J., & McGue, M. (1981). Familial studies of intelligence: A review. *Science, 212,* 1055–1059.

Boukydis, C. F. Z., & Burgess, R. L. (1982). Adult physiological response to infant cries: Effects of temperament, parental status, and gender. *Child Development, 53,* 1291–1298.

Bower, T. G. R. (1966). The visual world of infants. *Scientific American, 215,* 80–92.

Bower, T. G. R. (1989). *The rational infant.* New York: Freeman.

Bowerman, M. (1985). Beyond communicative adequacy: From piecemeal knowledge to an integrated system in the child's acquisition of language. In K. E. Nelson (Ed.), *Children's language* (Vol. 5, pp. 369–398). Hillsdale, NJ: Erlbaum.

Bowlby, J. (1969). *Attachment and loss: Vol. 1. Attachment.* New York: Basic Books.

Bowlby, J. (1973). *Attachment and loss: Vol. 2. Separation, anxiety, and anger.* New York: Basic Books.

Bowlby, J. (1980). *Attachment and loss: Vol. 3. Loss, sadness, and depression.* New York: Basic Books.

Bowlby, J. (1988a). Developmental psychiatry comes of age. *The American Journal of Psychiatry, 145,* 1–10.

Bowlby, J. (1988b). *A secure base.* New York: Basic Books.

Boyes, M. C., & Allen, S. G. (1993). Styles of parent-child interactions and moral reasoning in adolescence. *Merrill-Palmer Quarterly, 39,* 551–570.

Brackbill, Y., McManus, K., & Woodward, L. (1985). *Medication in maternity.* Ann Arbor: University of Michigan Press.

Brackbill, Y., & Nevill, D. D. (1981). Parental expectations of achievement as affected by children's height. *Merrill-Palmer Quarterly, 27,* 429–441.

Bradbard, M. R., Martin, C. L., Endsley, R. C., & Halverson, C. F. (1986). Influence of sex stereotypes on children's exploration and memory: A competence versus performance distinction. *Developmental Psychology, 22,* 481–486.

Bradley, R. H., & Caldwell, B. M. (1984). 174 children: A study of the relationship between home environment and cognitive development during the first 5 years. In A. W. Gottfried (Ed.), *Home environment and early cognitive development: Longitudinal research* (pp. 5–56). New York: Academic Press.

Bradley, R. H., Caldwell, B. M., Rock, S. L., Barnard, K. E., Gray, C., Hammond, M. A., Mitchell, S., Siegel, L., Ramey, C. D., Gottfried, A. W., & Johnson, D. L. (1989). Home environment and cognitive development in the first 3 years of life: A collaborative study involving six sites and three ethnic groups in North America. *Developmental Psychology, 25,* 217–235.

Brand, E., Clingempeel, W. E., & Bowen-Woodward, K. (1988). Family relationships and children's psychological adjustment in stepmother and stepfather families: Findings and conclusions from the Philadelphia Stepfamily Research Project. In E. M. Hetherington & J. D. Arasteh (Eds.), *Impact of divorce, single parenting, stepparenting on children* (pp. 299–324). Hillsdale, NJ: Erlbaum.

Brandenburg, N. A., Friedman, R. M., & Silver, S. E. (1990). The epidemiology of childhood psychiatric disorders: Prevalence findings from recent studies. *Journal of the American Academy of Child and Adolescent Psychiatry, 29,* 76–83.

Breitmayer, B. J., & Ramey, C. T. (1986). Biological nonoptimality and quality of postnatal environment as codeterminants of intellectual development. *Child Development, 57,* 1151–1165.

Breland, H. M. (1974). Birth order, family configuration, and verbal achievement. *Child Development, 45,* 1011–1019.

Bretherton, I. (1992a). The origins of attachment theory: John Bowlby and Mary Ainsworth. *Developmental Psychology, 28,* 759–775.

Bretherton, I. (1992b). Attachment and bonding. In V. B. V. Hasselt & M. Hersen (Eds.), *Handbook of social development: A lifespan perspective* (pp. 133–155). New York: Plenum Press.

Bretherton, I. (1993). From dialogue to internal working models: The co-construction of self in relationships. In C. A. Nelson (Ed.), *The Minnesota symposia on child psychology* (Vol. 26, pp. 237–264). Hillsdale, NJ: Erlbaum.

Bristol, M. M., Gallagher, J. J., & Schopler, E. (1988). Mothers and fathers of young developmentally disabled and nondisabled boys: Adaptation and spousal support. *Developmental Psychology, 24,* 441–451.

Brody, G. H., Stoneman, Z., McCoy, J. K., & Forehand, R. (1992). Contemporaneous and longitudinal associations of sibling conflict with family relationship assessments and family discussions about sibling problems. *Child Development, 63,* 391–400.

Brody, N. (1992). *Intelligence* (2nd ed.). San Diego, CA: Academic Press.

Broman, C. L. (1993). Race differences in marital well-being. *Journal of Marriage and the Family, 55,* 724–732.

Broman, S. H., Nichols, P. L., & Kennedy, W. A. (1975). *Preschool IQ: Prenatal and early developmental correlates.* Hillsdale, NJ: Erlbaum.

Broman, S. H., Nichols, P. L., Shaughnessy, P., & Kennedy, W. (1987). *Retardation in young children.* Hillsdale, NJ: Erlbaum.

Bronfenbrenner, U. (1979). *The ecology of human development.* Cambridge, MA: Harvard University Press.

Bronfenbrenner, U. (1989). Ecological systems theory. *Annals of Child Development, 6,* 187–249.

Bronfenbrenner, U., Alvarez, W. F., & Henderson, C. R., Jr. (1984). Working and watching: Maternal employment status and parents' perceptions of their three-year-old children. *Child Development, 55,* 1362–1378.

Bronson, G. W. (1991). Infant differences in rate of visual encoding. *Child Development, 62,* 44–45.

Brooks-Gunn, J. (1987). Pubertal processes and girls' psychological adaptation. In R. M. Lerner & T. T. Foch (Ed.), *Biological-psychosocial interactions in early adolescence* (pp. 123–154). Hillsdale, NJ: Erlbaum.

Brooks-Gunn, J., Guo, G., & Furstenberg, F. F., Jr. (1993a). Who drops out of and who continues beyond high school? A 20-year follow-up of black urban youth. *Journal of Research on Adolescence, 3,* 271–294.

Brooks-Gunn, J., Klebanov, P. K., Liaw, F., & Spiker, D. (1993b). Enhancing the development of low-birthweight, premature infants: Changes in cognition and behavior over the first three years. *Child Development, 64,* 736–753.

Brooks-Gunn, J., & Matthews, W. S. (1979). *He and she: How children develop their sex-role identity.* Englewood Cliffs, NJ: Prentice-Hall.

Brooks-Gunn, J., & Reiter, E. O. (1990). The role of pubertal processes. In S. S. Feldman & G. R. Elliott (Eds.), *At the threshold: The developing adolescent* (pp. 16–53). Cambridge, MA: Harvard University Press.

Brooks-Gunn, J., & Warren, M. P. (1985). The effects of delayed menarche in different contexts: Dance and nondance students. *Journal of Youth and Adolescence, 13,* 285–300.

Broverman, I. K., Broverman, D., Clarkson, F. E., Rosenkrantz, P. S., & Vogel, S. R. (1970). Sex-role stereotypes and clinical judgments of mental health. *Journal of Consulting and Clinical Psychology, 34,* 1–7.

Broverman, I. K., Vogel, S. R., Boverman, D. M., Clarkson, F. E., & Rosenkrantz, P. S. (1972). Sex role stereotypes: A current appraisal. *Journal of Social Issues, 28*(2), 59–79.

Brown, B. B. (1990). Peer groups and peer cultures. In S. S. Feldman & G. R. Elliott (Eds.), *At the threshold: The developing adolescent* (pp. 171–196). Cambridge, MA: Harvard University Press.

Brown, B. B., Clasen, D. R., & Eicher, S. A. (1986). Perceptions of peer pressure, peer conformity dispositions, and self-reported behavior among adolescents. *Developmental Psychology, 22,* 521–530.

Brown, R. (1965). *Social psychology.* New York: Free Press.

Brown, R. (1973). *A first language: The early stages.* Cambridge, MA: Harvard University Press.

Brown, R., & Bellugi, U. (1964). Three processes in the acquisition of syntax. *Harvard Educational Review, 334,* 133–151.

Brown, R., & Hanlon, C. (1970). Derivational complexity and order of acquisition. In J. R. Hayes (Ed.), *Cognition and the development of language* (pp. 155–207). New York: Wiley.

Brownell, C. A. (1986). Convergent developments: Cognitive-developmental correlates of growth in infant/toddler peer skills. *Child Development, 57,* 275–286.

Brownell, C. A. (1988). Combinatorial skills: Converging developments over the second year. *Child Development, 59,* 675–685.

Brownell, C. A. (1990). Peer social skills in toddlers: Competencies and constraints illustrated by same-age and mixed-age interaction. *Child Development, 61,* 836–848.

Brownell, C. A., & Brown, E. (1992). Peers and play in infants and toddlers. In V. B. V. Hasselt & M. Hersen (Eds.), *Handbook of social development: A lifespan perspective* (pp. 183–200). New York: Plenum Press.

Brownell, C. A., & Carriger, M. S. (1990). Changes in cooperation and self-other differentiation during the second year. *Child Development, 61,* 1164–1174.

Bryant, P. E., MacLean, M., Bradley, L. L., & Crossland, J. (1990). Rhyme and alliteration, phoneme detection, and learning to read. *Developmental Psychology, 26,* 429–438.

Buchanan, C. M., Maccoby, E. E., & Dornbusch, S. M. (1991). Caught between parents: Adolescents' experience in divorced homes. *Child Development, 62,* 1008–1029.

Buchanan, C. M., Maccoby, E. E., & Dornbusch, S. M. (1992). Adolescents and their families after divorce: Three residential arrangements compared. *Journal of Research on Adolescence, 2,* 261–292.

Buehler, J. W., Kaunitz, A. M., Hogue, C. J. R., Hughes, J. M., Smith, J. C., & Rochat, R. W. (1986). Maternal mortality in women aged 35 years or older: United States. *Journal of the American Medical Association, 255,* 53–57.

Bullock, M., & Lütkenhaus, P. (1990). Who am I? Self-understanding in toddlers. *Merrill-Palmer Quarterly, 36,* 217–238.

Bumpass, L. (1984). Children and marital disruption: A replication and update. *Demography, 41,* 71–82.

Burchinal, M., Lee, M., & Ramey, C. (1989). Type of day-care and preschool intellectual development in disadvantaged children. *Child Development, 60,* 128–137.

Burns, A. (1992). Mother-headed families: An international perspective and the case of Australia. *Social Policy Report, Society for Research in Child Development, 6*(1), 1–22.

Buss, A. (1989). Temperaments as personality traits. In G. A. Kohnstamm, J. E. Bates, & M. K. Rothbart (Eds.), *Temperament in childhood* (pp. 49–58). Chichester, England: Wiley.

Buss, A. H., & Plomin, R. (1984). *Temperament: Early developing personality traits*. Hillsdale, NJ: Erlbaum.

Buss, A. H., & Plomin, R. (1986). The EAS approach to temperament. In R. Plomin & J. Dunn (Eds.), *The study of temperament: Changes, continuities and challenges* (pp. 67–80). Hillsdale, NJ: Erlbaum.

Bussey, K., & Bandura, A. (1992). Self-regulatory mechanisms governing gender development. *Child Development, 63,* 1236–1250.

Byrnes, J. P., & Takahira, S. (1993). Explaining gender differences on SAT-Math items. *Developmental Psychology, 29,* 805–810.

Cairns, R. B. (1991). Multiple metaphors for a singular idea. *Developmental Psychology, 27,* 23–26.

Cairns, R. B., Cairns, B. D., Necherman, H. J., Ferguson, L. L., & Gariepy, J. (1989). Growth and aggression: 1. Childhood to early adolescence. *Developmental Psychology, 25,* 320–330.

California Assessment Program. (1980). *Student achievement in California schools: 1979–1980 annual report. Television and student achievement*. Sacramento: California State Department of Education.

Callahan, C. M., & Rivara, F. P. (1992). Urban high school youth and handguns: A school-based survey. *Journal of the American Medical Association, 267*(22), 3038–3042.

Calvert, S. L., & Huston, A. C. (1987). Television and children's gender schemata. *New Directions for Child Development, 38,* 75–88.

Campbell, R. L., & Bickhard, M. H. (1992). Types of constraints on development: An interactivist approach. *Developmental Review, 12,* 311–338.

Campbell, S. B. (1990). The socialization and social development of hyperactive children. In M. Lewis & S. M. Miller (Eds.), *Handbook of developmental psychopathology* (pp. 77–92). New York: Plenum Press.

Campbell, S. B., Cohn, J. F., Flanagan, C., Popper, S., & Meyers, T. (1992). Course and correlates of postpartum depression during the transition to parenthood. *Development and Psychopathology, 4,* 29–47.

Campbell, S. B., Pierce, E. W., March, C. L., & Ewing, L. J. (1991). Noncompliant behavior, overactivity, and family stress as predictors of negative maternal control with preschool children. *Development and Psychopathology, 3,* 175–190.

Campbell, S. B., & Taylor, P. M. (1980). Bonding and attachment: Theoretical issues. In P. M. Taylor (Ed.), *Parent-infant relationships* (pp. 3–24). New York: Grune & Stratton.

Campione, J. C., & Brown, A. L. (1984). Learning ability and transfer propensity as sources of individual differences in intelligence. In P. H. Brooks, C. McCauley, & R. Sperber (Eds.), *Learning and cognition in the mentally retarded*. Hillsdale, NJ: Erlbaum.

Campione, J. C., Brown, A. L., & Ferrara, R. A. (1982). Mental retardation and intelligence. In J. R. Sternberg (Ed.), *Handbook of human intelligence* (pp. 392–492). Cambridge: Cambridge University Press.

Campione, J. C., Brown, A. L., Ferrara, R. A., Jones, R. S., & Steinberg, E. (1985). Breakdowns in flexible use of information: Intelligence-related differences in transfer following equivalent learning performance. *Intelligence, 9,* 297–315.

Cantwell, D. P. (1990). Depression across the early life span. In M. Lewis & S. M. Miller (Eds.), *Handbook of developmental psychopathology* (pp. 293–310). New York: Plenum Press.

Capron, C., & Duyme, M. (1989). Assessment of effects of socio-economic status on IQ in a full cross-fostering study. *Nature, 340,* 552–554.

Capute, A. J., Palmer, F. B., Shapiro, B. K., Wachtel, R. C., Ross, A., & Accardo, P. J. (1984). Primitive reflex profile: A quantification of primitive reflexes in infancy. *Developmental Medicine and Child Neurology, 26,* 375–383.

Capute, A. J., Palmer, F. B., Shapiro, B. K., Wachtel, R. C., Schmidt, S., & Ross, A. (1986). Clinical linguistic and auditory milestone scale: Prediction of cognition in infancy. *Developmental Medicine and Child Neurology, 28,* 762–771.

Carey, S., & Bartlett, E. (1978). Acquiring a single new word. *Papers and Reports on Child Language Development, 15,* 17–29.

Caron, A. J., & Caron, R. F. (1981). Processing of relational information as an index of infant risk. In S. Friedman and M. Sigman (Eds.), *Preterm birth and psychological development* (pp. 219–240). New York: Academic Press.

Carter, C. S. (1988). Patterns of infant feeding, the mother-infant interaction and stress management. In T. M. Field, P. M. McCabe, & N. Schneiderman (Eds.), *Stress and coping across development* (pp. 27–46). Hillsdale, NJ: Erlbaum.

Carver, R. P. (1990). Intelligence and reading ability in grades 2–12. *Intelligence, 14,* 449–455.

Casey, M. B. (1986). Individual differences in selective attention among prereaders: A key to mirror-image confusions. *Developmental Psychology, 22,* 58–66.

Ceci, S. J., & Bruck, M. (1993). Suggestibility of the child witness: A historical review and synthesis. *Psychological Bulletin, 113,* 403–439.

Center for Educational Statistics. (1987). *Who drops out of high school? From high school and beyond.* Washington, DC: Office of Educational Research and Improvement, U.S. Department of Education.

Centers for Disease Control. (1993). Rates of cesarean delivery—United States, 1991. *Journal of the American Medical Association, 269*(18), 2360.

Centerwall, B. S. (1989). Exposure to television as a cause of violence. In G. Comstock (Ed.), *Public communication and behavior* (pp. 1–58). San Diego, CA: Academic Press.

Centerwall, B. S. (1992). Television and violence: The scale of the problem and where to go from here. *Journal of the American Medical Association, 267*(22), 3059–3063.

Cernoch, J. M., & Porter, R. H. (1985). Recognition of maternal axillary odors by infants. *Child Development, 56,* 1593–1598.

Chalfant, J. C. (1989). Learning disabilities: Policy issues and promising approaches. *American Psychologist, 44,* 392–398.

Chandler, M., & Moran, T. (1990). Psychopathology and moral development: A comparative study of delinquent and nondelinquent youth. *Development and Psychopathology, 2,* 227–246.

Chapa, J., & Valencia, R. R. (1993). Latino population growth, demographic characteristics, and educational stagnation: An examination of recent trends. *Hispanic Journal of Behavioral Sciences, 15,* 165–187.

Chen, X., Rubin, K. H., & Sun, Y. (1992). Social reputation and peer relationships in Chinese and Canadian children: A cross-cultural study. *Child Development, 63,* 1336–1343.

Cherlin, A. (1992a). Infant care and full-time employment. In A. Booth (Ed.), *Child care in the 1990s: Trends and consequences* (pp. 209–214). Hillsdale, NJ: Erlbaum.

Cherlin, A. J. (1992b). *Marriage, divorce, remarriage.* Cambridge, MA: Harvard University Press.

Chess, S., & Korn, S. J. (1980). Temperament and behavior disorder in mentally retarded children. *Journal of Special Education, 23,* 122–130.

Chess, S., & Thomas, A. (1984). *Origins and evolution of behavior disorders: Infancy to early adult life.* New York: Brunner/Mazel.

Chi, M. T. (1978). Knowledge structure and memory development. In R. S. Siegler (Ed.), *Children's thinking: What develops?* (pp. 73–96). Hillsdale, NJ: Erlbaum.

Chi, M. T. H., & Ceci, S. J. (1987). Content knowledge: Its role, representation, and restructuring in memory development. In H. W. Reese (Ed.), *Advances in child development and behavior* (Vol. 20, pp. 91–142). Orlando, FL: Academic Press.

Chi, M. T. H., Hutchinson, J. E., & Robin, A. F. (1989). How inferences about novel domain-related concepts can be constrained by structured knowledge. *Merrill-Palmer Quarterly, 35,* 27–62.

Chomsky, N. (1965). *Aspects of a theory of syntax.* Cambridge, MA: MIT Press.

Chomsky, N. (1975). *Reflections on language.* New York: Pantheon Books.

Chomsky, N. (1986). *Knowledge of language: Its nature, origin, and use.* New York: Praeger.

Chomsky, N. (1988). *Language and problems of knowledge.* Cambridge, MA: MIT Press.

Christophersen, E. R. (1989). Injury control. *American Psychologist, 44,* 237–241.

Chumlea, W. C. (1982). Physical growth in adolescence. In B. B. Wolman (Ed.), *Handbook of developmental psychology* (pp. 471–485). Englewood Cliffs, NJ: Prentice-Hall.

Cicchetti, D. (1989). Developmental psychopathology: Past, present, and future. In D. Cicchetti (Ed.), *The emergence of a discipline: Rochester symposium on developmental psychopathology* (Vol. 1, pp. 1–12). Hillsdale, NJ: Erlbaum.

Cicchetti, D., & Barnett, D. (1991). Attachment organization in maltreated preschoolers. *Development and Psychopathology, 3,* 397–411.

Cillessen, A. H. N., van IJzendoorn, H. W., van Lieshout, C. F. M., & Hartup, W. W. (1992). Heterogeneity among peer-rejected boys: Subtypes and stabilities. *Child Development, 63,* 893–905.

Clark, E. V. (1975). Knowledge, context, and strategy in the acquisition of meaning. In D. P. Date (Ed.), *Georgetown University round table on language and linguistics.* Washington, DC: Georgetown University Press.

Clark, E. V. (1977). Strategies and the mapping problem in first language acquisition. In J. Macnamara (Ed.), *Language learning and thought* (pp. 147–168). New York: Academic Press, 1977.

Clark, E. V. (1983). Meanings and concepts. In J. H. Flavell & E. M. Markman (Eds.), *Handbook of child psychology: Vol. 3. Cognitive development* (pp. 787–840). New York: Wiley.

Clark, E. V. (1987). The principle of contrast: A constraint on language acquisition. In B. MacWhinney (Ed.), *Mechanisms of language acquisition* (pp. 1–34). Hillsdale, NJ: Erlbaum.

Clark, E. V. (1990). On the pragmatics of contrast. *Journal of Child Language, 41,* 417–431.

Clarke, A. D. B. (1968). Learning and human development—the 42nd Maudsley lecture. *British Journal of Psychiatry, 114,* 161–177.

Clarke, A. M., & Clarke, A. D. B. (1976). *Early experience: Myth and evidence.* New York: Free Press.

Clarke-Stewart, A. (1987). The social ecology of early childhood. In N. Eisenberg (Ed.), *Contemporary topics in developmental psychology* (pp. 292–318). New York: Wiley-Interscience.

Clarke-Stewart, A. (1990). "The 'effects' of infant day care reconsidered" reconsidered: Risks for parents, children, and researchers. In N. Fox & G. G. Fein (Eds.), *Infant day care: The current debate* (pp. 61–86). Norwood, NJ: Ablex.

Clarke-Stewart, A. (1992). Consequences of child care for children's development. In A. Booth (Ed.), *Child care in the 1990s: Trends and consequences* (pp. 63–82). Hillsdale, NJ: Erlbaum.

Cnattingius, S., Berendes, H. W., & Forman, M. R. (1993). Do delayed childbearers face increased risks of adverse pregnancy outcomes after the first birth? *Obstetrics and Gynecology, 81,* 512–516.

Cohen, Y. A. (1964). *The transition from childhood to adolescence.* Chicago: Aldine.

Coie, J. D., & Cillessen, A. H. N. (1993). Peer rejection: Origins and effects on children's development. *Current Directions in Psychological Science, 2,* 89–92.

Colby, A., Kohlberg, L., Gibbs, J., & Lieberman, M. (1983). A longitudinal study of moral judgment. *Monographs of the Society for Research in Child Development, 48*(1–2, Serial No. 200).

Cole, D. A. (1991). Change in self-perceived competence as a function of peer and teacher evaluation. *Developmental Psychology, 27,* 682–688.

Cole, M. (1992). Culture in development. In M. H. Bornstein & M. E. Lamb (Eds.), *Developmental psychology: An advanced textbook* (3rd ed.) (pp. 731–789). Hillsdale, NJ: Erlbaum.

Cole, M., & Traupmann, K. (1981). Comparative cognitive research: Learning from a learning disabled child. In W. A. Collins (Ed.), *Aspects of the development of competence: The Minnesota symposia on child psychology* (Vol. 14, pp. 125–154). Hillsdale, NJ: Erlbaum.

Collin, M. F., Halsey, C. L., & Anderson, C. L. (1991). Emerging developmental sequelae in the "normal" extremely low birth weight infant. *Pediatrics, 88,* 115–120.

Collins, W. A. (Ed.). (1984). *Development during middle childhood: The years from six to twelve.* Washington, DC: National Academy Press.

Colombo, J. (1993). *Infant cognition: Predicting later intellectual functioning.* Newbury Park, CA: Sage.

Compas, B. E., Ey, S., & Grant, K. E. (1993). Taxonomy, assessment, and diagnosis of depression during adolescence. *Psychological Bulletin, 114,* 323–344.

Comstock, G. (1991). *Television and the American child.* San Diego, CA: A.cademic Press.

Conger, R. D., Conger, K. J., Elder, G. H., Jr., Lorenz, F. O., Simons, R. L., & Whitbeck, L. B. (1992). A family process model of economic hardship and adjustment of early adolescent boys. *Child Development, 63,* 526–541.

Connolly, K., & Dalgleish, M. (1989). The emergence of a tool-using skill in infancy. *Developmental Psychology, 25,* 894–912.

Cook, M., & Birch, R. (1984). Infant perception of the shapes of tilted plane forms. *Infant Behavior and Development, 7,* 389–402.

Cooper, R. P., & Aslin, R. N. (1990). Preference for infant-directed speech in the first month after birth. *Child Development, 61,* 1584–1595.

Crisafi, M. A., & Brown, A. L. (1986). Analogical transfer in very young children: Combining two separately learned solutions to reach a goal. *Child Development, 57,* 953–968.

Crittenden, P. M., Partridge, M. F., & Claussen, A. H. (1991). Family patterns of relationship in normative and dysfunctional families. *Development and Psychopathology, 3,* 491–512.

Crnic, K. A., Greenberg, M. T., Ragozin, A. S., Robinson, N. M., & Basham, R. B. (1983). Effects of stress and social support on mothers and premature and full-term infants. *Child Development, 54,* 209–217.

Crockenberg, S. (1987). Predictors and correlates of anger toward and punitive control of toddlers by adolescent mothers. *Child Development, 58,* 964–975.

Crockenberg, S. B. (1981). Infant irritability, mother responsiveness, and social support influences on the security of infant-mother attachment. *Child Development, 52,* 857–865.

Cromer, R. F. (1991). *Language and thought in normal and handicapped children.* Oxford, England: Basil Blackwell.

Crook, C. (1987). Taste and olfaction. In P. Salapatek & L. Cohen (Eds.), *Handbook of infant perception: Vol. 1. From sensation to perception* (pp. 237–264). Orlando, FL: Academic Press.

Crouter, A. C., & McHale, S. M. (1993). Familial economic circumstances: Implications for adjustment and development in early adolescence. In R. M. Lerner (Ed.), *Early adolescence: Perspectives on research, policy, and intervention* (pp. 71–91). Hillsdale, NJ: Erlbaum.

Csikszentmihalyi, M., & Larson, R. (1984). *Being adolescent: Conflict and growth in the teenage years.* New York: Basic Books.

Cunningham, A. S., Jelliffe, D. B., & Jelliffe, E. F. P. (1991). Breast-feeding and health in the 1980s: A global epidemiologic review. *Journal of Pediatrics, 118,* 659–666.

Cutrona, C. E., & Troutman, B. R. (1986). Social support, infant temperament, and parenting self-efficacy: A mediational model of postpartum depression. *Child Development, 57,* 1507–1518.

D'Alton, M. E., & DeCherney, A. H. (1993). Prenatal diagnosis. *New England Journal of Medicine, 328,* 114–118.

Damon, W. (1977). *The social world of the child.* San Francisco: Jossey-Bass.

Damon, W. (1983). The nature of social-cognitive change in the developing child. In W. F. Overton (Ed.), *The relationship between social and cognitive development* (pp. 103–142). Hillsdale, NJ: Erlbaum.

Dannemiller, J. L. (1989). A test of color constancy in 9- and 20-week-old human infants following simulated illuminant changes. *Developmental Psychology, 25,* 171–184.

Danner, F. W., & Day, M. C. (1977). Eliciting formal operations. *Child Development, 48,* 1600–1606.

Darlington, R. B. (1991). The long-term effects of model preschool programs. In L. Okagaki & R. J. Sternberg (Eds.), *Directors of development* (pp. 203–215). Hillsdale, NJ: Erlbaum.

Davidson, E. S., Yasuna, A., & Tower, A. (1979). The effect of television cartoons on sex-role stereotyping in young girls. *Child Development, 50,* 597–600.

Davies, G. M. (1993). Children's memory for other people: An integrative review. In C. A. Nelson (Ed.), *Memory and affect in development: The Minnesota symposia on child psychology* (Vol. 26, pp. 123–157). Hillsdale, NJ: Erlbaum.

DeCasper, A. J., & Fifer, W. P. (1980). Of human bonding: Newborns prefer their mothers' voices. *Science, 208,* 1174–1176.

DeCasper, A. J., & Spence, M. J. (1986). Prenatal maternal speech influences newborns' perception of speech sounds. *Infant Behavior and Development, 9,* 133–150.

de Chateau, P. (1980). Effects of hospital practices on synchrony in the development of the infant-parent relationship. In P. M. Taylor (Ed.), *Parent-infant relationships* (pp. 137–168). New York: Grune & Stratton.

Declercq, E. R. (1993). Where babies are born and who attends their births: Findings from the revised 1989 United States Standard Certificate of Live Birth. *Obstetrics and Gynecology, 81,* 997–1004.

DeLoache, J. S. (1989). The development of representation in young children. In H. W. Reese (Ed.), *Advances in child development and behavior* (Vol. 22, pp. 2–37). San Diego, CA: Academic Press.

DeLoache, J. S., & Brown, A. L. (1987). Differences in the memory-based searching of delayed and normally developing young children. *Intelligence, 11,* 277–289.

DeMeis, D. K., Hock, E., & McBride, S. L. (1986). The balance of employment and motherhood: Longitudinal study of mothers' feelings about separation from their first-born infants. *Developmental Psychology, 22,* 627–632.

Dempster, F. N. (1981). Memory span: Sources of individual and developmental differences. *Psychological Bulletin, 89,* 63–100.

Denham, S. A., & Holt, R. W. (1993). Preschoolers' likeability as cause or consequence of their social behavior. *Developmental Psychology, 29,* 271–275.

Dennis, W. (1960). Causes of retardation among institutional children: Iran. *Journal of Genetic Psychology, 96,* 47–59.

Deutsch, C. K., & Kinsbourne, M. (1990). Genetics and biochemistry in attention deficit disorder. In M. Lewis & S. M. Miller (Eds.), *Handbook of developmental psychopathology* (pp. 93–108). New York: Plenum Press.

de Villiers, P. A., & de Villiers, J. G. (1992). Language development. In M. H. Bornstein & M. E. Lamb (Eds.), *Developmental psychology: An advanced textbook* (3rd ed.) (pp. 337–418). Hillsdale, NJ: Erlbaum.

The Diagram Group. (1977). *Child's body.* New York: Paddington.

Dietrich, K. N., Krafft, K. M., Bornschein, R. L., Hammond, P. B., Berger, O., Succop, P. A., & Bier, M. (1987). Low-level fetal lead exposure effect on neurobehavioral development in early infancy. *Pediatrics, 80,* 721–730.

Dishion, T. J. (1990). The family ecology of boys' peer relations in middle childhood. *Child Development, 61,* 874–892.

Dishion, T. J., Patterson, G. R., Stoolmiller, M., & Skinner, M. L. (1991). Family, school, and behavioral antecedents to early adolescent involvement with antisocial peers. *Developmental Psychology, 27,* 172–180.

Dodge, K. A. (1990). Developmental psychopathology in children of depressed mothers. *Developmental Psychology, 26,* 3–6.

Dodge, K. A., Coie, J. D., Pettit, G. S., & Price, J. M. (1990). Peer status and aggression in boys' groups: Developmental and contextual analysis. *Child Development, 61,* 1289–1309.

Dodge, K. A., & Feldman, E. (1990). Issues in social cognition and sociometric status. In S. R. Asher & J. D. Coie (Eds.), *Peer rejection in childhood* (pp. 119–155). Cambridge: Cambridge University Press.

Dodge, K. A., & Frame, C. L. (1982). Social cognitive biases and deficits in aggressive boys. *Child Development, 53,* 620–635.

Dodge, K. A., Murphy, R. R., & Buchsbaum, K. (1984). The assessment of intention-cue detection skills in children: Implications for developmental psychopathology. *Child Development, 55,* 163–173.

Dornbusch, S. M., Carlsmith, J. M., Bushwall, S. J., Ritter, P. L., Leiderman, H., Hastorf, A. H., & Goss, R. T. (1985). Single parents, extended households, and the control of adolescents. *Child Development, 56,* 326–341.

Dornbusch, S. M., Gross, R. T., Duncan, P. D., & Ritter, P. L. (1987a). Stanford studies of adolescence using the National Health Examination Survey. In R. M. Lerner & T. T. Foch (Eds.), *Biological-psychosocial interactions in early adolescence* (pp. 189–206). Hillsdale, NJ: Erlbaum.

Dornbusch, S. M., Ritter, P. L., Liederman, P. H., Roberts, D. F., & Fraleigh, M. J. (1987b). The relation of parenting style to adolescent school performance. *Child Development, 58,* 1244–1257.

Downey, D. B., & Powell, B. (1993). Do children in single-parent households fare better living with same-sex parents? *Journal of Marriage and the Family, 55,* 55–71.

Downey, G., & Coyne, J. C. (1990). Children of depressed parents: An integrative review. *Psychological Bulletin, 108,* 50–76.

Dreyer, P. H. (1982). Sexuality during adolescence. In B. B. Wolman (Ed.), *Handbook of developmental psychology* (pp. 559–601). Englewood Cliffs, NJ: Prentice-Hall.

Duke, P. M., Carlsmith, J. M., Jennings, D., Martin, J. A., Dornbusch, S. M., Gross, R. T., & Siegel-Gorelick, B. (1982). Educational correlates of early and late sexual maturation in adolescence. *Journal of Pediatrics, 100,* 633–637.

Duncan, G. (1993). *Economic deprivation and childhood development.* Paper presented at the biennial meetings of the Society for Research in Child Development, New Orleans.

Dunham, P. J., Dunham, F., & Curwin, A. (1993). Joint-attentional states and lexical acquisition at 18 months. *Developmental Psychology, 29,* 827–831.

Dunn, J. (1992). Siblings and development. *Current Directions in Psychological Science, 1,* 6–9.

Dunn, J. (1993). *Young children's close relationships.* Newbury Park, CA: Sage.

Dunn, J., & McGuire, S. (1994). Young children's nonshared experiences: A summary of studies in Cambridge and Colorado. In E. M. Hetherington, D. Reiss, & R. Plomin (Eds.), *Separate social worlds of siblings: The impact of nonshared environment on development* (pp. 111–128). Hillsdale, NJ: Erlbaum.

Dunphy, D. C. (1963). The social structure of urban adolescent peer groups. *Sociometry, 26,* 230–246.

Dunst, C. J., Brooks, P. H., & Doxsey, P. A. (1982). Characteristics of hiding places and the transition to stage IV performance in object permanence tasks. *Developmental Psychology, 18,* 671–681.

Dwyer, T., & Ponsonby, A. (1992). Sudden infant death syndrome—insights from epidemiological research. *Journal of Epidemiology and Community Health, 46,* 98–102.

Dyk, P. H. (1993). Anatomy, physiology, and gender issues in adolescence. In T. P. Gullotta, G. R. Adams, & R. Montemayor (Eds.), *Adolescent sexuality* (pp. 35–56). Newbury Park, CA: Sage.

Dykens, E. M., Hodapp, R. M., & Leckman, J. F. (1994). *Behavior and development in Fragile X syndrome.* Thousand Oaks, CA: Sage.

Easterbrooks, M. A., Davidson, C. E., & Chazan, R. (1993). Psychosocial risk, attachment, and behavior problems among school-aged children. *Development and Psychopathology, 5,* 389–402.

Eaton, W. O., & Enns, L. R. (1986). Sex differences in human motor activity level. *Psychological Bulletin, 100,* 19–28.

Eccles, J. S., & Midgley, C. (1990). Changes in academic motivation and self-perception during early adolescence. In R. Montemayor, G. R. Adams, & T. P. Gullotta (Eds.), *From childhood to adolescence: A transitional period?* (pp. 134–155). Newbury Park, CA: Sage.

Egeland, B., & Sroufe, L. A. (1981). Attachment and early maltreatment. *Child Development, 52,* 44–52.

Eisenberg, N. (1986). *Altruistic emotion, cognition, and behavior.* Hillsdale, NJ: Erlbaum.

Eisenberg, N. (1988). The development of prosocial and aggressive behavior. In M. H. Bornstein & M. E. Lamb (Eds.), *Developmental psychology: An advanced textbook* (2nd ed.) (pp. 461–496). Hillsdale, NJ: Erlbaum.

Eisenberg, N. (1990). Prosocial development in early and mid-adolescence. In R. Montemayor, G. R. Adams, & T. P. Gullotta (Eds.), *From childhood to adolescence: A transitional period?* (pp. 240–268). Newbury Park, CA: Sage.

Eisenberg, N. (1992). *The caring child.* Cambridge, MA: Harvard University Press.

Eisenberg, N., Fabes, R. A., Schaller, M., & Miller, P. A. (1989). Sympathy and personal distress: Development, gender differences, and interrelations of indexes. *New Directions for Child Development, 44,* 107–126.

Eisenberg, N., & Mussen, P. H. (1989). *The roots of prosocial behavior in children.* Cambridge: Cambridge University Press.

Eisenberg, N., Shell, R., Pasternack, J., Lennon, R., Beller, R., & Mathy, R. M. (1987). Prosocial development in middle childhood: A longitudinal study. *Developmental Psychology, 23,* 712–718.

Ekman, P. (1972). Universals and cultural differences in facial expressions of emotion. In J. Cole (Ed.), *Nebraska symposium on motivation, 1971* (pp. 207–282). Lincoln: University of Nebraska Press.

Ekman, P. (1973). Cross-cultural studies of facial expression. In P. Ekman (Ed.), *Darwin and facial expression* (pp. 169–222). New York: Academic Press.

Elder, G. H., Jr. (1974). *Children of the Great Depression.* Chicago: University of Chicago Press.

Elder, G. H., Jr. (1981). Scarcity and prosperity in postwar childbearing: Explorations from a life course perspective. *Journal of Family History, 5,* 410–431.

Elder, G. H., Jr. (1984). Families, kin, and the life course: A sociological perspective. In R. D. Parke (Ed.), *Review of child development research: Vol. 7. The family* (pp. 80–136). Chicago: University of Chicago Press.

Elkind, D. (1967). Egocentrism in adolescence. *Child Development, 38,* 1025–1034.

Elkind, D., & Bowen, R. (1979). Imaginary audience behavior in children and adolescents. *Developmental Psychology, 15,* 38–44.

Elliott, R. (1988). Tests, abilities, race, and conflict. *Intelligence, 12,* 333–350.

Eme, R. F. (1979). Sex differences in childhood psychopathology: A review. *Psychological Bulletin, 86,* 374–395.

Emery, R. E. (1988). *Marriage, divorce, and children's adjustment.* Newbury Park, CA: Sage.

Entwisle, D. R. (1990). Schools and the adolescent. In S. S. Feldman & G. R. Elliott (Eds.), *At the threshold: The developing adolescent* (pp. 197–224). Cambridge, MA: Harvard University Press.

Entwisle, D. R., & Alexander, K. L. (1990). Beginning school math competence: Minority and majority comparisons. *Child Development, 61,* 454–471.

Entwisle, D. R., & Doering, S. G. (1981). *The first birth.* Baltimore: Johns Hopkins University Press.

Epstein, S. (1991). Cognitive-experiential self theory: Implications for developmental psychology. In M. R. Gunnar & L. A. Sroufe (Eds.), *Self process and development: The Minnesota symposia on child development* (Vol. 23, pp. 79–123). Hillsdale, NJ: Erlbaum.

Ericsson, K. A., & Crutcher, R. J. (1990). The nature of exceptional performance. In P. B. Baltes, D. L. Featherman, & R. M. Lerner (Eds.), *Life-span development and behavior* (Vol. 10, pp. 188–218). Hillsdale, NJ: Erlbaum.

Erikson, E. H. (1963). *Childhood and society.* New York: Norton.

Erikson, E. H. (1964). *Insight and responsibility.* New York: Norton.

Erikson, E. H. (1974). *Dimensions of a new identity: The 1973 Jefferson lectures on the humanities.* New York: Norton.

Erikson, E. H. (1980). *Identity and the life cycle.* New York: Norton (original work published 1959).

Eron, L. D. (1987). The development of aggressive behavior from the perspective of a developing behaviorism. *American Psychologist, 42,* 435–442.

Eron, L. D., Huesmann, L. R., & Zelli, A. (1991). The role of parental variables in the learning of aggression. In D. J. Pepler & K. H. Rubin (Eds.), *The development and treatment of childhood aggression* (pp. 169–188). Hillsdale, NJ: Erlbaum.

Escalona, K. S. (1981). The reciprocal role of social and emotional developmental advances and cognitive development during the second and third years of life. In E. K. Shapiro & E. Weber (Eds.), *Cognitive and affective growth: Developmental interaction* (pp. 87–108). Hillsdale, NJ: Erlbaum.

Espinosa, M. P., Sigman, M. D., Neumann, C. G., Bwibo, N. O., & McDonald, M. A. (1992). Playground behaviors of school-age children in relation to nutrition, schooling, and family characteristics. *Developmental Psychology, 28,* 1188–1195.

European Collaborative Study. (1991). Children born to women with HIV-1 infection: Natural history and risk of transmission. *The Lancet, 337,* 253–260.

Fagan, J. F., III. (1992). Intelligence: A theoretical viewpoint. *Current Directions in Psychological Science, 1,* 82–86.

Fagan, J. F., & Singer, L. T. (1983). Infant recognition memory as a measure of intelligence. In L. P. Lipsett (Ed.), *Advances in infancy research* (Vol. 2, pp. 31–78). Norwood, NJ: Ablex.

Fagard, J., & Jacquet, A. (1989). Onset of bimanual coordination and symmetry versus asymmetry of movement. *Infant Behavior and Development, 12,* 229–235.

Fagot, B. I., & Hagan, R. (1991). Observations of parent reactions to sex-stereotyped behaviors: Age and sex effects. *Child Development, 62,* 617–628.

Fagot, B. I., & Leinbach, M. D. (1989). The young child's gender schema: Environmental input, internal organization. *Child Development, 60,* 663–672.

Fagot, B. I., & Leinbach, M. D. (1993). Gender-role development in young children: From discrimination to labeling. *Developmental Review, 13,* 205–224.

Fagot, B. I., Leinbach, M. D., & O'Boyle, C. (1992). Gender labeling, gender stereotyping, and parenting behaviors. *Developmental Psychology, 28,* 225–230.

Falbo, T. (1992). Social norms and the one-child family: Clinical and policy implications. In F. Boer & J. Dunn (Eds.), *Children's sibling relationships: Developmental and clinical issues* (pp. 71–82). Hillsdale, NJ: Erlbaum.

Falbo, T., & Poston, D. L., Jr. (1993). The academic, personality, and physical outcomes of only children in China. *Child Development, 64,* 18–35.

Famularo, R., Stone, K., Barnum, R., & Whatron, R. (1986). Alcoholism and severe child maltreatment. *American Journal of Orthopsychiatry, 56,* 481–485.

Fantz, R. L. (1956). A method for studying early visual development. *Perceptual and Motor Skills, 6,* 13–15.

Farnham-Diggory, S. (1986). Time, now, for a little serious complexity. In S. J. Ceci (Ed.), *Handbook of cognitive, social, and neuropsychological aspects of learning disability* (Vol. 1). Hillsdale, NJ: Erlbaum.

Farnham-Diggory, S. (1978). *Learning Disabilities.* Cambridge, MA: Harvard University Press.

Farnham-Diggory, S. (1992). *The learning-disabled child.* Cambridge, MA: Harvard University Press.

Farran, D. C., Haskins, R., & Gallagher, J. J. (1980). Poverty and mental retardation: A search for explanations. *New Directions for Exceptional Children, 1,* 47–66.

Farrar, M. J. (1992). Negative evidence and grammatical morpheme acquisition. *Developmental Psychology, 28,* 90–98.

Farrington, D. P. (1991). Childhood aggression and adult violence: Early precursors and later life outcomes. In D. J.

Pepler & K. H. Rubin (Eds.), *The development and treatment of childhood aggression* (pp. 5–30). Hillsdale, NJ: Erlbaum.

Faust, M. S. (1983). Alternative constructions of adolescent growth. In J. Brooks-Gunn & A. C. Petersen (Eds.), *Girls at puberty: Biological and psychosocial perspectives* (pp. 105–126). New York: Plenum Press.

Featherman, D. L. (1980). Schooling and occupational careers: Constancy and change in worldly success. In J. O. G. Brim & J. Kagan (Eds.), *Constancy and change in human development* (pp. 675–738). Cambridge, MA: Harvard University Press.

Featherstone, H. (1980). *A difference in the family*. New York: Basic Books.

Feldman, S. S. (1987). Predicting strain in mothers and fathers of 6-month-old infants: A short-term longitudinal study. In P. W. Berman & F. A. Pedersen (Eds.), *Men's transitions to parenthood* (pp. 13–36). Hillsdale, NJ: Erlbaum.

Feldman, S. S., & Elliott, G. R. (Eds.). (1990). *At the threshold: The developing adolescent*. Cambridge, MA: Harvard University Press.

Fennelly, K. (1993). Sexual activity and childbearing among Hispanic adolescents in the United States. In R. M. Lerner (Ed.), *Early adolescence: Perspectives on research, policy, and intervention* (pp. 335–352). Hillsdale, NJ: Erlbaum.

Fernald, A. (1993). Approval and disapproval: Infant responsiveness to vocal affect in familiar and unfamiliar languages. *Child Development, 64*, 657–674.

Fernald, A., & Kuhl, P. (1987). Acoustic determinants of infant preference for motherese speech. *Infant Behavior and Development, 10*, 279–293.

Feshbach, S. (1970). Aggression. In P. H. Mussen (Ed.), *Carmichael's manual of child psychology* (Vol. 2, 3rd ed.) (pp. 159–260). New York: Wiley.

Fetterman, D. (1990, June). Wasted genius. *Stanford Magazine*, pp. 30–33.

Field, T. (1990). *Infancy*. Cambridge, MA: Harvard University Press.

Field, T., Healy, B., Goldstein, S., Perry, S., Bendell, D., Schanberg, S., Zimmerman, E. A., & Duhn, C. (1988). Infants of depressed mothers show "depressed" behavior even with nondepressed adults. *Child Development, 59*, 1569–1579.

Field, T. M. (1977). Effects of early separation, interactive deficits, and experimental manipulations on infant-mother face-to-face interaction. *Child Development, 48*, 763–771.

Field, T. M. (1978). Interaction behaviors of primary versus secondary caretaker fathers. *Developmental Psychology, 14*, 183–185.

Field, T. M. (1991). Quality infant day-care and grade school behavior and performance. *Child Development, 62*, 863–870.

Field, T. M., De Stefano, L., & Koewler, J. H. I. (1982a). Fantasy play of toddlers and preschoolers. *Developmental Psychology, 18*, 503–508.

Field, T. M., Healy, B., Goldstein, S., & Guthertz, M. (1990). Behavior-state matching and synchrony in mother-infant interactions of nondepressed versus depressed dyads. *Developmental Psychology, 26*, 7–14.

Field, T. M., Woodson, R., Greenberg, R., & Cohen, D. (1982b). Discrimination and imitation of facial expressions by neonates. *Science, 218*, 179–181.

Finkelstein, N. W. (1982). Aggression: Is it stimulated by day care? *Young Children, 37*, 3–9.

Fish, M., Stifter, C. A., & Belsky, J. (1991). Conditions of continuity and discontinuity in infant negative emotionality: Newborn to five months. *Child Development, 62*, 1525–1537.

Flanagan, C. A., & Eccles, J. S. (1993). Changes in parents' work status and adolescents' adjustments at school. *Child Development, 64*, 246–257.

Flavell, J. H. (1982). Structures, stages, and sequences in cognitive development. In W. A. Collins (Ed.), *The concept of development: The Minnesota symposia on child psychology* (Vol. 15, pp. 1–28). Hillsdale, NJ: Erlbaum.

Flavell, J. H. (1985). *Cognitive development* (2nd ed.). Englewood Cliffs, NJ: Prentice-Hall.

Flavell, J. H. (1986). The development of children's knowledge about the appearance-reality distinction. *American Psychologist, 41*, 418–425.

Flavell, J. H. (1992). Cognitive development: Past, present, and future. *Developmental Psychology, 28*, 998–1005.

Flavell, J. H. (1993). Young children's understanding of thinking and consciousness. *Current Directions in Psychological Science, 2*, 40–43.

Flavell, J. H., Everett, B. A., Croft, K., & Flavell, E. R. (1981). Young children's knowledge about visual perception: Further evidence for the Level 1–Level 2 distinction. *Developmental Psychology, 17*, 99–103.

Flavell, J. H., Green, F. L., & Flavell, E. R. (1989). Young children's ability to differentiate appearance-reality and Level 2 perspectives in the tactile modality. *Child Development, 60*, 201–213.

Flavell, J. H., Green, F. L., & Flavell, E. R. (1990). Developmental changes in young children's knowledge about the mind. *Cognitive Development, 5*, 1–27.

Flavell, J. H., Green, F. L., Wahl, K. E., & Flavell, E. R. (1987). The effects of question clarification and memory aids on young children's performance on appearance-reality tasks. *Cognitive Development, 2*, 127–144.

Flavell, J. H., Zhang, X.-D., Zou, H., Dong, Q., & Qi, S. (1983). A comparison of the appearance-reality distinction in the

People's Republic of China and the United States. *Cognitive Psychology, 15,* 459–466.

Fleming, A. S., Ruble, D. L., Flett, G. L., & Schaul, D. L. (1988). Postpartum adjustment in first-time mothers: Relations between mood, maternal attitudes, and mother-infant interactions. *Developmental Psychology, 24,* 71–81.

Floyd, R. L., Rimer, B. K., Giovino, G. A., Mullen, P. D., & Sullivan, S. E. (1993). A review of smoking in pregnancy: Effects on pregnancy outcomes and cessation efforts. *Annual Review of Public Health, 14,* 379–411.

Folven, R. J., & Bonvillian, J. D. (1991). The transition from nonreferential to referential language in children acquiring American Sign Language. *Developmental Psychology, 27,* 806–816.

Ford, M. E. (1982). Social cognition and social competence in adolescence. *Developmental Psychology, 18,* 323–340.

Fox, N. A., Kimmerly, N. L., & Schafer, W. D. (1991). Attachment to mother/attachment to father: A meta-analysis. *Child Development, 62,* 210–225.

Fraiberg, S. (1974). Blind infants and their mothers: An examination of the sign system. In M. Lewis & L. A. Rosenblum (Eds.), *The effect of the infant on its caregiver* (pp. 215–232). New York: Wiley.

Fraiberg, S. (1975). The development of human attachments in infants blind from birth. *Merrill-Palmer Quarterly, 21,* 315–334.

Fraiberg, S. (1977). *Insights from the blind.* New York: New American Library (Meridian Books).

Francis, P. L., Self, P. A., & Horowitz, F. D. (1987). The behavioral assessment of the neonate: An overview. In J. D. Osofsky (Ed.), *Handbook of infant development* (2nd ed.) (pp. 723–779). New York: Wiley-Interscience.

Frankel, K. A., & Bates, J. E. (1990). Mother-toddler problem solving: Antecedents in attachment, home behavior, and temperament. *Child Development, 61,* 810–819.

Freedman, D. G. (1979). Ethnic differences in babies. *Human Nature, 2,* 36–43.

Freeman, E. W., & Rickels, K. (1993). *Early childbearing: Perspectives of black adolescents on pregnancy, abortion, and contraception.* Newbury Park, CA: Sage.

Freud, S. (1905). *The basic writings of Sigmund Freud* (Brill, A. A., Trans.). New York: Random House.

Freud, S. (1920). *A general introduction to psychoanalysis* (Riviere, J., Trans.). New York: Washington Square Press.

Frey, K. S., & Ruble, D. N. (1992). Gender constancy and the "cost" of sex-typed behavior: A test of the conflict hypothesis. *Developmental Psychology, 28,* 714–721.

Fu, Y., Pizzuti, A., Fenwick, R. G., Jr., King, J., Rajnarayan, S., Dune, P. W., Dubel, J., Nasser, G. A., Ashizawa, T., de Jong, P., Wieringa, B., Korneluk, R., Perryman, M. B., Ep-

stein, H. F., & Caskey, C. T. (1992). An unstable triplet repeat in a gene related to myotonic muscular dystrophy. *Science, 225,* 1256–1258.

Furrow, D. (1984). Social and private speech at two years. *Child Development, 55,* 355–362.

Furstenberg, F. F., Jr. (1991). As the pendulum swings: Teenage childbearing and social concern. *Family Relations, 40,* 127–138.

Furstenberg, F. F., Jr., & Cherlin, A. J. (1991). *Divided families: What happens to children when parents part.* Cambridge, MA: Harvard University Press.

Gallagher, J. J., & Ramey, C. T. (1987). *The malleability of children.* Baltimore: Paul H. Brookes.

Ganchrow, J. R., Steiner, J. E., & Daher, M. (1983). Neonatal facial expressions in response to different qualities and intensities of gustatory stimuli. *Infant Behavior and Development, 6,* 189–200.

Garbarino, J., Dubrow, N., Kostelny, K., & Pardo, C. (1992). *Children in danger: Coping with the consequences of community violence.* San Francisco: Jossey-Bass.

Garbarino, J., Kostelny, K., & Dubrow, N. (1991). *No place to be a child: Growing up in a war zone.* Lexington, MA: Lexington Books.

Garbarino, J., & Sherman, D. (1980). High-risk neighborhoods and high-risk families: The human ecology of child maltreatment. *Child Development, 51,* 188–198.

Gardner, D., Harris, P. L., Ohmoto, M., & Hamasaki, T. (1988). Japanese children's understanding of the distinction between real and apparent emotion. *International Journal of Behavioral Development, 11,* 203–218.

Gardner, H. (1983). *Frames of mind: The theory of multiple intelligence.* New York: Basic Books.

Garland, A. F., & Zigler, E. (1993). Adolescent suicide prevention. Current research and social policy implications. *American Psychologist, 48,* 169–182.

Garmezy, N. (1993). Vulnerability and resilience. In D. C. Funder, R. D. Parke, C. Tomlinson-Keasey, & K. Widaman (Eds.), *Studying lives through time: Personality and development* (pp. 377–398). Washington, DC: American Psychological Association.

Garmezy, N., & Masten, A. S. (1991). The protective role of competence indicators in children at risk. In E. M. Cummings, A. L. Green, & K. H. Karraker (Eds.), *Life-span developmental psychology: Perspectives on stress and coping* (pp. 151–174). Hillsdale, NJ: Erlbaum.

Garmezy, N., & Rutter, M. (Eds.) (1983). *Stress, coping, and development in children.* New York: McGraw-Hill.

Garn, S. M. (1980). Continuities and change in maturational timing. In O. G. Brim, Jr., & J. Kagan (Eds.), *Constancy and change in human development* (pp. 113–162). Cambridge, MA: Harvard University Press.

Gecas, V., & Seff, M. A. (1990). Families and adolescents: A review of the 1980s. *Journal of Marriage and the Family, 52,* 941–958.

Gelman, R. (1972). Logical capacity of very young children: Number invariance rules. *Child Development, 43,* 75–90.

Gentner, D. (1982). Why nouns are learned before verbs: Linguistic relativity versus natural partitioning. In S. A. Kuczaj II (Ed.), *Language development: Vol. 2. Language, thought, and culture* (pp. 301–334). Hillsdale, NJ: Erlbaum.

Gerson, R. P., & Damon. W. (1978). Moral understanding and children's conduct. *New Directions for Child Development, 2,* 41–60.

Gesell, A. (1925). *The mental growth of the preschool child.* New York: Macmillan.

Gibson, D. R. (1990). Relation of socioeconomic status to logical and sociomoral judgment of middle-aged men. *Psychology and Aging, 5,* 510–513.

Gibson, E. J. (1969). *Principles of perceptual learning and development.* New York: Appleton-Century-Crofts.

Gibson, E. J., & Spelke, E. S. (1983). The development of perception. In J. H. Flavell & E. M. Markman (Eds.), *Handbook of child psychology: Vol. 3. Cognitive development* (pp. 1–76). New York: Wiley.

Gibson, E. J., & Walk, R. D. (1960). The "visual cliff." *Scientific American, 202,* 80–92.

Gilligan, C. (1982a). New maps of development: New visions of maturity. *American Journal of Orthopsychiatry, 52,* 199–212.

Gilligan, C. (1982b). *In a different voice: Psychological theory and women's development.* Cambridge, MA: Harvard University Press.

Gilligan, C. (1987). Adolescent development reconsidered. *New Directions for Child Development, 37,* 63–92.

Gilligan, C., & Wiggins, G. (1987). The origins of morality in early childhood relationships. In J. Kagan & S. Lamb (Eds.), *The emergence of morality in young children* (pp. 277–307). Chicago: University of Chicago Press.

Gleitman, L. R., & Gleitman, H. (1992). A picture is worth a thousand words, but that's the problem: The role of syntax in vocabulary acquisition. *Current Directions in Psychological Science, 1,* 31–35.

Gleitman, L. R., & Wanner, E. (1988). Current issues in language learning. In M. H. Bornstein & M. E. Lamb (Eds.), *Developmental psychology: An advanced textbook* (2nd ed.) (pp. 297–358). Hillsdale, NJ: Erlbaum.

Glueck, S., & Glueck, E. (1972). *Identification of pre-delinquents: Validation studies and some suggested uses of Glueck Table.* New York: Intercontinental Medical Book Corp.

Gnepp, J., & Chilamkurti, C. (1988). Children's use of personality attributions to predict other people's emotional and behavioral reactions. *Child Development, 50,* 743–754.

Goldberg, S. (1972). Infant care and growth in urban Zambia. *Human Development, 15,* 77–89.

Goldberg, W. A. (1990). Marital quality, parental personality, and spousal agreement about perceptions and expectations for children. *Merrill-Palmer Quarterly, 36,* 531–556.

Golden, M., & Birns, B. (1983). Social class and infant intelligence. In M. Lewis (Ed.), *Origins of intelligence: Infancy and early childhood* (2nd ed.) (pp. 347–398). New York: Plenum Press.

Goldfield, B. A., & Reznick, J. S. (1990). Early lexical acquisition: Rate, content, and the vocabulary spurt. *Journal of Child Language, 17,* 171–183.

Gonsiorek, J. C., & Weinrich, J. D. (1991). The definition and scope of sexual orientation. In J. C. Gonsiorek & J. D. Weinrich (Eds.), *Homosexuality: Research implications for public policy* (pp. 1–12). Newbury Park, CA: Sage.

Good, T. L., & Weinstein, R. S. (1986). Schools make a difference: Evidence, criticisms, and new directions. *American Psychologist, 41,* 1090–1097.

Goodsitt, J. V., Morse, P. A., Ver Hoeve, J. N., & Cowan, N. (1984). Infant speech recognition in multisyllabic contexts. *Child Development, 55,* 903–910.

Gopnik, A., & Astington, J. W. (1988). Children's understanding of representational change and its relation to the understanding of false belief and the appearance-reality distinction. *Child Development, 59,* 26–37.

Gopnik, A., & Meltzoff, A. (1987). The development of categorization in the second year and its relation to other cognitive and linguistic developments. *Child Development, 58,* 1523–1531.

Gopnik, A., & Meltzoff, A. N. (1992). Categorization and naming: Basic-level sorting in eighteen-month-olds and its relation to language. *Child Development, 63,* 1091–1103.

Gottlieb, G. (1976). Conceptions of prenatal development: Behavioral embryology. *Psychological Review, 83,* 215–234.

Gottman, J. M. (1986). The world of coordinated play: Same- and cross-sex friendship in young children. In J. M. Gottman & J. G. Parker (Eds.), *Conversations of friends: Speculations on affective development* (pp. 139–191). Cambridge: Cambridge University Press.

Granrud, C. E. (1986). Binocular vision and spatial perception in 4- and 5-month-old infants. *Journal of Experimental Psychology: Human Perception & Performance, 12,* 36–49.

Gratch, G. (1979). The development of thought and language in infancy. In J. D. Osofsky (Ed.), *Handbook of infant development* (pp. 439–461). New York: Wiley-Interscience.

Greenberg, J., & Kuczaj, S. A., II (1982). Towards a theory of substantive word-meaning acquisition. In S. A. Kuczaj II (Ed.), *Language development: Vol. 1. Syntax and semantics* (pp. 275–312). Hillsdale, NJ: Erlbaum.

Greenberg, M., & Morris, N. (1974). Engrossment: The newborn's impact upon the father. *American Journal of Orthopsychiatry, 44,* 520–531.

Greenberg, M. T., Calderon, R., & Kusche, C. (1984). Early intervention using simultaneous communication with deaf infants: The effect on communication development. *Child Development, 55,* 607–616.

Greenberg, M. T., Siegel, J. M., & Leitch, C. J. (1983). The nature and importance of attachment relationships to parents and peers during adolescence. *Journal of Youth and Adolescence, 12,* 373–386.

Greenberg, M. T., Speltz, M. L., & DeKlyen, M. (1993). The role of attachment in the early development of disruptive behavior problems. *Development and Psychopathology, 5,* 191–213.

Greenberger, E., & Goldberg, W. A. (1989). Work, parenting, and the socialization of children. *Developmental Psychology, 25,* 22–35.

Greenberger, E., & Steinberg, L. (1986). *When teenagers work: The psychological and social costs of adolescent employment.* New York: Basic Books.

Greenough, W. T. (1991). Experience as a component of normal development: Evolutionary considerations. *Developmental Psychology, 27,* 11–27.

Greenough, W. T., Black, J. E., & Wallace, C. S. (1987). Experience and brain development. *Child Development, 58,* 539–559.

Grenier, G. (1985). Shifts to English as usual language by Americans of Spanish mother tongue. In R. O. D. L. Garza, F. D. Bean, C. M. Bonjean, R. Romo, & R. Alvarez (Eds.), *The Mexican American experience: An interdisciplinary anthology* (pp. 347–358). Austin: University of Texas Press.

Grossmann, K., Grossmann, K. E., Spangler, G., Suess, G., & Unzner, L. (1985). Maternal sensitivity and newborns' orientation responses as related to quality of attachment in northern Germany. *Monographs of the Society of Research in Child Development, 50*(1–2, Serial No. 209), 233–256.

Grusec, J. E. (1992). Social learning theory and developmental psychology: The legacies of Robert Sears and Albert Bandura. *Developmental Psychology, 28,* 776–786.

Grusec, J. E., Saas-Kortsaak, P., & Simutis, Z. M. (1978). The role of example and moral exhortation in the training of altruism. *Child Development, 49,* 920–923.

Gullotta, T. P., Adams, G. R., & Montemayor, R. (Eds.). (1993). *Adolescent sexuality.* Newbury Park, CA: Sage.

Gunnar, M. R. (1990). The psychobiology of infant temperament. In J. Colombo & J. Fagen (Eds.), *Individual differences in infancy: Reliability, stability, prediction* (pp. 387–410). Hillsdale, NJ: Erlbaum.

Gunnar, M. R., Larson, M. C., Hertsgaard, L., Harris, M. L., & Brodersen, L. (1992). The stressfulness of separation among nine-month-old infants: Effects of social context variables and infant temperament. *Child Development, 63,* 290–303.

Guralnick, M. J., & Paul-Brown, D. (1984). Communicative adjustments during behavior-request episodes among children at different developmental levels. *Child Development, 55,* 911–919.

Guttentag, R. E., Ornstein, P. A., & Siemens, L. (1987). Children's spontaneous rehearsal: Transitions in strategy acquisition. *Cognitive Development, 2,* 307–326.

Gzesh, S. M., & Surber, C. F. (1985). Visual perspective-taking skills in children. *Child Development, 56,* 1204–1213.

Haan, N. (1981). Adolescents and young adults as producers of their own development. In R. M. Lerner & N. A. Busch-Rossnagel (Eds.), *Individuals as producers of their own development* (pp. 155–182). New York: Academic Press.

Hack, M., Breslau, N., Weissman, B., Aram, D., Klein, N., & Borawski, E. (1991). Effect of very low birth weight and subnormal head size on cognitive abilities at school age. *New England Journal of Medicine, 325,* 231–237.

Haith, M. M. (1980). *Rules that babies look by.* Hillsdale, NJ: Erlbaum.

Haith, M. M. (1990). Progress in the understanding of sensory and perceptual processes in early infancy. *Merrill-Palmer Quarterly, 36,* 1–26.

Hakuta, K. (1986). *Mirror on language: The debate on bilingualism.* New York: Basic Books.

Hakuta, K., & Garcia, E. E. (1989). Bilingualism and education. *American Psychologist, 44,* 374–379.

Hale, S., Fry, A. F., & Jessie, K. A. (1993). Effects of practice on speed of information processing in children and adults: Age sensitivity and age invariance. *Developmental Psychology, 29,* 880–892.

Halpern, D. F. (1992). *Sex differences in cognitive abilities.* Hillsdale, NJ: Erlbaum.

Hanna, E., & Meltzoff, A. N. (1993). Peer imitation by toddlers in laboratory, home, and day-care contexts: Implications for social learning and memory. *Developmental Psychology, 29,* 701–710.

Hanshaw, J. B., Scheiner, A. P., Moxley, A. W., Gaev, L., Abel, V., & Scheiner, B. (1976). School failure and deafness after "silent" congenital cytomegalovirus infection. *New England Journal of Medicine, 295,* 468–470.

Hardy-Brown, K., Plomin, R., & DeFries, J. C. (1981). Genetic and environmental influences on the rate of communicative development in the first year of life. *Developmental Psychology, 17,* 704–717.

Harkness, S., & Super, C. M. (1985). The cultural context of gender segregation in children's peer groups. *Child Development, 56,* 219–224.

Harris, M. (1992). *Language experience and early language development: From input to uptake.* Hove, England: Erlbaum.

Harris, P. L. (1989). *Children and emotion: The development of psychological understanding.* Oxford: Basil Blackwell.

Harris, P. L., Olthof, T., & Terwogt, M. M. (1981). Children's knowledge of emotion. *Journal of Child Psychology and Psychiatry, 22,* 247–261.

Harrison, A. O., Wilson, M. N., Pine, C. J., Chan, S. Q., & Buriel, R. (1990). Family ecologies of ethnic minority children. *Child Development, 61,* 347–362.

Harter, S. (1987). The determinations and mediational role of global self-worth in children. In N. Eisenberg (Ed.), *Contemporary topics in developmental psychology* (pp. 219–242). New York: Wiley-Interscience.

Harter, S. (1990). Processes underlying adolescent self-concept formation. In R. Montemayor, G. R. Adams, & T. P. Gullotta (Eds.), *From childhood to adolescence: A transitional period?* (pp. 205–239). Newbury Park, CA: Sage.

Harter, S., & Pike, R. (1984). The Pictorial Perceived Competence Scale for Young Children. *Child Development, 55,* 1969–1982.

Harter, S., & Whitesell, N. R. (1989). Developmental changes in children's understanding of single, multiple, and blended emotion concepts. In C. Saarni & P. L. Harris (Eds.), *Children's understanding of emotion* (pp. 81–116). Cambridge: Cambridge University Press.

Hartup, W. W. (1989). Social relationships and their developmental significance. *American Psychologist, 44,* 120–126.

Hartup, W. W. (1992). Peer relations in early and middle childhood. In V. B. V. Hasselt & M. Hersen (Eds.), *Handbook of social development: A lifespan perspective* (pp. 257–281). New York: Plenum Press.

Harvard Educational Letter. (1987, March). Adolescent health: Squander now, pay later. p. 4.

Harvard Educational Letter. (1992, July/August). Youth sports: Kids are the losers, pp. 1–3.

Harwood, R. L. (1992). The influence of culturally derived values on Anglo and Puerto Rican mothers' perceptions of attachment behavior. *Child Development, 63,* 822–839.

Haskins, R. (1985). Public school aggression among children with varying day-care experience. *Child Development, 56,* 689–703.

Haskins, R. (1989). Beyond metaphor: The efficacy of early childhood education. *American Psychologist, 44,* 274–282.

Hatano, G., Siegler, R. S., Richards, D. D., Inagaki, K., Stavy, R., & Wax, N. (1993). The development of biological knowledge: A multi-national study. *Cognitive Development, 8,* 47–62.

Hatchett, S. J., & Jackson, J. S. (1993). African American extended kin systems: An assessment. In H. P. McAdoo (Ed.), *Family ethnicity: Strength in diversity* (pp. 90–108). Newbury Park, CA: Sage.

Haviland, J. J., & Malatesta, C. Z. (1981). The development of sex differences in nonverbal signals: Fallacies, facts, and fantasies. In C. Mayo & N. M. Henley (Eds.), *Gender and nonverbal behavior* (pp. 183–208). New York: Springer-Verlag.

Hawley, T. L., & Disney, E. R. (1992). Crack's children: The consequences of maternal cocaine abuse. *Social Policy Report, Society for Research in Child Development, 6*(4), 1–22.

Hawton, K., & Goldacre, M. (1982). Hospital admissions for adverse effects of medicinal agents (mainly self-poisoning) among adolescents in the Oxford region. *British Journal of Psychiatry, 141,* 166–170.

Hayes, C. D. (1987). *Risking the future: Vol. 1. Adolescent sexuality, pregnancy, and childbearing.* Washington, DC: National Academy Press.

Hayes, C. D., Palmer, J. L., & Zaslow, M. J. (1990). *Who cares for America's children?* Washington, DC: National Academy Press.

Heagarty, M. C. (1991). America's lost children: Whose responsibility? *Journal of Pediatrics, 118,* 8–10.

Helms, J. E. (1992). Why is there no study of cultural equivalence in standardized cognitive ability testing? *American Psychologist, 47,* 1083–1101.

Henker, B., & Whalen, C. K. (1989). Hyperactivity and attention deficits. *American Psychologist, 44,* 216–223.

Henneborn, W. J., & Cogan, R. (1975). The effect of husband participation on reported pain and the probability of medication during labour and birth. *Journal of Psychosomatic Research, 19,* 215–222.

Hess, E. H. (1972). "Imprinting" in a natural laboratory. *Scientific American, 227,* 24–31.

Hetherington, E. M. (1989). Coping with family transitions: Winners, losers, and survivors. *Child Development, 60,* 1–14.

Hetherington, E. M. (1991a). The role of individual differences and family relationships in children's coping with divorce and remarriage. In P. A. Cowen & M. Hetherington (Eds.), *Family transitions* (pp. 165–194). Hillsdale, NJ: Erlbaum.

Hetherington, E. M. (1991b). Presidential address: Families, lies, and videotapes. *Journal of Research on Adolescence, 1,* 323–348.

Hetherington, E. M., & Camera, K. A. (1984). Families in transition: The process of dissolution and reconstitution. In R. D. Parke, R. N. Emde, H. P. McAdoo, & G. P. Sackett (Eds.), *Review of child development research: Vol. 7. The family* (pp. 398–440). Chicago: University of Chicago Press.

Hetherington, E. M., & Clingempeel, W. G. (1992). Coping with marital transitions: A family systems perspective. *Monographs of the Society for Research in Child Development, 57*(2–3, Serial No. 227).

Higgins, A. (1991). The just community approach to moral education: Evolution of the idea and recent findings. In W. M. Kurtines & J. L. Gewirtz (Eds.), *Handbook of moral behavior and development: Vol. 3. Application* (pp. 111–141). Hillsdale, NJ: Erlbaum.

Higgins, A., Power, C., & Kohlberg, L. (1984). The relationship of moral atmosphere to judgments of responsibility. In W. M. Kurtines & J. L. Gewirtz (Eds.), *Morality, moral behavior, and moral development* (pp. 74–108). New York: Wiley-Interscience.

Higgins, A. T., & Turnure, J. E. (1984). Distractibility and concentration of attention in children's development. *Child Development, 55,* 1799–1810.

Hill, J. P. (1988). Adapting to menarche: Familial control and conflict. In M. R. Gunnar & W. A. Collins (Eds.), *Development during the transition to adolescence: Minnesota symposia on child psychology* (Vol. 21, pp. 43–78). Hillsdale, NJ: Erlbaum.

Hinde, R. A., & Stevenson-Hinde, J. (1986). Relating childhood relationships to individual characteristics. In W. W. Hartup & Z. Rubin (Eds.), *Relationships and development* (pp. 27–50). Hillsdale, NJ: Erlbaum.

Hinde, R. A., Titmus, G., Easton, D., & Tamplin, A. (1985). Incidence of "friendship" and behavior toward strong associates versus nonassociates in preschoolers. *Child Development, 56,* 234–245.

Hines, M. (1982). Prenatal gonadal hormones and sex differences in human behavior. *Psychological Bulletin, 92,* 56–80.

Hinshaw, S. P., Lahey, B. B., & Hart, E. L. (1993). Issues of taxonomy and comorbidity in the development of conduct disorder. *Development and Psychopathology, 5,* 31–49.

Hirsch, H. V. B., & Tieman, S. B. (1987). Perceptual development and experience-dependent changes in cat visual cortex. In M. H. Bornstein (Ed.), *Sensitive periods in development: Interdisciplinary perspectives* (pp. 39–80). Hillsdale, NJ: Erlbaum.

Hirshberg, L. M., & Svejda, M. (1990). When infants look to their parents: 1. Infants' social referencing of mothers compared to fathers. *Child Development, 61,* 1175–1186.

Hirsh-Pasek, K., Trieman, R., & Schneiderman, M. (1984). Brown and Hanlon revisited: Mothers' sensitivity to ungrammatical forms. *Journal of Child Language, 11,* 81–88.

Hofferth, S. L. (1985). Updating children's life course. *Journal of Marriage and the Family, 47,* 93–115.

Hofferth, S. L. (1987a). Teenage pregnancy and its resolution. In S. L. Hofferth & C. D. Hayes (Eds.), *Risking the future: Adolescent sexuality, pregnancy, and childbearing. Working papers* pp. 78–92). Washington, DC: National Academy Press.

Hofferth, S. L. (1987b). Social and economic consequences of teenage childbearing. In S. L. Hofferth & C. D. Hayes (Eds.), *Risking the future: Adolescent sexuality, pregnancy, and childbearing. Working papers* (pp. 123–144). Washington, DC: National Academy Press.

Hoffman, H. J., & Hillman, L. S. (1992). Epidemiology of the sudden infant death syndrome: Maternal, neonatal, and postneonatal risk factors. *Clinics in Perinatology, 19*(4), 717–737.

Hoffman, L. W. (1984). Work, family, and the socialization of the child. In R. D. Parke (Ed.), *Review of child development research: Vol. 7. The family* (pp. 223–282). Chicago: University of Chicago Press.

Hoffman, L. W. (1989). Effects of maternal employment in the two-parent family. *American Psychologist, 44,* 283–292.

Hoffman, L. W., & Manis, J. D. (1978). Influences of children on marital interaction and parental satisfactions and dissatisfactions. In R. M. Lerner & G. B. Spanier (Eds.), *Child influences on marital and family interaction* (pp. 165–213). New York: Academic Press.

Hoffman, M. L. (1982). Development of prosocial motivation: Empathy and guilt. In N. Eisenberg (Ed.), *The development of prosocial behavior* (pp. 281–314). New York: Academic Press.

Hoffman, M. L. (1988). Moral development. In M. H. Bornstein & M. E. Lamb (Eds.), *Developmental psychology: An advanced textbook* (2nd ed.) (pp. 497–548). Hillsdale, NJ: Erlbaum.

Holden, C. (1987). Genes and behavior: A twin legacy. *Psychology Today, 21*(9), 18–19.

Holloway, S. D., & Hess, R. D. (1985). Mothers' and teachers' attributions about children's mathematics performance. In I. E. Sigel (Ed.), *Parental belief systems: The psychological consequences for children* (pp. 177–200). Hillsdale, NJ: Erlbaum.

Holmbeck, G. N., & Hill, J. P. (1991). Conflictive engagement, positive affect, and menarche in families with seventh-grade girls. *Child Development, 62,* 1030–1048.

Honzik, M. P. (1986). The role of the family in the development of mental abilities: A 50-year study. In N. Datan, A. L. Greene, & H. W. Reese (Eds.), *Life-span developmental psychology: Intergenerational relations* (pp. 185–210). Hillsdale, NJ: Erlbaum.

Hopkins, J., Marcus, M., & Campbell, S. B. (1984). Postpartum depression: A critical review. *Psychological Bulletin, 95,* 498–515.

Horowitz, F. D. (1987). *Exploring developmental theories: Toward a structural/behavioral model of development.* Hillsdale, NJ: Erlbaum.

Horowitz, F. D. (1990). Developmental models of individual differences. In J. Colombo & J. Fagen (Eds.), *Individual differences in infancy: Reliability, stability, prediction* (pp. 3–18). Hillsdale, NJ: Erlbaum.

Howard, J. (1978). The influence of children's developmental dysfunctions on marital quality and family interaction. In R. M. Lerner & G. B. Spanier (Eds.), *Child influences on marital and family interaction: A life-span perspective* (pp. 275–298). New York: Academic Press.

Howat, P. M., & Saxton, A. M. (1988). The incidence of bulimic behavior in a secondary and university school population. *Journal of Youth and Adolescence, 17,* 221–321.

Howes, C. (1983). Patterns of friendship. *Child Development, 54,* 1041–1053.

Howes, C. (1987). Social competence with peers in young children: Developmental sequences. *Developmental Review, 7,* 252–272.

Howes, C. (1990). Can the age of entry into child care and the quality of child care predict adjustment in kindergarten? *Developmental Psychology, 26,* 292–303.

Howes, C., & Matheson, C. C. (1992). Sequences in the development of competent play with peers: Social and pretend play. *Developmental Psychology, 28,* 961–974.

Howes, C., Phillips, D. A., & Whitebook, M. (1992). Thresholds of quality: Implications for the social development of children in center-based child care. *Child Development, 63,* 449–460.

Hubbard, F. O. A., & van IJzendoorn, M. H. (1987). Maternal unresponsiveness and infant crying: A critical replication of the Bell and Ainsworth study. In L. W. C. Tavecchio & M. H. van IJzendoorn (Eds.), *Attachment in social networks* (pp. 339–378). Amsterdam: Elsevier Science Publishers B. V. (North-Holland).

Hubel, D. H., & Weisel, T. N. (1963). Receptive fields of cells in striate cortex of very young, visually inexperienced kittens. *Journal of Neurophysiology, 26,* 994–1002.

Hudley, C., & Graham, S. (1993). An attributional intervention to reduce peer-directed aggression among African-American boys. *Child Development, 64,* 124–138.

Huesmann, L. R., Lagerspetz, K., & Eron, L. D. (1984). Intervening variables in the television violence-aggression relation: Evidence from two countries. *Developmental Psychology, 20,* 746–775.

Humphreys, L. G., Davey, T. C., & Park, R. K. (1985). Longitudinal correlation analysis of standing height and intelligence. *Child Development, 56,* 1465–1478.

Hunter, A. G., & Ensminger, M. E. (1992). Diversity and fluidity in children's living arrangements: Family transitions in an urban Afro-American community. *Journal of Marriage and the Family, 54,* 418–426.

Hunter, J. E., & Hunter, R. F. (1984). Validity and utility of alternative predictors of job performance. *Psychological Bulletin, 86,* 721–735.

Huntington, L., Hans, S. L., & Zeskind, P. S. (1990). The relations among cry characteristics, demographic variables, and developmental test scores in infants prenatally exposed to methadone. *Infant Behavior and Development, 13,* 533–538.

Hurwitz, E., Gunn, W. J., Pinsky, P. F., & Schonberger, L. B. (1991). Risk of respiratory illness associated with day-care attendance: A nationwide study. *Pediatrics, 87,* 62–69.

Huston, A. C. (1983). Sex-typing. In E. M. Hetherington (Ed.), *Handbook of child psychology: Vol. 4. Socialization, personality, and social development* (pp. 387–463). New York: Wiley.

Huston, A. C., Greer, D., Wright, J. C., Welch, R., & Ross, R. (1984). Children's comprehension of televised formal features with masculine and feminine connotations. *Developmental Psychology, 20,* 707–716.

Huston, A. C., Wright, J. C., Rice, M. L., Kerkman, D., & St. Peters, M. (1990). Development of television viewing patterns in early childhood: A longitudinal investigation. *Developmental Psychology, 26,* 409–420.

Hutt, S. J., Lenard, H. G., & Prechtl, H. F. R. (1969). Psychophysiological studies in newborn infants. In L. P. Lipsitt & H. W. Reese (Eds.), *Advances in child development and behavior* (Vol. 4, pp. 128–173). New York: Academic Press.

Hutto, C., Parks, W. P., Lai, S., Mastrucci, M. T., Mitchell, C., Munoz, J., Trapido, E., Master, I. M., & Scott, G. B. (1991). A hospital-based prospective study of perinatal infection with human immunodeficiency virus type 1. *Journal of Pediatrics, 118,* 347–353.

Hymel, S., Rubin, K. H., Rowden, L., & LeMare, L. (1990). Children's peer relationships: Longitudinal prediction of internalizing and externalizing problems from middle to late childhood. *Child Development, 61,* 2004–2021.

Ingram, D. (1981). Early patterns of grammatical development. In R. E. Stark (Ed.), *Language behavior in infancy and early childhood* (pp. 327–358). New York: Elsevier/North-Holland.

Inhelder, B., & Piaget, J. (1958). *The growth of logical thinking from childhood to adolescence.* New York: Basic Books.

Inoff-Germain, G., Arnold, G. S., Nottelmann, E. D., Susman, E. J., Cutler, G. B., Jr., & Chrousos, G. P. (1988). Relations between hormone levels and observational measures of aggressive behavior of young adolescents in family interactions. *Developmental Psychology, 24,* 129–139.

Isabella, R. A. (1993). Origins of attachment: Maternal interactive behavior across the first year. *Child Development, 64,* 605–621.

Isabella, R. A., Belsky, J., & von Eye, A. (1989). Origins of infant-mother attachment: An examination of interactional synchrony during the infant's first year. *Developmental Psychology, 25,* 12–21.

Istvan, J. (1986). Stress, anxiety, and birth outcomes. A critical review of the evidence. *Psychological Bulletin, 100,* 331–348.

Jacklin, C. N. (1989). Female and male: Issues of gender. *American Psychologist, 44,* 127–133.

Jackson, N. E., & Butterfield, E. C. (1986). A conception of giftedness designed to promote research. In R. J. Sternberg & J. E. Davidson (Eds.), *Conceptions of giftedness* (pp. 151–181). Cambridge: Cambridge University Press.

Janos, P. M., & Robinson, N. M. (1985). Psychosocial development in intellectually gifted children. In F. D. Horowitz & M. O'Brien (Eds.), *The gifted and talented: Developmental perspectives* (pp. 149–196). Washington, DC: American Psychological Association.

Jensen, A. R. (1980). *Bias in mental testing.* New York: Free Press.

Johnson, C., Lewis, C., Love, S., Lewis, L., & Stuckey, M. (1984). Incidence and correlates of bulimic behavior in a female high school population. *Journal of Youth and Adolescence, 13,* 15–26.

Johnston, J. R. (1985). Cognitive prerequisites: The evidence from children learning English. In D. I. Slobin (Ed.), *The crosslinguistic study of language acquisition: Vol. 2. Theoretical issues* (pp. 961–1004). Hillsdale, NJ: Erlbaum.

Jones, E. F., Forrest, J. D., Goldman, N., Henshaw, S. K., Lincoln, R., Rosoff, J. L., Westoff, C. F., & Wulf, D. (1986). *Teenage pregnancy in industrialized countries.* New Haven, CT: Yale University Press.

Jones, K. L., Smith, D. W., Ulleland, C. N., & Streissguth, A. (1973). Pattern of malformation in offspring of chronic alcoholic mothers. *The Lancet, 1,* 1267–1271.

Jordan, N. C., Huttenlocher, J., & Levine, S. C. (1992). Differential calculation abilities in young children from middle- and low-income families. *Developmental Psychology, 28,* 644–653.

Jorgensen, S. R. (1993). Adolescent pregnancy and parenting. In T. P. Gullotta, G. R. Adams, & R. Montemayor (Eds.), *Adolescent sexuality* (pp. 103–140). Newbury Park, CA: Sage.

Jung, C. G. (1916). *Analytical psychology.* New York: Moffat, Yard.

Jung, C. G. (1939). *The integration of personality.* New York: Holt, Rinehart and Winston.

Jusczyk, P. W., Cutler, A., & Redanz, N. J. (1993). Infants' preference for the predominant stress patterns of English words. *Child Development, 64,* 675–687.

Kagan, J. (1971). *Change and continuity in infancy.* New York: Wiley.

Kagan, J., Kearsley, R., & Zelazo, P. (1978). *Infancy: Its place in human development.* Cambridge, MA: Harvard University Press.

Kagan, J., Reznick, J. S., & Snidman, N. (1990). The temperamental qualities of inhibition and lack of inhibition. In M. Lewis & S. M. Miller (Eds.), *Handbook of developmental psychopathology* (pp. 219–226). New York: Plenum Press.

Kagan, J., Snidman, N., & Arcus, D. (1993). On the temperamental categories of inhibited and uninhibited children. In K. H. Rubin & J. B. Asendorpf (Eds.), *Social withdrawal, inhibition, and shyness in childhood* (pp. 19–28). Hillsdale, NJ: Erlbaum.

Kail, R. (1991a). Developmental change in speed of processing during childhood and adolescence. *Psychological Bulletin, 109,* 490–501.

Kail, R. (1991b). Processing time declines exponentially during childhood and adolescence. *Developmental Psychology, 27,* 259–266.

Kail, R., & Park, Y. (1992). Global developmental change in processing time. *Merrill-Palmer Quarterly, 38,* 525–541.

Kandel, E. R. (1985). Nerve cells and behavior. In E. R. Kandel & J. H. Schwartz (Eds.), *Principles of neural science* (2nd ed.) (pp. 13–24). New York: Elsevier.

Karmiloff-Smith, A. (1993, Spring). NeoPiagetians: A theoretical misnomer? *Society for Research in Child Development Newsletter, 3,* 10–11.

Kataria, S., Frutiger, A. D., Lanford, B., & Swanson, M. S. (1988). Anterior fontanel closure in healthy term infants. *Infant Behavior and Development, 11,* 229–233.

Kaye, K. (1982). *The mental and social life of babies: How parents create persons.* Chicago: University of Chicago Press.

Kazdin, A. E. (1993). Adolescent mental health. Prevention and treatment. *American Psychologist, 48,* 127–141.

Keating, D. P. (1980). Thinking processes in adolescence. In J. Adelson (Ed.), *Handbook of adolescent psychology* (pp. 211–246). New York: Wiley.

Keating, D. P., List, J. A., & Merriman, W. E. (1985). Cognitive processing and cognitive ability: Multivariate validity investigation. *Intelligence, 9,* 149–170.

Keefe, S. E., & Padilla, A. M. (1987). *Chicano ethnicity.* Albuquerque: University of New Mexico Press.

Keeney, T. J., Cannizzo, S. R., & Flavell, J. H. (1967). Spontaneous and induced verbal rehearsal in a recall task. *Child Development, 38,* 935–966.

Kellam, S. G., Ensminger, M. E., & Turner, R. J. (1977). Family structure and the mental health of children: Concurrent and longitudinal community-wide studies. *Archives of General Psychiatry, 34,* 1012–1022.

Kelley, M. L., Sanches-Hucles, J., & Walker, R. R. (1993). Correlates of disciplinary practices in working- to middle-class African-American mothers. *Merrill-Palmer Quarterly, 39,* 252–264.

Kempe, A., Wise, P. H., Barkan, S. E., Sappenfield, W. M., Sachs, B., Gortmaker, S. L., Sobol, A. M., First, L. R., Pursley, D., Reinhart, H., Kotelchuck, M., Cole, F. S., Gunter, N., & Stockbauer, J. W. (1992). Clinical determinants of the racial disparity in very low birth weight. *New England Journal of Medicine, 327,* 969–973.

Kendall-Tackett, K. A., Williams, L. M., & Finkelhor, D. (1993). Impact of sexual abuse on children: A review and synthesis of recent empirical studies. *Psychological Bulletin, 113,* 164–180.

Kessner, D. M. (1973). *Infant death: An analysis by maternal risk and health care.* Washington, DC: National Academy of Sciences.

Kestenbaum, R., Farber, E. A., & Sroufe, L. A. (1989). Individual differences in empathy among preschoolers: Relation to attachment history. *New Directions for Child Development, 44,* 51–64.

Kilpatrick, S. J., & Laros, R. K. (1989). Characteristics of normal labor. *Obstetrics and Gynecology, 74,* 85–87.

Kitchen, W. H., Doyle, L. W., Ford, G. W., Murton, L. J., Keith, C. G., Rickards, A. L., Kelly, E., & Callanan, C. (1991). Changing two-year outcome of infants weighing 500 to 999 grams at birth: A hospital study. *Journal of Pediatrics, 118,* 938–943.

Klaus, H. M., & Kennell, J. H. (1976). *Maternal-infant bonding.* St. Louis, MO: Mosby.

Kline, M., Tschann, J. M., Johnston, J. R., & Wallerstein, J. S. (1989). Children's adjustment in joint and sole physical custody families. *Developmental Psychology, 25,* 430–438.

Knight, G. P., Cota, M. K., & Bernal, M. E. (1993). The socialization of cooperative, competitive, and individualistic preferences among Mexican American children: The mediating role of ethnic identity. *Hispanic Journal of Behavioral Sciences, 15,* 291–309.

Kohlberg, L. (1964). Development of moral character and moral ideology. In M. L. Hoffman & L. W. Hoffman (Eds.), *Review of child development research* (Vol. 1, pp. 283–332). New York: Russell Sage Foundation.

Kohlberg, L. (1966). A cognitive-developmental analysis of children's sex-role concepts and attitudes. In E. E. Maccoby (Ed.), *The development of sex differences* (pp. 82–172). Stanford, CA: Stanford University Press.

Kohlberg, L. (1975). The cognitive-developmental approach to moral education. *Phi Delta Kappan,* pp. 670–677.

Kohlberg, L. (1976). Moral stages and moralization: The cognitive-developmental approach. In T. Lickona (Ed.), *Moral development and behavior: Theory, research, and social issues* (pp. 31–53). New York: Holt.

Kohlberg, L. (1978). Revisions in the theory and practice of moral development. *New Directions for Child Development, 2,* 83–88.

Kohlberg, L. (1980). *The meaning and measurement of moral development.* Worcester, MA: Clark University Press.

Kohlberg, L. (1981). *Essays on moral development: Vol. I. The philosophy of moral development.* New York: Harper & Row.

Kohlberg, L. (1984). *Essays on moral development: Vol. II. The psychology of moral development.* San Francisco: Harper & Row.

Kohlberg, L., & Candee, D. (1984). The relationship of moral judgment to moral action. In W. M. Kurtines & J. L. Gewirtz (Eds.), *Morality, moral behavior, and moral development* (pp. 52–73). New York: Wiley.

Kohlberg, L., & Elfenbein, D. (1975). The development of moral judgments concerning capital punishment. *American Journal of Orthopsychiatry, 54,* 614–640.

Kohlberg, L., & Higgins, A. (1987). School democracy and social interaction. In W. M. Kurtines & J. L. Gewirtz (Eds.), *Moral development through social interaction* (pp. 102–130). New York: Wiley-Interscience.

Kohlberg, L., Levine, C., & Hewer, A. (1983). *Moral stages: A current formulation and a response to critics. Contributions to human development, 10.* Basel: S. Karger.

Kohlberg, L., & Ullian, D. Z. (1974). Stages in the development of psychosexual concepts and attitudes. In R. C. Friedman, R. M. Richart, & R. L. Vande Wiele (Eds.), *Sex differences in behavior* (pp. 209–222). New York: Wiley.

Kohn, M. L. (1980). Job complexity and adult personality. In N. J. Smelser & E. H. Erikson (Eds.), *Themes of work and love in adulthood* (pp. 193–212). Cambridge, MA: Harvard University Press.

Kohn, M. L., & Schooler, C. (1983). *Work and personality: An inquiry into the impact of social stratification.* Norwood, NJ: Ablex.

Kolata, G. (1992, April 26). A parents' guide to kids' sports. *The New York Times Magazine,* pp. 12–15, 40, 44, 46.

Kopp, C. B. (1983). Risk factors in development. In M. M. Haith & J. J. Campos (Eds.), *Handbook of child psychology: Vol. 2. Infancy and developmental psychobiology* (pp. 1081–1188). New York: Wiley.

Kopp, C. B. (1990). Risks in infancy: appraising the research. *Merrill -Palmer Quarterly, 36,* 117–140.

Kopp, C. B., & Kaler, S. R. (1989). Risk in infancy: Origins and implications. *American Psychologist, 44,* 224–230.

Korn, S. J. (1984). Continuities and discontinuities in difficult/easy temperament: Infancy to young adulthood. *Merrill-Palmer Quarterly, 30,* 189–199.

Korner, A. F., Hutchinson, C. A., Koperski, J. A., Kraemer, H. C., & Schneider, P. A. (1981). Stability of individual differences of neonatal motor and crying patterns. *Child Development, 52,* 83–90.

Kotulak, R. (1990, September 28). *Chicago Tribune,* pp. 1, 16.

Kuczaj, S. A., II (1977). The acquisition of regular and irregular past tense forms. *Journal of Verbal Learning and Verbal Behavior, 49,* 319–326.

Kuczaj, S. A., II (1978). Children's judgments of grammatical and ungrammatical irregular past tense verbs. *Child Development, 49,* 319–326.

Kuhl, P. K., & Meltzoff, A. N. (1984). The intermodal representation of speech in infants. *Infant Behavior and Development, 7,* 361–381.

Kuhn, D. (1992). Cognitive development. In M. H. Bornstein & M. E. Lamb (Eds.), *Developmental psychology: An advanced textbook* (3rd ed.) (pp. 211–272). Hillsdale, NJ: Erlbaum.

Kuhn, D., Nash, S. C., & Brucken, L. (1978). Sex role concepts of two- and three-year-olds. *Child Development, 49,* 445–451.

Kupersmidt, J. B., & Coie, J. D. (1990). Preadolescent peer status, aggression, and school adjustment as predictors of externalizing problems in adolescence. *Child Development, 61,* 1350–1362.

Kurdek, L. A., & Krile, D. (1982). A developmental analysis of the relation between peer acceptance and both interpersonal understanding and perceived social self-competence. *Child Development, 53,* 1485–1491.

Kurtines, W. M., & Gewirtz, J. L. (Eds.). (1991). *Handbook of moral behavior and development* (Vol. 1, *Theory;* Vol. 2, *Research;* Vol. 3, *Application*). Hillsdale, NJ: Erlbaum.

La Freniere, P., Strayer, F. F., & Gauthier, R. (1984). The emergence of same-sex affiliative preferences among preschool peers: A developmental/ethological perspective. *Child Development, 55,* 1958–1965.

Lamb, M. E. (1981). The development of father-infant relationships. In M. E. Lamb (Ed.), *The role of the father in child development* (2nd ed.) (pp. 459–488). New York: Wiley.

Lamb, M. E., Frodi, A. M., Hwang, C., Frodi, M., & Steinberg, J. (1982). Mother- and father-infant interaction involving play and holding in traditional and nontraditional Swedish families. *Developmental Psychology, 18,* 215–221.

Lamb, M. E., Frodi, M., Hwang, C., & Frodi, A. M. (1983). Effects of paternal involvement on infant preferences for mothers and fathers. *Child Development, 54,* 450–458.

Lamb, M. E., Sternberg, K. J., & Prodromidis, M. (1992). Nonmaternal care and the security of infant-mother attachment: A reanalysis of the data. *Infant Behavior and Development, 15,* 71–83.

Lambert, C. (1993, March–April). The demand side of the health care crisis. *Harvard Magazine,* pp. 30–33.

Lamborn, S. D., Mounts, N. S., Steinberg, L., & Dornbusch, S. M. (1991). Patterns of competence and adjustment among adolescents from authoritative, authoritarian, indulgent, and neglectful families. *Child Development, 62,* 1049–1065.

Lamke, L. K. (1982a). Adjustment and sex-role orientation. *Journal of Youth and Adolescence, 11,* 247–259.

Lamke, L. K. (1982b). The impact of sex-role orientation on self-esteem in early adolescence. *Child Development, 53,* 1530–1535.

Langlois, J. H., Ritter, J. M., Roggman, L. A., & Vaughn, L. S. (1991). Facial diversity and infant preferences for attractive faces. *Developmental Psychology, 27,* 79–84.

Langlois, J. H., Roggman, L. A., Casey, R. J., Ritter, J. M., Rieser-Danner, L. A., & Jenkins, V. Y. (1987). Infant preferences for attractive faces: Rudiments of a stereotype? *Developmental Psychology, 23,* 263–369.

Langlois, J. H., Roggman, L. A., & Rieser-Danner, L. A. (1990). Infants' differential social responses to attractive and unattractive faces. *Developmental Psychology, 26,* 153–159.

Leach, P. (1983). *Babyhood* (2nd ed., rev.). New York: Knopf.

Leadbeater, B. J., & Dionne, J. (1981). The adolescent's use of formal operational thinking in solving problems related to identity resolution. *Adolescence, 16,* 111–121.

Leaper, C. (1991). Influence and involvement in children's discourse: Age, gender, and partner effects. *Child Development, 62,* 797–811.

Lederberg, A. R., & Mobley, C. E. (1990). The effect of hearing impairment on the quality of attachment and mother-toddler interaction. *Child Development, 61,* 1596–1604.

Lee, C. C. (1985). Successful rural black adolescents: A psychological profile. *Adolescence, 20,* 129–142.

Leon, G. R., Perry, C. L., Mangelsdorf, C., & Tell, G. (1989). Adolescent nutritional and psychological patterns and risk for the development of an eating disorder. *Journal of Youth and Adolescence, 18,* 273–282.

Lerner, J. V., & Galambos, N. L. (1986). Child development and family change: The influences of maternal employment in infants and toddlers. In L. P. Lipsitt & C. Rovee-Collier (Eds.), *Advances in infancy research* (Vol. 4, pp. 40–86). Norwood, NJ: Ablex.

Lerner, R. M. (1985). Adolescent maturational changes and psychosocial development: A dynamic interactional perspective. *Journal of Youth and Adolescence, 14,* 355–372.

Lerner, R. M. (1987). A life-span perspective for early adolescence. In R. M. Lerner & T. T. Foch (Eds.), *Biological-psychosocial interactions in early adolescence* (pp. 9–34). Hillsdale, NJ: Erlbaum.

Lester, B. M. (1987). Prediction of developmental outcome from acoustic cry analysis in term and preterm infants. *Pediatrics, 80,* 529–534.

Lester, B. M., & Dreher, M. (1989). Effects of marijuana use during pregnancy on newborn cry. *Child Development, 60,* 765–771.

Levano, K. J., Cunningham, G., Nelson, S., Roark, M., Williams, M. L., Guzick, D., Dowling, S., Rosenfeld, C. R., & Buckley, A. (1986). A prospective comparison of selective and universal electronic fetal monitoring in 34,995 pregnancies. *New England Journal of Medicine, 315,* 615–619.

Levitt, M. J., Guacci-Franco, N., & Levitt, J. L. (1993). Convoys of social support in childhood and early adolescence: Structure and function. *Developmental Psychology, 29,* 811–818.

Levy, G. D., & Fivush, R. (1993). Scripts and gender: A new approach for examining gender-role development. *Developmental Review, 13,* 126–146.

Lewis, C. C. (1981). How adolescents approach decisions: Changes over grades seven to twelve and policy implications. *Child Development, 52,* 538–544.

Lewis, M. (1990). Social knowledge and social development. *Merrill-Palmer Quarterly, 36,* 93–116.

Lewis, M. (1991). Ways of knowing: Objective self-awareness of consciousness. *Developmental Review, 11,* 231–243.

Lewis, M., Allesandri, S. M., & Sullivan, M. W. (1992). Differences in shame and pride as a function of children's gender and task difficulty. *Child Development, 63,* 630–638.

Lewis, M., & Brooks, J. (1978). Self-knowledge and emotional development. In M. Lewis & L. A. Rosenblum (Eds.), *The development of affect* (pp. 205–226). New York: Plenum Press.

Lewis, M., & Brooks-Gunn, J. (1979). *Social cognition and the acquisition of self*. New York: Plenum Press.

Lewis, M., & Miller, S. M. (Ed.). (1990). *Handbook of developmental psychopathology*. New York: Plenum Press.

Lewis, M. D. (1993). Early socioemotional predictors of cognitive competence at 4 years. *Developmental Psychology, 29*, 1036–1045.

Liben, L. S. (1978). The development of deaf children: An overview of issues. In L. S. Liben (Ed.), *Deaf children: Developmental perspectives* (pp. 3–20). New York: Academic Press.

Lickona, T. (1978). Moral development and moral education. In J. M. Gallagher & J. J. A. Easley (Eds.), *Knowledge and development* (Vol. 2, pp. 21–74). New York: Plenum Press.

Lickona, T. (1983). *Raising good children*. Toronto: Bantam Books.

Lillard, A. S., & Flavell, J. H. (1992). Young children's understanding of different mental states. *Developmental Psychology, 28*, 626–634.

Linney, J. A., & Seidman, E. (1989). The future of schooling. *American Psychologist, 44*, 336–340.

Lipsitt, L. P. (1982). Infant learning. In T. M. Field, A. Houston, H. C. Quay, L. Troll, & G. E. Finley (Eds.), *Review of human development* (pp. 62–78). New York: Wiley.

Livesley, W. J., & Bromley, D. B. (1973). *Person perception in childhood and adolescence*. London: Wiley.

Lockman, J. J., & Thelen, E. (1993). Developmental biodynamics: Brain, body, behavior connections. *Child Development, 64*, 953–959.

Loehlin, J. C. (1992). *Genes and environment in personality development*. Newbury Park, CA: Sage.

Loehlin, J. C., Horn, J. M., & Willerman, L. (1989). Modeling IQ change: Evidence from the Texas Adoption Project. *Child Development, 60*, 993–1004.

Long, J. V. F., & Vaillant, G. E. (1984). Natural history of male psychological health: Escape from the underclass. *The American Journal of Psychiatry, 141*, 341–346.

Longo, D. C., & Bond, L. (1984). Families of the handicapped child: Research and practice. *Family Relations, 33*, 57–65.

Lore, R. K., & Schultz, L. A. (1993). Control of human aggression: A comparative perspective. *American Psychologist, 48*, 16–25.

Lubinski, D., & Benbow, C. P. (1992). Gender differences in abilities and preferences among the gifted: Implications for the math-science pipeline. *Current Directions in Psychological Science, 1*, 61–66.

Luke, B., & Murtaugh, M. (1993). The racial disparity in very low birth weight. *New England Journal of Medicine, 328*, 285–286.

Luster, T., Boger, R., & Hannan, K. (1993). Infant affect and home environment. *Journal of Marriage and the Family, 55*, 651–661.

Luster, T., Rhoades, K., & Haas, B. (1989). The relation between parental values and parenting behavior: A test of the Kohn hypothesis. *Journal of Marriage and the Family, 51*, 139–147.

Luthar, S. S., & Zigler, E. (1992). Intelligence and social competence among high-risk adolescents. *Development and Psychopathology, 4*, 287–299.

Lykken, D. T., McGue, M., Tellegen, A., & Bouchard, T. J., Jr. (1992). Emergenesis: Genetic traits that may not run in families. *American Psychologist, 47*, 1565–1577.

Lyons, N. P. (1983). Two perspectives: On self, relationships, and morality. *Harvard Educational Review, 53*, 125–145.

Lyons-Ruth, K., Alpern, L., & Repacholi, B. (1993). Disorganized infant attachment classification and maternal psychosocial problems as predictors of hostile-aggressive behavior in the preschool classroom. *Child Development, 64*, 572–585.

Lytton, H., & Romney, D. M. (1991). Parents' differential socialization of boys and girls: A meta-analysis. *Psychological Bulletin, 109*, 267–296.

Maccoby, E. E. (1980). *Social development: Psychological growth and the parent-child relationships*. New York: Harcourt Brace Jovanovich.

Maccoby, E. E. (1984). Middle childhood in the context of the family. In W. A. Collins (Ed.), *Development during middle childhood: The years from six to twelve* (pp. 184–239). Washington, DC: National Academy Press.

Maccoby, E. E. (1988). Gender as a social category. *Developmental Psychology, 24*, 755–765.

Maccoby, E. E. (1990). Gender and relationships. A developmental account. *American Psychologist, 45*, 513–520.

Maccoby, E. E., Doering, C. H., Jacklin, C. N., & Kraemer, H. (1979). Concentrations of sex hormones in umbilical-cord blood: Their relation to sex and birth order of infants. *Child Development, 50*, 632–642.

Maccoby, E. E., & Jacklin, C. N. (1974). *The psychology of sex differences*. Stanford, CA: Stanford University Press.

Maccoby, E. E., & Jacklin, C. N. (1987). Gender segregation in childhood. In H. W. Reese (Ed.), *Advances in child development and behavior* (Vol. 20, pp. 239–288). Orlando, FL: Academic Press.

Maccoby, E. E., & Martin, J. A. (1983). Socialization in the context of the family: Parent-child interaction. In E. M. Hetherington (Ed.), *Handbook of child psychology: Vol. 4. Socialization, personality, and social development* (pp. 1–102). New York: Wiley.

Maccoby, E. E., & Mnookin, R. H. (1992). *Dividing the child: Social and legal dilemmas of custody*. Cambridge, MA: Harvard University Press.

MacDonald, K. (1992). Warmth as a developmental construct: An evolutionary analysis. *Child Development, 63*, 753–773.

Macfarlane, A. (1977). *The psychology of childbirth*. Cambridge, MA: Harvard University Press.

MacGowan, R. J., MacGowan, C. A., Serdula, M. K., Lane, J. M., Joesoef, R. M., & Cook, F. H. (1991). Breast-feeding among women attending women, infants, and children clinics in Georgia, 1987. *Pediatrics, 87*, 361–366.

Maclean, M., Bryant, P., & Bradley, L. (1987). Rhymes, nursery rhymes, and reading in early childhood. *Merrill-Palmer Quarterly, 33*, 255–281.

Madsen, W. (1969). Mexican Americans and Anglo Americans: A comparative study of mental health in Texas. In S. C. Plog & R. B. Edgerton (Eds.), *Changing perspectives in mental illness* (pp. 217–247). New York: Holt, Rinehart and Winston.

Magnusson, D., Stattin, H., & Allen, V. L. (1986). Differential maturation among girls and its relation to social adjustment: A longitudinal perspective. In P. B. Baltes, D. L. Featherman, & R. M. Lerner (Eds.), *Life-span development and behavior* (Vol. 7, pp. 136–173). Hillsdale, NJ: Erlbaum.

Main, M., & Cassidy, J. (1988). Categories of response to reunion with the parent at age 6: Predictable from infant attachment classifications and stable over a 1-month period. *Developmental Psychology, 24*, 415–426.

Main, M., & Hesse, E. (1990). Parents' unresolved traumatic experiences are related to infant disorganized attachment status: Is frightened and/or frightening parental behavior the linking mechanism? In M. T. Greenberg, D. Cicchetti, & E. M. Cummings (Eds.), *Attachment in the preschool years: Theory, research, and intervention* (pp. 161–182). Chicago: University of Chicago Press.

Main, M., Kaplan, N., & Cassidy, J. (1985). Security in infancy, childhood, and adulthood: A move to the level of representation. *Monographs of the Society for Research in Child Development, 50* (Serial No. 209), 66–104.

Main, M., & Solomon, J. (1990). Procedures for identifying infants as disorganized/disoriented during the Ainsworth Strange Situation. In M. T. Greenberg, D. Cicchetti, & E. M. Cummings (Eds.), *Attachment in the preschool years: Theory, research, and intervention* (pp. 121–160). Chicago: University of Chicago Press.

Malina, R. M. (1982). Motor development in the early years. In S. G. Moore & C. R. Cooper (Eds.), *The young child: Reviews of research* (Vol. 3, pp. 211–232). Washington, DC: National Association for the Education of Young Children.

Malina, R. M. (1990). Physical growth and performance during the transition years. In R. Montemayor, G. R. Adams, & T. P. Gullotta (Eds.), *From childhood to adolescence: A transitional period?* (pp. 41–62). Newbury Park, CA: Sage.

Malinosky-Rummell, R., & Hansen, D. J. (1993). Long-term consequences of childhood physical abuse. *Psychological Bulletin, 114*, 68–79.

Mangelsdorf, S. C. (1992). Developmental changes in infant-stranger interaction. *Infant Behavior and Development, 15*, 191–208.

Maratsos, M. (1983). Some current issues in the study of the acquisition of grammar. In J. H. Flavell & E. M. Markman (Eds.), *Handbook of child psychology: Vol. 3. Cognitive development* (pp. 707–786). New York: Wiley.

Marcia, J. E. (1966). Development and validation of ego identity status. *Journal of Personality and Social Psychology, 3*, 551–558.

Marcia, J. E. (1980). Identity in adolescence. In J. Adelson (Ed.), *Handbook of adolescent psychology* (pp. 159–187). New York: Wiley.

Marcus, G. F., Pinker, S., Ullman, M., Hollander, M., Rosen, T. J., & Fei, X. (1992). Overregularization in language acquisition. *Monographs of the Society for Research in Child Development, 57*(4, Serial No. 228).

Marcus, R. F. (1986). Naturalistic observation of cooperation, helping, and sharing and their association with empathy and affect. In C. Zahn-Waxler, E. M. Cummings, & R. Iannotti (Eds.), *Altruism and aggression: Biological and social origins* (pp. 256–279). Cambridge: Cambridge University Press.

Marean, G. C., Werner, L. A., & Kuhl, P. K. (1992). Vowel categorization by very young infants. *Developmental Psychology, 28*, 396–405.

Markestad, I. (1992). Sleeping position and crib death in Norway. *Tidsskrift for den norske laegeforening, 112*, 1427–1429.

Markman, E. M. (1989). *Categorization and naming in children: Problems of induction*. Cambridge, MA: MIT Press, Bradford Books.

Markman, E. M., & Hutchinson, J. (1984). Children's sensitivity to constraints on word meaning: Taxonomic vs. thematic relations. *Cognitive Psychology, 16*, 1–27.

Martin, C. L. (1991). The role of cognition in understanding gender effects. In H. W. Reese (Ed.), *Advances in child development and behavior* (Vol. 23, pp. 113–150). San Diego, CA: Academic Press.

Martin, C. L. (1993). New directions for investigating children's gender knowledge. *Developmental Review, 13*, 184–204.

Martin, C. L., & Halverson, C. F., Jr. (1981). A schematic processing model of sex typing and stereotyping in children. *Child Development, 52*, 1119–1134.

Martin, C. L., & Halverson, C. F., Jr. (1983). The effects of sex-typing schemas on young children's memory. *Child Development, 54*, 563–574.

Martin, C. L., & Little, J. K. (1990). The relation of gender understanding to children's sex-typed preferences and gender stereotypes. *Child Development, 61*, 1427–1439.

Martin, C. L., Wood, C. H., & Little, J. K. (1990). The development of gender stereotype components. *Child Development, 61,* 1891–1904.

Martin, E. P., & Martin, J. M. (1978). *The black extended family.* Chicago: University of Chicago Press.

Martorano, S. C. (1977). A developmental analysis of performance on Piaget's formal operations tasks. *Developmental Psychology, 13,* 666–672.

Marvin, R. S., & Greenberg, M. T. (1982). Preschoolers' changing conceptions of their mothers: A social-cognitive study of mother-child attachment. *New Directions for Child Development, 18,* 47–60.

Masataka, N. (1992). Motherese in a signed language. *Infant Behavior and Development, 15,* 453–460.

Massad, C. M. (1981). Sex role identity and adjustment during adolescence. *Child Development, 52,* 1290–1298.

Masten, A. S. (1989). Resilience in development: Implications of the study of successful adaptation for developmental psychopathology. In D. Cicchetti (Ed.), *The emergence of a discipline: Rochester symposium on developmental psychopathology* (Vol. 1, pp. 261–294). Hillsdale, NJ: Erlbaum.

Masten, A. S., Best, K. M., & Garmezy, N. (1990). Resilience and development: Contributions from the study of children who overcome adversity. *Development and Psychopathology, 2,* 425–444.

Matarazzo, J. D. (1992). Biological and physiological correlates of intelligence. *Intelligence, 16,* 257–258.

Mather, P. L., & Black, K. N. (1984). Heredity and environmental influences on preschool twins' language skills. *Developmental Psychology, 20,* 303–308.

Mathew, A., & Cook, M. (1990). The control of reaching movements by young infants. *Child Development, 61,* 1238–1257.

Maurer, D., & Maurer, C. (1988). *The world of the newborn.* New York: Basic Books.

McAdoo, H. P. (Ed.). (1993). *Family ethnicity: Strength in diversity.* Newbury Park, CA: Sage.

McBride, G. (1991). Nontraditional inheritance: 2. The clinical implications. *Mosaic, 22*(Fall), 12–25.

McCall, R. B. (1979). The development of intellectual functioning in infancy and the prediction of later IQ. In J. D. Osofsky (Ed.), *Handbook of infant development* (pp. 707–741). New York: Wiley-Interscience.

McCall, R. B., Appelbaum, M. I., & Hogarty, P. S. (1973). Developmental changes in mental performance. *Monographs of the Society for Research in Child Development, 38* (Serial No. 150).

McCall, R. B., & Carriger, M. S. (1993). A meta-analysis of infant habituation and recognition memory performance as predictors of later IQ. *Child Development, 64,* 57–79.

McCall, R. B., Evahn, C., & Kratzer, L. (1992). *High school underachievers.* Newbury Park, CA: Sage.

McCarthy, J., & Hardy, J. (1993). Age at first birth and birth outcomes. *Journal of Research on Adolescence, 3,* 374–392.

McCord, J. (1982). A longitudinal view of the relationship between parental absence and crime. In J. Gunn & D. P. Farrington (Eds.), *Abnormal offenders, delinquency, and the criminal justice system* (pp. 113–128). London: Wiley.

McCord, W., McCord, J., & Zola, I. K. (1959). *Origins of crime.* New York: Columbia University Press.

McCormick, K. F. (1992). Attitudes of primary care physicians toward corporal punishment. *Journal of the American Medical Association, 267,* 3161–3165.

McFalls, J. A., Jr. (1990). The risks of reproductive impairment in the later years of childbearing. *Annual Review of Sociology, 16,* 491–519.

McHale, S. M., & Lerner, R. M. (1990). Stages of human development. In R. M. Thomas (Ed.), *The encyclopedia of human development and education* (pp. 163–166). Oxford: Pergamon Press.

McKey, R. H., Condelli, L., Granson, H., Barrett, B., McConkey, C., & Plantz, M. (1985). *The impact of Head Start on children, families and communities (final report of the Head Start Evaluation, Synthesis and Utilization Project).* Washington, DC: CSR.

McLaughlin, B. (1984). *Second-language acquisition in childhood: Vol. 1. Preschool children* (2nd ed.). Hillsdale, NJ: Erlbaum.

McLloyd, V. (1993). *Research on childhood poverty: Exploring its relevance to current policy debates.* Paper presented at the biennial meetings of the Society for Research in Child Development, New Orleans.

Melson, G. F., Ladd, G. W., & Hsu, H. (1993). Maternal support networks, maternal cognitions, and young children's social and cognitive development. *Child Development, 64,* 1401–1417.

Meltzoff, A. N. (1988). Infant imitation and memory: Nine-month-olds in immediate and deferred tasks. *Child Development, 59,* 217–225.

Meltzoff, A. N., & Borton, R. W. (1979). Intermodal matching by human neonates. *Nature, 282,* 403–404.

Meltzoff, A. N., & Moore, M. K. (1983). Newborn infants imitate adult facial gestures. *Child Development, 54,* 702–709.

Mervis, C. B., & Mervis, C. A. (1982). Leopards are kitty-cats: Object labeling by mothers for their thirteen-month-olds. *Child Development, 53,* 267–273.

Meyer-Bahlburg, H. F. L., Ehrhardt, A. A., & Feldman, J. F. (1986). Long-term implications of the prenatal endocrine milieu for sex-dimorphic behavior. In L. Erlenmeyer-Kimling & N. E. Miller (Eds.), *Life-span research on the prediction of psychopathology* (pp. 17–30). Hillsdale, NJ: Erlbaum.

Miller, B. C., Christopherson, C. R., & King, P. K. (1993). Sexual behavior in adolescence. In T. P. Gullotta, G. R. Adams, & R. Montemayor (Eds.), *Adolescent sexuality* (pp. 57–76). Newbury Park, CA: Sage.

Miller, G. A. (1956). The magical number seven, plus or minus two: Some limits on our capacity for processing information. *Psychological Review, 63*, 81–96.

Millstein, S. G., & Litt, I. R. (1990). Adolescent health. In S. S. Feldman & G. R. Elliott (Eds.), *At the threshold: The developing adolescent* (pp. 431–456). Cambridge, MA: Harvard University Press.

Mischel, W. (1966). A social learning view of sex differences in behavior. In E. E. Maccoby (Ed.), *The development of sex differences* (pp. 56–81). Stanford, CA: Stanford University Press.

Mischel, W. (1970). Sex typing and socialization. In P. H. Mussen (Ed.), *Carmichael's manual of child psychology* (Vol. 2, pp. 3–72). New York: Wiley.

Mitchell, E. A., Ford, R. P. K., Steward, A. W., Taylor, B. J., Becroft, D. M. O., Thompson, J. M. D., Scragg, R., Hassall, I. B., Barry, D. M. J., Allen, E. M., & Roberts, A. P. (1993). Smoking and sudden infant death syndrome. *Pediatrics, 91*, 893–896.

Mitchell, P. R., & Kent, R. D. (1990). Phonetic variation in multisyllable babbling. *Journal of Child Language, 17*, 247–265.

Mitchell, R. (1992). *Testing for learning: How new approaches to evaluation can improve American schools.* New York: Free Press.

Moffitt, T. E. (1990). Juvenile delinquency and attention deficit disorder: Boys' developmental trajectories from age 3 to age 15. *Child Development, 61*, 893–910.

Money, J. (1987). Sin, sickness, or status? Homosexual gender identity and psychoneuroendocrinology. *American Psychologist, 42*, 384–399.

Montemayor, R., & Eisen, M. (1977). The development of self-conceptions from childhood to adolescence. *Developmental Psychology, 13*, 314–319.

Montpetit, R. R., Montoye, H. J., & Laeding, L. (1967). Grip strength of school children, Saginaw, Michigan—1964. *Research Quarterly, 38*, 231–240.

Moon, C., & Fifer, W. P. (1990). Syllables as signals for 2-day-old infants. *Infant Behavior and Development, 13*, 377–390.

Moore, E. G. J. (1986). Family socialization and the IQ test performance of traditionally and transracially adopted black children. *Developmental Psychology, 22*, 317–326.

Moore, K. A., Myers, D. E., Morrison, D. R., Nord, C. W., Brown, B., & Edmonston, B. (1993). Age at first childbirth and later poverty. *Journal of Research on Adolescence, 3*, 393–422.

Moore, K. L. (1988). *The developing human: Clinically oriented embryology* (4th ed.). Philadelphia: W. B. Saunders.

Moores, D. F. (1985). Early intervention programs for hearing impaired children: A longitudinal assessment. In K. E. Nelson (Ed.), *Children's language* (Vol. 5, pp. 159–196). Hillsdale, NJ: Erlbaum.

Morgan, M. (1982). Television and adolescents' sex role stereotypes: A longitudinal study. *Journal of Personality and Social Psychology, 43*, 947–955.

Morgan, M. (1987). Television, sex-role attitudes, and sex-role behavior. *Journal of Early Adolescence, 7*, 269–282.

Morrison, D. M. (1985). Adolescent contraceptive behavior: A review. *Psychological Bulletin, 98*, 538–568.

Morrongiello, B. A. (1988). Infants' localization of sounds along the horizontal axis: Estimates of minimum audible angle. *Developmental Psychology, 24*, 8–13.

Morrongiello, B. A., Fenwick, K. D., & Chance, G. (1990). Sound localization acuity in very young infants: An observer-based testing procedure. *Developmental Psychology, 26*, 75–84.

Morse, P. A., & Cowan, N. (1982). Infant auditory and speech perception. In T. M. Field, A. Houston, H. C. Quay, L. Troll, & G. E. Finley (Eds.), *Review of human development* (pp. 32–61). New York: Wiley.

Mortimer, J. T., Finch, M., Shanahan, M., & Ryu, S. (1992). Work experience, mental health, and behavioral adjustment in adolescence. *Journal of Research on Adolescence, 2*, 25–57.

Mosher, F. A., & Hornsby, J. R. (1966). On asking questions. In J. S. Bruner, R. R. Olver, & P. M. Greenfield (Eds.), *Studies in cognitive growth* (pp. 68–85). New York: Wiley.

Munro, G., & Adams, G. R. (1977). Ego-identity formation in college students and working youth. *Developmental Psychology, 13*, 523–524.

Munroe, R. H., Shimmin, H. S., & Munroe, R. L. (1984). Gender understanding and sex role preference in four cultures. *Developmental Psychology, 20*, 673–682.

Murray, J. L., & Bernfield, M. (1988). The differential effect of prenatal care on the incidence of low birth weight among blacks and whites in a prepaid health care plan. *New England Journal of Medicine, 319*, 1385–1391.

Murray, J. P. (1980). *Television & youth: 25 years of research and controversy.* Stanford, CA: The Boys Town Center for the Study of Youth Development.

Myers, B. J. (1987). Mother-infant bonding as a critical period. In M. H. Bornstein (Ed.), *Sensitive periods in development: Interdisciplinary perspectives* (pp. 223–246). Hillsdale, NJ: Erlbaum.

Naeye, R. L., & Peters, E. C. (1984). Mental development of children whose mothers smoked during pregnancy. *Obstetrics and Gynecology, 64*, 601–607.

Nash, S. C. (1975). The relationship among sex-role stereotyping, sex-role preference, and the sex difference in spatial visualization. *Sex Roles, 1*, 15–32.

National Center for Health Statistics (1984, September 28). Advance report on final natality statistics, 1982. *Monthly Vital Statistics Report, 33*(6), Supplement.

Neimark, E. D. (1982). Adolescent thought: Transition to formal operations. In B. B. Wolman (Ed.), *Handbook of developmental psychology* (pp. 486–502). Englewood Cliffs, NJ: Prentice-Hall.

Nelson, C. A. (1987). The recognition of facial expression in the first two years of life: Mechanisms of development. *Child Development, 58,* 889–909.

Nelson, K. (1973). Structure and strategy in learning to talk. *Monographs of the Society for Research in Child Development, 38* (Serial No. 149).

Nelson, K. (1977). Facilitating children's syntax acquisition. *Developmental Psychology, 13,* 101–107.

Nelson, K. (1985). *Making sense: The acquisition of shared meaning.* New York: Academic Press.

Nelson, K. (1988). Constraints on word learning. *Cognitive Development, 3,* 221–246.

Newcomb, A. F., Bukowski, W. M., & Pattee, L. (1993). Children's peer relations: A meta-analytic review of popular, rejected, neglected, controversial, and average sociometric status. *Psychological Bulletin, 113,* 99–128.

Newcombe, N. S., & Baenninger, M. (1989). Biological change and cognitive ability in adolescence. In G. R. Adams, R. Montemayor, & T. P. Gullotta (Eds.), *Biology of adolescent behavior and development* (pp. 168–194). Newbury Park, CA: Sage.

Nightingale, E. O., & Goodman, M. (1990). *Before birth: Prenatal testing for genetic disease.* Cambridge, MA: Harvard University Press.

Nilsson, L. (1990). *A child is born.* New York: Delacorte Press.

Norton, A. J., & Glick, P. C. (1986). One parent families: A social and economic profile. *Family Relations, 35,* 9–18.

Nottelmann, E. D., Susman, E. J., Blue, J. H., Inoff-Germain, G., Dorn, L. D., Loriaux, D. L., Cutler, G. B., Jr., & Chrousos, G. P. (1987). Gonadal and adrenal hormone correlates of adjustment in early adolescence. In R. M. Lerner & T. T. Foch (Eds.), *Biological-psychosocial interactions in early adolescence* (pp. 303–324). Hillsdale, NJ: Erlbaum.

Nowakowski, R. S. (1987). Basic concepts of CNS development. *Child Development, 58,* 568–595.

O'Brien, M. (1992). Gender identity and sex roles. In V. B. V. Hasselt & M. Hersen (Eds.), *Handbook of social development: A lifespan perspective* (pp. 325–345). New York: Plenum Press.

O'Brien, S. F., & Bierman, K. L. (1988). Conceptions and perceived influence of peer groups: Interviews with preadolescents and adolescents. *Child Development, 59,* 1360–1365.

O'Connor, S., Vietze, P. M., Sandler, H. M., Sherrod, K. B., & Altemeier, W. A. (1980). Quality of parenting and the mother-infant relationships following rooming-in. In P. M. Taylor (Ed.), *Parent-infant relationships* (pp. 349–368). New York: Grune & Stratton.

Offord, D. R., Boyle, M. H., & Racine, Y. A. (1991). The epidemiology of antisocial behavior in childhood and adolescence. In D. J. Pepler & K. H. Rubin (Eds.), *The development and treatment of childhood aggression* (pp. 31–54). Hillsdale, NJ: Erlbaum.

O'Hara, M. W., Schlechte, J. A., Lewis, D. A., & Varner, M. W. (1992). Controlled prospective study of postpartum mood disorders: Psychological, environmental, and hormonal variables. *Journal of Abnormal Psychology, 100,* 63–73.

Oller, D. K. (1981). Infant vocalizations: Exploration and reflectivity. In R. E. Stark (Ed.), *Language behavior in infancy and early childhood* (pp. 85–104). New York: Elsevier/North-Holland.

Olshan, A. F., Baird, P. A., & Teschke, K. (1989). Paternal occupational exposures and the risk of Down syndrome. *American Journal of Human Genetics, 44,* 646–651.

Olson, H. C., Sampson, P. D., Barr, H., Streissguth, A. P., & Bookstein, F. L. (1992). Prenatal exposure to alcohol and school problems in late childhood: A longitudinal prospective study. *Development and Psychopathology, 4,* 341–359.

Olson, S. L., Bates, J. E., & Kaskie, B. (1992). Caregiver-infant interaction antecedents of children's school-age cognitive ability. *Merrill-Palmer Quarterly, 38,* 309–330.

O'Neill, D. K., Astington, J. W., & Flavell, J. H. (1992). Young children's understanding of the role that sensory experiences play in knowledge acquisition. *Child Development, 63,* 474–490.

Osofsky, J. D. (Ed.). (1987). *Handbook of infant development.* New York: Wiley-Interscience.

Overton, W. F., & Reese, H. W. (1973). Models of development: Methodological implications. In J. R. Nesselroade & H. W. Reese (Eds.), *Life-span developmental psychology: Methodological issues* (pp. 65–86). New York: Academic Press.

Overton, W. F., Ward, S. L., Noveck, I. A., Black, J., & O'Brien, D. P. (1987). Form and content in the development of deductive reasoning. *Developmental Psychology, 23,* 22–30.

Padilla, A. M., Lindholm, K. J., Chen, A., Duran, R., Hakuta, K., Lambert, W., & Tucker, G. R. (1991). The English-only movement: Myths, reality, and implications for psychology. *American Psychologist, 46,* 120–130.

Page, D. C., Mosher, R., Simpson, E. M., Fisher, E. M. C., Mardon, G., Pollack, J., McGillivray, B., de la Chapelle, A., & Brown, L. G. (1987). The sex-determining region of the human Y chromosome encodes a finger protein. *Cell, 51,* 1091–1104.

Paikoff, R. L., & Brooks-Gunn, J. (1990). Physiological processes: What role do they play during the transition to adolescence? In R. Montemayor, G. R. Adams, & T. P. Gullotta (Eds.), *From childhood to adolescence: A transitional period?* (pp. 63–81). Newbury Park, CA: Sage.

Palkovitz, R. (1985). Fathers' birth attendance, early contact, and extended contact with their newborns: A critical review. *Child Development, 56,* 392–406.

Papousek, H., & Papousek, M. (1991). Innate and cultural guidance of infants' integrative competencies: China, the United States, and Germany. In M. H. Bornstein (Ed.), *Cultural approaches to parenting* (pp. 23–44). Hillsdale, NJ: Erlbaum.

Parke, R. D., & Tinsley, B. R. (1981). The father's role in infancy: Determinants of involvement in caregiving and play. In M. E. Lamb (Ed.), *The role of the father in child development* (2nd ed.) (pp. 429–458). New York: Wiley.

Parke, R. D., & Tinsley, B. R. (1984). Fatherhood: Historical and contemporary perspectives. In K. A. McCluskey & H. W. Reese (Eds.), *Life-span developmental psychology: Historical and generational effects* (pp. 203–248). Orlando, FL: Academic Press.

Parmelee, A. H., Jr. (1986). Children's illnesses: Their beneficial effects on behavioral development. *Child Development, 57,* 1–10.

Parmelee, A. H., Jr., & Sigman, M. D. (1983). Perinatal brain development and behavior. In M. M. Haith & J. J. Campos (Eds.), *Handbook of child psychology: Vol. 2. Infancy and developmental psychobiology* (pp. 95–156). New York: Wiley.

Parmelee, A. H., Jr., Wenner, W. H., & Schulz, H. R. (1964). Infant sleep patterns from birth to 16 weeks of age. *Journal of Pediatrics, 65,* 576–582.

Parsons, J. E., Adler, T. F., & Daczala, C. M. (1982). Socialization of achievement attitudes and beliefs: Parental influences. *Child Development, 53,* 310–321.

Passman, R. H., & Longeway, K. P. (1982). The role of vision in maternal attachment: Giving 2-year-olds a photograph of their mother during separation. *Developmental Psychology, 18,* 530–533.

Patterson, C. J., Kupersmidt, J. B., & Vaden, N. A. (1990). Income level, gender, ethnicity, and household composition as predictors of children's school-based competence. *Child Development, 61,* 484–494.

Patterson, G. R. (1975). *Families: Applications of social learning to family life.* Champaign, IL: Research Press.

Patterson, G. R. (1980). Mothers: The unacknowledged victims. *Monographs of the Society for Research in Child Development, 45* (Serial No. 186).

Patterson, G. R., Capaldi, D., & Bank, L. (1991). An early starter model for predicting delinquency. In D. J. Pepler & K. H. Rubin (Eds.), *The development and treatment of childhood aggression* (pp. 139–168). Hillsdale, NJ: Erlbaum.

Patterson, G. R., DeBaryshe, B. D., & Ramsey, E. (1989). A developmental perspective on antisocial behavior. *American Psychologist, 44,* 329–335.

Paxton, S. J., Wertheim, E. H., Gibbons, K., Szmukler, G. I., Hillier, L., & Petrovich, J. L. (1991). Body image satisfaction, dieting beliefs, and weight loss behaviors in adolescent girls and boys. *Journal of Youth and Adolescence, 20,* 361–379.

Pederson, D. R., Moran, G., Sitko, C., Campbell, K., Ghesquire, K., & Acton, H. (1990). Maternal sensitivity and the security of infant-mother attachment: A Q-sort study. *Child Development, 61,* 1974–1983.

Pedlow, R., Sanson, A., Prior, M., & Oberklaid, F. (1993). Stability of maternally reported temperament from infancy to 8 years. *Developmental Psychology, 29,* 998–1007.

Pegg, J. E., Werker, J. F., & McLoed, P. J. (1992). Preference for infant-directed over adult-directed speech: Evidence from 7-week-old infants. *Infant Behavior and Development, 15,* 325–345.

Pence, A. R. (Ed.). (1988). *Ecological research with children and families: From concepts to methodology.* New York: Teachers College Press.

Pennington, B. F., Bender, B., Puck, M., Salbenblatt, J., & Robinson, A. (1982). Learning disabilities in children with sex chromosome anomalies. *Child Development, 53,* 1182–1192.

Penrod, S. (1993). The child witness, the courts, and psychological research. In C. A. Nelson (Ed.), *Memory and affect in development: The Minnesota symposia on child psychology* (Vol. 26, pp. 159–170). Hillsdale, NJ: Erlbaum.

Perner, J. (1991). On representing that: The asymmetry between belief and desire in children's theory of mind. In D. Frye & C. Moore (Eds.), *Children's theories of mind: Mental states and social understanding* (pp. 139–156). Hillsdale, NJ: Erlbaum.

Petersen, A. C. (1987). The nature of biological-psychosocial interactions: The sample case of early adolescence. In R. M. Lerner & T. T. Foch (Eds.), *Biological-psychosocial interactions in early adolescence* (pp. 35–62). Hillsdale, NJ: Erlbaum.

Petersen, A. C., Compas, B. E., Brooks-Gunn, J., Stemmler, M., Ey, S., & Grant, K. E. (1993). Depression in adolescence. *American Psychologist, 48,* 155–168.

Petersen, A. C., Sarigiani, P. A., & Kennedy, R. E. (1991). Adolescent depression: Why more girls? *Journal of Youth and Adolescence, 20,* 247–272.

Petersen, A. C., & Taylor, B. (1980). The biological approach to adolescence. In J. Adelson (Ed.), *Handbook of adolescent psychology* (pp. 117–158). New York: Wiley.

Peterson, G. H., Mehl, L. E., & Leiderman, P. H. (1979). The role of some birth-related variables in father attachment. *American Journal of Orthopsychiatry, 49,* 330–338.

Petitto, L. A. (1988). "Language" in the prelinguistic child. In F. S. Kessell (Ed.), *The development of language and language researchers: Essays in honor of Roger Brown* (pp. 187–222). Hillsdale, NJ: Erlbaum.

Phillips, K., & Fulker, D. W. (1989). Quantitative genetic analysis of longitudinal trends in adoption designs with application to IQ in the Colorado Adoption Project. *Behavior Genetics, 19,* 621–658.

Phinney, J. S. (1990). Ethnic identity in adolescents and adults: Review of research. *Psychological Bulletin, 108,* 499–514.

Phinney, J. S., & Rosenthal, D. A. (1992). Ethnic identity in adolescence: Process, context, and outcome. In G. R. Adams, T. P. Gullotta, & R. Montemayor (Eds.), *Adolescent identity formation* (pp. 145–172). Newbury Park, CA: Sage.

Piaget, J. (1932). *The moral judgment of the child.* New York: Macmillan.

Piaget, J. (1952). *The origins of intelligence in children.* New York: International Universities Press.

Piaget, J. (1954). *The construction of reality in the child.* New York: Basic Book (original work published 1937).

Piaget, J. (1970). Piaget's theory. In P. H. Mussen (Ed.), *Carmichael's manual of child psychology* (Vol. 1, 3rd ed.) (pp. 703–732). New York: Wiley.

Piaget, J. (1977). *The development of thought: Equilibration of cognitive structures.* New York: Viking Press.

Piaget, J., & Inhelder, B. (1969). *The psychology of the child.* New York: Basic Books.

Pianta, R., Egeland, B., & Erickson, M. F. (1989). The antecedents of maltreatment: Results of the Mother-Child Interaction Research Project. In D. Cicchetti & V. Carlson (Eds.), *Child maltreatment* (pp. 203–253). Cambridge: Cambridge University Press.

Pick, H. L., Jr. (1986). Reflections on the data and theory of cross-modal infancy research. In L. P. Lipsitt & C. Rovee-Collier (Eds.), *Advances in infancy research* (Vol. 4, pp. 230–239). Norwood, NJ: Ablex.

Pickens, J., & Field, T. (1993). Facial expressivity in infants of depressed mothers. *Developmental Psychology, 29,* 986–988.

Pinker, S. (1987). The bootstrapping problem in language acquisition. In B. MacWhinney (Ed.), *Mechanisms of language acquisition* (pp. 399–442). Hillsdale, NJ: Erlbaum.

Pitkin, R. M. (1977). Nutrition during pregnancy: The clinical approach. In M. Winick (Ed.), *Nutritional disorders of American women.* New York: Wiley.

Plomin, R. (1989). Environment and genes: Determinants of behavior. *American Psychologist, 44,* 105–111.

Plomin, R., & DeFries, J. C. (1985). *Origins of individual differences in infancy: The Colorado Adoption Project.* Orlando, FL: Academic Press.

Plomin, R., Loehlin, J. C., & DeFries, J. C. (1985). Genetic and environmental components of "environmental" influences. *Developmental Psychology, 21,* 391–402.

Plomin, R., & McClearn, G. E. (Eds.). (1993). *Nature, nurture & psychology.* Washington, DC: American Psychological Association.

Plomin, R., Pedersen, N. L., McClearn, G. E., Nesselroade, J. R., & Bergeman, C. S. (1988). EAS temperaments during the last half of the life span: Twins reared apart and twins reared together. *Psychology and Aging, 3,* 43–50.

Plomin, R., & Rende, R. (1991). Human behavioral genetics. *Annual Review of Psychology, 42,* 161–190.

Plomin, R., Rende, R., & Rutter, M. (1991). Quantitative genetics and developmental psychopathology. In D. Cicchetti & S. L. Toth (Eds.), *Internalizing and externalizing expressions of dysfunction: Rochester symposium on developmental psychopathology* (pp. 155–202). Hillsdale, NJ: Erlbaum.

Porter, J. R., & Washington, R. E. (1993). Minority identity and self-esteem. *Annual Review of Sociology, 19,* 139–161.

Poulson, C. L., Nunes, L. R. D., & Warren, S. F. (1989). Imitation in infancy: A critical review. In H. W. Reese (Ed.), *Advances in child development and behavior* (Vol. 22, pp. 272–298). San Diego, CA: Academic Press.

Powell, B., & Steelman, L. C. (1982). Testing an undertested comparison: Maternal effects on sons' and daughters' attitudes toward women in the labor force. *Journal of Marriage and the Family, 44,* 349–355.

Power, C., & Peckham, C. (1990). Childhood morbidity and adulthood ill health. *Journal of Epidemiology and Community Health, 44,* 69–74.

Power, C., & Reimer, J. (1978). Moral atmosphere: An educational bridge between moral judgment and action. *New Directions for Child Development, 2,* 105–116.

Power, T. G., Gershenhorn, S., & Stafford, D. (1990). Maternal perception of infant difficultness: The influence of maternal attitudes and attributions. *Infant Behavior and Development, 13,* 421–437.

Prechtl, H. F. R., & Beintema, D. J. (1964). *The neurological examination of the full-term newborn infant: Clinics in developmental medicine, 12.* London: Hinemann.

Pulkkinen, L. (1982). Self-control and continuity in childhood delayed adolescence. In P. Baltes & O. Brim (Eds.), *Life span development and behavior* (Vol. 4, pp. 64–107). New York: Academic Press.

Pye, C. (1986). Quiche Mayan speech to children. *Journal of Child Language, 13,* 85–100.

Pyle, R., Mitchell, J., Eckert, E., Halverson, P., Neuman, P., & Goff, G. (1983). The incidence of bulimia in freshman college students. *International Journal of Eating Disorders, 2,* 75–85.

Quiggle, N. L., Garber, J., Panak, W. F., & Dodge, K. A. (1992). Social information processing in aggressive and depressed children. *Child Development, 63,* 1305–1320.

Raja, S. N., McGee, R., & Stanton, W. R. (1992). Perceived attachments to parents and peers and psychological well-being in adolescence. *Journal of Youth and Adolescence, 21,* 471–485.

Ramey, C. T. (1992). High-risk children and IQ: Altering intergenerational patterns. *Intelligence, 16,* 239–256.

Ramey, C. T. (1993). A rejoinder to Spitz's critique of the Abecedarian experiment. *Intelligence, 17,* 25–30.

Ramey, C. T., & Campbell, F. A. (1987). The Carolina Abecedarian Project: An educational experiment concerning human malleability. In J. J. Gallagher & C. T. Ramey (Eds.), *The malleability of children* (pp. 127–140). Baltimore: Paul H. Brookes.

Ramey, C. T., & Haskins, R. (1981a). The modification of intelligence through early experience. *Intelligence, 5,* 5–19.

Ramey, C. T., & Haskins, R. (1981b). Early education, intellectual development, and school performance: A reply to Arthur Jensen and J. McVicker Hunt. *Intelligence, 5,* 41–48.

Ramey, C. T., Lee, M. W., & Burchinal, M. R. (1989). Developmental plasticity and predictability: Consequences of ecological change. In M. H. Bornstein & N. A. Krasnegor (Eds.), *Stability and continuity in mental development* (pp. 217–234). Hillsdale, NJ: Erlbaum.

Ramey, C. T., Yeates, K. W., & Short, E. J. (1984). The plasticity of intellectual development: Insights from inventive intervention. *Child Development, 55,* 1913–1925.

Rappoport, L. (1972). *Personality development: The chronology of experience*. Glenview, IL: Scott, Foresman.

Ree, M. J., & Earles, J. A. (1992). Intelligence is the best predictor of job performance. *Current Directions in Psychological Science, 1,* 86–89.

Reisman, J. E. (1987). Touch, motion, and proprioception. In P. Salapatek & L. Cohen (Eds.), *Handbook of infant perception: Vol. 1. From sensation to perception* (pp. 265–304). Orlando, FL: Academic Press.

Reisman, J. M., & Shorr, S. I. (1978). Friendship claims and expectations among children and adults. *Child Development, 49,* 913–916.

Remafedi, G. (1987a). Adolescent homosexuality: Psychosocial and medical implications. *Pediatrics, 79,* 331–337.

Remafedi, G. (1987b). Male homosexuality: The adolescent's perspective. *Pediatrics, 79,* 326–30.

Renouf, A. G., & Harter, S. (1990). Low self-worth and anger as components of the depressive experience in young adolescents. *Development and Psychopathology, 2,* 293–310.

Report of National Institute. (1993). Report of National Institute of Child Health and Human Development workshop on Chorionic Villus sampling and limb and other defects, October 20, 1992. *Teratology, 48,* 7–13.

Rest, J. R. (1983). Morality. In J. H. Flavell & E. M. Markman (Eds.), *Handbook of child psychology: Vol. 3. Cognitive development* (pp. 556–629). New York: Wiley.

Rest, J. R., & Thoma, S. J. (1985). Relation of moral judgment development to formal education. *Developmental Psychology, 21,* 709–714.

Rholes, W. S., & Ruble, D. N. (1984). Children's understanding of dispositional characteristics of others. *Child Development, 55,* 550–560.

Ricciuti, H. N. (1993). Nutrition and mental development. *Current Directions in Psychological Science, 2,* 43–46.

Rice, M. L. (1989). Children's language acquisition. *American Psychologist, 44,* 149–156.

Rice, M. L., Huston, A. C., Truglio, R., & Wright, J. (1990). Words from "Sesame Street": Learning vocabulary while viewing. *Developmental Psychology, 26,* 421–428.

Richman, A. L., Miller, P. M., & LeVine, R. A. (1992). Cultural and educational variations in maternal responsiveness. *Developmental Psychology, 28,* 614–621.

Richters, J., & Pellegrini, D. (1989). Depressed mothers' judgments about their children: An examination of the depression-distortion hypothesis. *Child Development, 60,* 1068–1075.

Riegel, K. F. (1975). Adult life crises: A dialectic interpretation of development. In N. Datan & L. H. Ginsberg (Eds.), *Lifespan developmental psychology: Normative life crises* (pp. 99–128). New York: Academic Press.

Rierdan, J., & Koff, E. (1991). Depressive symptomatology among very early maturing girls. *Journal of Youth and Adolescence, 20,* 415–425.

Rierdan, J., & Koff, E. (1993). Developmental variables in relation to depressive symptoms in adolescent girls. *Development and Psychopathology, 5,* 485–496.

Rierdan, J., Koff, E., & Stubbs, M. L. (1989). Timing of menarche, preparation, and initial menstrual experience: Replication and further analysis in a prospective study. *Journal of Youth and Adolescence, 18,* 413–426.

Roberts, C. W., Green, R., Williams, K., & Goodman, M. (1987). Boyhood gender identity development: A statistical contrast of two family groups. *Developmental Psychology, 23,* 544–557.

Roberts, R. E., & Sobhan, M. (1992). Symptoms of depression in adolescence: A comparison of Anglo, African, and Hispanic Americans. *Journal of Youth and Adolescence, 21,* 639–651.

Robinson, H. B. (1981). The uncommonly bright child. In M. Lewis & L. A. Rosenblum (Eds.), *The uncommon child* (pp. 57–82). New York: Plenum Press.

Robinson, J. L., Kagan, J., Reznick, J. S., & Corley, R. (1992). The heritability of inhibited and uninhibited behavior: A twin study. *Developmental Psychology, 28,* 1030–1037.

Robinson, N. M., & Janos, P. M. (1986). Psychological adjustment in a college-level program of marked academic acceleration. *Journal of Youth and Adolescence, 15,* 51–60.

Roche, A. F. (1979). Secular trends in human growth, maturation, and development. *Monographs of the Society for Research in Child Development, 44* (3–4, Serial No. 179).

Rodning, C., Beckwith, L., & Howard, J. (1991). Quality of attachment and home environments in children prenatally exposed to PCP and cocaine. *Development and Psychopathology, 3,* 351–66.

Rogers, J. (1991). Nontraditional inheritance: 1. Mechanisms Mendel never knew. *Mosaic, 22*(Fall), 3–11.

Rogers, J. L. (1984). Confluence effects: Not here, not now! *Developmental Psychology, 20,* 321–331.

Rohner, R. P., Kean, K. J., & Cournoyer, D. E. (1991). Effects of corporal punishment, perceived caretaker warmth, and cultural beliefs on the psychological adjustment of children in St. Kitts, West Indies. *Journal of Marriage and the Family, 53,* 681–693.

Rollins, B. C., & Feldman, H. (1970). Marital satisfaction over the family life cycle. *Journal of Marriage and the Family, 32,* 20–27.

Rolls, B. J., Fedoroff, I. C., & Guthrie, J. F. (1991). Gender differences in eating behavior and body weight regulation. *Health Psychology, 20,* 133–142.

Rooks, J. P., Weatherby, N. L., Ernst, E. K. M., Stapleton, S., Rosen, D., & Rosenfield, A. (1989). Outcomes of care in birth centers: The national birth center study. *New England Journal of Medicine, 321,* 1804–1811.

Rose, S. A., & Ruff, H. A. (1987). Cross-modal abilities in human infants. In J. D. Osofsky (Ed.), *Handbook of infant development* (2nd ed.) (pp. 318–362). New York: Wiley-Interscience.

Rosenbaum, J. E. (1984). *Career mobility in a corporate hierarchy.* New York: Academic Press.

Rosenbaum, J. E. (1991). Are adolescent problems caused by school or society? *Journal of Research on Adolescence, 1,* 301–322.

Rosenblith, J. F., & Sims-Knight, J. E. (1989). *In the beginning: Development in the first two years of life.* Newbury Park, CA: Sage.

Ross, G., Kagan, J., Zelazo, P., & Kotelchuck, M. (1975). Separation protest in infants in home and laboratory. *Developmental Psychology, 11,* 256–257.

Rothbart, M. K. (1989a). Temperament in childhood: A framework. In G. A. Kohnstamm, J. E. Bates, & M. K. Rothbart (Eds.), *Temperament in childhood* (pp. 59–75). Chichester, England: Wiley.

Rothbart, M. K. (1989b). Biological processes in temperament: In G. A. Kohnstamm, J. E. Bates, & M. K. Rothbart (Eds.), *Temperament in childhood* (pp. 77–110). Chichester, England: Wiley.

Rotheram-Borus, M. J., Rosario, M., & Koopman, C. (1991). Minority youths at high risk: Gay males and runaways. In M. E. Colten & S. Gore (Eds.), *Adolescent stress: Causes and consequences* (pp. 181–200). New York: Aldine de Gruyter.

Rovee-Collier, C. (1986). The rise and fall of infant classical conditioning research: Its promise for the study of early development. In L. P. Lipsitt & C. Rovee-Collier (Eds.), *Advances in infancy research* (Vol. 4, pp. 139–162). Norwood, NJ: Ablex.

Rovee-Collier, C. (1993). The capacity for long-term memory in infancy. *Current Directions in Psychological Science, 2,* 130–135.

Rovet, J., & Netley, C. (1983). The triple X chromosome syndrome in childhood: Recent empirical findings. *Child Development, 54,* 831–845.

Rowe, I., & Marcia, J. E. (1980). Ego identity status, formal operations, and moral development. *Journal of Youth and Adolescence, 9,* 87—99.

Rubin, K. H., Fein, G. G., & Vandenberg, B. (1983). Play. In E. M. Hetherington (Ed.), *Handbook of child psychology: Vol. 4. Socialization, personality, and social development* (pp. 693–774). New York: Wiley.

Rubin, K. H., Hymel, S., Mills, R. S. L., & Rose-Krasnor, L. (1991). Conceptualizing different developmental pathways to and from social isolation in childhood. In D. Cicchetti & S. L. Toth (Eds.), *Internalizing and externalizing expressions of dysfunction: Rochester symposium on developmental psychopathology* (Vol. 2, pp. 91–122). Hillsdale, NJ: Erlbaum.

Ruble, D. N. (1987). The acquisition of self-knowledge: A self-socialization perspective. In N. Eisenberg (Ed.), *Contemporary topics in developmental psychology* (pp. 243–270). New York: Wiley-Interscience.

Ruble, D. N., Balaban, T., & Cooper, J. (1981). Gender constancy and the effects of sex-typed televised toy commercials. *Child Development, 52,* 667–673.

Ruble, T. L. (1983). Sex stereotypes: Issues of change in the 1970's. *Sex Roles, 9,* 397–402.

Russell, G. (1982). Shared-caregiving families: An Australian study. In M. E. Lamb (Ed.), *Nontraditional families* (pp. 139–172). Hillsdale, NJ: Erlbaum.

Russell, J. A. (1989). Culture, scripts, and children's understanding of emotion. In C. Saarni & P. L. Harris (Eds.), *Children's understanding of emotion* (pp. 293–318). Cambridge: Cambridge University Press.

Rutter, D. R., & Durkin, K. (1987). Turn-taking in mother-infant interaction: An examination of vocalizations and gaze. *Developmental Psychology, 23,* 54–61.

Rutter, M. (1978a). Family, area and school influences in the genesis of conduct disorders. In L. Hersov, M. Berber, & D. Schaffer (Eds.), *Aggression and antisocial behavior in childhood and adolescence* (pp. 95–114). Oxford: Pergamon Press.

Rutter, M. (1978b). Early sources of security and competence. In J. S. Bruner & A. Garton (Eds.), *Human growth and development* (pp. 33–61). London: Oxford University Press.

Rutter, M. (1983). School effects on pupil progress: Research findings and policy implications. *Child Development, 54,* 1–29.

Rutter, M. (1987). Continuities and discontinuities from infancy. In J. D. Osofsky (Ed.), *Handbook of infant development* (2nd ed.) (pp. 1256–1296). New York: Wiley-Interscience.

Rutter, M. (1989). Isle of Wight revisited: Twenty-five years of child psychiatric epidemiology. *Journal of the American Academy of Child and Adolescent Psychiatry, 28,* 633–653.

Rutter, M. (1990). Commentary: Some focus and process considerations regarding effects of parental depression on children. *Developmental Psychology, 26,* 60–67.

Rutter, M., & Garmezy, N. (1983). Developmental psychopathology. In E. M. Hetherington (Ed.), *Handbook of child psychology: Vol. 4. Socialization, personality, and social development* (pp. 775–912). New York: Wiley.

Rutter, M., Tizard, J., & Whitmore, K. (1981). *Education, health and behaviour.* Huntington, NY: Krieger (originally published 1970).

Ryan, A. S., Rush, D., Krieger, F. W., & Lewandowski, G. E. (1991). Recent declines in breast-feeding in the United States, 1984 through 1989. *Pediatrics, 88,* 719–727.

Sack, W. H., Mason, R., & Higgins, J. E. (1985). The single parent family and abusive child punishment. *American Journal of Orthopsychiatry, 55,* 252–259.

Sagi, A. (1990). Attachment theory and research from a cross-cultural perspective. *Human Development, 33,* 10–22.

Sagi, A., van IJzendoorn, M. H., & Koren-Karie, N. (1991). Primary appraisal of the Strange Situation: A cross-cultural analysis of preseparation episodes. *Developmental Psychology, 27,* 587–596.

Saigal, S., Szatmari, P., Rosenbaum, P., Campbell, D., & King, S. (1991). Cognitive abilities and school performance of extremely low birth weight children and matched term control children at age 8 years: A regional study. *Journal of Pediatrics, 118,* 751–760.

Sameroff, A., Seifer, R., Barocas, R., Zax, M., & Greenspan, S. (1987). Intelligence quotient scores of 4-year-old children: Social-environmental risk factors. *Pediatrics, 79,* 343–350.

Sameroff, A. J. (1983). Developmental systems: Contexts and evolution. In W. Kessen (Ed.), *Handbook of child psychology: Vol. 1. History, theory, and methods* (pp. 237–294). New York: Wiley.

Sapir, E. (1929). The status of linguistics as a science. *Language, 5,* 207–214.

Sattler, J. M. (1988). *Assessment of children.* San Diego: Jerome M. Sattler.

Saunders, W. L., & Shepardson, D. (1987). A comparison of concrete and formal science instruction upon science achievement and reasoning ability of sixth grade students. *Journal of Research in Science Teaching, 24,* 39–51.

Savage-Rumbaugh, E. S. (1990). Language acquisition in a nonhuman species: Implications for the innateness debate. *Developmental Psychobiology, 23,* 599–620.

Savage-Rumbaugh, E. S., Murphy, J., Sevcik, R. A., Brakke, K. E., Williams, S. L., & Rumbaugh, D. M. (1993). Language comprehension in ape and child. *Monographs of the Society for Research in Child Development, 58*(3–4, Serial No. 223).

Scafidi, F. A., Field, T. M., Schanberg, S. M., Bauer, C. R., Tucci, K., Roberts, J., Morrow, C., & Kuhn, C. M. (1990). Massage stimulates growth in preterm infants: A replication. *Infant Behavior and Development, 13,* 167–188.

Scarr, S., & Eisenberg, M. (1993). Child care research: Issues, perspectives, and results. *Annual Review of Psychology, 44,* 613–644.

Scarr, S., & Kidd, K. K. (1983). Developmental behavior genetics. In M. M. Haith & J. J. Campos (Eds.), *Handbook of child psychology: Vol. 2. Infancy and developmental psychobiology* (pp. 345–434). New York: Wiley.

Scarr, S., & McCartney, K. (1983). How people make their own environments: A theory of genotype → environment effects. *Child Development, 54* 424–435.

Scarr, S., & Weinberg, R. A. (1983). The Minnesota adoption studies: Genetic differences and malleability. *Child Development, 54,* 260–267.

Scarr-Salapatek, S. (1976). An evolutionary perspective on infant intelligence: Species patterns and individual variations. In M. Lewis (Ed.), *Origins of intelligence* (pp. 165–198). New York: Plenum Press.

Schaefer, E. S. (1989). Dimensions of mother-infant interaction: Measurement, stability, and predictive validity. *Infant Behavior and Development, 12,* 379–393.

Schaefli, A., Rest, J. R., & Thoma, S. J. (1985). Does moral education improve moral judgment? A meta-analysis of intervention studies using the Defining Issues Test. *Review of Educational Research, 55,* 319–352.

Schaie, K. W. (1983). What can we learn from the longitudinal study of adult psychological development? In K. W. Schaie (Ed.), *Longitudinal studies of adult psychological development* (pp. 1–19). New York: Guilford Press.

Schank, R. C., & Abelson, R. (1977). *Scripts, plans, goals, and understanding.* Hillsdale, NJ: Erlbaum.

Schlesinger, H. S., & Meadow, K. P. (1972). *Sound and sign.* Berkeley: University of California Press.

Schneider, M. L. (1992). The effect of mild stress during pregnancy on birthweight and neuromotor maturation in rhesus monkey infants (*Macaca mulatta*). *Infant Behavior and Development, 15,* 389–403.

Schneider, W., & Bjorklund, D. F. (1992). Expertise, aptitude, and strategic remembering. *Child Development, 63,* 461–473.

Schneider, W., & Pressley, M. (1989). *Memory development between 2 and 20*. New York: Springer-Verlag.

Schoendorf, K. C., Hogue, C. J. R., Kleinman, J. C., & Rowley, D. (1992). Mortality among infants of black as compared with white college-educated parents. *New England Journal of Medicine, 326*, 1522–1526.

Schoendorf, K. C., & Kiely, J. L. (1992). Relationship of sudden infant death syndrome to maternal smoking during and after pregnancy. *Pediatrics, 90*, 905–908.

Schramm, W. F., Barnes, D. E., & Bakewell, J. M. (1987). Neonatal mortality in Missouri home births, 1978–84. *American Journal of Public Health, 77*, 930–935.

Scollon, R. (1976). *Conversations with a one-year-old*. Honolulu: University of Hawaii Press.

Sears, P. S., & Barbee, A. H. (1977). Career and life satisfactions among Terman's gifted women. In J. C. Stanley, W. C. George, & C. H. Solano (Eds.), *The gifted and the creative* (pp. 28–66). Baltimore: Johns Hopkins University Press.

Sears, R. R., Maccoby, E. E., & Levin, H. (1977). *Patterns of child rearing*. Stanford, CA: Stanford University Press (originally published 1957 by Row, Peterson).

Seidman, D. S., Ever-Hadani, P., & Gale, R. (1989). The effect of maternal weight gain in pregnancy on birth weight. *Obstetrics and Gynecology, 74*, 240–246.

Seitz, V. (1988). Methodology. In M. H. Bornstein & M. E. Lamb (Eds.), *Developmental psychology: An advanced textbook* (2nd ed.) (pp. 51–84). Hillsdale, NJ: Erlbaum.

Selman, R. L. (1980). *The growth of interpersonal understanding*. New York: Academic Press.

Sepkoski, C. (1987). *A longitudinal study of the effects of obstetric medication*. Paper presented at the biennial meetings of the Society for Research in Child Development, Baltimore.

Serbin, L., Moskowitz, D. S., Schwartzman, A. E., & Ledingham, J. E. (1991). Aggressive, withdrawn, and aggressive/withdrawn children in adolescence: Into the next generation. In D. J. Pepler & K. H. Rubin (Eds.), *The development and treatment of childhood aggression* (pp. 55–70). Hillsdale, NJ: Erlbaum.

Serbin, L. A., Powlishta, K. K., & Gulko, J. (1993). The development of sex typing in middle childhood. *Monographs of the Society for Research in Child Development, 58*(2, Serial No. 232).

Shaffer, D., Garland, A., Gould, M., Fisher, P., & Trautman, P. (1988). Preventing teenage suicide: A critical review. *Journal of the American Academy of Child and Adolescent Psychiatry, 27*, 675–687.

Shaffer, D., Garland, A., Vieland, V., Underwood, M., & Busner, C. (1991). The impact of curriculum-based suicide prevention programs for teenagers. *Journal of the American Academy of Child and Adolescent Psychiatry, 30*, 588–596.

Shantz, C. U. (1983). Social cognition. In J. H. Flavell & E. M. Markman (Eds.), *Handbook of child psychology: Vol. 3. Cognitive development* (pp. 495–555). New York: Wiley.

Sheldon, W. H. (1940). *The varieties of human physique*. New York: Harper.

Shelton, B. A. (1990). The distribution of household tasks. Does wife's employment status make a difference? *Journal of Family Issues, 11*, 115–135.

Sherrod, K. B., O'Connor, S., Vietze, P. M., & Altemeier, W. A. I. (1984). Child health and maltreatment. *Child Development, 55*, 1174–1183.

Shonkoff, J. P. (1984). The biological substrate and physical health in middle childhood. In W. A. Collins (Ed.), *Development during middle childhood: The years from six to twelve* (pp. 24–69). Washington, DC: National Academy Press.

Shore, C. (1986). Combinatorial play, conceptual development, and early multiword speech. *Developmental Psychology, 22*, 184–190.

Shweder, R. A., Mahapatra, M., & Miller, J. G. (1987). Culture and moral development. In J. Kagan & S. Lamb (Eds.), *The emergence of morality in young children* (pp. 1–82). Chicago: University of Chicago Press.

Siebert, J. M., Hogan, A. E., & Mundy, P. C. (1986). On the specifically cognitive nature of early object and social skill domain associations. *Merrill-Palmer Quarterly, 32*, 21–36.

Siegal, M. (1987). Are sons and daughters treated more differently by fathers than by mothers? *Developmental Review, 7*, 183–209.

Siegel, L. S. (1993). Phonological processing deficits as the basis of a reading disability. *Developmental Review, 13*, 246–257.

Siegler, R. S. (1976). Three aspects of cognitive development. *Cognitive Psychology, 8*, 431–520.

Siegler, R. S. (1978). The origins of scientific reasoning. In R. S. Siegler (Ed.), *Children's thinking: What develops?* (pp. 109–150). Hillsdale, NJ: Erlbaum.

Siegler, R. S. (1981). Developmental sequences within and between concepts. *Monographs of the Society for Research in Child Development, 46*(2, Serial No. 189).

Sigman, M., Neumann, C., Carter, E., Cattle, D. J., D'Souza, S., & Bwibo, N. (1988). Home interactions and the development of Embu toddlers in Kenya. *Child Development, 59*, 1251–1261.

Silverstein, L. B. (1991). Transforming the debate about child care and maternal employment. *American Psychologist, 46*, 1025–1032.

Simmons, R. G., Blyth, D. A., & McKinney, K. L. (1983). The social and psychological effects of puberty on white females. In J. Brooks-Gunn & A. C. Petersen (Eds.), *Girls at puberty: Biological and psychosocial perspectives* (pp. 229–272). New York: Plenum Press.

Simmons, R. G., Burgeson, R., & Reef, M. J. (1988). Cumulative change at entry to adolescence. In M. R. Gunnar & W. A. Collins (Eds.), *Development during the transition to adolescence: Minnesota symposia on child psychology* (Vol. 21, pp. 123–150). Hillsdale, NJ: Erlbaum.

Simons, R. L., Robertson, J. F., & Downs, W. R. (1989). The nature of the association between parental rejection and delinquent behavior. *Journal of Youth and Adolescence, 18,* 297–309.

Skinner, B. F. (1957). *Verbal behavior.* New York: Prentice-Hall.

Slaby, R. G., & Frey, K. S. (1975). Development of gender constancy and selective attention to same-sex models. *Child Development, 46,* 849–856.

Slaughter-Defoe, D. T., Nakagawa, K., Takanishi, R., & Johnson, D. J. (1990). Toward cultural/ecological perspectives on schooling and achievement in African- and Asian-American children. *Child Development, 61,* 363–383.

Slobin, D. I. (1985a). Introduction: Why study acquisition crosslinguistically? In D. I. Slobin (Ed.), *The crosslinguistic study of language acquisition: Vol. 1. The data* (pp. 3–24). Hillsdale, NJ: Erlbaum.

Slobin, D. I. (1985b). Crosslinguistic evidence for the language-making capacity. In D. I. Slobin (Ed.), *The crosslinguistic study of language acquisition: Vol. 2. Theoretical issues* (pp. 1157–1256). Hillsdale, NJ: Erlbaum.

Smetana, J. G. (1990). Morality and conduct disorders. In M. Lewis & S. M. Miller (Eds.), *Handbook of developmental psychopathology* (pp. 157–180). New York: Plenum Press.

Smetana, J. G., Killen, M., & Turiel, E. (1991). Children's reasoning about interpersonal and moral conflicts. *Child Development, 62,* 629–644.

Smith, D. W. (1978). Prenatal life. In D. W. Smith, E. L. Bierman, & N. M. Robinson (Eds.), *The biologic ages of man* (2nd ed.) (pp. 42–62). Philadelphia: W. B. Saunders.

Smith, D. W., & Stenchever, M. A. (1978). Prenatal life and the pregnant woman. In D. W. Smith, E. L. Bierman, & N. M. Robinson (Eds.), *The biologic ages of man* (2nd ed.) (pp. 42–77). Philadelphia: W. B. Saunders.

Smoll, F. L., & Schutz, R. W. (1990). Quantifying gender differences in physical performance: A developmental perspective. *Developmental Psychology, 26,* 360–369.

Snarey, J. R. (1985). Cross-cultural universality of social-moral development: A critical review of Kohlbergian research. *Psychological Bulletin, 97,* 202–232.

Snarey, J. R., Reimer, J., & Kohlberg, L. (1985). Development of social-moral reasoning among kibbutz adolescents: A longitudinal cross-sectional study. *Developmental Psychology, 21,* 3–17.

Snyder, L. (1978). Communicative and cognitive abilities and disabilities in the sensorimotor period. *Merrill-Palmer Quarterly, 24,* 161–180.

Soken, N. H., & Pick, A. D. (1992). Intermodal perception of happy and angry expressive behaviors by seven-month-old infants. *Child Development, 63,* 787–795.

Sonnenschein, S. (1986). Development of referential communication skills: How familiarity with a listener affects a speaker's production of redundant messages. *Developmental Psychology, 22,* 549–552.

Sontag, L. W., Baker, C. T., & Nelson, V. L. (1958). Mental growth and personality development: A longitudinal study. *Monographs of the Society for Research in Child Development, 23* (Serial No. 68).

Sosa, R., Kennell, J. H., Klaus, M. H., Robertson, S., & Urrutia, J. (1980). The effect of a supportive companion on perinatal problems, length of labor and mother-infant interaction. *New England Journal of Medicine, 303,* 597–600.

Spelke, E. S. (1979). Exploring audible and visible events in infancy. In A. D. Pick (Ed.), *Perception and its development: A tribute to Eleanor J. Gibson* (pp. 221–236). Hillsdale, NJ: Erlbaum.

Spelke, E. S. (1982). Perceptual knowledge of objects in infancy. In J. Mehler, E. C. T. Walker, & M. Garrett (Eds.), *Perspectives on mental representation* (pp. 409–430). Hillsdale, NJ: Erlbaum.

Spelke, E. S. (1985). Perception of unity, persistence, and identity: Thoughts on infants' conceptions of objects. In J. Mehler & R. Fox (Eds.), *Neonate cognition* (pp. 89–113). Hillsdale, NJ: Erlbaum.

Spelke, E. S. (1991). Physical knowledge in infancy: Reflections on Piaget's theory. In S. Carey & R. Gelman (Eds.), *The epigenesis of mind: Essays on biology and cognition* (pp. 133–169). Hillsdale, NJ: Erlbaum.

Spelke, E. S., & Owsley, C. J. (1979). Intermodal exploration and knowledge in infancy. *Infant Behavior and Development, 2,* 13–27.

Spelke, E. S., von Hofsten, C., & Kestenbaum, R. (1989). Object perception in infancy: Interaction of spatial and kinetic information for object boundaries. *Developmental Psychology, 25,* 185–196.

Spence, J. T., & Helmreich, R. L. (1978). *Masculinity and femininity.* Austin: University of Texas Press.

Spencer, M. B., & Dornbusch, S. M. (1990). Challenges in studying minority youth. In S. S. Feldman & G. R. Elliott (Eds.), *At the threshold: The developing adolescent* (pp. 123–146). Cambridge, MA: Harvard University Press.

Spieker, S. J., & Booth, C. L. (1988). Maternal antecedents of attachment quality. In J. Belsky & T. Nezworski (Eds.), *Clinical implications of attachment* (pp. 95–135). Hillsdale, NJ: Erlbaum.

Spiker, D. (1990). Early intervention from a developmental perspective. In D. Cicchetti & M. Beeghly (Eds.), *Children with Down syndrome: A developmental perspective* (pp. 424–448). Cambridge: Cambridge University Press.

Spiker, D., Ferguson, J., & Brooks-Gunn, J. (1993). Enhancing maternal interactive behavior and child social competence in low birth weight, premature infants. *Child Development, 64,* 754–768.

Spitze, G. (1988). Women's employment and family relations: A review. *Journal of Marriage and the Family, 50,* 595–618.

Sroufe, L. A. (1979). The coherence of individual development: Early care, attachment, and subsequent developmental issues. *American Psychologist, 34,* 834–841.

Sroufe, L. A. (1983). Infant-caregiver attachment and patterns of adaptation in preschool: The roots of maladaption and competence. In M. Perlmutter (Ed.), *Minnesota symposium on child psychology* (Vol. 16, pp. 41–84). Hillsdale, NJ: Erlbaum.

Sroufe, L. A. (1988). The role of infant-caregiver attachment in development. In J. Belsky & T. Nezworski (Eds.), *Clinical implications of attachment* (pp. 18–40). Hillsdale, NJ: Erlbaum.

Sroufe, L. A. (1989). Pathways to adaptation and maladaptation: Psychopathology as developmental deviation. In D. Cicchetti (Ed.), *The emergence of a discipline: Rochester symposium on developmental psychopathology* (pp. 13–40). Hillsdale, NJ: Erlbaum.

Sroufe, L. A. (1990). A developmental perspective on day care. In N. Fox & G. G. Fein (Eds.), *Infant day care: The current debate* (pp. 51–60). Norwood, NJ: Ablex.

Sroufe, L. A., Carlson, E., & Schulman, S. (1993). Individuals in relationships: Development from infancy through adolescence. In D. C. Funder, R. D. Parke, C. Tomlinson-Keasey, & K. Widaman (Eds.), *Studying lives through time: Personality and development* (pp. 315–342). Washington, DC: American Psychological Association.

Sroufe, L. A., Egeland, B., & Kreutzer, T. (1990). The fate of early experience following developmental change: Longitudinal approaches to individual adaptation in childhood. *Child Development, 61,* 1363–1373.

Sroufe, L. A., & Rutter, M. (1984). The domain of developmental psychopathology. *Child Development, 55,* 17–29.

Stanovich, K. E. (1993). A model for studies of reading disability. *Developmental Review, 13,* 225–245.

Starfield, B. (1991). Childhood morbidity: Comparisons, clusters, and trends. *Pediatrics, 88,* 519–526.

Starfield, B., & Pless, I. B. (1980). Physical health. In O. G. Brim, Jr., & J. Kagan (Eds.), *Constancy and change in human development* (pp. 272–324). Cambridge, MA: Harvard University Press.

Stattin, H., & Klackenberg-Larsson, I. (1993). Early language and intelligence development and their relationship to future criminal behavior. *Journal of Abnormal Psychology, 102,* 369–378.

Stein, Z., Susser, M., Saenger, G., & Morolla, F. (1975). *Famine and human development: The Dutch hunger winter of 1944–1945.* New York: Oxford University Press.

Steinberg, L. (1988). Reciprocal relation between parent-child distance and pubertal maturation. *Developmental Psychology, 24,* 122–128.

Steinberg, L. (1990). Interdependence in the family: Autonomy, conflict and harmony in the parent-adolescent relationship. In S. S. Feldman & G. R. Elliott (Eds.), *At the threshold: The developing adolescent.* Cambridge, MA: Harvard University Press.

Steinberg, L., & Dornbusch, S. M. (1991). Negative correlates of part-time employment during adolescence: Replication and elaboration. *Developmental Psychology, 27,* 304–313.

Steinberg, L., Dornbusch, S. M., & Brown, B. B. (1992a). Ethnic differences in adolescent achievement: An ecological perspective. *American Psychologist, 47,* 723–729.

Steinberg, L., Elmen, J. D., & Mounts, N. S. (1989). Authoritative parenting, psychosocial maturity, and academic success among adolescents. *Child Development, 60,* 1424–1436.

Steinberg, L., Fegley, S., & Dornbusch, S. M. (1993). Negative impact of part-time work on adolescent adjustment: Evidence from a longitudinal study. *Developmental Psychology, 29,* 171–180.

Steinberg, L., Lamborn, S. D., Dornbusch, S. M., & Darling, N. (1992b). Impact of parenting practices on adolescent achievement: Authoritative parenting, school involvement, and encouragement to succeed. *Child Development, 63,* 1266–1281.

Steinberg, L., Mounts, N. S., Lamborn, S. D., & Dornbusch, S. D. (1991). Authoritative parenting and adolescent adjustment across varied ecological niches. *Journal of Research on Adolescence, 1,* 19–36.

Steiner, J. E. (1979). Human facial expressions in response to taste and smell stimulation. In H. W. Reese & L. P. Lipsitt (Eds.), *Advances in child development and behavior* (Vol. 13, pp. 257–296). New York: Academic Press.

Stenchever, M. A. (1978). Labor and delivery. In D. W. Smith, E. L. Bierman, & N. M. Robinson (Eds.), *The biologic ages of man* (2nd ed.) (pp. 78–86). Philadelphia: W. B. Saunders.

Sternberg, R. J. (1986). *Intelligence applied.* New York: Harcourt Brace Jovanovich.

Sternberg, R. J., & Davidson, J. E. (1985). Cognitive development in the gifted and talented. In F. D. Horowitz & M. O'Brien (Eds.), *The gifted and talented: Developmental perspectives* (pp. 37–74). Washington, DC: American Psychological Association.

Sternberg, R. J., & Davidson, J. E. (Eds.) (1986). *Conceptions of giftedness.* Cambridge: Cambridge University Press.

Sternberg, R. J., & Suben, J. G. (1986). The socialization of intelligence. In M. Perlmutter (Ed.), *Perspectives on intellectual development: The Minnesota symposia on child psychology* (Vol. 19, pp. 201–236). Hillsdale, NJ: Erlbaum.

Sternberg, R. J., & Wagner, R. K. (1993). The g-ocentric view of intelligence and job performance is wrong. *Current Directions in Psychological Science, 2,* 1–5.

Stevenson, H. W. (1988). Culture and schooling: Influences on cognitive development. In E. M. Hetherington, R. M.

Lerner, & M. Perlmutter (Eds.), *Child development in life span perspective* (pp. 241–258). Hillsdale, NJ: Erlbaum.

Stevenson, H. W., & Chen, C. (1989). Schooling and achievement: A study of Peruvian children. *International Journal of Educational Research, 13,* 883–894.

Stevenson, H. W., Chen, C., Lee, S., & Fuligni, A. J. (1991). Schooling, culture, and cognitive development. In L. Okagaki & R. J. Sternberg (Eds.), *Directors of development* (pp. 243–268). Hillsdale, NJ: Erlbaum.

Stevenson, H. W., & Lee, S. (1990). Contexts of achievement: A study of American, Chinese, and Japanese children. *Monographs of the Society for Research in Child Development, 55*(1–2, Serial No. 221).

Stevenson, H. W., Lee, S., Chen, C., Lummis, M., Stigler, J., Fan, L., & Ge, F. (1990). Mathematics achievement of children in China and the United States. *Child Development, 61,* 1053–1066.

Steward, M. S. (1993). Understanding children's memories of medical procedures: "He didn't touch me and it didn't hurt!" In C. A. Nelson (Ed.), *Memory and affect in development: The Minnesota symposia on child psychology* (Vol. 26, pp. 171–225). Hillsdale, NJ: Erlbaum.

Stewart, J. F., Popkin, B. M., Guilkey, D. K., Akin, J. S., Adair, L., & Flieger, W. (1991). Influences on the extent of breast-feeding: A prospective study in the Philippines. *Demography, 28,* 181–199.

Stewart, R. B., Cluff, L. E., & Philp, R. (1977). *Drug monitoring: A requirement for responsible drug use.* Baltimore: Williams & Wilkins.

Stigler, J. W., Lee, S., & Stevenson, H. W. (1987). Mathematics classrooms in Japan, Taiwan, and the United States. *Child Development, 58,* 1272–1285.

Stigler, J. W., & Stevenson, H. W. (1991, Spring). How Asian teachers polish each lesson to perfection. *American Educator,* pp. 12–20, 43–47.

Stipek, D. (1992). The child at school. In M. H. Bornstein & M. E. Lamb (Eds.), *Developmental psychology: An advanced textbook* (3rd ed.) (pp. 579–625). Hillsdale, NJ: Erlbaum.

Stipek, D., & Gralinski, H. (1991). Gender differences in children's achievement-related beliefs and emotional responses to success and failure in math. *Journal of Educational Psychology, 83,* 361–371.

Stoneman, Z., Brody, G. H., & Burke, M. (1989). Sibling temperaments and maternal and paternal perceptions of marital, family, and personal functioning. *Journal of Marriage and the Family, 51,* 99–113.

Storfer, M. D. (1990). *Intelligence and giftedness.* San Francisco: Jossey-Bass.

Stoutjesdyk, D., & Jevne, R. (1993). Eating disorders among high performance athletes. *Journal of Youth and Adolescence, 22,* 271–282.

St. Peters, M., Fitch, M., Huston, A. C., Wright, J. C., & Eakins, D. J. (1991). Television and families: What do young children watch with their parents? *Child Development, 62,* 1409–1423.

Strassberg, Z., Dodge, K. A., Bates, J. E., & Pettit, G. S. (1992). The longitudinal relation between parental conflict strategies and children's sociometric standing in kindergarten. *Merrill-Palmer Quarterly, 38,* 477–493.

Streissguth, A. P., Aase, J. M., Clarren, S. K., Randels, S. P., LaDue, R. A., & Smith, D. F. (1991). Fetal alcohol syndrome in adolescents and adults. *Journal of the American Medical Association, 265,* 1961–1967.

Streissguth, A. P., Barr, H. M., & Sampson, P. D. (1990). Moderate prenatal alcohol exposure: Effects on child IQ and learning problems at age 7 $1/2$ years. *Alcoholism: Clinical and Experimental Research, 14,* 662–669.

Streissguth, A. P., Barr, H. M., Sampson, P. D., Darby, B. L., & Martin, D. C. (1989). IQ at age 4 in relation to maternal alcohol use and smoking during pregnancy. *Developmental Psychology, 25,* 3–11.

Streissguth, A. P., Landesman-Dwyer, S., Martin, J. C., & Smith, D. W. (1980). Teratogenic effects of alcohol in humans and laboratory animals. *Science, 209,* 353–361.

Streissguth, A. P., Martin, D. C., Barr, H. M., Sandman, B. M., Kirchner, G. L., & Darby, B. L. (1984). Intrauterine alcohol and nicotine exposure: Attention and reaction time in 4-year-old children. *Developmental Psychology, 20,* 533–541.

Streissguth, A. P., Martin, D. C., Martin, J. C., & Barr, H. M. (1981). The Seattle longitudinal prospective study on alcohol and pregnancy. *Neurobehavioral Toxicology and Teratology, 3,* 223–233.

Striegel-Moore, R. H., Silberstein, L. R., & Rodin, J. (1986). Toward an understanding of risk factors for bulimia. *American Psychologist, 41,* 246–263.

Strobino, D. M. (1987). The health and medical consequences of adolescent sexuality and pregnancy: A review of the literature. In S. L. Hofferth & C. D. Hayes (Eds.), *Risking the future: Adolescent sexuality, pregnancy, and childbearing. Working papers* (pp. 93–122). Washington, DC: National Academy Press.

Sue, S., & Okazaki, S. (1990). Asian-American educational achievements: A phenomenon in search of an explanation. *American Psychologist, 45,* 913–920.

Super, C. M., & Harkness, S. (1982). The infant's niche in rural Kenya and metropolitan America. In L. Adler (Ed.), *Issues in cross-cultural research* (pp. 47–56). New York: Academic Press.

Swedo, S. E., Rettew, D. C., Kuppenheimer, M., Lum, D., Dolan, S., & Goldberger, E. (1991). Can adolescent suicide attempters be distinguished from at-risk adolescents? *Pediatrics, 88,* 620–629.

Szapocznik, J., & Kurtines, W. M. (1993). Family psychology and cultural diversity: Opportunities for theory, research and application. *American Psychologist, 48,* 400–407.

Taffel, S. M., Placek, P. J., & Liss, T. (1987). Trends in the United States cesarean section rate and reasons for the 1980–85 rise. *American Journal of Public Health, 77,* 955–959.

Takei, Y., & Dubas, J. S. (1993). Academic achievement among early adolescents: Social and cultural diversity. In R. M. Lerner (Ed.), *Early adolescence: Perspectives on research, policy, and intervention* (pp. 175–190). Hillsdale, NJ: Erlbaum.

Tamis-LeMonda, C., & Bornstein, M. H. (1987). Is there a "sensitive period" in human mental development? In M. H. Bornstein (Ed.), *Sensitive periods in development: Interdisciplinary perspectives* (pp. 163–182). Hillsdale, NJ: Erlbaum.

Tannen, D. (1990). *You just don't understand.* New York: William Morrow.

Tanner, J. M. (1978). *Fetus into man: Physical growth from conception to maturity.* Cambridge, MA: Harvard University Press.

Tanner, J. M., Hughes, P. C. R., & Whitehouse, R. H. (1981). Radiographically determined widths of bone, muscle and fat in the upper arm and calf from 3–18 years. *Annals of Human Biology, 8,* 495–517.

Taylor, M., Cartwright, B. S., & Carlson, S. M. (1993a). A developmental investigation of children's imaginary companions. *Developmental Psychology, 29,* 276–285.

Taylor, R. D., Casten, R., & Flickinger, S. M. (1993b). Influence of kinship social support on the parenting experiences and psychosocial adjustment of African-American adolescents. *Developmental Psychology, 29,* 382–388.

Tellegen, A., Lykken, D. T., Bouchard, T. J., Wilcox, K. J., Segal, N. L., & Rich, S. (1988). Personality similarity in twins reared apart and together. *Journal of Personality and Social Psychology, 54,* 1031–1039.

Teller, D. Y., & Bornstein, M. H. (1987). Infant color vision and color perception. In P. Salapatek & L. Cohen (Eds.), *Handbook of infant perception: Vol. 1. From sensation to perception* (pp. 185–236). Orlando, FL: Academic Press.

Terman, L. (1916). *The measurement of intelligence.* Boston: Houghton Mifflin.

Terman, L. (1925). *Genetic studies of genius: Vol. 1. Mental and physical traits of a thousand gifted children.* Stanford, CA: Stanford University Press.

Terman, L., & Merrill, M. A. (1937). *Measuring intelligence: A guide to the administration of the new revised Stanford-Binet tests.* Boston: Houghton Mifflin.

Terman, L., & Oden, M. (1947). *Genetic studies of genius: Vol. 4. The gifted child grows up.* Stanford, CA: Stanford University Press.

Terman, L., & Oden, M. (1959). *Genetic studies of genius: Vol. 5, The gifted group at mid-life.* Stanford, CA: Stanford University Press.

Tew, M. (1985). Place of birth and perinatal mortality. *Journal of the Royal College of General Practitioners, 35,* 390–394.

Thal, D., & Bates, E. (1990). Continuity and variation in early language development. In J. Colombo & J. Fagen (Eds.), *Individual differences in infancy: Reliability, stability, prediction* (pp. 359–385). Hillsdale, NJ: Erlbaum.

Thelen, E. (1981). Rhythmical behavior in infancy: An ethological perspective. *Developmental Psychology, 17,* 237–257.

Thelen, E. (1984). Learning to walk: Ecological demands and phylogenetic constraints. In L. P. Lipsitt & C. Rovee-Collier (Eds.), *Advances in infancy research* (Vol. 3, pp. 213–260). Norwood, NJ: Ablex.

Thelen, E. (1989). The (re)discovery of motor development: Learning new things from an old field. *Developmental Psychology, 25,* 946–949.

Thelen, E. (1992). Development as a dynamic system. *Current Directions in Psychological Science, 1,* 189–193.

Thelen, E., & Adolph, K. E. (1992). Arnold L. Gesell: The paradox of nature and nurture. *Developmental Psychology, 28,* 368–380.

Thomas, A., & Chess, S. (1977). *Temperament and development.* New York: Brunner/Mazel.

Thomas, R. M. (Ed.). (1990). *The encyclopedia of human development and education: Theory, research, and studies.* Oxford: Pergamon Press.

Thomas, R. M. (1990a). Motor development. In R. M. Thomas (Ed.), *The encyclopedia of human development and education: Theory, research, and studies* (pp. 326–330). Oxford: Pergamon Press.

Thomas, R. M. (1990b). Body image and body language. In R. M. Thomas (Ed.), *The encyclopedia of human development and education: Theory, research, and studies* (pp. 377–378). Oxford: Pergamon Press.

Thomas, R. M. (1990c). Basic concepts and applications of Piagetian cognitive development theory. In R. M. Thomas (Ed.), *The encyclopedia of human development and education: Theory, research, and studies* (pp. 53–55). Oxford: Pergamon Press.

Thompson, S. K. (1975). Gender labels and early sex role development. *Child Development, 46,* 339–347.

Thorne, B. (1986). Girls and boys together . . . but mostly apart: Gender arrangements in elementary schools. In W. W. Hartup & Z. Rubin (Eds.), *Relationships and development* (pp. 167–184). Hillsdale, NJ: Erlbaum.

Thornton, A. (1990). The courtship process and adolescent sexuality. *Journal of Family Issues, 11,* 239–273.

Timmer, S. G., Eccles, J., & O'Brien, K. (1985). How children use time. In F. T. Juster & F. P. Stafford (Eds.), *Time, goods, and well being* (pp. 353–369). Ann Arbor: Institute for Social Research, The University of Michigan.

Tobin-Richards, M. H., Boxer, A. M., & Petersen, A. C. (1983). The psychological significance of pubertal change: Sex differences in perceptions of self during early adolescence. In J. Brooks-Gunn & A. C. Petersen (Eds.), *Girls at puberty: Biological and psychosocial perspectives* (pp. 127–154). New York: Plenum Press.

Tomasello, M., & Mannle, S. (1985). Pragmatics of sibling speech to one-year-olds. *Child Development, 56,* 911–917.

Tomlinson-Keasey, C., Eisert, D. C., Kahle, L. R., Hardy-Brown, K., & Keasey, B. (1979). The structure of concrete operational thought. *Child Development, 50,* 1153–1163.

Trehub, S. E., Bull, D., & Thorpe, L. A. (1984). Infants' perception of melodies: The role of melodic contour. *Child Development, 55,* 821–830.

Trehub, S. E., & Rabinovitch, M. S. (1972). Auditory-linguistic sensitivity in early infancy. *Developmental Psychology, 6,* 74–77.

Trehub, S. E., Thorpe, L. A., & Morrongiello, B. A. (1985). Infants' perception of melodies: Changes in a single tone. *Infant Behavior and Development, 8,* 213–223.

Tremblay, R. E. (1991). Commentary. Aggression, prosocial behavior, and gender: Three magic words, but no magic wand. In D. J. Pepler & K. H. Rubin (Eds.), *The development and treatment of aggression* (pp. 71–78). Hillsdale, NJ: Erlbaum.

Tronick, E. Z., Morelli, G. A., & Ivey, P. K. (1992). The Efe forager infant and toddler's pattern of social relationships: Multiple and simultaneous. *Developmental Psychology, 28,* 568–577.

Tuna, J. M. (1989). Mental health services for children: The state of the art. *American Psychologist, 44,* 188–199.

Tunmer, W. E., Herriman, M. L., & Nesdale, A. R. (1988). Metalinguistic abilities and beginning reading. *Reading Research Quarterly, 23,* 134–158.

Turiel, E. (1966). An experimental test of the sequentiality of developmental stages in the child's moral judgment. *Journal of Personality and Social Psychology, 3,* 611–618.

Turkheimer, E., & Gottesman, I. I. (1991). Individual differences and the canalization of human behavior. *Developmental Psychology, 27,* 18–22.

Umberson, D., & Gove, W. R. (1989). Parenthood and psychological well-being: Theory, measurement, and stage in the family life course. *Journal of Family Issues, 10,* 440–462.

Underwood, M. K., Coie, J. D., & Herbsman, C. R. (1992). Display rules for anger and aggression in school-age children. *Child Development, 63,* 366–380.

Ungerer, J. A., & Sigman, M. (1984). The relation of play and sensorimotor behavior to language in the second year. *Child Development, 55,* 1448–1455.

United States Bureau of the Census. (1992). *Statistical Abstract of the United States: 1992* (112th ed.). Washington, DC: U.S. Government Printing Office.

Upchurch, D. M. (1993). Early schooling and childbearing experiences: Implications for post-secondary school attendance. *Journal of Research on Adolescence, 3,* 423–443.

Urban, J., Carlson, E., Egeland, B., & Sroufe, L. A. (1991). Patterns of individual adaptation across childhood. *Development and Psychopathology, 3,* 445–460.

Valdez-Menchaca, M. C., & Whitehurst, G. J. (1992). Accelerating language development through picture book reading: A systematic extension to Mexican day care. *Developmental Psychology, 28,* 1106–1114.

Vandenberg, B. (1984). Developmental features of exploration. *Developmental Psychology, 20,* 3–8.

Van de Perre, P., Simonen, A., Msellati, P., Hitimana, D., Vaira, D., Bazebagira, A., Van Goethem, C., Stevens, A., Karita, E., Sondag-Thull, D., Dabis, F., & Lepage, P. (1991). Postnatal transmission of human immunodeficiency virus type 1 from mother to infant. *New England Journal of Medicine, 325,* 593–598.

van IJzendoorn, M. H., Goldberg, S., Kroonenberg, P. M., & Frenkel, O. J. (1992). The relative effects of maternal and child problems on the quality of attachment: A meta-analysis of attachment in clinical samples. *Child Development, 63,* 840–858.

van IJzendoorn, M. H., & Kroonenberg, P. M. (1988). Cross-cultural patterns of attachment: A meta-analysis of the Strange Situation. *Child Development, 59,* 147–156.

Vellutino, F. R. (1987). Dyslexia. *Scientific American, 256,* 34–41.

Vernon, P. A. (Ed.). (1987). *Speed of information-processing and intelligence.* Norwood, NJ: Ablex.

Vernon, P. A., & Mori, M. (1992). Intelligence, reaction times, and peripheral nerve conduction velocity. *Intelligence, 16,* 273–288.

Victoria Infant Collaborative Study Group. (1991). Eight-year outcome in infants with birth weight of 500–999 grams: Continuing regional study of 1979 and 1980 births. *Journal of Pediatrics, 118,* 761–767.

Vihko, R., & Apter, D. (1980). The role of androgens in adolescent cycles. *Journal of Steroid Biochemistry, 12,* 369–373.

Vorhees, C. F., & Mollnow, E. (1987). Behavioral teratogenesis: Long-term influences on behavior from early exposure to environmental agents. In J. D. Osofsky (Ed.), *Handbook of infant development* (2nd ed.) (pp. 913–971). New York: Wiley-Interscience.

Vuchinich, S., Bank, L., & Patterson, G. R. (1992). Parenting, peers, and the stability of antisocial behavior in preadolescent boys. *Developmental Psychology, 28,* 510–521.

Vygotsky, L. S. (1962). *Thought and language.* New York: Wiley.

Wachs, T. D., Bishry, Z., Sobhy, A., McCabe, G., Galal, O., & Shaheen, F. (1993). Relation of rearing environment to adaptive behavior of Egyptian toddlers. *Child Development, 64,* 586–604.

Waddington, C. H. (1957). *The strategy of the genes*. London: Allen & Son.

Wahlström, J. (1990). Gene map of mental retardation. *Journal of Mental Deficiency Research, 34,* 11–27.

Wald, E. R., Guerra, N., & Byers, C. (1991). Frequency and severity of infections in day care: Three-year follow-up. *Journal of Pediatrics, 118,* 509–514.

Waldrop, M. F., & Halverson, C. F. (1975). Intensive and extensive peer behavior: Longitudinal and cross-sectional analysis. *Child Development, 46,* 19–26.

Walker, H., Messinger, D., Fogel, A., & Karns, J. (1992). Social and communicative development in infancy. In V. B. Van Hasselt & M. Hersen (Eds.), *Handbook of social development: A lifespan perspective* (pp. 157–181). New York: Plenum Press.

Walker, L. J. (1980). Cognitive and perspective-taking prerequisites for moral development. *Child Development, 51,* 131–139.

Walker, L. J. (1989). A longitudinal study of moral reasoning. *Child Development, 60,* 157–160.

Walker, L. J., de Vries, B., & Trevethan, S. D. (1987). Moral stages and moral orientations in real-life and hypothetical dilemmas. *Child Development, 58,* 842–858.

Wallerstein, J. (1989, January 22). Children after divorce: Wounds that don't heal. *The New York Times Magazine,* pp. 19–21, 41–44.

Wallerstein, J. S. (1984). Children of divorce: Preliminary report of a ten-year follow-up of young children. *American Journal of Orthopsychiatry, 54,* 444–458.

Walters, R. H., & Brown, M. (1963). Studies of reinforcement of aggression: 3. Transfer of responses to an interpersonal situation. *Child Development, 34,* 563–571.

Walton, G. E., Bower, N. J. A., & Bower, T. G. R. (1992). Recognition of familiar faces by newborns. *Infant Behavior and Development, 15,* 265–269.

Walton, G. E., & Bower, T. G. R. (1993). Amodal representation of speech in infants. *Infant Behavior and Development, 16,* 233–253.

Waterman, A. S. (1985). Identity in the context of adolescent psychology. *New Directions for Child Development, 30,* 5–24.

Watson, J. D., & Crick, F. H. C. (1953). Molecular structure of nucleic acid: A structure for deoxyribose nucleic acid: *Nature, 171,* 737–738.

Watson, M. W., & Getz, K. (1990a). Developmental shifts in Oedipal behaviors related to family role understanding. *New Directions for Child Development, 48,* 5–28.

Watson, M. W., & Getz, K. (1990b). The relationship between Oedipal behaviors and children's family role concepts. *Merrill-Palmer Quarterly, 36,* 487–506.

Waxman, S., & Gelman, R. (1986). Preschoolers' use of superordinate relations in classification and language. *Cognitive Development, 1,* 139–156.

Waxman, S. R., & Hall, D. G. (1993). The development of a linkage between count nouns and object categories: Evidence from fifteen- to twenty-one-month-old infants. *Child Development, 64,* 1224–1241.

Waxman, S. R., & Kosowski, T. D. (1990). Nouns mark category relations: Toddlers' and preschoolers' word-learning biases. *Child Development, 61,* 1461–1473.

Webster-Stratton, C., & Hammond, M. (1988). Maternal depression and its relationship to life stress, perceptions of child behavior problems, parenting behaviors and child conduct problems. *Journal of Abnormal Child Psychology, 16,* 299–315.

Wechsler, D. (1974). *Manual for the Wechsler Intelligence Scale for Children, Revised.* New York: Psychological Corp.

Wegman, M. E. (1990). Annual summary of vital statistics— 1989. *Pediatrics, 86,* 845–847.

Wegman, M. E. (1991). Annual summary of vital statistics— 1990. *Pediatrics, 88,* 1081–1092.

Wegman, M. E. (1992). Annual summary of vital statistics— 1991. *Pediatrics, 90,* 835–845.

Weinberg, R. A. (1989). Intelligence and IQ: Landmark issues and great debates. *American Psychologist, 44,* 98–104.

Weinberg, R. A., Scarr, S., & Waldman, I. D. (1992). The Minnesota transracial adoption study: A follow-up of IQ test performance. *Intelligence, 16,* 117–135.

Weiss, B., Dodge, K. A., Bates, J. E., & Pettit, G. S. (1992). Some consequences of early harsh discipline: Child aggression and a maladaptive social information processing style. *Child Development, 63,* 1321–1335.

Weisz, J. R., Sigman, M., Weiss, B., & Mosk, J. (1993). Parent reports of behavioral and emotional problems among children in Kenya, Thailand, and the United States. *Child Development, 64,* 98–109.

Wellman, H. M. (1982). The foundations of knowledge: Concept development in the young child. In S. G. Moore & C. C. Cooper (Eds.), *The young child: Reviews of research* (Vol. 3, pp. 115–134). Washington, DC : National Association for the Education of Young Children.

Wellman, H. M. (1988). First steps in the child's theorizing about the mind. In J. W. Astington, P. L. Harris, & D. R. Olson (Eds.), *Developing theories of mind* (pp. 64–92). New York: Cambridge University Press.

Wen, S. W., Goldenberg, R. L., Cutter, G. R., Hoffman, H. J., Cliver, S. P., Davis, R. O., & DuBard, M. D. (1990). Smoking, maternal age, fetal growth, and gestational age at delivery. *American Journal of Obstetrics and Gynecology, 162,* 53–58.

Werker, J. F., & Tees, R. C. (1984). Cross-language speech perception: Evidence for perceptual reorganization during the first year of life. *Infant Behavior and Development, 7,* 49–63.

Werner, E. E. (1986). A longitudinal study of perinatal risk. In D. C. Farran & J. D. McKinney (Eds.), *Risk in intellectual and psychosocial development* (pp. 3–28). Orlando, FL: Academic Press.

Werner, E. E., Bierman, J. M., & French, F. E. (1971). *The children of Kauai.* Honolulu: University of Hawaii Press.

Werner, E. E., & Smith, R. S. (1982). *Vulnerable but invincible: A study of resilient children.* New York: McGraw-Hill.

Werner, E. E., & Smith, R. S. (1992). *Overcoming the odds: High risk children from birth to adulthood.* Ithaca, NY: Cornell University Press.

Werner, H. (1948). *Comparative psychology of mental development.* Chicago: Follett.

Werner, L. A., & Gillenwater, J. M. (1990). Pure-tone sensitivity of 2- to 5-week-old infants. *Infant Behavior and Development, 13,* 355–375.

Whitehurst, G. J., Falco, F. L., Lonigan, C. J., Fischel, J. E., De-Baryshe, B. D., Valdez-Menchaca, M. C., & Caulfield, M. (1988). Accelerating language development through picture book reading. *Developmental Psychology, 24,* 552–559.

Whiting, B. B., & Edwards, C. P. (1988). *Children of different worlds: The formation of social behavior.* Cambridge, MA: Harvard University Press.

Wiesenfeld, A. R., Malatesta, C. Z., & DeLoach, L. L. (1981). Differential parental response to familiar and unfamiliar infant distress signals. *Infant Behavior and Development, 4,* 281–296.

Wilcox, A. J., Weinberg, C. R., O'Connor, J. F., Baird, D. D., Schlatterer, J. P., Canfield, R. E., Armstrong, E. G., & Nisula, B. C. (1988). Incidence of early loss of pregnancy. *New England Journal of Medicine, 319,* 189–194.

Williams, E., Radin, N., & Allegro, T. (1992). Sex role attitudes of adolescents reared primarily by their fathers: An 11-year follow-up. *Merrill-Palmer Quarterly, 38,* 457–476.

Williams, J. E., & Best, D. L. (1990). *Measuring sex stereotypes: A multination study* (rev. ed.). Newbury Park, CA: Sage.

Willig, A. (1985). Meta-analysis of studies on bilingual education. *Review of Educational Research, 55,* 269–317.

Willows, D. M., & Ryan, E. B. (1986). The development of grammatical sensitivity and its relationship to early reading achievement. *Reading Research Quarterly, 21,* 253–266.

Wilson, M. N. (1986). The black extended family: An analytical consideration. *Developmental Psychology, 22,* 246–258.

Wilson, M. N. (1989). Child development in the context of the black extended family. *American Psychologist, 44,* 380–385.

Winick, M. (1980). *Nutrition in health and disease.* New York: Wiley.

Woodward, A. L., & Markman, E. M. (1991). Review. Constraints on learning as default assumptions: Comments on Merriman & Bowman's "The mutual exclusivity bias in children's word learning." *Developmental Review, 11,* 137–163.

World Health Organization. (1981). *Contemporary patterns of breast-feeding: Report on the WHO collaborative study on breast-feeding.* Geneva: World Health Organization.

Yonas, A. (1981). Infants' responses to optical information for collision. In R. N. Aslin, J. R. Alberts, & M. R. Peterson (Eds.), *Development of perception: Psychobiological perspectives: Vol. 2. The visual system* (pp. 313–334). New York: Academic Press.

Yonas, A., & Owsley, C. (1987). Development of visual space perception. In P. Salapatek & L. Cohen (Eds.), *Handbook of infant perception: Vol. 2. From perception to cognition* (pp. 80–122). Orlando, FL: Academic Press.

Youngblade, L. M., & Belsky, J. (1992). Parent-child antecedents of 5-year-olds' close friendships: A longitudinal analysis. *Developmental Psychology, 28,* 700–713.

Zahn-Waxler, C., & Radke-Yarrow, M. (1982). The development of altruism: Alternative research strategies. In N. Eisenberg (Ed.), *The development of prosocial behavior* (pp. 109–138). New York: Academic Press.

Zajonc, R. B. (1983). Validating the confluence model. *Psychological Bulletin, 93,* 457–480.

Zajonc, R. B., & Marcus, G. B. (1975). Birth order and intellectual development. *Psychological Review, 82,* 74–88.

Zametkin, A. J., Nordahl, T. E., Gross, M., King, A. C., Semple, W. E., Rumsey, J., Hamburger, S., & Cohen, R. M. (1990). Cerebral glucose metabolism in adults with hyperactivity of childhood onset. *New England Journal of Medicine, 323,* 1361–1366.

Zaslow, M. J., & Hayes, C. D. (1986). Sex differences in children's responses to psychosocial stress: Toward a cross-context analysis. In M. E. Lamb, A. L. Brown, & B. Rogoff (Eds.), *Advances in developmental psychology* (Vol. 4, pp. 285–238). Hillsdale, NJ: Erlbaum.

Zelazo, N. A., Zelazo, P. R., Cohen, K. M., & Zelazo, P. D. (1993). Specificity of practice effects on elementary neuromotor patterns. *Developmental Psychology, 29,* 686–691.

Zeskind, P. S., & Ramey, C. T. (1981). Preventing intellectual and interactional sequelae of fetal malnutrition: A longitudinal, transactional, and synergistic approach to development. *Child Development, 52,* 213–218.

Zigler, E., & Hall, N. W. (1989). Physical child abuse in America: Past, present, and future. In D. Cicchetti & V. Carlson (Eds.), *Child maltreatment* (pp. 38–75). Cambridge: Cambridge University Press.

Zigler, E., & Hodapp, R. M. (1991). Behavioral functioning in individuals with mental retardation. *Annual Review of Psychology, 42,* 29–50.

Zoccolillo, M. (1993). Gender and the development of conduct disorder. *Development and Psychopathology, 5,* 65–78.

CREDITS

1: Laura Dwight; 3: Emily Strong/The Picture Cube; 4: Paul Conklin; 10: David Young-Wolff/Photo Edit; 13: Daemmrich/The Image Works; 16: Myrleen Ferguson/Photo Edit; 18: Laura Dwight; 19: Don Smetzer/Tony Stone Images; 30: Laura Dwight; 37: Ricardo De Aratanha/The Image Bank; 39: Petit Format/Nestlé/SS/Photo Researchers; 40: Photo Researchers; 41: Tony Freeman/Photo Edit; 48 (top left): Petit Format/Nestlé/SS/Photo Researchers; 48 (top right): Petit Format/Nestlé/SS/Photo Researchers; 48 (bottom left): Petit Format/Nestlé/SS/Photo Researchers; 48 (bottom right): Petit Format/Nestlé/SS/Photo Researchers; 52: Laura Dwight; 63: Laura Dwight; 71: M. Richards/Photo Edit; 74: S.I.U./Peter Arnold, Inc.; 77: David Young-Wolff/Photo Edit; 79: Hyman/Stock Boston; 84 (all): *From The Neurological Examination of the Full Term Newborn Infant,* by Heinz F. R. Prechtl, Second Edition; *A Manual for Clinical Use* from the Department of Developmental Neurology, University of Groningen; *Clinics in Developmental Medicine,* No. 63, 1977. Spastics International Medical Publications, now MacKeith Press; London: William Heinemann Medical Books Ltd.; Philadelphia: J. B. Lippincott Co. Printed in England by The Lavenham Press Ltd., Lavenham, Suffolk; 85: Photo Researchers; 86: Laura Dwight; 87: Laura Dwight; 89: Jeffry W. Myers/Stock Boston; 95: Laura Dwight; 101: Richard Hutchings/Photo Edit; 103: Jim Whitmer; 104: Myrleen Ferguson/Photo Edit; 105: Daemmrich/The Image Works; 116 (top): Elizabeth Crews/The Image Works; 116 (center): Laura Dwight; 116 (bottom): Laura Dwight; 119: Gale Zucker/Stock Boston; 124: Brent Jones; 130: Tom McCarthy/Photo Edit; 134: Laura Dwight; 135: Laura Dwight; 137: Michael Newman/Photo Edit; 140: Laura Dwight; 141: Enrique Ferorelli Enterprises, Inc.; 144: Elizabeth Hatton/The Stock Market; 147: Laura Dwight; 150: Laura Dwight; 151 (all): Zimbel/Monkmeyer Press Photo Service; 156 (top): Myrleen F. Cate/Photo Edit; 156 (bottom): Richard Hutchings/Photo Edit; 161: Laura Dwight; 163: Daemmrich/The Image Works; 165: Laura Dwight; 167 (top): Bob Daemmrich; 167 (bottom): Bob Daemmrich/Stock Boston; 169: Laura Dwight; 172: Paul Conklin/Photo Edit; 175: R. Crandall/Stock Boston; 177: David Young-Wolff/Photo Edit; 180: Elizabeth Crews/The Image Works; 190: Bob Daemmrich/The Image Works; 192: Peter Southwick/Stock Boston; 193: Laura Dwight; 195 (top): Sam Falk/NYT Pictures; 196 (left): Laura Dwight; 196 (right): Laura Dwight; 199: Elizabeth Crews/The Image Works; 202: From Carolyn Rovee-Collier, *Current Directions in Psychological Science,* 2(4), 130–135. 1993; 204: Laura Dwight; 212: R. Sidney/The Image Works; 216 (left): Laura Dwight; 216 (center): Elizabeth Crews/The Image Works; 216 (right): John Eastcott/YVA Momatiuk/The Image Works; 220: Laura Dwight; 227: Laura Dwight; 229: H. S. Terrace/Anthro-Photo; 231: Elizabeth Crews/The Image Works; 239: Laura Dwight; 241: Roy Kirby/Stock Boston; 242: Miro Vintoniv/Stock Boston; 243: Suzanne Haldane/Stock Boston; 250: Laura Dwight; 251: Laura Dwight; 253: Tony Freeman/Photo Edit; 257: Bob Daemmrich; 259: Myrleen Ferguson/Photo Edit; 260: Bob Daemmrich; 263: Jerry Howard/Positive Images; 267: Tony Freeman/Photo Edit; 269: Andy Snow; 271: Bob Daemmrich/Stock Boston; 274: Laura Dwight; 276: Jeff I. Greenberg/Photo Edit; 278: M. Heron/Monkmeyer Press Photo Service; 282: Tony Freeman/Photo Edit; 288: Bob Daemmrich; 290: Laura Dwight; 292: Laura Dwight; 296: Daniel Laine/Actuel; 297: Daemmrich/The Image Works; 299: Michael Newman/Photo Edit; 300: Lawrence Migdale/Photo Researchers; 302: Willie Hill/The Image Works; 305: Brent Jones; 308: Jerry Howard/Positive Images; 313: S. Roessler/The Stock Market; 315: Frank Siteman/The Picture Cube; 317 (left): Laura Dwight; 317 (right): Laura Dwight; 318: Laura Dwight; 323: Winter/The Image Works; 324: Laura Dwight; 330: Elizabeth Crews/The Image Works; 332: Laura Dwight; 333: Jerry Howard/Positive Images; 339: Laura Dwight; 344: John Coletti/The Picture Cube; 348: Laura Dwight; 349 (all): Photos from *Unmasking the Face* by Paul Ekman and Wallace V. Friesen, Prentice Hall, 1975; 351: Esther Shapiro/Photo Researchers; 357: Peter Menzel/Stock Boston; 358: J. C. Francolon/Gamma-Liaison; 363: Willie Hill, Jr./The Image Works; 365: Tony Freeman/Photo Edit; 366: MacDonald/Photo Edit; 373: John Lund/PhotoFile; 375: Bob Daemmrich; 377: Myrleen Ferguson/Photo Edit; 381: Brent Jones; 386: Joan Clifford/The Picture Cube; 390: Timothy Eagan/Woodfin Camp & Associates; 392: Bill Aron/Photo Edit; 394: Phil Borden/Photo Edit; 395: David Young-Wolff/Photo Edit; 397: Joyce Marshall/*Fort Worth Star-Telegram*//SIPA-Press; 402: Lawrence Migdale/Stock Boston; 405: Jim Harrison/Stock Boston; 407: Daemmrich/Stock Boston; 410: Milt and Joan Mann/Cameramann International, Ltd.; 414: Bob Daemmrich; 416: Hache/Photo Researchers; 423: Burt Glinn/Magnum Photos; 425: John Neubauer/Photo Edit; 426: Brent Jones; 427: Bob

Name Index

Abelson, R., 346
Achenbach, T. M., 435, 438, 439, 443, 447
Adams, G. R., 133, 294
Adams, M. J., 252
Adler, A., 20
Adler, T. F., 186
Adolph, K. E., 5
Ainsfeld, M., 201
Ainsworth, M. D. S., 315, 319, 325
Aksu-Koc, A. A., 247
Al Awad, A. M. E. L., 392
Alexander, K. L., 177
Allegro, T., 308
Allen, S. G., 383
Allesandri, S. M., 290
Alpern, L., 329
Amato, P. R., 393
Anderson, C. L., 80
Andersson, B., 405, 406
Apter, D., 113
Arcus, D., 262
Aslin, R. N., 8, 9, 137, 140, 158, 245, 475
Astbury, J., 79
Astington, J. W., 205, 206
Astone, N. M., 119
Attie, I., 125, 126
Avis, J., 205

Bachman, J. G., 414
Baenninger, M., 120
Bailey, J. M., 335
Baird, P. A., 52, 63
Bakewell, J. M., 77
Balaban, T., 304
Baldwin, D. A., 242
Bamford, F. N., 4, 90
Bandura, A., 17, 19, 200, 267, 269, 270, 271, 272, 305, 307
Bank, L., 11, 467
Barenboim, C., 352
Barkley, R. A., 440, 441
Barnard, K. E., 79, 80, 92, 177
Barnes, D. E., 77
Barnes, H. L., 381
Barnett, D., 326, 394
Barr, H. M., 59, 129
Barrett, G. V., 411
Bartlett, E., 242

Bartsch, K., 213
Bates, E., 96, 230, 231, 235, 244, 247, 250, 466
Bates, J. E., 177, 266, 287, 329
Baumrind, D., 378, 381, 382
Baydar, N., 172, 405
Bearison, D. J., 468
Becker, J. A., 243
Beckwith, L., 60
Bedard, J. A., 212
Bee, H. L., 79, 80
Bell, D. C., 381
Bell, L. G., 381
Bellinger, D., 61
Bellugi, U., 235
Belsky, J., 82, 316, 329, 406, 407
Bem, S. L., 309
Benbow, C. P., 184
Bender, B., 52
Berberian, K. E., 321
Berch, D. B., 52
Berendes, H. W., 63
Berg, J. M., 56
Berk, L. E., 243
Berkowitz, G. S., 63
Bernal, M. E., 428
Berndt, T. J., 333, 353, 365
Bernfield, M., 65
Bertenthal, B. I., 110
Betancourt, H., 12
Bettes, B. A., 246
Bickhard, M. H., 5
Bierman, J. M., 424
Bierman, K. L., 330
Bigelow, B. J., 354
Binet, A., 165
Birch, R., 148
Birns, B., 176
Bivens, J. A., 243
Bjorklund, D. F., 212, 223
Black, B., 338
Black, J. E., 49, 109
Black, K. N., 249
Block, J., 282, 298, 383
Bloom, L., 236
Blyth, D. A., 121
Boer, F., 387, 400
Bond, L., 458

Bonvillan, J. D., 231
Booth, A., 433
Booth, C. L., 326
Bornschein, R. L., 10
Bornstein, M. H., 27, 35, 137, 140, 226, 255
Borton, R. W., 147
Bouchard, T. J., Jr., 7, 264
Boukydis, C. F. Z., 95
Bowen, R., 472
Bowen-Woodward, K., 393
Bower, N. J. A., 142
Bower, T. G. R., 142, 147, 158
Bowerman, M., 247
Bowlby, J., 20, 279, 280, 282, 314, 318
Boxer, A. M., 121
Boyes, M. C., 383
Boyle, M. H., 24, 25, 336
Brackbill, Y., 76, 104
Bradbard, M. R., 304
Bradley, L., 252
Bradley, R. H., 177
Brand, E., 393
Brandenburg, N. A., 435
Breitmayer, B. J., 82, 480
Bretherton, I., 231, 320, 325, 343
Bristol, M. M., 458
Brody, G. H., 172, 387, 388
Brody, N., 175, 183, 184, 188
Broman, C. L., 422, 425
Broman, S. H., 176, 422, 447, 448
Bromley, D. B., 351, 352
Bronfenbrenner, U., 11, 12, 375, 396
Bronson, G. W., 141
Brooks, J., 151
Brooks-Gunn, J., 67, 81, 114, 122, 125, 126, 172, 289, 405, 411, 461, 473
Broverman, I. K., 303
Brown, A. L., 221, 222, 448
Brown, B. B., 333, 385
Brown, E., 330
Brown, M., 269
Brown, R., 228, 235, 237, 238, 244, 248
Brownell, C. A., 204, 248, 330, 466
Bruck, M., 211
Brucken, L., 308
Bryant, P. E., 252
Buchanan, C. M., 394, 396
Buchshbaum, K., 347
Buehler, J. W., 63
Bukowski, W. M., 338
Bull, D., 146
Bullock, M., 290
Bumpass, L., 281, 390
Burchinal, M., 180, 181
Burgeson, R., 472
Burgess, R. L., 95
Burke, M., 387
Burns, A., 391
Buss, A. H., 7, 95, 263, 265
Bussey, K., 307
Butterfield, E. C., 453

Byers, C., 93
Byrnes, J. P., 184

Cairns, R. B., 336, 477
Calderon, R., 454
Caldwell, B. M., 177
Callahan, C. M., 423
Calvert, S. L., 307
Camaioni, L., 231
Campbell, D., 83
Campbell, F. A., 180
Campbell, R. L., 5
Campbell, S. B., 316, 442, 467
Campione, J. C., 222, 448
Campos, J. J., 110
Candee, D., 365
Capaldi, D., 26, 467
Capron, C., 175, 176
Capute, A. J., 231
Carey, S., 242
Carlson, E., 329
Carlson, S. M., 196
Caron, A. J., 141
Caron, R. F., 141
Carriger, M. S., 153, 466
Carter, C. S., 92
Cartwright, B. S., 196
Carver, R. P., 172
Casey, R. J., 148
Cassidy, J., 327, 389
Casten, R., 398
Ceci, S. J., 211, 212
Centerwall, B. S., 419
Cernoch, J. M., 139
Chance, G., 138
Chandler, M., 366
Chapa, J., 427
Chazan, R., 423
Chen, C., 409
Chen, X., 338
Cherlin, A. J., 391, 395, 400, 401, 403
Chess, S., 266
Chi, M. T. H., 212
Chilamkurti, C., 351
Chomsky, N., 246
Christophersen, E. R., 124
Christopherson, C. R., 117
Cicchetti, D., 326, 437
Cillessen, A. H. N., 338
Clark, E. V., 239, 241, 242
Clarke, A. D. B., 476
Clarke, A. M., 476
Clarke-Stewart, A., 404, 406, 407
Clasen, D. R., 333
Claussen, A. H., 318
Clingempeel, W. E., 391, 392, 393
Cluff, L. E., 57
Cnattinguis, S., 63
Cogan, R., 77
Coie, J. D., 336, 338, 340
Colby, A., 355, 359

Cole, D. A., 299
Cole, M., 12, 35,433
Collin, M. F., 80
Collin, W. A., 483
Colombo, J., 167
Compas, B. C., 461
Comstock, G., 416, 417
Conger, R. D., 397
Connolly, K., 128
Cook, F. H., 148
Cook, M., 431
Cooper, J., 304
Cooper, R. P., 245
Cota, M. K., 428
Cournoyer, D. E., 380
Cowan, N., 144
Coyne, J. C., 443
Crick, F. H. C., 41
Crisafi, M. A., 221
Crittenden, P. M., 318
Crnic, K. A., 398
Crockenberg, S., 284, 285, 398
Cromer, R. F., 239
Crook, C., 138
Crouter, A. C., 374
Crutcher, R. J., 212
Csikszentmihalyi, M., 332
Cunningham, A. S., 92, 93
Curwin, A., 242
Cutler, A., 230
Cutrona, C. E., 398

Daczala, C. M., 186
Daher, M., 138
Dalgleish, M., 128
D'Alton, M. E., 52
Damon, W., 353, 366
Dannemiller, J. L., 148
Danner, F. W., 215
Darlington, R. B., 180
David, R., 13
Davidson, C. E., 423
Davidson, E. S., 307
Davidson, J. E., 453
Davies, G. M., 211
Day, M. C., 215
DeBaryshe, B. D., 11, 12
DeCasper, A. J., 145, 146
DeCherney, A. H., 52
Declercq, E. R., 77
DeFries, J. C., 178, 249, 359
DeKlyen, M., 439
DeLoach, L. L., 91
DeLoache, J. S., 210, 222, 448
DeMeis, D. K., 397
Denham, S. A., 338
Dennis, Wayne, 130
Depinet, R. L., 411
Descartes, R., 45
De Stefano, L., 196
Deutsch, C. K., 442

de Villers, J. G., 238, 255
de Villers, P. A., 238, 255
Dietrich, K. N., 61
Dionne, J., 474
Dishion, T. J., 11, 340
Disney, E. R., 60
Dodge, K. A., 339, 346, 443
Doering, C. H., 77
Dornbusch, S. M., 295, 383, 384, 385, 386, 393, 395, 396, 415, 422, 426, 428, 431
Downey, D. B., 394
Downey, G., 443
Doxsey, P. A., 151
Dreher, M., 95
Dreyer, P. H., 335
Dubas, J. S., 411
Dubrow, N., 422, 433
Duncan, G., 422
Dunham, F., 242
Dunham, P. J., 242
Dunn, J., 343, 400
Dunphy, D. C., 333
Dunst, C. J., 151
Durkin, K., 243
Duyme, M., 175, 176
Dwyer, T., 94
Dyk, P. H., 117
Dykens, E. M., 52

Earles, J. A., 411
Easterbrooks, M. A., 423
Eaton, W. O., 97
Eccles, J., 330
Eccles, J. S., 397, 472
Edelbrock, C. S., 435, 443
Edwards, C. P., 26, 305
Egeland, B., 29, 318, 426, 478
Eggebeen, D., 406
Ehrhardt, A. A., 50, 308
Eicher, S. A., 333
Eisen, M., 291, 292
Eisenberg, N., 312, 336, 337, 343, 361, 364, 365, 404, 406
Ekman, Paul, 348
Elder, G. H., Jr., 374
Elfenbein, D., 355
Elkind, D., 472
Elliott, G. R., 483
Elliott, R., 184, 188
Elmen, J. D., 383
Eme, R. F., 457
Enns, L. R., 97
Ensminger, M. E., 390
Entwisle, D. R., 77, 177, 411
Epstein, H. F., 10
Erickson, M. F., 318
Ericsson, K. A., 212
Erikson, E. H., 20, 21, 33, 273, 276, 277, 278, 279, 287, 293, 333
Eron, L. D., 337, 340, 418, 419, 439
Escalona, K. S., 467
Espinosa, M. P., 129
Evahn, C., 411

Ever-Hadani, P., 62
Ey, S., 461
Eyres, S. J., 92

Fagan, J. F., III, 165, 183
Fagot, B. I., 301, 305
Falbo, T., 388
Famularo, R., 318
Farber, E. A., 351
Farnham-Diggory, S., 450, 451, 452, 461
Farran, D. C., 176
Farrar, M. J., 246
Farrington, D. P., 340, 439
Faust, M. S., 121
Featherman, D. L., 411
Featherstone, H., 458
Fedoroff, I. C., 125
Fein, G. G., 196
Feldman, E., 308, 347
Feldman, H., 82
Feldman, J. F., 50
Feldman, S. S., 273, 483
Fennelly, K., 117, 118
Fenwick, K. D., 138
Ferguson, J., 81
Fernald, A., 144, 230
Ferrara, R. A., 448
Feshbach, S., 336
Fetterman, D., 453
Field, D. E., 92, 196
Field, T., 99
Field, T. M., 196, 201, 318, 406
Fifer, W. P., 87, 145
Filardo, E. K., 467
Finkelhor, D., 378
Finkelstein, N. W., 406
Fivush, R., 306
Flanagan, C. A., 397
Flavell, E. R., 204
Flavell, J. H., 151, 194, 204, 206, 212, 213, 225, 229, 345, 475, 476
Fleming, A. S., 83
Flickinger, S. M., 398
Floven, R. J., 231
Floyd, R. L., 57
Ford, M. E., 364
Forman, M. R., 63
Fox, N. A., 328
Fraiberg, S., 318
Frame, C. L., 339
Frankel, K. A., 266, 329
Frantz, R. L., 135
Freeman, E. W., 117, 119
French, F. E., 424
Freud, S., 20, 21, 33, 275, 276, 279, 289
Frey, K. S., 301, 306
Friedman, R. M., 435
Fry, A. F., 218
Fu, Y., 42
Fulker, D. W., 175
Furrow, D., 243
Furstenberg, F. F., Jr., 119, 172, 391, 395, 401, 411

Galambos, N. L., 397
Gale, R., 62
Gallagher, J. J., 176, 188, 422, 458
Ganchrow, J. R., 138
Garbarino, J., 318, 422, 423, 433
Garcia, E. E., 240
Gardner, D., 205
Gardner, H., 173
Garland, A. F., 444
Garmezy, N., 14, 172, 423, 437, 438
Garn, S. M., 123, 128
Gauthier, R., 304
Gecas, V., 323
Gelman, R., 206, 207
Gershenhorn, S., 267
Gerson, R. P., 366
Gesell, A. L., 5, 6, 33
Getz, K., 280
Gibson, E. J., 140, 155, 156, 359
Gillenwater, J. M., 138
Gilligan, C., 363
Gleitman, H., 233
Gleitman, L. R., 233, 236
Glick, P. C., 390
Glueck, H., 377
Glueck, S., 377
Gnepp, J., 351
Godhart, A. W., 387
Goldacre, M., 444
Goldberg, S., 152
Goldberg, W. A., 394, 397
Golden, M., 176
Goldfield, B. A., 233
Gonsiorek, J. C., 335
Good, T. L., 412
Goodman, M., 52, 69
Goodsitt, J. V., 144
Gopnik, A., 205, 207, 239
Gottesman, I. I., 182, 477
Gottlieb, G., 154
Gottman, J. M., 331, 332
Gove, W. R., 82
Graham, S., 347
Gralinski, H., 410
Granrud, C. E., 148
Grant, K. E., 461
Gratch, G., 150
Green, F. L., 204
Greenberg, J., 77, 239, 439, 454
Greenberg, M. T., 321, 324
Greenberger, E., 397, 414, 416
Greenough, W. T., 6, 49, 109
Grenier, G., 427
Grossmann, K., 327
Grusec, J. E., 269, 270, 287
Guerra, N., 93
Gullota, T. P., 133
Gunnar, M. R., 261, 264, 321
Guralnick M. J., 204
Guthrie, J. F., 125
Guttentag, R. E., 210

Gzesh, S. M., 194

Haan, N., 467, 473
Haas, B., 421
Hack, M., 80
Hagan, R., 305
Haith, M. M., 5, 136, 141, 158
Hakuta, K., 240, 255
Hale, S., 218
Hall, D. G., 239
Hall, N. W., 318
Halsey, C. L., 80
Halverson, C. F., Jr., 306
Hammond, M., 389
Hammond, M. A., 79
Hanlon, C., 244
Hanna, E., 201
Hannan, K., 265
Hans, S. L., 95
Hansen, D. J., 378
Hanshaw, J. B., 480
Hardy, J., 64
Hardy-Brown, K., 249
Harkness, S., 4, 331, 467
Harris, M., 242, 255
Harris, P. L., 205, 351
Harrison, A. O., 429
Hart, E. L., 438
Harter, S., 291, 297, 298, 312, 348, 474
Hartup, W. W., 314, 330, 343
Haskins, R., 176, 180, 406, 422
Hatano, G., 430
Hatchett, S. J., 425
Haviland, J. J., 457
Hawley, T. L., 60
Hawton, K., 444
Hayes, C. D., 67, 404, 408
Heagarty, M. C., 56, 65
Helmreich, R. L., 309, 310
Helms, J. E., 27
Henker, B., 440, 441
Henneborn, W. J., 77
Herbsman, C. R., 336
Hersen, M., 312
Hess, E. H., 9
Hess, R. D., 186
Hesse, E., 326, 389
Hetherington, E. M., 265, 281, 391, 392, 393
Higgins, A., 367
Higgins, A. T., 156
Higgins, J. E., 318
Hill, J. P., 322
Hillman, L. S., 94
Hinde, R. A., 330, 383
Hines, M., 50
Hinshaw, S. P., 438
Hirsch, H. V. B., 9
Hirsh-Pasek, K., 244
Hock, E., 397
Hodapp, R. M., 52
Hofferth, S. L., 119, 389

Hoffman, H. J., 94
Hoffman, L. W., 82, 397
Hoffman, M. L., 349
Hogan, A. E., 466
Holloway, S. D., 186
Holmbeck, G. N., 322
Holt, R. W., 338
Honzik, M. P., 171
Hopkins, J., 83
Horn, J. M., 175
Horowitz, F. D., 14, 15
Howard, J., 60, 458
Howat, P. M., 125
Howes, C., 196, 406
Hsu, H., 398
Hubel, D. H., 154
Hudley, C., 347
Huesmann, L. R., 337, 419
Hughes, P. C. R., 108
Humphreys, L. G., 120
Hunter, A. G., 390
Hunter, J. E., 411
Hunter, R. F., 411
Huntington, L., 95
Hurwitz, J. E., 93
Huston, A. C., 307, 416
Hutchinson, J., 241
Huttenlocher, J., 176
Hymel, S., 445

Ingram, D., 237
Inhelder, B., 21, 199
Inoff-Germain, G., 322
Isabella, R. A., 316, 328
Istvan, J., 64
Ivey, P. K., 320

Jacklin, C. N., 184, 304, 331
Jackson, J. S., 425
Jackson, N. E., 453
Janos, P. M., 453
Jelliffe, D. B., 92
Jelliffe, E. F. P., 92
Jensen, A. R., 183
Jessie, K. A., 218
Jevne, R., 125
Johnson, C., 125
Jones, E. F., 118
Jones, K. L., 58
Jordan, N. C., 176
Jorgensen, S. R., 118
Jung, C. G., 20
Juscyk, P. W., 230

Kagan, J., 153, 261, 262, 265, 320
Kail, R., 218
Kandel, E. R., 48
Kaplan, N., 327, 389
Karmiloff-Smith, A., 203
Kaskie, B., 177
Kataria, S., 107

Kaye, K., 87
Kazdin, A. E., 127
Kean, K. J., 380
Kearsley, R., 320
Keating, D. P., 215, 221
Keefe, S. E., 428
Kellam, S. G., 390, 393
Kelley, M. L., 422
Kempe, A., 62, 65
Kendall-Tackett, K. A., 378
Kennedy, R. E., 445
Kennedy, W. A., 176, 422
Kennell, J. H., 74, 315–316
Kent, R. D., 230
Kessner, D. M., 64, 67
Kestenbaum, R., 149, 351
Kidd, K. K., 42, 52, 53, 175, 183, 264, 448
Kiely, J. L., 94
Killen, M., 363
Kilpatrick, S. J., 73
Kimmerly, N. L., 328
King, P. K., 117
Kinsbourne, M., 442
Kitchen, W. H., 79
Klackenberg-Larsson, I., 172
Klaus, H. M., 74, 315
Kline, M., 281
Knight, G. P., 428
Koewler, J. H. I., 196
Koff, E., 121, 122
Kohlberg, L., 305, 306, 355, 357, 358, 359, 360, 361, 362, 363, 365, 366, 367, 368
Kohn, M. L., 397
Koopman, C., 335
Kopp, C. B., 51, 56, 66
Koren-Karie, N., 327
Korn, S. J., 266
Korner, A. F., 91
Kosowski, T. D., 241
Kostelny, K., 422, 433
Kotulak, R., 422
Kratzer, L., 411
Kreutzer, T., 29, 478
Krile, D., 364
Kroonenberg, P. M., 326
Kuczaj, S. A., II, 238, 239
Kuhl, P. K., 144, 147
Kuhn, D., 219, 226, 308
Kupersmidt, J. B., 340, 422
Kurdek, L. A., 364
Kusche, C., 454

Ladd, G. W., 398
La Freniere, P., 304
La Gaipa, J. J., 354
Lagerspetz, K., 419
Lahey, B. B., 438
Lamb, M. E., 35, 226, 255, 318, 324, 407, 408
Lambert, C., 13
Lamborn, S. D., 383
Lamke, L. K., 310

Lang, M. E., 82
Langlois, J. H., 143
Laros, R. K., 73
Larson, R., 332
Leach, P., 99
Leadbeater, B. J., 474
Leaper, C., 332, 341
Lederberg, A. R., 459
Lee, C. C., 426
Lee, M., 180, 181
Lee, S., 183
Leiderman, P. H., 77
Leinbach, M. D., 301, 305
Leitch, C. J., 324
Leon, G. R., 126
Lerner, J. V., 397
Lerner, R. M., 16, 104, 121
Lester, B. M., 95
Levano, K. J., 78
Levin, H., 269
Levine, C., 358
LeVine, R. A., 178
Levine, S. C., 176
Levitt, M. J., 323
Levy, G. D., 306
Lewis, C. C., 214
Lewis, M., 289, 290, 461
Lewis, M. D., 177
Liben, L. S., 454
Lickona, T., 343
Lillard, A. S., 206
Linney, J. A., 412
Lipsitt, L. P., 87
Liss, T., 73
List, J. A., 221
Litt, I. R., 124, 125
Little, J. K., 306
Livesley, W. J., 351, 352
Lockman, J. J., 128
Loehlin, J. C., 175, 178
Loevinger, J., 20
Long, J. V. F., 424
Longeway, K. P., 321
Longo, D. C., 458
Lopez, S. R., 12
Lore, R. K., 13
Lubinski, D., 184
Luke, B., 62
Luster, T., 265, 421
Luthar, S. S., 172
Lütkenhaus, P., 290
Lykken, D. T., 264
Lyons, N. P., 363
Lyons-Ruth, K., 329
Lytton, H., 305

McAdoo, H. P., 433
McBride, G., 44
McBride, S. L., 397
McCall, R. B., 153, 171, 411
McCarthy, J., 64

McCartny, K., 285
McClearn, G. E., 35
Maccoby, E. E., 64, 269, 304, 306, 322, 331, 341, 377, 382, 394, 396, 401
McCord, J., 377
McCord, W., 377
McCormick, K. F., 380
MacDonald, K., 377
McFalls, J. A., Jr., 63
Macfarlane, A., 73, 74, 77
McGee, R., 324
MacGowan, C. A., 93
McGue, M., 7
McGuire, S., 388
McHale, S. M., 16, 374
McKey, R. H., 180
McKinney, J. D., 121
McLaughlin, B., 240
MacLean, M., 252, 253
McLloyd, V., 421
McLoed, P. J., 245
McManus, K., 76
Madsen, W., 428
Magnusson, D., 121
Magzamen, S., 467
Mahapatra, M., 361
Main, Mary, 326, 327, 389
Malatesta, C. Z., 91, 457
Malina, R. M., 106, 114, 115, 129, 133
Malinosky-Rummell, R., 378
Mangelsdorf, S. C., 321
Manis, J. D., 82
Mannle, S., 243
Maratsos, M., 237
Marcia, J. E., 293, 474
Marcus, G. B., 179
Marcus, G. F., 238
Marcus, M., 83
Marcus, R. F., 335
Marean, G. C., 144
Markestad, I., 94
Markman, E. M., 241
Martin, C. L., 306, 307
Martin, E. P., 425
Martin, J. A., 382
Martorano, S. C., 213, 214
Marvin, R. S., 321
Masataka, N., 245
Mason, R., 318
Massad, C. M., 310
Masten, A. S., 172, 423, 446
Matarazzo, J. D., 223
Mather, P. L., 249
Matheson, C. C., 196
Matthews, W. S., 67
Maurer, C., 76, 99
Maurer, D., 76, 99
Meadow, K. P., 455
Mehl, L. E., 77
Meltzoff, A. N., 147, 201, 239
Merriman, W. E., 221
Mervis, C. A., 241

Mervis, C. B., 241
Meyer-Bahlburg, H. F. L., 50, 308
Midgley, C., 472
Miller, B. C., 117
Miller, G. A., 211
Miller, S. M., 461
Millstein, S. G., 124, 125
Mischel, W., 305
Mitchell, E. A., 94
Mitchell, R., 170, 230
Mnookin, R. H., 394, 401
Mobley, C. E., 459
Moffitt, T. E., 441
Mollnow, E., 53, 57, 60
Money, J., 50, 309
Montemayor, R., 133, 291, 292
Moon, C., 87
Moore, C., 53
Moore, E. J. K., 183
Moore, K. A., 119
Moores, D. F., 454
Moos, R. H., 444
Moran, T., 366
Morelli, G. A., 320
Morgan, M., 307
Morris, N., 77
Morrison, D. M., 117
Morrongiello, B. A., 138, 146
Morse, P. A., 144
Mortimer, J. T., 416
Mounts, N. S., 383
Muir, J. E., 212
Mundy, P. C., 466
Munro, G., 294
Munroe, R. H., 301
Munroe, R. L., 301
Murphy, R. R., 347
Murray, J. L., 65
Murray, J. P., 417
Murtough, M., 62
Mussen, P. H., 364
Myers, B. J., 316

Naeye, R. L., 58
Nash, S. C., 308
Needleman, H. L., 61
Neimark, E. D., 213
Nelson, C. A., 144
Nelson, K., 233, 234, 242, 246, 250
Netley, C., 52
Nevill, D. D., 104
Newcomb, A. F., 338
Newcombe, N. S., 120
Newman, V., 393
Nichols, P. L., 176, 422
Nightingale, E. O., 52, 69
Nilsson, L. A., 70
Norton, A. J., 390
Nottelmann, E. D., 111
Nowakowski, R. S., 109
Nunes, L. R. D., 201

O'Boyle, C., 305
O'Brien, K., 330
O'Brien, M., 304, 312
O'Brien, S. F., 330
O'Connell, B., 230
O'Connor, S., 316
Oden, M., 453
Offord, D. R., 24, 25, 336
O'Hara, M. W., 83
Okazaki, S., 182
Oller, D. K., 230
Olshan, A. F., 52
Olson, D. H., 381
Olson, H. C., 59
Olson, S. L., 177
Olthof, T., 351
O'Neill, D. K., 206
Ornstein, P. A., 210
Osofsky, J. D., 99, 158, 287, 483
Overton, W. F., 215, 283
Owsley, C., 141, 145

Padilla, A. M., 240, 428
Page, D. C., 44
Paikoff, R. L., 473
Palkovitz, R., 77
Palmer, J. L., 404
Papousek, M., 317
Pardo, C., 433
Park, Y., 218
Parke, R. D., 77, 317
Parmelee, A. H., Jr., 49, 124
Parsons, J. E., 186
Partridge, M. F., 318
Passman, R. H., 321
Pattee, L., 338
Patterson, C. J., 422
Patterson, G. R., 11, 12, 26, 269, 378, 379, 467
Paul-Brown, D., 204
Peckham, C., 124
Pederson, D. R., 328
Pedlow, R., 265
Pegg, J. E., 245
Pellegrini, D., 389
Pence, A. R., 401
Pennington, B. F., 66
Perner, J., 205
Peters, E. C., 58
Petersen, A., 125
Petersen, A. C., 121, 443, 445, 461
Petersen, M. R., 121
Peterson, G. H., 77
Petitto, L. A., 231
Philip, R., 57
Phillips, D. A., 175
Phinney, J. S., 295
Piaget, J., 21, 150, 164, 191, 192, 193, 194, 195, 199, 252, 272, 355, 467, 479
Pianta, R., 318
Pick, A. D., 147, 155
Pike, R., 291

Pillard, R. C., 335
Pinker, S., 244
Pitkin, R. M., 62
Placek, P. J., 73
Pless, I. B., 124
Plomin, R., 7, 35, 95, 178, 181, 249, 263, 264, 265
Ponsonby, P. H., 94
Porter, J. R., 139, 425
Poston, D. L., Jr., 388
Poulson, C. L., 201
Powell, B., 308, 394
Power, C., 124, 267, 367
Pressley, M., 218, 226
Prodromidis, M., 407
Pulkkinen, L., 383
Pye, C., 246
Pyle, R., 125

Quiggle, N. L., 339

Rabinovitch, M. S., 144
Racine, Y. A., 24, 25
Radin, N., 308
Radke-Yarrow, M., 335
Ramey, C. T., 61, 82, 180, 181, 188, 404, 450, 480
Ramsey, E., 11, 12
Rappaport, L., 275
Redanz, N. J., 230
Ree, M. J., 411
Reef, M. J., 472
Reese, H. W., 283
Reimer, J., 359, 367
Reisman, J. E., 139, 331
Reiter, E. O., 114
Remafedi, G., 335
Rende, R., 7, 181
Renouf, A. G., 298
Repacholi, B., 329
Rest, J. R., 359, 360, 367
Reznick, J. S., 233, 262
Rhoades, K., 421
Rholes, W. S., 351
Ricciuti, H. N., 61
Rice, M. L., 255, 417
Richman, A. L., 178
Richters, J., 389
Rickels, K., 117, 119
Riegel, K. F., 463
Rierdan, J., 121, 122
Rieser-Danner, L. A., 143
Rivara, F. P., 423
Roberts, C. W., 308
Roberts, R. E., 443
Robertson, S., 377
Robinson, H. B., 452
Robinson, J. L., 263
Robinson, N. M., 453
Roche, A. F., 129
Roding, C., 60
Rogers, J. L., 44, 179, 265
Roggman, L. A., 143

Rohner, R. P., 380
Rollins, B. C., 82
Rolls, B. J., 125, 126
Romney, D. M., 305
Rooks, J. P., 77
Rosario, M., 335
Rose, S. A., 146
Rosenbaum, P., 411, 412
Rosenblith, J. F., 47, 60, 70, 76, 483
Rosenthal, D. A., 295
Ross, Gail, 324
Rothbart, M. K., 95, 261
Rotheram-Borus, M. J., 335
Rovee-Collier, C., 87, 202, 203
Rovet, J., 52
Rovine, M., 82, 406
Rowe, I., 474
Rubin, K. H., 196, 338
Ruble, D. N., 291, 304, 306, 351
Ruff, H., 146
Russell, G., 318
Rutter, D. R., 7, 243, 265, 318
Rutter, M., 14, 96, 265, 412, 437, 438, 459, 478
Ryan, A. S., 93
Ryan, E. B., 252

Sack, W. H., 318
Sadovnick, A. D., 63
Sagi, A., 327
St. Peters, M., 417
Sameroff, A., 375, 423
Sampson, P. D., 59
Sanches-Hucles, J., 422
Sapir, E., 13
Sarigiani, P. A., 445
Sattler, J. M., 172
Saunders, W. L., 198
Savage-Rumbough, E. S., 229
Saxton, A. M., 125
Scafidi, F. A., 81
Scarr, S., 7, 42, 52, 53, 175, 183, 264, 285, 404, 406, 408, 448
Scarr-Salapatek, S., 477
Schaefer, E. S., 377
Schaefli, A., 367
Schafer, W. D., 328
Schaie, K. W., 24
Schank, R. C., 346
Schlesinger, H. S., 455
Schneider, M. L., 64
Schneider, W., 218, 223, 226
Schneiderman, M., 244
Schoendorf, K. C., 65, 94
Schooler, C., 397
Schopler, E., 458
Schramm, W. F., 77
Schulenberg, J., 414
Schulman, S., 329
Schultz, L. A., 13, 108
Scollon, R., 232
Sears, R. R., 269
Seff, M. A., 323

Seidman, D. S., 62
Seidman, E., 412
Seitz, V., 35
Selman, R. L., 345, 353, 354, 364
Sepkoski, C., 77
Serbin, L., 340
Shaffer, D., 444
Shantz, C. U., 352, 368
Sheldon, W. H., 105
Shelton, B. A., 396
Shepardson, D., 198
Sherman, D., 318
Shimmin, H. S., 301
Shonkoff, J. P., 111
Shore, C., 230, 248
Shorr, S. I., 331
Short, E. J., 180
Shweder, R. A., 361
Siebert, J. M., 466
Siegal, M., 305
Siegel, J. M., 324
Siegel, L. S., 451
Siegler, R. S., 217, 219
Siemens, L., 210
Sigman, M., 177, 248
Sigman, M. D., 49
Silver, S. E., 435
Silverstein, L. B., 408
Simmons, R. G., 121, 472
Simon, T., 165
Simons, R. L., 377
Sims-Knight, J. E., 47, 60, 70, 76, 483
Singer, L. T., 183
Skinner, B. F., 244
Slaby, R. G., 301
Slaughter-Defoe, D. T., 429
Slobin, D. I., 5, 246, 247
Smetana, J. G., 363, 366
Smith, D. W., 123
Smith, L. B., 140
Smith, R. S., 119, 172, 424
Smoll, F. L., 108
Snarey, J. R., 358, 359, 360
Snidman, N., 262
Snyder, L., 231, 248, 321
Sobhan, M., 443
Soken, N. H., 147
Solomon, J., 326
Sonuga-Barke, E. J. S., 392
Sosa, R., 77
Spelke, E. S., 145, 147, 149, 155, 156
Speltz, M. L., 439
Spence, J. T., 310
Spence, M. J., 146
Spencer, M. B., 295, 426, 428
Spieker, S. J., 326
Spiker, D., 81, 450
Spitze, G., 396
Sroufe, L. A., 29, 281, 285, 325, 328, 329, 351, 407, 426, 437, 459, 478, 480
Stanovich, K. E., 451

Stanton, W. R., 324
Starfield, B., 124
Stattin, H., 121, 172
Steelman, L. C., 308
Stein, Z., 61
Steinberg, J., 431
Steinberg, L., 322, 383, 384, 385, 386, 414, 415, 416
Steiner, J. E., 138, 139
Stemmler, M., 461
Sternberg, K. J., 407
Sternberg, R. J., 173, 183, 453
Stevenson, H. W., 182, 183, 185, 409, 429
Stevenson-Hinde, J., 383
Stewart, R. B., 57, 93
Stigler, J., 183, 185
Stiles, K. M., 61
Stipek, D., 410
Stoneman, Z., 387
Stoutjesdyk, D., 125
Strassberg, Z., 347
Strayer, F. F., 304
Streissguth, A., 59
Striegel-Moore, R. H., 126
Strobino, D. M., 64
Stubbs, M. L., 122
Suben, J. G., 183
Sue, S., 182
Sullivan, M. W., 290
Sun, Y., 338
Super, C. M., 4, 331, 467
Surber, C. F., 194
Swedo, S. E., 444
Szapocznik, J., 376

Taffel, S. M., 73
Takahira, S., 184
Takei, Y., 411
Tal, J., 27
Tamis-LeMonda, C., 10, 27
Tannen, D., 343
Tanner, J. M., 47, 66, 107, 108, 111, 112, 120, 123, 133
Taylor, M., 196
Taylor, P. M., 316
Taylor, R. D., 398
Tees, R. C., 144, 145
Tellegen, A., 264
Teller, D. Y., 137
Terman, L., 453
Terwogt, M. M., 351
Teschke, K., 52
Tew, M., 77
Thal, D., 250
Thelen, E., 5, 86, 128
Thoma, S. J., 367
Thomas, A., 266
Thomas, R. M., 35, 105, 226
Thompson, S. K., 301
Thorne, B., 331
Thornton, A., 334
Thorpe, L. A., 146
Tieman, S. B., 9

Timmer, S. G., 330
Tinsley, B. R., 77, 317
Tizard, J., 443
Tobin-Richards, M. H., 121
Tomasello, M., 243
Tower, A., 307
Traupmann, K., 433
Treffers, P. D. A., 387
Trehub, S. E., 144, 146
Tremblay, R. E., 340
Trevethan, S. D., 359
Trieman, R., 244
Tronick, E. Z., 320
Troutman, B. R., 398
Turiel, E., 363, 367
Turkheimer, E., 182, 477
Turner, R. J., 390
Turnure, J. E., 156

Ullian, D. Z., 305
Umberson, D., 82
Ungerer, J. A., 248
Upchurch, D. M., 119
Urban, J., 329

Vaden, N. A., 422
Vaillant, G. E., 424
Valdez-Menchaca, M. C., 245
Valencia, R. R., 427
Vandenberg, B., 155, 196
Van de Perre, P., 56
Van Hasselt, V. B., 312
van IJzendoorn, M. H., 318, 326
Vellutino, F. R., 451
Vernon, P. A., 221
Vihko, R., 113
Volterra, V., 231
von Eye, A., 316
von Hofsten, C., 149
Vorhees, C. F., 53, 57, 60
Vuchinich, S., 11, 26
Vygotsky, Lev S., 21

Wachs, T. D., 13, 27
Waddington, C. H., 477
Wahlström, J., 53
Wald, E. R., 93
Waldman, I. D., 183
Waldrop, M. F., 332
Walker, H., 318
Walker, L. J., 359, 360, 363, 368
Walker, R. R., 422
Wallace, C. S., 49, 109
Wallerstein, J. S., 391
Walters, R. H., 269
Walton, G. E., 142, 147
Wanner, E., 236
Warren, S. F., 201
Washington, R. E., 425
Waterman, A. S., 294
Watson, J., 41

Watson, M. W., 280
Waxman, S., 206, 239, 241
Webster-Straton, C., 389
Wechsler, D., 167
Wegman, M. E., 65, 94, 124
Weinberg, C. R., 7, 175, 183
Weinberg, R. A., 182
Weinrich, J. D., 335
Weinstein, R. S., 412
Weisel, T. N., 154
Weiss, B., 347
Wellman, H. M., 205, 207
Wen, S. W., 63
Werker, J. F., 144, 145, 245
Werner, E. E., 64, 66, 67, 119, 172, 424, 481
Werner, H., 22
Werner, L. A., 138
Whalen, C. K., 440, 441
Whitehouse, R. H., 108
Whitehurst, G. J., 245
Whitesell, N. R., 348
Whiting, B. B., 26, 305
Whitmore, K., 443
Wiesenfeld, A. R., 91
Wiggins, G., 363
Willerman, L., 175

Williams, E., 308
Williams, L. M., 378
Willows, D. M., 252
Wilson, M. N., 425, 426
Winick, M., 62
Wittig, B. A., 325
Wood, C. H., 306
Woodward, A. L., 241
Woodward, L., 76

Yasuna, A., 307
Yeates, K. W., 180
Yee, I. M. L., 63
Yonas, A., 140, 154
Youngblade, L. M., 329

Zahn-Waxler, C., 335
Zajonc, R. B., 179
Zametkin, A. J., 442
Zaslow, M. J., 67, 404, 455
Zelazo, N. A., 131
Zelazo, P., 320
Zelli, A., 337, 419
Zeskind, P. S., 61, 95, 480
Zigler, E., 52, 172, 318, 444
Zoccolillo, M., 439
Zola, I. K., 377

SUBJECT INDEX

Note: Italicized page numbers indicate material in boxes, figures, and tables.

Accommodation, 22, 192–193, 200
Achievement tests, 167–169
  sample items from, *168*
Achievers, 410–411
Acuity, 136
  auditory development and, 138
  visual skills and, 136–137
Adaption process, 22
  atypical child and family, 458
  Piaget's theories and, 191–193
Adolescence, 415. *See also* Puberty
  ability in school and, 410
  age at first date, *335*
  aggressive behavior and, 438–439
  androgyny in, 309–310
  black teenagers and, 426
  body image and, *126*
  cliques and, 333
  cognitive development in, 213–215, 474
  conduct disorders in, 438
  depression and, 435, 445
  describing other people and, 352
  eating disorders and, 125–126
  equilibration and, 193
  ethnic identity in, *295*
  family conflict and, 322–324
  friendships and, 353–354
  health habits in, 126–128
  homosexuality and, *335*
  hormones and, 111–112
  identity and, 292–293
  illness and health, 124–126
  impact of employment on, 414–416
  impact of television on, 416–420
  intimate relationships and, 333, 473
  peer relationships and, 332–334
  pregnancy, 118–119, *120*
  psychopathology and, 435
  self-concept and, 291–292
  sexuality and, 117–118
  smoking and, *127*
  social isolation and, 445
  suicide and, *444*
  summary development of, *471*
Adopted children, 183

  IQ scores of, *176*
  temperament and, 263
Adrenal androgen, 111
Adult stages, 279
Affectional bond, 315
Affordances, 155
African-Americans, 425–426
  child-rearing style of, 385–386
  ethnicity, 425–426
  extended families of, 426
  IQ test and, 183
  low-birth-weight babies and, 79
  sexual activity and, 117
Age and moral reasoning, 359
Aggression, 336–337
  adolescent-onset, 438–439
  childhood-onset, 438
  as conduct disorder, 438
  day care and, 406
  desensitization and viewing violence, 420
  popularity and, 338–340
  reinforcement theory and, 272
  sex differences and, 439
  teacher ratings of, *337*
  teenage employment and, 414
  television's effects on, 418–420
AIDS, 56–57
Alcohol
  adolescent suicide and, *444*
  prenatal development and, 58–59
  Streissguth's studies on, 59
Alpha-fetoprotein test (AFP), 54
Altruism, 334
Altruistic children, *337*
Amniocentesis, 54
Amnion, 47
Analgesics, 74
Anal stage, 274
Androgyny, 309–310
Anesthesia, 74–75
Animism, 431
Anorexia nervosa, 125–126
Anoxia, 78–79
Apgar score, 81
Appearance and reality, 204–205

Asian-Americans, 428–429
    child-rearing styles of, 385–386
    extended families and, 429
    mathematics ability and, 182–183
Aslin's models, 8, 129–130, 475–476
Aspirin, 60–61
Assimilation, 22, 192, 200
Attachment
    Bowlby's model and, 279–280
    child–parent bond and, 319–321, 406–408
    cross-cultural comparisons, 320, 327
    definition of, 315
    effects of day care, 406–408
    elementary-school years and, 321–322
    horizontal relationships and, 330–337
    individual differences and, 325–329
    long-term consequences of, 328–329
    parents' bond to child, 315–318
    peer-relationship differences and, 338–341
    preschool stage and, 321–322
    secure-insecure classification, 325–329
    security of, 281, 407
    stability of classification, 326–328
Attachment behavior, 315
    blind children and, 459
    deaf children and, 459
    infant and mother, 463–465
    internal models and, 10
    meshing, 316–317
Attention deficit hyperactivity disorder (ADD), 439–442
Attunement, 9, 130, 154
Atypical development
    childhood psychopathology and, 438–442
    effect on family, 458–459
    incidence of, 435–436
    intellectual, 447–453
    physical, 454–455
    sex differences and, 455–458
Auditory development
    acuity in, 138
    deafness and, 454, 459
    detecting sound locations, 138
    discriminating speech sounds and, 144–145
    listening and, 144–146
Authoritarian rearing style, 382
    Asian-Americans and, 430
    Hispanic-Americans and, 428
Authoritative rearing style, 383
    effective school settings and, 414
    stress and, 424
Autonomy, Erikson's stage of, 278
Autosomes, 44
Axon, 48

Babbling, 230
Babinsky reflex, 85
Ballet dancers, 122, 123
Bandura's theory, 19–20, 22
Basic trust, 277
Bayley Scales for Infant Development, 167
Behavior

    of altruistic children, 337
    attachment and, 10, 315–317, 459, 463–465
    competitive, 340
    criminal, 340, 438, 439, 441
    empathetic understanding and, 364
    friendship and, 364–365
    moral judgment and, 365–367
    physical changes and, 115–119
    prosocial, 334, 336, 361–362
    sex-role behavior, 300, 303–304
Behavior genetics, 6–7
Behavior problems. See Problem behavior
Bilingual children, 240
    Hispanic families and, 427
Biological approach to personality
    basic propositions and, 261–262
    consistency of temperament and, 265
    environmental interactions and, 265
    inheritance of temperament and, 263
    psychological connections, 263–264
    strengths, weaknesses, and implications of, 266–267
Biological theories, 17, 33, 261–267
Birth
    assessing the newborn, 81
    cesarean section and, 57, 78
    choices, 74–77
    drugs during delivery, 74–76
    father's presence at, 77
    first greeting in, 73–74
    location of, 76–77
    problems at, 78–81
    stages of labor and, 72–73
Blacks. See African-Americans
Blastocyst, 46
Blindness
    attachment and, 456, 459
    childhood and, 454–455, 459
    intervention and, 455
Body image, 126
Bone development, 106–107
Bowlby's attachment model, 279–280
Braille, 455
Brain
    development of, 109
    fetal development and, 48–49
    learning disorders and, 451
    prenatal malnutrition and, 61
    thyroid hormone and, 110
Brain damage, 448–449
    hyperactivity and, 441
    mental retardation and, 448–449
    sleeping patterns and, 90
Breast-feeding
    versus bottle-feeding, 92
    cultural and class differences in, 93
    infant–mother attachment and, 463–464
Bronfenbrenner's ecological development approach, 375–377
Bulimia, 125

Canalization, 477
Caring, ethic of, 363–364

Categorical self, 289

Cephalocaudal process, 107

Cesarean section, 57, 78

Child abuse, *318, 378*

Childhood. *See also* Preschool period; School-age child; Stages of
  development
  attention deficit hyperactivity disorder and, 439–442
  blindness and, 454–455, 459
  conduct disorders in, 438–439
  deafness and, 454, 459
  depression, 442–445
  giftedness and, 452–453
  hyperactivity in, 440–442
  learning disorders and, 450–451
  mental retardation and, 447–450
  psychopathologies of, 435
  stress and, 445

Child rearing, 381–386
  authoritarian style, 382
  authoritative styles, 383
  effect on child, 386–386
  ethnic groups and, 385–386
  neglecting style, 383
  permissive style, 382
  Sternberg-Dornbusch studies on, 383–386

Child to parent relationships, 319–321

Chorionic villus sampling (CVS), *54*

Chromosomal anomalies, 66, 448

Chromosomes, 41
  dominant and recessive genes and, 42–44
  genotypes and phenotypes, 45–46
  males and females, 44
  twins and siblings, 44–45

Classical conditioning, 17–18, 86

Classification
  and development of word meanings, 239–241
  expertise and, 212–213
  illustration of ablity, *198*
  preschool period, 206–207
  types of, 197

Cliques, 333

Clustering, *210*

Cocaine, prenatal development and, 60

Cognitive development, 470. *See also* IQ (intelligence quotient);
    IQ tests
  in adolescence, 213–215, 474
  attachment and, 463, 466
  Bandura's theories and, 19
  from birth to 18 months, 466
  concrete operational stage and, 469
  day care and, 404–405
  elementary-school years and, 469, 470
  expertise and, 212–213
  giftedness and, 452–453
  heredity and, 181–182
  in infancy, 200–203
  language and, 239, 247, 466
  mental retardation and, 448
  negatives effects of TV on, 417–418
  Piaget's theories on, 21–22, 191–200
  play and, *196*

preschool years and, 203–208, 468
  racial differences in, 182–183
  school experience and, 409
  sex differences in, 183–186
  sex-role development and, 305–307
  Sternberg's triarchic theory of intelligence and, 173–175
  theories on, 21–22, 33
  views of intelligence and, 164–165

Cohort, 25

Colic, 94

College students
  identity and, 294
  moral judgment and behavior, 365

Color constancy, 148

Color vision, 137–138

Combinational skills, 466

Commitment in adolescence, 293

Communalism, 425

Communication
  within families, 381
  and self-direction, 243–244

Competence, 167

Competitiveness, 340

Componential intelligence, 173, 181

Conception, 40–41
  genetics of, 41–46

Concrete operational stage, 197–198, 215
  cognitive development and, 469
  elementary-school period and, 469
  Piaget's cognitive-developmental theory, 197–198

Conditioned stimuli, 17

Conduct disorders, 438–439

Confucianism, 429

Conservation, 194, 200
  preschool period and, 206–207
  types of, *197*

Constraints
  inborn biases and, 5
  on word learning, 241–243

Constructive play, *196*

Constructivism, 199–200
  language development and, 247–248

Contextual intelligence, 174

Contextualist paradigm, 376

Contraceptives, 117–118

Control, parents' methods of, 378–381

Control group, 28

Conventional morality, 357

Cooing, 230

Correlation, 31, 34

Cortex, 109

Criminal behavior, 438
  aggressiveness and, 340
  childhood-onset conduct disorders and, 439
  hyperactivity/delinquency and, 441

Critical period, 9

Cross-cultural study, 26–27

Cross-modal transfers, 146–147

Cross-sectional study, 24–26, 33

Cross-sex children, 308–309

Crowds, 333

Crying, 91–92, 94–45
Cultural influences, 12–14
  breast-feeding and, 93
  children's early words and, 234
  cross-cultural studies, 27
  economic variations and, 421
  overview of, 430–432
  temperament and, 96
Culture, 12
Cumulative deficit, 176
Cystic fibrosis, 53
Cytomegalovirus (CMV), 56, 57, 480

Day care, 62, 402–404
  aggressive behavior and, 406
  child–parent attachment and, 406–408
  effect on cognitive development, 404–405
  ideal setting, 409
  IQ and, 405
  peer relationships and, 330
  quality of, 406
Deafness
  in childhood, 454, 459
  children of deaf parents, 231
Decentering, 468
Deductive logic, 198
  in formal operational stage, 199
Defense mechanisms, 276, 282
Delinquincy, 416
  childhood-onset conduct disorders and, 439
  criminality and, 441
  hyperactivity and, 442
Delivery, 74–76
Dendrites, 48
  "pruning the arbor," 48, 218, 468, 474
Deoxyribonucleic acid (DNA), 41
Dependent variable, 28
Depression
  in adolescents, 442, 445
  in childhood, 442–447
  family system and, 445
  physical development and, 121–122
  postpartum, 83
Depth perception, 140–141
Desensitization to violence, 420
Developmental change, 15–16
Developmental psychopathology, 436–447
  externalizing problems and, 438–442
  internalizing problems, 442–447
  vulnerability and resilience, 446
Developmental stages, 16. See also Stages of development
Diagnostic and Statistical Manual of Mental Disorders (DSM-III-R), 438–439
Diet
  eating disorders and, 125–126
  malnutrition and, 61
  physical development and, 129
  prenatal development and, 61–62
Diethylstilbestrol (DES), 60
Difficult child, 95
Dilation, 72

Discipline, 382
Discriminating speech sounds and voices, 144–146
Diseases
  brain damage and, 448
  inherited, 53
  of mother and prenatal development, 55–57
  placenta and, 47
  prenatal, 55–57
Dishabituation, 87, 135
Divorce, 389–395
  Hispanic-Americans and, 427
  impact of, 391–393
  legal and living arrangements, 394–395
  Oedipal period and, 281
  softening effects of, 396
Dizygotic twins, 45
Dolls, 196, 302
Dominant genes, 42–44
Doubt, 278
Down syndrome, 51–52, 66, 435
  mother's age and, 52
  sex-chromosome anomalies and, 52
Drinking. *See* Alcohol
Dropouts, school, 411–412
  Hispanics and, 428
  pregnancy and, 412
  social class and, 411
Drugs
  for hyperactivity, 441
  pregnancy and, 57–60
  teenage suicide and, 125, 444
  use at delivery, 74–76
Dyslexia, 450

Early words, language development and, 232–235
Easy child, 95
Eating, 92
Eating disorders, 125–126
Ecological perspective, 11–14
Ecology of development
  Bronfenbrenner's approach and, 375–377
  family interaction and, 377–381
  systems theory of, 375
Ectomorphic body type, 105
Effacement, 72
Ego, 20
Egocentrism, 194, 200, 472
  decentering thinking and, 468
  preoperational child and, 199
  preschooler and, 204
Eisenberg's model of prosocial reasoning, 361–362
Elaboration, 210
Elementary-school years
  abilities with logic and, 198
  attachment theory, 321–322
Embryo, 47
Embryonic stage, 46–47
Emotional disturbances, 438
Emotional tone of family, 377
Empathy, 349–351
  stages of, 350

Empiricism, 135
  perceptual development and, 154–155
Employment
  father's job and family, 373–374, 397
  impact on adolescents, 414–416
  mother's employment and family, 395–397
  teenage delinquency and, 416
Endocrine glands, 110
Endomorphic body type, 105
Environment
  biological approach to personality and, 265
  gender schema and, 309
  language and, 250
  physical development and, 129–131
  social class and, 421
  temperament and, 265
Environmental influence models, 7–9
Environmental toxins, 52
Equilibration, 22, 193
Erikson's psychosocial stages, 21
  compared to Freud's psychosexual stages, 274
  identity in adolescence and, 292–293
  personality development and, 276–279
  strengths and weaknesses of, 281–283
Estradiol, 111, 473
Estrogen, 111
Ethics, 31
  children, rearing altruistic, 337
  Kohlberg on, 356
Ethnic group, 425
Ethnic identity in adolescence, 295
Ethnicity, 424–430
  African-Americans, 425–426
  Asian-Americans, 428–429
  Hispanic-Americans and, 427–428
  perspective on, 430
Ethological theory, 279
Executive processes, 220–221
Existential self, 289
Expectations
  family and, 378
  pubertal change and, 121
Experience, 9–10
  child's growth and, 104
  learning theories and, 18
Experiential intelligence, 173
Experimental designs, 27–29
Experimental group, 28
Experiments, 27
Expertise, 212–213
Expressive language, 231, 251
Expressive style, 234
Extended Black Family, The (Martin and Martin), 425
Extended families, 392
  African-Americans and, 426
  Asian-Americans and, 429
  Hispanic-Americans and, 427–428
Externalizing problems, 438

Faces, babies' perception of, 142–144
Facial expression, newborn's responses and, 139

Facilitation effect, 8–9
Fallopian tube, 40
Family
  in African-American subculture, 425–426
  child-rearing styles, 381–386
  child's characteristics and, 387
  communication patterns in, 381
  conflict in, 322–324
  divorce and, 389–395
  effect of atypical child on, 458–459
  effect of poverty on, 421–422
  emotional tone of, 377
  in Hispanic-American subculture, 427–428
  IQ and, 176–179
  legal and living arrangements, 394–395
  mother's employment and, 395–397
  parents' characteristics and, 387–389
  siblings and, 387–389
  stepparents and, 393–394
  stress and, 445
Family day care, 404
Family policy, 408
Fat development, 108
Fathers
  father–child bonds, 317–318, 324–325
  job effect on family and, 373–374, 397
  Oedipal stage and, 275
  poverty and, 422
  presence at delivery, 77
Fetal alcohol syndrome (FAS), 58
Fetal stage, 48–49
  hormones and, 110
  major milestones in, 48
Fetus, 47
  prenatal diagnosis of, 54
Fictive kin, 427–428
First pretend play, 196
Fixation, 281
Fontanels, 107
Foreclosure, 293
Formal operational stage, 474
  logic in, 198–199
  and Piaget's cognitive-developmental theory, 198–199
Fragile-X syndrome, 52
Fraternal twins, 45
  temperament and, 263
Freud's psychosexual stages, 20–21, 274–277
  development of, 275
  differences from Erikson's theories, 274
  divorce and, 281
  strengths and weaknesses of, 281–283
Friendship
  adolescents and, 332–334, 353–354
  behavior and, 364–365
  infants and preschoolers, 330
  schoolchildren and, 330–332

Gametes, 41
Gender
  aggression and, 439
  atypical development and, 455–458

Gender (*Continued*)
  caring ethic and, 363–364
  child's self-perception of, 308–309
  cross-sex children and, 308–309
  differences in physical development, 119–123
  eating disorders and, 125–126
  effects of divorce and, 281, 392
  genetics and, 44
  hormones in adolescence and, 111–112
  infants and, 96–97
  IQ and, 184–186
  Oedipus conflict and, 275, 280–281
  personality and physical development, 121–122
  physical growth and, 120
  prenatal development and, 66–67
  sexual development and, 112–115
Gender concept
  androgyny and, 309–310
  cross-sex children and, 308–309
  defined, 300
  developmental patterns and, 301–303
Gender constancy, 301
Gender identity, 301
Gender schema theory, 306–307
Gender stability, 301
Genes, 41
Genetic errors, 51–54
Genetics
  behavior genetics, 6–7
  dominant and recessive genes, 42–44
  genotypes and phenotypes, 45–46
  language development and, 249–250
  males and females, 44
  prepregnancy testing and, 54
  Rh factor and, 56
  twins and siblings, 44–45
Genital herpes, 56, 57
Genital stage, 276
Genotype, 41, 45–46
Germinal stage, 46–47
Gesell's maturational theory, 17
Gestation period, 46, 47
Gestural language, 231–232
Gibson's perceptual development theory, 155–156
Giftedness, 452–453
Gilligan's ethic of caring, 363–364
Glial cells, 48, 109
Gonadotropic hormones, 111
Grammar
  complex sentences at 30–48 months, 238–239
  explosion at 27–36 months, 237–238
  first sentences at 18–20 months, 235–237
Grief, 458
Growth, 6. *See also* Physical development
Guilt, 278

Habituation, 87–88, 135
  perception and, 153
Head Start, 179–180
Health and illness
  adolescence and, 124–125
  early and middle childhood, 124
Hearing. *See* Auditory development
Hearing-impaired children, 454
Heredity. *See also* Genetics
  effect on IQ, 181–182
  versus environment, 4
  inherited diseases, 53
  language and, 249–250
  personality traits and, *264*
  physical development and, 128
  retardation and, 448
  temperament and, 263
Herpes simplex, 57
Heterosexuality, *335*
Heterozygosity, 42
Hispanic-Americans, 427–428
  child-rearing style, 385–386
  extended families and, 427–428
  school dropouts, 428
  sexual activity and, 117
Holophrases, 235
Homicide among teens, 124
Homosexuality, *335*
Horizontal relationships, 314
  between children, 330–337
Hormones
  in adolescence, 111–112
  from birth to adolescence, 110–111
  cross-sex children and, 308–-309
  estrogen, 111
  gonadotropic hormones, 111
  prenatal, 110, 308
  puberty and, 112–115
Horowitz's model, *15*
Hostility and abuse, *378*
Huntington's disease, 53
Hyperactivity, 439–442
  diagnostic criteria for, *440*
  positron-emission tomography (PET), 442
Hypothalamus gland, 111

Id, 20
Identical twins, 45
Identification, 276, 282–283
  sex-role development and, 301–303
  visual skills and, 141–142
Identity
  adolescence and, 292–293
  Erikson's stage of, 279
Identity achievement, 293
Identity diffusion, 293
Imitation, 200–202
  language and, 244
Implantation, 47
Imprinting, 9
Inborn biases and constraints, 5
Inborn error of metabolism, 448
Independent variable, 28
Induction effect, 9
Inductive logic, 198, 215
Industry, Erikson's stage of, 279

Infants, 89. *See also* Birth; Prenatal development
  auditory development and, 138
  breast- versus bottle-feeding, 92
  child–parent attachment, 319–321, 406–408
  cognitive development and, 200–203
  cross-modal transfer and, 146–147
  crying and, 91–92, 94–45
  day care and, 62, 407
  eating and, 92
  first-year health and death, 93–94
  gender differences and, 66–67, 96
  hearing and, 138
  hearing-impaired, 454
  imprinting and, 9
  IQ and, 167
  low birth weight (LBW), 15, 79
  manipulative skills and, 115
  memory and, 202–203
  motion and, 139
  motor skills and, 85–86
  movement and manipulative skills of, *116*
  movement skills and, 115
  operant conditioning and, 136
  parent–child attachment, 315–318, 463–465
  peer relationships, 329–332
  preference technique and, 135
  prelinguistic phase and, 229–232
  psychosexual stages and, 274–277
  psychosocial stages and, 276–279
  reflexes and, 82–84
  self-concept and, 289
  sensitive period of, 10
  sex differences and, 96–97
  simultaneous developments in, *464*
  sleeping and, 90
  smell and, 138–139
  states of consciousness and, 89
  sudden infant death syndrome (SIDS) and, 94
  taste and, 138–139
  temperament of, 95–96
  touch and, 139
  very low birth weight and, *80*
  visual skills, 136–138
Infant tests, 167
Inferiority, 279
Inflections, 235, 237–238
Information processing, 217–223
  as approach to intelligence, 165
  developmental approaches to, 217–218
  individual differences in, 221–222
  strategies for remembering and, *210*
Initiation rituals, 296
Initiative, Erikson's stage of, 278
Innateness theories, language and, 246–247
Inner-city poverty, 422–423
Insecure attachments. *See* Secure and insecure attachments
Instrumental conditioning, 18
Intelligence, 164–165. *See also* Cognitive development; IQ (intelligence quotient)
Internalizing problems, 442–447
Internal models of experience, 10–11

Interviews, 30
Intimacy, 354, 363
  adolescents and, 333, 473
  cliques and, 333
  between girls, 340
Intrinsic reinforcement, 19
IQ (intelligence quotient), 9, 31, 166, 248. *See also* IQ test
  academic performance and, 410
  day care and, 405
  expertise and, 223
  explaining differences in, 175–181
  FAS and, 58–59
  general cognitive development and, 368
  Head Start program and, 179–180
  heredity and, 181–182
  inception of, 166
  information processing and, 221–222
  language development and, 153, 377
  low birth weight and, 15
  mental retardation and, 448–449
  prenatal nutrition and, 63
  race differences in, 182–183
  sex differences and, 184–186
IQ tests, 223, 434
  early tests, 165–166
  limitations of, 173
  modern versions of, 167
  predictive value of, 172–173
  rationale for, 186–187
  stability of scores and, 169–171
  Stanford-Binet test, 165–166
  versus Sternberg's triarchic theory, 173–175

Klinefelter's syndrome, 52
Kohlberg's stages of moral development, 355–359, 355–361, *356*
  applying to education, 367
  behavior and, 365–367
  critique of, 360–361
  Gilligan's criticism of, 363
  sequence of stages, 359–360
  universality of, 360

Labor, stages of, 72–73
Langlois' studies on babies' preferences, *143*
Language, 466
  auditory development and, 144–145
  bilingual children and, *240*
  constructivist theories and, 247–248
  developing grammar, 235–239
  differences in style, 250–251
  early gestures and, 231–232
  early perception of, 230
  early sounds, 230–231
  environmental theories and, 245–246, 250
  explanation of, 228–229
  first words, 232–235
  hearing impaired and, 454
  imitation and reinforcement, 244
  individual differences and, 248–251
  innateness theories and, 246–247
  IQ and, 153

Language (*Continued*)
  learning disabilities and, 451–452
  pragmatics and, 243
  prelinguistic stage and, 229–232
  reading and, 252–253
  and self-control, 243–244
  word meanings and, 239–243
Latency stage, 276
Law and order orientation, 357
Lead, 61
Learning disorders
  definitions and labels, 450–451
  nature of, 451–452
Learning principles, home application of, 268
Learning theories, 17–20. *See also* Social learning theories
  Bandura's theories and, 19–20
  classical conditioning and, 17–18, 86
  habituation and, 87–88, 135
  language development and, 244
  operant conditioning and, 18–19, 86
  personality development and, 267–273
  schematic learning, 87
Libido, 20
Listening
  discriminating individual voices and, 145–146
  discriminating speech sounds and, 144–145
  prenatal, 146
Locus of genes, 41
Logic, 198
  in concrete operational stage, 197–198
  in formal operational stage, 198–199
  teenagers and, 215
Longitudinal study, 24, 26
Low birth weight (LBW), 15, 79, 480

Maintenance pattern, 8
Manipulative skills, 115, *116*
Marriage, black families and, 425
Masturbation, 276
Mathematics
  race and ability in, 183
  sex and ability in, 184–186
Maturation, 5–6
  physical development and, 128
Mean length of utterance (MLU), 248
Medulla, 109
Meiosis, 41
Memory
  of child witness, *211*
  in infancy, 202–203
  measuring capacity of, *218*
  strategies for remembering, *210*, 211–212
Menarche, 113, 123, 129
Mental age, 166
Mental development, 120–121
Mental retardation, 435
  assessment of, 447
  causes of, 448–450
  cognitive functioning and, 448
  definitions and labels, 450–451
  fetal alcohol syndrome and, 58–59

genetic causes, 51–52
  IQ scores and, 447
Mesomorphic body type, 105
Metacognition, 206
  executive process and, 220–221
Metamemory, 206
Midbrain, 109
Mind, theory of, 205–206
Miscarriage, 41
Mitosis, 41
Modeling, 10, 19
  personality development and, 270–271
Monozygotic twins, 45
Morality
  Eisenberg's model of prosocial reasoning, 361–362
  Gilligan's ethic of caring, 363–364
  Kohlberg's stages of development, 355–361
Moral judgment, 365–367
Moral reasoning, 359
Moratorium, 293
Moro reflex, 84, 87–88
Motherese, 245
Mother–infant interaction, 324–325
  breast-feeding and, 92, 463–464
  low birth weight (LBW) and, 79
  trust and, 277–278
Mothers
  attachment of blind babies and, *456*
  childbirth and, 72–81
  child custody and, 394–395
  child's attachment to, 324–325
  job's effect on family, 395–397
  Oedipal stage and, 276, 280–281
  postpartum depression and, 83
  poverty and, 422
  weight gain in pregnancy, *62*
Motion, sense of, 139
Motor development, 115–116
Motor skills, 85–86
  development of, *116*
Movement skills, 115
Multiple sclerosis, 110
Muscle development, 107–108
Muscular dystrophy, *53*
Myelin, 110
Myelinization, 110

Naming explosion, 233–234
National Longitudinal Study of Youth, 405
Nativism, 135
  perceptual development and, 153–154
Nature-nurture debate, 4–5, 33
  interactions between both, 14–15
  nature side of equation, 5–7, 33
  nurture side of equation, 7–14, 33
Negative reinforcement, 18
Negatives, 238
Neglecting style of child rearing, 383
Nervous system
  child development and, 108–110
  composition of, 109–110

Nervous system (*Continued*)
  postembryonic development of, 48–49
Neurons, 48–49, 109
  single developed, *50*
Newborn. *See also* Birth; Infants; Prenatal development
  adapting to, 82
  assessment of, 81
  habituation, 87–88
  motor skills of, 85–86
  perceptual skills of, 85
  reflexes of, 82–85
  and schematic learning, 87
  social skills and, 88
Nurture. *See* Nature-nurture debate

Object concept, 148–152, 200
Object constancy, 148
Objective self, 289–291
Object perception, 149
Object permanence, 149–151
  in Zambian infants, *152*
Observation, research through, 29–30
Observational learning, 19
Oedipus conflict, 276, 280–281
One-child policy (China), 388
Operant conditioning, 18–19, 86, 136
Operations, 193
Oral stage, 274
Ossification, 107
Ovaries, *111, 112*
Overextension, language and, 241
Overregularization, 238
Ovum, 40

Parenting. *See* Child rearing
Parents. *See also* Family; Fathers; Mothers
  adapting to newborns, 82
  blind children and, 457
  characteristics of, 389–389
  child abuse and, *318, 378*
  childhood depression and, 443–444
  effect of jobs on family, 395–397
  of hyperactive children, 441–442
  methods of control and, 378–381
  reading to children, *245*
  restrictiveness, 379
  social support to, 400–401
Parent to child relationships, 315–318
  adolescence and, 322–324
  preschool and elementary-school years, 321–322
Partial reinforcement, 19
Peer relationships, 330–334
  adolescence and, 332–334
  day care and, 330
  individual differences in, 338–341
  infants and, 330
  popularity and rejection, 338–340
  preschoolers and, 330
  school-age children and, 330–332
  sex differences and, 340–341
Perceptual constancies, 147–148

Perceptual development, 134–136
  auditory skills and, 138, 144–146
  constancies and, 147–148
  cross-modal transfer and, 146–147
  explanations of, 153–156
  looking and, 140–141
  methods of studying, 135–136
  object concept and, 148–152
  senses of touch and motion, 139–140
  smelling and tasting, 138–139
  speed and efficiency, 152–153
  visual skills and, 136–138
Perceptual skills, 85
Performance, 168
Performance tests, *170*
Permissive rearing style, 382
Personality. *See also* Temperament
  Bowlby's attachment model and, 279–280
  defined, 260
  effect of day care on, 406
  Erikson's psychosocial stages and, 276–279
  Freud's psychosexual stages and, 274–277
  heredity and, 264
  learning approaches to, 267–273
  major views of, 260–261
  modeling and, 270–271
  psychoanalytic theories and, 273
  rate of development and, 121–122
  reinforcement and, 269–270
  synthesis of theories, 283–285
Perspective taking, 204
Phallic stage, 275–276
Phenotypes, 45–46
Phenylketonuria (PKU), *53*, 448
Phonemic awareness, 252
Physical development, 129–131
  adolescents and, 124–125
  of bones, 105–106
  environmental effects on, 129–131
  fat and, 108
  height and weight changes and, 105–106
  heredity and, 128
  hormones and, 110–112
  individual differences and, 119–123
  maturation and, 128
  of muscles, 107–108
  nervous system and, 108–110
  racial differences and, 123
  reasons for studying, 104–105
  secular trends and, 129
  sexual maturity and, 112–115
  social class and, 123
Piaget's cognitive-developmental theory, 21–22
  adaption process and, 22, 191–193
  concrete operations stage, 197–198
  constructivism and, 199–200
  direct tests of, 208
  formal operational stage, 198–199
  influences of, 199–200
  operations and, 193
  preoperational stage, 194–197

Piaget's cognitive-developmental theory *(Continued)*
   qualitative change and, 200
   sensorimotor stage and, 193–194
   sex-role development and, 305
Pituitary gland, 111
Placenta, 47
Play
   children's sports and, *118*
   gender schema and, 306
   through Piaget's cognitive stages, *196*
   preschoolers and, *196*, 329–330
   school-age children and, 330
   sex-role behavior and, 304
   toys and, 304–306
Popularity, 338–340
   reading others' feelings and, *347*
Positive reinforcement, 18
Positron-emission tomography (PET), 442
Postpartum depression, 83
Poverty
   Asian-Americans and, 429
   black families and, 426
   chronic stress and, 423–424
   effect on children, 421–422
   effect on families, 421–422
   inner-city, 422–423
   IQs and, 15, 422
   low-birth-weight babies and, 15
   physical development and, 129
   prenatal behavior and, 422
Pragmatics, 243
Preconventional morality, 355–356
Preference technique, 135
Pregnancy. *See also* Birth; Prenatal development
    and drugs, 57–60
   genetic testing before, *54*
   mother's diseases during, 55–57
   mother's weight gain during, *62*
   school dropouts and, 412
   smoking during, 57–58
   teenage, 118–119, *120*
   teratogens and, 39
Prelinguistic phase, 229–232
Premature infants, 79
Prenatal development, 47
   age of mother and, 63–64
   conception, 40–41
   critical stages in, *55*
   diet/nutrition and, 61–62
   embryonic stage, 46–47
   emotional state of mother, 64
   fetal stage, 48–49
   gender differences in, 66–67
   genetic errors and, 51–54
   germinal stage, 46–47
   hormones and, 110
   length and height and, 49
   nervous system and, 48–49
   number of pregnancies and, 64
   poverty and, 422
   risks and consequences of problems in, 65–66

   sexual differentiation and, 49–51
   social class and, 67
   teratogens and, 54–61
Prenatal diagnosis of fetus, *54*
Preoperational stage, 194–197
Prepregnancy genetic testing, *54*
Preschool period, 203–204
   appearance and reality, 204–205
   attachments and, 321–322
   cognitive development in, 203–208
   conservation and classification, 206–207
   Head Start and, 179–180
   IQ and, 10
   parallel development during, *467*
   peer relationships and, 330
   perspective taking and, 204
   play and, *196*, 330
   preoperational stage and, 194
   sex-role development and, 306
   theories of mind, 205–206
Preterm infant, 79
Primary sex characteristics, 112
Primitive reflex, 83
Principled morality, 357–359
Principle of contrast, 242
Problem behavior, 435
   attention-deficit hyperactivity disorder and, 439–442
   conduct disorders, 438–439
   cultural influences and, 437
   depression and, 121–122
   temperament and, *266*
Problem solving, 219–220
Prosocial behavior, 334, 336, 361–362
Prosocial reasoning, 361–362
Proximodistal process, 107
Psychoanalytic theories, 20–21, 33
   evidence and application of, 280–281
   personality development and, 273–283
   strengths and weaknesses of, 281–283
Psychometric approach, 164
Psychopathology. *See* Developmental psychopathology
Psychosexual stages, 21, 274–277, *275*
Psychosocial stages, 21, *277*, *278*–279
Puberty, *472*, *473*. *See also* Adolescence
   changes for boys, 114–115
   changes for girls, 113–114, 470
   hormonal changes and, 112–115
   physical development and, 108, 121, 474
   psychosexual development and, 276–277
   psychosocial development and, 279
   sexual maturity and, 112–115
   Tanner's stages of, *113*
Punishment, 18
   spanking, *380*

Qualitative change, 15, 200
Quantitative change, 15
Quasi experiment, 34
Questionnaires, 30
Questions, 238

Race
    and ability in mathematics, 183
    IQ and, 182–183
    physical development and, 123
Reading
    to children, *245*
    language and, 252–253
    learning disorders and, 451
    perceptual development and, 148
Reasoning. *See also* Logic
    moral, 359
    prosocial, 361–362
Receptive language, 231
Recessive diseases, *45*
Recessive genes, 42–44
Reciprocity, 470
Referential style, 234, *251*
Reflexes, 82–85
Rehearsal strategies, 209–210
Reinforcement, 18–19
    aggression and, 272
    cross-sex children and, 308–309
    intrinsic, 19
    language development and, 244
    negative, 18
    partial, 19
    personality development and, 269–270
    positive, 18
Rejection, 338–340
Religion
    African-American families and, 426
    Buddhist system, 431
Repetition, motherese and, 245
Research, on development, 23–24
    analysis of results, 30–32, 34
    cross-cultural designs, 26–27
    cross-sectional designs and, 24–26, 33
    ethical issues and, *31*
    experimental designs and, 27–29
    longitudinal design and, 26
    methods for, 29–30
Research analysis, 30–32, 34
Research methods, 29–30
Resilience, 14–15, 33
    developmental psychopathology and, 446
Responses of others, child's growth and, 104
Responsiveness, 377–378
Restrictiveness, 379
Rh factor, *56*
Ritalin, 441
Role confusion, 279
Role flexibility, 425
Rubella, 56

Schema, 200
    gender identity and, 306–307
    newborns and, 463
Schematic learning, 87
Schemes, 191–192
Scholastic Apptitude Tests (SATs), 184
School-age child

attachments and, 321–322
    expertise and, 212–213
    memory and strategy development, 208–209
    parallel changes in, 469
    peer relationships and, 331–332, 469
    Piaget's ideas and, 208, 469
    rehearsal strategies, 209–210
    self-concept and, 291–292, 469
Schools
    guns in, 422–423
    impact of, 408–409
    inner-city poverty and, 422
    performance tests and, *170*
    quality of, 412–414
    self-judgments and, 409–411
Secondary sex characteristics, 112
Secular trends, 129
Secure and insecure attachments, 325–326, 424
    cross-cultural comparisons, *327*
    day care and, 406–408
    definitions and, 325
    long-term consequences of, 328–329
    origins of, 328
    stability and, 326–328
Sedatives, 74
Seeing. *See* Visual skills
Self-awareness, 289–291
Self-concept, 272
    child's growth and, 105
    defined, 288–289
    developmental patterns of, 289–296
    individual differences and, 296–299
    personality development, 269–271
    sex-role behavior and, 300, 303–304
    sex-role concepts and, 300–303
    sex-role stereotypes and, 301–303, 307–310
    summary of, 299
Self-control, language and, 243–244
Self-efficacy, 329
Self-esteem, 296–297
    androgyny and, 310
    authoritarian rearing style and, 384
    consequence of variation, 298
    consistency over time, 297–298
    gifted children and, 452–453
    late adolescence and, 473
    origins of differences, 298–299
Self-selection, 415–416
Semantics, 228
Sensitive period, 10
Sensorimotor play, *196*
Sensorimotor stage, 193–194
Sentences
    complex, 238–239
    first, 235–237
Sequential design, 24
Sex chromosomes, 44
    anomalies in, 52
Sex differences
    aggressive behavior and, 439
    atypical development and, 455–458

Sex differences *(Continued)*
 body images among adolescents, *126*
 infants and, 96–97
 IQ and, 184–186
 peer relationships and, 331–332, 340–341
 physical development and, 112–115
 prenatal, 49–51
Sex-role behavior, 300
 androgyny and, 309–310
 cross-sex children and, 308–309
 development of, 303–304
 divorce and, *281*
Sex-role concept, 300
Sex roles
 defined, 300
 developmental patterns and, 301–304
Sex-role stereotypes
 defined, 300
 development of, 301–303
 global context and, *303*
 individual differences and, 307–310
 on TV, *307*
Sex-typed, 300
Sexual activity, 117–118, 473
Sexual development, 112–113
 in boys, 114–115
 in girls, 113–114
Sexual differentiation, 49–51
Sexuality
 adolescents and, 117–118
 Freud's psychosexual stages and, 20–21, 274–277
 sexual maturity and, 112–115
Shame, 278
Shape constancy, 148
Siblings, 387–389
Sickle-cell anemia, 42, *53*
Sign language, 454
Simultaneous developments, *466*
 in infants, *464*
Single-gene defects, 53
Size constancy, 148
Sleeping, 90
Slow-to-warm-up child, 95
Small-for-date infant, 79
Smell, sense of, 138–139
Smoking
 pregnant mothers and, 57–58
 relationship to SIDS, 94
 teenagers and, *127*, 415
Social class. *See also* Poverty
 physical development and, 123
 poverty effects on children, 421–422
 prenatal development and, 67
 school dropouts and, 411
Social cognition, 344–345
 cognitive side of, 345–346
 cross-cultural comparisons and, 348–349
 describing other people and, 351–352
 development of empathy, 349–351
 Eisenberg's model of prosocial reasoning, 361–362
 general cognitive development, 368

 Gilligan's ethic of caring, 363–364
 Kohlberg's stages of moral development, 355–361
 morality of actions and, 354–355
 moral judgment and behavior, 365–367
 reading others' feelings and, 346–348
 social side of, 346
 thinking about relationships and, 352–354
Social cognitive theory, 19
Social contract orientation, 358
Social development
 attachment theory and, 314–315
 child's attachment to parents, 319–325
 differences in peer relationships, 338–341
 horizontal relationships between children, 330–337
 parent to child bond, 315–318
 quality differences in attachments, 325–329
Social isolation, 445
Social learning theories
 personality development and, 269–271
 sex-role development and, 305
Social referencing, 144
Social skills, 88
Sociodramatic play, 196
Spanking, 380
Sports for children, *118*
Stages, 481
Stages, concept of, 200
Stages of development. *See also* Adolescence; Preschool period; School–age child
 adolescence (12 to 20), 470–474
 Aslin's models and, 475–476
 birth to 18 months, 463–466
 elementary school years (6 to 12), 468–470
 individual differences in, 480–481
 major influences on, 475–476
 nature of change, 480–481
 preschool years (18 months to 6 years), 466–468
 systems theory and, 463
 timing and, 476–478
Stanford-Binet test, 165–166
States of consciousness, 89
Stepparent families, 393–394
Stereotyping. *See* Sex-role stereotypes
Sternberg-Dornbusch studies, 383–386
Sternberg's triarchic theory of intelligence, 173–175
Strange situation, 325–326
 day care and, 407
Stress, *423–424*
 child abuse and, *378*
 vulnerability and, 446
Subjective self, 289
Substitute pretend play, *196*
Sucking reflex, 84
Sudden infant death syndrome (SIDS), 94
Suicide, *444*
 among teenagers, 125
Superego, 20
Symbiotic relationship, 289
Symbols, 463
 language as, 228–229
Sympathy, 349

Synapse, 49
Syntax, 228
Systematic searching, *210*
Systems theory, 375, 463

Taste, sense of, 138–139
Tay-Sachs disease, *53*
Teenage pregnancy, 118–119, *120*
Telegraphic speech, 235
Television
    adolescent viewing patterns, 416
    aggression and, 418–420
    negative effects of, 417–418
    positive educational effects of, 417
    sex-role stereotypes, *307*
Temperament, 95–96, 261–267
    basic propositions and, 261–262
    behavior problems and, *266*
    consistency over time, 265
    difficult child, 95
    easy child, 95
    environmental interactions, 265
    inheritance and, 263
    psychological connections, 263–264
    slow-to-warm-up child, 95
    twins and, *263*
    variations among infants, 95–96
Teratogens, 9
    diseases and drugs, 54–61
    during pregnancy, 39
    prenatal development and, 51
Testes, 112, *113*
Testis-determining factor (TDF), 44
Testosterone, 111, 473
Tests and testing. *See also* IQ tests
    achievement tests, 167–169, *168*
    Alpha-fetoprotein test (AFP), *54*
    amniocentesis, *54*
    Apgar score, 81
    Bayley Scales for Infant Development, 167
    performance tests, *170*
    prenatal diagnosis of fetus, *54*
    Scholastic Apptitude Tests (SATs), 184
    Sternberg's triarchic theory and, 173–175
Theories of development, 16–17
    biological, 17, 33, 261–267
    cognitive, 21–22, 305–307
    comparison of, 22–23
    learning theories. *See* Learning theories
    psychoanalytic theories. *See* Psychoanalytic theories
Theory of mind, 205–206

Thyroid hormone (thyroxine), 110
Time, 32
Touch, sense of, 139
Toys. *See* Play
Tracking, 137
Tranquilizers, 74
Transitivity principle, 212
Triarchic theory of intelligence, Sternberg's, 173–175
Trust versus mistrust, 277–278
Turner's syndrome, 52
Twins, 44–45
    IQ scores of, 175
    temperament, *263*

Ultrasound test, *54*
Umbilical cord, 47
Unconditioned response, 17
Unconditioned stimulus, 17
Underachievers, 411
Universality, moral development and, 360
Uterus, 40

Vertical relationships, 314
Very low-birth-weight infants, 79
    long-term outcomes of, 80
Visual cliff, 140
Visual skills. *See also* Blindness
    acuity of, 136–137
    color vision, 137–138
    depth perception and, 140–141
    identifying objects and, 141–142
    perception of faces and, 142–144
    tracking and, 137
Vocabulary
    child at 14–19 months, *232*
    day care and, 405
    first words, 232–235
    motherese and, 245–246
    word meanings and, 239–243
Vulnerability, 14–15, 33, 480
    developmental psychopathology and, 446

Walking, 115
Warmth versus hostility, 377
Wechsler Intelligence Scale for Children (WISC), 167
Weight and height changes, 105–106
Words
    child's first, 232–233
    development of meanings, 239–243
    later learning of, 234–235
    learning constraints and, 241–243
    naming explosion and, 233–234